W9-CCX-964

For Reference

Not to be taken from this room

Opera Production II

A Handbook

QUAINTANCE EATON

with Production Problems in Handel's Operas

by RANDOLPH MICKELSON

UNIVERSITY OF MINNESOTA PRESS · MINNEAPOLIS

© Copyright 1974 by the University of Minnesota.
All rights reserved.

Printed in the United States of America
at Jones Press, Minneapolis.

Published in the United Kingdom and India by the Oxford University
Press, London and Delhi, and in Canada
by the Copp Clark Publishing Co. Limited, Toronto

Library of Congress Catalog Card Number: 61-16843

ISBN 0-8166-0689-7

Opera Production I: A Handbook by Quaintance Eaton,
originally published by the University of Minnesota Press,
will be available from Da Capo Press,
New York, in April 1974.

Memorial Library
Mars Hill College
Mars Hill, N. C.
DISCARD

PREFACE

THE PREFACE to the first volume outlined briefly the plan and potential usefulness of its contents. I can do no better than repeat its substance, with a few minor changes.

This book is designed to be useful to all opera producers, to students, writers, and performers, and also to those who, not actively concerned with the production of opera, nevertheless have a lively curiosity about the art. A book of fact rather than critical judgment, it reveals the many elements that make up more than 350 operas.

The producer can find in these pages all the information essential for judging which operas are suited to his equipment—or even, by virtue of period, style, and story, to his temperament. How to stage a work is left to him. But by quick scanning he can determine all that is basic for production: the number and importance of settings; the size of orchestra, chorus, ballet; the number of singers, their relative importance and individual requirements. He can learn where to get musical materials. Then, if he should want to consult a fellow producer, he can readily discover others who have performed a given work in America.

The student and writer will benefit from the easy accessibility of facts, clearly presented. Furthermore, the student and writer, together with the general reader, can marvel at the amazing complexity of an opera production.

Historical material anchors the reader in the necessary knowledge of period (when the composer lived, when the opera was first presented, and the time in which the story takes place), source of libretto, and any unusual circumstances of performance or revision. This information, however, has been compressed into capsule form because the book is a practical guide rather than a historical or musicological treatise.

Performers can tell at a glance the suitability of roles to their talents. Vocal and acting demands are set forth; in most cases exact ranges are given, as well as details of other requirements.

In a truly opera-minded society, the so-called general reader would be placed first instead of last. The orchid of opera would be as widely and as lovingly cultivated as the simplest country garden. In spite of the phenomenal growth in opera production, chiefly in workshops and colleges, and the

R
782.07
E140

760442

enormous public created by long-playing recordings, America is not yet an operatic country in that all participants in opera production can make a full-time living at it, and that audiences accept opera as a pleasurable matter of course. Failing that desirable state, we can hope that facts about the art we serve will find an audience outside the limited professional circle, if only because they enjoy a peep behind the scenes, which often proves irresistible to even the least knowledgeable. Perhaps by luring novices backstage, and revealing some of those mysteries that are unsuspected from the other side of the curtain, we may gain new customers out front.

QUAINTANCE EATON

New York
December 1972

ACKNOWLEDGMENTS

THE SECOND VOLUME of *Opera Production* progressed in fits and starts over the period between the signing of the contract with the University of Minnesota Press and the final delivery of the manuscript. The long delay, regretted no less sharply by the author than by her mentor, the late James S. Lombard, had several causes, chiefly economic. Contributing mightily was the dearth of eager researchers, anxious to toil long hours over troublesome details for little or no recompense. It would be too discouraging to recall in full the early misadventures, when too many all-too-sanguine helpers decided abruptly that the assignments they had been brooding over for months were after all not the attractive prospect they had envisioned. So they returned their lists and the search began all over again, until finally there was nothing to do but give up on the idea of such regular assistants as had been at hand for the first volume.

Still, this is no one-man job, and some help has indeed been forthcoming. I am eternally grateful for it. John W. Freeman of *Opera News* did the basic work on most of the Czech repertoire. Mrs. Alan Wagner, who had been a stalwart for the first volume, managed to outline a few of the early Verdis and others even though she had moved to California. More recently, Felix Popper was a tower of strength, not only in the Richard Strauss operas he admires so much, but in providing statistics from the New York City Opera (Hans Sondheimer had previously supplied some timings), and John Grande, the librarian of the Metropolitan Opera, sent along vital information about the Met's repertoire.

From other companies assistance arrived when data were needed about particular performances: from Osbourne W. McConathy of the Opera Company of Boston; Marcus L. Overton, Lyric Opera of Chicago; John M. Ludwig, Center Opera, Minneapolis; George M. Schaefer, St. Paul Opera; John O. Crosby, Santa Fe Opera; Arthur G. Cosenza, New Orleans Opera; David Lloyd, Lake George Opera Festival; and Norman Lloyd, Oberlin College. These are evidenced in my correspondence; I hope I have not missed anyone; if so, apologies.

Individuals supplying necessary information include: Christopher Keene for *Yerma* and *Melusine*, which he conducted at Santa Fe; Naomi Ornest and Kurt Saffir for Haydn's *Armida*; William Spada for *Marina*; Ben Weber for *Mefistofele*, *Doktor Faust*, and *Moses und Aron*; Karoly Köpe for the two Szokolay and the Salieri operas; Noel Gillespie for most of Meyerbeer, some Bellini, and others that had performances in Washington, D.C.; Robert Lawrence for *La Navarraise*, *Le Jongleur de Notre Dame*, *La Juive*, and *La Damnation de Faust*; the late Robert Sabin for *Zerrissene*; and Miss Belle Schiller for allowing me to hear Russian and Czech recordings.

The musicologist-librarian Sirvart Poladian-Kachie not only worked on *Khovantschina* and *I Puritani* but vouchsafed much valuable information about the particular requirements of Handel. This preceded some collaboration with Randolph Mickelson, who in addition to persuading me that several charmers lurked in ignored shelves filled with Auber, Adam, Marschner, and the like, poured out such a wealth of pertinent data on Handel that I persuaded him to write the helpful suggestions that appear at the end of the Introduction.

Composers were willing to assist—naturally, one would think, although a couple of exceptions still bother me—as noted in the Introduction. Those who came through with details are, alphabetically: Joyce Barthelson, Jack Beeson, Richard Brooks, Richard Cumming (and his librettist, Henry Butler), John Eaton, Myron S. Fink, Grant Fletcher, Hans Werner Henze, Peggy Glanville-Hicks, Ian Hamilton, Lee Hoiby, the widow of Frederick Jacobi, Martin Kalmanoff, Ernest Kanitz, Ulysses Kay, Ellis Kohs, Marvin David Levy, Normand Lockwood, the late Douglas Moore, Sam Morgenstern, Thomas Pasatieri, Vittorio Rieti, Ned Rorem, Elie Siegmeister, Stanley Silverman, Robert Starer, Lester Trimble, Isaac Van Grove, James Wade, and Malcolm Williamson. Again, I apologize if I've overlooked anyone.

Without the wholehearted cooperation of the publishers, this task would be impossible. So let me thank them all and try to name them: Rosalie Calabrese of ACA; Bob Holton and Bob Beatey of Belwin-Mills; Henson Markham of Boosey & Hawkes (now of Salabert); Arthur Cohn of MCA; John Owen Ward of Oxford University Press (now of Boosey & Hawkes); Kurt Michaelis of C. F. Peters; Ursula Eastman of Theodore Presser; and George Sturm of G. Schirmer, all of whom sent scores cheerfully to whatever point I needed them. Then for some typing in an emergency I am deeply grateful to Richard Mealey, director of the New York City Opera Guild, and to my friend and colleague Barbara Fischer-Williams.

Libraries were again a bulwark of available knowledge; I recall specially the Music Division of the Library for the Performing Arts at Lincoln Center, the Redwood Library of Newport, R.I., and the Harwood Foundation of Taos, N.M.

It was indeed in that beautiful New Mexico valley where Taos lies, surrounded by the unforgettable mountains, that I accomplished most of the final work during the summers of 1971 and 1972. For this haven I am indebted to Henry Sauerwein, Jr., director of the Helene Wurlitzer Foundation of New Mexico, who provided an ideal place to work in some of the most fascinating surroundings in the world.

viii

Although the active participation of the Committee for the Development of Opera that sponsored the first volume was no longer forthcoming, warm encouragement was offered on many occasions by members of that band of producers and authorities, as well as by the dozens of company directors who insisted, much to the author's gratification, in labeling *Opera Production I* the bible of the opera world. Many, many times have they vowed how eagerly they awaited the second volume.

Well, here it is! I only hope it fulfills their anticipations and those of my patient publisher and editor. If only Jim Lombard had lived to share in whatever approbation comes along!

Q. E.

CONTENTS

xii

SHORT OPERAS

INDEXES

Opera Production II

THIS BOOK *is compact—highly condensed and codified. It will be essential, therefore, for the reader to familiarize himself with the method of condensation and codification by reading and perhaps rereading this introduction.*

INTRODUCTION

After the first volume of *Opera Production* appeared and settled down into the hands of many of this nation's opera producers and opera lovers, the chief criticism that wafted back to the author was that some opera or group of operas had not been included. I had tried to fend this off by the following paragraph:

"In the matter of selection, it will prove impossible to please everyone, as always. I expect any number of accusations of sins of omission. There is sure to be a cry: 'Why not more Handel?' Lesser-known works of well-known composers will be cited—those of Gounod, Smetana, Wolf-Ferrari, Bizet. Many attractive names did not make our marquee at all—Berlioz, Fauré, Janáček, and Korngold among them."

The need to supply these missing links and other omissions inspired this second volume, especially as revivals of Handel, the Czech works, Berlioz, and even Meyerbeer seemed to catch the producers' and the public's attention. Then the field opened up so broadly that once again it became a matter of elimination and choice, and in spite of the inclusion of such seemingly forgotten or "manifestly" inconsequential ventures as the works of Lortzing, Marschner, Respighi, Auber, and a dozen others, there will no doubt be an anguished cry of "Why not so-and-so?" I offer no excuses except one—the long-postponed publication date at last threatened to become a literal "dead" line, and I had to stop somewhere. As it is, in order to justify the boast that all the gaps mentioned had been filled in, Korngold's *Die tote Stadt* barely made it under the wire. I had intended ignoring it until I wanted to quote verbatim the paragraph above.

Some of the entries may seem far-out, some trifling, some unjustified for one reason or another. But there are always producers who want to put on a work that no one else considers; they will find plenty herein. After all, taste is as individual as the ear of the beholder, to scramble a cliché.

Let me single out a few works that I consider potential prizes in the treasure hunt, although some are manifestly thorny. The two operas by the Hungarian Szokolay; the comparatively unknown Czech Petrovics and Penderecki entries; several of the British school—Sir Michael Tippett, Ian Hamilton, Malcolm Williamson, Gordon Crosse, and Nicholas Maw; some of the redoubtable Teutons—Kelemann, Zimmerman, Killmayer. Orff and Henze we have always with us.

3

And who can account for the recent popularity of Delius? I feel like daring someone to put on, at last, Sessions's *Montezuma* and to stage Busoni's *Doktor Faust*—but perhaps a hero has already taken the dare. Perhaps the presence here of some of these challenging works may stimulate performance. These are not recommendations, to be sure, but rather represent the joy of a researcher unearthing treasures that may be unknown by the generality. After the work I did on it, I should be pleased to witness a performance of Rafael Kubelik's *Cornelia Faroli*. Half seriously, I asked the late and mourned Göran Gentele if he might possibly mount the work of his artistic director. He laughed, and answered that he thought it might be considered improper just then.

As for the Americans, they crowd in upon us in ever increasing torrents—a miracle, when producing opportunities seem to wane and not wax in this generation of our performing arts discontent. One or two turn out works in such profusion that it becomes almost an embarrassment of (possible) riches—how many to include?

And on the other hand, suppose a composer has toiled over one or more scores and the compiler of this volume has repeatedly asked him or her to submit them or answer a questionnaire and the answers are willing but vague and the material never appears—how to account for their omission? An author-editor's patience is not quite inexhaustible. Those composers who did cooperate are listed in the Acknowledgments.

It seems to me in retrospect that I was in a time machine, darting back to pick up early Mozart, Verdi, Wagner, Puccini, as many Offenbach as possible, and certain hitherto omitted Bellini, Rossini, Donizetti, Massenet, Rimsky-Korsakov, Weber, and others, and seesawing back and forth for Strauss, Stravinsky, Prokofiev, Martinu, and so on; then venturing into fairly uncharted spaces for later Britten and some of the unknowns. For other gems, oddities, discoveries, and duty calls, I leave you to the mercies of the indices and the book itself.

Many omissions I have already explained on the grounds of time (although there were several quite willful and arbitrary ones), but a word is due the lack of certain categories. A few examples that might be classified as "children's" opera, or Christmas or religious works, or operettas and musical comedies, will be found, generally for their intrinsic worth, but the categories themselves have been omitted—understandably so, I believe. Other volumes would be required to do them justice, and in fact, the recent Central Opera Service listing of repertoires includes dozens of examples of the first two, so I refer you to that invaluable institution and to Maria F. Rich, editor of the *Central Opera Service Bulletin*.

Now for the specifics and the explanation of each section of the material. Much of this is repeated from the first volume because it remains pertinent; some data are changed or eliminated.

One of the first criteria for performance is the duration of a work: a producer needs to know whether an opera will fill an entire evening or must

4

be paired with another. For this reason, operas are separated into two classifications, long and short, under which categories titles appear alphabetically.

For practical purposes the line of demarcation between the long and the short was set arbitrarily at 90 minutes. Operas of a minimum length of one and a half hours may fill an evening or be combined with a shorter work. Still, you may be surprised to find *Dantons Tod* (78 minutes), *Katya Kabanová* (88 minutes), and *Die Kluge* (90 minutes) in the short list, since often they stand alone in performance. Once again there are more long works than short covered.

All titles are listed alphabetically in the table of contents under the divisions Long and Short. Every effort has been made to avoid ambiguity and to facilitate finding an opera even at the expense of many repetitions. Both the original titles (except the Russian, which are given in English alone, since I believe Russian phonetics are apt to look ridiculous and convey poorly a true pronunciation) and their English translations appear, and in a few cases a third title in another language or a variant translation is shown, both in the entry itself and in the table of contents. Thus one can find *The Stag King* and *Il Re Servo* as well as *König Hirsch*. With the exception of the Russians, Czechs and Hungarians, the original title has been given precedence at the head of each entry, followed by the English translation and by any variants.

Both duration and orchestrations, incidentally, proved the most elusive to pin down. After countless questions about both (even involving appeals to Europe), I had to give up in many cases. (The answers would come back: "It's full-length," or "a full evening." And silence on the matter of orchestra.) Information on both was occasionally gleaned from that bulwark against ignorance, G. E. Lessing's *Handbuch des Opern-Repertoires* and other German sources in the Library of the Performing Arts at Lincoln Center, but comparable volumes for the French and Italian repertoire seem nonexistent. Consequently, I beg to be excused for omissions in these categories—I tried for years and on two continents! At least we are certain in most cases that the opera *is* full-length, although I must confess that occasionally I have my doubts about that 90-minute demarcation.

Introductory Paragraph. This includes the name of the composer and his dates; the original language, author, and source of the libretto; the commission, if any; the place and date of the premiere; versions or adaptations; classification of drama and of the structure and style of the music; place and time of the action; number of acts and scenes; overall timing.

Designation in a dramatic sense is made—"tragedy," "comedy," "farce," etc.—with occasional qualification, such as "historical drama" or "Oriental farce." (Note the absence of such classifications as "opéra comique," "operetta," and "opera seria," which are used only occasionally to clarify a historical reference.)

Musical description or classification proved to be one of the most difficult tasks: to describe structure, style, and mood without resorting to opinion, still preserving the individuality of each opera. Certain formulas resulted after long experiment and discussion.

Structurally, operas are divided into two broad categories: (1) those with mainly set numbers (often specified as arias, duets, ensembles, etc.); these may be separated by recitatives, either patter (*secco*) or accompanied, or they may be closely knit into the orchestral texture; (2) those which are "composed-through," expressed here as "continuous texture," where the orchestral web is unbroken and often of highest importance, and set numbers do not appear or are inseparable from the texture. The presence of overture or prelude and of orchestral interludes is generally noted.

Unusual difficulties of orchestra are indicated. Harmonic properties are often touched upon, particularly where specific influences are apparent: folk, dissonance, atonality, polytonality, twelve-tone (serial technique), aleatoric, microtonal. There are contemporary idioms difficult to encapsule, and explanations may not tell the whole story; for this I beg pardon and only hope that the somewhat skeletal descriptions will prove adequate to stimulate curiosity and further investigation on the part of the producer.

Style, when not otherwise labeled, is to be inferred from the description of story, structure, and orchestral and vocal specifications. "Verismo" (the characteristic of the Italian realistic school), is indicated where applicable.

Classifications of vocal line include melodious; patterned after speech (I usually avoid the term "parlando"); declamatory; florid. The general description is particularized under individual roles.

I have not attempted to suggest staging beyond the specifications of locale and time; to accept any one authority would be unfair, while to compare several would require more space than is available.

Act and Scene Divisions. This is generally a separate entry for long operas, but is incorporated in the introductory paragraph of many short ones. Where different versions exist, these have been specified if possible.

Timings by Acts. At best, timings are only approximate, as every performance is subject to fluctuation because of cuts or individual tastes. Overall duration, as well as timing by acts and occasionally scenes, is based upon information from the Metropolitan Opera, New York City Opera, and other companies, and from publishers and composers. In too many cases, no timings were available for various reasons, among them the lack of contemporary performances.

Synopsis of Plot. To write a short synopsis of an opera and keep it clear and sensible is very difficult. To attain to any literary distinction in such writing is virtually impossible. Outlining the story by acts soon proved impractical for reasons of space. Very few operas can be thus clarified in neat compartments. Of course, more detail is given for new or unfamiliar operas, which form the bulk of the contents.

No matter how spare the outline of the plot, I tried to introduce each major character in order to establish relationships and relative importance.

Roles. These are divided into major, lesser, speaking, mute and bit. The character's name, type of voice, vocal requirements, and range are listed.

Information about requirements for any specific role can be seen at a glance in the various sections. The type of voice, with few exceptions, ap-

6

pears in every instance; often special problems are mentioned: the need for agility, sustained tone, high or low tessitura, and so on. Where no special requirements appear, the role may be presumed to call for average vocal abilities and portrayal of the character as revealed in the synopsis.

The exact compass of a role does not represent the complete picture of a vocal characterization, but it serves as a useful signpost. Extremes of range are most often indicated, together with mention of tessitura and optional notes. Occasionally only the top or bottom extreme is given. Where the range is omitted, no special problem exists.

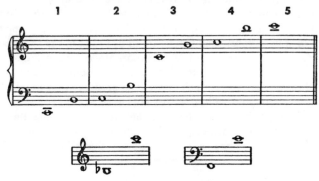

The accompanying key to range symbols has been simplified from the older method, and employs capital letters throughout, numbering the ranges from 1 to 5, beginning with low C. The upper part of the accompanying illustration is the key to the range symbols. The lower part shows, on the left, a sample soprano range (Bb2 to C5) and, on the right, a sample bass range (F1 to E3).

Chorus. To show the minimum chorus required, the parts have been divided into, for example, SSAATTBB. This means that at some point the score shows two lines each for soprano, alto, tenor, and bass. Occasionally specific information is given about the desirability of large forces, the special duties of the chorus, the division into several choruses, the characters the chorus must portray. The number and complexity of this last requirement will indicate to the producer the necessity for supers, which generally have not otherwise been specified. The musical importance of the chorus is noted occasionally in the introductory paragraph.

Ballet. The genre and the approximate number of dancers required, where available, are listed. The place in the opera and whatever detailed information appears in the score or is known from experience also appear.

Production Problems or Notes. Although each producer or director may want to solve his problems for himself, certain problems are inherent in some operas, such as the elaborate Meyerbeer productions and various apotheoses, apparitions, and disappearances. Wherever a production problem is implicit in or vital to the story, it is mentioned. Several operas require quick changes of scene during musical interludes of prescribed length; this fact is noted.

Orchestra. Complete instrumentation, including stage requirements, is given (*Stage* means instruments either onstage or behind the scenes). Doubling instruments are shown in parentheses, e.g., 2 fl (picc) means that the second flute doubles piccolo. Wherever possible, the number of percussion players is given rather than a complete list of percussion instruments, although this appears occasionally.

Material. Getting the music for performance of an opera may not be so simple as one might imagine. The producer will probably want to rent all the musical materials as few companies own their own music. Going about this has become more complicated by reason of the state of flux in which the music publishing industry has found itself in the past decade. Firms have merged or gone out of business, so that the former list hardly applies. The publishers of works represented herein are to be found in the list of abbreviations. I refer you once again to COS for more up-to-date information.

Because the repertoire collected here is often obscure or new, publishers have not always been easy to track down. The producer may indeed find that he has to resort to public libraries for copies of vocal scores, or to composers or fellow producers—if the latter are inclined to share the treasures they have gleaned so painstakingly. Furthermore, few of these old or new operas will be found in the only rental library that still exists—Mapleson. The Kalmus catalogue contains several, but Tams-Witmark no longer handles opera material.

Upon the advice of most of the publishers consulted, I have omitted some of the details that formerly appeared under "Material," giving only the publisher (abbreviated), in which case it is taken for granted that all the material is for rent. Because prices fluctuate so wildly—mostly upward—I was asked not to include the cost of vocal scores. Where the notation "VS*" appears, it means that the vocal score is for sale. Otherwise it is on a rental basis.

Information about librettos or translations is seldom included, because Central Opera Service valiantly provides these matters in its highly efficient bulletins. After all, *Opera Production I* was planned as a supplement to the COS Manual, and as the latter expanded and served producers and public in so many fields, the necessity for such material under hard cover decreased.

The omission of the section covering production photographs was decided upon for two reasons: the repertoire and the lack of research assistance. Many of the works included have not been given in the United States, as a quick glance at the index of *Opera News* proved. The second reason is even more cogent: I must plead poverty as far as this type of associate diggers is concerned.

Similarly, performance data are limited, for essentially similar reasons. Venturesome producers will be happy to know that many of the treasures lurking in these pages will come as novelties to the American public. And even those that have been seen here and there are not completely documented; a selection from the COS bulletins and certain producers seemed sufficient to let you know the work had been done at least once.

8

Performing companies are not cued by number as before, but are abbreviated in the text clearly enough (it is hoped) for the reader to identify them. Still, yet again, I ask that you consult the COS list of performing units, which is kept up to date, as mine cannot be.

The index by composers, the final element in the book, gives original titles only again, except for the Russians, Czechs, and Hungarians. It offers, first, a convenient check on the length of the opera: after each title is an L (for long) or an Sh (for short).

Since the size of the orchestra often proves a determining factor for producers (especially in workshops), this information is given in the index by composers as a symbol after each title: SO means a small orchestra; MO a medium orchestra; LO a large orchestra. SO includes the chamber orchestra or even smaller ensemble. MO often approximates the usual "Mozart" orchestra or the Rossini orchestra of *Otello*. When winds and brass exceed pairs (except for the usual three trombones), when the percussion is augmented, or when unusual instruments or stage instruments are added, the orchestra has been designated as LO. The producer will of course want to turn to the opera in question for more detailed study of orchestral requirements.

Because the number of operas covered fully is substantially larger than in the first volume, no supplementary list appears. Instead, here is a brief notice of works known to be in preparation, possibly of interest to the ambitious producer, or new works too late to be included in full.

Bloch's *Macbeth*, for some years rather controversial, has recently come into focus, particularly with a fine production by the Juilliard American Opera Center in May 1973. Although too late to include in the regular contents, I should like to mention it as eminently viable. With its continuous texture (in a moderately large orchestra) which is reminiscent of Debussy, Wagner and Strauss, yet stamped with the individuality later to become so powerful, its two strong characterizations and dramatic construction, and the English version by Alex Cohen and the composer after Edmond Fleg's libretto, which retains actual lines as well as the flavor of Shakespeare, this *Macbeth* offers a great deal to an ambitious producer. The Macduff scene was omitted in the Juilliard version, which brought the duration to about two hours.

OPERAS IN PREPARATION OR TOO LATE

Beeson, Jack. *Cap'n Jinks of the Horse Marines.* Libretto in English by Sheldon Harnick, based on the play by Clyde Fitch. "Comedy in music." Setting: New York City in the 1870's. Two or three acts (approx 120 min). Major Roles: lyr-col s, c, t, lyr bar, bs bar, bs, one deaf-and-dumb character; 10 minor roles. Medium orchestra.

Britten, Benjamin. *Death in Venice.* Based on Thomas Mann's novel. Premiere scheduled for Aldeburgh Festival, June 16, 1973. American premiere: Metropolitan Opera, October 18, 1974.

Crosse, Gordon. *The Story of Vasco*. Libretto by Ted Hughes based on Georges Schehadé's play, *L'Histoire de Vasco*. Setting: An unspecified war, mid-19th century; French military costumes.

Crosse, Gordon. *The Wheel of the World*. Based on Chaucer's *Canterbury Tales*. Extended new version at Aldeburgh Festival, June 5, 1973.

Hamilton, Ian. *The Catiline Conspirators*. After Ben Jonson. Premiere scheduled for 1974.

Henderson, Alva. *Medea*. Premiere: San Diego, November 29, 1972.

Kohs, Ellis B. *Rhinoceros*. After Ionesco's play. Four singers, three actors, chamber ensemble, and eight-track tape system. About 75 min.

Maderna, Bruno. A modern *Satyricon*. To be published by Salabert. American premiere: Tanglewood, August 2, 1973.

Mayer, William. *A Death in the Family*. Adapted by composer from the play *All the Way Home* by Tad Mosel, which was based on James Agee's novel, *A Death in the Family*. Full length.

Pasatieri, Thomas. *The Seagull*. Libretto by Kenward Elmslie, based on Chekhov. Premiere scheduled for Houston, March 5, 1974.

Reif, Paul. *Portrait in Brownstone*. Libretto by Henry Butler after the novel by Louis Auchincloss. Drama. Setting: New York City, 1900–1965. Continuous texture, atonal, vocal lines melodic and declamatory. Two acts, seventeen scenes (150 min). Vocal score in draft only.

NEW OPERAS COMMISSIONED FOR BICENTENNIAL, 1976

Floyd, Carlisle. Title to be announced. Houston. Premiere: March 1976.

Ginastera, Alberto. *Barrabas*. New York City Opera. Premiere: 1976.

Henderson, Alva. *The Unforgiven*. (Indians in Texas.) San Diego, tentative.

Kastle, Leonard. *The Pariahs*. (Whaling era.) Seattle. Premiere: Summer 1976.

Kirchner, Leon. *Henderson, the Rain King*. (After Saul Bellow.) New York City Opera. Premiere: 1976.

London, Edwin. Title to be announced (on Lincoln). Lake George. Premiere: Summer 1976.

Pasatieri, Thomas. *Ines de Castro*. (14th-century Portugal.) Baltimore. Premiere: February 1976.

Penderecki, Krzystof. Title to be announced. Chicago. Premiere: 1976.

Seigmeister, Elie. Title to be announced (on Louisiana history). Shreveport Symphony. Premiere: 1976.

NOTE: Hawaii will commission a new original Hawaiian opera. Other new operas planned are the following: Gerhard Track, *Minnequa*. Pueblo Civic Symphony, January 1976. Dexter Morrill, Colgate University, 1976. Also: Sousa, *El Capitan*, at Dallas; Barton, *The Disappointment* (first American Opera) by After Dinner Co.; MacFeeley, *They Nobly Dar'd*, rewriting commissioned by New England Regional Opera; Meyerowitz, *Emily Dickinson*, in first professional performances by Goldovsky Opera.

10

PRODUCTION PROBLEMS IN HANDEL'S OPERAS

by Randolph Mickelson

A THOROUGH study of how to prepare a Handelian opera score for performance would take several large volumes. I will therefore limit myself here to making a few salient points, both specific and general, and to indicating a list of necessary reading.

No conductor should, in my opinion, attempt a performance of Handelian or, indeed, any other 18th-century work—Haydn and Mozart included—without having first read and absorbed the pertinent material contained in Quantz's *On Playing the Flute*, which is fortunately available in an excellent English translation by E. B. Reilly (New York: Free Press). Other suggested reading is Tartini's treatise on the violin, *Traité des agréments de la musique*, E. R. Jacobi, editor, with English translation by C. Girdlestone (Celle, 1961); and Tosi's *The Italian School of Florid Song* (London, 1743; New York: Johnson Reprint, 1969, facsimile edition). Also helpful are the examples of ornaments and cadenzas in H.-P. Schmitz, *Die Kunst der Verzierung im 18. Jahrhundert* (Kassel: Bärenreiter, 1965).

This is only a beginning list, and although it will not provide a complete solution to the problems, it will indicate to an imaginative and unafraid conductor the paths in which he can give free play to his musicality.

To supplement this reading list with my own thoughts and findings, the result of experience both in performing and recording situations as well as in research in the literally hundreds of other authoritative sources, I shall discuss the size and treatment of the orchestra and the appropriate voices and singing styles.

The instrumental balance of 18th-century opera orchestras was radically different from that of the modern orchestra. Although a larger orchestra may be required because of the modern theater's greater size and—an important difference—the sunken orchestra pit (Handel's orchestra played on the level of what is today called the "orchestra seats"), it is imperative that the 18th-century balance of sonority be preserved. If it is not, Handel's orchestration (he knew what he was doing) will be weakened, and the grand effects of, for example, the massed woodwinds will be transformed into chamber music.

In Handel's time, the most important Italian repertory opera houses in Europe had a virtually standardized string section of six first violins, six sec-

11

ond violins (the two violin lines are always of equal importance), three violas (the viola part is always subservient and often merely doubles the bass line at the octave), four celli, and two double basses. The large number of bass instruments is crucial. Eighteenth-century music is, to a greater degree than music of another period, constructed over the bass line, which must, therefore, be substantial. Two harpsichords were used; 18th-century harpsichords were loud. (If yours are feeble, I suggest amplification so that the singers, as well as the audience, can hear them.) Four oboes—crucial!—and three bassoons were customary. Flutes, trumpets, drums, horns, etc., when required, were used, one per part. Handel seems to have preferred four bassoons but otherwise followed his Continental contemporaries. For a large theater, this list might be enlarged to ten first violins, ten second violins, five violas, six celli, three or four double basses, six oboes, and six (!) bassoons.

I shall now indicate some specific pitfalls in the Handelian scoring, and, in doing so, shall refer to the popular *Giulio Cesare* (see *Opera Production I*).

First of all, the German Handel Society edition by Chrysander, which was recently reprinted by Gregg Press of New Jersey, offers the only available Handel opera scores that are not either tampered with or downright mutilated.

Handel did not always indicate when the oboes and bassoons should play, but an indication like the *tutti* (p. 8) often means that they should. In other places, he says *tutti violini*, which means that they shouldn't. However, even when the oboes and bassoons play in an aria, they must be silent when the part has a *p*. You will find that there is usually such an orchestra *p* during the singing. Be guided in the end by the writing in each piece and by how it sounds in your theater.

The oboes and bassoons almost always play together. The exceptions are given by Handel. In the aria (p. 45), we have *violini unisoni*—no oboes— then in bar 11, the bassoons play. The reason Handel wrote *violini unisoni* was to indicate that, although the bassoons play, the oboes do not. The effect is rather grotesque and is an excellent musical characterization of the Egyptian general's rather rough protestations of love for Cleopatra.

When there are violin but no viola parts, as on page 34, the violas should *not* be silent but should double the celli an octave higher. Adjust the viola part so that it does not go higher than the vocal or violin line, by dropping an octave at such places.

Following Quantz, add trills and appogiaturas copiously to the violin parts. They add a great brilliance and were expected by Handel. Flute parts, like the one on page 15, should have even more trills than the violins. I suggest, for example, bar 1, trill on the C♯; bar 2 on the A; bar 3 on the A; bar 4 on the G. When the text mentions birds (see p. 60), an abundance of trills is indicated. When the words are sad, add appogiaturas instead. Let the text guide you in all of these matters. If the opera seems too long, cut an occasional *da capo*, but cut the middle section as well or the aria will end in the wrong key. There is evidence that Handel did this too. I think, however, that it is a grave mistake to rearrange the order of the arias. For example, in a performance of *Cesare* I heard the arias of Cleopatra switched around, so that "Piangeró la sorte mia" was relocated from the last act to the first. Cleopatra's music deepens in emotional intensity as the opera progresses, and this misplacement of her tragic utterance is equivalent to switching "Addio del passato" to the first act of *La Traviata*.

In the opening of the second act of *Cesare*, the use of the onstage orchestra antedates that of *Don Giovanni* by sixty-four years. It is a pity to dispense with the spectacular stage effect of the princely garden entertainment with which Handel and Cleopatra hope to bedazzle, charm, and seduce Caesar—and the audience. There is a model mountain in the garden, which, to everyone's surprise, suddenly splits open to disclose Cleopatra and the exotic (Egyptian?) orchestra. Baroque operas were, and should be, full of baroque stage effects; they were and should be grand entertainment, not a deadly serious bore; and a lot of stylized posing is no substitute for a few opening mountains, disappearing palaces, flying gods and goddesses, and even some live birds (see *Rinaldo*, Act I, Scene 6).

Another point related to keeping the enjoyment level high is the choice of tempi. Such words as *allegro* and *adagio* meant something very different in Handel's time from what they mean today. *Andante*, for instance, meant precisely that: going, or, in other words, "Don't Let It Drag." Now it indicates a slowish tempo. I have heard Caesar's "Va tacito e nascosto" (p. 40), for example, sung like a dirge, exactly the opposite of Handel's warning— Keep It Moving. Without going into a whole study of this subject, I would advise conductors to follow their musical feelings, rather than the misleading tempo words and, in general, to take the fastest tempi that singers will allow. Even slow arias should go surprisingly fast. The slowness is usually in the words, not in the notes.

The casting of these operas is not so great a problem as some think. The brisk tempi and the correct orchestration will help the singers a great deal to feel the style and expressiveness of this music. First and foremost, singers must not only understand every word of the recitatives and of the arias, but they must be able to declaim them in an expressive way, as a good Shakespearean actor would do. These operas are not static, but they do contain soliloquies; and, like *Hamlet* or *Macbeth*, they will collapse if the words are not rendered with the utmost sensitivity to their meaning and emotional impact. Remember, Handel did not say to his company, "Listen, Verdi and Puccini haven't been born yet, so cool it." All the descriptions of 18th-century singing indicate that it was liberally peppered with sobs, gasps, *crescendi, diminuendi*—in fact, all the devices of expressive singing. At the same time, charm was an important ingredient of 18th-century culture, and some of Handel's music is frankly coy. Therefore, the singer should be guided by the words and music and be coy in the coy arias (p. 30, 38), storm in the rage arias (p. 67), trill often in the bird arias (p. 59), and deliver the great soliloquies (p. 82) with the intensity and theatricality of a fine Shakespearean actor. In general, the singer must find the predominant effect or emotion of each aria, get as far into it as he can, and not be timid—or worse—tepid.

13

In casting Handel's prima donna roles, a good point of reference is that Bellini's *Norma* is one of the last operas that, while Romantic, still embodies much of the 18th-century *opera seria* tradition. Since there is a more or less living tradition of performance practice for *Norma*, a comparison will be helpful. For instance, note the importance of dramatic declamation in the recitatives. The vocal writing of the part of Norma is very similar to that of Cleopatra and, indeed, to all the music that Handel wrote for Francesca Cuzzoni. The heavy dramatic arias or sections of arias are low and sustained (compare "Piangeró la sorte mia" and "In mia man' al fin tu sei"). But when the drama turns to rage, the tessitura sails up (not *too* high), and the writing becomes somewhat florid—neither Cleopatra nor Norma has to sing music as florid as Semiramide's. This similarity is borne out by the fact that most of today's important Normas have had striking success with Cleopatra as well.

Therefore, I would say that to cast a Cuzzoni role, look for a soprano who could sing and act a fine Norma. For the parts written for Anna Strada, Alcina for example, the tessitura is rather higher, but the singer's strong points should be similar.

A word about casting the castrato parts. It is absolutely unsuitable (*pace* Lang et al.!) to give them to a bass or baritone. The tessitura of castrato roles is low, and a lot of coloratura sung by a bass on the lowest notes of his voice will sound like gargling, no matter how great a singer he is. Besides, this practice will also transpose the vocal part down an octave, thereby often forcing a singer to sing below the bass line of the orchestra, which will do a horrifying violence to the harmony. Handel's own solution to this problem when a castrato was not available was to give the part to a female alto or mezzo-soprano, making appropriate transpositions. Another possibility is that, in the unlikely event that a tenor is available with the requisite agility, size of voice, and heroic timbre, the castrato parts be given to him; be sure that the part is suitably transposed. The mezzo-soprano is still the best bet, however; and if any doubt remains, imagine a bass singing Mozart's Cherubino, Rossini's Arsace, or (perish the thought!) Strauss's Octavian.

On the question of vocal ornamentation, space permits only a few words. Most arias require a cadenza at the end of each section, making a total of three. They should show off the best notes and vocal tricks of the singer, be sung on one breath, and should be arranged so that the third cadenza is the flashiest. On the point of the *da capo* ornaments, they should amount to almost a total rewrite of the vocal line. An audience cannot be asked to sit through thirty-odd arias, each of which is sung twice in relentless succession. There exist in old books and manuscripts many examples of the way in which the *da capo*'s were rewritten; but unfortunately, almost none of these examples has found its way into modern print. It has taken me some years and much travel to assemble my collection of such material, and therefore there is no better solution I can offer a conductor or producer who, because of other obligations, must be a relatively casual student of this music, other than to advise him not to be timid, to use every bit of musical and compositional skill at his disposal, and to remember that baroque music should be *baroque.*

Here I think I should quote Tosi, the most authoritative author of Handel's time: "In the first part [of an aria] nothing is required but the simplest ornaments of good taste and few, so that the composition remains simple, plain, and pure; in the second, they expect that to this purity some artful graces be added, by which a connoisseur can hear that the ability of the singer is greater; and, in the repeat of the first part, he that does not vary it for the better is no great master."

BIOGRAPHICAL NOTE: Randolph Mickelson is a musicologist, conductor, and vocal coach, specializing in the style of early music. He has prepared the scores of Shield's *Rosina,* Graun's *Montezuma,* and Bononcini's *Griselda* for Richard Bonynge and Joan Sutherland, many songs for Montserrat Caballé, as well as Handel's *Giulio Cesare,* and ornamented the arias for her prize-winning Rossini Rarities record. Other artists who have consulted him on early operas are Martina Arroyo, Grace Bumbry, Fiorenza Cossotto, Justino Diaz, Marilyn Horne, Evelyn Lear, Luciano Pavarotti, Ruggiero Raimondi, Katia Ricciarelli, Renata Scotto, and Beverly Sills. Among other theaters, Milan's La Scala has featured his work, notably the revival of Rossini's *L'Assedio di Corinto.* Q. E.

Long Operas

LONG OPERAS

🎬 Adriana Lecouvreur

Music by Francesco Cilèa (1866–1950). Libretto in Italian by Arturo Colautti, from the play by Eugène Scribe and Ernest Legouvé. Premiere: Milan, November 6, 1902. Romantic drama based on historical characters. Accompanied recitatives, set numbers, conventional harmonies. Brief prelude to each act. Setting: Paris, 1730. Four acts (130 min).

ACT I: Greenroom of the Comédie Française (36 min). ACT II: A villa outside Paris (32 min). ACT III: Palace of the Prince de Bouillon (28 min). ACT IV: Adriana's house (34 min).

Synopsis. Before the evening performance, Adriana confesses to her mentor, the stage director Michonnet, that she loves a soldier (in reality Maurizio, the Count of Saxony), forestalling Michonnet's own declaration of love for her. Maurizio is playing a double game: the Princess de Bouillon is his mistress. The Prince himself, with an actress for a mistress, invites the company to her villa after the show. Maurizio, accepting an invitation from the Princess, breaks his date with Adriana—but the entire intrigue comes to a head in the villa. Maurizio, by now in love with Adriana, is uneasy with the Princess, and manages to hide her when the others appear—she should not be seen in such company. When Adriana enters and discovers his true identity, Maurizio enlists her help to smuggle the Princess incognito out of the villa. Michonnet gives Adriana a bracelet the Princess drops in her flight; this, together with a bunch of violets Adriana has given Maurizio and he has, in turn, handed to the Princess when she questions him suspiciously, play crucial parts in the tragedy that ensues. Maurizio is still on a secret political mission when the Prince gives a great ball, and the Princess, recognizing by her voice that Adriana is her rival, watches the reaction of the actress when the news of Maurizio's wounding in a duel is announced. But it is false news; Maurizio enters and relates his recent triumphs in battle. A festive ballet on the Judgment of Paris is performed, at the end of which Paris presents the prize not to Venus but to the Princess. The latter begins to goad Adriana, who produces the bracelet in revenge, but it has no effect. Now the actress is asked to perform, and recites a speech from Racine's *Phèdre*, using Racine's words to brand the Princess a strumpet, provoked by Maurizio's fickleness in again flirting with the Princess. She is escorted out in disgrace, and retires from the theater. Spending her birthday ill and alone, she is touched by the visit of Michonnet with a precious gift, and also by the visit of four colleagues, who beg her to return. Another gift arrives: the faded bouquet she has given Maurizio with a card from him. Deeply hurt, she presses the flowers to her face and thus seals her fate. For the bouquet has been poisoned by the Princess and the card forged. Too late, Maurizio, summoned by Michonnet, arrives; Adriana dies in his arms.

Major Roles. ADRIANA LECOUVREUR (s); needs dramatic flair; sustained lyric singing; C3 to B♭4. PRINCESS DE BOUILLON (m-s); strong personality; B2 to A4. MAURIZIO (t); dramatic style; E2 to B3. MICHONNET (bar); B♭1 to G♭3.

Lesser Roles. MLLE JOUVENOT, actress (s). MLLE DANGEVILLE, actress (m-s). POISSON, actor (t). QUINAULT, actor (bs). ABBÉ DE CHAZEUIL, a frivolous priest (t). PRINCE DE BOUILLON (bs).

Bit Role. MAJORDOMO (sp).

Chorus. SSATTBB. Ladies, gentlemen, servants.

Ballet. In Act III.

Orchestra. 2 fl, picc, 2 ob, Eng hrn, 2 cl, 2 bsn, 4 hrn, 3 trp, 3 trb, tuba, timp, perc, harp, cel, strings.

Material. Bel (Son).

Performances. Met: 1968–69. Conn. Op. (Hartford): 10.18.69.

Die Aegyptische Helena · Helen in Egypt

Music by Richard Strauss (1864–1949). Libretto in German by Hugo von Hofmannsthal. Premiere: Dresden, June 6, 1928. Revised for Vienna (1933), with cuts and substitutions; addition of trio. Symbolical drama, based on a fragment of Euripides. Continuous texture; difficult vocal line. Brief prelude. Setting: near Egypt, after the Trojan War (1193–1184 B.C.). Two acts (150 min).

ACT I: Islet of Aithra near Egyptian coast. ACT II: Palm grove at foot of Atlas.

Synopsis. According to this story, Helen was never in Troy; a double was substituted for her, while the famous beauty was sent to Atlas in Africa. Before the curtain, Menelaus has recovered his wife after the Trojan War, but determines to put her to death because of the bloodshed she has caused. Before he can accomplish this, his ship is wrecked at the command of a sorceress, Aithra, daughter of an Egyptian king and beloved of the god Poseidon. Aithra has learned of Helen's plight from an Omniscient Sea-shell (Poseidon's emissary). Entering Aithra's palace, Menelaus attempts to carry out his vow, but Aithra causes him to hear once again the battle sounds of Troy, and he rushes out, then returns in the belief that he has killed both Paris and Helen. The sorceress meanwhile has given Helen a potion which brings forgetfulness of evil, and shows her just waking to convince Menelaus that she has never been to Troy. The newly reunited couple are wafted to a land at the foothills of the Atlas Mountains, where the names of Helen and

Troy have never been heard. Menelaus is still troubled by his imagined murder of Helen, and believes the beautiful woman with him to be a phantom. A wandering sheik Altair and his son Da-Ud approach the couple, and at once bow down to this loveliest of women. It is the old story repeated: Troy could happen again. Menelaus is jealous, but consents to go hunting with Da-Ud, soon, however, slaying the young man, who reminds him of Paris. Meanwhile, Helen has obtained the antidote to the forgetfulness potion, and persuades Menelaus to drink it with her. She has chosen the harder way: to make Menelaus forgive her misdeeds rather than to be deluded into believing her innocent. At once he sees her as real and attempts to kill her. But she wins him with her smile. Altair brings his forces to conquer Menelaus and Helen, but Aithra once more intervenes. The child Hermione appears, asking her father Menelaus, Where is my beautiful mother? This is a further bridge for the reunion of the two; they enter upon a new life.

Major Roles. HELENA (dram s); high tessitura; A2 to C5 (one C♯5). MENELAUS (dram t); sustained; B♭1 to B3. AITHRA (s); sustained; some coloratura; trill; A♭2 to sustained C5 (one D5 in ensemble). ALTAIR (bar); F1 to F♯3. DA-UD (t); D2 to G♯3. SEA-SHELL (c); A♭2 to D4.

Lesser Roles. SERVANTS (s and m-s).

Bit Roles. HERMIONE (s). ARMED YOUTHS (t).

Chorus. SATB. Warriors, slaves, eunuchs. Six small solos: Elves (s, s, c); Altair's slaves (s, s, m-s).

Orchestra. 4 fl, 2 ob, Eng hrn, 3 cl, bs cl, 3 bsn, 6 hrn, 6 trp, 4 trb, tuba, timp, perc, 2 harp, cel, organ, cembalo, strings. *Stage*: 6 ob, 6 cl, 2 tamb, 4 tri, timp, 4 hrn, 2 trp, 2 trb (deleted in revised vers).

Material. B & H. VS (g)*.

Performances. Bost. Sym.: 3.26.65 (conc). Litt. Orch. (NYC): 4.11.67 (conc).

🜨 L'Africaine · L'Africana · The African Maid

Music by Giacomo Meyerbeer (1791–1864). Libretto in French by Eugène Scribe. Premiere: Paris, April 28, 1865. Romantic tragedy on a grand scale. Accompanied recitatives, set arias, and ensembles. Requires mature vocal techniques and stamina in all roles. Overture; interludes before Acts II, III, and IV. Conventional harmonic structure. Some exotic Eastern flavor. Setting: Lisbon, a ship at sea, and India, early 16th century. Five acts, six scenes (145 min).

ACT I: Portuguese royal council chamber, Lisbon (40 min). ACT II: A prison cell (30 min). ACT III: Aboard Don Pedro's ship at sea (20 min). ACT IV: Outside an Indian palace (35 min). ACT V i: Garden of Selika's palace (10 min); ii: A promontory overlooking the sea (10 min).

Synopsis. Inez, daughter of the Portuguese Admiral Don Diego, loves Vasco da Gama, who is presumed lost in a sea disaster but returns, bringing two natives of a new land he has discovered. They are the Indian queen Selika and her attendant Nelusco. Don Diego wishes Inez to marry Don Pedro, president of the royal council. Upon Vasco's return Don Pedro orders him jailed on charges of insulting the council, which turned down Vasco's proposal to explore the new land. Selika, her rank unknown to the Portuguese, also loves Vasco, and finds her way to his prison cell to confess her love and to warn him of Nelusco's dangerous jealousy. Inez agrees to marry Don Pedro, thus freeing Vasco from jail. Don Pedro sets out to explore the new land himself, taking Inez, with Selika and Nelusco as guides. Nelusco plans to blow up the ship. Knowing this, Vasco outfits his own ship and overtakes Don Pedro at sea. His attempts to warn Don Pedro are rebuffed, and Vasco is seized. A storm drives the ship aground, and savages, at Nelusco's command, slay all but a few, who are taken prisoner. Selika is welcomed back as queen. She prevents Vasco's murder by claiming he is her husband. The marriage rites are barely celebrated when Inez arrives, and Vasco's love for her is rekindled. Rather than have the lovers killed, the understanding Selika orders Nelusco to provide them with a ship in which to return to Portugal. As they sail away, Selika breathes deeply from a poison-laden mancanilla tree and dies. Nelusco finds her body and himself shares her death.

Major Roles. INEZ (dram s); high tessitura; extremely florid throughout; B2 to C5. SELIKA (s); florid, low tessitura (might be undertaken by a true dram m-s); Ab2 to B4. VASCO DA GAMA (dram t); high tessitura; dramatic; florid; C2 to B3. NELUSCO (bar); florid; A1 to F#3 (G3 opt). DON PEDRO (bs); florid; F1 to E3. DON DIEGO (bs); F1 to E3.

Lesser Roles. ANNA, Inez' attendant (m-s). DON ALVAR, a council member (t). GRAND INQUISITOR (bs). HIGH PRIEST OF BRAHMA (bar).

Chorus. SSAATTBB. Priests, inquisitors, soldiers, sailors, Indians, attendants, ladies. Solo quartet for TTBB in Act III.

Ballet. Indian March and ballet, Act IV.

Orchestra. 2 picc, 2 fl, 2 ob, Eng hrn, 2 cl, bs cl, 4 bsn, Eb sax, 4 hrn, 2 corn, 2 trp, 3 trb, tuba, timp (3), perc (3), harp, strings. *Stage:* 2 ob, 2 hrn, 2 bsn, 2 harp, harm, dr, bells, 2 little sax, 4 sop sax, 4 alto sax, 2 bar sax, 4 trp, 6 bs sax.

Production Problems. Ship scene requires lengthwise section showing between-decks areas and cabin interiors. Storm.

Material. Bel (Ri).

Performances. Op. Orch. of N.Y.: 4.20.72 (conc). San Fran.: 11.3.72.

🖾 Agamemnon

Music by Iain Hamilton (1922–). Libretto in English by the composer after translation by Philip Vellacott of Aeschylus's *Agamemnon*. Unperformed. Tragedy. Contemporary idiom. Vocal line difficult; often patterned after speech; declamatory. No overture. Brief interludes between scenes. Setting: The palace of Atreus, ancient Greece. Two acts (approx 100 min).

ACT I: Before the palace, with immense statues of Zeus, Apollo, and Hermes. ACT II: Same, but from a different angle, statue of Apollo more prominent.

Synopsis. The populace reviews the events that have followed from Agamemnon's sacrifice of his daughter Iphigenia in order to receive a favorable wind to Troy. Clytemnestra predicts the fall of Troy; soon afterward, Agamemnon returns in triumph, bringing the Trojan princess Cassandra as a prize. Cassandra's prophecy of doom is disregarded, and the murder of Agamemnon is accomplished, with Clytemnestra and the weak Aegisthus triumphant. The fate of the House of Atreus is sealed in one more act of violence and impiety.

Major Roles. CLYTEMNESTRA (dram s); very difficult; needs strength throughout wide range; A♯2 to B4. AGAMEMNON (bs); G1 to E3. CASSANDRA (s); needs strength at both ends of range; B2 to B4. WATCHMAN (t); D♭2 to A3. HERALD (bar); G1 to F3.

Lesser Roles. AEGISTHUS (t); C2 to G♯3. CALCHAS (bs); from chorus.

Chorus. SATTBB. Very important; plays a major role. Often divided. Attendants, soldiers, guards.

Orchestra. fl (picc), ob (Eng hrn), cl (bs cl), hrn, trp, trb, perc, piano, harp, 2 vln, vla, cel, cb.

Material. Pr.

🎝 Alcina

Music by George Frideric Handel (1685–1759). Libretto in Italian after the fairy tale by Ariosto (arr. by Antonio Marchi). Premiere: London, April 16, 1735. Elaborate set pieces; difficult and florid vocal lines. Overture. Setting: Imaginary kingdom. Three acts, seven scenes.

ACT I i: Deserted place surrounded by high precipitous mountains, a cave at the foot; ii: Anteroom to Alcina's apartments. ACT II i: Magnificent hall in Alcina's palace; ii: Palace garden; iii: Subterranean magic chamber. ACT III i: Vestibule in palace; ii: Exterior of palace.

Synopsis. Handel's sorcerer is a woman, with the gentle Bradamante as a foil (Bradamante is disguised as a youth, however). Ruggiero, a Christian knight betrothed to Bradamante, falls in love with Alcina, while the sorcerer's sister Morgana in turn falls for Bradamante. Morgana's lover, Oronte, becomes jealous. The Paladin Astolfo has been bewitched by Alcina, but is rescued by his son Oberto, when Ruggiero finally breaks the magic urn in Alcina's enchanted courtyard, restoring his sanity and reuniting himself with Bradamante. (To add to the confusion, Ruggiero is played by a woman.)

Major Roles. ALCINA (s); needs flexibility; trill; C3 to B♭4. RUGGIERO (s or m-s); florid; trill; B2 to A4. MORGANA (s); flexible; trill; E3 to B4. BRADAMANTE (c); some fioratura; trill; A2 to E4. ORONTE (t); florid; E2 to A3. MELISSO, governor for Bradamante (bs); B1 to E3. OBERTO (s); flexible; E3 to A4.

Chorus. SATB. Important.

Ballet. Vital. As elaborate as possible.

Production Difficulties. Should be imaginatively staged; elaborate sets possible; transformation scene where mountain breaks asunder and reveals Alcina's palace; destruction of palace.

Orchestra. 2 fl, picc, 2 ob, 2 bsn, 2 hrn, cembalo, strings.

Material. German Handel Soc. VS (i and g)*. G Sc (Bä).

🎵 Amerika · America

Music by Ellis B. Kohs (1916–   ). Libretto by the composer in German and English, after the Edwin Muir translation of the novel by Franz Kafka, and the dramatization by Max Brod. No staged production as of August 1973. Abridged, semi-staged concert version with two pianos and percussion by Western Opera Theater (traveling unit of San Francisco Opera), May 19, 1970, Los Angeles; repeat, San Francisco, May 27, 1970. Tragicomedy; fantasy. Music expressive of character; set numbers embedded in continuous texture; serial and tonal in varying degrees, depending upon dramatic requirements; vocal line patterned after speech; some declamation, quasi-recitative, rhythmic and normal dialogue. Some mime. No overture; brief interludes between scenes. Setting: In or near New York City, just before World War I. Expressionistic, single split-level scene desirable. Three acts, eleven scenes (145 min).

Synopsis. (ACT I i) Karl Rossmann, having been seduced by a maidservant in his native Prague, is sent to America by his parents to avoid scandal. He is unexpectedly met by his uncle, Senator Edward Jacob, who looks after him and furthers his education. (ii) Invited by Jacob's friend Pollunder to visit him and his daughter Clara, Karl accepts over his uncle's protests. (iii) He finds he cannot cope with Clara's playful advances and asks Pollunder to let him return to his uncle. However, a letter from Senator Jacob, brought by Mr. Green, forbids him to return or to communicate. (ACT II i, ii) Karl begins his wanderings. He meets Robinson and Delamarche, two tramps seeking employment, but shakes them off and finds work in a fine hotel where (iii) he is befriended by the Manageress and becomes very attached to her secretary Therese. One day (iv) Robinson appears, creates an uproar for which Karl is unjustly blamed by the Head Waiter and the Bell Captain, and Karl is ultimately dismissed. (ACT III i) Karl accompanies Robinson to the apartment of Brunelda, with whom Robinson and Delamarche are living, turns down an invitation to be their servant, and escapes. (ii Interlude). He secures a job (iii) with the Nature Theater of Oklahoma, and meets Therese again, as she is a recruiter for the company. They must part, but hope to reunite. (iv) As Karl boards a train, bound for an uncertain future, he experiences visions of his recent encounters.

Major Roles. KARL ROSSMANN (lyr-dram t); exacting dramatic requirements; must appear youthful; constantly on stage; C2 (one A1) to B♭3. ROBINSON

24

(high light t); needs versatility for comedy, mock-tragedy; florid; C2 to C4. DELAMARCHE (lyr bar); romantic type (may double with Stoker); A1 to E3. POLLUNDER (dram bar); (may double with Staff Manager); G1 to F3. SENATOR JACOB (bs); light, capable of humor (may double with Bell Captain); A♭1 to E3. CLARA (col s); coquette, yet capable of jiu-jitsu expertise; C3 to C5. THERESE (lyr-dram s); young, fresh, naive; D3 to A4. MANAGERESS (m-s); motherly type; D3 to G♯4. BRUNELDA (c); dramatic, sexy; G♯2 to D4.

Lesser Roles. STOKER (bar); (doubles with Delamarche). STAFF MANAGER (bar); (doubles with Pollunder). BELL CAPTAIN (bs); heavy, ruthless (doubles with Sen. Jacob). CAPTAIN (bs); heavy, jovial (doubles with Head Waiter). HEAD WAITER (bs); military type (doubles with Captain).

Bit Roles. MR. GREEN (sp); (doubles with The Husband). THE HUSBAND (sp); (doubles with Mr. Green). MAIDSERVANT (s); (doubles with Wife). WIFE (sp); (doubles with Maidservant). RENNELL, bellboy (t); (doubles with First Clerk). FIRST CLERK (t); (doubles with Rennell).

Supers. Large number: passengers, crew, officers, hotel guests, offstage voices, job applicants, a stranger, taxi driver, head purser, railway conductor, servants, clerks, maids, two bellboys, three "angels," three clerks (many doubles).

Orchestra. 2 fl (picc), 2 ob (Eng hrn), 2 cl (bs cl), bsn (cont bsn), alto sax, ten sax, bar sax, 2 hrn, trp, trb (ten), tuba, perc (traps, sn dr, xyl, tri, wd blk), 9 strings (2.2.2.2.1). *Stage*: brass band (may be pre-taped): 2 trp, 2 hrn, bar hrn, 3 trb, 2 tuba, sn dr, bs dr with cym; 4 buglers.

Material. Pr.

⚑ L'Amico Fritz · Friend Fritz

Music by Pietro Mascagni (1863–1945). Libretto in Italian by P. Suardon (N. Daspurao) after Erckmann-Chatrian's novel. Premiere: Rome, November 1, 1891. Romantic comedy. Melodic; set pieces. Prelude; intermezzo between Acts II and III. Setting: contemporary Alsace. Three acts (approx 92 min).

ACT I: Fritz's dining room. ACT II: Orchard near a farm. ACT III: Same as I.

Synopsis. Fritz, a rich bachelor landowner, complains to his friend Rabbi David that still another couple has asked him for a dowry. It is his 40th birthday, and other friends, Hanezo and Federico, come to congratulate him. David goes to tell the young couple of their good luck. Fritz laughs at him, but David prophesies that his friend will be married within a year. Caterina, the housekeeper, brings Suzel, daughter of one of Fritz's tenants, to give him flowers. Beppe fiddles outside and is asked to come in and sing for the company. Suzel leaves; David comments that she will no doubt marry soon; Fritz protests she is too young, and David repeats his wager that Fritz himself will marry—the prize is one of Fritz's vineyards. In the orchard, Suzel is picking cherries; when Fritz enters, they sing the melodious "cherry" duet. Friends take Fritz on a drive, but David stays behind and tells Suzel

25

the story of Isaac and Rebecca, appropriate to the situation. When Fritz returns, David tests him by announcing he has found a husband for Suzel. Fritz realizes he must love her, but leaves without saying anything. Suzel is desolate. An intermezzo that has become very popular leads to the third act, which shows Fritz distraught. Beppe tries to comfort him with a new song, but it is about unhappy love, and disturbs Fritz still further. He refuses David's request to consent to Suzel's wedding. She begs him to save her from a loveless match, and he finally admits his own love for her. David wins the bet.

Major Roles. FRITZ KOBUS (t); E2 to Bb3. SUZEL (s); C3 (one B2 with B3 opt) to B4. BEPPE (m-s); D3 to G4. DAVID (bar); high tessitura; D2 to F3.

Lesser Roles. HANEZO (bs); G1 to E3. FEDERICO (t); E2 to G3. CATERINA (s); D3 to E4.

Orchestra. (Manh. Sch. perf). 3 fl (picc), 2 ob, 2 cl, 2 bsn, 4 hrn, 2 trp, 3 trb, tuba, perc, harp, strings. *Stage*: ob.

Material. Bel (Son). Map. VS: G Sc*; Pet (f)*.

Performances. Rittenhouse Op. Soc., (Phila.): 5.61. San Fran. Op. Guild: 6.63. Ruffino (NYC): 4.25.70. Manh. Sch. (NYC): 5.15.70. Bel Canto (NYC): 2.14.71.

🎵 Andréa del Sarto

Music by Daniel Lesur (1908–   ). Libretto in French by the composer after Alfred de Musset. Premiere: Marseille, January 24, 1969. Tragedy, based on historical characters. Melodic; richly textured harmonies; set numbers; recitative. Overture. Interludes between I i and ii; II i and ii. Setting: Florence in 1531. Two acts, four scenes (120 min).

ACT I i: Courtyard of Del Sarto's villa (35 min); ii: Lucrèce's chamber (31 min). ACT II i: Terrace of garden overlooking Florence (11 min); ii: Grand hall in the villa (43 min).

Synopsis. Andréa del Sarto's wife Lucrèce, secretly the mistress of Andréa's most trusted friend and pupil, Cordiani, is preparing to run away with her lover. The old concierge Grémio tries to apprehend Cordiani, who kills him. Andréa discovers the seducer to be the one painter in whom he believes the future of his art to repose, and forgives him, but orders him to leave Italy. Cordiani tries to see Lucrèce a last time but is discovered, and Andréa's disgrace becomes public. A duel ensues in which Cordiani does not defend himself and is gravely wounded. Repudiating Lucrèce, Andréa lives alone in despair, at last learning that Cordiani has recovered and taken Lucrèce away. Andréa sends his youngest pupil after them with the message: "Why fly so precipitately? The widow of Andréa del Sarto can marry Cordiani." Then he drinks poison. But the remorseful Lucrèce and Cordiani separate forever.

Major Roles. ANDRÉA DEL SARTO, Florentine painter (bar); sustained;

26

dramatic; B1 to F3. LUCRECE, his wife (lyr s); C♯3 to B4. SPINETTE, follower of Lucrèce (col s); E3 to D♭5. CORDIANI, pupil and friend of Andréa (lyr t); D2 to B♭3. LIONEL, old pupil (bs); A♭1 to F3. GRÉMIO, concierge (bs); DAMIEN, pupil-friend of Cordiani (bar "Martin"); B1 to D♭3. CÉSAR-IO, young pupil of Andréa (light t); top G3.

Chorus. TTB; SM-SM-SA in II ii only. Pupils, models, valets, servants, women of village.

Ballet. Gagliarda and pavane in II ii.

Orchestra. 3 fl (2 picc), 2 ob, Eng hrn, 2 cl, bs cl, 2 bsn, cont bsn, 4 hrn, 2 trp, 2 trb, tuba, timp, perc (4): 2 cym susp, 2 cym, 2 antique cym, 2 gongs, tam-tam, tri, Basque dr, bs dr, side dr, ten dr, 2 tom-tom, xyl, vib, bells; cel, 1 or 2 harp, strings.

Material. Pet (Chou). VS*.

🎵 L'Ange de Feu · The Flaming Angel

Music by Serge Prokofiev (1891–1953). Libretto in Russian by the composer after a novel by Valery Briussov. Premiere: Paris, November 25, 1954 (concert form); stage premiere: Venice Festival, September 14, 1955. Medieval tragedy with supernatural elements and philosophical concepts. Overall symphonic development; leading motives are used; many dissonances and key changes; uncommon orchestral coloration. No overture; interludes between scenes in Act II. Voice parts extremely difficult because treated as instruments. Setting: Germany, principally Cologne, 16th century. Five acts, seven scenes (107 min).

ACT I: Attic of an inn (30 min). ACT II i: A room in Cologne (17 min); ii: A fantastic interior, crowded with books, stuffed birds, skeletons, chemical instruments (6 min); iii: Steep bank of the Rhine (14 min). ACT III: Street with Heinrich's house, unfinished Cologne Cathedral in background (7 min). ACT IV: Quiet garden in Cologne with tables and benches (15 min). ACT V: Convent undercroft with stone arches; door leading to outside (18 min).

Synopsis. The knight Ruprecht, returning to Germany from Italy, finds a small room in a slatternly inn. His neighbor is Renata, whose terrified cries cause Ruprecht to break down her door and eventually quiet her. She tells of a vision she had at seven when an angel named Madiel absorbed her whole life, marking her for a saint. But when she begs him to be hers in flesh as well as spirit, he leaves her in fury. Later he promises to return in the guise of a man. She thinks she recognizes him in young Count Heinrich, but he will not acknowledge his identity as Madiel. Ruprecht determines to seduce her, though the Innkeeper denounces her as a witch, and brings a fortune-teller who sees a vision of blood. Ruprecht and Renata depart hastily, the knight forever caught up in the girl's fate. In Cologne, she practices magic with the help of Glock, who also takes Ruprecht to the astrologer Agrippa of Nettescheim. On his way home, he encounters Renata outside

Heinrich's house. She claims he has insulted her, and incites Ruprecht to a duel, but while he is entering the house, Heinrich appears at a window as an angel. When Ruprecht returns, saying that Heinrich has accepted his challenge, Renata has changed her mind. Ruprecht is wounded in the duel, which causes Renata remorse; he recovers slowly. Once again, Renata leaves him to enter a convent, after attempting suicide. In his perplexity, he seeks a beergarden, where Mephistopheles and Faust are dining. Mephistopheles swallows a small boy, then produces him when the innkeeper complains. They invite Ruprecht to join them and depart. Renata is questioned in the convent by the Abbess and the Inquisitor, who suspect her of causing certain demonic manifestations. A terrible scene of hysteria, possession, and exorcism follows, in which groups of nuns turn on the Inquisitor. As Renata and the others reach the highest frenzy, Ruprecht, who has appeared on the gallery with Faust, tries to throw himself over, but is restrained by Mephistopheles. Guards burst in as a dazzling ray of sunlight penetrates the undercroft, and the Inquisitor pins Renata with his staff and orders her to be tortured and burned.

Major Roles. RENATA (dram s); extremely difficult and long role (86 min onstage); demands volatile and impassioned acting; B2 to Bb4 (one C5). RUPRECHT (bar); also difficult; Ab1 to F#3 (one G3 with D3 opt). MEPHISTOPHELES (t); expected to be buffo then heroic; D2 to A3. FAUST (bar); C2 to E3.

Lesser Roles. (All demand expert singing and acting.) INNKEEPER (m-s). FORTUNE-TELLER (s). JACOB GLOCK (t). AGRIPPA (t). THE INQUISITOR (bs). LABORER; MATTHEW, Ruprecht's second in the duel; ABBESS; PHYSICIAN; INNKEEPER. COUNT HEINRICH (mute).

Chorus. SATB. Extremely complicated; often divided; several solo parts.

Orchestra. 3 fl, 3 ob, 3 cl, 3 bsn, 4 hrn, 3 trp, 3 trb, tuba, 2 hrp, timp, perc, strings.

Material. B & H.

Performances. NYCO: 9.22.65 (Amer prem), etc. Lyr. Op. of Chic.: 12.3.66, etc.

⚜ Antigonae

Music by Carl Orff (1895–   ). Libretto after play by Sophocles, German translation by Friedrich Hölderlin. Premiere: Salzburg, August 9, 1949. Musical play, combining the myths of Apollo and Dionysus, the former in dynamic psalmody and the manner of Gregorian chant, the latter in dance and rhythmic reiteration of chants in single tones. Occasional melismatic ariosos; important chorus; massive orchestra. Several orchestral interludes. Setting: Ancient Thebes. Three parts (158 min).

Synopsis. During the siege of Thebes, two brothers, fighting on opposite sides, were both killed. King Creon decrees that Polynices, who fought with the enemy, shall not be buried, but left to the ravens. His sister Antigonae defies the command, but is caught by the watchman and condemned to death. Creon's son Haemon, Antigonae's betrothed, attempts to save her, but it is the prophecy of old Tiresias that great misfortune will befall if she is killed that stays the King's hand. Still it is too late: Antigonae has killed herself, followed by Haemon and Ismène, Creon's wife. The king is left alone, mourning.

Major Roles. ANTIGONAE (s); needs strength at extremes of range; wide skips (one of 2 octaves); much low tessitura; F2 to Bb4. ISMENE (s); B2 to G4. CREON (bs); extremely high tessitura; G1 to A3. HAEMON (t); Bb1 to C4. TIRESIAS (t); florid passages; C2 to Bb3.

Lesser Roles. MESSENGER (bs); F1 to Gb3. EURYDICE (s or m-s); C3 to A4. WATCHMAN (t); high tessitura; C2 to sustained Bb3.

Chorus. TB. Needs agility; several solos.

Orchestra. 6 pianos (with variety of sounding devices), 4 harp, 9 cb, 6 fl (picc), 6 ob (3 Eng hrn), 6 trp (mute), 7–8 timp (one with high A), 59 perc (10–15 players).

Material. Bel (Sch).

Performances. Litt. Orch. (NYC—conc): 4.68.

◤ Antony and Cleopatra

Music by Samuel Barber (1910–   ). Libretto in English, adapted by Franco Zeffirelli from the play by William Shakespeare. Premiere: Metropolitan Opera, New York, September 16, 1966. Tragedy. Music in difficult contemporary idiom; occasional lyrical lines; vocal line often patterned after speech. No overture. Five orchestral interludes. One scene accompanied entirely by percussion. Recitative is improvised for character in I vii over stick dance. Three acts, 16 scenes (114 min).

ACT I i: The Empire; ii: Cleopatra's palace; iii: Senate in Rome; iv: Cleopatra's palace; v: Caesar's palace; vi: Cleopatra's palace; vii: Roman galley (45 min). ACT II i: Caesar's palace; ii: Cleopatra's palace garden; iii: Antony's camp; iv: Outside Antony's tent; v: Battlefront at Actium; vi: Cleopatra's palace; vii: Battlefield; viii: Antony's ruined tent (41 min). ACT III: The Monument (28 min).

Synopsis. The libretto closely follows the play in action.

Leading Roles. CLEOPATRA (s); difficult intervals; sustained; dramatic; Bb2 to B4. ANTONY (high bs); high tessitura; G1 (one F1 with C2 opt, one E1) to G3. CAESAR (dram t); high tessitura; Eb2 to Bb3 (one C4 with G3 opt). ENOBARBUS, Antony's friend (bs); Gb1 to F3. OCTAVIA (lyr s); E#3 to Bb4. CHARMIAN, Cleopatra's attendant (m-s); Bb2 to G#4 (one Ab4 with F4 opt).

Lesser Roles. IRAS, Cleopatra's attendant (c). DOLABELLA (bar). MARDIAN, a eunuch (high t); has considerable falsetto. SOOTHSAYER (bs). THIDIAS (t or high bar). Senators: AGRIPPA (bs); LEPIDUS (buf t); MAECENAS (bar). EROS, Antony's shield bearer (young t or high bar). Antony's officers: CANDIDUS (bar); DEMETRIUS (low t); SCARUS (bs); DECRETAS (bs). A RUSTIC (bar or bas). MESSENGER (t). ALEXAS, Cleopatra's attendant (bs). VOICE OFFSTAGE (s); top C♯5 and D5.

Chorus. SSATB; very elaborate; many divisions; extremes of range; several solos. People of the Empire, Cleopatra's attendants, Senators, guards, watchmen, soldiers.

Ballet. As elaborate as possible. In I iv Egyptian girls play cymbals, antique clappers, tambourines; dance to three untuned drums. Stick dance of sailors and slaves in I vii.

Orchestra. 3 fl (2 picc, alto fl), 2 ob, Eng hrn, 2 cl, bs cl, 2 bsn, cont bsn, 4 hrn, 3 trp, 3 trb, tuba, timp, perc (6), piano, cel, 2 harp, strings. *Stage*: 4 trp, 4 trb, perc, Spanish guit, Ondes Martinot.

Material. G Sc.

♬ Arden Muss Sterben · Arden Must Die

Music by Alexander Goehr (1932–   ). Libretto in German by Erich Fried, based freely on anonymous 16th-century play, *Arden of Faversham*. Commissioned by the Hamburg State Opera. Premiere: Hamburg, March 5, 1967. Satire (elements of *Beggar's Opera* and Gilbert & Sullivan). Contemporary harmony; vocal lines difficult. Many ensembles. Brief prelude; interludes between Act I i and ii. Setting: Faversham and environs; London, 16th century. Two acts, nine scenes, epilogue (104 min).

ACT I i: Arden's house; ii: Alice's bedroom; iii: The marshes; iv: Arden's house. ACT II i: A street in London near St. Paul's; ii: Alice and others on opposite side of stage, iii: A house in a dark street; iv: The murderers and Mrs. Bradshaw; Arden's dining room; Epilogue.

Synopsis. Arden, a wealthy businessman, is marked for death by all the others except Mrs. Bradshaw, who acts throughout as an innocent who condemns but condones the various schemes to bring about Arden's demise. His wife Alice has a lover, Mosbie, who is the brother of her maid Susan, and has been a humble tailor. Susan and her lover Michael, the manservant, do not plot their master's death actively but would welcome it for financial gain. Alice enlists Green and Reede, landowners ruined by Arden, but also employs two notorious murderers, Shakebag and Black Will, to do the deed. Their first attempt fails as they lose Arden and his friend Franklin in the dark and fog, and Shakebag falls in the river. They lose again as Arden and Franklin remain safe in a London inn. Their third try succeeds, as they fall on Arden at a banquet in his house while he is celebrating his reunion with his false wife and friends. But their callous joy is shortlived; Franklin brings retribution with the Mayor and police. The spoken Epilogue points the moral: we others are not guilty like Alice and her colleagues, but "far further off and much better organized."

Major Roles. ARDEN (bs); E♯1 to E3. FRANKLIN (bs); F♯1 to C3. ALICE (m-s); A♭2 (one G2) to B♭4. MOSBIE (t); C♯2 to B♭3. SUSAN (s); needs

30

flexibility; G2 to B♭4. MICHAEL (t); needs flexibility; C♯2 to B3 (C4 in ensemble). MRS. BRADSHAW, a neighbor (c); G2 to F♯4. GREENE (bar); B1 to E3. REEDE (bs); low E1 (one D1 with D2 opt). SHAKEBAG (t); B♭1 to B3. BLACK WILL (bs); F1 to E♭3.

Lesser Roles. FERRYMAN (bs); E♭1 to D♭3. SHEPHERD (s). MAYOR OF FAVERSHAM (bar); G1 to G3. APPRENTICE (sp); *Sprechstimme.*

Chorus. SATB. Market people. TB. Six constables.

Orchestra. picc, 2 fl (picc), 2 ob (Eng hrn), Eng hrn, 2 cl (E♭ cl, basset hrn), bs cl, 3 bsn (cont bsn), 4 hrn, 3 trp, 3 trb, tuba, timp, 2 harp, elec piano, organ, cembalo, acc, perc (4), strings. *Stage:* string 5-tet.

Material. Bel (Sch). VS (g, e)*. Tr: Geoffrey Skelton.

ᛗ Ariane et Barbe Bleu · Ariadne and Blue Beard

Music by Paul Dukas (1865–1935). Libretto in French after Maeterlinck's play of the same name. Premiere: Paris, May 10, 1907. Fantastic tale. Expressive orchestration in continuous texture; vocal line patterned after speech. Brief preludes to each act. Setting: Blue Beard's castle. Three acts. ACT I: Hall in castle, with large center door, three smaller doors on each side. ACT II: Vast subterranean vaulted hall with adjoining passage. ACT III: Same as I.

Synopsis. An angry crowd outside the castle comments on the growing suspicion that Blue Beard has murdered his five wives and now plans the same fate for his sixth, Ariane. The new bride enters with her frightened nurse, and immediately proceeds to disobey her husband, seeking to discover his secret by using a forbidden gold key and discarding six silver ones. The nurse, however, opens one door after another with the silver keys, disclosing fabulous gems. Ariane is not above pausing to apostrophize the diamonds in a dazzling aria, but soon reverts to her original purpose. The seventh door opens on darkness and a dull moaning sound. Blue Beard intervenes; their quarrel brings further outbursts from the crowd, whereupon Ariane steps outside to reassure them. At last, Ariane is able to penetrate to the dark chamber and rescue the five captive wives. Blue Beard returns and is wounded by the aroused villagers. When Ariane opens the doors, they deliver her tightly bound husband to her. She cuts the bonds, but refuses to remain. The five other women stay with their lord, declining freedom.

Major Roles. BLUE BEARD (bs); A♯1 to C3. ARIANE (m-s); some high tessitura; G♯2 to A♯4. NURSE (c); A♭2 to F♯4.

Lesser Roles. The five wives (no range problems): SELYSETTE (m-s); YGRAINE (s), one B4; MÉLISANDE (s); BELLANGERE (s), one B4; ALLADINE (mime). OLD PEASANT (bs). TWO PEASANTS (t and bs).

Chorus. TTBB. Peasants. Several solos.

Orchestra. 3 fl (2 picc), 2 ob, Eng hrn, 2 cl, bs cl, 3 bsn, cont bsn, 4 hrn, 3 trp, 3 trb, tuba, timp, perc, 2 harp, cel, strings.

Material. Du. VS (f, e).

🎵 Ariodante

Music by George Frideric Handel (1685–1759). Libretto in Italian by Antonio Salvi. Premiere: London, January 8, 1735. Spectacular drama. Expressive orchestra makes great use of dance forms; vocal line customarily florid. Overture and sinfonias at intervals. Setting: Scotland. Three acts, twelve scenes (approx 130 min [Washington performance]).

ACT I i: Ginevra's room; ii: Outdoors; iii: A palace garden; iv: In the country. ACT II i: Back of the palace; ii: Room in the palace; iii: King's chamber. ACT III i: In the forest; ii: Room in the palace; iii: Battleground; iv: Dark room; v: Festival hall.

Synopsis. Polinesso, his suit rejected by Ginevra, decides to use Dalinda, her friend, as a pawn to achieve his goal of attaining the kingdom. The King, delighted at Ariodante as a son-in-law, orders Odoardo to prepare the wedding. Lurcanio, Ariodante's brother, loves Dalinda, but she has become involved with Polinesso and rejects him. Dalinda impersonates Ginevra in a rendezvous, and Ariodante, believing Ginevra faithless, disappears. Ginevra is in disgrace. Ariodante in hiding saves Dalinda from assassins sent by Polinesso, who hopes to dispose of her now that his victory is in sight. Meanwhile, the King will forgive Ginevra only if a knight fights and wins a duel for her honor. Polinesso volunteers, and Lucarnio takes his challenge and wounds him mortally. Ariodante and Dalinda return and expose the plot. The kingdom rejoices.

Major Roles. KING OF SCOTLAND (bs); florid passages; trill; needs strength throughout wide range; G1 (one F1) to Eb3 (one F3). GINEVRA, his daughter (col s); considerable fioratura; trill; E3 to A4. ARIODANTE (m-s or c); many coloratura passages; wide range emotionally and vocally; trill; C3 (one B2) to A4. DALINDA (lyr s); needs flexibility; E3 to G4 (one Bb4). POLINESSO, Duke of Albania (c orig; trill; A2 to D4—one E4); bs-bar. LURCANIO (t); D#2 to G3 (one A3).

Lesser Role. ODOARDO, King's councillor (bar).

Chorus. SATB. Courtiers, farmers, in Acts I and III.

Ballet. Very elaborate, after each act.

Orchestra. 2 fl, 2 ob, 2 bsn, 2 hrn, 2 trp, strings, continuo (vcl, cb, cembalo). Strings can be enlarged, ob, bsn, cembalo added).

Material. Gr. G Sc (Bä).

Performances. Handel Soc. (NYC): 3.29.71 (NYC prem—conc). JFK Center (Wash.): 9.14.71.

🎵 Armida

Music by Antonin Dvořák (1841–1904). Libretto in Czech by Jaroslav Vrchlický, after Tasso. Premiere: Prague, March 25, 1904. Mystic drama with religious overtones. Set numbers. Nationalistic flavor. Overture. Setting: Damascus and environs in time of crusades. Four acts (157 min).

32

ACT I: Hydraot's palace. ACT II: The crusaders' camp. ACT III: Armida's enchanted gardens. ACT IV: Oasis in the desert.

Synopsis. There are many differences between this and the story of Gluck's opera. Ismen, the magical ruler, who has long sought Armida's hand, proposes that she tempt the crusaders to their ruin. She falls genuinely in love with Rinald, one of the crusaders, who returns her passion in spite of the warnings of Peter the Hermit. Ismen creates many difficulties for the two lovers, finally delivering the Archangel Michael's shield to the Knights Sven and Ubald, who use its magic powers to bring Rinald back to his crusade. In a fierce battle, Rinald kills Ismen and another warrior in black armor, only to discover that this victim is Armida.

Major Roles. HYDRAOT, King of Damascus (bs). ARMIDA, his daughter (s). ISMEN (bar). BOHUMIR, crusade leader (bar). PETER THE HERMIT (bs). RINALD (t).

Lesser Roles. GERNAND (bs), DUDO (t), UBALD (bs), SVEN (t), ROGER (t), other knights. HLASATE (bs). MUEZIN (bar). SIRENA (s).

Chorus. SSAATTBB.

Orchestra. picc, 2 fl, 2 ob, Eng hrn, 2 cl, bs cl, 2 bsn, cont bsn, 4 hrn, 3 trp, 3 trb, tuba, harp, timp, perc, strings.

Material. B & H (Artia). VS (cz)*. G Sc (Bä).

🎵 Armida

Music by Franz Josef Haydn (1732–1809). Libretto in Italian by Jacopo Durandi, after Tasso. Commissioned by Esterhazy. Premiere: Esterhaz, February 26, 1784. Medieval heroic drama, based on fantasy. Set numbers; conventional harmony; vocal line almost invariably florid. Overture. Setting: Damascus during crusades. Three acts, six scenes (140 min).

ACT I i: Interior of castle; ii: Encampment on mountainside; iii: Interior of castle (50 min). ACT II i: Interior of castle; ii: Encampment (60 min). ACT III: Enchanted wood (30 min).

Synopsis. Acting on the orders of her uncle Idreno, ruler of Damascus, the sorceress Armida has cast a spell over the heroic crusader Rinaldo, causing him to abandon his efforts to liberate Jerusalem. Rinaldo's fellow crusaders, led by Ubaldo and Clotarco, are encamped outside Idreno's castle waiting to rescue Rinaldo. But he has fallen completely under Armida's spell, and she returns his love, much to her uncle's dismay. Idreno promises Rinaldo the hand of Armida if he defeats the invaders encamped without. When he discovers their true identity, he refuses. Idreno orders Zelmira, the Egyptian sultan's daughter held prisoner in the castle, to entice the crusaders inside to be slaughtered. She is reluctant, especially after meeting Clotarco, to whom she is attracted. Armida suggests that Clotarco be sent to bring Ubaldo for negotiations. Ubaldo agrees, and persuades Rinaldo to forsake Armida, whereupon the sorceress faints. When she regains consciousness, Rinaldo has gone, and she swears vengeance, following Rinaldo

33

to the encampment and reawakening the spell. Ubaldo tells his friend that the only way to escape Armida is to cut down the magic myrtle in the wood. A group of nymphs, led by Zelmira, urge him to return to the castle, but in spite of their pleas and the threats of Armida, who suddenly appears, followed by an attack by the Furies, he finally succeeds in cutting down the myrtle. The opera ends with a sextet in which all the principals bemoan the injustice of a world in which love must always submit to honor and duty.

Roles. ARMIDA (dram-col s); extremely high tessitura; sustained; difficult fiorature; D♯3 to C5. ZELMIRA (lyr-col s); problems equal to Armida, but shorter role, less heroic; C3 to C5. RINALDO (dram t); low tessitura; difficult florid passages; wide skips; extreme contrasts in mood which must sustain tension; B♭1 to A3. UBALDO (lyr t); exceptionally low register; moderately difficult fiorature; needs expressive acting; B♭1 to A3. CLOTARCO (lyr t); no vocal difficulties; only one aria; D2 to A3. IDRENO (dram bar with low range or bs with high); many wide downward skips; sustained; florid; F♯1 to G3 (extreme occurs within two bars).

Orchestra. fl, 2 ob, 2 cl (only in crusaders' march when ob tacet) 2 bsn, 2 hrn, timp only in one aria, cembalo, strings.

Material. G. Henle*. G Sc (Bä). Tr: Naomi Ornest and Kurt Saffir.

🖋 Aroldo

Music by Giuseppe Verdi (1813–1901). Libretto in Italian by Francesco Maria Piave. Premiere: Rimini, August 16, 1857. (*Aroldo* is an adaptation of *Stiffelio*, first performed in Trieste in 1850.) Romantic melodrama. Accompanied recitative, set arias and numbers. Conventional harmonic structure. Overture. Setting: England and Scotland, 1189–1192 (Third Crusade). Four acts, five scenes (125 min).

ACT I i: Egberto's castle in Kent (22 min); ii: Another room in the castle (28 min). ACT II: Graveyard of the castle (31 min). ACT III: Egberto's castle (23 min). ACT IV: Banks of Loch Lomond (21 min).

Synopsis. Mina, wife of the Saxon warrior Aroldo, was seduced by Godvino, another knight, while her husband was on a crusade. Aided by her father Egberto, the penitent Mina tries to hide her indiscretion in order to preserve Aroldo's happiness. Eventually Aroldo learns the truth. He is about to duel with Godvino when his close friend Briano, a religious hermit, bids Aroldo to forgive. Egberto, prevented from suicide by Briano, kills Godvino to avenge his own honor. Sadly Mina signs a bill of divorce when Aroldo insists, but vows her eternal love for him. Aroldo retires to Loch Lomond with Briano to become a hermit. Exiled for Godvino's murder, Egberto and Mina are caught in a storm on Loch Lomond and cast ashore. Aroldo would deny them shelter but Briano again intervenes. The couple are reunited at last.

Major Roles. MINA (dram s); difficult, florid, demanding great agility

34

and polished technique; B♭2 to C5. AROLDO (t); florid; C2 to B♭3. EGBERTO (bar); florid; F1 to G3.

Lesser Roles. GODVINO (t). BRIANO (bs).

Bit Roles. ELENA, Mina's cousin (m-s). ENRICO, another cousin (t). JORG, Aroldo's servant (mute).

Chorus. SSATTBB. Ladies and gentlemen of Kent, knights, pages, heralds, harvesters, shepherds, huntsmen.

Orchestra. 2 fl, 2 ob, 2 cl, 2 bsn, 4 hrn, 2 trp, 3 trb, tuba, timp, perc, org, bells, strings. *Stage:* band.

Material. Bel (Ri).

Performances. Amato (NYC): 3.7.61.

✄ Attila

Music by Giuseppe Verdi (1813–1901). Libretto in Italian by Temistocle Solera, based on a play by Zacharias Werner. Premiere: Venice, March 17, 1846. Historical melodrama. Conventional harmonic structure. Accompanied recitative, set arias and numbers. Brief prelude to Act I. Setting: Italy, mid-5th century. Prologue, three acts, seven scenes (New Orleans production: 100 min).

Prologue: Ruins of Aquileia (15 min). ACT I: Shores of Adriatic Sea (15 min). ACT II i: Attila's camp (15 min); ii: Attila's tent (16 min). ACT III i: Attila's camp (9 min); ii: Banquet hall (15 min); iii: Roman camp (15 min).

Synopsis. Attila, leader of the Huns, invades Italy and captures the city of Aquileia. Odabella, daughter of the late Lord of Aquileia, pretends loyalty to the conqueror, while secretly vowing vengeance. Ezio, envoy of the Roman Empire, bargains unsuccessfully with Attila for Italy's deliverance. Foresto, beloved of Odabella, mistakes her motives and reproaches Odabella for abandoning him and his faithful followers. She convinces him of her true intentions. Despite a warning vision, Attila continues his assault on Rome, until the vision returns; he then declares a truce. Foresto and Ezio secretly plan to surround and massacre the Huns. Attila entertains the Romans despite another warning omen. At a banquet he is served wine which Foresto has poisoned, but Odabella, who has other ideas of vengeance, prevents him from drinking the wine. She then convinces Attila to spare Foresto's life in return for her disclosure which saved Attila's life. Foresto again misunderstands Odabella's actions, upbraids her, and leaves. Ezio returns to Rome with news of the truce's termination, while Attila plans to marry Odabella as her reward for saving his life. Foresto and Ezio continue to plot against the Huns. Neither believes in Odabella's good faith until Attila discovers her in the Romans' company. Odabella stabs Attila through the heart as Roman soldiers rush in.

Major Roles. ODABELLA (dram s); florid, abounding in a great variety of technical difficulties; high tessitura; frequent demands at top of range;

35

Bb2 to C5. FORESTO (t); high tessitura; B1 to Bb3. EZIO (bar); B1 to G3. ATTILA (bs); F♯1 to F3.

Lesser Roles. ULDINO (t), young Briton slave of Foresto. LEONE (bs).

Chorus. SSAATTBB. Odabella's attendants, virgins and children, Druid priestesses, Roman and Hun soldiers, refugees.

Orchestra. 2 fl, 2 ob, 2 cl, 2 bsn, 4 hrn, 2 trp, 3 trb, tuba, timp, perc, bells, harp, strings. *Stage:* band.

Material. Bel (Ri).

Performances. New Orleans Op.: 10.9.69. Newark: 10.20.72.

⬛ Aufstieg und Fall der Stadt Mahagonny · Rise and Fall of the City of Mahagonny · Mahagonny

Music by Kurt Weill. Libretto in German by Bertolt Brecht. Premiere: Leipzig, March 1930. Satiric tragicomedy, moralistic implications. Continuous texture, embodying songs and dialogue; deceptively simple harmonies; theatricality of highest importance; considerable influence of jazz; significant ensembles. Brief prelude. Setting: the fictional Alabama town of Mahagonny, sometime in the 1920's. Three acts, many scenes (may be suggested by lights, projections, etc.) (approx 120 min).

ACT I i: A desert waste; ii: Outskirts of Mahagonny; iii: A metropolis; iv: The road to Mahagonny; v: Mahagonny; vi: Jenny's room; vii: The tavern; viii: The pier; ix: Outside the tavern; x: Mahagonny; xi: The wall. ACT II i: The wall; ii: Eating; iii: Loving; iv: Fighting; v: Drinking; vi: In Mahagonny. ACT III i: A cell; ii: Courtroom; iii: A room in Mahagonny; iv: The same; v: Outside Mahagonny.

Synopsis. This bitter satire, with its roots in the disillusioned Germany of the 1920's, possesses contemporary values in the scathing denunciation of the human condition. The story is not so much realistic as symbolic, the characters representing various aspects of man's character and weaknesses. Mahagonny is the town founded by three fleeing convicts, Trinity Moses, Fatty, and Leocadia Begbick, and gradually overrun with the dregs of humanity, threatened with a natural cataclysm, a hurricane, reprieved, and continuing its materialistic existence. To Mahagonny come Alaska miners, headed by Jimmie Mahoney, who represents the only good and free spirit in the play. But for the ultimate sin, the lack of money, he is condemned to die. The other chief character is Jenny, the pleasant prostitute. Hers is the outstanding song, "Moon of Alabama."

Major Roles. (All need style and theatrical ability more than conventional vocal equipment). LEOCADIA BEGBICK (c or m-s). FATTY (t). TRINITY MOSES (bar). JENNY (s). JIM MAHONEY (t). JACK (t). BILLY BANKBOOK (bar). ALASKA WOLF JOE (bs). TOBY HIGGINS (t).

Chorus. SATB. Six girls, six men singled out.

Orchestra. 2 fl, ob, cl, alto sax, ten sax, 2 bsn (cont bsn), 2 hrn, 3 trp, 2

36

trb, tuba, timp, perc, piano, harm ad lib, banjo, bs guit, bandoneon. *Stage*: (Can be drawn from orchestra.) 2 fl, picc, 2 cl, 3 sax, 2 bsn, 2 hrn, 2 trp, 2 trb, tuba, perc, piano, zither, xyl ad lib, banjo, bandoneon.

Material. Pr (UE).

Performances. Stratford (Ont) Fest.: July 1965 (N. Amer prem). Carmen Capalbo production: NYC, March 1970. Op. Soc of Wash.: 2.15.73. Bost. Op.: 4.13.73.

⚑ Bartleby

Music by Walter Aschaffenburg (1927–   ). Libretto in English by Jay Leyda, based on the story by Herman Melville. Premiere: Oberlin College Conservatory, November 12, 1964. Drama. Music has contemporary feeling; expressive, strong, complicated orchestra. Vocal line patterned after speech. Setting: New York, 1840's. Overture after Prologue. Prologue, two acts, five scenes; interludes (approx 110 min).

Prologue: In Lawyer's chambers. ACT I i: Lawyer's office; Interlude; ii: Same as i, Saturday afternoon a few days later. ACT II i: Same as I i, the following Sunday evening; Interlude: a street, some weeks later; ii: The office, now empty; Interlude: The Lawyer; iii: Courtyard of New York City Tombs prison.

Synopsis. The Lawyer, his clerks Trodden and Nippers, and office boy Ginger, cannot understand the new scrivener Bartleby. Bartleby gradually withdraws from the office routine, "preferring not to" do any of his tasks. When the exasperated Lawyer dismisses him, Bartleby "prefers not to" leave; instead, the Lawyer moves his office. Bartleby, besieged by the Landlord, other tenants, cleaning women, and onlookers, still does not budge until he is taken to prison. There, in spite of the intervention of the Lawyer, who still cannot rid himself of a feeling of responsibility for the strange man, Bartleby "prefers not to" eat, and collapses in death, as enigmatic as ever.

Major Roles. LAWYER (bar); long and exacting role; difficult intervals; some high sustained passages; A1 to F#3. BARTLEBY (t); not much singing but impressive, impassive characterization; F2 to G3. TRODDEN (bs); F#1 to D3. NIPPERS (buf t); E2 to Ab3. GINGER (s); Eb3 to Gb4; has a whistling passage.

Lesser Roles. LANDLORD (bs-bar). MRS. CUTLETS, a grubwoman (c).

Bit Parts. TURNKEY (bs). THE CLIENT (mute). POLICEMAN (mute).

Chorus. SATB. Tenants, cleaning women, scriveners, office boys, offstage congregation at vespers. Offstage prisoners: TBB.

Orchestra. 2 fl (picc), 2 ob, 2 cl (bs cl), 2 bsn, 2 hrn, 2 trp, trb (t bs), timp, harp, piano, strings (6 or 5, 6 or 5, 4, 4, 3 or 2). Perc: sn dr, bs dr with cym, cym, susp cym, tamb, tam-tam, tri, wd bl, xyl.

Material. Pr. VS*.

♬ The Bassarids

Music by Hans Werner Henze (1926–   ). Libretto in English by W. H. Auden and Chester Kallman, based on *The Bacchae* by Euripides. Premiere (in German): Salzburg Festival, August 6, 1966. Classical tragedy; designated opera seria by composer. Music falls into two contrasting phases, each with own themes and chords and tone-rows: the harsher Thebes music, including Pentheus; and Dionysus music, more voluptuous; vocal lines extremely difficult; tricky ensembles. No overture. Setting: Courtyard of Royal Palace in ancient Thebes and Mount Cytheron. One act, divided into four sections like symphonic movements, with an Intermezzo ("Judgment of Calliope") in Part III (approx 150 min).

Synopsis. Cadmus, who founded Thebes after the adventure of sowing the dragon's teeth that sprang up as warriors, has just abdicated in favor of his grandson Pentheus, son of Agave. The populace is greeting its new monarch, but runs off to Mount Cytheron when news arrives that Dionysus has come. This god is the son of Cadmus's daughter, Semele, by Zeus. Her tomb is at one side of the stage and her cult still exists, although there is a strong faction that disbelieves. It is this conflict that animates the story. Cadmus, Agave, the ancient, blind prophet Tiresias, and the old slave Beroe discuss Dionysus and Pentheus, who has shut himself away in fasting and prayer. The result of his vigil is made known when a Captain of the Guard (with whom both Agave and her sister Autonoe attempt a flirtation) proclaims a royal edict forbidding the belief that Zeus had a son by Semele. Pentheus himself extinguishes the flame on Semele's tomb and decrees death to anyone attempting to relight it. Offstage, to a stringed instrument, a voice (Dionysus) invites everyone to Mount Cytheron. Agave and Autonoe obey as if hypnotized. Pentheus orders the Captain to round up everyone on Cytheron, vowing to extirpate the cult of Dionysus. Beroe prays to the Mother Goddess for his protection.

Into the Judgment Hall the Captain brings his prisoners, among whom are Agave and Autonoe, Tiresias, a woman slave with her daughter, and a Stranger. All are in trance; Agave babbles her Cytheron experience and is sent to house arrest with her sister; the woman and her daughter are tortured. Beroe recognizes the Stranger as Dionysus, but Pentheus will not listen to her warning. Dionysus' forces are too much for Pentheus; the flame on Semele's tomb is restored, the prisoners freed, and an earthquake shakes the palace. Pentheus is tempted by the Stranger to see in a mirror what is going on on Cytheron. The audience sees an Intermezzo which depicts Pentheus' fantasies, dominated by repressed sex. All the characters are dressed as in a pastoral play of an 18th-century French court, performing "The Judgment of Calliope" as a flippant charade, using Roman names for the Olympians. Pentheus, torn with disgust, is nevertheless hypnotized by the Stranger and goes to Cytheron himself, dressed in one of his mother's robes. There he witnesses Dionynesian dances and is pursued by a band of maenads, who tear him apart.

38

Major Roles. DIONYSUS (also VOICE and STRANGER) (t); high tessitura; needs flexibility; C♯2 to B♭3; B3 has F or F♯3 opt. PENTHEUS (bar); high tessitura; difficult intervals; sustained, dramatic; B1 to F♯3; one G♯3 (G♯2 opt). CADMUS (bs); A♭1 to E3. TIRESIAS (t); B♭1 to B♭3 (also CALIOPE). CAPTAIN (bar); G1 to F3 (also ADONIS). AGAVE (m-s); trill; B♭2 to A4; B♭4 has F4 opt (also VENUS). AUTONOE (spin s); trill; needs flexibility; F3 to C5 (also PROSERPINE). BEROE (m-s); G♯2 to E4. Singers in Intermezzo use the extremes of their ranges.

Lesser Roles. SLAVE (mute). HER DAUGHTER (mute).

Chorus. SSAATTBB. Bassarids (maenads and bacchants), citizens, guards, servants, musicians.

Orchestra. 4 fl, 2 ob, 2 Eng hrn, 4 cl (cont sax, E♭ cl, double cont sax), bs cl (cont sax, ten sax), 4 bsn (cont bsn), 6 hrn, 4 trp (bs trp), 3 trb, 2 tuba (cont bs tuba), timp, elaborate perc, 2 harp, 2 cel, 2 piano, strings. *Stage*: 4 trp (from pit), 2 mandolin, guit.

Reduced Version. 4 fl, 2 ob, 2 Eng hrn, 4 cl, 4 bsn, 4 hrn, 4 trp, 3 trb, tuba, timp, perc, harp, cel, pianino, strings.

Production Problems. Elaborate changes of scenery; production of head of Pentheus; earthquake and holocaust.

Material. Bel (Sch), VS (g, e)*.

Performances. Sante Fe: 8.7.68 (Amer prem). USC: 4.12.69.

🎵 La Battaglia di Legnano · The Battle of Legnano

Music by Giuseppe Verdi (1813–1901). Libretto in Italian by Salvatore Cammarano, based on a proud chapter in Italian history. Premiere: Rome, January 26, 1849. Patriotic melodrama. Accompanied recitative, set arias and numbers. Conventional harmonic structure. Overture and short introduction to Acts I, II, and III. Setting: Milan, 1176. Four acts, seven scenes (110 min).

ACT I i: Outside Milan; ii: A shady spot. ACT II: Como. ACT III i: Crypt of a Milan cathedral; ii: Lida's apartment; iii: Arrigo's room. ACT IV: Milan.

Synopsis. Citizens of Lombardy have formed a league to repel the invaders, led by Frederic Barbarossa, and they assemble in Milan. Arrigo, leader of the Veronese contingent, who has been wounded and imprisoned, returns and is welcomed by his old friend Rolando, a Milanese duke. All present swear to defend Italy. Lida, Rolando's wife, is wooed by Marcovaldo, a German prisoner who was freed by her husband. She spurns his advances. While Rolando attends a war council, Arrigo, who had been Lida's lover before her marriage, reproaches Lida for her choice. Lida claims all thought Arrigo was dead. He is unconvinced, and leaves. Barbarossa appears at Como with a huge German army, and sends Arrigo and Rolando back to Milan to report Italy's impending doom. They defy him in a burst of patriotism. Arrigo joins the select group of Death Riders which Rolando leads. Fearing her lover's death, Lida writes him a compromising letter. Rolando bids his wife and son a touching farewell, and asks Arrigo to watch over them if he is killed. As they leave Marcovaldo calls Rolando aside and shows him Lida's letter to Arrigo, which he has intercepted. Rolando swears vengeance on the lovers. Receiving no reply to her letter, Lida visits Arrigo, proclaims her undying love, and says they must part. Rolando surprises the pair. Preferring to doom Arrigo to a life of dishonor rather than instant death, he locks them in the room. Ashamed of his absence from the Death Riders, Arrigo jumps out the window shouting "Long live Italy!" The Austrian army is defeated at Legnano, and Barbarossa is personally felled by the mortally wounded Arrigo. At Arrigo's request he is dragged into the Milan cathedral where he expires kissing his country's flag, having first convinced Rolando of Lida's fidelity and received forgiveness.

Major Roles. LIDA (s); much florid music; C♯3 to C♯5. ARRIGO (t); A1 to B♭3. ROLANDO (bar) florid, staccato passages, trills; B♭1 to G♭3.

Lesser Roles. MARCOVALDO (bar). FREDERIC BARBAROSSA (bs).

Bit Roles. FIRST CONSUL (bs). SECOND CONSUL (bs). PODESTA OF COMO (bar). IMELDA (m-s) Lida's maid. HERALD (t).

Chorus. SSATTBB. Lida's serving women, warriors, magistrates, dukes, Milanese citizens, senators, town fathers of Como, priests.

Orchestra. 2 fl, 2 ob, 2 cl, 2 bsn, 4 hrn, 2 trp, 3 trb, tuba, timp, perc, bells, harp, strings.

Material. Bel (Ri).

🎵 Béatrice

Music by André Messager (1853–1929). Poem in French by Robert de Flers and Gaston A. de Caillavet after Charles Nodier. Premiere: Monte Carlo, March 21, 1914. "Lyric legend." Melodious. Set numbers. Short preludes before each act. Setting: 16th-century Sicily and Calabria. Four acts.

ACT I: A convent court. ACT II: A terrace beside the sea, below a garden. ACT III: A poor fisherman's cabaret on the Calabrian shore. ACT IV: Same as I.

Synopsis. Béatrice, a rebel in the convent because she worships the Virgin even over God, tells the priest how the Virgin answered her prayer to spare the life of Lorenzo, a relative who has been like a brother to her and who has been wounded in the war with the Turks. She promised to take the veil if her prayer were answered. A Gypsy, succored by the convent, disturbs her by prophesying that her life would be one of love. Lorenzo, not understanding her vow, returned to the army and she has not seen him since. Now he gains entrance disguised as a beggar in order to rescue her. She is proof against his ardent pleas, but he returns with two men who overpower her and carry her away. The statue of the Virgin comes alive and takes her place. In a luxurious villa, Lorenzo has tired of Béatrice, although she has grown to love him passionately. He invites convivial comrades for an evening of merrymaking, but Béatrice remains aloof, protesting her love at such length that he drinks to a capricious Venus. Fabrice, one of the revelers, proposes a visit to the beach. Everyone leaves but Lorenzo and Musidora, who is ready for a flirtation. Lorenzo responds by a long embrace which Béatrice, returning, sees, then retreats. Lorenzo promises to join Musidora in Palermo within the hour. Béatrice upbraids her lover, but he coolly leaves her. In despair, she summons the merrymakers and offers herself first to one then another, swearing to live only for pleasure. In a fisherman's tavern, the Gypsy predicts bad fortune. Lorenzo enters and tells of four years of wandering. The Gypsy offers to bring a fabulous dancer, Ginevra, who has turned men's heads to the point of duelling. Lorenzo, left alone by his comrade, recognizes the dancer as Béatrice, and begs her to return to him. Disillusioned, she refuses so definitely that he goes. As the fishermen return, Béatrice feverishly promises to dance for them and give herself to each in turn. At the end of her dance, the men fight over her and Beppo is killed. The others turn on Béatrice, but at last leave her. In her remorse, she hears an invisible choir singing the Hymn to the Virgin, and slowly follows the imaginary voices. Entering the convent court, almost collapsing with fatigue, she prays God for punishment, then notices that the Virgin has taken her place. The Virgin places her cloak on Béatrice's shoulders, tells her she is forgiven, and mounts her altar once again. Béatrice at first is reluctant to accept dispensation, but the voice of the Virgin bespeaks a miracle, which the sisters accept and receive Béatrice in their company again.

Major Roles. BÉATRICE (dram s); C3 to B4. THE VIRGIN (s); F3 to A4. MUSIDORA (m-s); C3 to G♭4. THE GYPSY (m-s or c); A2 to G♭4. MOTHER SUPERIOR (m-s); C3 to F4. LORENZO (t); C2 to B♭3.

Lesser Roles. FROSINE, LÉLIA, SISTERS ODILE, BLANDINE, MONIQUE (all s). TIBÉRIO (bar). PRIEST (bs). FABRICE (t). FABIO (t). BEPPO (bar).

Bit Parts. GARDENER (t). FISHERMAN (t).

Chorus. SATB. Nuns, fishermen, angels.

Orchestra. 3 fl, 2 ob, Eng hrn, 2 cl, bs cl, 3 bsn, 4 hrn, 3 trp, 3 trb, tuba, timp, bells, tri, bs dr, harp, org (ad lib), strings.

Material. B & H VS*.

🔲 Beatrice di Tenda · Beatrice of Tenda

Music by Vincenzo Bellini (1801–1835). Libretto in Italian by Felice Romani, possibly based on novel, *Il Castello di Binasco,* by Diodata Saluzzo-Roero. Commissioned by Teatro la Fenice, Venice. Premiere: Venice, March 16, 1833. Historical drama. Set numbers, accompanied recitative; conventional harmony with considerable melisma. Prelude. Growing sophistication in orchestra color. Chorus functions as Greek chorus, commentator and participant. Vocal lines dramatic, melodic, some florid and some declamatory. Long, intricate ensembles. Setting: Castle of Binasco, near Milan, 1418. Two acts, six scenes (approx 152 min).

ACT I i: Inner courtyard of castle; ii: Agnese's apartments; iii: The park; iv: Remote gallery in the castle. ACT II i: Great hall; ii: Dungeon.

Synopsis. After the death of the Count, his widow Beatrice of Tenda has married Filippo Maria Visconti, Duke of Milan. Younger than she, Filippo has tired of Beatrice and loves Agnese del Manio, a lady-in-waiting. Agnese, however, loves Orombello di Ventimiglia, who himself is enamored of Beatrice. In this tangled web, Agnese discovers Orombello's passion and schemes to concoct evidence against Beatrice, both political and personal. Beatrice and Orombello are arrested; the latter confesses, implicating Beatrice, who does not break down even under torture. She is led to execution, after forgiving Agnese, who has confessed.

Major Roles. FILIPPO (bar); dramatic; needs some flexibility; high tessitura; Bb1 to F3. BEATRICE (spin s); needs both dramatic and coloratura ability; high tessitura; trill Bb2 to C5 (2 D5). AGNESE (spin s); high tessitura; C#3 to Bb4. OROMBELLO (lyr-dram t); coloratura passages; high tessitura; C#2 (1 Bb1) to A3.

Lesser Roles. ANICHINO, friend of Orombello (t). RIZZARDO DEL MAINO, confidant of Filippo (bar or bs).

Chorus. SSATTBB, often divided. Courtiers, soldiers, populace, etc.

Orchestra. 2 fl, 2 ob, 2 cl, 2 bsn, 4 hrn, 2 trp, 3 trb, timp, perc, harp, strings.

Material. Bel (Ri). VS out of print.

Performances. Amer. Op. Soc. (NYC): 2.21.61; 3.1.61 (conc).

✍ Béatrice et Bénédict · Beatrice and Benedict

Music by Hector Berlioz (1803–1869). Libretto in French by the composer after Shakespeare's *Much Ado about Nothing*. Commissioned by the Baden-Baden Theater. Premiere: Baden-Baden, August 9, 1862 (in French). German revision with recitatives replacing dialogue by Felix Mottl; premiere: Carlsruhe, April 6, 1888. German revision by J. Stransky and W. Keefeld; premiere: Leipzig, March 27, 1913. Women's trio and offstage chorus in Act II added for the published score a few weeks after the premiere. Sentimental-historical comedy. Set numbers, dialogue. Overture; entr'acte before Act II. Typical Berlioz harmonies with special brass sound. Melodic; vocal line with florid and declamatory passages. Setting: Messina, Sicily; 16th century. Two acts (approx 135 min).

ACT I: Grounds of the Governor's palace (approx 80 min). ACT II: Large hall in the palace (approx 55 min).

Synopsis. General Don Pedro and his lieutenants Claudio and Bénédict are returning to Messina after a victory over the Moors. Hero, younger daughter of Messina's Governor Leonato, celebrates her reunion with her fiancé Claudio, while her sister Béatrice renews her customary witty bickering with Bénédict. Bénédict scouts the possibility of marriage, while Don

Pedro and Claudio resolve to trap him. Somarone, the music master, conducts a "wedding cantata," which spoofs academicians and pedagogues, musical and literary. Bénédict is tricked into realizing that he may love Béatrice after all. His avowal surprises Béatrice, who is tempted to return his affection, and even signs a contract. But the two fall to quarreling again, ending however with a love duet in which they state that they have signed a temporary truce until tomorrow.

Major Roles. BÉATRICE (lyr-col m-s); florid passages; C#3 to B4. HERO (s); florid; high tessitura; C#3 to B4. BÉNÉDICT (t); needs great flexibility; C#2 to B3. URSULA, Hero's nurse (c); G2 to F4. SOMARONE (buf-bs); must be good actor; B1 to F3.

Lesser Roles. CLAUDIO (bar). DON PEDRO (bs). LEONATO (mute, character part).

Bit Parts (all sp). MESSENGER; SCRIVENER; TWO SERVANTS.

Chorus. SSATTBB. Considerable counterpoint; some florid soprano passages. Townspeople, officers, attendants, musicians, courtiers.

Ballet. Short Sicilienne in Act I; an improvisation in Act II.

Orchestra. 2 fl (picc), 2 ob (Eng hrn), 2 cl, 2 bsn, 4 hrn (preferably 2 natural, 2 valve), 2 trp, 2 corn à pist (1 ad lib), 3 trb, timp, guit, perc, 2 harp, tamb, strings. *Stage*: 2 ob, 2 bsn, 2 trp, corn à pist, tamb, large dr, cym, 2 small dr, 2 guit.

Material. Ox (E vers by Geoffrey Dunn).

Performances. Litt. Orch. (NYC): 3.60 (Amer prem—conc). Op. Soc. of Wash.: 6.3.64 (Amer stage prem). Manh. Sch. (NYC): 5.65. Los Ang. Philh.: 4.70.

⩗ Beatrix Cenci

Music by Alberto Ginastera (1916–   ). Libretto in Spanish by William Shand and Alberto Girri, based on real personages. Commissioned by the Opera Society of Washington, D.C. Premiere: Washington, September 10, 1971. Historical melodrama. Dissonant contemporary idiom, difficult vocal line, largely declamatory; some song speech, dialogue. Setting: Rome and Petrella, end of 16th century. Two acts, fourteen scenes (95 min).

ACT I i: Antechamber, Cenci Palace, Rome; ii: Cenci's apartments; iii: Lucrecia's apartments; iv: Gardens of the palace; v: Banquet hall; vi: Beatrix's bedroom; vii: Bernardo's room. ACT II i: Terrace, Castle of Petrella; ii: Passageway; iii: Dining hall; iv: Antechamber, then bedroom; v: Cenci Palace, Rome; vi: Prison, Castel Sant' Angelo; vii: Prison cell.

Synopsis. The cruel Count Francesco Cenci, excoriated by the people and feared by his daughter Beatrix and his second wife Lucrecia, orders his servant Andrea to arrange a masked ball at which he intends to "celebrate" the death of his two sons. Beatrix seeks escape by sending a letter to the Pope with her former suitor, Orsino, who has taken holy orders. But Orsino treacherously tears up the letter. At the ball, Beatrix is partnered in a sen-

43

suous dance by her father, to her ultimate horror. The guests leave in dismay although Beatrix pleads with them not to abandon her, her stepmother and her little brother Bernardo. Orsino returns and lies about the letter, saying that the Pope has rejected Beatrix's plea. He leaves Beatrix to be assaulted by her father. In exile in the decaying castle at Petrella, Beatrix is advised by her older brother Giacomo to avenge her disgrace by killing her father, and hires two assassins, Olimpio and Marzio. Lucrecia gives Cenci a sleeping potion, delivering him to the assassins, who, however, lose their courage until Beatrix threatens them. They stab the Count, whose last act is to tear at Beatrix's dress. Months later, Orsino announces that the Count's body has been found, one of the assassins has been killed and the other has confessed. Beatrix is arrested, bound, and tortured. She prepares to die, then recoils in horror as she contemplates meeting her father in hell; but finally composes herself and goes to the scaffold.

Major Roles. COUNT FRANCESCO CENCI (bs); F1 (E1 in song speech) to G3. BEATRIX (lyr s); needs flexibility; difficult intervals, wide skips; B2 to B4. LUCRECIA (c); difficult intervals; A♭2 to B4. BERNARDO (boy s); needs flexibility; low F2. ORSINO (t); C2 to A3.

Lesser Roles. ANDREA (bar); G1 to E♭3. GIACOMO (bs-bar); A1 to G3. OLIMPIO and MARZIO (sp).

Bit Role. A GUARD (bs).

Chorus. SATB. Also speaks. Nobles, guards, judges, servants, etc.

Ballet. Can be in I v.

Orchestra. 3 fl (picc), 3 ob, 3 cl, 2 bsn, cont bsn, 4 hrn, 4 trp, 4 trb, tuba, harp, organ, cel, mandolin, timp, perc (elaborate, including xyl, vib), strings. Sound effects, including howling of dogs, on tape.

Production Problems. Films and projections may be used.

Material. B & H.

Performances. NYCO: 3.14.73.

🎵 The Beggar's Opera

Version of John Gay's ballad opera by Daniel Pinkham (1923–   ). Commissioned by Cambridge Drama Festival. Premiere: Cambridge, Mass., 1955. Historical comedy. Set numbers; pseudo-Baroque style. Adaptation of the traditional story by Richard Baldrich. Setting: London, 18th century. Four acts (180 min).

Major Roles. MR. PEACHUM, MRS. PEACHUM, POLLY, CAPTAIN MACHEATH, LOCKIT, LUCY, etc. Many lesser roles.

Chorus. SATB. Small.

Orchestra. fl, ob, hrn, trp, timp, harpsichord, strings (12 players altogether).

Material. ACA.

44

🎭 Der Belagerungzustand · The Siege

Music by Milko Kelemen (1924–   ). Libretto in German by the composer and Joachim Hess after Albert Camus' novel, *The Plague*. Premiere: Hamburg, January 13, 1970. Difficult intervals; voices and several instruments often required to sing or play one quarter tone above or below written notes; unconventional harmonies; *Sprechstimme* combined with singing. Setting: A town, any time, any place. Prologue and two acts (120 min).

Scenes: After audience is seated, Pest and the Secretary station themselves at stage left and right with bridge between. Curtain rises on lively city scene, which changes by means of projections from a Square, with churchyard and adminstrative offices in center, to a city silhouette, and back.

Synopsis. Inhabitants of a town, terrified by a comet, react feverishly with a summer celebration, but soon are thrown into a deeper panic by deaths caused by the Plague. Among the characters are Victoria and Diego, who love each other; Nada, a drunkard with contempt for everything; and the Governor, who is impotent to save the situation and eventually flees. The Plague becomes the State, and nobody can escape. His Secretary marks down the victims in a little book. Nada, because he is "Nothing," is appointed to a high post. Diego, actively opposing the Plague, seeks shelter in the Judge's house, but the latter fears infection and sends him away. Victoria leaves with him. After two brushes with the Secretary, Diego defies her and learns her secret. The man without fear will be saved. But Victoria has fallen. Diego offers his life for hers, but will not meet the Plague's condition that he and Victoria leave town. He sacrifices himself for Victoria and the people, and the Plague is forced to go—for the moment.

Major Roles. THE PLAGUE (bar); very difficult; needs flexibility, strength and sinister characterization; G#1 to G3 (one Ab3). SECRETARY (c or m-s); F#2 to G#4 (many passages octave higher opt). DIEGO (t); C#2 to Bb3. VICTORIA, Judge's daughter (s); needs great flexibility; many difficult intervals; C#3 to Bb4 (B4 with B3 opt; C5 with A4 opt). NADA (high t); florid passages; Eb2 to B3, C4, C#4 and Db4 with lower opt; also touches D4. JUDGE (bar); G#1 to E3. HIS WIFE (m-s); C#3 to F#4. GOVERNOR (bs); F1 to E3. MUNICIPAL COUNSELLOR I (high bar). MUNICIPAL COUNSELLOR II (t). FISCHER (bs); Ab1 to Eb3.

Lesser Roles. OFFICER (t). PARSON (t). BIG MAN (bar). PRAYING WOMAN (s).

Chorus. SSSSSSSSSTTTTTBBBBBB. Very important and difficult; some solos; often divided: eight S and eight C solos; twelve women in church, etc. Many improvised passages. Men, women, counsellors, police, drunkards. Remains on stage throughout, creating production problem.

Orchestra. 3 fl (picc), 3 ob (Eng hrn), 2 cl, Eb cl (bs cl), 3 bsn (cont bsn), 4 hrn, 3 trp, 3 trb, tuba, harp, cembalo, cel, elec organ, piano, glock, 4 timp, very complicated perc (2 players at right, 3 at left including 6 typewriters [or simulated]); strings. Electronic effects in several scenes. Loudspeakers required.

Material. Pet (Lit). Three tapes supplied for offstage voices and sounds. No projection slides supplied.

🎭 Benvenuto Cellini

Music by Hector Berlioz (1803–1869). Libretto in French by Léon de Wailly and Auguste Barbier. Premiere: Paris, September 10, 1838. Romantic drama. Melodious, set numbers, recitative, elaborate orchestra, rhythmically complex; important ensembles and chorus. Overture; also between scenes i and ii in Act II the "Roman Carnival" overture is played. Setting: Rome, 1532. Three acts, four scenes (approx 150 min).

ACT I: Room in Balducci's house. ACT II i: Courtyard of a tavern; ii: Piazza di Colonna. ACT III: Before Cellini's house, foundry in background.

Synopsis. Cellini, the Florentine goldsmith, has been summoned by the Pope to Rome, and has fallen in love with Teresa, daughter of the Papal treasurer, Balducci. The two plan to elope during the carnival; Cellini will wear a white monk's hood, his apprentice Ascanio a brown one. They are overheard by Fiermosca, the Pope's sculptor and Balducci's favorite as a suitor for his daughter. Cellini, impoverished, agrees to complete his statue of Perseus by morning in exchange for a stipend from the Pope, delivered by Balducci. In the excitement and bustle of the carnival, Cellini and Ascanio attempt to abduct Teresa, but Fieramosca and Pompeo (a hireling) are similarly disguised. A riot breaks out in which Cellini stabs Pompeo, but the white-robed Fieramosca is arrested in his stead. Cellini is safe for the moment, but disaster converges on him from several quarters: Balducci accuses him of the murder, Fieramosca believes he has abducted Teresa, and Cardinal Salvati arrives to see the "Perseus." But at the threat of another supplanting him in finishing the statue, Cellini declares that he will cast it then and there. Throwing in all his completed works, he at last has enough metal; the "Perseus" (one of the glories of Florence) is completed, to everyone's satisfaction, and Cellini wins his bride.

Major Roles. BALDUCCI (bs); trill on A1; F1 to Eb3. TERESA (s); needs flexibility; some florid passages and high tessitura; C3 to B4. BENVENUTO CELLINI (t); high tessitura; C2 to C4 (several) and Db4. ASCANIO (m-s); B2 to B4. FIERAMOSCA (bar); Bb1 to F3 (one Ab3 with F3 opt).

Lesser Roles. POMPEO (bar). FRANCESCO (t), BERNARDINO (bs), Cellini's workmen. INNKEEPER (t). OFFICER (bar).

Chorus. SATTBB. Workmen, maskers, citizens, monks.

Orchestra. 2 fl (2 picc), 2 ob, 2 cl, 4 bsn, 4 hrn, 4 trp, 2 pist, 3 trb, tuba, timp, perc, harp, strings.

Production Difficulty. Casting statue. Big crowd scenes.

Material. Ka (French edit 1863). VS: Pet (f)*.

Performances. Litt Orch. (NYC): 3.22.65 (conc). Cleve. Inst.: 5.27.70.

46

Die Bernauerin · The Ballad of Agnes Bernauer

Music by Carl Orff (1895–   ). Libretto in Bavarian dialect by composer after 15th-century story. Premiere: Stuttgart, June 15, 1947. Musical play. In composer's rhythmic, repetitive style; considerable dialogue, *Sprechstimme*, small amount of solo vocal line largely declamatory. Chorus very important. Brief preludes to Acts I and II. Setting: Munich and vicinity, 15th century. Prologue and two acts, eleven scenes (115 min).

Prologue: Curtain with fantastic Bavarian heraldic emblems. ACT I i: Bathhouse in Augsburg; ii: Inn in Munich; iii: A street, shadowy image of the Virgin; iv: Castle Voheburg (45 min). ACT II (Curtain with Duke Albrecht's seal); i: Two burghers before curtain; ii: Albrecht's castle at Straubing; iii: Chancellery in Munich; iv: Corner of a dark church in Munich; v: Castle Straubing; vi: Witches' den; vii: Open field (70 min).

Synopsis. Young Albrecht, Duke of Bavaria and Count of Voheburg, persists in marrying Agnes, daughter of the bathhouse proprietor Bernauer, in spite of the objections of his father, the old Duke, and of his friends. The old Duke, outraged, has Agnes abducted and drowned as a witch.

Major Roles (all in rhythmic speech except Agnes, who sings in Act II). ALBRECHT. AGNES.

Lesser Roles. YOUNG ADELIGE, Albrecht's friend. KASPAR BERNAUER. DUKE ERNST, Albrecht's father. CHANCELLOR. CAPTAIN. JUDGE. BAILIFF. MONK. SERVANT GIRL (mute). TWO MUNICH BURGHERS. FIVE WITCHES (men's voices). HERALD. FRENCH STREET SINGER (t).

Chorus. SSAATTBB. *Sprechstimme* in Act II. Solo t in orchestra; solo s from above. People, warriors, guests at bathhouse.

Orchestra. 3 fl (picc), 3 ob (Eng hrn), 3 cl, bs cl, 2 bsn, cont bsn, 4 hrn, 3 trp, 3 trb, tuba, timp (7 kettles), perc: bs dr, 3 side dr, tri, ratchet, castanets, 3 cym, clash and suspended, tam-tam, xyl, 2 glock, metallophone, tub bells. In Witches' scene, in addition to above: 2 piano, 8–10 stone plates, bs xyl, 2 small timp, cym (1 clash, 2 suspended), large and small tamtam, bs dr, big dr, ratsche, 8–10 various rattles. *Stage*: organ, 2 piano, large tam-tam, bs dr, at least 6 side dr, at least 3 ten dr, 2 bells, F3, F♯4.

Material. Bel (Sch). Authorized English adapt.: Fritz André Kracht.

Performances. Univ. of Kansas City: 3.21.68 (Amer prem).

Der Besuch der Alten Dame · The Visit of the Old Lady

Music by Gottfried von Einum. Libretto in German by Friedrich Dürrenmatt after his play. Commissioned by the Vienna Staatsoper. Premiere: Vienna, May 23, 1971. Tragedy. Tonal harmonies, melodious yet dramatic vocal line with some declamation, powerfully evocative orchestra. Setting: The small, mid-European town of Güllen; the present. Three acts, ten scenes, linked with interludes (135 min).

ACT I i: Railway station platform; ii: Interior of Golden Apostle Inn; iii:

47

Konrad's Village Wood; iv: Inn dining room. ACT II i: Alfred Ill's shop in the square, hotel balcony at one side; ii: Station platform. ACT III i: Petersen's barn; ii: Ill's shop, greatly spruced up; iii: The wood; iv: Railway station.

Synopsis. Into the dilapidated little town of Güllen arrives a former villager, now a wealthy woman of the world: Claire Zachanassian. Her entourage includes her seventh husband, a butler, two gum-chewing ruffians, and a pair of blind eunuchs. The townsfolk, smartened up as far as possible to greet her, are not left long in ignorance of her mission. When she was a girl, she tells them, Alfred Ill had made her pregnant and then lied about it and got her driven out of town. She had become a prostitute, then married many times, notably a rich Armenian. Now she has come back for "justice." She will give the town a cool million on one condition: that Ill is killed.

The immediate reaction is righteous horror, but the signs of corruption soon appear. The first evidence is everyone's acquisition of new finery—on credit. Ill begins to sense that the town is turning against him. Claire calmly watches, managing to take two new husbands and dispose of as many, and revealing that the two eunuchs are former Gülleners who lied about her at the trial and whom she found and had castrated and blinded. The certainty grows in Ill. Even his best friend, the upright Schoolmaster, and his family begin to show enmity. The inevitable happens, in the midst of great fanfare from press and worldwide attention. Claire has her victim, ostensibly dead from too great excitement. The town has its money—and thorough degradation. Only Ill has gained—in resolute character and even a trace of nobility.

Major Roles. CLAIRE ZACHANASSIAN (m-s); needs great power; forcefulness throughout range. ALFRED ILL (high bar); strong dramatic requirements. HIS WIFE (lyr s). HIS DAUGHTER (s). HIS SON (t). THE MAYOR (dram t). THE PRIEST (bs bar). THE SCHOOLMASTER (bar).

Lesser Roles. THE BUTLER (light t). KOBY and LOBY, blind eunichs (t, t). THE DOCTOR (bar). THE POLICEMAN (bs-bar). HOFBAUER (t). HELMESBERGER (bar). CLAIRE'S HUSBAND NO. IX (t). TWO WOMEN (s, s). STATIONMASTER (bs-bar). RAILWAY GUARD (bs). CONDUCTOR (t). CAMERAMAN (bs). Mute: HUSBAND VII, TOBY and ROBY (ruffians), REPORTER (sp).

Chorus. SATB. Townspeople.

Orchestra. 2 fl, picc, 2 ob, 2 cl, 2 bsn, 4 hrn, 3 trp, 3 trb, tuba, timp, perc (tamb, cym, side dr, ten dr, bs dr, tam-tam, tri), guit, strings. *Stage*: tub bells, station bell, fire bell.

Material. B & H. VS*.

Performances. San Fran.: 10.25.72 (Amer prem).

🎵 Black Widow

Music by Thomas Pasatieri (1945–   ). Libretto in English by the composer, based on the novel *Dos Madres* by Miguel de Unamuno. Premiere:

Seattle, March 2, 1972. Tragedy. Continuous texture; melodic; vocal line florid; conventional harmonies. Six interludes. Setting: A Spanish town, early 20th century. Three acts, seven scenes (approx 120 min).

ACT I (45 min); ACT II (45 min); ACT III (30 min).

Synopsis. The beautiful young widow Raquel is obsessed with the desire to bear a child, but cannot. She involves her wealthy lover Juan in a plot: he shall marry Berta, a young girl desperately in love with him, and give Raquel any child of the marriage. The opera shifts from reality to surreality as Juan dies, and Berta becomes helpless and insane. Raquel shelters Berta, then gives her money to marry again, advising her that "it's no good to be a widow."

Major Roles. RAQUEL (m-s or dram s); extremely demanding both lyrically and dramatically; needs remarkable agility and strength for 14-minute monologue at end of Act I. BERTA (lyr s); high tessitura; some florid passages. JUAN (lyr bar); difficult role dramatically; must have exceptional acting ability. MARTA, Berta's mother (m-s). PEDRO, Berta's father (t).

Orchestra. 2 fl (picc), 2 ob (Eng hrn), 2 cl (bs cl), 2 bsn (cont bsn), 2 hrn, 2 trp, 2 trb, tuba, perc (2), harp, strings.

Material. Bel.

🎵 Blood Wedding · Vérnász

Music by Sandor Szokolay (1931–   ). Libretto in Hungarian by Gyula Illyés, based on the Lorca play, *Bodas de Sangre.* Premiere: Budapest, October 31, 1964. Tragedy. Music governed by dramatic necessity, employing occasional serialism; deliberate attempt to incorporate Spanish idiom, but pervaded by Hungarian flavor: strong folk mood. Continuous texture, embodying well-defined scenes. Vocal line extremely difficult; largely melodious; considerable *Sprechstimme.* Brief prelude; interludes for all scene changes. Setting: rural Spain, late 19th–early 20th century. Three acts, seven scenes (approx 135 min).

ACT I i: Home of the Groom; ii: Home of Leonardo; iii: Interior of Bride's home (45 min). ACT II i: Another room in Bride's home; ii: Banquet in patio (35 min). ACT III i: Desolate landscape; ii: A white dwelling (55 min).

Synopsis. A young Spanish girl prepares for her wedding, but is still disturbed by her attraction to her former fiancé, Leonardo, who has married another woman. He also cannot forget his former sweetheart, and is compelled to ride his horse nightly to her farm, although they never meet. At the dawn of her wedding day, Leonardo finally confronts her, and their pent-up passions explode and they confess they have never ceased to love each other. The Groom's mother, although her misgiving has been based on an old feud between the two families, was not wrong in disapproving her son's marriage. As the guests arrive, Leonardo slips away. The bridal procession returns from church for the wedding feast. At the height of the celebration, it is discovered that the bride and Leonardo are missing. Leonardo's wife enters, shrieking that the couple has eloped on horseback. Ancient hatreds flare, and the company sets off to take vengeance. The hapless lovers are gradually overtaken; the bride escapes, but Leonardo stays to face the outraged Groom. Both perish in a duel (not seen), and the two bodies are brought in in a funeral procession.

Major Roles. THE MOTHER OF THE GROOM (dram c); very sustained, needs strength at extremes of range; high tessitura. THE BRIDE (dram s); extremely difficult; demands great stamina, strength throughout range. LEONARDO (dram bar); high tessitura; forceful; F1 to G3. THE GROOM (dram t). LEONARDO'S WIFE (lyr-spin s). LEONARDO'S MOTHER-IN-LAW (c). BRIDE'S SERVANT (s). NEIGHBOR (s). FATHER OF THE BRIDE (bs).

Lesser Roles. THREE WOODCUTTERS (bar, bs-bar, bs). DEATH (c). THE MOON (high t); sustained high tessitura. BEST MAN (bar). TWO BRIDESMAIDS (s, m-s).

Chorus. SSAATTB: wedding guests. Large chorus indispensable. Women, men, mixed, children; at times combined.

Ballet. Flamenco dancers in wedding scene; number according to availability.

Orchestra. 3 fl (picc), 3 ob (Eng hrn), 3 cl (bs cl), 3 bsn (cont bsn), 4 hrn, 3 trp, 3 trb, tuba, harp, cel, xyl, perc (3), timp, pipe organ, strings.

Material. B & H. Tr: Károly Köpe.

Performances. Amer prem scheduled at Ohio St. Univ. (Columbus): 5.17.73 (Amer prem).

Boccaccio

Music by Franz von Suppé (1819–1895). Libretto in German by F. Zell (Camillo Walzell) and Richard Genée. Premiere: Vienna, February 1, 1879. Modern version with libretto by Alfred Rott and Frederick Schreyvogel and musical adaptation by Anton Paulig and Rudolf Kattnigg, 1951. Operetta. Melodious; set numbers. Setting: Florence and its environs, 1331. Three acts.

ACT I: A piazza. ACT II: A street, flanked by the houses of Fiammetta and Isabella. ACT III: The palace and gardens of the Duke of Tuscany.

Synopsis. The men of Florence are up in arms against the piquant love stories of young Boccaccio which all too clearly reveal the true identity of their sinful characters. They determine to burn the books. Meanwhile, the barber Scalza's pretty wife Beatrice is entertaining a gallant, Leonetto, who calls on Boccaccio for help when the barber arrives home. Leonetto and Boccaccio engage in a mock duel which gets them out of the scrape. Another intrigue is in process between Prince Pietro of Palermo, visiting incognito the cooper's wife Isabella, and mistaken for Boccaccio. When his identity is revealed, apologies are in order, but the book burning goes on, the men enlisting the help of a beggar, who is Boccaccio himself. In this disguise he watches Fiammetta, adopted daughter of the grocer Lambertuccio and his

50

wife Peronella—but in reality the illegitimate daughter of the Duke of Tuscany, who decides to marry her to Prince Pietro.

Boccaccio and Fiammetta genuinely love each other, and finally are united after various skirmishes and misunderstandings, Prince Pietro relinquishing his claims and renewing his pursuit of Isabella.

Major Roles. GIOVANNI BOCCACCIO (m-s); needs acting ability and great charm. PIETRO, Prince of Palermo (t). BARBER SCALZA (bs). BEATRICE, his wife (s). COOPER LOTTERINGHI (bar). ISABELLA, his wife (s). GROCER LAMBERTUCCIO (bar). PERONELLA, his wife (s). FIAMMETTA (lyr s).

Lesser and Bit Roles. LEONETTO (t). Boccaccio's friends: TOFANO, CHICHIBIO, GUIDO, CISTI, FEDERICO, RINIERI, GIOTTO. A STRANGER. BUTLER OF THE DUKE OF TUSCANY. A PEDDLER. MISTRESS JANCOFIORE. ELISA, her niece. MARIETTA, a young girl. MISTRESS NONA PULCI. AUGUSTINA, ELENA, ANGELICA, her daughters.

Chorus. SATB. Lotteringhi's workers, journeyman coopers, beggars, serving maids.

Pantomime. (Act III) Pantaleone, Brighella, Pulcinella, Colombine, Arlechino, Scarpino, Narcissino.

Material. Map.

🎭 Bomarzo

Music by Alberto Ginastera (1916–   ). Libretto in Spanish by Manuel Mujica Lainez after his novel. Commissioned by the Washington (D.C.) Opera Society. Premiere: Washington, May 19, 1967. Melodrama. Serial technique, with aleatoric and microtonal sections; many eccentric orchestral effects. Vocal line difficult, mostly recitative, occasionally melodic. Prelude, fourteen interludes, necessitating quick scene changes. Setting: Bomarzo, Florence, Rome, 16th century. Two acts, fifteen scenes (131 min).

ACT I i: Bomarzo Castle park ("The Potion"); ii: Room in Castle ("Pier Francesco's Childhood"); iii: Pier Francesco's Study ("The Horoscope"); iv: Chamber of Pantasilea, Florence ("Pantasilea"); v: Countryside in Bomarzo ("The Tiber"); vi: Great hall in castle ("Pier Francesco Orsini, Duke of Bomarzo"); vii: Terrace and garden of castle ("Fiesta at Bomarzo"); vii: Pier Francesco's study ("The Portrait by Lorenzo Lotto") (82 min). ACT II i: Palace of Galeazzo Farnese, Rome ("Julia Farnese"); ii: Bridal chamber, Bomarzo ("The Bridal Chamber"); iii: Same, at a distance ("The Dream"); iv: Gallery of castle ("The Minotaur"); v: Garden of castle ("Maerbale"); vi: Silvio's studio in castle ("The Alchemy"); vii: Park of castle, same as I i ("The Park of the Monsters") (49 min).

Synopsis. Pier Francesco Orsini, Duke of Bomarzo (sometimes called Vicino), drinks a potion that his astrologer Silvio de Narni has said would make him immortal. Instead, it is a fatal poison. As he dies, the events of his life pass before him. A stunted hunchback, he spent a miserable childhood, bedeviled by his brothers Girolamo and Maerbale. They force him to wear women's clothes; his father, instead of rescuing him, drags him into a haunted room where a skeleton seems to dance and menace him. Diana Orsini, his grandmother, hails him as Duke as the astrologer weaves a potent charm and the peacocks cry to foretell a death. His father has been wounded in battle. The young man is sent to the courtesan Pantasilea in Florence, but the experience in her room of mirrors, reflecting thousandfold his horrid image, completely unnerves him. His brother Girolamo ridicules his horoscope, but falls from a promontory on the Tiber and hits his head on a rock. The new Duke courts the beautiful Julia Farnese, but is chagrined when she prefers his brother Maerbale. In a macabre dance festival, erotic and terrifying dreams pass before the Duke, who then visits his portrait, so idealized that seeing his actual self in a mirror destroys his peace of mind and makes his image appear to be the devil. Still courting Julia, he spills a glass of wine on her dress and counts it a premonition of death. After their marriage, Bomarzo finds himself impotent and dreams that his courtiers capture Julia and offer him what he could not attain in life. Then he flees to the gallery where he embraces the marble statue of the Minotaur. As years go by, he becomes sure Julia is unfaithful with Maerbale. He sets his beloved servant Abdul on his brother and has him killed. Silvio mixes the magic potion while Bomarzo's nephew Nicholas watches. The boy poisons the drink. A young shepherd signals in the garden that the park of Bomarzo forgives him for transforming its rocks into gigantic monsters (these exist in reality and were the inspiration for the novel). Bomarzo dies in his "Sacred Wood."

Major Roles. PIER FRANCESCO ORSINI (t); extremely demanding role; high tessitura very exposed; very difficult intervals; needs strength at extremes of range; C2 (B♭1 in song speech) to A3. SILVIO DE NARNI (bar); high tessitura; C2 (A♭1 in song speech) to G3. GRAN CORRADO ORSINI, Pier's father (bs); A♭1 to F3. GIROLAMO (bar); C2 to G3. MAERBALE (bar); G1 (G2 opt) to F♯3. NICHOLAS ORSINI (c or t); c, C3 to G♯4; t, B♭2 to G♯3. JULIA FARNESE (s); C♯3 to A♯4. PANTALISEA (m-s); C3 to G♯4. DIANA ORSINI (c); G2 to G4.

Lesser Roles. MESSENGER (bar). SHEPHERD BOY (child), PIER FRANCESCO, GIROLAMO and MAERBALE as children (mimes.) SKELETON (d).

Chorus. SATB. Prelates, courtiers, pages, servants, astrologers.

Ballet. Erotic dance in I vii.

Orchestra. 2 fl (picc), 2 ob (Eng hrn), 2 cl (cl E♭, 2 bs cl), 2 bsn (cont bsn), 3 hrn, 3 trp, 3 trb, 4 timp, mandolin, harp, clavicembalo, piano (cel), harpsichord, strings (vla d'amore), xyl, perc (3): bells, 3 crotale, 6 dr susp, 5 bongos, 5 cowbells, 3 tamb, 2 thin metal sheets, Japanese wind chimes (3 sizes), laiiiro, glock, 3 tri, 3 tam-tams, 5 tom-toms, 5 temple bl, bells, whip, 3 low Chinese gongs, military dr (1 with snares, 1 without), t dr, bass dr, 5 wd bl, Japanese yoshigi (sharp cracking noise), ratchet.

Materials. B & H. VS*.

Performances. NYCO: 3.14.68; 9.26.68; 10.19.69, etc.

🎵 Boulevard Solitude

Music by Hans Werner Henze (1926–   ). Libretto in German by Grete Weil, after scenario by Walter Jockisch. Premiere: Hanover, February 17, 1952. Tragedy, loosely based on Prévost's novel *Manon Lescaut*. Music eclectic, individualistic twelve-tone idiom, some melody, jazz elements, a little *Sprechstimme*. Brief prelude. Important interludes. Setting: Paris, just after World War II. Two acts, seven scenes (approx 120 min).

ACT I i: Railroad station in large French city; ii: Small loft; iii: Lilaque's elegant boudoir; iv: University library. ACT II i: Dope dive; ii: Lilaque's house, split stage showing foyer and bedroom; iii: in front of prison.

Synopsis. Armand, a young student, and Manon become lovers, but Armand soon is jealous and Manon discontented with poverty. Lescaut procures men for his sister Manon, who leaves Armand for Lilaque. But brother and sister are kicked out after money is missing. Armand laments the loss of Manon while his friend Francis extolls learning. Armand and Manon are reunited, but once again she leaves him and he becomes a dope addict. In a dive, Lescaut, his junkie, appears with Manon's next prospect, Lilaque's son, and Manon seeks Armand, but he is too far gone. She leaves a message for him to come to Lilaque's apartment, Lescaut steals a painting, but Lilaque the father catches the trio. Manon shoots Lilaque; Lescaut escapes, and Lilaque the son discovers Manon with the revolver in her hand. She is taken to prison. Armand, waiting outside to see her as she is being transferred to another prison, accepts the fact that his life is ended without her.

Major Roles. MANON LESCAUT (high s); difficult vocal line; Eb3 to B4. ARMAND DES GRIEUX (lyr t); C2 to B3. LESCAUT (bar); considerable high tessitura; B1 to G3. LILAQUE, SR., rich capitalist (high buf t); F#2 to B3.

Lesser Roles. FRANCIS (bar); B1 to F3. LILAQUE, JR. (bar); G#1 to G#3.

Chorus. SSATB; brief children's chorus.

Ballet. Much of action is choreographed. Mimes: Maid, dope addicts, cigarette boy, flower girl, students, newsboys, beggars, servants, police, servant of Lilaque, Jr.

Orchestra. 2 fl (2 picc), ob, Eng hrn, cl, bs cl, 2 bsn, 4 hrn, 4 trp (jazz trp), 3 trb, tuba, timp, perc (2 small dr, big dr, large and small cym, tam-tam, xyl, vib, glock, claves, maracas, harp, piano, mandolin, strings.

Material. Bel (Sch). VS*. Tr: Norman Platt.

Performances. Santa Fe: 8.2.67 (Amer prem). Manh. Sch. (NYC): 5.13.72.

🎵 Brandenburgers in Bohemia · Branibori v Cechách

Music by Bedřich Smetana (1824–1884). Libretto in Czech by Karel Sabina. Premiere: Prague, January 5, 1866. Patriotic drama. Melodious, with nationalistic color. Set pieces, recitative. Brief prelude. Setting: Bohemia, 1279. Three acts (149 min).

Synopsis. Otto of Brandenburg has assumed the regency of Bohemia after the death of Otakar II and pillages the countryside, also imprisoning the Crown Prince. The news is brought to the country seat of the Burgomaster of Prague, Wolfram Olbromovíc, by his daughter Ludiše's lover, Junoš. Wolfram hurries to Prague, whereupon Ludiše and her sisters Vlčenka and Děčana are kidnapped by the German Tausendmark (who loves Ludiše), with the help of the Brandenburgers. Ludiše escapes but is recaptured. Tausendmark accuses the vagabond Jíra of the kidnapping; Jíra is condemned to death. A command from Otto that his troops must leave Bohemia must be obeyed, but first a ransom is demanded for Ludiše, which proves the innocence of Jíra, because he is imprisoned. The Burgomaster still trusts Tausendmark, however, and commissions him to rescue the sisters. The German's plan to carry off Ludiše once again is foiled by the Prague populace under Junoš and Jíra. Freedom comes simultaneously to the Burgomaster's daughters and the kingdom of Bohemia.

Major Roles. WOLFRAM (bs); needs strength at bottom of range; F1 to Eb3. JUNOS (t); D2 to B3. JAN TAUSENDMARK (bar); high tessitura; Bb1 to Gb3. JIRA (t); C♯2 to A3 (one Bb3 in ensemble). LUDISE (s); C3 to firm C5. VLCENKA (s); top Ab4 (can take C5 with Ludiše). DECANA (m-s); G2 to F♯4. (two sisters sing mostly in ensemble). KMET (bs); F1 to F3.

Lesser Roles. OLDRICH ROKYCANSKY (bar); G♯1 (G1 opt G2) to E3. VARNEMAN (t); top A3. BIRIC (bs).

Chorus. SSAATTBB. Very important. Citizens, servants, Brandenburg soldiers, etc.

Ballet. Act I.

Orchestra. 2 fl, 2 ob, 2 cl, 2 bsn, 4 hrn, 2 trp, 3 trb, tuba, perc, strings.

Material. B & H (HM).VS*.

📖 Il Campiello · The Campiello

Music by Ermanno Wolf-Ferrari (1876–1948). Libretto in Italian by Mario Ghisalberti after a play by Carlo Goldoni. Premiere: Milan, February 12, 1936. Lyric comedy. Highly melodious; traditional harmonies; continuous texture with set numbers embedded; vocal line often patterned after speech; occasional dialogue; recitatives; important ensembles. Brief preludes to each act. Setting: Venice, 1700, the piazza Il Campiello. Three acts.

Synopsis. The Piazza Campiello is rife with disturbances, lovers' quarrels, jealousy, animosity between two old ladies (played by tenors for the incongruous effect), and just ordinary noise, which causes Fabrizio, uncle of Gasparina, to decide to move. The Cavalier Astolfi, who wanders in now and then, seems the only one who can make peace. He courts Gasparina, and wins Fabrizio's consent, whereupon the girl sings a sad farewell to her beloved Campiello, which will miss her.

Major Roles. (All need flexibility for rapid patter). GASPARINA, young clockmaker (s); uses the sound "z" instead of "s"; D3 to B4. FABRIZIO DEI

54

Memorial Library
Mars Hill College
Mars Hill, N. C.

RITORTI, her uncle (bs); Bb1 to E3. DONA CATE PANCIANA, old woman (buf t);
C2 to B3 (fals D4 with lower opt). LUCIETA, her daughter (s); C3 to several firm C5's. DONA PASQUA POLEGANA, old woman (buf t); C2 to Bb3 (one
C5 fals). GNESE, her daughter (s); C3 to C5. ANZOLETO, Lucieta's betrothed
(bs); A1 to E3. ZORZETO, Gnese's betrothed (t); C2 to B3. ORSOLA (m-s);
top G#4. THE CAVALIER ASTOLFI (bar); top F3.

Lesser Roles. SANSUGA (mute). ORBI (mute). WAITER at inn (mute). GIO-
VANNI (d). PORTERS (mute).

Chorus. SATBB.

Ballet. Celebrating various foods; folk-like.

Orchestra. 2 fl (picc), 2 ob, 2 cl, 2 bsn, 4 hrn, 3 trp, 3 trb, tuba, timp,
perc, harp, piano, org, chimes, cel, strings. *Stage:* bells.

Material. Bel (Ri).

🦋 I Capuleti ed i Montecchi · The Capulets and the Montagues

Music by Vincenzo Bellini (1801–1835). Libretto in Italian by Felice Romani after Shakespeare. Premiere: Venice, March 11, 1830. Tragedy. Set
numbers, recitatives, very melodious vocal line; important ensembles. Overture (Sinfonia). Setting: Verona, 13th century. Two acts, six scenes (125
min). The last scene of an opera by Vaccaj on the same subject (and by the
same librettist) was often substituted for Bellini's (see below). Bellini used
music from a prior unsuccessful opera, *Zaira*, but it is difficult to detect.

ACT I i: A gallery in the palace of Capellio. ii: Giulietta's room. iii:
Courtyard of Capellio's palace. ACT II i: Apartment in palace. ii: Secluded
spot near palace. iii: Tomb of the Capulets.

Synopsis. At a gathering of the Guelphs (Capulets), a proposal of peace
with the Ghibellines (Montagues) is made, but rejected by Capellio and
Tebaldo, leaders. Tebaldo volunteers to destroy the enemy's leader, Romeo,
and Capellio promises him the hand of his daughter, Giulietta. The family
doctor Lorenzo tries to intervene, knowing that Romeo and Giulietta have
secretly met and fallen in love, but is rejected. Romeo appears in the guise
of a Ghibilline ambassador and proposes peace through a marriage between
Giulietta and himself, but is furiously refused. In her apartment, Giulietta
bewails her coming marriage, but refuses to abandon her father when Romeo
enters and suggests flight. He escapes through a secret passage at the approach of Capellio and Tebaldo. Romeo plots to rescue his love by force,
but in the ensuing battle, Lorenzo persuades Giulietta to take the fateful
potion which will simulate death. However, he is arrested by Capellio before
he can inform Romeo. Tebaldo challenges Romeo to a duel, but they are
interrupted by the funeral procession of Giulietta. Left alone by her tomb,
Romeo takes poison, and is discovered dying as Giulietta revives. She herself
dies of a broken heart.

Bellini's last scene has a chorus mourning Giulietta, Romeo's suicide, and

55

760442

Giulietta's awakening in time to join her lover in a duet before his death. It ends with Lorenzo, Capellio, and the chorus. Vaccaj's scene ends with Romeo's death. The music is of course quite different, Vaccaj's in set, developed pieces, while Bellini's is mostly recitative, gathering dramatic force up to the duet.

Major Roles. CAPELLIO (bs), the principal Capulet; A♭1 to E♭3. GIULIETTA (s); florid; D3 to C5. ROMEO (m-s); needs flexibility; G2 to B4. TEBALDO (t); A♭1 to E3. LORENZO (bs); A♭1 to E3.

Chorus. TTB (SATB in Vaccaj). Capuletti, Montecchi, soldiers, armorers, damsels.

Orchestra. 2 fl, 2 ob, 2 cl, 2 bsn, 4 hrn, 2 trp, 3 trb, tuba, timp, perc: bs dr, cym, dr, tri; harp, strings. *Stage*: 2 fl, 2 cl, 2 bsn, 2 hrn, 2 trp, trb, dr, bs dr.

Material. Bel (Ri). Map.

Performances. Amer. Op. Soc. (NYC): 4.28.64 (conc). Phila. Lyr.: 10.22.68.

🎵 Cardillac

Music by Paul Hindemith (1895–1963). Libretto in German by the composer and Ferdinand Leon after the latter's play based on E. T. A. Hoffmann's "Das Fraulein von Scudero." Premiere: Dresden, November 9, 1926. Melodrama. Revised version premiere: Zurich, June 20, 1952. Revision modifies abstract character of original by greater psychological impact and drama, with flowing, dramatic orchestra and important recitatives alternating with melodic passages, set numbers and ensembles. In original, Lully's opera *Phaeton* is performed in Act III, which is omitted in revision. Setting: Paris, end of 17th century. Four acts (five scenes in original) (approx 113 min).

ACT I: Paris square. ACT II: Singer's room. ACT III: Cardillac's room. ACT IV: Square outside Opéra.

Synopsis. Cardillac, the famous jeweler, loves his creations so much that he cannot bear to part with them. After each sale, he murders the purchaser. These crimes have stirred all Paris. The latest is a cavalier who has bought a belt for a prima donna. With a rich Marquis the singer visits the jeweler and recognizes the belt, which the Marquis buys. An officer takes the belt as bait, and gives it to Cardillac's daughter. Meanwhile, Cardillac's partner, who loves the daughter, has been suspected of the murders and is accused, but the sight of the belt on his daughter drives Cardillac mad and he confesses.

Major Roles. CARDILLAC (bar); brilliant acting role; some sustained high tessitura; B♭1 to F3. HIS DAUGHTER (s); C♯3 to A4 (one B4). CARDILLAC'S APPRENTICE (t); C♯2 to A3. FIRST SINGER AT OPERA (s); sustained; B♭2 to B♭4.

Lesser Roles. OFFICER (bs); G♯1 to E3. YOUNG CAVALIER (t); D2 to A3.

In Lully opera (no range problems): KLYMENE (c); PHAETON (t); APOLLO (bs). RICH MARQUIS (mute). TENOR(s).

Chorus. SATB. Citizens, theater personnel.

Ballet. In opera scene.

Orchestra. fl, 2 picc, ob, Eng hrn, 2 cl, bs cl, ten sax, 2 bsn, cont bsn, hrn, 2 trp, 2 trb, bs tuba, piano, perc (4), strings. *Stage:* fl, ob, bsn, harp, cembalo, vln, vla, vcl, cb.

Material. Bel (Sch). VS*.

Performances. Santa Fe: 7.26.67 (Amer prem). USC: 4.17.71.

✍ Carry Nation

Music by Douglas Moore (1893–1969). Libretto in English by William North Jayme. Written for Centennial of University of Kansas; premiere: Lawrence, Kans., April 28, 1966. Historical drama. Conservative harmonies; flowing melodies, with some folk flavor. Set pieces. Brief prelude; one orchestral interlude. Setting: Kansas and Missouri, mid-19th, turn of 20th century. Prologue and two acts, seven scenes (123 min).

Prologue: A plush "joint" in Topeka. ACT I i: Parlor of Carry's parents' home in Belton, Mo.; ii: Belton churchyard; iii: Belton barn decorated for hoedown (62 min). ACT II i: Charles and Carry's home in Holden, Mo.; ii: Mother's bedroom; iii: Saloon in Holden; iv: Easter, churchyard in Belton (61 min).

Synopsis. The story, except for the prologue, is Carry's early history, leading up to her first "ordination" with Bible and hatchet, which is shown in the Topeka saloon. The opera opens with Carry cleaning house in preparation for a boarder, her father reading from the Bible. Her mother's mind is obviously failing, and her father has turned to Carry all his emotional nature. Charles, the new boarder, interrupts this scene, making a gallant speech but soon collapsing. The mother offers brandy, but the father angrily declares there shall be no spirits in the house. Charles is persuaded to kneel in prayer with the household. The beginning of an attraction between the two young people is noticed, hopefully by the mother, apprehensively by the father. In the churchyard, Charles rebels at the women's self-abasement, and is about to take a drink when Carry enters. There is a scene of wooing and an embrace, discovered by the father, who sends Carry to church and reviles Charles. The latter taunts the older man with his unnatural love for Carry, then at his further outburst, deliberately drinks from a flask. The father orders him to leave. But at a barn dance, he returns to tell Carry he has a chance to practice in Holden, Mo. The father is furious, but frustrated by the mother, who foolishly plays *grande dame.* Charles, flushed with the drink, publicly proposes to Carry, who accepts him amid the congratulations of the crowd.

At a sewing bee, well-meaning ladies gossip about Charles's weakness and leave when he enters. To Carry's protests, he promises not to drink, whereupon she tells him of their coming child. In the mother's bedroom, she is far gone in fantasy, playing with Carry's toys. She shows the father Carry's letter about the baby, and in spite of her protests, he determines to go to his daughter. His wife collapses, calling him a destroyer.

Charles has passed out in a saloon. Carry enters and shatters his bottle. The other men go out, and the father appears. Carry finally decides to go home. In the churchyard, Carry reads a letter from Charles saying all is well, but the father shatters her hopes by bringing a telegram notifying her of his death. She sinks to her knees to pray, then exclaims: "Someone has to pay!" She faces the audience, her pastel cloak falling to reveal the black dress of the prologue, while a chorus comes on stage, "an army advancing." A Bible is placed in one of Carry's hands, a hatchet in the other, "the act of ordination."

Major Roles. CARRY NATION (m-s); C3 to Ab4. FATHER (bs-bar); C2 to F3. MOTHER (s); C3 to C5. CHARLES (bar).

Lesser Roles. CHURCHYARD CARETAKER; BEN, livery man in Belton; PREACHER (offstage); at hoedown, YOUNG MAN, GIRL, BOY, and THE TOASTER; TWO WOMEN at sewing bee; TWO MEN in saloon; CITY MARSHAL.

Chorus. SATB.

Ballet. Hoedown dancers; boy tap dancer in saloon.

Orchestra. 2 fl (picc), 2 ob, (Eng hrn), 2 cl (bs cl), 2 bsn, 3 hrn, 2 trp, 2 trb, timp, perc, harp, strings.

Material. Ga. VS*.

Performances. Wichita, Kansas City, Kans., San Fran. Spring Op.: 1966. NYCO: March, April 1968.

🎵 Castor et Pollux · Castor and Pollux

Music by Jean-Philippe Rameau (1683–1764). Libretto in French by P. J. Bernard. Premiere: Paris, October 24, 1737. Classic drama. Extremely melodic; rich harmonies; vocal line ornamented; recitatives and set pieces. Brief overture also used as entr'acte between Prologue and Act I. Setting: Sparta, entrance to Hades and Elysian fields in ancient times. Prologue, five acts.

Prologue: Abandoned field near Mt. Olympus. Entr'acte and Tambourin. ACT I: Tomb of the Spartan Kings. Entr'acte: Gavotte. ACT II: Vestibule of Temple of Jupiter. Entr'acte: Allemande. ACT III: Entrance to Hades. Entr'acte: Chaconne. ACT IV: Elysian Fields. ACT V: Near Sparta.

Synopsis. Pollux, with the approval of his father Jupiter, enters Hades to try to restore his twin brother Castor to earth. The price is high: he himself must remain below. Phébé, who loves him, tries to restrain him, but Télaire, whom he loves (but who secretly loves Castor), urges him on. The exchange is made, but the grieving Castor says he will remain on earth but one day. Jupiter, moved, restores Pollux to earth, and makes him and Castor immortal.

Major Roles. MINERVE (s); needs flexibility; D3 to G4. VÉNUS (s); can

58

double with Happy Spirit; D3 to A4. L'AMOUR (t); needs flexibility; can double with Castor; F2 to B♭3 (one C4). MARS (bs); A1 to E3; can double with Athlete II. TELAIRE (s); sustained, noble; trill; C3 to A4. PHEBE (s); needs sustained strength as well as lyric line; trill; D3 to A4. POLLUX (bar or bs); sustained, also flexible; needs strength at extremes of range; much low tessitura; G1 to F3.

Lesser Roles. JUPITER (bs). A1 to E3. HIGH PRIEST (t); D2 to G3. FOLLOWER OF HEBE (s); D♯3 to A4. A PLANET (s). MERCURY (mute). ATHLETE I (high t). ATHLETE II (bs); can double with Mars. HAPPY SPIRIT (s); can double with Vénus. CASTOR (t); can double with L'Amour. A PLANET (s); can double with Minerve.

Chorus. SSATB. The Graces (Followers of Vénus); The Arts (Followers of Minerve); The Pleasures (Followers of L'Amour). Athletes, Priests, Demons, Specters, Monsters, Happy Spirits, etc.

Ballet. Very important. All entr'actes and during opera.

Orchestra. 2 fl, 2 ob, 2 bsn, trp, harpsichord, strings.

Material. Du (El-V).

Performances. Litt. Orch. (NYC): 1.11.65 (conc).

🎭 Caterina Cornaro

Music by Gaetano Donizetti (1797–1848). Libretto in Italian by Giacomo Sacchèro, originally titled *La Regina di Cipro.* Premiere: Naples, January 12, 1844. Revised by Rubino Profeta; premiere: Naples, May 28, 1972. Lyric historical tragedy. Some conventional passages alternating with new idiom that anticipates Verdi; vocal line both dramatic and lyrical; set numbers. Setting: Venice and Nicosia, 1472. Prologue and two acts, five scenes.

Prologue i: Ballroom of the Cornaro palace in Venice; ii: Caterina's apartment. ACT I i: A square in Nicosia; ii: A room in the royal palace. ACT II: Hall of the royal palace.

Synopsis. Caterina Cornaro is about to wed the young French nobleman Gerardo when the festivities are halted by Mocenigo, a member of the ruling Council of Ten, who tells Caterina's father Andrea that for political reasons she must marry Lusignano, King of Cyprus. Gerardo tries to rescue Caterina, but having been warned of his danger, she repulses him for his own sake. In Nicosia, Mocenigo has been appointed Venetian ambassador and plots with Strozzi to take over Cyprus but is alarmed at the news Gerardo has been seen in Nicosia and makes an abortive attempt to assassinate the Frenchman. Gerardo is saved by none other than Lusignano, who reveals Caterina's innocent part in the political marriage. The two men vow friendship, and the King even grants Gerardo an audience with Caterina. Both realize they must renounce their love. Mocenigo, attempting to denounce Caterina, is arrested but manages to give the signal for a rebellion against the King. In the battle, Lusignano is fatally wounded, and Caterina takes over the reins of government.

Major Roles. CATERINA (dram-col s); florid, with high tessitura but not extreme ranges, wide skips. GERARDO (t); needs flexibility. LUSIGNANO (bar); some florid passages. ANDREA CORNARO (bs). MOCENIGO (bs).

Lesser Roles. STROZZI (t). MATILDA, Caterina's confidante (s). A COURTIER (t).

Chorus. SATB. Nobles, soldiers, etc. High, light tenors.

Orchestra. 2 fl, picc, 2 ob, 2 cl, 2 bsn, 4 hrn, 2 trp, 3 trb, bs trb, timp, bs dr, harp, strings.

Material. May be rented from San Carlo, Naples.

Performances. Op. Th. of N.J. (NYC): 4.15.73 (Amer prem).

🦫 Cendrillon · Cinderella

Music by Jules Massenet (1842–1912). Libretto in French by Henri Cain after the fairy tale by Charles Perrault. Premiere: Paris, May 24, 1899. Highly melodious; conventional harmonies. Brief overture. Setting: transferred to Louis XIII period. Four acts, six scenes (180 min).

ACT I: Large room in the home of Mme de la Haltière. ACT II: Festival hall and gardens in King's palace. ACT III i: Same as I; ii: Home of the Fairy. ACT IV i: Terrace of Cendrillon's country home; ii: King's court.

Synopsis. The story follows the fairy tale as far as the return from the King's ball, where the Prince has ignored the two stepsisters and become entranced by Cendrillon. The women are quarreling over the unknown, and in response to Cendrillon's question about what the Prince had said of her, lie, and say that he had called her ugly enough to be hanged. Cendrillon faints, and her father determines to take her to the country to recover. The scene changes to the fairy's home, where the Prince and Cendrillon wander side by side in the meadow, separated by a flowery hedge. Neither can see the other until the fairy waves her wand. They fall into a magic sleep. In the country home, Cendrillon babbles of the ball and the prince in her sleep, but only her father hears. He makes her believe she has dreamed it all, but when the stepmother announces that all girls are to proceed to court so that the Prince can find his unknown love, Cinderella knows it is real. And the slipper fits.

Major Roles. CENDRILLON (s); C3 to Bb4 (touches C5, one D5 with A4 opt). PANDOLPHE, her father (bs); a little dialogue; A1 to F3. MME DE LA HALTIERE (c); some florid passages; trill, buffa action; Bb2 to F4. NOÉMIE, her daughter (s); some florid passages; trill; C3 to C5. DOROTHÉE, the other daughter (m-s); florid; trill; C3 to A4. FAIRY GODMOTHER, (col s); very florid; high tessitura; trill; B2 to F5. PRINCE (t—orig falcon or dram s); C2 to Bb3. MAJORDOMO OF ENTERTAINMENT (bar); C2 to Eb3. DEAN OF FACULTY (t); D2 to G3. KING (bar); C2 to E3.

Lesser Role. PRIME MINISTER (bs).

Bit Role. HERALD (sp).

Chorus. SSATTBB. Occasionally in four parts. Servants, doctors, ministers, young girls, courtesans; six spirits. (4 s, 2 c).

Ballet. Act II. Fairies in III ii. March of Princesses before IV ii.

Orchestra. 3 fl, 2 ob, 2 cl, 2 bsn, 4 hrn, 2 trp, 3 trb, timp, timbals, perc (4) 2 harp. *Stage*: lute, vla d'amore, trp, fl de cristal.

Material. Pr (Heu).

Performances. Amato Op. in Brief (NYC): 12.14.63. Manh. Sch. (NYC): 5.14.71.

⚜ Col. Jonathan the Saint

Music by Dominick Argento (1927–   ). Libretto in English by John Olon. Premiere: Denver, December 31, 1971. Ironic drama. Continuous texture, atmospherically dramatic; set numbers embedded; traditional harmonies; vocal line melodious. Interlude of waltzes between Acts II and III. Setting: Tidewater country of Maryland, after Civil War. Four acts, spoken Prologue (140 min).

ACT I: "Ruin and Recollection," Hall of Lyonesse. ACT II: "Arias and Irritation," Terrace overlooking Chesapeake Bay. Waltz Interlude. ACT III: "Dancing and Tableaux," The restored terrace. ACT IV: "The Demon Lover," Reconstructed hall.

Synopsis. The mansion Lyonesse has been partially burned in a raid by Union soldiers, the leader of which, Col. Jonathan Gilourin, has returned out of a sense of responsibility and curiosity. The house has been converted into a hotel by the elderly Allegra Harper and her niece Daisy. Sabrina, Daisy's sister and owner of Lyonesse, returns from a three-year search for news of her dead Confederate soldier husband, whom Jonathan strongly resembles. Allegra counts on this circumstance to attract Sabrina, but she is indifferent to Jonathan and remains in a dream world where only her husband's words of farewell have meaning. Jonathan, now in love with Sabrina, helps rebuild the house and coaxes Daisy, who has fallen in love with him herself, to reveal the farewell words of Sabrina's husband, which he quotes to her. Still immersed in make-believe, she yields to him. They marry, and he restores the house to its private status. But Sabrina is increasingly drawn to the world of shadows, and meets the ghost of her former husband, pledging her immortal love to him, forever re-enacting their last goodbye. Still, she lives in the present, trying to reassure Jonathan, whose suspicions are only partially lulled. Throughout the story, the three black servants—unstereotyped characters—Henry, Mary Chairs, and Cleopatra, her niece, play an important part, as does the skipper of the *Bay Belle*, Captain Gerome K. Mullikin.

Major Roles. ALLEGRA HARPER, aged 60 (lyr col s); some florid passages; trill; C3 to B4. DAISY, aged 18 (m-s); G2 to G4. COL. JONATHAN GILOURIN (dram t); sustained, forceful, some melisma; C#2 to Bb3. SABRINA (dram s); sustained; needs flexibility for several passages; B2 to B4. HENRY (bar); A1

61

to G♭3. CLEOPATRA (s); top G4. MARY CHAIRS, aged 80 (m-s); no range problem. CAPT. GEROME K. MULLIKIN (bs-bar); needs flexibility; A1 to F♯3.

Lesser Roles. THE CONFEDERATE SOLDIER (lyr t); top A3. From chorus: THREE LADIES (s, s, c); OLD GENTLEMAN (lyr t); PLAIN GIRL (s); PRETTY GIRL (c); SERVANT (bar).

Chorus. SATB. Excursionists, dancers, guests.

Ballet. Important, for waltzes, polkas, etc.

Orchestra. 2 fl, 2 ob, 2 cl, 2 bsn, 3 hrn, 2 trp, trb, perc (3), harp, strings. *Stage*: cl, corn, piano, vln, vcl.

Material. B & H.

⚑ Cornelia Faroli

Music by Rafael Kubelik (1914–   ). Libretto in Czech by Dalibor Faltis. Premiere: Augsburg, August 1972. Historical drama. Vocal line largely declamatory, some lyrical passages; orchestra important in interludes, subordinated to voices; contemporary harmony; considerable dialogue, some accompanied. No overture. Setting: Venice and Verona, 16th century. Six scenes (160 min).

Scene i: Aretino's palace in Venice. ii: A square in Verona. iii: Titian's country house. iv: Same. v: Same. vi: Residence of the Spanish Ambassador.

Synopsis. In the banquet hall of the worldly satirist Aretino, Venice's fair women gather to do him homage. His friend, the painter Titian, is hailed for his portrait of Aretino, and so impressed is the Spanish Ambassador Mendoza that he commissions Titian to paint Charles V and the late Queen Isabella. Titian protests that the miniature of the queen is not adequate, and prefers a living model, an ideal face. In search for such a worthy model, he visits Verona, and comes on a horrible scene. A witch is being burnt. The painter is so struck by the beauty of the unfortunate victim that he determines to rescue her. It seems that if a respectable citizen will offer to marry her, she may be saved. Titian assumes a false name and carries off the girl. In his country studio, Cornelia sits for the portrait, worshiping the painter. Aretino visits, admiring both the painting and the model. To show off Cornelia, Titian invites the Venetian women, who, however, display malicious envy and hatred, to the extent of ripping off Cornelia's finery and tearing at her hair. Titian intervenes, furious. For the first time he sees Cornelia as more than an impersonal model. While he is away in town, Aretino visits, heaping gifts on Cornelia which she refuses, saying that Titian is going to marry her. Vengefully, Aretino reveals that Titian is already married and has children. Cornelia is stunned, and resolves to leave. Embracing Titian passionately, she rushes out and disappears. Titian would follow her, but is dissuaded by his servant Rodrigo. The painting at last is exhibited in the Spanish Ambassador's house, to everyone's admiration. A judge from Verona, Salvado, remarks on its resemblance to a beautiful witch whom he has sentenced to the stake, where indeed she had gone, obstinately silent. Aretino saves the difficult situation by saying that the judge must be deluded. The Ambassador proposes a toast to Titian, who is only half-comforted by Aretino's assurance that Cornelia will live—in his art.

Major Roles. PIETRO ARETINO (t); needs flexibility; difficult intervals; G1 to B3. TITIAN (bar); Ab1 to A3. CORNELIA FAROLI (s); sustained; needs strength and flexibility for florid passages, difficult intervals; Bb2 to firm C5's. Her voice is taped for passage which requires two voices. HORTADO DE MENDOZA (bs); A1 to E3.

Lesser Roles. Four women who sing mostly in ensemble: MARIETTA (s); some high passages, top C5; SOFIE (s); ANGELA (m-s); COUNTESS CATERINA (c). ENRICO SALVADO (bs); Bb1 to E♯3. INQUISITOR (bs); also taped.

Chorus. SSAATTBB. Several small solos.

Orchestra. 2 fl, 2 ob, 3 cl, 2 sax, 2 bsn, 4 hrn, 3 trp, 2 trb, tuba, timp, perc (3), harp, cembalo, strings.

Material. Pet (Lit). VS (g).

✠ Crime and Punishment · Bun és Bunhődes

Music by Emil Petrovics (1930–   ). Adapted from Dostoevsky's novel by Gyula Maár; libretto in Hungarian, English translation by Eva Rácz. Premiere: Budapest, October 26, 1969. Psychological drama. Rondo form. Orchestration spare, but with large amount of instrumental color; freely treated twelve-tone harmonies; continuous texture. Vocal lines mostly declamatory; occasional lyrical passages. Brief prelude; very brief occasional orchestral interludes; action is continuous within acts. Setting: Russian town, time unspecified but probably late 19th century. Three acts, 29 scenes.

Production Note. The premiere production used a structure of iron pipes on both sides of stage, with steps to upper levels. The center was left free, representing the street. Various portions were lighted as the action shifts.

ACT I: Old Woman's Flat; A taproom; Raskolnikov's room; Old Woman's room; Raskolnikov's room; Street; Police station. ACT II: Raskolnikov's room; Street; Cafe frequented by prostitutes; Street; Raskolnikov's room; Old Woman's room; Street; Taproom; Street; Raskolnikov's room; Street; Magistrate's office; Street. ACT III: Street; Sonya's room; Street; Raskolnikov's room; Street; Magistrate's office; Street; Raskolnikov's room; Street.

Synopsis. The action follows the novel closely, with the elimination of many characters, including Raskolnikov's sister and mother. The brilliant student, crazed by poverty and dogged by ambition to pursue his studies, murders the Old Woman, a money lender, and her sister Lizaveta, meets a young prostitute Sonya, whom he trusts with his confidence after she reads to him the Biblical story of Lazarus. All the while he seeks to repent and confess and finally, in an oratorio-like scene while the populace comments and Sonya recites the Lazarus story, kneels and confesses before the world.

63

Major Roles. RASKOLNIKOV (bs or bs-bar); extremely taxing; never off-stage; jaggedly declamatory; needs strength throughout range; G1 to E3 (two F#3, one F#3). His inner thoughts are expressed through his taped voice. SONYA (s); some lyrical passages; C3 to A4 (occasional Bb4; one B4). OLD WOMAN (m-s); A2 to E4. SVIDRIGUYLOV (bar); Bb1 to G3; G fals.

Lesser Roles. (Character roles of some difficulty). DRUNK (t). RAZUMIHIN (bar); top G3. BEGGAR WOMAN (s); some high tessitura. HURDY-GURDY MAN (t); one lyrical song. MAGISTRATE (t); needs flexibility; top Ab3. MARMELA-DOV, dissolute civil servant (bar); top F#3. JUNIOR OFFICER (t); top A3. SERVANT GIRL (c); G2 to Eb4. INSPECTOR (bar); taxing; needs flexibility; top G3.

Other Lesser Roles. STUDENT (t); C2 to A3. OFFICER (bar); A1 to Db3. DOCTOR (bs); G#1 to E3. POLICEMAN (t). HOUSE PAINTER (t). GAUDILY DRESSED WOMAN (s); top B4.

Bit Roles. STRANGER (t). SECOND GENTLEMAN (bar). TWO WORKERS (t, bar). MAN IN BLACK (bs).

Mute Roles. LIZAVETA. WELL-FED GENTLEMAN. CONCIERGE. TWO HOUSE PAINTERS.

Chorus. SATTBB, divided into SATB, TTBB. Very important.

Orchestra. Large, without any extreme demands.

Material. B & H. VS (h).

✍ The Crucible

Music by Robert Ward (1917–   ). Libretto in English by Bernard Stambler, based on the play by Arthur Miller. Commissioned by the New York City Opera. Premiere: New York, October 26, 1961. Historical drama. Set numbers knit into continuous texture. Orchestral interludes. Setting: Salem, Massachusetts, 1692. Four acts, five scenes (110 min).

ACT I: Home of the Reverend Samuel Parris, showing living room and Betty's bedroom (31 min). ACT II: Kitchen–dining room of John Proctor's farmhouse (27 min). ACT III i: Secluded spot in forest; ii: Town meeting-house (28 min). ACT IV: Town blockhouse (24 min).

Synopsis. Several parishioners have gathered in the Reverend Parris' home, apprehensively discussing possible witchcraft. Parris' daughter Betty, her cousin Abigail Williams, and a slave, Tituba, have been caught dancing in the forest with other girls. Abigail seems the center of the trouble. She has been discharged from service by Goody (good wife) Elizabeth Proctor, who suspects she has seduced John Proctor. To seek divine help, a psalm is sung, driving Betty, hitherto in a stupor, into hysterics. Reverend Hale, skilled in dealing with witches, arrives, and forces Tituba into a confession of consorting with the Devil. Betty recovers, whereupon all but Abigail resume the psalm. Abigail sings of her pact with the Devil, and receives a sign that she must report all others in league with the power of darkness.

64

John Proctor learns that if he exposes Abigail, she will reveal their adultery. Mary Warren, their current servant, returns from court and reports that many have been arrested, one woman to hang. A warrant is served upon Elizabeth, who has been accused by Abigail of using a witch's poppet (doll) to kill her. Such a doll is discovered. John remembers that Mary has made it and stuck the needle in its heart, with Abigail's knowledge. Mary acknowledges this, but Elizabeth is taken away. John determines that Mary shall testify, even if Abigail reveals all. He meets the girl that evening, but refuses her pleas to abandon Elizabeth. She threatens exposure.

In the courtroom, Judge Danforth presides, ordering Giles Corey to jail and torture for refusing to name witnesses to his charge of witchcraft against Thomas Putnam. Proctor presents Mary's testimony that the girls' "Crying-Out-Against-Witches" was a fraud, alleging that Abigail has used the emotional outbreak as an opportunity to destroy Elizabeth. Then he confesses his adultery. Elizabeth denies it, thinking to help, but makes him out a perjurer. The girls, led by Abigail, fall into hysterical frenzy, causing Mary to repudiate her testimony. They accuse Proctor of being "The Devil's Man."

Abigail steals money from her uncle and offers to help John escape prison. He refuses. Hale and Parris try to persuade Danforth to postpone hanging John and Rebecca Nurse; he will not. Elizabeth and John, left alone, rise above the wreckage of their lives. John first thinks he will confess, then decides against it when he learns that his confession must be written and will be displayed publicly. Rebecca, on her way to the gallows, inspires him by her steadfastness, and he joins her as Elizabeth blesses him.

Major Roles. JOHN PROCTOR (bar); difficult dramatically and vocally; G1 to G♯3. ELIZABETH PROCTOR (m-s); requires strong acting; A2 to G♯4 (B♭4 opt). ABIGAIL WILLIAMS (s); taxing role requiring youthful appeal over menace; C3 to C5. REVEREND JOHN HALE (bs); F♯1 to F♯3. JUDGE DANFORTH (dram t); extremes of range; harsh, forceful actor; B1 to B3.

Lesser Roles. REVEREND SAMUEL PARRIS (t). TITUBA (c); dark timbre; preferably black and alert actress. REBECCA NURSE (c); must act as very elderly. GILES COREY (t); elderly, contentious, characterization more important than voice. MARY WARREN (s); needs wide range and vocal agility.

Minor Roles. ANN PUTNAM (s). THOMAS PUTNAM (bar). EZEKIEL CHEEVER (t).

Bit Roles. FRANCIS NURSE (bs). SARAH GOOD (s). BETTY PARRIS (m-s). RUTH PUTNAM (col s). SUSANNA WALCOTT (c). MERCY LEWIS (c). MARTHA SELDON (s). BRIDGET BOOTH (s).

Chorus. SATB. Townspeople, bailiffs.

Orchestra. 2 fl (picc), 2 ob (Eng hrn), 2 cl (bs cl), 2 bsn (cont bsn opt), 4 hrn, 2 trp, tenor trb, bs trb, timp, perc (1), harp, strings. Short segment of taped sound opt for 40 seconds of Act III.

Material. Hi (Ga). VS (e, g)*.

Performances. A great many, including San Fran., Seattle, many colleges, university groups, and European productions.

▨ La Cubana, or A Life for Art

Music by Hans Werner Henze (1926–   ). Libretto in German by Hans Magnus Enzensberger; English libretto and lyrics by Mel Mandel. Commissioned by WNET/13 Opera Theater, New York. Premiere: WNET, (scheduled for) December 1973. "A Cruel and Obscene Vaudeville." Eclectic score, drawing on widely varied elements; some dissonance, some melody; vocal lines dramatic and difficult; *Sprechstimme* and dialogue interspersed with songs, choruses, etc. Setting: Havana, 1905 to 1959 ("Time is collapsed . . . memory and reality are indistinguishable as we move from the present into Rachel's illusive and elusive past"). Prologue, five tableaux, four "intermezzos," epilogue (approx 105 min uncut; less than 90 min on TV).

Prologue, intermezzos, and epilogue: Rachel's dingy apartment in Havana, 1959. Tableau i: The shabby Tivoli cabaret, 1906; ii: A square in Havana, 1910; iii: A dusty square in a little Cuban town, 1914; iv: Rachel's dressing room in the Alhambra Theater, 1927; onstage; the dressing room; v: Square in front of the Alhambra Theater, 1935.

Synopsis. The aged Rachel, a decrepit music-hall star and actress, broods over the past as her old servant Ofelia warns her of a revolution going on outside. She embarks on the first of a series of flashbacks to her glamorous career. First she remembers her affair with the wealthy young Eusebio. Then in 1910 the comet appeared, frightening everyone; also an exquisitely evil pimp, Yarini, caught Rachel's attention but was killed. In 1914, Rachel is with a provincial circus and in love with Paco, a circus artist; their performance is disrupted by the black revolutionary El Cimarron. Some years later, Rachel has become a great star in the Alhambra Theater. Before and after her performance in *Fresh Flesh* (in which she impersonates a man [Teodoro] in order to get at a former lover, Alberto, who is with his wife), Rachel becomes involved with a young revolutionary, Federico, and defies a powerful Senator on his behalf, staying with him through the dissolution of the theater, a revolutionary demonstration, and her own downfall. In the epilogue, a hurricane is imminent, and Rachel fearfully prepares for death, dressing up in old finery to the tune of her first song played on a scratchy record.

Major Roles. YOUNG RACHEL (lyr s); needs highly dramatic acting ability; also appears as TEODORO. Rachel's lovers: EUSEBIO, PACO, FEDERICO (bar). OLD RACHEL (sp); dram actress. LUCILE, a beautiful young whore; also the young wife in the play, *Fresh Flesh* (m-s). ALBERTO (also YARINI) (t). DON ALFONSO, circus director (also TELESCOPE MAN) (bs-bar). EL CIMARRON (bs-bar). A CRITIC (also THEATER DIRECTOR) (t). OFELIA (sp).

Lesser Roles. THE SENATOR. LOTOT, a gangster. TWO GENTLEMEN. THIRTEEN WITNESSES, who double as circus and music hall performers, waiters, Cimarrones, a rehearsal pianist, students, beggars, musicians, stagehands, peasants, a cleaning woman, casket carriers, an archbishop, etc. Most of these appear as chorus of Witnesses between scenes.

Orchestra. Stage: 2 fl (2 picc), 2 ob, 2 cl (E♭ cl, bs cl), alto sax, 2 trp, 2 ten tuba, bs tuba, bamboo fl, ocharina, mouth harmonica, 3 Jewsharps, man-

dolin, guit, ten banjo, marimbula, glock, bs dr with cym, prepared piano, 3 vln, vcl, cb. Six actors play toy instruments (whistle, 2 pot lids, 2 bicycle hrn, comb, ratchet). *Backstage*: fl (picc), 2 cl (bs cl), alto sax, ten sax, corn, 2 trp, trb, bs tuba, ten banjo, acc or harm, pianola with prepared roll, piano, vln, vcl, cb, org ad lib. Perc (4): (1) high voodoo dr, cabaca, cacavella; (2) waldteufel, andeira, pedal maracas, (3) dr with plywood top, holzröhren-klapper; (3) medium voodoo dr, chocolo, metal whip; (4) low voodoo dr, tramboline, 5 metal sounds (anvils or bars); Trinidad steel dr played by 1.
Material. Bel.

The Cunning Little Vixen · Príhody Lisky Bystrousky

Music by Leoš Janáček (1854–1928). Libretto in Czech by the composer after a short story by Rudolf Tésnohlídek. Premiere: Brno, November 6, 1924. Fairy tale. Music strongly rooted in Moravian folk tunes; vocal line rhythmic, patterned after speech, longer melodious passages although no conventional set numbers. Short preludes to Acts I, II; several interludes, notably Act III, i and ii. Setting: a forest in fairy-tale time. Three acts, ten scenes.

ACT I i: A forest ("How they caught the vixen, Sharpears"); ii: Forester's cottage ("Sharpears in the yard"); iii: The same ("Sharpears, the politician, runs away"). ACT II i: Same as I i ("Sharpears, the usurper of property"); ii: Village inn; iii: The wood ("Sharpears's excursions"); iv: Sharpears's lair ("Sharpears's wooing and mating"). ACT III i: Edge of the forest ("Sharpears's death"); ii: Village inn; iii: The forest in spring ("Baby Sharpears").

Synopsis. The Forester interrupts a dance by forest creatures, falls asleep but wakens in time to catch Sharpears, the pretty vixen, and take her home. She languishes in captivity, tormented by the dog Lapák, the Forester's son Pepík and his friend Frantík, and, after a futile attempt to escape, by the cock and hens. At last she bites through the rope that imprisons her and runs off to the forest. Restored to her mischievous ways, she dispossesses the badger. In the inn, the unpopular Priest, who resembles the badger, escapes as angry peasants come after him. He has seduced the gypsy girl brought to the village by the Forester. This girl has also captivated the Schoolmaster, but chooses to marry the poacher Harašta. Sharpears is wooed by the handsome fox Goldenmane; they are married by the woodpecker. One fine day the fox family is at play when Harašta appears with stolen chickens. Sharpears lures him away; her cubs fall to the feast. The poacher returns, fires at the cubs, who are protected by their mother. She falls dead. Later at the inn, the Forester and the Schoolmaster talk; the former has heard that Harašta gave his bride a fox muff and he mourns Sharpears; the latter is more concerned with the loss of the gypsy. The Forester goes to the forest to be comforted by the awakening of nature after her winter sleep. He again dozes; when he wakes, the creatures of the forest are near. Among them is a vixen cub. The cycle is complete.

Major Roles. FORESTER (bar); considerable high tessitura; F♯1 to F♯3. HIS WIFE (c); E3 to A4. SCHOOLMASTER (t); E♭2 to A3. PRIEST (bs); A♭1 to F♭3. HARASTA (bs) A♭1 to F♯3. VIXEN (s); high trills; C♯3 to D♭5. THE FOX, GOLDENMANE (t or s); D♯2 or 3 to B3 or 4.

Lesser Roles. LAPAK, Forester's Dog (m-s). PASAK, innkeeper (t); HIS WIFE (s); BADGER (bs); ROOSTER (s); HEN (s); SCREECHOWL (c); JAY (s); WOODPECKER (c). SHARPEARS as cub (child s); PEPÍK, FRANTÍK, CRICKET, GRASSHOPPER, MOSQUITO, FROG (boy s).

Chorus. SATB; children. Peasants, hens, fox cubs, forest birds, animals.
Ballet. Children as animals.
Orchestra. 4 fl, 3 ob, 3 cl, 3 bsn, 4 hrn, 3 trp, 3 trb, tuba, timp, perc, harp, cel, strings.
Production Problems. Cast is partly human, partly animal; difficult to make believable. Quick scene changes.
Material. Pr (UE).
Performances. Mannes Coll. (NYC): 5.7.64 (Amer prem).

🎬 Dalibor

Music by Bedřich Smetana (1824–1884). Libretto in German by Josef Wenzig (Czech translation by Ervin Spindler). Premiere: Prague, May 16, 1868. Patriotic drama. Set numbers, arias, recitatives, in continuous texture. No overture; brief preludes to Acts II and III; brief interludes between II ii and iii; III ii and iii. Setting: Prague, 15th century. Three acts, seven scenes (155 min).

ACT I: Judgment Hall of king's castle (50 min). ACT II i: Street below castle; ii: House of Benes, jailor, inside castle; iii: Dalibor's cell (55 min). ACT III i: Throne room; ii: Dalibor's cell; iii: Open place before castle (50 min).

Synopsis. The theme, which came to be considered a truly nationalistic expression, contains obvious parallels to Beethoven's *Fidelio.* The legendary hero, Dalibor, revenges the murder of his friend Zdenek by slaying the murderer, the Burgrave of Ploskovice. The Burgrave's sister, Mlada, accuses Dalibor in a hearing before Vladislav, King of Bohemia, but is immediately struck by the hero's proud, manly bearing. Softened by a growing love for him, she pleads vainly for his freedom. With Jitka, an orphan befriended by Dalibor, she plans to release him from his life sentence, and enters the prison in man's costume, becoming the assistant of Benes, the jailer. In his cell, Dalibor has a vision of Zdenek, who plays his violin once more. Dalibor asks for a violin, which Mlada brings him. In a powerful and beautiful duet the two discover their love. The king is warned by Benes and Budovij, Captain of the Guard, that a popular uprising in favor of Dalibor is in the making; Benes has discovered the plans of his assistant, who has disappeared.

The king reluctantly condemns Dalibor to death. Mlada, Jitka, and Dalibor's squire, Vitek, prepare to storm the prison. Mlada is wounded and is carried out by Dalibor, who, when he sees their hopeless situation, stabs himself. (An alternative ending shows Dalibor executed before the rescue party reaches him, with Mlada killed in the rescue attempt.)

Major Roles. DALIBOR (t); high tessitura; Eb2 to Bb3 (several B3, G♯3 opt; one C4, Ab3 opt). MLADA (s); some high tessitura; B2 (one A♯2, C♯3 opt) to B4 (one C5, Ab4 opt). KING VLADISLAV (bar); C2 (one B1, B2 opt) to F3. BUDIVOJ (bar); B1 to F3. BENES (bs); F1 (one E1, E2 opt) to F3. VITEK (t); E2 to B3. JITKA (s); needs agility; high tessitura; C3 to C5.

Lesser Role. ZDENEK'S GHOST (mute).

Chorus. SATB. Nobles, soldiers, men, women.

Orchestra. picc, 2 fl, 2 ob, 2 cl, 2 bsn, 4 hrn, 2 trp, 3 trb, tuba, timp, perc, harp, strings. *Stage*: 4 (8) trp, 3 trb, tuba, bells.

Material. B & H. VS (cz)*. GSc (Bä).

🎭 La Damnation de Faust · The Damnation of Faust

Music by Hector Berlioz (1803–1869) Libretto in French by the composer, loosely after Goethe; originally a choral work, *Eight Scenes from the Life of Faust.* Premiere: Paris, December 6, 1846. Dramatic legend. Music is episodic; orchestra very important; vocal line melodious. No overture; several orchestral interludes. Setting: medieval Germany and Hungary. Four parts, twelve scenes (under 120 min).

I: Hungarian plain. II i: Faust's study; ii: The cave of Auerbach at Leipzig; iii: Groves and prairies on bank of Elba. III i: Marguerite's chamber; ii: In front of Marguerite's house; iii: Marguerite's chamber. IV i: Marguerite's chamber; ii: Forest and caves; iii: Plains, mountains, valleys; iv: Hell; Epilogue: Earth.

Synopsis. Faust is bored with nature, observing simple country folk. The Hungarian March ends the first part. To the older Faust appears Méphistophélès, who promises Faust the gamut of experience and transports him to Auerbach's Cellar, where the revelry becomes unbridled. Méphistophélès induces a vision of Marguerite for Faust, who awakens to find the real maiden, and seduces her. Will-o'-the-wisps dance in the garden. The lovers part as the villagers approach. Méphistophélès gives Marguerite a sleeping potion for her mother; it is poison, and the girl is accused of her mother's murder. Faust signs a paper which he believes is to free Marguerite from prison, but in reality he has sold his soul to the Devil. Méphistophélès and his prey take a wild ride through eerie country, ending in the abyss. Spirits of the pit exult over Faust's downfall, while the soul of Marguerite is greeted by a heavenly choir.

Major Roles. MARGUERITE (m-s); C3 to A4 (one Bb4). FAUST (t); D2 to C♯4. MEPHISTOPHELES (bar or bs); A1 to F3 (one A3 with F♯3 opt; many opt notes higher or lower). BRANDER (bs); needs flexibility for Song of the Rat; A1 to D3.

Chorus. SS(or A)TTBB. Very important. Sometimes divided. Basses have D1. Peasants, soldiers, church choir, drinkers, students, bourgeois, demons, etc.

Ballet. Very important. Sylphs; Will-o'-the-Wisps.

Orchestra. 2 fl, picc, 2 ob, Eng hrn, 2 cl, bs cl, 4 bsn, 4 hrn, 2 trp, 2 corn à pist, 3 trb, 2 tuba, 2 harp, 8 (or 4) timp (4 or 2 players), bs dr, cym, sn dr, tam-tam, strings.

Material. Map.

Performances. Caramoor (N.Y.) Fest. 6.16.62. Wayne St. Univ. (Detroit): 4.24.69. Ravinia (Chic.): 6.28.69. Oakland Sym.: 12.2.69. Saratoga Fest.: 8.20.71. Berkshire Fest.: 8.22.71. N.Y. Phil.: 11.8.73 (conc).

🎭 Daphne

Music by Richard Strauss (1864–1949). Libretto in German by Josef Gregor. Premiere: Dresden, October 15, 1938. Bucolic tragedy. Continuous texture, with occasional arias inset. Brief overture. Setting: Peneios's hut, Mt. Olympus visible; antiquity. One act (105 min).

Synopsis. Daphne, the daughter of Peneios and Gaea, is more sympathetic to the natural world than to humanity. She has no wish to marry, although her childhood playmate, Leukippos, entreats her. Gaea insists that she attend the festival in honor of the god Dionysus, traditional time for lovers' mating. She refuses; two maids console Leukippos and dress him in Daphne's discarded festival raiment. Peneios predicts that one day Apollo will return to earth. His wife and the shepherds ridicule him while a strange herdsman appears, as if in confirmation of his prophecy. It is, of course, Apollo. Peneios sends for Daphne, who is immediately drawn to the stranger, as he is amazed by her beauty. He assures her that she will never be parted from the sun, which she adores. Half in a dream, she puts a blue cloak on his shoulders and allows him to embrace her. The herdsman, who has called her "Sister," now proclaims his love for her, to her confusion and dismay. Leukippos, in maiden's garments, persuades her to join the dance, but the stranger protests, and disrupts the feast with a thunderclap, revealing Leukippos's true identity and himself as Apollo. Daphne now feels doubly betrayed and refuses both suitors, whereupon Apollo kills Leukippos. Then, regretfully, he apologizes to his fellow god, Dionysus, for slaying one of his followers, and also to Zeus for interfering in mortals' affairs. To keep his promise to Daphne, he turns her into one of the laurel trees she loves. From her branches will be cut the wreaths for heroes.

Major Roles. PENEIOS, a fisherman (bs); A1 to E3. GAEA (c); E♭2 to F4. DAPHNE (dram s); high tessitura; florid; dramatic attacks on B4; B♭2 to C5. LEUKIPPOS (t); C♯2 to B3 (one attack on C4). APOLLO (t); very taxing; considerable high tessitura; C♯2 to B3.

Lesser Roles. FOUR SHEPHERDS: (bar) C2 to E3; (t) D2 to G♯3; (bs) D2 to E♭3; (bs) C2 to A♭2. TWO MAIDS: (s) G2 to B4; (s) B♯2 to A4.

Chorus. SATB. Shepherds, maskers, maids.

Ballet. At feast for Dionysus; as elaborate as desired.

Orchestra. 3 fl, 2 ob, Eng hrn, 3 cl, basset hrn, bs cl, 3 bsn, cont bsn, 4 hrn, 3 trp, 3 trb, tuba, timp, perc, 2 harp, org, strings. *Stage:* Alpine hrn.

Material. B & H. StS*. VS (g)*. Tr: Maria Massey Pelikan.

Performances. Litt. Orch (Bklyn): 10.7.60; (NYC): 10.10.60 (conc—Amer prem). Santa Fe: 7.29.64 (Amer stage prem). Pittsb. Sym.: 6.26.70 (TV tape). Amer. Sym. (NYC): 11.29.70 (conc). San Fran. Sym.: 12.70 (conc).

🖾 Debora e Jaele · Deborah and Jaele

Music by Ildebrando Pizzetti (1880–1968). Libretto in Italian by the composer. Premiere: Milan, December 16, 1922. Drama drawn from biblical story. Continuous texture; no rigid forms; vocal line a "sung declamation." Short prelude; prelude to Act III. Setting: Israel in biblical times. Three acts (135 min).

ACT I: Square of Nephthali in city of Kèdesh. ACT II: Palace of Sisera at Harosceth. ACT III: Encampment of Keniti.

Synopsis. The Jewish forces, beaten by Sisera, captain and King of Canaan, consult the prophetess Deborah, telling her of Sisera's cruelty. Hever cools their spirits by recounting Sisera's power. His wife, Jaele, is reviled because she is suspected of having been Sisera's lover, but Deborah, finally appearing, takes her part and promises imminent revenge. Barak, commander of the Jewish army, is willing to fight, but not against such odds. Deborah tells him to take his army to Mt. Tabor and prepare to fall on Sisera; he will not have the ultimate glory, however, because of his doubts. In Sisera's camp, the commander is revealed to be a man of honor and integrity, punishing a brute and scorning the advances of Hever, who has come as a spy. Sisera sends everyone away when a lady, who is Jaele by the tokens she sends, arrives. She tells him she has repented of refusing his love before; he believes her and her tale of the small size of the Jewish army, but a messenger brings an exactly opposite account, and Jaele confesses her treachery. Sisera refuses to punish her, and she is about to yield to him when the voice of Mara, whose children have been murdered by soldiers, restores her to duty. Sisera sets her free. After the Jewish victory, Sisera seeks refuge in Jaele's tent. The libretto differs from the biblical account in that Jaele's motive for slaying Sisera is to save him from falling alive into his enemies' hands.

Major Roles. DEBORA (m-s); requires some flexibility; A2 to G4. JAELE (dram s); B♭2 (G2 with G3 opt) to C5. MARA (m-s). A2 to A4. HEVER THE KENITE (bar); A1 to E♯3. KING SISERA (t); C2 to B♭3.

Lesser Roles. NABI, Prince of Nephthali (bar). BARAK, commander of Jewish forces (bs). AZRAEL (t). SHILLEM (t). JESSER, a fool (bar). ADONISEK, a

71

captain of Sisera (bar). TALMAI (bar). SLAVE (t). SHEPHERD (bar). PIRAM (bar). JAFIA (t) BLIND MAN (bs).

Chorus. SSAATTBBB. Very important; several solo parts. Old Men, Captains, Guards, Citizens.

Orchestra. 3 fl, 3 ob, 3 cl, 3 bsn, 4 hrn, 3 trp, 2 trb, tuba, timp, perc, cel, bells, tam-tam, harp, strings. *Stage:* Several instruments.

Material. Bel (Ri).

The Decision

Music by Thea Musgrave (1928–   ). Libretto in English by Maurice Lindsay after a television play by Ken Taylor, based on a true incident in Ayrshire. Premiere: London, November 30, 1967. Continuous texture embodying a few set numbers. Vocal line patterned after speech. Brief prelude, several interludes. Setting: Meningtown, about 1835. Three acts, eighteen scenes: should be continuous, possibly using drop curtain or blackouts or revolving stage or projections (approx 120 min).

ACT I i: Square of mining town, dominated by slag heap and wheel of winding gear; ii: Low gallery section of coal face with iron tracks; iii: Pithead, with stage divided by high wall with big iron gates; winding gear, etc., inside pithead, road leading to gates; iv: Gallery, same as ii; v: Flashback twenty years, outdoors with Brown visible in front of transparency; vi: Gallery; vii: Flashback ten years, Aunt's cottage; viii: Gallery. ACT II i: Pithead, next day; ii: Gallery; iii: Flashback six years, a wood; iv: Flashback five years, Wayson's cottage; v: Interior of church; vi: Outside manager's office. ACT III: An unused gallery, ten days later; ii: The Square; iii: Gallery; iv: Pithead.

Synopsis. John Brown, trapped in the mine, sees his life in flashbacks: the warning of his father; the indecision and final marriage of his girl Kate to Wayson, mine foreman; the secret meeting with her. Kate bears a stillborn child and Wayson threatens her with public condemnation and judgment. She dies of fever and fright. The Minister condemns John publicly. In the present, rescue attempts are called off by Wayson, but John's father and the miners continue to try. Wayson sends them away but hears knocking from the mine and to salve his conscience determines to rescue John himself against the Manager's orders. While rescuers' voices near, John tries to find a way out, but hallucinations of his Father, Kate, Aunt, and the Minister prevent. He is rescued, but dies almost immediately. Wayson, repentant, extols his memory, and the crowd mourns.

Major Roles. JOHN BROWN (bar); Ab1 (Gb1 with B1 opt) to F♯3. KATE, his girl (m-s); needs flexibility; Ab2 to G4 (one A4 with E4 opt). JOHN'S FATHER (bs-bar); G1 to E3. WAYSON (t); E2 to A3. KATE'S AUNT (c); A2 to E4. MANAGER OF THE PIT (bs); C2 to E3 (D3 opt); F3 in song-speech. MINISTER (bs); C2 to Eb3.

Lesser Roles. JACK and JIM (2 t); need flexibility for drunken song. PRE-

72

CEPTOR (t); can double with Jack or Jim. THREE MINERS (2 bar, bs). FOUR MINERS' WIVES (2 s, 2 c).

Chorus. SATTBB. Important. Miners and their women.

Orchestra. 2 fl (2 picc), 2 ob, 2 cl, bs cl, 2 bsn, cont bsn, 4 hrn, 3 trp, trb, tuba, timp, perc, harp, strings.

Material. G Sc (Che).

⚑ Deidamia

Music by George Frideric Handel (1685–1759). Libretto in Italian by Paolo Antonio Rolli. Premiere: London, January 10, 1741. Pseudo–historical-mythological drama. Simple harmonic structure, classical forms, set numbers, patter recitatives; vocal line agile, often florid, requires great flexibility. Overture. Sinfonia before Act III. Setting: the Greek island of Skyros, before the Trojan War (about 1200 B.C.). Three acts, ten scenes (approx 150 min).

ACT I i: Vestibule of the palace near the harbor, with access to the altar of Hercules; ii: Pavilion, with view of countryside; iii: Chamber in palace. ACT II i: Garden; ii: Hunting party; iii: Forest. ACT III i: Ground floor chamber; ii: Galleria; iii: Apartment; iv: Imperial hall.

Synopsis. Because the Oracle had prophesied that Achilles would meet his death at an early age, his parents have disguised him as a girl (Pirra), and sent him to Skyros to live with the daughters of their friend King Lycomedes. Deidamia, the princess, falls in love with Achilles. Ulysses (under the assumed name of Antilocus), Fenice, King of Argos, and Nestor come to Skyros to enlist the help of Lycomedes in the Trojan War. Also Ulysses suspects that Achilles may be hiding here, and without Achilles, the Oracle has said, the war cannot be won. At a hunting party, the hero betrays himself by his prowess in the chase, Ulysses discloses his identity and his mission, and the warriors depart, leaving Deidamia grieving for Achilles.

Major Roles. DEIDAMIA (col s); florid; high tessitura; sudden change of registers; C3 to Bb4. ACHILLES (s); light, rapid, spirited; passionate and military passages; F3 to A4. ULYSSES (dram-col c); taxing; sustained, florid, extremely dramatic as well as cantabile; D3 (touches C3) to G4 (touches A4). NEREA, Deidamia's friend (s); light, flexible, wide skips; B2 to A4.

Lesser Roles. FENICE (bs); broad; bravura; C2 to F3. LYCOMEDES (bs); dramatic; G1 to E3.

Chorus. SATB. Hunters, courtiers, and ladies of the court.

Ballet. Ad lib.

Orchestra. 2 ob, 2 bsn, 2 hrn, 2 trp, timp, lute, 2 harpsichords, strings. *Stage:* hunting hrns.

Material. German Handel Soc.; Handel's complete works; Leipzig, 1885; reprinted by Gr. G Sc (Bä).

Performances. Hartt Coll. (Hartford): 2.25.59. Univ. of Ind.: 10.11.69.

73

🎭 The Devil and Kate · Čert a Káča

Music by Antonín Dvořák (1841–1904). Libretto in Czech by the composer and Adolf Wenig. Premiere: Prague, National Theater, November 2, 1899. Folktale comedy; robust, colorful, humorous, with strong rhythm and lyric line. Overture. Setting: Czechoslovakia in legendary times. Three acts (105 min).

ACT I: Porch of a village inn (55 min). ACT II: In Hell (26 min). ACT III: Hall in the Princess's castle (24 min).

Synopsis. At a county fair, peasants joke about the strong-minded spinster Kate and her eagerness for a husband. A stranger appears—Marbuel, an assistant devil to Lucifer—on the mission of finding out whether the local Princess and her steward deserve to go to Hell. Courting Kate for information, he invites her to accompany him home; when she accepts, the ground opens and they disappear in a cloud of smoke. The shepherd Jirka, though he does not want Kate for himself, determines to rescue her. Amid revelries in Hell, Kate quickly gains the upper hand through her bossiness and garrulity, and refuses to be rescued. At length Marbuel succeeds in getting rid of her. Jirka, sent to fetch the Princess to Hell, saves her by persuading her to abolish serfdom. Kate helps by again terrifying Marbuel when he appears, and all ends happily.

Major Roles. KATE (m-s); top A4. PRINCESS (dram s); B♭2 to B4. MARBUEL (bs or bs-bar); sinister, suave, comic; top E3. JIRKA (t); robust; also lyric; top B♭3.

Lesser Roles. KATE'S MOTHER (c). CHAMBERMAID (s). LUCIFER (bs). GATEKEEPER (bar). MARSHAL (bar). MUSICIAN (bar).

Chorus. SATB (Acts I and III). TTBB (Act II).

Orchestra. 2 fl, picc, 2 ob, Eng hrn, 2 cl, bs cl, 2 bsn, cont bsn, 4 hrn, 3 trp, 3 trb, tuba, timp, perc, harp, strings.

Material. VS: Orbis, Prague, B & H (cz).

🎭 The Devil's Wall · Čertova Stěna

Music by Bedřich Smetana (1824–1884). Libretto in Czech by Eliška Krásnohorská. Premiere: Prague National Theater, October 29, 1882. Romantic comedy; supernatural story elements comparable to *Der Freischütz*; songful, often folklike, plentiful ensembles. Brief prelude. Setting: Vyšší Brod on the Vltava (Danube), site of the so-called Devil's Wall—a picturesque rock formation said to be left over from a satanic attempt to dam the river; 13th century. Three acts (139 min).

ACTS I and II: Rozmberk (Rosenberg), castle of Vok Vítkovic. ACT III: Banks of the river.

Synopsis. The noble Vok, once unhappy in love, has foresworn marriage—to the dismay of his friends, who think he should have an heir and are trying in vain to interest him in eligible girls. His friend Jarek wants to marry

74

Kutuška but cannot, having sworn not to wed until Vok does. The devil Rarach teases the villagers and subjects Jarek to trials on his knightly quests. Meanwhile, Vok is named guardian of Hedvika, daughter of his former sweetheart, who has recently died. He falls in love with her and eventually wins her, after threatening to join monastic orders. Rarach, scheming against the new monastery in the area, tries to flood it by building a wall in the river, but is thwarted by Hedvika, who warns the villagers, and by a penitent hermit, Beneš, who invokes the power of the Cross. Hedvika is united with Vok and Jarek with Kutuška.

Major Roles. VOK VITKOVIC (bar); grand seigneur; top Gb3, fairly frequent E3. JAREK (t); top Bb3. RARACH (bs); G1 to E3. BENES (bs). MICHALEK (lyr t); top A3. ZAVIS (lyr t). HEDVIKA (s); top B4. KATUSKA (s); top A4.

Chorus. SATB. Episodes not extended but atmospherically important.

Material. VS (cz): B & H.

🦋 Doktor Faust · Doctor Faust

Music by Ferruccio Busoni (1866–1924). Libretto in German by the composer, after Marlowe's *Doctor Faustus.* Premiere: Dresden, May 21, 1925. Philosophical melodrama. Some set numbers incorporated into continuous texture; free chromatic as well as tonal harmonies; Wagnerian-type melody; often patterned after speech; occasionally florid and declamatory. Orchestral prelude; ends with chorus backstage singing the word *Pax.* Setting: medieval Wittenberg, other locales (see tableaux). Left unfinished, the work was completed by Busoni's pupil, Philip Jarnach. Divided into tableaux, with orchestral interlude.

Prologue I: Narrator in front of curtain; Prologue II: Faust's study; Prologue III: The same, night. Intermezzo: Chapel in Munster Cathedral. Tableau I: Ducal court in Parma. Symphonic intermezzo: Sarabande. Tableau II: Inn in Wittenberg. Tableau III: Street in Wittenberg.

Synopsis. Doktor Faust makes his philosophical and magical arrangement with Mephistopheles and seduces the maiden Margaret (who does not appear in the opera). In a cathedral in Munster, accompanied by the pervading sound of organ music, a soldier prays for vengeance on the man who has seduced his sister. Mephistopheles removes him by causing him to be killed by other soldiers for murder of their captain. (This scene is omitted in concert versions.) Faust attends the wedding of the Duke of Parma to a beautiful young girl, and after enchanting the royal pair and the guests with his magical projections, makes off with the Duchess. The Devil is present in all these scenes in a variety of disguises (see under *Roles*). After an extended and solemn sarabande, Faust is seen in an inn, drinking and then quarreling with his students, who divide into Catholic and Protestant factions. They quiet down when Faust tells him of his one true love, a Duchess. Mephistopheles enters, saying that the Duchess has died and sent him a memento. He places at Faust's feet the corpse of a new-born baby, retells Faust's romantic story in unromantic terms, and sets fire to the baby, which is seen to be only straw. From the smoke he summons Helen of Troy, then leaves Faust alone. Faust still dreams of beauty, but it eludes him, and shadowy figures warn him his hour has come. In a street, students congratulate Wagner, who has succeeded Faust as Rector of the University. Faust enters and sees a beggar woman, who hands him a dead child. It is the Duchess. He tries to pray, but is denied. On the crucifix he sees Helen of Troy, and cries out in horror. (At this point, Busoni's score ends.) Faust uses his last power to redeem himself, and in dying, does so, as a youth arises from his body. Mephistopheles is left with only an empty skin.

Major Roles. DOKTOR FAUST (bar); some high tessitura; G♯1 to G3. MEPHISTOPHELES (t); high tessitura; sings also Man in Black, Monk, Herald, Chaplain, Spirit Voice, Courier. NIGHTWATCHMAN; C2 to C4. WAGNER (bar); low tessitura; F♯1 to D♭3. DUCHESS OF PARMA (s); needs flexibility; C♭3 to C♭5. DUKE OF PARMA (t); C2 to G3.

Lesser Roles. MASTER OF CEREMONIES (bs). GIRL'S BROTHER (bar). LIEUTENANT (t). THREE STUDENTS from Cracow (t, 2 bs). THEOLOGIAN (bs). JURIST (bs). DOCTOR OF NATURAL HISTORY (bar). FOUR STUDENTS from Wittenberg (4 t). Spirit voices: GRAVIS (bs), LEVIS (bs), ASMODUS (bar), BEELZEBUB (t), MEGARUS (t) (can be drawn from chorus).

Chorus. SSATTBB. Churchgoers, Soldiers, Courtiers, Hunters, Catholic and Lutheran Students, Country people.

Ballet. In Parma court scene.

Orchestra. 2 fl, picc, 2 ob (Eng hrn), 2 cl, bs cl, 3 bsn (cont bsn, 5 hrn, 3 trp, 3 trb, tuba, timp, perc, 2 harp, cel, org, strings. *Stage*: 2 hrn, 3 trp, trb, vln, vla, vcl, glock.

Material. AMP (BH). VS*.

Performances. Amer. Op. Soc. (NYC): 12.11.64 (conc—Amer prem).

🎵 Le Domino Noir · The Black Domino

Music by Daniel François Auber (1782–1871). Libretto in French by Eugène Scribe. Premiere: Paris, December 2, 1837. Light opera. Tuneful; alternates between a can can type of music and religious melodies, with occasional Spanish influences, such as the bolero of the overture. Voices are light with no range problems; all require trills. Setting: Madrid. Three acts (105 min).

ACT I: A masked ball (35 min). ACT II: Another ball (40 min). ACT III: The convent (30 min).

Synopsis. Angèle, about to become an abbess in Madrid, yields to temptation and attends a masked ball, where she falls in love with Horace of Massarene, a young nobleman. In hopes of meeting him again, she goes to another party, and is barely saved by her mask from exposure. After

76

further complications, she is released from her vows by the Queen and is free to marry her lover.

Major Roles. ANGÉLE (s or m-s); needs agility and grace and stylish acting; A2 to Ab4. HORACE (t); needs strength at bottom of range; A1 to G3.

Lesser Roles. JACINTHE (m-s). JULIANO (t); high tessitura. GIL PEREZ (light bs). LORD ELFORT (bs). BRIGETTE LA TOURIERE (m-s or s). URSULE (m-s or s).

Chorus. SA (nuns) TB (soldiers; combined at end).

Orchestra. 2 fl (2 picc), 2 ob, 2 cl, 2 bsn, 4 hrn, 2 trp, 3 trb, timp, perc, harp, strings. *Stage:* 2 fl, 2 ob, 2 cl, 2 bsn, 2 hrn, 2 trp, 2 trb, harp, strings.

Material. Map.

🎭 Don Quichotte · Don Quixote

Music by Jules Massenet (1842–1912). Libretto in French by Henri Cain after play by Le Lorrain based on Cervantes. Premiere: Monte Carlo, February 19, 1910. Highly melodious; set numbers, ensembles; some dialogue. Prelude with chorus. Brief prelude to Acts II, IV; entr'actes between II and III, IV and V; orchestral passage during windmill scene in Act II. Setting: Spain in the Middle Ages. Five acts (120 min).

ACT I: Public Square, Inn at left; Dulcinea's house at right. ACT II: The Windmills. ACT III: The Sierra. ACT IV: Dulcinea's House. ACT V: Death of Don Quichotte.

Synopsis. Don Quichotte and his companion ride into the square where the throng is praising the beauty of Dulcinea. Don Quichotte serenades the lady, arousing the jealousy of Juan, but a duel is prevented by Dulcinea herself. She promises the Don to be his love if he will recover a necklace stolen by brigands. He begins his travels, tilting at the windmills, then is captured by the brigands, who are so impressed by his courtliness, courage, and love for Dulcinea that they give him the necklace and free him. Dulcinea, amazed and delighted at the return of the necklace, listens to the Don's profession of love, but tells him her past, and begs him to forget her. He goes to his death, weary and disillusioned, bequeathing his most priceless possession, an "island of dreams," to his faithful squire, Sancho Panza.

Major Roles. DON QUICHOTTE (bs); one of the great roles in the repertoire; requires high degree of acting; A1 to E3. SANCHO (bar); trill; Ab1 to E3. DULCINEA (c); some fioratura; Ab2 to G4 (one A4). JUAN (t); D2 to G♯3.

Lesser Roles. PEDRO (s); Bb3 to Bb4. GARCIA (s); C3 to G4. RODRIGUEZ (t); D2 to Bb3.

Bit Roles. TWO SERVANTS (2 bar). BANDIT CHIEF (sp). FOUR BANDITS (sp).

Chorus. SAATTBB. Nobles, Ladies, Dulcinea's Friends, Bandits, etc.

Orchestra. 3 fl, 3 ob, 3 cl, 3 bsn, 4 hrn, 3 trp, 3 trb, timp, perc (4), 2 harp, guit, strings. *Stage:* 11 instruments.

Material. Pr (Heu).

Performances. Hartt. Coll. (Hartford): 2.17.65. San Diego Op.: 4.21.68. Houston Op.: 5.6.69.

◪ Don Rodrigo

Music by Alberto Ginastera (1916–   ). Libretto in Spanish by Alejandro Casona. Commissioned by the Municipality of Buenos Aires. Premiere, Colon, Buenos Aires, July 24, 1964. Historical-legendary drama. Twelve-tone music, embodying speech with prosodic rhythm, with music, with relative pitch, and with singing; also melodic singing; recitative. Vocal line with difficult intervals. No overture; six interludes between scenes. Setting: Toledo, 8th century. Three acts, nine scenes (95 min).

ACT I i: Rodrigo's palace in Toledo ("The Victory") (12 min); ii: The Basilica ("The Coronation") (11 min); iii: The Vault of Hercules ("The Secret") (5 min). ACT II i: Rodrigo's gardens ("Love") (11 min); ii: Florinda's bedchamber ("The Outrage") (11 min); iii: The same ("The Message") (6 min). ACT III i: Rodrigo's bedchamber ("The Dream") (12 min); ii: The battlefield of Guadalete ("The Battle") (9 min); iii: A small hermitage ("The Miracle") (18 min).

Synopsis. Returning in triumph from the defeat of the rebels who blinded his father, Rodrigo sees Florinda, the daughter of his comrade Count Julian, Governor of Africa, and promises her father to treat her as a daughter if he will allow her to stay at court. Rodrigo is crowned in the Basilica, swearing to take Spain as his wife. When Florinda hands him the crown, it falls to the floor. Disregarding this sinister omen, he places the crown on his own head. As thirty-third king, he breaks tradition by not adding his own padlock to a mysterious chest in the Vault of Hercules, but instead breaks it open to satisfy his curiosity. Inside he finds an Arab flag and a curse on the king who profanes the mystery: he shall be the last of his dynasty and his country shall be sacked by Moors. His followers flee, and Rodrigo is left stricken. Attended by his tutor Teudiselo, Rodrigo spies Florinda disrobing and bathing in a fountain. His approach startles her into flight. As she sings at bedtime, Florinda's room is invaded by Rodrigo, who overpowers her. But the love so brutally won turns to anger when Rodrigo forsakes her. She writes her father a bitter note, begging him to come to avenge her. Rodrigo has a premonitory dream, which comes true in Africa, as Julian arms to invade Spain. On the battlefield, the African troops charge seven times against Rodrigo, who is wounded in his right arm. Nevertheless, he grasps his sword in his left hand to meet the eighth charge, which brings defeat. He manages to reach a small hermitage, where as a penitent he accuses himself of causing the death of his people. Florinda finds him and tells him his soldiers will raise Spain again. He dies in her arms, and the bells of Spain ring out in a miracle: Florinda cries: "It is all Spain that is answering—it is the hand of the Lord!"

Major Roles. FLORINDA (dram s); Ab2 (Ab3 opt; touches G2 in song

78

speech) to C5. DON RODRIGO (dram t); high tessitura; sustained, also needs flexibility; Bb1 (Ab1 in song speech) to C4 (Bb3 opt). DON JULIAN (bar); needs strength in extremes of range; Ab1 to G#3, Ab3 has Ab2 opt. TEUDISE-LO (bs); Eb1, C#1 has C#2 opt, to F3. FORTUNA, Florinda's servant (m-s); Bb2 to F4.

Lesser Roles. TWO MAIDENS (s, m-s). BISHOP (bar). BLIND HERMIT (bar). TWO PAGES (t, bar). TWO LOCKSMITHS (t, bar). THREE MESSENGERS (t, bar, c). VOICE IN DREAM (bs). RAPAZ, young boy (t). ZAGALA, young girl (s).

Chorus. SSAATTBB. Once divided. Very important. Also speaking chorus. Heralds, pages, maidens, ladies, noblemen, captains, soldiers, watchmen, Arab soldiers, peasants, shepherds, woodcutters, craftsmen, etc.

Orchestra. 3 fl (picc), 3 ob (Eng hrn), 3 cl (bs cl), 3 bsn (cont bsn), 6 hrn, 4 trp, 4 trb, tuba, timp (2), perc (6): includes 3 tamb, 3 crotale, 3 tri, 3 small susp cym, 3 tam-tam, 2 cym, big dr, whip, 25 bells; glock, cel, mandolin, vla d'amore, harp, strings. *Stage*: 12 hrn, 8 trp.

Production Problems. Distribution of instruments throughout auditorium.

Material. B & H. VS (s).

Performances. NYCO (N. Amer prem): 2.22.66; 10.7.70, etc.

🎵 Le Donne Curiose · Inquisitive Women

Music by Ermanno Wolf-Ferrari (1876–1948). Libretto in Italian by Luigi Sugana after a play by Carlo Goldoni. Premiere: Munich, November 27, 1903. Comedy. Many ensembles, fairly complicated; a few ariettas; melody patterned after rapid speech. Orchestra light, refined. Overture. Intermezzo between Act II i and ii. Setting: Venice, mid-18th century. Three acts, six scenes.

ACT I i: A club for men only; ii: A room in Ottavio's house. ACT II i: A room in Lelio's house; ii: Ottavio's house. ACT III i: Street outside club; ii: Club foyer to dining room.

Synopsis. Ottavio's wife Beatrice and Lelio's wife Eleanora have grown unbearably curious about the club where their husbands spend so much time, and where the presence of women is forbidden. Beatrice is certain that gambling is the chief attraction; Eleanora insists that the men are alchemists and trying to convert base metal to gold. Rosaura, daughter of Beatrice and Ottavio, thinks that women are secretly smuggled into the men's retreat, while the maid Colombina holds out for treasure hunting. The four women determine to see for themselves. By several ruses they obtain three sets of keys. Colombina dresses as a man to obtain entrance, but is found out by Pantalone, the gruff bachelor who is the club's leading spirit. Rosaura's fiancé Florindo has given her his keys but spurns her when he discovers the dishonorable use she is prepared to put them to. Finally the four women resort to bribery and threats. Pantalone's servant Arlecchino, who has his eye on Colombina, reluctantly admits them to the sacred premises. They spy through the dining room door and discover that their men, far from engaging in ne-

79

farious pursuits, are eating a delicious dinner. The women's eagerness precipitates them through the door, to the initial horror and eventual acceptance of the men. All join in dancing and merriment, and the women are even welcomed into the secret, the password, "Here's to Friendship."

Major Roles. OTTAVIO (bs); G1 to E3. FLORINDO (lyr t); C2 to B3. PANTALONE (buf bs); wide skips, needs high falsetto; G1 to F3. ARLECCHINO (bs); Ab1 to E3. BEATRICE (m-s); trill; A2 to G4. ROSAURA (lyr s); several coloratura passages; C3 to B4 (one Cb5, one C5). COLOMBINA (lyr s); C3 to Bb4 (one C5). ELEANORA (m-s); some high tessitura; C3 to Bb4. LELIO (bar); A1 to F#3.

Lesser Roles. Friends of Pantalone: LEANDRO (t); E2 to G3; LUNARDO (bar); ASDRUBALL (t); ALMORO (t); ALVISE (t); MENEGO (bs); MOMOLO (bs).

Bit Roles. TWO GONDOLIERS (bar). SERVANT (mute).

Chorus. SATB (offstage). Gondoliers, populace.

Orchestra. 2 fl, 2 ob, 2 cl, 2 bsn, 2 hrn, 2 trp, harp, perc (1–2), timp, strings. *Stage:* mandolins.

Material. G Sc (Wein).

Performances. Henry St. Sett. (NYC): 6.1.63.

🎭 I Due Foscari · The Two Foscari

Music by Giuseppe Verdi (1813–1901). Libretto in Italian by Francesco Maria Piave, based on the play, *The Two Foscari,* by Lord Byron. Premiere: Rome, November 3, 1844. Melodrama. Highly melodic; conventional harmonies. Prelude. Setting: Venice, 1457. Four acts (or three, with five scenes) (105 min).

ACT I: Council chamber. ACT II i: Jacopo's dungeon; ii: Council chamber. ACT III i: St. Mark's Square; ii: Doge's apartments (According to Rome Opera performance).

Synopsis. The powerful Venetian Council of Ten tries the Doge's son Jacopo for murder, and condemns him to renewed exile in spite of his wife Lucrezia's plea to his father, who is impotent to help him. Lucrezia visits her husband in prison, as does his father, but they cannot prevent his punishment. During Carnival in St. Mark's Square, a galley ship arrives to bear Jacopo away. The Doge laments the loss of all of his sons and rejoices when the real murderer is found and Jacopo is proclaimed innocent. But it is too late: Jacopo falls dead at the moment of disclosure. The Council of Ten demands the Doge's abdication. Although he had tried twice to retire, he now refuses, but they give him no choice. He hands his crown and mantle to a senator and collapses as bells toll for his successor. His chief enemy Loredano marks his account paid.

Major Roles. FRANCESCO FOSCARI, Doge of Venice (bar). JACOPO, his son (t). LUCREZIA CONTARINI, Jacopo's wife (s). JACOPO LOREDANO, member of the Council of Ten (bs).

80

Lesser Roles. BARBARIGO, Senator (t). PISANA, friend of Lucrezia (s). OFFICER OF THE COUNCIL OF TEN (t). SERVANT OF DOGE (bs). Mute: MESSER GRANDE. TWO SMALL SONS OF JACOPO. OFFICER. JAILOR.

Chorus. SATB. Senators, councilors, etc. Merrymakers. People of Venice.

Ballet. Possible in Act III i.

Orchestra. 2 fl, 2 ob, 2 cl, 2 bsn, 4 hrn, 2 trp, 3 trb, tuba, timp, perc, harp, strings.

Material. Bel (Ri).

Performances. Rome Opera (NYC): 7.1.68.

✎ Elegy for Young Lovers

Music by Hans Werner Henze (1926–   ). Libretto in English by W. H. Auden and Chester Kallman. Premiere: Schwetzingen Festival, May 20, 1961 (in German); premiere in English, Glyndebourne, England, July 13, 1961. Tragedy. Individual synthesis of neo-classicism and serialism, elaborate and exotic orchestral color though small except percussion; set pieces in short, titled sections, each a unit; vocal line difficult but melodious. Some spoken dialogue; also singing speech on three pitch levels. Extended orchestral interlude at scene change in Act III. Setting: Austrian Alps; early 20th century. Three acts (152 min).

ACT I (Emergence of the Bridegroom) Parlor and terrace of Der Schwarze Adler, inn in Austrian Alps. Snowcapped peak of Hammerhorn visible. ACT II (Emergence of the Bride) Same as I. ACT III (Man and Wife) Same as I until set divides in half and rolls offstage. Mountain backstage moves forward. Hammerhorn behind scrim in blizzard. Later a spotlight reveals dressing table behind scrim, then reading desk on stage center. Finally scrim becomes backdrop of Mt. Parnassus.

Synopsis. Every year, the self-centered poet, Gregor Mittenhofer, returns to the same Alpine inn to observe (clinically) the visions of the elderly Hilda Mack, who has been driven mad by the death of her husband on the Hammerhorn forty years ago. The poet incorporates these visions into his poems. He brings with him a young mistress, Elisabeth Zimmer; a middle-aged secretary, Carolina, Grafin von Kirchstetten; his physician, Dr. Wilhelm Reischmann; and the latter's son, Toni. Hilda is returned to sanity by the discovery of her husband's body in a glacier; the poet's inspiration is gone. He stage-manages a trip into the mountains by Elisabeth and Toni, to seek a certain flower. The two young people, already in love, wander too far. When a blizzard suddenly comes up, they are caught. The poet, who could have saved them, is pleased at finding a new inspiration. His poem is finished.

Major Roles. GREGOR MITTENHOFER (bar); high tessitura; G1 to G3, one G♯3 (G♯2 opt). HILDA MACK (col s); florid and difficult with wide skips, high tessitura, trills (one on C5); B2 to E5 (two sustained F♯5, opt F♯4). ELISABETH ZIMMER (s); B2 to B4. CAROLINA (c); trill; G♯2 to A4. DR. WILHELM

81

REISCHMANN (bs); F1 to G3. TONI (lyr t); C2 to Bb3 (one C#4, opt Ab3 or C4).

Bit Roles. JOSEF MAUER, Alpine guide (sp). SERVANTS (mute).

Orchestra. fl (picc, alto fl, fl dolce), Eng hrn (ob), cl (bs cl), alto sax, bsn, hrn, trp, trb, timp, perc (3—glock, cel, musical saw, marimba, vibraharp, mandolin, chittara), harp, piano (without lid), 2 vln, vla, vcl, cb, bells on tape.

Production Problems. Movable stage advisable. Snowstorm.

Material. Bel (Sch). VS (e, g).

Performances. Juill. (NYC): 4.29.65 (Amer prem). Univ. of Ind.: 3.2.68.

☘ Ernani

Music by Giuseppe Verdi (1813–1901). Libretto in Italian by Francesco Maria Piave, after the play by Victor Hugo. Premiere: Teatro la Fenice, Venice, March 9, 1844. Tragedy. Highly melodious; dramatic; set numbers; conventional harmonies; extended ensembles. Brief prelude. Setting: Spain, early 16th century. Four acts, five scenes (104 min).

ACT I i: The mountains of Aragon; ii: Elvira's apartment in Don Ruy de Silva's castle (40 min). ACT II: Great hall in the castle (27 min). ACT III: A sepulchral vault in the Cathedral at Aix-la-Chapelle (21 min). ACT IV: Terrace of Ernani's castle (16 min).

Synopsis. Don Ruy Gomez de Silva discovers his ward, Elvira, whom he hopes to marry, in the company of two rivals, the young Ernani (really John of Aragon), whom she favors, and Don Carlos, the King. The King commands Silva to let Ernani go, but later, believing him dead, Elvira consents to marry her aging guardian. Ernani returns, disguised as a monk, and in spite of offering to sacrifice his life, is protected by Silva on his honor as a host. He hides Ernani from the King, who threatens to execute him, and carries off Elvira. Ernani goes to her rescue, first handing Silva his hunting horn with the promise that he will kill himself if ever Silva blows it. The King is proclaimed Emperor and pardons all conspirators, restoring Ernani's lands and titles. Ernani and Elvira are about to be married when Silva takes his revenge by blowing the horn. Ernani stabs himself.

Major Roles. ERNANI, bandit chief (John of Aragon) (t); sustained; trill; extremes of range (A1 and Bb3 in one passage); otherwise Bb1 to A3 (2 Bb3 in ensembles, with Gb3 opt). DON CARLO, King of Castile (bar); consistently high tessitura; some florid passages; A1 to G3. DON RUY GOMEZ DE SILVA (bs): both sustained and florid; G1 to F3. ELVIRA (s); sustained; high tessitura; considerable coloratura; trill; Bb2 to (many) C5.

Lesser Roles. GIOVANNA, Elvira's maid (s). DON RICCARDO, esquire to the King (t). JAGO, esquire to Silva (bs).

Chorus. SSATTBB. Mountaineers, bandits, cavaliers, followers of Silva, servants of Elvira, people of Lega, Spanish nobles and ladies.

Ballet. In Act I i and III.

Orchestra. 2 fl, 2 ob, 2 cl, bs cl, 2 bsn, 4 hrn, 2 trp, 3 trb, tuba, timp, perc, harp, strings. *Stage*: 3 trp. Band (not at Met).

Material. Bel (Col). Map. Pr. Ka.

Performances. Met: 1956–57; 62–63; 64–65; 70–71. San Fran.: 9.13.68. Op. Guild, Greater Miami: 1.25.71.

▶ Euryanthe

Music by Carl Maria von Weber (1786–1826). Libretto in German by Helmina von Chezy. Premiere: Vienna, October 25, 1823. Romantic drama. Continuous texture, with dramatic recitatives and set numbers woven in; extended arias, ensembles; full orchestration of great power and color; vocal line both melodic and declamatory; overture. Setting: France, 12th century. Three acts, six scenes (140 min).

ACT I i: Hall in royal palace (25 min); ii: Entrance to Tomb in Garden of Palace of Nevers (40 min). ACT II i: Garden of Palace of Nevers (15 min); ii: Hall in royal palace (20 min). ACT III i: A wild, rocky gorge (20 min); ii: Open field near Palace of Nevers (20 min).

Synopsis. Lysiart of Foret, a knight in the retinue of King Louis VI of France, jealously maligns the faith of all women and challenges Adolar, another knight, to a wager that his own betrothed, Euryanthe of Savoy, is no exception. Their entire possessions are staked. Eglantine of Puiset, Euryanthe's handmaiden, loves Adolar and helps Lysiart betray Euryanthe by persuading her to reveal Adolar's family secret: his sister Emma has committed suicide after her lover's death in battle. Eglantine steals a ring from Emma's tomb, and with this evidence, Lysiart proves Euryanthe's faithlessness. Adolar gives up all his estates to Lysiart, and follows Euryanthe to a rocky gorge, where he would slay her but is prevented by the attack of a serpent, which Euryanthe manages to avert. He abandons her to her fate, but when the King and a hunting party discover her, she is able to convince the monarch of her innocence. Eglantine and Lysiart are about to be married but Eglantine is tormented by her conscience. Adolar arrives and challenges Lysiart to a duel, but the King forbids them to fight, and tells Adolar that Euryanthe has died with his name on her lips. Eglantine then bursts forth with the whole story of her and Lysiart's perfidy, and Lysiart stabs her. Euryanthe enters, and the lovers are reunited.

Major Roles. EURYANTHE OF SAVOY (dram s); needs strength throughout wide range; dramatic expressiveness; flexibility; C3 to C♯5. EGLANTINE OF PUISET (m-s); many florid passages; dramatic strength; A♯2 to C5. COUNT ADOLAR OF NEVERS (t); needs heroic quality; strength throughout range; E2 to B♭3. COUNT LYSIART OF FORET (bar); both sustained and flexible; violent quality; G1 to F3. (These four roles are prophetic of Wagner's early operas; Eglantine and Lysiart particularly call to mind Ortrud and Telramund. They are as demanding as Wagner roles, as extended and powerful.)

83

Lesser Roles. KING LOUIS VI OF FRANCE (bs); comparable in many ways to a Wagnerian King. RUDOLPH, a knight (t). BERTHA (s).

Chorus. SATTBB. Ladies, nobles, knights, hunters, peasants. Very important.

Orchestra. 2 fl, 2 ob, 2 cl, 2 bsn, 4 hrn, 2 trp, 3 trb, timp, strings. *Stage*: 2 picc, 2 ob, 2 cl, 2 bsn, 4 hrn, 4 trp, 3 trb, timp.

Material. Map.

Performances. Litt. Orch. (NYC): 10.27.70 (conc).

✄ The Excursions of Mr. Broucek · Vylety Páne Brouckovy

Music by Leoš Janáček (1854–1928). Libretto in Czech by Victor Dyk and F. S. Procházka after a novel by Svatopluk Cech. Premiere: Prague, July 12, 1920. Satire. First part ("to the Moon") is simpler, employing waltz rhythms and ironic contrasts; second part ("in the 15th century") is more lyrical and with greater harmonic richness. Overture and interludes. Setting: Prague and the Moon, 20th and 15th centuries. Two acts, nine scenes (116 min).

Prague, 1920: Scenes i, iv, v, ix. On the Moon: Scenes ii, iii. Prague, 1420: Scenes vi, vii, viii.

Synopsis. Mathias Brouček, complacent, stupid, greedy, uncultured bourgeois of early 20th-century Prague, has a drunken fantasy in which he sees himself as a hero confronting the V.I.P.'s of the Moon, who are in reality only his neighbors and servants transformed. Then he transports himself and "retinue" to early Hussite Prague, (which the Emperor Sigmund is besieging) where his antics are equally ridiculous. His character remains the same, but each of the others assumes different identity (generally upgraded) in both "dream" sequences, indicated by M (Moon) and P2 (early Prague).

Major Roles. MATHIAS BROUCEK (t); top Bb3. MAZAL (t); top Bb3; younger painter (M, BLANKYTNY, poet; P2, PETRIK, Kunka's bridegroom). SACRISTAN OF ST. VEIT (bs); (M, LUNOBAR, scholar; P2, DOMSIK, bellringer of Tein Church). MALINKA, his daughter (s); (M, ETHEREA, Lunobar's daughter; P2, KUNKA, Bellringer's daughter).

Lesser Roles. VIRFEL, innkeeper (bs); (M, CAROSKVOUCI, intellectual patron; P2, KOSTKA, Town Councillor). BUSBOY in Virfel's inn (s); (M, MINISTER OF CULTURE; P2, A SCHOLAR). FANNY NOVAK, Brouček's housekeeper (c); (M, MINISTER OF FOOD; P2, FRANTISKA, bellringer's housekeeper). A STREETCAR CONDUCTOR (t); (M, MINISTER OF TRANSPORTATION; P2, WATCHMAN). GUEST AT THE INN (M, REPRESENTATIVE OF MOON REPUBLIC). BYSTANDER (M, MOON MAID). P2 only: VACEK WITH THE IRON HAND (bar).

Chorus. TTBB. Burghers and armed forces. Children's chorus.

Orchestra. 4 fl (picc), 2 ob, Eng hrn, 2 cl, bs cl, 2 bsn, cont bsn, 4 hrn, 3 trp, 4 trb, tuba, timp, perc, cel, glock, bagpipe, org, harp, strings.

Material. PR (UE).

Ezio

Music by George Frideric Handel (1685–1759). Libretto in Italian by Pietro Metastasio. Premiere: London, January 15, 1732. Historical drama. Simple harmonic structure; vocal line almost entirely florid, great deal of melisma. Brief overture; brief "sinfonia" before Act II. Setting: Rome, A.D. 5th century. Three acts, five scenes.

ACT I: Roman Forum. ACT II i: Garden of Emperor Valentiniano III's palace on Palatine Hill; ii: Gallery of statues. ACT III i: Vestibule of prison; ii: Ancient Campidoglia.

Synopsis. Ezio, general in the army of Caesar, returns triumphant from a campaign against Attila. He is engaged to Fulvia, daughter of the patrician Massimo, who, however, is the secret enemy of Prefect Varo, Ezio's friend. The emperor, in love with Fulvia, schemes against Ezio, while his sister, Onoria, secretly in love with the general, arouses Fulvia's jealousy. Ezio is thrown into prison, but the complicated palace intrigue is made to end happily with his return to Fulvia, after a riotous mob scene in which the people storm the imperial bastions.

Major Roles. (All need flexibility, trills). VALENTINIANO III (bs, orig. male c); A1 to D3. FULVIA (s); B2 to A4. EZIO (bar, orig. male c); B♭1 to D3. ONORIA (m-s or c); C3 to D4. MASSIMO (t); most important part, with several elaborate arias; C2 to A3. VARO (bs); F1 to F3. Difficult role.

Orchestra. 2 fl, 2 hrn, 2 ob, 2 bsn, trp, trb, timp, strings (6, 6, 4, 3, 2). Continuo: harpsichord, vcl. cb.

Material. G Sc (Bä)

Performances. Actors' Op. (NYC): 3.22.59; 5.11.59 (conc). Handel Soc. of N.Y.: 1.30.73.

La Favorite · La Favorita · The Favorite

Music by Gaetano Donizetti (1797–1848). Libretto in French by Alphonse Royer and Gustave Vaëz after *Le Comte de Commingues* by D'Arnaud, reworked by Eugène Scribe. Premiere: Paris Opéra, December 2, 1840. (Originally intended for the Théâtre de la Renaissance and titled *L'Ange de Niside*, it was expanded from three acts to four for the Opéra.) Since sung in many languages, chiefly Italian. Romantic drama. Highly melodious, set numbers, ensembles, recitatives. Overture. Setting: Spain, the Kingdom of Castile, 1340. Four acts, five scenes.

ACT I i: Hall in the monastery; ii: The island of St. Leon. ACT II: Gardens of the palace of the Alcazar. ACT III: A salon in the palace. ACT IV: Cloisters of the monastery.

Synopsis. Leonora, the mistress of King Alfonso XI of Castile, has fallen deeply in love with Fernando, a young novice in the Monastery of St. James, who renounces his vocation for her. Not knowing her position, he accepts a commission from the King and is victorious in battle with the Moors. He asks for the hand of Leonora, and the King, though reluctant to give her up, decides that this is the solution to his own predicament—he has been threatened with Papal excommunication if he does not restore his rightful wife to her position. Leonora, doubtful of Fernando's love if he knows the truth, nevertheless sends a letter to him by her servant Ines, who, however, is intercepted by Don Gasparo, the King's minister, so that Fernando marries Leonora in ignorance. He is soon enlightened by the jeers of the court, and repudiates his bride and his honors, returning to the monastery, where Baldassare, the Prior, welcomes him. Leonora, disguised as a novice, seeks him out and wins his pardon and reawakens his love. But it is too late; she dies in his arms.

Major Roles. LEONORA DI GUZMAN (s or m-s); florid passages; sustained, dramatic; A2 to Bb4. ALFONSO XI (bar); high tessitura; needs great flexibility; trill; C2 to F3. FERNANDO (t); high tessitura; E2 to C#4. BALDASSARE (bs); F1 to Fb3.

Lesser Roles. DON GASPARO (t); D2 to F#3. INES (s); some florid passages; C3 to Bb4.

Bit Role. A GENTLEMAN (t).

Chorus. SATB. Gentlemen and ladies of the court, pages, guards, mountaineers, monks, soldiers.

Ballet. Act II, as elaborate as desired.

Orchestra. 2 fl, 2 ob, 2 cl, 2 bsn, 4 hrn, 2 trp, 3 trb, tuba, timp, perc, org, harp, strings. *Stage*: band.

Material. Bel (Ri). Map.

Performances. Dallas Civic Op.: 11.26.69. San Fran.: 9.7.73.

🎭 Feathertop

Music by Joyce Barthelson. Libretto in English by the composer adapted from story by Hawthorne. Concert premiere: New York, January 26, 1968. Folk fantasy-satire. Continuous texture; conventional 20th-century harmony; melodic. Overture (9 min). Setting: a New England village, 18th century. Prologue, two acts, four scenes, epilogue (96 min).

Prologue: Mother Rigby's hut in forest (5 min). ACT I i: Garden adjoining Gookin's house, noon of same day; ii: Mother Rigby's hut, early afternoon (47 min). ACT II i: Gookin drawing room, partial view of garden, late afternoon; ii: same, early evening (39 min). Epilogue: Mother Rigby's hut, late evening (5 min).

Synopsis. Mother Rigby, a mischievous witch, has brought to life a scarecrow with a feather in his hat. He passes for the elegant Lord Feathertop and courts Polly Gookin, to the awe of neighbors. The only dissenters are children, who recognize him as a pumpkinhead, and Polly's sweetheart, Daniel, who feels he is a phony. Just as Polly is about to accept his suit, his lordship is exposed by a truth-revealing mirror and flees to Mother Rigby. He loses the life-giving pipe she has placed between his lips and collapses into the sticks and straws of the scarecrow. Mother Rigby reflects that there is many a man succeeding with no more wits than this, and sails off on her broomstick, black bats and black cats in tow.

Major Roles. MOTHER RIGBY (m-s); B♭2 to G4. JUDGE GOOKIN (bs); F1 to D3. POLLY GOOKIN (lyr s); E♭3 to B♭4. LORD FEATHERTOP (t); E2 to A♯3. DANIEL (bar); C2 to F♯3.

Lesser Role. SMALL BOY (boy s).

Bit Roles. PRUDENCE (s), PRISCILLA (s), KATE (c), friends of Polly.

Chorus. SSATB, children. Villagers.

Ballet. Three dancers: Broom, Tongs, Kettle (puppets cleaning up hut in I ii).

Orchestra. 2 fl (picc), ob, 2 cl, bsn, 2 hrn, 2 trp, 2 trb, perc, xyl, bells, strings.

Material. Fi.

Performances. Met Studio (conc with narrator; tape available).

✍ Fedora

Music by Umberto Giordano (1867–1948). Libretto in Italian by Arturo Caulotti after the play by Victorien Sardou. Premiere: Milan, November 17, 1898. Romantic tragedy. Melodious, with dramatic climaxes; occasional nationalistic flavor (Russian, Swiss tunes, French waltz, Polish song). Very brief prelude. Setting: St. Petersburg, Paris, and Switzerland, late 19th century. Three acts.

ACT I: Count Vladimir Andreievich's drawing room in St. Petersburg. ACT II: Fedora's house in Paris. ACT III: Fedora's chalet outside village of Thun, Switzerland.

Synopsis. Count Vladimir Andreievich is carried, wounded, into his house, where his fiancée Princess Fedora Romanov has called to see him. When he dies, Fedora vows to avenge him. Suspicion falls on Count Loris Ipanov. At a party in her Paris house, Fedora welcomes Countess Olga and her friend, the pianist Boleslao Lazinski. Then Fedora sets her plot in motion, asking the help of De Siriex, French Foreign Secretary, sending a message to Russian authorities, and drawing from Loris the admission that he was in truth responsible for the Count's death, although there are mitigating circumstances. Telling him to return that night with proof, she commands Grech, the police officer, to kidnap Loris and take him back to Russia. But she changes her mind when Loris proves that he had killed Vladimir only after the Count had wounded him. Loris had discovered that his wife, who had since died, was having an affair with the Count. Fedora spirits Loris away to Switzerland and they marry. Loris is still haunted by unknown spies, for Fedora's plot is still in force. Olga and de Siriex arrive; the latter tells Fedora that Vladimir's brother and friend, whom she had betrayed along with Loris, have died in prison and the shock has killed Loris' mother. The same news reaches Loris from his friend Doctor Borov, who adds that a woman has been responsible. Discovering that it was Fedora, Loris becomes violent, but Fedora takes poison and dies in his arms as he forgives her.

Major Roles. PRINCESS FEDORA ROMANOV (s); C3 to A4 (one Bb4, one C5, both with octave opt). COUNT LORIS IPANOV (t); C#2 to A3 (one Bb3). DE SIRIEX (bar); needs some flexibility; D#2 to F#3. COUNTESS OLGA SUKAREV (s); C#3 to A4 (one opt Bb4). GRECH (bs); C2 to E3.

Lesser Roles. BOROV (bar); top F3. CIRILLO, coachman (bar). LOREK, surgeon (bar). DIMITRI, groom (c). DESIRE, valet (t). LITTLE SAVOYARD (m-s). BARON ROUVEL (t). BOLESLAO LAZINSKI (mime; can be played by actual pianist).

Chorus. SATB. Several small solos: NICOLA, SERGIO, grooms (t, b); BOY. Servants, gentlemen, ladies.

Orchestra. picc, 2 fl, 2 ob, Eng hrn, 2 cl (bs cl), 2 bsn, 4 hrn, 3 trp, 3 trb, timp, bs dr, cym, tri, sistra, tamb, tam-tam, bells (can be elec), harp, strings.

Material. Bel (Son). VS (i, e)*.

Performances. Dallas Civic Op.: 11.26.69. Op. Orch. of N.Y.: 12.6.70 (conc). Ruffino Op. (NYC): 3.31.71. Op. Th. of N.J. (Newark): 11.12.71.

🎭 Die Feen · The Fairies

Music by Richard Wagner (1813–1883). Libretto in German by the composer after Gozzi's *La Donna Serpente*. Premiere: Munich, June 29, 1888. Blend of fantasy and reality; some comedy. Set numbers, conventional harmonies; important ensembles. Overture; brief prelude to Act III. Setting: mythical kingdom. Three acts, eleven scenes.

ACT I i: Fairy garden; ii: Wild desert; iii: Garden and palace; iv: Festive procession of the fairies. ACT II i: Hall in Arindal's palace; ii: An empty space. ACT III i: Festive hall; ii: Cleft in underworld kingdom; iii: Another part of the kingdom; iv: Rock in magic grotto; v: Fairy palace.

Synopsis. Prince Arindal of Tramond loves the beautiful Ada for many years, though he does not know her identity. When finally he asks her, she disappears, since she was a supernatural being who desired to become human, but was forced to protect her true status. The Prince in despair follows her to her underworld kingdom and remains there to rule with her, relinquishing his humanity.

Major Roles. ADA (s); needs flexibility; D3 to C5. ARINDAL (t); high tessitura; some florid passages; top A3 (touches Bb3). LORA, his sister (s); needs flexibility; top firm C5. MORALD, her lover (bar); top F#3.

Lesser Roles. FAIRY KING (bs); top E3. GORNOT, hunter (buf bs); top E3. DROLLA, Lora's maid (s); top A4. GUNTHER, courtier of Tramond (buf t). HARALD, Arindal's commander-in-chief (bs). FARZANA and ZEMIRA, fairies (s, s). TWO CHILDREN (Arindal's and Ada's) (mute). MESSENGER (t). MAGIC VOICE (bs).

Chorus. SSATB. Fairies, travelers, warriors, ghosts, etc.

Ballet. As elaborate as desired.

Orchestra. Picc, 2 fl, 2 op, 2 cl, 2 bsn, 4 hrn, 2 trp, 3 trb, timp, perc, harp, strings. *Stage*: 2 fl, 2 cl, 2 trp, 4 trb.
Material. BH.

🎵 La Fiamma · The Flame

Music by Ottorino Respighi (1879–1936). Libretto in Italian by Claudio Guastalla after *The Witch* by G. Wiers Jenssen. Premiere: Rome, January 23, 1934. Melodrama. Conventional harmonies enriched by exotic flavor; melodious; vocal line dramatic, highly charged; continuous texture with set numbers embedded. Brief preludes to each act. Setting: Ravenna in the last year of the 7th century. Three acts.

ACT I: Basilio's villa, between the coast and deep pine woods. ACT II: Palace of Teodorico in Ravenna: gallery at left rear; ancient room through an arch at lower right; center resplendent with Byzantine decoration. ACT III: Multiple scene; Donello's chamber in arch backed by curtain; curtain opens to reveal forecourt of basilica; curtain opens further to reveal basilica of San Vitale.

Synopsis. Silvana, whose mother has been suspected of witchcraft, has been married to the Exarch of Ravenna, Basilio, whose mother, the Greek Eudossia, hates her. When Eudossia's presence is removed, the girls of the court chatter merrily, but Silvana is oppressed and longs for freedom. Left alone in the garden, she is approached by Agnes di Cervia, an old associate of her mother's, who is trying to escape from a mob bent on sending her to the stake for a murder. Silvana reluctantly sends her to the gallery for safety, but she is nevertheless discovered and carried away to torture and death. Meanwhile, Donello, Basilio's son by his first wife, returns from Byzantium and is welcomed by the court maids and also by Silvana. The two young people discover a bond of sympathy from their early days, but the advent of the mob breaks off their reunion. Donello entertains the maids with naughty tales of the cult of Venus; one of the girls, Silvana's favorite Monica, has fallen in love with him and given herself to him. Silvana discovers this and banishes Monica to a nunnery. Donello reveals to his father that Agnes had called on Silvana before she died, and Basilio then remembers that his attraction to his wife seemed to be flavored by witchcraft. When he discusses this with Silvana, she reacts strangely: perhaps she does after all possess dark powers. To test this, she summons Donello by her will and the two become lovers. Eudossia discovering them, tells Donello that he has been summoned again to Byzantium; half relieved, he goes. Basilio, suddenly feeble, tries to win Silvana's attention, but she turns on him in such a rage of scorn and denunciation that he dies of shock. This is exactly Eudossia's triumph; calling Silvana before the Bishop, she witnesses the young woman's eventual breakdown and tacit confession of guilt. There is no doubt that Agnes's fate will also overtake Silvana.

Major Roles. EUDOSSIA (m-s); A♭2 to B♭4. BASILIO (high bar). DONELLO (t); Eb2 to Bb3. SILVANA (s); high tessitura; needs flexibility; C3 to Bb4. AGNES (m-s); Bb2 to A4. MONICA (s); C#3 to Bb4. AGATA (s); C3 to Bb4. LUCILLA (m-s); Bb2 to G4. SABINA (m-s); G2 to F#4.

Lesser Roles. ZOE (m-s). THE BISHOP (bs). THE EXORCIST (bs). A MOTHER (s). A CLERK (t).

Chorus. SSSAATTBB. Very important. Several solos. Boys' chorus. All need wide range and flexibility. Maids, clergy, followers, crowd, scholars, etc.

Orchestra. 3 fl, 3 ob, 3 cl, 3 bsn, 4 hrn, 3 trp, 3 trb, tuba, timp, perc, harp, strings. *Stage*: Some instruments.

Material. Bel (Ri).

📓 Fille de l'Homme · Daughter of Man

Music by Pierre Capdeville (1906–   ). Libretto in French by Jean de Beer. Commissioned by the State, 1960. Premiere: Bordeaux, November 9, 1967. Lyric tragedy. Expressive, violent orchestra; dissonant, animated. Vocal line partly patterned after speech; difficult intervals; some speech song. No overture; prelude to Act III. Setting: a town in southern Italy, winter 1943–1944. Three acts (approx 100 min).

ACT I: Carlotta's apartment. ACT II: Vestibule of entrance to Franciscan convent with doors leading to street, chapel, and cloister. ACT III: House of Captain Alfano.

Synopsis. Carlotta's lover, Captain Tibaldo Alfano, is accused of being a traitor by Colonel Rizzo, who demands that she kill him. He has sold his comrades to buy her an expensive necklace, the Colonel insists. At 2 A.M. Carlotta seeks the help of Father Bruno, begging him to come with her to administer last rites to Tibaldo, whom she intends to kill. Father Bruno is horrified. Carlotta leaves, maintaining that hers is the hardest duty and throwing down the necklace. She begs him to meet her at 6 o'clock at Tibaldo's house. Father Bruno contemplates the necklace with dismay as the monks file past into the chapel, singing a hymn. Later in Tibaldo's house, Carlotta hides a gun as Father Bruno enters. She accuses Tibaldo, who pleads his innocence, but eventually tries to escape, bumping into Carlotta, who shoots him. The Colonel telephones; Carlotta tells him her mission is accomplished, then collapses as Father Bruno prays for her.

Major Roles. CARLOTTA, aged about 27 (lyr-dram s); needs strength for sustained upper range; B2 (E2 in declamation) to B4. CAPTAIN TIBALDO ALFANO, 30 (dram t); B1 (D2 opt) to A3. FATHER BRUNO (bar); Ab1 (one G1 with G2 opt) to G3. COLONEL RIZZO, 50 (bs); E#1 to F3.

Chorus. Invisible soldiers TB. Franciscan monks TBB.

Orchestra. 3 fl (picc), 2 ob, Eng hrn, 2 cl, bs cl, 2 bsn, cont bsn, 4 hrn, 3 trp, 2 trb, tuba, timp, perc: xyl, vib, tam-tam, tamb provençal, military dr, bs dr, cym, susp cym; 2 harp, piano, cel, strings. *Stage*: glock.

Material. Pet (Chou). VS*.

90

🎵 La Fille de Madame Angot · The Daughter of Madam Angot

Music by Charles Lecocq (1832–1918). Book and lyrics by Clairville, Giraudin, and Konig. Premiere: Brussels, December 4, 1872. Operetta. Comedy. Melodious; dialogue, set numbers, recitatives. Brief overture. Brief interludes between acts. Setting: Paris under the Directorate, after the Revolution. Three acts (150 min).

ACT I: A market square. ACT II: Mlle Lange's drawing room. ACT III: Outside a dance hall. Epilogue.

Synopsis. A story rich in complications and about-faces. Clairette, daughter of the late adventurous Mme Angot (who has even charmed the Sultan away from his harem), has been adopted by the market folk, and is about to be married to the man of their choice, the barber Pomponnet. She is, however, in love with the Royalist poet, Ange Pitou, who has just written a satirical song about Mlle Lange, the actress-mistress of Barras, head of the Directorate. Larivaudière, the secret lover of Lange, bribes the poet not to make the song public. But knowing that every time Pitou performs he is arrested, Clairette boldly sings the controversial ditty and achieves her aim, to be imprisoned and thus postpone the wedding. Furthermore, there is some doubt about her paternity, as she was born in the harem. Lange is curious about Clairette and uses Barras' influence to have her sent for. Pomponnet, dressing Lange's hair, insists that Clairette is innocent; the culprit is Pitou. He goes to fetch the song in proof. Clairette and Lange discover that they were school friends. But now Ange Pitou arrives, also summoned by Lange. Between them springs up an instant attraction. The arrival of the jealous Larivaudière prompts Lange to an unwittingly true story that it is Clairette who loves the poet. She convinces Larivaudière that Pitou's sympathy is necessary, as they too, with Barras, are in reality conspiring for the Royalists. Pomponnet returns and is immediately arrested for possessing a copy of the song. A meeting of the Royalists is scheduled for midnight at Lange's home. Threatened by Hussars sent to arrest them, they turn the conspiratorial session into a merry ball, in which the Hussars join. Clairette discovers that Lange cherishes tender emotions for her poet, and plans to trap them. But at last, Clairette realizes that Pomponnet, who was arrested for her sake, is really for her, and she gives Pitou to Lange for nothing—exactly what he is worth.

Major Roles. CLAIRETTE ANGOT (s); C♯3 to B4. POMPONNET (t); D2 to D4. ANGE PITOU (t); D2 to A3. MLLE LANGE (m-s); B2 to A4. LARIVAUDIERE (bar); B♭1 to F3.

Lesser Roles. JAVOTTE (s), AMARANTE (s), market women. GUILLAUME (t), CADET (t), BUTEUX (bs), market men. LOUCHARD, police officer. HERSILIE, Lange's servant. BABET, Clairette's servant. TRENITZ, officer of the Hussars.

Chorus. SATTB. Market men and women, citizens, Hussars.

Ballet. Waltz, principals and chorus, Act II. Ball, Act III.

91

Material. Map. VS: B & H (f, e)*.
Performances. Radio City Music Hall (NYC): 11.29.50, etc. CBC-TV: 1.69.

La Fille du Régiment · The Daughter of the Regiment

Music by Gaetano Donizetti (1797–1848). Libretto in French by Jules-Henri Vernoy de Saint-Georges and Jean-Françaix-Alfred Bayard. Premiere: Paris Opéra-Comique, February 11, 1840. Often performed in Italian as *La Figlia del Reggimento*. Romantic comedy. Highly melodious; set numbers; French dialogue set as recitative for Italian version. Overture. Setting: Mountains in the Swiss Tyrol, about 1815. Two acts (115 min).

ACT I: A Tyrolean landscape (75 min). ACT II: Hall in the Castle of Birkenfeld (40 min).

Synopsis. Marie, the darling of the 21st Regiment of Grenadiers, which adopted her after finding her abandoned on the battlefield as a child, is happy with her life and extremely fond of her special foster father, the old top sergeant Sulpice. She expresses her delight in a number called the Rataplan, in which she drums with rolls and flourishes. She tells Sulpice about a young Swiss named Tonio who has rescued her from a precipice and whom she loves. Tonio himself decides to join the regiment, since they have decided Marie shall marry no one outside. But her identity is revealed as the niece of the Marquise of Birkenfeld, who takes her into the aristocratic life of the castle and arranges a marriage with the son of the Duchess of Crakenthorp. Marie is not happy, and finally brings the Marquise to acknowledge that she is her own love child, and to allow her marriage to Tonio.

Major Roles. MARIE (col s); considerable coloratura; trill; must be able to play drum solo; C3 to B4. TONIO (t); D2 to (many) C4. SULPICE (buf bs); B♭1 to F3. MARQUISE OF BIRKENFELD (m-s); B♭2 to F♯4.

Lesser Roles. DUCHESS OF CRAKENTHORP (sp). HORTENSIO, steward to the Marquise (bs—at Met. buf t). CORPORAL (bs). PEASANT (t). NOTARY (mute).

Chorus. SSATTB. Soldiers, Swiss villagers, servants of Marquise.

Orchestra. 2 fl (2 picc), 2 ob (2 Eng hrn), 2 cl, 2 bsn, 4 hrn, 2 trp, 3 trb, perc, timp, strings.

Met Orchestra. 2 fl (picc), 2 ob (Eng hrn), 2 cl, 2 bsn, 4 hrn, 2 trp, 3 trb, tuba, timp, perc, strings. *Stage:* 2 trp, side dr, piano (played onstage).

Material. Bel. Map. (Met uses Bonynge French vers.) Ka.

Performances. Phila. Lyr.: 1966–1967. Amer. Op. Soc. (NYC): 2.13.70 (conc). Op. Co. of Boston: 2.21.70; 1.9.73. Denver Lyric Op.: 5.17.70. Met.: 2.17.72 etc. Cin. Summ. Op.: 7.25.73. Seattle Op.: 9.13.73. Chic. Lyric Op.: 10.20.73 etc.

La Finta Giardiniera · The False Gardener

Music by Wolfgang Amadeus Mozart (1756–1791). Libretto in Italian attributed to Raniero da Calzabigi. Premiere: Munich, January 13, 1775. Revised twice with German text. Later performances in Europe and the United States brought further revisions. Comedy. Conventional structure with set numbers, recitatives, ensembles. Overture. Setting: Lagonero, middle 18th century. Three acts, eight scenes (approx 150 min).

ACT I i: Garden of the Podestá's house; ii: A hall in the Podestá's palace; iii: A corner in the garden. ACT II i: Winter garden; ii: A grotto in the woods. ACT III i: A room in the Podestá's palace; ii: A deserted fountain; iii: Garden.

Synopsis. A year before the story opens, the Marchese Violante has been stabbed in a fit of jealousy by her fiance, Count Belfiore, who has left her for dead and departed from Milan. Violante sets off to find him, and learning that he has been betrothed to Arminda, niece of the Podestá (ruler) of Lagonero, hires out as the Podestá's gardener named Sandrina. The plot is immediately complicated by persons' falling in love impossibly: Ramiro, a young knight, with Arminda; Arminda with Belfiore; Nardo (Violante's servant Roberto in disguise) with the maid Serpetta, who has set her cap for her master the Podestá, who casts a covetous eye at "Sandrina." Before the couples can be sorted out, with only the Podestá left alone, much confusion ensues.

Major Roles. MARCHESE VIOLANTE (SANDRINA) (s). COUNT BELFIORE (t); some florid passages. ARMINDA (s). SERPETTA (lyr s). PODESTA, DON ANCHISE (buf bar). RAMIRO (m-s). NARDO (ROBERTO) (bs-bar).

Lesser Role. DOCTOR (sp).

Orchestra. 2 fl, 2 ob, 2 cl, 2 bsn, 4 hrn, 2 trp, timp, strings.

Material. G Sc (Bä).

Performances. New England Op. Th.: 1950. Op. Co. of Boston: Hunter Coll. (NYC): 5.68. Chamber Op. of Colon Th. (Washington, D.C.): 5.27.71.

La Finta Semplice · The False Simpleton

Music by Wolfgang Amadeus Mozart (1756–1791). Libretto in Italian from Carlo Goldoni, elaborated by Mario Coltellini. Premiere: Salzburg, May 1, 1769. Comedy. Melodious; set numbers, recitative. Overture; brief intermezzo before Act III. Setting: Cremona. Three acts (110 min).

ACT I: A garden, with alley of trees leading to facade of country chateau. ACT II: Room in Cassandro's house. ACT III: Garden.

Synopsis. A clever woman, pretending to be a simpleton, maneuvers two shy bachelors, one her brother, into marrying girls they wanted but did not dare approach.

Roles. (No range problems.) ROSINA, a Hungarian baroness (s); needs flexibility; trill; top Bb4. CAPTAIN FRACASSO, her brother (t). NINETTA, chambermaid (s); trill; top A4. DONNA GIACENTA (s). DON POLIDORO, her brother (t); top Bb3. DON CASSANDRO, brother of last two, a rich landowner (bs). SIMONE, servant (bs).

93

Orchestra. 2 fl, 3 ob, 2 bsn, 2 hrn, strings.
Material. Bel (Ri).

✍ Fra Diavolo · Brother Devil

Music by Daniel François Auber (1782–1871). Libretto in French by Eugène Scribe. Premiere: Paris, January 28, 1830. Comedy-drama. Highly melodious; conventional harmonies; set numbers. Setting: An inn near Rome, 1830. Three acts (110 min).

ACT I: Matteo's Inn, near Terracina. ACT II: Zerlina's bedroom. ACT III: In the hills near Terracina.

Synopsis. The notorious bandit Fra Diavolo, posing as the Marchese San Marco, has aroused the jealousy of the traveling Lord Cockburn by his behavior toward Lady Cockburn in an encounter on the road. The two bandits Giacomo and Beppo have taken Lord Cockburn's jewels, but cannot find his money. In an aside, the Marchese informs them it is hidden in the lady's dress. The bandits plan a further assault on the couple, using as a vantage point the room of the innkeeper's daughter Zerlina, who is being forced to marry the rich Francesco although she is in love with the dragoon officer Lorenzo. Lorenzo has recovered the jewels and given the reward money to Zerlina. Now he comes to her rescue as the bandits are about to stab her. Still in the character of the Marchese, Fra Diavolo also inspires jealousy in Lorenzo by his presence in Zerlina's room. Nevertheless, Lorenzo and Zerlina are married. Diavolo leaves orders for his followers in a hollow tree, but during the wedding procession, Giacomo and Beppo are arrested and Diavolo is forced to appear in his rightful guise. He is shot, and falls into the abyss. (Originally the bandit was merely arrested, not killed.)

Major Roles. FRA DIAVOLO (t). Swashbuckling role. LORD COCKBURN (bar). PAMELA, his wife (m-s). ZERLINA (s); has famous aria "Oui, c'est demain." LORENZO (t). GIACOMO (t). BEPPO (bs).

Lesser Roles. MATTEO (bs). FRANCESCO, a farmer (bs). A MILLER (bs).

Chorus. SATB. Dragoons, servants, peasants.

Orchestra. 2 fl (2 picc), 2 ob, 2 cl, 2 bsn, 4 hrn, 2 trp, 3 trb, timp, perc, strings. *Stage*: 4 hrn, 2 trp, 3 trb, glock.

Material. Bel (Sch). Map. Ka.

Performances. Hunter Coll. (NYC): 5.10.56. San Fran.: 11.22.68 etc. Rittenhouse Op. Soc. (Phila.): 2.10.71.

✍ Francesca da Rimini · Francesca of Rimini

Music by Riccardo Zandonai (1883–1944). Libretto in Italian adapted by Tito Ricordi from the play by Gabriele d'Annunzio. Premiere: Turin, February 19, 1914. Tragedy. Highly melodious, continuous texture, voice often patterned after speech. No overture. Setting: Ravenna and Rimini, end of the 13th century. Four acts, five scenes (125 min).

ACT I: Court in the house of the Polentani adjacent to a garden, in Ravenna. ACT II: Interior of fortified tower in the house of the Malatesti, Rimini. ACT III: Tower room with frescoes depicting adventures of Tristan with curtained alcove. ACT IV i: Octagonal hall of gray stone, overlooking mountains, with grated door leading to subterranean prison; ii: Tower room with alcove.

Synopsis. Francesca, daughter of Guido da Polenta, must marry Giovanni, known as Gianciotto, "The Lame," son of Malatesta da Verrucchio, but because of his ugliness, his brother Paolo "The Fair" is substituted at an introduction. The two young people fall deeply in love. After the marriage, Francesca visits a tower from which war is being waged by the Guelphs against the Ghibellines and chides Paolo for the fraud. He pleads innocence. They are interrupted by the advent of a third brother, the young Malatestino, who has lost an eye in battle, and is henceforth called "The One-Eyed." Gianciotto brings the news that the war is won and that Paolo has been elected Captain of the People in Florence. Paolo departs for that city. In her tower room, Francesca is reading from the story of Lancelot and Guinevere to her women, who dance and sing in celebration of spring. A slave whispers to Francesca, who dismisses her women to receive Paolo, who has returned from Florence, unable to bear absence from her. They kiss in ecstasy. But Malatestino, who himself has a guilty passion for Francesca, discovers their love and betrays them to Gianciotto. The husband surprises the lovers and slays them both.

Major Roles. FRANCESCA (s); lyrical and also intensely dramatic; C3 to B4 (one C5). SAMARITANA, her sister (m-s); E3 to A4. OSTASIO, her brother (bar); D2 to G3. GIANCIOTTO (bar); extremely high tessitura; B1 to many firm G3's. PAOLO (t); E2 to B3. MALATESTINO (t); E2 (C2 with C3 opt) to A3 (one opt Bb3).

Lesser Roles. Francesca's women: BIANCOFIORE (s), must be short in stature; GARSENDA (s); DONELLA (s); ALTICHIARA (m-s); the slave SMARAGDI (m-s). SER TOLDO BERARDENGO (t); can double with ARCHER. JESTER (bar); can double with TOWER WARDEN. VOICE OF PRISONER OFFSTAGE; top Cb4.

Chorus. SSAATTBB. Women of court, archers.

Orchestra. 4 fl, 3 ob, 3 cl, 3 bsn, 4 hrn, 3 trp, 3 trb, tuba, timp, perc, cel, bells, harp, strings. Op. Orch. of N.Y. performance added instruments originally called for: lute, vla pomposa, bs fl, and shawm.

Material. Bel (Col).

Performances. Op. Orch. of N.Y.: 3.22.73 (conc).

📧 From the House of the Dead · Z Mrtvého Domu

Music by Leoš Janáček (1854–1928). Libretto in Czech by the composer after *The House of the Dead* by Feodor Mikhailovich Dostoevsky. Premiere: Brno, Czechoslovakia, April 12, 1930 (posthumous, with "adaptations" by Břetislav Bakala and Osvald Chlubna). Premiere of original version: Prague, National Theater, April 24, 1964. Prison drama, predominantly male cast. Declamatory, often harsh style, mixing folklike vigor with atonal tendencies; pungent, compressed, emotionally intense. Setting: Ostrogg prison camp on the river Irtysch in Siberia, Tsarist times (ca.1850). Three acts, four scenes (100 min).

ACT I: Prison courtyard in winter (35 min). ACT II: Riverbank in summer, a year and a half later (30 min). ACT III i: Prison hospital, winter; ii: Same as Act I (35 min).

Synopsis. Alexander Petrovich Gorianchikov arrives at the camp in Siberia and is humiliated by the commandant for being a political prisoner and sophisticate. The other prisoners recall their past and celebrate a holiday from their dismal life by enacting a crude play about Don Juan and his servant Kedril. Gorianchikov befriends one of the prisoners, Alyei, a sensitive young Tartar, and teaches him to write. At length Gorianchikov ends his term and must leave his friend behind, as the prisoners release an eagle whose broken wing they have been nursing; it flies away, a symbol of the indomitable human spirit.

Major Roles. GORIANCHIKOV (bar); sympathetic character, observer and confessor, well bred. ALYEI (t); top B3. SHISHKOV, a murderer (bar); long narrative in Act III; top Gb3.

Lesser Roles. SHAPKIN (bar); SKURATOV (t); several other prisoners of assorted age and physique. COMMANDANT (bs). PROSTITUTE, female prisoner (s or m-s). FOUR MEN, FOUR WOMEN, in pantomime Don Juan play (mute).

Chorus. TTBB. Atmospheric background passages, important to mood but not of sustained length.

Orchestra. 4 fl (3 picc), 2 ob, Eng hrn, 3 cl (bs cl), 3 bsn (cont bsn), 4 hrn, 3 trp, bs trp (ten tuba), 3 trb, tuba, timp, perc, cel, harp, strings.

Material. Pr (UE).

Performances. NET-TV: 1969–1970; 11.20.70.

✄ The Gambler

Music by Serge Prokofiev (1891–1953). Libretto in Russian by the composer, based on the novel by the same name by Dostoevsky. Premiere: Brussels, April 29, 1929. A few set pieces embodied in continuous texture; recitative; vocal line not very melodious, inflected after speech. Difficult ensembles. Brief prelude; entr'actes IV i and ii, with chorus ii and iii. Setting: the fashionable Central European gambling spa, Roulettenberg, 1865. Four acts, six scenes.

ACT I: Garden adjoining a Casino. ACT II: Main lounge of the Grand Hotel Casino. ACT III: Drawing room adjoining Casino. ACT IV i: Alexis's room; ii: Large gambling hall; iii: Alexis's room.

Synopsis. Alexis, tutor to the children of a retired General, gambles for the General's stepdaughter Pauline, whom he loves, and loses. He boasts that if he had his own money he would win, being a Tatar; he could achieve no other good fortune because he is the younger son of a good family. The General, in straitened circumstances, has borrowed from a wealthy and elegant Marquis, and presumably promised his stepdaughter in marriage as payment. He himself is engaged to a worldly, voluptuous demimondaine, Blanche. He rests his hopes on the death of his ancient grandmother. Alexis, who has confessed his love to Pauline, defiantly accepts her challenge to do something foolish, which takes the form of taunting a rich Baron and his wife. The General is horrified, because any breath of scandal will jeopardize his relationship with Blanche, who has already made herself conspicuous by begging money from the Baron. Alexis comes almost to the point of a duel, and asks a rich Englishman, Astey, to second him. Into this complicated situation arrives the Grandmother in a sedan chair, showing warmth to Pauline and Alexis, but disowning the General. She indulges in a gambling spree which bankrupts her in cash, although she still owns a considerable estate. Withdrawing, she invites Pauline to stay, leaving the General in despair. Blanche deserts the General for wealthy Prince Nilsky. The Marquis departs, leaving a politely sarcastic note for Pauline; her fortune and the General's are gone. She goes to Alexis, resolved to act like a human being and to offer herself to him. He is elated, but, seized with an idea, rushes out to secure money and begins to play roulette. In a scene of mounting excitement, he breaks the bank. Staggering back to his small room, he dazedly contemplates his new fortune, and does not at first see that Pauline is there watching him. He presses money on her, which she accepts, but only to throw it in his face, disillusioned and embittered by his attitude. After her departure, Alexis immediately forgets her in gloating over his winnings. The gambler's nature has overpoweringly asserted itself.

Major Roles. THE GENERAL (bs); dramatic, imposing presence; some high tessitura; needs strength in both extremes of range; G#1 (one F1) to E3. PAULINE (s); Db3 to A4 (one B4). ALEXIS (t); sustained; Bb1 to Bb3 (final B3, G opt). GRANDMOTHER (m-s); dominating, haughty; Bb2 to G4. MARQUIS (t); C2 to A3. MR. ASTLEY (bar); C2 to Eb3. BLANCHE (c); D3 to G4.

Lesser Roles. PRINCE NILSKY (t); needs falsetto; C3 to B5. BARON WURMERHELM (bs). POTAPICH, Grandmother's servant (bar).

Bit Roles. DIRECTOR (bs). CROUPIERS (t-t). FAT ENGLISHMAN (bs). TALL ENGLISHMAN (bs). PAINTED LADY (s). PALE LADY (s). LA DAME COMME-CI, COMME-CA (m-s). OLD LADY (m-s). OLD SUSPICIOUS LADY (c). RECKLESS GAMBLER (t). SICKLY GAMBLER (t). HUNCHBACK GAMBLER (t). UNLUCKY GAMBLER (bar). OLD GAMBLER (bs). SIX GAMBLERS (2 t, 2 bar, 2 bs). Mute: HOTEL CLERK; BARONESS WURMERHELM; MANAGER; BELLBOY; FEODOR, THEODOR, and MARTHA (Grandmother's servants).

Chorus. SATB. Players, hotel guests, servants, porters; voices behind curtain or in pit during IV ii, iii.

Orchestra. 3 fl, 3 ob, 3 cl, 3 bsn, 4 hrn, 3 trp, 3 trb, tuba, timp, perc, 2 harp, strings. *Stage:* piano IV iii, with 2 croupiers' voices.

Material. B & H (Paris).

Performances. 85th St. Playhouse (NYC): 4.2.57, etc.

🎵 I Gioielli della Madonna · The Jewels of the Madonna

Music by Ermanno Wolf-Ferrari (1876–1948). Libretto in Italian by C. Zangarini and E. Golesciani. Premiere (in German as *Der Schmuck der Madonna*): Berlin, December 23, 1911. Premiere in Italian: Chicago, January 16, 1912 (American premiere). Melodrama. Continuous texture; melodious, many ensembles. No overture. Intermezzo between Act II and III. Setting: Contemporary Naples. Three acts (125 min).

ACT I: Square in Naples by the sea (45 min). ACT II: Carmela's garden (45 min). ACT III: A haunt of the Camorra (35 min).

Synopsis. Maliela has been adopted by Carmela as a baby and lives with the old lady and her blacksmith son Gennaro. She is restless and untamed, and longs to escape to a more exciting life. The attentions of the head of the Camorra, the handsome Rafaele, at first seem not to appeal to her, but she gradually melts and promises to meet him. He vows that for her he would even steal the jewels from the Madonna who has been carried past in a procession. Maliela taunts Gennaro with Rafaele's vow to steal the jewels, and he goes off to perform this unholy deed; then when he shows them to Maliela, she yields to his lovemaking. Next day, she goes to Rafaele, who has boasted to his carousing comrades that he will be the first man in her life. When he discovers that she has given herself to Gennaro, he casts her aside contemptuously. The jewels fall from her robe; as Gennaro enters madly, she flings them at his feet. The crowd recoils in superstition. Maliela goes to drown herself, and Gennaro plunges a knife into his heart.

Major Roles. GENNARO (t); C2 to B♭3 (B3 has G3 opt). CARMELA (m-s); C3 to A♭4. MALIELA (dram s); needs great intensity and vivid acting; considerable flexibility; trill; C♯3 to B4 (one C5). RAFAELE (bar); acting role; considerable high tessitura; C2 to F♯3.

Lesser Roles. BIASCO, a scribe (bs). Camorrists: CICCILLO (buf t); ROCCO (bs). Friends of Camorrists: STELLA (s), top C5; SERENA (c); CONCETTA (s); GRAZIA ("LA BIONDINA"), dancer (s). TOTONNO, young peasant (t).

Chorus. SSATTBB, children; often divided; several solos. People, vendors, Camorrists, Neapolitan characters, etc.

Ballet. In Acts I and II.

Orchestra. picc, 2 fl, 2 ob, Eng hrn, 2 cl, bs cl, 2 bsn, cont bsn, 4 hrn, 3 trp, 3 trb, tuba, timp, perc, glock, harp, guit, mandoline, strings.

Material. Pr (Wein).

Performances. Rittenhouse Op. Soc. (Phila.): 4.12.62.

🎵 Il Giuramento · The Oath

Music by Saverio Mercadante (1795–1870). Libretto in Italian by Gaetano Rossi, based on Victor Hugo's *Angelo*. Premiere: Milan, March 10, 1837.

Melodrama. The first of the composer's "reform" operas in which he deleted cabalettas and crescendos and employed newly rich harmonies and modulations, decidedly influencing Verdi. Set numbers; important ensembles; melodious as well as dramatic vocal line. Very brief orchestral prelude, choral prelude to both acts. Setting: Syracuse, Sicily, 14th century. Two (can be three) acts, five scenes (approx 105 min).

ACT I i: Elaisa's palace; ii: Bianca's apartment. ACT II i: Square near Manfredo's palace; ii: Tombs of the Counts of Syracuse; iii (or III): Elaisa's palace.

Synopsis. The story bears a strong resemblance to *La Gioconda* because of its identical origin; however, there are minor differences. Elaisa, who loves Viscardo de Benevente, discovers that he loves Bianca, wife of Manfredo. The traitorous Brunoro arranges a rendezvous with Bianca for Viscardo. Elaisa, confronting the lovers, is recognized by Bianca as the daughter of the man whose life she once saved; Elaisa remembers her oath to reward her father's savior, and protects Bianca when Manfredo bursts in, summoned by Brunoro. In a battle with the troops of Agrigento, Brunoro is killed. Bianca is also supposed to have died, but in reality is hidden by Manfredo in the family tomb, where he comes to kill her. But Elaisa substitutes a sleeping potion for the intended poison and spirits Bianca to her own palace. Viscardo, believing Elaisa an accomplice in Bianca's "death," stabs her, but she reveals the truth and Bianca and Viscardo are united.

Major Roles. VISCARDO (t); needs flexibility; top B3. MANFREDO (bar); high tessitura; B1 to F3. ELAISA (dram s); needs flexibility for florid passages; trill; D3 to firm C5. BIANCA (m-s); sustained, dramatic; wide skips; trill; needs agility as well as strength; A♭2 to B4.

Lesser Roles. BRUNORO (t); top G3. ISAURA, Bianca's maid (s).

Chorus. SSATTB. Very important. Gentlemen, armed cavaliers, dignitaries, ladies, artisans, pages, fishermen, guards, servants, a majordomo.

Ballet. As desired in I i.

Orchestra. 2 fl, 2 ob, 2 cl, 2 bsn, 4 hrn, 2 trp, 3 trb, tuba, timp, perc (2), harp, strings. *Stage*: 2 fl, 2 ob, 3 cl, 2 hrn, 3 trp, 2 trb, harp.

Material. Bel (Col). Map.

Performances. Juill. (NYC): 5.15.70.

☙ Gloriana

Music by Benjamin Britten (1913–   ). Libretto in English by William Plomer. Dedicated to Her Majesty Queen Elizabeth II; composed for Coronation. Premiere: London, June 8, 1953. Drama based on history. Melodic; strong Elizabethan flavor; continuous texture with set numbers embedded. Vocal line wryly melodious; difficult intervals; odd inflections and prosody. Brief overture. Important choruses. Setting: England in later years of Elizabeth I's reign (1558–1603). Three acts, eight scenes.

ACT I i: Outside a tilting ground; ii: Queen's anteroom in Nonesuch. ACT.

II i: Guildhall in Norwich; ii: Garden of Essex's house in the Strand; iii: Great room in Whitehall Palace. ACT III i: Queen's anteroom in Nonesuch; ii: Street in City of London; iii: Room in Whitehall Palace.

Synopsis. Elizabeth reconciles Essex and Mountjoy, who fight in boisterous rivalry. Cecil advises her to be cautious, saying: "The art of government is in procrastination, silence, and delay." Essex pleads his suit to Elizabeth and excoriates Raleigh and Cecil, who oppose his claim to be Deputy for Ireland. Elizabeth, much taken by Essex, prays to retain her will and honor as a monarch and to subdue her womanly impulses. At Norwich a masque is given in honor of the visiting Queen. Essex and his lady, Mountjoy and Lady Rich (Essex's sister), plan to defy the Queen in the matter of Essex's appointment. At a grand levée, the Queen takes the ladies off to change linen after a strenuous dance, and reappears wearing Lady Essex's overelaborate gown, which looks grotesque on her. She goes to change, leaving Lady Essex and the others shaken by the insult. When the Queen returns in her own garb she astonishes the assemblage by giving Essex the desired Irish command. Later Essex breaks in on the Queen at her dressing table with news of virtual failure. On Cecil's advice, Elizabeth decides to imprison her former favorite. Essex is proclaimed a traitor in the streets to the amazement of the populace. The Queen signs the death warrant in spite of the importunities of Mountjoy, Lady Rich, and Lady Essex. Then as a procession of phantom kings and queens passes by, she stands in twilight reverie and addresses a spoken plea to her people, claiming her deeds to be their interest. She admits to Cecil and to the Archbishop that she is ready to die.

Major Roles. ELIZABETH (s); needs some flexibility; dialogue; Bb2 to Bb4. ROBERT DEVEREUX, Earl of Essex (t); needs flexibility; wide skips; dramatic tension in high tessitura; C2 to A3. FRANCES, COUNTESS OF ESSEX (m-s); G2 to F4. CHARLES BLOUNT, LORD MOUNTJOY (bar); difficult intervals; A1 to F3. PENELOPE, LADY RICH (s); some sustained passages; Bb2 to Bb4 (one B4, one C5). SIR ROBERT CECIL (bar); some dialogue; B1 to F3. SIR WALTER RALEIGH (bs); F1 to Eb3. HENRY CUFFE, satellite of Essex (bar); F#1 to F#3 (one G3, G2 opt).

Lesser Roles. LADY-IN-WAITING (s); D3 to B4. RECORDER OF NORWICH (bs); G1 to C3. HOUSEWIFE (m-s). SPIRIT OF MASQUE (t); short role but important; florid; high tessitura; F2 to A3. MASTER OF CEREMONIES (t). CITY CRIER (bar); high Db.

Chorus. SSATTB. Boys with broken voices. Citizens, maids of honor, ladies, gentlemen of household, courtiers, masquers, old men, men and boys in Essex's following, councellors.

Ballet. Choral dances in II i; Morris Dance, Coranto in II iii. Dancers: Time, Concord, country girls, rustics, fishermen, Morris dancer.

Actors. Pages, ballad singer's runner, St. John Harington, French Ambassador, Archbishop of Canterbury, Phantom Kings and Queens.

Orchestra. 3 fl (2 picc), 2 ob, Eng hrn, 2 cl, bs cl, 2 bsn, cont bsn, 4 hrn, 3 trp, 3 trb, tuba, timp, perc, harp, strings. *Stage*: I i trp (multiples of 3);

100

II iii orchestra for dances: 5 strings and/or 5 woodwinds, pipe (fl), tabor (small side dr without sn); III ii gittern; III iii side dr, cym, bs dr, wind machine, harp.

Material. B & H. VS*.

Performances. Cincin. May Fest.: 5.9.56 (Amer prem).

⚜ The Golden Lion

Music by Gerald Kechley (1919–   ). Libretto in English by Elwyn Kechley. Premiere: University of Washington, Seattle, April 28, 1959; revised December 1959. Drama. Continuous texture with arias embedded; some exotic flavor; vocal line largely melodious; some declamation. Interlude between Act I ii and iii. Setting: Constantinople, 800. Two acts, six scenes (115 min).

ACT I i: The throne room; ii: Courtyard; iii: Throne room; iv: Throne room. ACT II i: Throne room; ii: Nunnery.

Synopsis. A struggle goes on in 9th-century Byzantium between two factions to choose an Empress for the pleasure-loving Emperor Theophilus. Amos, a false monk and very powerful, favors Theodora; the Patriarch John and the Empress-Dowager have chosen the young and naive Casia. Theophilus is enchanted by Casia and gives her the bell which is symbolic of the golden apple he will later formally bestow upon his final choice. But many intrigues intervene; Amos steals the bell and tells Casia the Emperor has given it to Theodora; she accuses the Emperor of treachery, and in a rage he gives the apple to Theodora, an irrevocable choice. Theophilus repents the marriage, and with Amos's conniving, intends to free Casia from the nunnery she has entered. Amos attempts to murder John to take his place, but to save the Patriarch's life, Theodora renounces her throne and exposes Amos. Casia refuses to leave her sanctuary, and Theophilus, at last brought to his senses, determines to rule justly with Theodora by his side and their son Michael as his heir. The golden lion with which Amos sought to propitiate the Emperor has roared in vain.

Major Roles. THEOPHILUS (bar); must be archer; A1 to F♯3 (one G♭3, one G3). THEODORA (s or m-s); C♯3 to A3. AMOS (t); must be archer; C2 to A♭3. CASIA (s); needs flexibility; C♯3 to B4. JOHN (bs); G♯1 to G♭3. EMPRESS-DOWAGER (m-s); A2 to G4.

Lesser Roles. THREE LADIES (s, s, m-s). THREE MONKS (t, bar, bs).

Chorus. SSATB (offstage). BB (monks offstage).

Orchestra. 2 fl, cl, bsn, hrn, trp, trb, perc, piano, strings. *Stage*: bells.

Material. Pr.

Performances. Univ. of Wash. (Seattle): 3.5.68.

⚜ Griechische Passion · The Greek Passion

Music by Bohuslav Martinu (1890–1959). Libretto in German by the composer, adapted from the novel by Nikos Kazantzakis. Premiere: Zurich, June

9, 1961. Music drama. Fresh use of traditional harmonies, rhythms, and melodies, with Greek melodies inspired by folk song and Orthodox liturgy woven into continuous texture. Vocal line largely melodious, also patterned after speech; some dialogue. Brief prelude; interludes between II ii and iii; III i and ii, ii and iii. Setting: The village of Lycovrissi and the Sarakina Mountains, older times. Four acts, nine scenes (approx 120 min).

ACT I: Square in Lycovrissi, a village on the slope of the Sarakina Mountains, Easter morning. ACT II i: Yannakos's little house and stable with donkey, opposite Katerina's garden; ii: By the fountain of St. Vassily; iii: Desolate mountain spot. ACT III i: Manolios's cottage on the mountain slope; ii: Small room in Katerina's house; iii: Mountain road. ACT IV i: The square, with church; ii: The mountain.

Synopsis. Priest Grigoris, dominating force in the village, selects actors for the Passion: Manolios, strong and humble shepherd, already saintlike, for Christ; Yannakos, the sturdy, warm-hearted peddler, for the Apostle Peter; Michelis, son of the arrogant village leader, Archon Patriarcheas, himself handsome and sensitive, for the Apostle John; Kostandis, crabby owner of the café, as Apostle James; Panait, wild and undisciplined saddler, as Judas (he protests violently of course). The Widow Katerina, generous with her person as well as her possessions, is a natural choice for Mary Magdalen. As they all react in their various ways to the assignments, the sound of a band of refugees from the Turks is heard, led by Priest Fotis, one of the great-souled. Although individuals, namely Manolios and Katerina, receive them with compassion, Grigoris rejects them, using as an excuse that the dying Despinio has cholera. Manolios advises them to seek shelter on the mountain, and they depart.

Yannakos chides Katerina for flirting with Manolios, when it is Panait who loves her—and anyway, Manolios is engaged to young Lenio, beautiful love child of old Patriarcheas. The miser Ladas approaches Yannakos, offering gold if he will rifle the possessions of the refugees. Yannakos on his way up the mountain meets Manolios and warns him of Katerina's designs on him. She approaches him, but he evades her. Led by Fotis, the refugees plan a new village on the mountain; Yannakos, deeply moved, confesses his sin and is forgiven.

Manolios dreams of Lenio and her constant demand for a date for their marriage, and also of the importunate Katerina. His shepherd boy Nikolio plays his pipe, distracting Manolios, and entrancing Lenio, who has come to talk to Manolios. Nikolio carries off Lenio, while Manolios goes to Katerina, but resists temptation and leaves her. Manolios implores the villagers to give of their substance to the refugees, but his Christ-like bearing infuriates the elders, and as the village celebrates the wedding of Lenio and Nikolio, Manolios is excommunicated for blasphemy and killed by the crowd, led by Panait. On Christmas Eve on the mountain, Priest Fotis and the refugees celebrate the birth of Christ and pray for Manolios.

Major Roles. GRIGORIS (bs); G1 to E3. MANOLIOS (t); top A3. YANNAKOS

102

(t); F2 to G3. KATERINA (m-s or s); D3 to A4. FOTIS (bar); C2 to F3. KOSTANDIS (bs). PANAIT (t); top A♭3. LENIO (s); top B♭4.

Lesser Roles. MICHELIS (t). DESPINIO (col s); top C5 (B♭4 opt). NIKOLIO (t); should play or simulate playing flute. ADONIS, the barber (t). ARCHON PATRIARCHEAS (bs). OLD MAN (bs). OLD WOMAN (c). Speaking roles: LADAS; NARRATOR.

Chorus. SATTB. Very important; often doubled. Villagers, refugees, boys.

Orchestra. 3 fl, 3 ob, 3 cl, 3 bsn, 4 hrn, 3 trp, 3 trb, tuba, timp, perc, harp, strings. *Stage:* acc, flûte-à-bec, harm, cl, vln, bells.

Material. Pr (UE).

📌 The Growing Castle

Music by Malcolm Williamson (1931–   ). Libretto in English by the composer after Strindberg's *Dream Play.* Commissioned by Dynevor Center. Premiere: Dynevor Castle, South Wales, August 13, 1968. Allegorical fantasy. Melodic, mostly conventional harmonies; set numbers embedded in continuous texture. Setting: Heaven and Earth; no time specified, although suggestion is of 20th century. Two acts, eight scenes (110 min).

ACT I i: The Upper Air, later the Castle; ii: Theater alley; iii: Lawyer's office, later the Church; Lawyer's house. ACT II i: Foulstrand with sulphur pools, later Fairhaven; ii: Fingal's Cave; iii: The University; iv: Wilderness.

Synopsis. Agnes, a daughter of the gods, comes to earth and encounters numerous adventures with mankind. She feels pity for an Officer and his dying Mother, who quarrel over past injustices; later the Officer appears before a theater crying for his love Emilia and trying to open a forbidden door. Agnes takes the place and the shawl of the theater Janitress; the shawl is painful to wear, but it is her talisman to receive the confidences of human beings. A Lawyer attempts to relieve her of its burden. He takes her and the Officer to church to receive laurel crowns but is himself rejected. Agnes promises him a finer crown, but her compassion changes to human love, and they marry, but soon hate each other. Agnes's misery is epitomized by a servant Kristina, who frantically pastes up every crevice in the house so that no air may enter. The Officer rescues Agnes, leaving the Lawyer to return to his first hell. In gloomy Foulstrand, the voices of lovers are heard from nearby Fairhaven as Agnes and the Officer wander through the sulphuric miasma. The Officer hopes to be a teacher, but the Schoolmaster foils his pretensions to adulthood. Agnes pities mankind again as Ugly Edith pours out her woes. The Lawyer tries to drag Agnes back to her duty and suffering, but she resists, hoping to set free the miserable beings around her, before returning to whence she came. The Lawyer reminds her of One who came before on such a mission and was hanged on a cross. She retreats to far-off Fingal's Cave to meditate, but is disturbed by the supplications of a Poet, who wishes to reach the ear of God. Agnes cannot follow his vision, which becomes a shipwreck, with sailors dying because they see the Savior

103

walking over the water, then changes several times until at last Agnes is in an Alley of the University. The Chancellor and Deans of the four faculties dispute over the opening of the door. As Agnes chides them for their doubts and dissension, the door opens of itself, revealing a radiance but nothing else. Believing themselves cheated, the Deans would stone Agnes, but, again resisting the plea of the Lawyer to return to her mundane duties and her child, she takes the Poet into the Wilderness. In their dialogue, they realize that love is suffering; that Agnes's greatest suffering came from living; that though they may feel love for each other, Agnes must return to carry the lamentations of man, which she has shared, to the throne.

Roles. All twenty-eight may be sung by four singers; some parts are more difficult than others; in the more demanding, intervals are wide, and strength is needed at extremes of ranges. The roles are distributed as follows: AGNES (s); longest and most exacting; Bb2 to B4. M-s (G2 to Ab4): MOTHER, JANITRESS, UGLY EDITH, DAMNED SOUL IN FOULSTRAND, POET, CHORISTER, KRISTINA, LOVER IN FAIRHAVEN. Bar I: (F1 to F♯3): BILLSTICKER, LAWYER, SCHOOLMASTER, FIRST SAILOR, BLIND MAN, CHANCELLOR, CHORISTER, LOVER IN FAIRHAVEN. Bar II (F1—one D1 at bottom of portamento—to F♯3—G4 in fals): OFFICER AXEL, SECOND SAILOR, DAMNED SOUL IN FOULSTRAND, DEAN OF THEOLOGY, DEAN OF PHILOSOPHY, DEAN OF MEDICINE, DEAN OF LAW (using alternate masks), CHORISTER, LOVER IN FAIRHAVEN.

Orchestra. Piano, harpsichord, Gaelic harp (opt), side dr, tamb, large gong.

Production Problems. Quick changes of scene demand ingenuity and probably expert lighting, possibly projections. Stage directions often imply motivations, etc., difficult to realize, such as "vibrant with sexual excitement she scarcely understands"; "the storm at sea is reflected in the faces"; "she must think up an answer," etc.

Material. B & H (Wein). VS*.

Performances. Caramoor Fest. (Amer prem): 7.3.70. Montreal: 2.5.71. Toronto: 2.9.71.

🎵 Guillaume Tell · William Tell

Music by Gioachino Rossini (1792–1868). Libretto in French by V. J. Etienne de Jouy and Hippolyte L. F. Bis, based on the play of the same name by Johann Christoph Friedrich von Schiller (assisted by the composer and Armand Marrast). Italian text by Calisto Bassi. Premiere: Paris, August 3, 1829. Patriotic drama. Set numbers; recitative; important choruses; advanced (for Rossini) harmonic structure; considerable use of ranz des vaches (Alpine horn tunes). Overture (Sinfonia); orchestral interlude in Act I; Passo a sei (ballet); Passo a tre with yodel chorus in Act III. Setting: Switzerland, fourteenth century. Originally four acts; reduced to three (currently restored to four, six scenes) (approx 210 min).

ACT I: Tell's chalet on Lake Lucerne. ACT II: A deep valley near Brunner.

ACT III i: A ruined chapel near Gessler's palace; ii: The market square of Altdorf. ACT IV i: Outside Melcthal's house; ii: Tell's chalet.

Synopsis. Two Swiss patriots, William Tell and Walter Fürst, are struggling to free their countrymen from Austrian oppression. On the day of the Shepherd Festival, Ruedi, a fisherman, sings of the beauty of the country; the town patriarch, Melcthal, blesses lovers except his own son, Arnold, who has fallen in love with the Princess Mathilde, daughter of the Hapsburg tyrant, Gessler. Austrian guards arrive in search of a shepherd, Leuthold, who has killed a soldier to protect his daughter. Tell helps Leuthold to escape. The soldiers take Melcthal as a hostage. Arnold tells Mathilde that he will abandon his country for her, but learning from Tell that his father has been killed, repents and joins the gathering clans in rebellion. During the celebration of the centenary of Austrian rule, Tell and his son Jemmy refuse to bow to Gessler's hat as the sign of his sovereignty. Gessler orders Tell to shoot an apple off the head of Jemmy. He coolly does so, then informs Gessler that a second arrow was reserved for him if the shot had failed. He sends the boy to tell his mother, Hedwig, to light the beacons of revolution. She cannot reach the mountains to carry this out, but instead sets fire to their own house as the signal. Tell is arrested but escapes, shooting Gessler with his second arrow. The victorious Swiss join the happy Tell family and the reunited Arnold and Mathilde.

Roles. WILLIAM TELL (bar); needs power at both extremes of range; considerable high tessitura; wide skips; F1 to G♯3. ARNOLD (t); many dramatic passages, high tessitura; quite florid; B♭1 to C4 (one C♯4). MATHILDE (s); very florid; needs trill; B2 to C5. MELCTHAL (bs); E1 to E3. JEMMY (m-s); several coloratura passages; B2 to C5. HEDWIG (c); A♭2 (one G2) to A4. WALTER FURST (bs); E♭1 to E3. RUEDI (fisherman) (t); some brilliant coloratura; E2 to C4. LEUTHOLD (bs); D♭2 to E3. GESSLER (bs); F1 to F3. RUDOLPH, Gessler's henchman (t); B1 to B3.

Bit Role. A HUNTER (t or bar); can be from chorus.

Chorus. SSATTBB. Very important. Three choruses in Act II. Soldiers, pages, shepherds, fishermen, Swiss patriots, dancers, Mathilde's serving women.

Ballet. In Acts I and III. As elaborate as desired.

Orchestra. 2 fl, 2 ob, 2 cl, 2 bsn, 4 hrn, 4 trp, 3 trb, tuba, timp, perc, bells, 2 harp, strings. *Stage*: 4 hrn.

Material. Bel (Col). VS (i)*. Pr. Map.

Performances. Litt. Orch. (NYC): 3.18.63 (conc). Op. Orch. of N.Y.: 3.13.72 (conc).

🎭 Hamlet

Music by Sándor Szokolay (1931–   ). Libretto in Hungarian by Janos Arany and the composer, adapted directly from Shakespeare. Premiere: Budapest, October 19, 1968. Tragedy. Composer uses dodecaphonic techniques freely and "with certain restrictions has synthesized the music of the Vienna school with that of Bártok and Stravinsky." No closed arias; the famous monologues begin as speech and develop into singing; some *Sprechstimme* as well as dialogue; vocal line extremely difficult. Brief prelude and interludes. Setting: Elsinore, Denmark, 14th century. Three acts, eleven scenes.

ACT I i: Platform before castle of Elsinore (interlude: Funeral March); ii: Hall of State in castle; iii: Room in Polonius's house; iv: The platform. ACT II i: Room in Polonius's house; ii: Room in castle. ACT III i: Room in castle; ii: Gertrude's chamber; iii: Another room in castle; iv: Church graveyard; v: Hall in castle.

Synopsis. Follows play closely, with certain excisions.

Major Roles. CLAUDIUS, King of Denmark (bar); very difficult; high tessitura; needs strength at extremes of range; G#1 to A3. HAMLET (t); strenuous and difficult; some high tessitura; C2 (B#1 in *Sprechstimme*) to A#3 (one Bb3). GERTRUDE (c); F2 to G4. HORATIO (bar); some wide skips; G#1 to G3. POLONIUS (bs); F1 to Eb3. LAERTES (t); C#2 (C2 in *Sprechstimme*) to Bb3. OPHELIA (s); C3 to A4. GHOST OF HAMLET'S FATHER (bs); F1 (one E1) to E3 (touches F3).

Lesser Roles. ROSENCRANZ and GUILDENSTERN (t, t); almost always sing together. MARCELLUS (bs); F1 (one E1) to Eb3. BERNARDO (bs); G1 to E3. FRANCESCO (bs); G#1 to D3. TWO GRAVEDIGGERS (t, bar). PRIEST (bs-bar). OSRICK (t). A NOBLEMAN (t). LUCIANUS (bar). PLAYER KING, PLAYER QUEEN, 1ST PLAYER, MESSENGER (rhythmic prose roles). CORNELIUS, VOLTEMAND (mute).

Chorus. SATB. Many divisions, especially in women's chorus, i.e.: S, M-S, C; S, M-S, C, C, etc. Ladies and gentlemen of Court, followers, officers, soldiers, players.

Orchestra. Presumed large.

Material. B & H (Artesius, Budapest; Sch). VS (g).

🎵 Hamlet

Music by Ambroise Thomas (1811–1896). Libretto in French by Michel Carré and Jules Barbier. Based on Shakespeare. Premiere: Paris, March 9, 1868. Romantic tragedy. Set numbers; conventional harmonies; highly melodious. Brief prelude; entr'actes between Acts II and III; with ballet before IV. Setting: Elsinore, Denmark, 14th century. Five acts, seven scenes (180 min).

ACT I i: Throne room in Elsinore Castle; ii: The ramparts. ACT II i: Palace gardens. ii: Hall in the palace; ACT III: Room in the palace. ACT IV: The lake. ACT V: The graveyard.

Synopsis. At the festivities marking the crowning of Queen Gertrude, who has married her late husband's brother Claudius, her son Hamlet enters, brooding and bitter. Nevertheless he assures Ophelia, daughter of

106

Polonius, of his love. Her brother Laertes announces his departure on a mission for the King. Hamlet sullenly refuses to join the celebrants at a ball. Horatio and Marcellus, watching at the ramparts, tell Hamlet they have seen the ghost of his father. The ghost reveals his murder by Claudius and urges his son to revenge. Hamlet ignores Ophelia, who asks permission of Gertrude to leave the court. The King is convinced Hamlet is mad. Hamlet announces that he has arranged a play. Alone with the players, he instructs them in their roles, then leads them in a Bacchic drinking song. The play mimes Hamlet's father's death, and the King's reaction confirms Hamlet's suspicions; he accuses his stepfather, but the court ignores him, believing him to be insane. Hamlet ponders his future in an abridged version of the famous soliloquy. Suspecting Polonius of complicity, he vents his anger on Ophelia, also on the Queen, who is spared by the apparition of the ghost, who chides Hamlet for his laxity. Ophelia, distraught, wanders among the guests at a *fête champêtre* on the shores of a lake and, left alone, enters the water. Hamlet muses near a grave; his questions to the philosophical gravediggers are interrupted by Laertes, who engages Hamlet in a duel. A funeral cortege enters; Hamlet realizes Ophelia is dead. He kills the King, then stabs himself. (This is the "Covent Garden" ending, written for the London premiere in 1869. The original elevated Hamlet to the throne.)

Major Roles. HAMLET (bar); some high tessitura; trill; C#2 to G#3 (several firm F#3). CLAUDIUS (bs); Eb1 (Eb2 opt) to F3 (D3 opt); one E3 with F# opt; OPHELIA (s); florid; trill; exceptionally difficult mad scene; several variations by Carvallo, one to D5; one firm E5, one with C#5 opt. GERTRUDE (m-s); needs flexibility; A#2 to Bb4 (one B4 with B3 opt). LAERTES (t); F2 to A3.

Lesser Roles. HORATIO (bs). POLONIUS (bs). MARCELLUS (t). GHOST (bs). TWO GRAVEDIGGERS (bar, t). Pantomime: PLAYER KING, PLAYER QUEEN, PLAYER VILLAIN; PAGES.

Chorus. SSTTBB. Cavaliers, Ladies, Soldiers, Players, Servants, Peasants.

Ballet. Long and elaborate in Act IV, part with chorus.

Orchestra. 2 fl, 2 ob, 2 cl, bs cl, bar sax, 2 bsn, 4 hrn, 2 corn, 2 trp, 3 trb, bs tuba, timp, perc, 2 harp, strings. *Stage*: fl, cl, hrn, 3 trp, 4 trb, bs trb, perc (4), 2 harp, cannon.

Material. Pr.

Performances. Manh. Sch. (NYC): 5.4.67.

🎭 The Hanging Judge

Music by Normand Lockwood (1906–   ). Libretto in English by Russell Porter. Commissioned for Denver University Centennial. Premiere: Denver, March 1964. Civil War frontier drama. Continuous texture of conventional harmonies, some set numbers; vocal line patterned after speech, some melody. Setting: An American frontier, 1861. Three acts, twelve scenes.

ACT I i: A "sociable" under the trees in May; ii: Tables removed during

107

blackout, replaced by pulpit. ACT II i: Frontier courtroom; ii: Interior of Shannon's home; iii: Governor's room in hotel. ACT III i: A square dance; ii: General's headquarters; iii: Shannon's home; iv: Fort Bison; v: Court-martial; vi: A pulpit; vii: A cell.

Synopsis. Minister Shannon urges peace on his congregation at a picnic supper to welcome the Presiding Elder, as a meeting is to be held next day to try to counteract the evil forces of Bardwell and his rough gang. The simple festivities are interrupted by Bardwell's men, who overturn tables and taunt the company. But Shannon will not permit counterviolence and the crowd leaves. Overhearing adverse criticism of his stand, Shannon suffers grievous doubts, not allayed by the congratulations of the town prostitute, Rheba, who gives him two pistols for protection. When he is shot in the shoulder by one of Bardwell's gang and kills the hoodlum, the crowd backs him. His experience turns Shannon into a "hanging judge," but he still cannot reach Bardwell. Rheba gives him a list, headed by Bardwell, of men who have bought up guns and ammunition in order to foil the attempt to raise a militia by the Governor, who is about to arrive, hoping to turn back an attack by the Confederate Army. This brings the war to the western frontier and the Governor demands loyalty to the Union. Shannon, who has been asked to resign as judge by his former best friend Raleigh, adds the latter's name to the list of traitors. Shannon becomes a colonel, but grows restive as no war seems near. He is ordered to a western fort to protect the Indians, but his false sense of mission, stimulated by Rheba's suggestions, leads him to command a massacre of the Indian camp. He even shoots pointblank four chiefs taken prisoner. He is court-martialed, but begs for one day to return to his pulpit. Only Rheba comes to hear him. Recognizing her voice, which he had mistaken for God's, he kills her. At the end, he still protests that God commanded him, and that might was right.

Major Roles. BROTHER SHANNON (bar); top F♯3 (one G3). ELIZABETH, his wife (m-s); low F2. RHEBA (s or m-s). RALEIGH (bar or bs).

Lesser Roles. SARAH, Raleigh's wife. PRESIDING ELDER, JOSIAH WEBB. BARDWELL (t). LEADER OF BARDWELL GANG (bar or bs). GOVERNOR (bar).

Bit Roles. TWO SOLDIERS (sp). ORDERLY (bar). VOICE BEHIND SCENE (sp). TWO OFFICERS (t, bs). GENERAL (t). MAJOR (bar or bs). CAPTAIN (bar or bs). LIEUTENANT (t). GUARD (t). FOUR INDIAN CHIEFS (mute).

Chorus. SATB. Men, women, children, "town girls," Indians. Several solos.

Orchestra. 2 fl, ob, 2 cl, 2 bsn, 2 hrn, 2 trp, 2 trb, timp, perc, strings. *Stage*: acc.

Material. ACA.

🎵 Hans Heiling

Music by Heinrich Marschner (1796–1861). Libretto in German by Edouard Devrient. Premiere: Berlin, May 24, 1833. Romantic drama with supernatural elements, after a legend. Set numbers, arias, recitative, ensembles, some dialogue. Highly melodious; conventional harmonies. Overture; storm music; wedding march in Act III. For Vienna, the following were added: elaborate aria for Anna in Act II; difficult arias for Hans and Konrad in Act III; new duet. Setting: Legendary Germany. Prologue and three acts, six scenes (150 min).

Prologue: The depths of the earth. ACT I i: Anna's house; ii: Village festival. ACT II i: The forest; ii: Anna's house. ACT III i: A ravine in the mountains; ii: The village.

Synopsis. Hans Heiling, King of the gnomes, falls in love with a mortal, Anna, and forswears his kingdom. His mother gives him a magic book and beautiful diamonds; the latter help his cause with Anna and her mother Gertrud. But his quiet demeanor puzzles the girl and when she finds the magic book, she demands that he destroy it, and with it goes the last power he has retained over the gnomes. At a village festival, Anna's former lover Konrad provokes Heiling, who in turn rouses Anna's resentment. In the forest, the girl broods over her bridegroom, who has disappointed her, and longs for Konrad. The Queen appears, reveals to Anna Heiling's origin, and begs her to send him back. She turns to Konrad, and when Heiling returns, rejects him, saying that she knows who he is. He throws his dagger at Konrad and disappears, trying to return to his kingdom. The gnomes refuse, but the Queen pardons him. He has not repented wholly, however, for at the wedding of Anna and Konrad, he tries to be revenged. Once more the Queen intervenes, this time succeeding in winning her son back to his rightful place, forgetting and forgiving the mortals.

Major Roles. THE QUEEN (s); C♯3 to A4. HANS HEILING (bar); considerable high tessitura; florid passages; G1 to F♯3. ANNA (s); needs flexibility; trill; top B4; KONRAD (t); some florid passages; several B3; C4. GERTRUD (c); no range problems.

Lesser Roles. STEPHAN, smith (bs). NIKLAS (sp).

Chorus. SATB.

Orchestra. Presumed medium.

🎭 Heracles

Music by John Eaton (1935–   ). Libretto in English by Michael Fried. Radio premiere: RAI, Turin, Italy, October 10, 1968. Stage premiere: Indiana University, Bloomington, April 15, 1972. Revisions: Act II divided into two acts. Epic drama. Set numbers knit into continuous texture; extended tonality; difficult orchestral interludes; vocal line melodic. Setting: Ancient Greece. First version, three acts, eight scenes; second version, four acts, eight scenes (195 min).

Revised version: ACT I, i, ii, iii: Oechalia, dawn to midday (75 min). ACT II i, ii: Trachis, dawn to afternoon (55 min); ACT III i, ii: Trachis, afternoon to dusk (35 min). ACT IV: Oechalia, midday (30 min).

109

Synopsis. After his victory over King Eurytus, Heracles is acclaimed as savior by the people of Oechalia. His lieutenant and false friend Lichas leads the chorus of praise. Only Iole, daughter of the dead king, remains silent for a while, then denounces Heracles and is carried away by attendants. Heracles enters the temple of his father Zeus to pray for heroic sons now that his labors are done, being dissatisfied with his timid son Hyllus by his wife Deianira. When the oracle prophesies that a virgin born of an enemy shall bear heroic sons to a son of Zeus, Heracles interprets this to mean Iole. Lichas, eavesdropping, taunts Heracles with superstition, and makes his own plans, which include Iole's seduction. He is successful in arranging a rendezvous with the maid and, when Heracles discovers them, is saved by a bolt of lightning striking at the hero's feet. Heracles sends Lichas to Deianira in Trachis with news of his victory. Meanwhile, a second oracle, believed by Deianira, states that Heracles will return to Trachis in tranquility or die. Deianira has a charm which should prevent Heracles from loving another: some drops of the blood of the centaur Nessus whom Heracles has killed. She impregnates a robe with this blood and entrusts it to Lichas, who believes that he can win either by the efficacy of the charm or its potentiality as a death trap, for still another oracle has said that no living being can kill Heracles. Deianira discovers that a portion of the robe she has daubed with blood has burst into flame and sends Hyllus to warn Lichas, then goes to take her own life. But it is too late: the robe burns Heracles at the moment of his triumph. When Hyllus exposes Lichas and Iole, Lichas seeks escape on the altar of Zeus but is struck dead by a bolt of lightning. Learning of the death of his wife, and confronted bravely by his son, Heracles now realizes the truth of all three oracular pronouncements: he will die now that his labors are done, but from no living hand; the third prophecy will be fulfilled if Hyllus marries Iole. He praises Zeus's wisdom and mounts a funeral pyre.

Major Roles. HERACLES (bar); high dram passages; F1 to A3 (Bb3 opt). LICHAS (t); wide skips, mercurial changes in articulation; must be good actor; C2 to B3 (C4, C♯4, D4 opt); HYLLUS (t); some florid passages; C2 to B3 (C♯4 opt). DEIANIRA (m-s); needs great stamina; G2 (D2 opt) to A4 (Bb4 opt). IOLE (s); B2 to C♯5 (D5 opt).

Lesser Roles. OLD WOMAN (s); high tessitura. YOUNG GIRL (s); high tessitura. MESSENGER (bs).

Bit Roles. TWO SOLDIERS (bar, t).

Chorus. SSATTB. An ensemble of leaders of the people of Oechalia; very difficult polyphony. BB. Priests. SATB. Soldiers, people of Oechalia. SSAA. Deianira's attendants.

Ballet. Possible at beginning of Act II.

Orchestra. picc, 3 fl (picc), 3 ob, Eng hrn, 3 cl, Eb cl, bs cl, 3 bsn, cont bsn, sarrusophone (or cont bsn), 8 hrn (4 opt), 3 trp, 3 trb, bs trb, tuba, 2 harps (8 possible), piano, cel, vib, timp, perc (6), strings. *Stage*: ten dr, at least 2 trp.

110

Material. Shawnee Press, Delaware Water Gap, Pa. Tr (i): Mario Bertoncini; (g): Ernest Kaiser.

🎵 Hérodiade · Herodias

Music by Jules Massenet (1842–1912). Libretto in French by Paul Milliet and Henri Gremont (Georges Hartmann) after Flaubert. Premiere: Brussels, December 19, 1881. Partly rewritten, Italian version, given in Paris three years later. Tragedy. Highly melodious; important chorus. Brief prelude. Setting: Galilee and Jerusalem, circa A.D. 30. Four acts, seven scenes (approx 120 min).

ACT I: Outer court of Herod's palace. ACT II i: Herod's chamber; ii: Square of Jerusalem. ACT III i: Phanuel's dwelling; ii: The holy temple. ACT IV i: A dungeon; ii: Great hall in palace.

Synopsis. Several differences exist between this story and that of Salome (Strauss). The chief point is John the Baptist's kindness to Salome, who does not know that her mother is Herodias. The Chaldean Phanuel promises to help Salome in her search. Hérode, who is pursuing Salome, is confronted by Hérodiade, who complains of the prophet Jean's denunciation of her. Jean, entering at this moment, repeats his diatribe, and they retreat hastily. Salome rushes in, joyful at finding the man who has previously befriended her; he rejects her proffered affection. In the Tetrarch's chamber, he longs for Salome and will not heed Phanuel's warning against his profligate life. He sings of his "fleeting vision" (*Vision fugitive*). Urged on by Phanuel, Hérode harangues the populace to throw off the Roman yoke. They are interrupted by the arrival of Vitellius, the Roman proconsul, whose suspicions of treason are lulled by Hérode's declaration that the restoration of the temple is all the priests desire. Vitellius promises this shall be done. At the entrance of Jean, Hérode tells Vitellius that the prophet is a disturber anxious for power. Jean retorts that all power is from God. In an inner room, Phanuel consults the stars and informs Hérodiade that Salome is her daughter. Hérodiade exclaims that Salome is rather her rival. In the temple, Salome, despairing because Jean has been jailed, is offered help by Hérode, but repulses him. The priests urge that Vitellius condemn Jean, but the proconsul turns the proceedings over to Hérode, who is infuriated by Salome's intercession and sentences Jean to death. Salome joins Jean in prison and wins his reluctant admiration and affection by her devotion. But he bids her save herself. The High Priest secretly offers Jean a pardon if he will join Hérode against Rome, but he refuses. Hérode and Hérodiade entertain Vitellius with dancing. Salome appears, but Hérode is deaf to her entreaty for Jean's pardon, and calls the executioner, who presently appears with a bloody sword. Salome turns on Hérodiade and is about to stab her, when Hérodiade claims her as a daughter; whereupon Salome stabs herself.

Major Roles. HÉRODE (bar); consistently high tessitura; sustained, forceful, passionate; C♯2 to G♭3 (one G3 with G2 opt). JEAN (t); D2 to B♭3 (one

111

opt B3, one opt C4). PHANUEL (bs); G1 to E♭3 (E3 opt A2). VITELLIUS
(bar); C2 to E♭3. SALOME (s); B2 to one firm C5 (two C5 opt C4). HÉROD-
IADE (m-s); A2 to B♭4 (one C♭5).

Lesser Roles. HIGH PRIEST (bar). VOICE (t). YOUNG BABYLONIAN (s).

Chorus. SSTTBB. Merchants, Jewish and Roman soldiers, priests, Levites,
temple attendants, sailors, overseers, scribes. Many supers advisable.

Orchestra. picc, 2 fl, 2 ob, Eng hrn, 3 cl, 2 bsn, alto sax, contrabs sax, 4
hrn, 2 corn, 2 trp, 4 trb, tuba, timp, perc, 2 harp, strings. *Stage*: 9 parts.

Material. Pr (Heu).

Performances. Amer. Op. Soc. (NYC): 2.10.63 (conc).

🎼 Horspfal

Music by Eric Stokes (1930–   ). Libretto in English by Alvin Greenberg.
Commissioned by the Center Opera Association, Minneapolis. Premiere:
Minneapolis, February 15, 1969. Premiere with revised orchestration: New
York, May 28, 1971. Tragicomic satire and fantasy on historical themes.
Continuous texture, embodying set numbers. Mixture of styles—folk, reli-
gious, patriotic, polytonality, dissonance, etc. Setting: a bed; from long ago
until very recently. Two acts (110 min).

ACT I: The Bed, as the home of the American Indian (65 min). ACT II:
The same (45 min).

Synopsis. The Indian's pristine home is invaded by a succession of spoil-
ers: Betsy Ross and the D.A.R. ("Dancers and Revelers") Girls: the archeolo-
gist John Eliot, looking for the "Lost Ruins of Mankind"; choir singers and
their director; a band of crows; an ethno-musicologist, who rips the bed-
sheets with her dance then believes the Indian's moans to be his ethnic song;
a surveying team; a real estate agent; Aus-Sam-Jaw, who launches into an
oration; two sociologists; Wild Bill Hickock and a football team; the
painter Frederick Remington, a census taker, and a folk singer. Each in his
own way exploits the Indian, who is wrapped in Betsy's red-white-and-blue
flag and delivered to the tourists. His home goes up in figurative flames.

Major Roles. INDIAN (dram bar); sustained; B♭1 to F3. CROWS: (s) C3 to
B♭4 (c or m-s), B2 to E4; (t), C2 to G3 or A3; (bar), B♭1 to G3; multi-
lingual. All crows must have vaudeville talent, song-and-dance, mime, team-
work.

Lesser Roles. JOHN ELIOT (t); powerful, dramatic; B♭1 to B♭3; can dou-
ble as Real Estate Agent, then must be able to sing jazz. REAL ESTATE AGENT
(t); jazz style; C♭2 to A3. BETSY ROSS (col s); A2 (touches E2) to G4.
D.A.R. LADIES (s, m-s). AUS-SAM-JAW (high bar); sustained, grandiloquent.
ETHNO-MUSICOLOGIST (s); can double with Census Taker. TWO SOCIOLO-
GISTS (m-s), can double as crowd member in Act II; (bar), can double with
Frederick Remington in Act II. CENSUS TAKER (s); Act II only. FREDERICK
REMINGTON (bar); Act II only. POLITICIAN (t); declamatory style like that
of keynoters at national convention. WILD BILL HICKOCK (bs-bar); strong

112

low range to **D1**. CHOIR DIRECTOR (t); little singing but important as leader. Tourist family: MOM (s); DAD (bs); JUNIOR (boy s); F3 to E♭4 in finale.

Bit Roles. GEOLOGIST (bs-bar); can be from chorus. FOLK SINGER (s); can be from chorus.

Chorus. Team: at least 9 men, 3 high, 3 medium, 3 low. Surveyors, football team, forty-niners, oil riggers, backstage sound effects, etc. Choir: SAB, hymn singers, some action in crowd scenes. Crowd: mixed; much in stylized *Sprechstimme.*

Orchestra. 2 fl (2 picc, 2 recorder), 2 cl E♭ (2 B♭ ten sax), 2 trp B♭, 2 trb, tuba, piano, perc (2–3) strings (minimum 8 vln, 4 vcl, 2 cb). *Stage*: harm or electronic org (played by choir director). Note: 1, preferably 2 assistant conductors required.

Production Note. Film and still production essential.

Material. Eric Stokes, Music Dep't. Univ. of Minn., Minneapolis 55455. Or Minnesota Opera Co., 1812 S. Sixth St., Minneapolis 55404.

Performances. Hunter Coll. (NYC): 5.28.71.

✄ Les Huguenots · The Huguenots

Music by Giacomo Meyerbeer (1791–1864). Libretto in French by Eugène Scribe and Emile Deschamps. Premiere: Paris, February 29, 1836. Historical drama. One of the great lavish spectacles that requires lavish mountings and virtuoso singers. Elaborate orchestration; difficult florid vocal lines; many dramatic effects; important ensembles. Brief overture. Setting: Touraine and Paris, 1572. Five acts, six scenes (160 min).

ACT I: Hall in the castle of the Comte de Nevers, Touraine. ACT II: A garden in the Queen's castle. ACT III: A square in Paris, chapel and inns. ACT IV: An apartment in De Nevers's castle. Entr'acte and ball. ACT V i: A ballroom; ii: A churchyard.

Synopsis. The core of the story is the massacre of the Huguenots on St. Bartholomew's Day in Paris, in August 1572. Peace between the Catholics and Huguenots is finally to be declared on the occasion of the marriage of Queen Marguerite de Valois. Count de Nevers therefore includes in a banquet to his Catholic friends the Huguenot nobleman Raoul de Nangis. When each is called on to relate an amorous adventure, Raoul tells of an unknown beauty he cannot forget. A lady is announced; Raoul recognizes her as his unknown. She is Valentine, Nevers's betrothed, who asks Nevers to release her from the vow. As it is the Queen's wish, Nevers accedes. The Queen's Page, Urbain, summons Raoul to an interview with the Queen, his eyes blindfolded. The Queen brings Valentine and Raoul together, but Raoul refuses the betrothal since he believes Valentine still to be attached to Nevers. Valentine, deeply hurt, marries Nevers. Her father, the Comte de St. Bris, swears vengeance, challenges Raoul to a duel, and arranges to have him set on by assassins. But the Queen intervenes, and Raoul learns the truth about Valentine. He secretly says goodbye to her and overhears

113

the plot for the massacre of Huguenots. The signal is to be the tolling of the bell of St. Germain; the monks consecrate the swords of the conspirators in a stirring ceremony. Raoul leaves his love to join the victims, and with his servant and companion Marcel, who is wounded, seeks refuge in a church. Valentine finds him with the news that Nevers has been killed; she may marry him if he will convert to Catholicism. He refuses, whereupon she declares herself of his faith, and Marcel pronounces nuptials over the couple. St. Bris discovers them, and as the trio defy the Cross of Lorraine, murders them all.

Major Roles. All need great dramatic strength and flexibility for difficult passages. MARGUERITE DE VALOIS (dram col s); considerable fioratura; trill; C3 (one B2) to C5. VALENTINE (dram col s); high tessitura; needs strength at extremes of wide range; fioratura; trill; long and demanding role; C3 (one Bb2) to C5. RAOUL DE NANGIS (t); dram; needs great flexibility as well as strength over wide range; trill; C2 (one B1) to C4 (one D4). COMTE DE NEVERS (bar); dram as well as flexible; A1 (one G1) to E3 (one F3). COMTE DE ST. BRIS (bar or bs-bar); dram and flexible; F1 (one E1) to E3. MARCEL (bs); considerable floridity; wide range; many trills; E1 (2 C1) to E3. URBAIN (m-s or c); needs flexibility; trill; in added aria, Non, non, non, vous n'avez jamais, A2 (one G2, one F2) to B4.

Lesser Roles. Catholic Noblemen: COMTE DE TAVANNES (t). COMTE DE COSSE (t). COMTE DE MERU (bs). COMTE DE RETZ (bar). MAUREVERT (bs); solo. BOIS ROSÉ, Huguenot soldier (t); top Ab4. PAGE OF NEVERS (s). LADIES OF HONOR (s, s, m-s). HUGUENOT SOLDIERS (t, bs). ARCHER (t). THREE MONKS (t, t, bs). TWO GYPSIES (s, s).

Chorus. SSAATTBB. Aristocrats, soldiers, populace.

Ballet. Acts II and III.

Orchestra. picc, 2 fl, 2 ob (2 Eng hrn), 2 cl, 2 bsn, 4 hrn, 4 trp, 3 trb, tuba, timp, perc, harp, strings, vla d'amore. *Stage:* picc, cl F, 6 cl C, 2 ob, 2 bsn, 4 hrn, 4 trp, corn, 2 trb, tuba, small & bs dr, cym, tri, glock.

Material. Bel (Ri). Map.

Performances. Amer. Op. Soc. (NYC): 5.14.69 (conc).

✙ L'Infidelita Delusa · Deceit Outwitted

Music by Franz Josef Haydn (1732–1809). Libretto in Italian by Marco Coltellini. Premiere: Esterhazy, July 26, 1773. Comedy. Highly melodic. Set numbers, arias, and ensembles. Patter recitative translated as dialogue for English and German. Overtures (sinfonia) before each act. Setting: Italy, early 18th century. Two acts, three scenes (approx 120 min).

ACT I i: Countryside, Filippo's house in foreground, others visible; ii: Room in Vespina's and Nanni's house. ACT II: Room in Filippo's house.

Synopsis. A network of conflicting loves. Nancio, a wealthy countryman, and the elderly Filippo plan that the latter's daughter Sandrino will marry Nancio; she agrees, although she loves Nanni, who has wooed her for three years. Nanni and his sister Vespina (who loves Nancio) threaten vengeance. Nancio bewails the artificiality of city women and the unlikelihood of happiness with one. Sandrina counsels Nancio to marry Vespina, but he retorts he now loves Sandrina. Vespina overhears and strikes him. A fracas ensues. Vespina dresses as an old woman and tells Nanni she will stop the match. She informs Filippo that his daughter has been married to and betrayed by Nancio. Filippo believes the tale and rejects Nancio, now completely bewildered. Vespina next disguises herself as a German servant whose master will marry Sandrina. Nancio is piqued by Filippo's finding a richer man. Vespina now impersonates the nobleman, Marquis of Ripafratta, who has no intention of marrying Sandrina but will give her to his servant. Nancio thinks this delicious revenge. Vespina's final masquerade is as a notary, who marries Sandrino to Nanni, disguised as the servant, then reveals the whole bag of trickery. Nancio yields to her, and the wedding ceremony is doubled.

Major Roles. VESPINA (s); needs flexibility; trill; C3 to C5 (touches C#5). SANDRINA (s); some coloratura; trill; D3 (one Bb2) to C5. FILIPPO (t); high tessitura; C2 to B3 (one C4, C3 opt). NANCIO (t); Bb1 to C4 (one C4 in opt passage with Bb3 top). NANNI (bs); needs strength at extremes of range; F1 to F#3 (one G3, one A3). Note: Another name, such as Silvio may be substituted in Eng vers.

Orchestra. 2 ob, 2 bsn, 2 hrn, 2 or 4 trp, timp, piano, strings.

Material. Pr (UE). VS (e—Andrew Porter)*. Haydn-Mozart Press, Salzburg, edited by H. Robbins Landon.

Performances. St. Univ. of Iowa (Iowa City): 3.11.63 (Amer prem). Detroit Inst. of Arts: 4.30.65. Op. Soc. of Wash.: 1966. Princeton Univ. Op. Th.: 12.70. San Fran. St. Coll.: 3.14.70. Lake George: 7.20.71.

🎵 The Insect Comedy

Music by Martin Kalmanoff (1920–   ). Libretto in English by Lewis Allan, based on the play by Karel and Josef Capek. Unperformed at writing. Fantasy-satire. Music varies from quasi-operetta (Act I) through free tonality and irregular rhythms (Act II) to stark dissonance (Act III). Because of fantasy elements, mixed media is appropriate. Three acts.

Synopsis. Disillusioned with the world, a man gets drunk and lies down in a field. In his fantasy, he sees the world taken over by insects: butterflies who do nothing; a businessman fly; a factory of ants, who believe war is inevitable. The arrogant winner of this war claims to be ruler of the world. In an epilogue, the hero has learned so much that he can go back to his fellow men and tell them everything. But death intervenes, in spite of the man's plea for just an hour of grace, and he dies without imparting his valuable knowledge.

Roles. VAGRANT (bar); Bb1 to G3. PROFESSOR (t); D2 to Bb3. FELIX (t); C2 to C4. IRIS (s); Bb2 to C5. CHRYSALIS (s); Eb3 to C5. CHNEUMON FLY (bar); C2 to E3. BEETLE (bs); F#1 to E3. MRS. BEETLE (m-s); D3 to Ab4.

115

CRICKET (t); C2 to A3. MRS. CRICKET (m-s); C3 to F4. SCIENTIST (t); F♯2 to B♭3.

Orchestra. 2 fl (picc), 2 ob (Eng hrn), cl, bs cl, 2 bsn (cont bsn), 4 hrn, 2 trp, 3 trb, tuba, timp, perc, harp, strings.

Material. Composer: 392 Central Park West, New York, N.Y. 10025.

🎵 Intermezzo

Music by Richard Strauss (1864–1949). Libretto in German by the composer. Premiere: Dresden, November 4, 1924. Domestic comedy, said to be patterned after the composer's own life. Continuous texture; vocal line patterned after speech; occasional set numbers interwoven; some dialogue. Twelve symphonic interludes. Setting: Contemporary Berlin and Vienna. Two acts, thirteen scenes (approx 120 min).

ACT I i: Robert's dressing room; ii: Toboggan track; iii: Inn at Grundlsee; iv: Notary's house; v: Storch's sitting room; vi: Baron's room in the Notary's house; vii: Storch's dining room; viii: Child's bedroom. ACT II i: Commercial Councillor's house (the skat game); ii: Notary's office; iii: In the Prater, Vienna; iv: Christine's dressing room; v: Dining room.

Synopsis. Conductor Robert Storch and his chatterbox wife Christine begin one of their usual arguments as he is packing for a trip to Vienna. She deplores his job, which keeps him around the house too much; he retorts that it is truly creative. She brings up the sore point of his less distinguished ancestry, whereupon he rushes off to breakfast. The maid Anna comes to help Christine pack, and suggests that her evident boredom might be relieved by going tobogganing. Robert returns, and another storm blows up, interrupted by the maid's announcement that the sledge has arrived to take him to the station. A dozen activities absorb Christine, until a friend phones, inviting her to go tobogganing. At the local sledge run, she collides with the young Baron Lummer. They meet later, going dancing to many lovely waltzes in the Grundlsee inn. She takes him under her wing, renting a room for him at the Notary's house, writing her husband enthusiastically about him. She is determined to dominate the young man as she cannot rule her husband. He importunes her for financial help; she replies that her husband will take care of that, but this does not satisfy him.

In his room, he meditates on this anomalous relationship; then sends away a young girl named Resi, with whom he might really be in love, because he fears the landlady's gossip. He writes Christine a letter asking for 1,000 marks, then bursts in on her as she reads it. She sends him away to clean off the snow, then receives a letter from a servant. It is addressed to her husband, but she opens it, to find what she takes for a love letter. Furiously she sends the Baron away, refusing his help, and sends her husband a telegram, saying all is over. She creeps in to her sleeping child, and wakes him with her recriminations; he hotly defends his father. Robert receives the telegram at a skat game with cronies and leaves in haste. His four friends re-

116

turn to their game. Christine consults the Notary about a divorce, but he refuses to proceed without consulting Robert. Robert is agonizing over his problem when another conductor, Stroh, confesses that it is he who should have received the letter. In a frenzy of packing, Christine at last consents to receive Stroh and is finally convinced of her husband's innocence. There are several additional twists to their reconciliation, but eventually it occurs.

Major Roles. CHRISTINE STORCH (s); extremely taxing; Bb2 to B4. ROBERT STORCH (bar); high tessitura; A1 to G3. BARON LUMMER (t); D2 to A3.

Lesser Roles. ANNA (s); C3 to G4. NOTARY (bar); Gb1 to E3. NOTARY'S WIFE (s); G3 to G4. Skat Players: CONDUCTOR STROH (t); C2 to A3; BUSINESSMAN (bar); A1 to G3; JUDGE (bar); B1 to Eb3; SINGER (bs); Bb1 to E3. LITTLE FRANZL (sp).

Bit Roles. RESI, THERESE, MARIE, COOK (sp).

Orchestra. 2 fl, 2 ob, 2 cl, 2 bsn, 3 hrn, 2 trp, 2 trb, perc, timp, piano, harp, strings.

Material. B & H. VS*.

Performances. Litt. Orch. (NYC): 2.11.63 (conc—Amer prem).

☒ Iris

Music by Pietro Mascagni (1863–1945). Libretto in Italian by Luigi Illica. Premiere: Rome, November 22, 1898. Melodrama. Orchestra tinged with naturalistic and Oriental effects; vocal line melodious. Prelude. Setting: Japan, 19th century. Three acts.

ACT I: Home of Iris near city. ACT II: Interior of Green House in the Yoshiwara. ACT III: The Sewer.

Synopsis. An opening "Hymn to the Sun" depicts the dawn. The beautiful Iris is desired by Osaka, a wealthy degenerate, who kidnaps the girl under cover of a marionette show brought to her cottage by Kyoto, proprietor of a house of ill fame. They leave money for Iris's blind father, thus legalizing the abduction and leading the old man to believe his daughter has gone voluntarily to the Yoshiwara, the prostitutes' quarter. Osaka cannot awaken Iris to passion and is bored with her innocence. To win him back, Kyoto dresses Iris in transparent robes and sets her on a balcony for all to see. Osaka capitulates, but before he can reach her, she has heard her father's voice and called out to him. Still believing her there under her own volition, he throws mud at her. In despair, she jumps to her death in the sewer below. Ragpickers and scavengers uncover her body and strip it of jewels. She is not yet dead, however, and rouses just long enough to apostrophize the sun and nature. The sewer seems to change to a field of blossoms as she sinks to death.

Major Roles. IL CIECO, Iris's blind father (bs); some dialogue; Ab1 to Eb3. IRIS (s); C3 to B4. OSAKA (t); E2 to Bb3. KYOTO (bar); B1 to F3 (one F#3).

Lesser Roles. GEISHA (s). DEALER (t). RAGPICKER (t).

Chorus. SSAATTBB. Ragpickers, shopkeepers, geishas, laundry girls, citi-

117

zens, strolling players. Three women representing Beauty, Death, the Vampire. A young girl.

Orchestra. 3 fl, 3 ob, 3 cl, 3 bsn, 4 hrn, 3 trp, 3 trb, tuba, timp, perc, bells, 2 harp, strings.

Material. Bel (Col). VS (i)*.

Performances. Opera Guide Co., Casa Ital. (NYC): 2.24.63.

🎵 Irmelin

Music by Frederick Delius (1862–1934). Libretto in English by the composer. Premiere: Oxford, England, May 4, 1953. Romance. Highly melodic, traditional harmonies; vocal line lyrical. Preludes to each act and to Act III ii; interludes in Act II. Setting: Fairy-tale kingdom. Three acts, six scenes.

ACT I: Irmelin's room in the castle. ACT II i: Swamp in the forest; ii: Hall in Rolf's stronghold; iii: In the mountains. ACT III i: Hall in the castle; ii: Outside the castle.

Synopsis. The Princess Irmelin refuses all suitors proposed by her father, waiting for the love of her dreams. The very day she is forced to be betrothed to an unwanted knight, her love appears in the person of Nils, presumably a prince bewitched by the cohorts of the robber Rolf and forced to tend his swine. The two recognize each other as true mates, and wander off together in the wood.

Major Roles. IRMELIN (lyr s); sustained line; B2 to A4 (one firm B4, one firm C5). THE KING (bs); C2 to E3. NILS (t); B1 to A3 (one B♭3 opt). ROLF (bs-bar); C2 to F3.

Lesser Roles. THREE KNIGHTS (bar, t, bs). A MAID (m-s). VOICE IN THE AIR (s). SERVANT (bar). WOMAN (s).

Chorus. SSAATTBB. Robbers, knights, guests, women, wood nymphs, girls and boys.

Orchestra. 3 fl, 2 ob, Eng hrn, 2 cl, bs cl, 3 bsn, 4 hrn, 3 trp, trb, 3 tuba, timp, perc, harp, strings.

Material. B & H. VS*.

🎵 The Jacobin · Jakobín

Music by Antonin Dvořák (1841–1904). Libretto in Czech by Marie Cervinkové-Riegrové. Premiere: Prague, February 12, 1889. Revised 1897. Folk drama. Melodic, nationalistic flavor; set numbers in continuous texture; important ensembles. Brief preludes to Acts I, II. Setting: A small town, 1793. Three acts (119 min).

ACT I: Small town fair. ACT II: Schoolmaster's house. ACT III: Count Harasova's estate.

Synopsis. Bohuš, son of Count Harasova, returns with his wife Julie to

118

his home after living through the French Revolution, only to find that his cousin Adolf is to succeed him as his father's heir. Adolf has accused Bohuš of being a Jacobin, and he is later discovered and arrested. Meanwhile, a secondary plot develops with the courtship of young George and the Schoolmaster's daughter Terinka, who is also wooed by the pretentious steward Philip. Bohuš's difficulties are resolved when Count Harasova hears Julie singing a lullaby his late wife used to sing; he summons his son, rejects his nephew, and allows George and Terinka to marry.

Major Roles. COUNT HARASOVA (bs); top Eb. BOHUS, his son (bar); C#2 to F#3. ADOLF, his nephew (bar); top F. JULIE, Bohuš's wife (s); B2 to B4 (two firm C5 in ensemble). PHILIP, a steward (high bs); needs flexibility, trill; top E3. GEORGE (Jírí) (t); top B3. BENDA, schoolmaster (t); top G3. TERINKA, his daughter (lyr-col s); both sustained and florid; top C5.

Lesser Role. LOTINKA, housekeeper (c).

Chorus. SSAATB. Important. Sings Mass in Act I.

Ballet. Of folk character, at end of opera.

Orchestra. 2 fl (2 picc), picc, 2 ob, Eng hrn, 2 cl, bs cl, 2 bsn, cont bsn, 4 hrn, 2 trp, 3 trb, tuba, harp, timp, perc, tri, strings (2.1.1.1.1).

Material. B & H. VS (cz)*.

🔰 Jenufa

Music by Leoš Janáček (1854–1928). Libretto in Czech by the composer after a story by Gabriella Preissová. Premiere: Brno, January 21, 1904. Drama. Music flavored with Slovak songs and dances; declamatory; vocal line patterned after speech, restless melodic line; very few sustained sections. Brief preludes to Acts I, II and III. Setting: Moravia in 19th century. Three acts (104 min).

ACT I: Grandmother Buryja's mill in the mountains (35 min). ACT II: Kostelnicka's living room (42 min). ACT III: The same (27 min).

Synopsis. Of two stepbrothers, grandsons of Grandmother Buryja, Laca is secretly in love with Jenufa, foster daughter of Kostelnicka, a widow of Grandmother's son. Jenufa, however, is openly attached to Stewa, handsomer of the two brothers, and is even bearing his child. News comes that Stewa has been deferred in the army draft, and he follows soon after, extremely drunk. A gay dance is interrupted by Kostelnicka, who tells Stewa that only if he can stay sober for a year may he marry Jenufa. This is disastrous to Jenufa, who pleads with Stewa, but he is evasive. After he leaves, Laca returns, taunts Jenufa, and at last slashes her viciously across the face. Jenufa's baby is born, but Kostelnicka aids her to keep it secret. She begs Stewa to marry Jenufa now, but he admits that he has made a contract to marry Karolka, the mayor's daughter. Kostelnicka at last confesses Jenufa's sin to Laca, hoping he will marry her. But he is reluctant. Desperate, Kostelnicka takes the baby and drowns him. Laca yields to his love for Jenufa, and she agrees to marry him. But Kostelnicka's foreboding persists through

119

all the wedding preparations, and is justified when the baby's body is discovered. She confesses, and goes out with the Mayor. Laca and Jenufa at last find understanding through their suffering.

Major Roles. GRANDMOTHER BURYJA (c); Cb3 to G4. LACA (t); high tessitura; D♯2 to Cb4. STEWA (t); some high tessitura; Db2 to Bb3. KOSTELNICKA (s); very dramatic; wide skips; Bb2 to Cb5. JENUFA (s); some high tessitura; sustained, dramatic; B2 to Cb5.

Lesser Roles. OLD FOREMAN at the mill (bar); Ab1 to F3. MAYOR (bs); top F♯3. HIS WIFE (m-s). KAROLKA, his daughter (m-s); Eb3 to Bb4.

Bit Roles. MAID (m-s). BARENA, maid (s). JANO, shepherd boy (s). AUNT (c).

Chorus. SATTBB. Musicians, Village People, Recruits.

Ballet. Peasant dance in Act I.

Orchestra. picc, 2 fl, 2 ob, Eng hrn, 2 cl, bs cl, 2 bsn, cont bsn, 4 hrn, 2 trp, 3 trb, bs tuba, timp, perc, harp, strings. *Stage:* String quintet, 2 hrn, bells, toy trp.

Material. Pr (UE).

Performances. Litt. Orch. (NYC): 11.1.66 (conc). USC: 12.7.69 (Eng). Ind. Univ.: 10.21.72.

🎵 Jeremiah

Music by Myron S. Fink (1932–   ). Libretto in English by Earlene Hamel Hawley. Premiere: Binghamton, N.Y., May 25, 1962. Religious drama. Set numbers knit into continuous texture; conventional dissonant harmonies; vocal line melodic. Preludes to Acts I and III; interludes in Act IV. Setting: Southern Illinois, 1880's. Four acts, six scenes (145 min).

ACT I i: Interior of Stephens home; ii: Same (55 min). ACT II: A hotel interior and street corner in neighboring town (30 min). ACT III: The Stephens home (25 min). ACT IV i: Interior of a church; ii: Same (35 min).

Synopsis. Jeremiah Stephens, a religious fanatic, quarrels with his wife Rebecca and turns to their young boarder, the schoolteacher Deborah Carter, for consolation. Jeremiah's son Samuel also falls in love with Deborah and takes her to a neighboring town, where they are followed and denounced by Jeremiah. Rebecca urges Samuel and Deborah to flee, but Samuel's ardor frightens Deborah, who is almost against her will attracted to Jeremiah. They read the Songs of Solomon together and kiss passionately. Deborah confesses her sin before the congregation, but refuses to tell the elder Amos the identity of her partner. The congregation accuses Samuel, who defends himself by naming his father. Jeremiah acknowledges his guilt but declares himself superior to their judgment. He asks God for guidance and opens the Bible to the sacrifice of Isaac. Samuel, come to seek peace with his father, becomes the victim of Jeremiah's megalomania, as the father strangles the son and stands triumphantly over his body.

Major Roles. JEREMIAH STEPHENS (dram bar); high tessitura; considerable sustained singing alternating with strong dramatic action; florid passages in Act IV; B1 to G3. REBECCA STEPHENS (dram or spin-lyr s); sustained; much dramatic recitative; A2 to C5. SAMUEL STEPHENS (lyr t); D2 to C4 (opt Bb3). DEBORAH CARTER (lyr m-s); G#2 to G#4.

Lesser Roles. NAOMI, a neighbor (s); only in Act I. SARAH, a neighbor (m-s or c—only in Act I). AMOS (bs—only in Act IV).

Bit Roles. TWO YOUNG MEN, A YOUNG WOMAN (from chorus; Act II). TWO MEN, A WOMAN (sp; Act IV i).

Chorus. SATB. Townspeople, courting couples, congregation.

Ballet. Act II, round dance, square dance, waltz.

Orchestra. 2 fl (picc), 2 ob, 2 cl, 2 bsn, 3 hrn, 2 trp, 3 trb, tuba, timp (3), cym, xyl (opt), harp, strings.

Material. Composer: 340 Riverside Drive, New York, N.Y. 10025.

♬ Le Jongleur de Notre Dame · The Juggler of Notre Dame

Music by Jules Massenet (1842–1912). Libretto in French by Maurice Léna. Miracle play. Premiere: Monte Carlo, February 18, 1902. Melodious; considerable dramatic effect. Massenet wrote the title role for a tenor, and never approved Mary Garden's appropriation of it. Brief preludes before Acts I and II; orchestral interlude leads to Act III without pause. Setting: the Abbey of Cluny in Burgundy, 14th century. Three acts (approx 120 min).

ACT I: Square at Cluny. ACT II: Cloister. ACT III: Chapel.

Synopsis. Jean, a poor juggler, tries to collect money in a lively spring market-day fair, but attracts no attention until he sings a sacrilegious drunkard's song, which enrages the populace and horrifies the Prior. Jean reluctantly abandons his freedom, urged by the Prior, only when he is promised food along with salvation. He follows the Prior and the cook Boniface into the Abbey. The monks, including a painter, a poet, a musician, and a sculptor, quarrel over the best way to glorify the Virgin. Jean is sad because he knows no way. Boniface reassures him by saying that even his vegetables and spices honor Her. In the deserted chapel, Jean kneels before the statue of the Virgin, telling her he will do homage to her through his performance. He proceeds to juggle until the Prior and the monks enter and denounce him. The statue of the Virgin comes alive, and blesses her juggler, who dies happily at her feet.

Major Roles. JEAN (t or s); F2 to A3 (or F3 to A4). BONIFACE (bar); B1 to F3. PRIOR (bs); Ab1 to Eb3.

Lesser Roles. Monks: POET (t); G2 to A3. PAINTER (bar); D2 to F3. MUSICIAN (bar); C2 to F3. SCULPTOR (bs); G1 to Db3. TWO ANGELS (s, m-s). THE VIRGIN (A Vision).

Chorus. SATBB, divided into many parts. Solos: Crier Monk (bar); Wag (bar); Tipsy Man (bs); Knight (t); Voice (bar). Monks, Angel

Voices, Knights, Townsfolk, Country Folk; Hucksters; Clerks; Beggars.

Ballet. Possible in Act I.

Orchestra. 2 fl, picc, 2 ob, Eng hrn, 2 cl, bs cl, 2 bsn, cont bsn, 4 hrn, 3 trp, 3 trb, tuba, timp, perc, 1 or 2 harp, strings, vla d'amore. *Stage*: 5 instruments.

Material. Pr (Heu). VS*. Map.

Performances. Ill. Op. Guild (Chic.):12.18.63. Friends of French Op. (NYC): 4.26.67.

🎭 La Juive · The Jewess

Music by Jacques François Halévy (1799–1862). Libretto in French by Eugène Scribe. Premiere: Paris, February 25, 1835. Melodrama. Highly melodius; recitative; set numbers; many important ensembles; chorus prominent. (Adolphe Nourrit, who created the role of Eléazar, is said to have partially rewritten certain portions, notably the famous aria, "Rachel, quand du Seigneur.") Two versions of overture, one long, one short and leading directly to stage action. Brief prelude to Act II. Funeral March Act V. Of two editions, Lemoine contains entire score, with long overture; Choudens omits important scenes. Most of these were restored in a concert version by Robert Lawrence and the Friends of French Opera (New York, 1964). Setting: Constance, Switzerland; 1414. Original version (Lemoine) shows five acts, six scenes (approx 150 min).

ACT I (Te Deum): Square in Constance, showing church and Eléazar's shop. ACT II (Passover): Room in Eléazar's house. ACT III i: The palace (sometimes omitted); ii: The Emperor's gardens. ACT IV: Prison. ACT V: Tent, with view of scaffold and fiery cauldron.

Synopsis. In Scribe's original story, Brogni as chief magistrate has banished Eléazar from Rome, thus saving his life after he has been condemned to death as a usurer. In a siege by Neapolitans, Brogni's house was burnt; his wife was killed and his daughter disappeared. Deeply affected, Brogni joined the Church, rising to the office of Cardinal, president of the Council. As the opera opens, the church choir chants a Te Deum in honor of the Emperor's forthcoming visit. Léopold, Prince of the Empire, who has just scored a victory over the Hussites, has previously fallen in love with Eléazar's daughter, Rachel, and has been accepted by Eléazar as a workman under the name of Samuel. Ruggiero, provost of Constance, discovers Eléazar working, although it is a Christian holiday. Eléazar is saved by the entrance of Brogni, who recognizes him. Léopold serenades Rachel, who invites him to the Passover celebration that evening. A crowd gathers; Eléazar and Rachel are rescued once more by the intervention of Léopold, who has been recognized by the sergeant Albert. Rachel wonders at his power over the Christians. In Act II, she worries still more at his refusal of un-

122

leavened bread. The Princess Eudoxie, Léopold's wife, calls on Eléazar to buy a chain for her husband. Léopold, overhearing, is conscience-stricken. Still, he loves Rachel, and, even though he confesses his Christianity, she almost yields. Eléazar, mollified at last by his daughter's pleas, consents to her marriage, but his fury returns when Léopold admits that he is unable to marry.

In the scene often omitted, Rachel has followed Léopold to the palace, although she still does not guess his identity. She begs Eudoxie to be allowed to serve as a slave for one day only; the Princess agrees. The festival for the Emperor begins. After a ballet, Eléazar and Rachel bring the chain to Eudoxie, who is about to place it around Léopold's neck, when Rachel denounces him. Brogni condemns the two Jews and Léopold to death. Eudoxie begs Rachel to withdraw her charge against Léopold to save him. After agonized reflection, Rachel agrees. The Cardinal then implores Rachel to renounce Judaism in order to save herself. She refuses. Eléazar also refuses a similar plea and reveals at last that a Jew had saved Brogni's daughter. In spite of Brogni's anguish, Eléazar will not tell him where the girl is (she is, of course, Rachel), though he is torn by his knowledge that he is allowing Rachel to go to her death under false pretenses. In his greatest moment of torture, crowds howling for the execution of the Jews determine him to sacrifice Rachel. Léopold's sentence has been commuted to banishment, but Eléazar and Rachel are led to the scaffold. Eléazar gives Rachel one last chance to abjure her faith, but when she disdains the idea, she is thrown into the cauldron. At the very moment she is consumed by flames, Eléazar turns to Brogni and cries: "There is your daughter!" then proceeds inflexibly to his own death.

Major Roles. (All extremely difficult, high or low tessitura; ranges based on complete score.) PRINCESS EUDOXIE (col s); very florid; trill; B♭2 to D5 (B♭4 opt), otherwise C5. RACHEL (dram s); needs flexibility, strength in extremes of range; trill; A♭2 (A♭3 opt), otherwise A2 to D5 (B♭4 opt), otherwise C5. ELÉAZAR (dram t); sustained intensity; D2 to C4. CARDINAL DE BROGNI (bs); needs power in extremes of range; trill; touches E1, one firm E♭1 to F3. LÉOPOLD (high t); extremely high tessitura; florid; trill; D2 to D4.

Lesser Roles. RUGGIERO (bar); A1 to F3. ALBERT (bs); B1 to E3.

Bit Roles. HERALD (bar). OFFICER (t). MAJORDOMO (bar). EXECUTIONER (bar).

Chorus. SATTBB; particularly large male group. Small solos.

Ballet. Waltz in Act I; longer pantomime ballet in Act III ii.

Orchestra. 2 fl (picc), 2 ob (2 Eng hrn), 2 cl, 2 bsn, 4 hrn, 4 trp, 3 trb, tuba, harp, organ, timp, perc (3), strings. *Stage:* anvil, chimes, thunder dr, sn dr.

Material. Pet (Chou). VS (f or g)*. Map.

Performances. Friends of French Op. (NYC—conc): 3.12.64; (Bklyn) 3.17.64. New Or.: 10.18.73.

✣ Der Junge Lord · The Young Lord

Music by Hans Werner Henze (1926–   ). Libretto in German by Inge-borg Bachmann from a fable, "The Sheik of Alexandria and His Slaves," by Wilhelm Hauff. Commissioned by the Deutsche Oper, Berlin. Premiere: Berlin, April 7, 1965. Satiric comedy. Contemporary idiom reverting occasionally to traditional tonality, with frequent dissonance, intricate orchestration and rhythms; avowedly eclectic. Vocal line angular and patterned after speech. Very brief prelude; important interludes. Setting: the little German town of Hulsdorf-Gotha, 1830. Two acts, six scenes (138 min).

ACT I i: The main square; ii: The Baroness von Greenweasel's salon; iii: Main square, with circus troupe. ACT II i: Main square, a winter evening; ii: Reception at Sir Edgar's house; iii: Grand Ball at the Town Casino.

Synopsis. The townspeople of Hulsdorf-Gotha are bewildered by the long-awaited Englishman, Sir Edgar, his strange luggage and exotic entourage. In the confusion, Luise, the richest girl in town, and Wilhelm, a student, converse for the first time. Luise is desperate because her duenna, Baroness Greenweasel, plans for her to marry Sir Edgar, whom she expects for tea. When the Turkish page Jeremy brings a refusal from the Englishman, the Baroness determines to make life impossible for him. Sir Edgar offends the other townspeople by giving money to a visiting circus, members of which he invites into his house after refusing to associate with natives. Children torment Jeremy, who escapes into Sir Edgar's house, from which horrible screams are heard. The awakened populace is calmed, however, by the Secretary's explanation that the screams were merely lamentations of young Lord Barrat, Sir Edgar's nephew, who is pained by the lessons in German he is taking in order to be presented to the townsfolk. At last, Sir Edgar gives a reception, and all profess to be charmed by young Barrat, imitating and flattering him, until Wilhelm, dismayed by the visitor's behavior toward Luise, insults him. Luise faints; Wilhelm leaves in disgrace. At a ball, it is presumed that the engagement of Barrat and Luise will be announced. Soon the company is imitating Barrat's increasingly wild dance, even to tearing off clothing. At this denouement, Barrat is revealed in his true character—an ape from the circus. In the ensuing consternation, Sir Edgar and his secretary depart, and Luise and Wilhelm are reconciled.

Major Roles. SIR EDGAR (mime). SECRETARY (bar); B1 to F♯3 (G4 fals). LORD BARRAT (high char t); C♯2 to G3. (some high passages like screams). BARONESS VON GREENWEASEL (m-s); G♭2 to A♭4. LUISE, her ward (s); C3 to D5. IDA, her friend (light s); F3 to F5. WILHELM (lyr t); C2 to A3.

Lesser Roles. BEGONIA, a Creole cook (m-s); F♯2 to B♭4. THE BURGOMASTER (bs-bar); G♭1 to F♯3. CHIEF MAGISTRATE HARETHRASHER (bar); A♭1 to F♯3. TOWN COMPTROLLER SHARP (bar); A♭1 to F♯3. PROFESSOR VON MUCKER (buf t); D2 to B3. FRAU VON HOOFNAIL (m-s); A♭2 to F♯4. FRAU HARE-THRASHER (high s); C3 to D5. PARLORMAID (s); B♭2 to F♯4. AMINTORE LA ROCCA, circus director (dram t); C♯2 to F♯3. LAMPLIGHTER (bar); A♭1 to D♯3.

Mimes: M. LA TRUIARE, master of music, dancing, and deportment; MEA-
DOWS, the butler; JEREMY, Sir Edgar's Turkish page; SCHOOLMASTER; STREET-
SWEEPER; TWO MEN with brushes and paints.

Dancers. Circus performers: Rosita, the Cloud-Walking Maiden, tightrope
dancer from the Two Sicilies; Brimbilla, juggler from perilous Istria; Vul-
cano, fire-eater from Milan; Adam, the monkey.

Chorus. SATB. Ladies and gentlemen, young people of good society, common people, children.

Orchestra. 2 fl (picc), 2 ob, 2 cl, 2 bsn, 4 hrn, 2 trp, 2 trb, tuba, timp,
perc (6 players), harp, cel, piano, guit, 2 mandoline (ad lib), strings. *Stage*:
(I i) 2 picc, 2 ob, 2 cl, 2 trp, 2 trb, tuba, bs dr with cym, tri, marching lyre
chimes (picc, ob, perc opt). (I ii) piano. (I iii) trp, bs dr with cym, military dr, tamb, cym, tri. (II i) 2 tub bells. (II iii) picc, cl, trp, vln, vcl, cb,
bs dr, sn dr, tri.

Material. Bel (Sch).

Performances. San Diego: 2.17.67 (Amer prem). Houston: 12.67.
NYCO: 3.28.73, etc.

◪ Katerina Ismailova

Music by Dimitri Shostakovich (1906–   ). Libretto in Russian by A.
Preiss and the composer, based on a story by Nikolai Leskov. Original title,
Lady Macbeth of Mtsensk. Premiere: Moscow, January 22, 1934. Revised
1962; premiere: Moscow, January 8, 1963. Socio-domestic drama. Eclectic
in style, some folk references, parodies of familiar works. Set numbers embedded in continuous texture; vocal line largely patterned after speech. No
overture; interludes between all scenes. Setting: a provincial town in pre-
Revolutionary Russia. Four acts, nine scenes (eight in NYCO production)
(135 min).

ACT I i: The Ismailov courtyard (18 min); ii: The same (9 min); iii:
Katerina's bedroom (16 min). ACT II i: Same as I i (24 min); ii: Same as
I iii (20 min). ACT III i: Same as I i (9 min); ii: Police station (omitted by
NYCO); iii: Same as I i (9 min). ACT IV: Banks of a lake on the road to
Siberia (30 min).

Synopsis. Katerina, the bored wife of a rich provincial merchant, Zinovy
Borisov Ismailov, takes as a lover one of her husband's workmen, Sergei.
When they are discovered by her father-in-law, Boris Timofeyevich, she
poisons him with mushrooms. Then when her husband comes home unexpectedly, she incites Sergei to murder him and they hide the body in the
cellar, where it is discovered by the village drunk. He informs the police,
who arrest the couple as they are about to be married and send them to Siberia. On the road, Katerina becomes jealous of a female convict and throws
her in the lake, jumping in after her. (A comic scene in the police station
was omitted in the NYCO production.)

Major Roles. KATERINA ISMAILOVA (dram s); sustained, highly dramatic;

125

B2 to Bb4. SERGEI (dram t); D2 to Bb3. BORIS TIMOFEYEVICH ISMAILOV (high bass); some low tessitura opt; G1 (G2 opt) to F3. ZINOVY BORISOVICH IS-MAILOV (t); E2 to Bb3.

Lesser Roles. AKSINYA, a worker (s); C3 to Bb4 (continuous screams at Ab4). VILLAGE DRUNK (t); top Bb3. SONYETKA, a convict (c); A2 to Eb4. POLICE INSPECTOR (bs); C2 to F3. PRIEST (bs).

Bit Roles. NIHILIST (t). OLD CONVICT (bs). SERGEANT (bs). SENTRY (bs). POLICEMAN (bs). FEMALE CONVICT (s). STEWARD (bs). MILLHAND (bs). PORTER (bs). COACHMAN (t). TWO WORKMEN (t, t). GHOST OF BORIS (chorus bs).

Chorus. SAATBB. Workers, wedding guests, policemen, men and women convicts.

Orchestra. 2 fl, picc, 2 ob, Eng hrn, 2 cl, bs cl, Eb cl, 2 bsn, cont bsn, 4 hrn, 3 trp, 3 trb, tuba, timp, perc (2), cel, strings.

Material. MCA (Le). VS (r and e; tr E. Downes). Tr: Julius Rudel.

Performances. San Fran. (Amer prem new vers): 10.23.64. NYCO: 3.4.65; 4.12.70 etc.

🎵 Khovanshchina · The Khovansky Plot

Music by Modeste Petrovitch Mussorgsky. Libretto in Russian by the composer and V. V. Stassov. Premiere: St. Petersburg, February 21, 1886. Completed and orchestrated by Rimsky-Korsakov; official premiere: November 7, 1911. Version by Dimitri Shostakovich, Premiere: Leningrad, November 25, 1960 (the version used below). Historical-religious tragedy. Continuous texture embodying a few set numbers, accompanied recitative. Conventional harmonies; strong Russian color through folk-style harmonies and orchestration. Vocal line follows natural declamation of Russian language combined with melody. Prelude, entr'acte between IV i and ii. Setting: In and near Moscow in the time of Peter the Great, particularly during the period of struggle to enforce reforms, 1682–1689. Five acts, six scenes (144 min—Chicago perf).

ACT I: The Red Square in Moscow. ACT II: Golitsin's estate. ACT III: Army encampment near Bielgorod quarter of Moscow. ACT IV i: Banquet hall of Prince Khovansky; ii: St. Basil's Cathedral Square, Moscow. ACT V: Hermitage of Old Believers in forest outside Moscow.

Synopsis. The sprawling story depicts the struggle between three factions: Old Russia, as represented by Prince Ivan Khovansky, leader of the Streltsy (archers); the Sectarians, Old Believers led by Dosifei, whose help is enlisted by Khovansky; and the New Russia being inculcated by Peter the Great, the chief leader being Prince Vassily Golitsin. In Red Square, Kuzka and other archers jest and brag. The Boyar Shaklovity, a spy for the Tsar, dictates a letter to the Scrivener, warning the Tsar of a plot by the Khovanskys. The old prince enters, hailed by the crowd, and accuses the boyars of making trouble; his address seems somewhat ambiguous as he claims to be crushing

126

the enemies of the Tsar. His son Andrei drags in a German girl whom he has kidnapped, and who continues to reject his advances. Their altercation is interrupted by Marfa, an Old Believer, who has once been Andrei's lover and who cannot forget him. Dosifei attempts to make peace, but Prince Ivan at this juncture casts a lustful eye on Emma and orders her taken to his palace. Andrei tries to stab the girl rather than lose her, but Dosifei parts them and entrusts Emma to Marfa. Ivan then appoints his son a colonel and orders a march against the Kremlin.

On Prince Golitsin's estate, the councillor and former lover of the Regent Sophie reads a letter from her, wondering if he can still trust her. He has sent his colleague Varsonofiev to fetch Marfa, and when she enters, demands that she cast his horoscope. When she divines his ruin, he orders Varsonofiev to have her drowned. Prince Ivan Khovansky is announced; his visit turns into a fierce quarrel. Dosifei again makes peace just as Marfa rushes in, having been rescued by the Tsar's bodyguard. Shaklovity brings a message that the Regent has proclaimed the Khovanskys traitors and ordered their arrest.

At the Streltsy headquarters, Marfa broods on her lost love. Susanna, a fanatical Old Believer, denounces her as a sinner. Dosifei comforts Marfa, suggesting she concentrate on her troubled country. As they leave, Shaklovity enters, expressing hope that the Russian people may be freed from oppressive rule—he apparently plays both sides. He hides as the rowdy Streltsy march in, singing bawdy songs. Kuzka taunts the women folk, and a remarkable double antiphonal choral dialogue ensues. The Scrivener runs in, screaming that the Tsar's mercenaries have burned his house and are attacking the Streltsy quarters. Prince Khovansky refuses to lead the resistance, counseling temporary submission to the Tsar.

In his banqueting hall, the old prince listens to the singing maidservants to dispel his gloom, then watches the Persian dancing slaves, ignoring the warning sent him by Golitsin. Shaklovity brings an invitation to a council meeting with the Regent, but treacherously stabs Khovansky as the old man is ready to depart.

A crowd in St. Basil's Square watches Prince Golitsin going to his exile. Dosifei hears that Peter has ordered the execution of Old Believers, and resolves on mass suicide. Marfa tells Andrei that Emma is safely married to the man she loves. Andrei threatens to have his Streltsy kill her as a sorceress, but she tells him of his father's death, and bids him call the Streltsy. They appear, bearing the instruments of their own execution. When he learns of his own probable fate, Andrei begs Marfa to save him. She takes him out, as a Tsar's herald, Streshniev, brings reprieve for the Streltsy.

The Old Believers gather at their hermitage in a pine forest. They build a funeral pyre and ascend it with lighted torches, Dosifei leading them in prayer. Andrei rebels at self-sacrifice, calling constantly for Emma, but is drawn to the pyre by Marfa. The Tsar's troops arrive too late and fall back in horror at the human holocaust.

127

Major Roles. IVAN KHOVANSKY (bs); B♭1 to E3. MARFA (c); requires equal strength throughout entire range; both lyric and dramatic; often high tessitura; G2 to G4. ANDREI KHOVANSKY (t); high tessitura; touches D♭2 to B♭3. VASSILY GOLITSIN (t); high tessitura; D2 to B♭3. DOSIFEI (bs); A1 to F3; requires strong D♭3 to F3. SHAKLOVITY (bar); touches B♭1 and G3; equal strength throughout C2 to F3.

Lesser Roles. EMMA (s); touches G♭3 and C♭5. SCRIVENER (t); E2 to B♭3. SUSANNA (s); C3 to A4.

Bit Roles. VARSONOFIEV (bar). KUZKA (t). STRESHNIEV (t). THREE STRELTSY (bs, bs, t).

Chorus. SSAATTBB in many combinations and doublings; children's chorus. Extremely important, as in *Boris Godunov.* Moscovite people, Streltsy, wives and children; Old Believers, Persian slaves, servants, Tsar's bodyguard.

Ballet. Persian dances in IV i.

Orchestra. 2 fl, picc, 2 ob, Eng hrn, 2 cl A and B♭, bs cl, 2 bsn, cont bsn, 4 hrn, 3 trp B♭, 3 trb, tuba, 2–4 harp, piano, timp, perc (including tri, tamb, cym, dr, tam-tam, glock, bells), cel, strings. *Stage*: hrns, trps, trbs.

Material. Bessel (Paris).

Performances. Met 1949–1950. Lyr. Op. Chic.: 9.26.69, etc.

⚑ King Priam

Music by Sir Michael Tippett (1905–   ). Libretto in English by the composer, after Homer. Premiere: Coventry, June 5, 1962. Tragedy. Spare orchestration, contemporary idiom; vocal line patterned after speech, but with some aria types. Prelude with offstage chorus. Setting: ancient Troy and Sparta, before and during Trojan War. Three acts, ten scenes, six interludes.

ACT I i: Near Paris's cradle; Interlude: Nurse, Old Man, Young Guard; ii: The hunt; Interlude: Nurse, Old Man, Young Guard, then Wedding Guests; iii: Sparta, Helen and Paris, The Golden Apple. ACT II i: Walls of Troy; Interlude: Old Man, Hermes, Chorus; ii: Achilles's tent; Interlude: Old Man, Hermes, Chorus; iii: Walls of Troy. ACT III i: Andromache's home; Interlude: Serving Women; ii: Priam's room; Interlude: orchestra; iii: Achilles's tent; Interlude: Hermes as Messenger of Death; iv: Before an altar.

Synopsis. The story of the Trojan War is told with many psychological insights. Queen Hecuba's dream is interpreted by the Old Man as an augury that her newborn child, Paris, will be the cause of King Priam's death. The King gives orders to kill the baby but communicates his reluctance to the Young Guard, who gives the infant to a shepherd to rear. When Paris is grown, he meets his elder brother Hector and the King at a hunt, and is welcomed by Priam. Hector and Paris are antipathetic; as the former weds Andromache, Paris departs for Greece, where he falls under the spell of King Menelaus's fabled wife, Helen. Hermes, messenger of the Gods, who appears at critical junctures but refuses partisanship to all, brings Paris a golden apple, which he is fated to give to one of three goddesses, the warlike Athene, the motherly Hera, or the beautiful Aphrodite, goddess of love. He chooses Aphrodite, who allows him to kidnap Helen, thus incurring the deadly wrath of the other two goddesses.

The war now becomes inevitable. Before the walls of Troy, Hector berates Paris for cowardice, then sets off for battle. As they wait for news, Hecuba and Andromache bitterly castigate Helen, who serenely proclaims her immunity to censure because of her gift of inspiring love through her parentage, Zeus and Leda. Meanwhile the Greek Achilles refuses to fight because Agamemnon has stolen the girl given the hero as a reward for slaying Andromache's father and brothers in Thebes. But he lends his armor to his friend Patroclus, whom Hector kills, then strips of the armor.

The Trojans' triumph is short-lived. The enraged Achilles kills Hector and mutilates his body. Paris brings the news to Priam, who curses him, wishing he had killed this son since it is Hector who is dead and not himself as the augury foretold. Priam then seeks out Achilles and kisses the hands that killed his son. Achilles, moved to pity, allows the stricken father to take Hector's body. They exchange prophecies: Priam foretells that Paris will kill Achilles; Achilles names his own son, Neoptolemus as Priam's slayer, while Agamemnon will kill Paris. Priam at last realizes that vengeance is vain and longs only for his own death. Hermes comments on the mysteries of the story as seen through "mirror upon mirror," as a "timeless music played in time." Helen, the symbol of love and dissension, is the only one spared; Priam gently sends her back to Greece and composes himself at the altar for the death that soon comes to him at the hands of Achilles' son.

Major Roles. PRIAM, HECUBA, ANDROMACHE, PARIS, HERMES, NURSE, and HELEN have melismatic passages that require flexibility and sustained power. PRIAM (bs-bar); G♯1 to E3. HECUBA (dram s); D♭3 to A4. HECTOR (bar); some flexibility; C2 to F3. ANDROMACHE (lyr-dram s); B2 to A4. PARIS (as boy s, D3 to F♯4; as t, C2 to A3); high tessitura. HELEN (m-s); some wide skips; B♭2 to A♭4. ACHILLES (heroic t); sustained; flexibility for war cry; D2 to B♭3. PATROCLUS (light bar); B1 to E3.

Lesser Roles. HERMES (high, light t); E2 to B♭3. NURSE (m-s); B♭2 to F4. OLD MAN (bs); F1 to D3. YOUNG GUARD (lyr t); C2 to A3. (By masks, costumes or gestures, the above become chorus and declaim, though no declamation in character.) ATHENE, HERA, APHRODITE (s, s, m-s).

Chorus. Size at discretion of producer. SSATTBB. Some solo parts. Hunters, wedding guests, serving women, etc. Comments; smaller groups carry on narrative. Men need flexibility for war cry.

Orchestra. 2 fl (picc), ob, Eng hrn, 2 cl, bs cl, bsn, cont bsn, 4 hrn, 4 trp, 2 trb, tuba, timp, perc, guit, piano, (cel), harp, strings. *Before curtain*: trp.

Material. Bel (Sch). VS*.

129

🗽 The Kiss · Hubicka

Music by Bedřich Smetana (1824–1884). Libretto in Czech by Eliška Krásnohorská after a story by Karolina Svetlá. Premiere: Prague, November 7, 1876. Romantic comedy. Highly melodic, lyrical, frequently folkloristic; lively duets and ensembles comparable to *The Bartered Bride*. Overture. Setting: a small Czech town, mid-nineteenth century. Two acts, three scenes (150 min).

ACT I: Room in the cottage of the Palouckýs in the Krkonose Mountains of Bohemia. ACT II i: A mountain pass near the border; ii: Martinka's farmyard.

Synopsis. Lukáš, left a widower with a baby, wants to marry his old sweetheart Vendulka Paloucký. Her father agrees but warns the pair that their stubborn hotheadedness makes them a bad match. Indeed, they quarrel at once—over the appropriateness of a kiss to seal their engagement. Vendulka feels it would be disrespectful to the memory of Lukáš's first wife, so he leaves in anger. Vendulka and Martinka experience an adventure with smugglers near the border, then return to the latter's house where a happy ending is effected with a surprise turn when Lukáš at first refuses the kiss Vendulka now offers freely.

Major Roles. VENDULKA (s); top B4. LUKAS (t); makes first entrance on Ab3; top Bb3, opt C4. TOMAS, Lukáš's brother-in-law (bar); florid; top F♯3. PALOUCKY (bs); trill; coloratura and patter; A1 to E3. BARBARA, friend of Vendulka (m-s) (only in Manhattan production). BARCA, farmhand (t); coloratura; wide skips; trill; C♯2 to B3 (not in Manhattan performance). MARTINKA (c); low A2.

Lesser Roles. MATOUS, an old smuggler (bs). STRAZNIK (t).

Chorus. SATB.

Orchestra. 2 fl (2 picc), 2 ob, 2 cl, 2 bsn, 4 hrn, 2 trp, 3 trb, timp, perc, strings.

Material. B & H (H-M).

Performances. Manh. Sch. (NYC): 12.11.71.

🗽 The Knot Garden

Music by Sir Michael Tippett (1905–   ). Libretto in English by the composer. Premiere: London, December 2, 1970. Psychological drama. Tonal though unconventional harmonies; set numbers embedded in continuous texture; complicated orchestral score; most vocal lines contain wide skips, difficult intervals, floridity. Brief prelude; interludes between each act. Setting: Contemporary English rose garden and labyrinth, the latter not actual but suggested by lighting, etc.; should shift and even spin. Three acts (approx 100 min).

ACT I: "Confrontation." ACT II: "Labyrinth." ACT III: "Charade."

Synopsis. The psychoanalyst Mangus is discovered on his couch in the center of a storm. As it clears, he rises, proclaims himself to be Prospero. Dissolve to Thea in her garden. She and her husband Faber are set in their ways, but Faber secretly covets Flora, their ward. Enter Mel, a young black writer, and Dov, his white friend, in costume as Caliban and Ariel. Thea draws Mel away and Dov is jealous, but attracted to Faber. Denise, Thea's freedom-fighter sister, enlists the sympathy of the two young men by describing the torture that brought about her disfigurement; this takes the form of a blues session. Flora joins in, then Faber, then Thea, each with his own preoccupation, at last Mangus in an enormously complicated septet. In "Labyrinth" the maze seems to suck in characters from upstage and eject them downstage, as if they were in a puppet show manipulated by Mangus. First, Denise and Thea, as in a nightmare, sing separately of their fears; then Faber and Denise, denying that they have anything in common; then Faber with Flora, who escapes him in terror; then Thea, who horsewhips Faber to his knees; she is replaced by Dov. Faber is whirled away as he attempts to kiss Dov, and Mel comes on. Mel and Dov play a scene like a song-and-dance number, Mel rejecting Dov's attempt to regain their former affectionate status. Denise and Mel are the next encounter; her fierce spirit and sympathy for his cause wins him, but she is whirled away and Dov reappears to recriminate Mel, and is thrown downstage. Thea returns; Mel is whirled away; Flora, fleeing Faber, is projected to the forestage where the nightmarish atmosphere clearing, she is comforted by Dov. While he sings, the garden forms about them and they appear as lovers. Mel breaks the spell and the garden fades.

In "Charade," all but Thea and Denise assume characters in *The Tempest*, but the play is broken off by Mangus, who explains that there is no magic, only the power of love. Denise and Mel go off, followed reluctantly by Dov. Flora dances off alone to her future. Thea and Faber remain, their "enmity transcended in desire."

Major Roles. FABER, a civil engineer, about 35 (bar); robust; must whistle; B♭1 to F3 (A♭4 fals). THEA, his wife (dram m-s); needs great flexibility; B2 to A4. FLORA, their ward (light high s); adolescent quality; some florid passages; trill; C3 to B♭4 (touches C5). DENISE, Thea's sister (dram s); needs flexibility; one taxing aria; some melisma; awkward intervals; C3 to D♭5. MEL (lyr bs-bar); B♭1 (one G1) to F3. DOV, a musician (lyr t); one difficult aria with florid passages; C2 to B♭3 (touches B3). MANGUS (bar); high tessitura; both sustained and flexible; G♯1 to G3.

Chorus. Offstage voices speak and whistle in Act III.

Orchestra. 2 fl, 2 ob, 3 cl, 2 bsn, 4 hrn, 2 trp, 3 trb, tuba, timp, perc (5— sn dr, bs dr, ten dr, cym, susp cym, tamb, tub bells, wd bl, temple bl, metal bar or heavy tri, claves, whip, castanets, small rattle, xyl, vib, glock, jazz kit), harp, piano, cel, elec guit, elec harpsichord, strings.

Material. Bel (Sch). VS*.

131

⚓ Koanga

Music by Frederick Delius (1862–1934). Libretto in English by C. F. Keary after George Washington Cable's novel, *The Grandissimes*. Premiere: Elberfeld, March 30, 1904. Revised by Sir Thomas Beecham and Edward Agate; premiere: London, September 23, 1935. Tragedy. Consonant harmonies, with exotic flavor; vocal line melodic, set numbers mingled with passages patterned after speech; important ensembles. Brief preludes to Acts I, III; chorus prelude behind curtain before Act II. Setting: A Louisiana plantation on the Mississippi River, last half of 18th century. Prologue, three acts, five scenes, epilogue (approx 120 min).

Prologue: Verandah of southern plantation house. ACT I: Fields of sugar cane, a forest behind them. ACT II: Terrace before main entrance to Don José's house. ACT III i: Glade in dense forest, ground rising to hills at right; ii: Vision of plantation; iii: Chapel, Negro cabins, with houses at back. Epilogue: Same as Prologue.

Synopsis. Uncle Joe, an old slave, tells this story to plantation girls. An African prince, Koanga, is brought to the plantation of Don José Martinez, precipitating a tragedy. His marriage to Palmyra, a mulatto who is acting as maid to Don José's wife Clotilda (although she is in reality Clotilda's sister), is arranged, to the anger of the overseer Simon Perez, who covets Palmyra. Clotilda also opposes the marriage, but Palmyra and Koanga have fallen deeply in love. At the wedding ceremony, Perez kidnaps Palmyra, whereupon Koanga escapes to the forest and invokes voodoo powers to plague the Perez plantation. He returns to find Palmyra stricken also, and kills Perez, but is himself slain, whereupon Palmyra dies by her own hand.

Major Roles. DON JOSÉ MARTINEZ (bs); G1 to E♭3. SIMON PEREZ (t); C♭2 to A3. KOANGA (bar); extremely high tessitura and dramatic passages; B♭1 to (many) F3, G3, one A♭3, one A3. PALMYRA (s); both lyric and dramatic passages; needs strength; B♭2 to B♭4.

Lesser Roles. UNCLE JOE (bs). CLOTILDA (c). RANGWAN, voodoo priest (bs). Planters' daughters: RENÉE, HÉLÈNE, JEANNE, MARIE (s); AURORE, HORTENSE, OLIVE, PAULETTE (c); sing mostly in ensemble.

Chorus. SSAATTBB. Very important. Negro slaves, Creole dancers, servants.

Ballet. Creole dance Act II; wild voodoo dance Act III.

Orchestra. 3 fl, 3 ob, 3 cl, bs cl, 3 bsn, cont bsn, 4 hrn, 3 trp, 3 trb, tuba, timp, perc, strings.

Material. B & H.

Performances. Delius Ass'n. of Fla.: 1.31.63 (conc). Op. Soc. of Wash.: 12.18.70 (Amer stage prem).

☙ König Hirsch · Il Re Cervo · The Stag King (or, Die Irrfahrten der Wahrheit)

Music by Hans Werner Henze (1926–). Libretto in German by Heinz von Cramer after Gozzi's *Re Cervo*. Premiere: Berlin, September 23, 1956; revised and shortened for Cassel, 1963. Fairy tale. Strong dramatic impulse in music allied to lyrical feeling; subtle rhythms; vocal line both declamatory and melodious; some set numbers embedded in continuous texture; *Sprechstimme* and dialogue. Preludes to each act. Setting: a southern province, a Venice between wood and sea. Three acts (approx 110 min).

ACT I: Hall in the castle (50 min). ACT II: The wood (25 min). ACT III: A square in the city (35 min).

Synopsis. The young King, Leandro, who has been left in the woods and brought up by animals, has returned to his kingdom despite the machinations of his Royal Chancellor Tartaglia and is about to choose a bride. The flighty Scollatera offers herself, but is frightened at doing anything by herself, and summons three mirror selves to back her up. Leandro leaves his animal friends reluctantly, but is promised assistance by two statues in his castle, who will laugh when anyone tells a lie. Scollatera's insincerity is revealed by this laughter, but Costanza is greeted with silence. However, this beautiful girl has been primed by Tartaglia to hate Leandro, and though it is a case of love at first sight between the two young people, Costanza's vow to kill the King is revealed by Tartaglia, who takes her off to prison. Leandro renounces his kingdom and, led by the magician Cigoletti, returns to the forest, where he is sought by six foolish alchemists, Checco, a melancholy minstrel, and Coltellino, a bashful assassin whom Tartaglia has commissioned to kill Leandro. Tartaglia wounds a mighty stag, whose body Leandro assumes. Then Tartaglia takes on the appearance of Leandro and returns to instigate a reign of terror. People in the city do not lose hope, but whisper that when a stag walks through the streets, murderers will die. Costanza, who has been freed, meets the stag but is chased away by Tartaglia. The animal returns however, and all is set right as Coltellino kills Tartaglia, believing him to be the King. Leandro resumes his own form and exchanges promises of eternal love with Costanza.

Major Roles. LEANDRO (t); C2 to A3 (Bb3 with G#3 opt). COSTANZA (s); C3 to Bb4; one firm B4, one C#5 opt. TARTAGLIA (bs-bar); needs strength at extremes of long range; many G1, F#1, F1, E1, Eb1, D1 with higher opt to many F3, F#3, firm Gb3 with some lower opt; trill on F#3 (F#2 opt). SCOLLATELLA I (col s); needs great flexibility; trill; C3 to D5. SCOLLATELLA II (mirror entity) (soubrette); SCOLLATELLA III (m-s); SCOLLATELLA IV (c); these last three sing mostly in ensemble. CHECCO (buf t); Bb1 to A3. COLTELLINO (buf t); needs flexibility; top A3; C4 has C3 opt.

Lesser Roles. CIGOLETTI (sp). THE STAG (mute). SIX ALCHEMISTS (clown-actors, with singing ad lib). TWO STATUES (s, s).

Chorus. SSATBB. Often divided. Voices of wood-nymphs (solo s, m-s, c, t, bs). Voices of people (solo s, m-s, c, t, bar, bs). Four women (can double with 3 Scollatellas and one wood-nymph). Three solo t. In Act III, three men's chorus. Ghosts, Moors, pages, animals, soldiers, servants, sedan-chair bearers, hunters, children ad lib.

Ballet. Animals, masquers.

Orchestra. 2 fl (picc), 2 ob (Eng hrn), 2 cl (bs cl), 2 bsn (cont bsn), 3 hrn, 2 trp, small antique trb (ad lib), 2 trb, timp, perc, piano, cel, harp, guit, mandolin, glock, organ (harm ad lib), strings. *Stage*: 2 hrn, 3 trp, tub bells, glock, org, mandolin, vib, perc (mil dr, bs dr, 2 cym, tri, 3 tom-tom, large tambour, tam-tam).

Material. Bel (Sch). VS*.

Performances. Santa Fe: 8.4.65 etc. (Amer prem).

🎵 Kumana

Music by Ernest Kanitz (1894–   ). Libretto in English by Jane Marshal. Not yet staged. American society comedy. Lyric, satirical, occasionally exotic; set numbers; tonality mixed with atonality. Setting: Fashionable waterfront colony, summer in early 1950's. One act, five scenes (approx 120 min).

Scene i: Beach at colony; ii–v: Various locations around the Smith mansion.

Synopsis. Kumana, early-orphaned daughter of American missionaries, has been brought up by natives of the Pacific island for which she is named When the island is evacuated for atomic tests, the U.S. government sends her to her aunt Rosalie Smith, a wealthy widow. Kumana's naiveté throws her relatives into confusion; she mistakes a coming-out party for a mating festival and shocks the guests with a mating dance. Then she tries to adopt a foundling left on the Smiths' doorstep, and proposes to her aunt's gardener, Tom, who is sent away believing the baby to be Kumana's. Next the girl proposes to Andrew, a society painter and fiancé of her cousin Gwen; then Roger, a rich, good-natured drunkard, agrees to take her, baby and all. Tom, learning the truth from the maid Molly, saves the situation by pretending to be the father of the baby.

Major Roles. TOM (high bar); A1 to E3 (G3 opt). KUMANA (lyr s); C♯3 to G♯4 (B4 opt). ROSALIE VAN RUTHERFORD SMITH (dram s); B2 to A♯4. GWEN (c); B♭2 to G4. FREDERICK SMITH, Rosalie's son (bar); C♯2 to E3. ANDREW (lyr t); D2 to D♭3. ROGER (bs); A1 to D3.

Lesser Roles. VICTORIA, Fred's fiancée (high m-s); E3 to G♯4. MOLLY (high s); E♭3 to A4. TWO POLICEMEN (bs, buf t). FOUR MOTHERS, of debutantes (2 s, 2 c). 3 STAGS (buf t, bar, bs). Some doubling possible.

Chorus. SATB. Mothers, stags, other guests.

Orchestra. 2 fl, ob, 2 cl, bsn, 2 hrn, trp, trb, timp, perc (2–3), piano, cel, harp, strings (5.3.2.2.1).

Material. Composer.

134

⚅ The Last Savage

Music by Gian-Carlo Menotti (1911–   ). Libretto in Italian by the composer. Commissioned by the Théatre National de l'Opéra Comique, Paris. Premiere: Paris, April 2, 1963. English version: George Mead. Premiere: Metropolitan Opera, New York, January 23, 1964. Revised, 1972. Comedy. Continuous texture embodying set numbers; conventional harmonies; vocal line melodious; important ensembles; interludes. Setting: India and Chicago, the present. Three acts, four scenes.

ACT I i: The palace of the Maharajah of Ragaputana, somewhere near the Himalayas; ii: Courtyard in the palace. ACT II: Living room of Kitty's house in Chicago. ACT III: Forest in India.

Synopsis. The Maharajah desires his son Prince Kodanda to marry Kitty, daughter of the millionaire Scattergood, but Kitty is determined to consummate her career as an anthropologist by capturing an Abominable Snowman, and the Prince is not willing to give up his playboy status. The two fathers persuade a simple stableboy, Abdul, to impersonate a wild man (for the consideration of $1 down, $99,999 at the end of the assignment), and Abdul unwillingly leaves his sweetheart Sardula, one of the palace maids, who soon consoles herself with the prince. Abdul is duly captured and brought back to Chicago, where he becomes the butt of sensation-seeking socialites and journalists and is subjected to various indignities at the hands of "civilization." Kitty's attempts to teach him more personal matters are not unwelcome, but cannot compensate for the savagery of other strange groups—artists, businessmen, tax experts, and so on—and Abdul flees. Kitty is inconsolable and pursues him to his native forest. When finally recaptured, he refuses the money due him, which impresses Kitty all the more; she resolves to stay with him in his primitive home. But even while the two lovers at last are together, Kitty signals her father, who sends a procession to their sylvan retreat bearing all the modern comforts of home. Who is civilizing whom?

Major Roles. KITTY (col s); considerable fioratura; trill; many firm high notes; C3 to E♭5. ABDUL (bar); top G3. SARDULA (lyr s); top C5. PRINCE KODANDA (t); top B♭3. MR. SCATTERGOOD (bs-bar); some flexible passages. MAHARAJAH (bs). MAHARANEE (c).

Lesser Roles. TWO INDIAN SCHOLARS (t, bar). TWO AMERICAN TAILORS (t, bar). ENGLISH TAILOR (t). ROMAN CATHOLIC PRIEST (bs). BLACK PROTESTANT MINISTER (bar). GREEK ORTHODOX PRIEST (t). RABBI (t). PHILOSOPHER (bar). PHYSICIAN (bar). PAINTER (t). POET (t). COMPOSER (bar). CONCERT SINGER (s). BUSINESS WOMAN (s).

Chorus. SSATBB.

Orchestra. 3 fl, 2 ob, 3 cl, 3 bsn, 4 hrn, 3 trp, 3 trb, tuba, timp, perc, 2 harp, piano, strings. *Stage:* hrn, trp, string trio.

Material. Bel (Col).

Performances. Hawaiian Op. Th.: 2.2.73.

🎵 Lavinia

Music by Henry Barraud (1900–   ). Libretto in French by Félicien Marceau. Premiere: Aix en Provence, July 20, 1961. Satirical comedy. Melodious. Overture; prelude to Act II. Setting: contemporary Naples. Three acts.

All three acts take place in an alley in Naples.

Synopsis. Fat Gennaro, fruit seller, and his friend, thin Peppino, scrap iron vendor, sing of the sweetness of their lazy southern life. Gennaro presses a gift of fruit on Carluccio, a worldly society reporter, believing him to be in love with Maria-Stella, his daughter. This is affirmed in a meeting of the two young people. A neighbor announces the birth of a child to Gennaro and the rejoicing is general until Gennaro learns it is another girl. All dispute what she shall be named. Rejecting all their suggestions, Gennaro decides on Lavinia. Neighbor Pasqualina says sarcastically (quoting *La Bohème*), "She can say, 'I'm called Lavinia, but I don't know why.'" (Other direct quotes include the Flower Song from *Carmen*.) All promise christening presents, but Carluccio, broke at the end of the month, offers only a paragraph in his column. This enraptures Gennaro, who sees in the publicity the future of Lavinia, even marriage to a rich American with two yachts, and—greatest luxury of all—a bathroom. His sudden dreams of fortune go to his head, and he refuses Maria-Stella's hand to Carluccio. All the neighbors are puzzled over the columnist's mythological reference to Aeneas as the father of Lavinia, and conclude that Gennaro has been cuckolded. His enormous wife, Nunziatina, indignantly denies the charge. Gennaro is brought to his senses when Carluccio explains the reference, but the neighbors still believe the worst and threaten to boycott the cuckold. Carluccio solves the problem by moving the entire family to another part of the city, but Gennaro stipulates that not one word of the young couple's marriage appear in the paper.

Major Roles. GENNARO (bs); A1 to F3. NUNZIATINA (c); A♯2 to F4. MARIA-STELLA (s); D3 to A♭4. CARLUCCIO (bs); some flamboyance; C2 to G3. PEPPINO (t); C2 to B♭3. PASQUALINA (s); C3 to A4.

Lesser Roles. ROSINA (s), GEMMA (c), COSTANZO (bs), CARMINE (bs), neighbors.

Orchestra. fl (picc), ob (Eng hrn), cl, bsn, hrn, trb, timp, perc (3), cel, piano, harp, strings.

Material. B & H. VS (f)*. Tr: Virginia Card.

🎵 The Legend of the Invisible City of Kitezh and the Maiden Fevronia

Music by Nikolai Rimsky-Korsakov (1844–1908). Libretto in Russian by V. I. Belsky. Premiere: St. Petersburg, February 20, 1907. Fantasy with moralistic overtones. Exotic orchestral coloring; deeper lyrical quality than in earlier operas; vocal line melodious. Prelude relies heavily on folk themes. Setting: A mythical kingdom on the Volga River, 6,751 years after the crea-

136

tion of the world. Four acts, six scenes (approx 190 min). Prelude: "Praise of Solitude."

ACT I: A wild and isolated forest near the Volga. ACT II: Lesser Kitezh. ACT III i: Greater Kitezh; Interlude: "The Battle of Kerzhenetz" (orch); ii: Forest clearing near a lake. ACT IV i: In the Kerzhenetz wood; Interlude: Pilgrimage to the Invisible City; ii: In the invisible city.

Synopsis. Fevronia, who seems to be the symbol of a pantheist saint, who by her kindness and forbearance wins the right to enter the "New Jerusalem" (the Sacred Invisible City) is discovered in the forest where she is most at home among her friends, the birds and animals. Prince Vsevolod, lost during a hunt, comes upon the maiden and falls in love with her, giving her a token ring when he departs. One of his followers, Fedor Poyarok, reveals his true identity. When Fevronia goes to Kitezh for the wedding, she is mocked by the rich, who incite Grischka Kouterma, the village drunk, to plague her. But the dissenters are drowned out in the general merriment, a typical Russian fair scene. The sound of Tartars' horns strikes a terrifying note, and the invaders soon appear, seeking a way to the citadel city, Greater Kitezh. Grischka turns traitor, and the Tartars kidnap Fevronia. In the Greater city, a blind huntsman, victim of the Tartars, accuses Fevronia of Grischka's sin; the old Prince Juri comments sadly on the decline of glory; warriors prepare to defend the city, and Prince Vsevolod leads a battalion to war. But the invaders are foiled by a dense golden fog which hides the sacred city and carries it up to Paradise. In the forest, the Tartars accuse Grischka of betrayal and tie him to a tree, then the chieftans fight over Fevronia and one is killed. Grischka begs Fevronia to free him, confessing his betrayal of her and the city. Magnanimously, the girl does so, and Grischka carries her off into the forest, while the Tartars awake to find the beleaguered city in its fog shroud mirrored in the lake. Superstitiously, they flee. Exhausted, Fevronia can go no further. Grischka has become hysterical with weird visions and the sound of Greater Kitezh's bells, and runs off pursued by nightmares. Fevronia has a vision of Vsevolod, and realizes he has been killed in battle. The voices of Paradise Birds Sirin and Alkonost lead her to Kitezh and Paradise.

Major Roles. FEVRONIA (s); longest role; lyr but needs stamina; C3 to A4. GRISCHKA KOUTERMA (t); important character role; top A3 (one firm A♯3, one B♭3). PRINCE JURI (bs); low tessitura; F1 (one firm E1) to E♭3. PRINCE VSEVOLOD JURIVICH (t) top A♭3. FEDOR POYAROK (bar); top F3. OTROK, a youth (m-s).

Lesser Roles. GUSLEE PLAYER (bs). BEAR TRAINER (t). TWO MEN (t, bs). BYEDAI (bs), BOUROUNDAI (bs), Tartar heroes. BLIND HUNTSMAN (bar). SIRIN (s), ALKONOST (c); Voices of Paradise Birds.

Chorus. SSAATTBB. Very important. Several solos. Prince's attendants, revelers, boyars, etc.

Ballet. Possible in wedding scene.

Orchestra. 3 fl (3 picc), alto fl, 2 ob, Eng hrn, 2 cl, bs cl, 2 bsn, cont bsn,

137

4 hrn, 3 trp, 3 trb, tuba, timp, perc, 2 harp, strings. *Stage*: ten, bs tuba, bells.

Material. Pet.

🎭 Die Liebe der Danae · The Love of Danae

Music by Richard Strauss (1864–1949). Libretto in German by Josef Gregor, from a sketch by Hugo von Hofmannsthal. Premiere: Salzburg, August 14, 1952. A "joyful myth." Continuous texture, rich orchestration, embodying several arias. No overture. Instrumental interludes between Act I i and ii ("Rain of Gold"); I ii and iii ("Dance of Pagans"); in Act II; between Act III i and ii, ii and iii. Prelude to Act III. Setting: Antiquity. Three acts, eight scenes (approx 165 min).

ACT I i: Throne room of King Pollux; ii. Danae's bedroom; iii: Pillared hall in the palace; iv: Harbor. ACT II: Danae's bedroom. ACT III i: Country road in the Orient; ii: Mountain forest; iii: Midas's hut.

Synopsis. To restore the impoverished realm of King Pollux, his daughter Danae will wed Midas, the richest man in the world. Danae dreams of a shower of gold, and is immediately attracted to an emissary of Midas, although he is not the person she saw in her dream (in reality it is Midas himself, simply dressed). When Midas's ship arrives, it is Jupiter who wears Midas's golden raiment and who has taken his place in order to court Danae. Danae's four cousins, each a queen who has been loved by Jupiter, penetrate his disguise, but do not betray him to Danae, for they sympathize with his need to deceive Juno. Each longs for his return to her, but he is in serious pursuit of Danae. He warns Midas that if he does not live up to his bargain (in return for the power to change everything he touches to gold, he has promised to obey Jupiter implicitly), he will be transformed back into a donkey-driver. Midas, however, cannot resist an embrace of Danae, who does not understand the mystery of his disguise, but already loves him. His touch is fatal: Danae turns to a golden statue. Jupiter will restore her to human form, but only for himself. Midas insists that she be allowed to choose. Her voice is immediately heard, choosing Midas. The two begin a new life in humble poverty. Jupiter is now beseiged by the four queens, led to him by Mercury, but renounces them and all earthly love. He is not allowed to forget earth, however, for Pollux and his nephews and creditors find him and demand reparation for his deception. Mercury suggests a shower of gold, which scatters the claimants successfully. Jupiter tries once more to sway Danae, but her staunchness finally commands his admiration. He leaves her to Midas.

Major Roles. JUPITER (bar); long, difficult part; much high tessitura; wide skips; G1 to G3. DANAE (s); needs strength at both ends of range; B2 to D♭5. MIDAS (t); sustained; dramatic; high tessitura; C2 to C♯4. MERCURY (t); C2 to B♭3. POLLUX (t); E♭2 to B3.

Lesser Roles. Four Queens (sing often as quartet): SEMELE (s); top C5;

138

EUROPA (s); ALKMENE (m-s); LEDA (c); low E♭2. FOUR KINGS, nephews of Pollux (2 t, 2 bs). FOUR WATCHMEN (bs).

Chorus. SSATTBB. Creditors, servants, followers of Pollux and Danae, townsfolk.

Orchestra. 3 fl, picc, 2 ob, Eng hrn, 3 cl, basset hrn, bs cl, 3 bsn, cont bsn, 6 hrn, 4 trp, 4 trb, tuba, 2 harp, cel, piano, timp, perc, strings.

Material. B & H. VS (g)*. Tr: Dennis Wakeling.

Performances. USC: 4.5.64 (Amer prem).

☙ Lizzie Borden

Music by Jack Beeson (1921–   ). Libretto in English by Kenward Elmslie, based on a scenario by Richard Plant; subtitled *A Family Portrait in Three Acts*, based on the legends surrounding the alleged New England murderess. Premiere: New York, March 25, 1965. Commissioned by the Ford Foundation. Lyric drama. Musical style varies from relatively simple evocations of late 19th-century hymnody to complex serial procedures. Arias, ensembles, and unaccompanied recitative are combined with continuous texture. Prelude to Act I is identical with that to Act II and is used also as interlude at climax. Setting: Fall River, Massachusetts, in the eighties. Three acts, five scenes, epilogue (117 min).

ACT I i: Living room and hall (showing staircase) of Borden house; ii: Girls' room and adjoining garden (32 min). ACT II: Living room (40 min). ACT III i: Girls' room and garden; ii: Living room. Epilogue: Living room, some years later (45 min).

Synopsis. During a choir rehearsal in the Borden house, the Reverend Harrington asks Lizzie for a donation to save Old Harbor Church. She advises him to speak to Abbie, her stepmother, who can persuade Andrew Borden to anything. Borden interrupts the rehearsal. Lizzie asks for a new gown, but is told to make do with one from the attic. The family assembles for lunch. Lizzie, planning for her sister Margret to escape the house by accepting Captain Jason MacFarlane's proposal of marriage, arranges that the minister should bring the captain to the house to meet Borden. During the evening, Abbie persuades her husband to buy her a new piano and to do over the house, removing all traces of his first wife, Evangeline. A family quarrel is interrupted by the arrival of the minister and the captain. Andrew mocks Jason's proposal and offers Lizzie instead. He forbids Lizzie to see the preacher again or to continue her machinations in behalf of Margret. While Abbie and Andrew are out celebrating their wedding anniversary, Jason persuades Margret to elope. Lizzie puts on Evangeline's wedding gown, which she has been remodeling for Margret. Entranced by her mirror image, she loses herself in fantasies and is caught and taunted by Abbie. Lizzie realizes that in sending Margret away, she will be left alone with her parents. She confesses to Jason that his letters have meant a great deal to her, and begs to keep them. Abbie witnesses the scene, and after Jason leaves, orders Lizzie around like a servant, then goes upstairs for a nap. Lizzie follows, snatching a weapon from the wall. Andrew returns; Lizzie, still in her mother's wedding dress, now stained with blood, demently imagines herself a young bride. She follows her horrified father into the bedroom. Several years pass. The Reverend Harrington returns a donation to Lizzie; the congregation has refused it, even though the jury had found her innocent of her parents' murders. As she closes the shutters, children circle the house, mocking her and her alleged deed.

Major Roles. LIZZIE (m-s); taxing vocally, needs exceptional gifts as singing actress; G2 (opt Bb2) to Bb4. ABBIE (spin-col s); dramatic ability necessary; middle-aged, plump; B2 to C#5. MARGRET (lyr s); C3 to C5. ANDREW BORDEN (bs-bar); strong musical, dramatic characterization; warmth not useful; G1 to F#3.

Lesser Roles. CAPTAIN JASON MAC FARLANE (lyr bar); Bb1 to F#3. REVEREND HARRINGTON (t); D2 to G3.

Chorus. SA; small chorus of children, young people.

Orchestra. 2 fl (picc), 2 ob (Eng hrn), 2 cl (bs cl), 2 bsn, 2 hrn, 2 trp, 2 trb, 2 tuba (t, bs), timp, perc (2), harp, harm, strings.

Material. B & H. VS*.

Performances. NET: 1966–1967. Univ. of Iowa: 12.67.

I Lombardi alla Prima Crociata · The Lombards at the First Crusade

Music by Giuseppe Verdi (1813–1901). Libretto in Italian by Temistocle Solera from the epic poem by Tommaso Grossi. Premiere: Milan, February 11, 1843. Historical drama. Conventional harmonies; set numbers; highly expressive; vocal lines both dramatic and lyrical. Brief prelude with chorus. Setting: Milan, Antioch, Jerusalem, and vicinity, 1099. Four acts, eleven scenes. The acts are titled: I: "La Vendetta" (The Revenge); II: "L'uomo della caverna" (The Man in the Cave); III: "La Conversione" (The Conversion); IV: "Il santo sepolcro" (The Holy Sepulchre).

ACT I i: Piazza di Sant' Ambrogio, Milan; ii: Gallery in the palace of Folco. ACT II i: Hall in the palace of Acciano, Antioch; ii: Entrance to a cave; iii: Women's quarters in Acciano's palace. ACT III i: Valley of Jehoshaphat; ii: Arvino's tent in Lombard camp; iii: Grotto near banks of the Jordan. ACT IV i: Cave in hills outside Jerusalem; ii: Lombard camp; iii: Arvino's tent.

Synopsis. Pagano, who has been banished because he tried to kill his brother Arvino, successful in winning the hand of Viclinda, whom Pagano also loved, now returns to Milan, outwardly repentant. As Arvino is proclaimed leader of the Lombard crusaders, Pegano and his henchman Pirro plan to abduct Viclinda and kill Arvino. But Pagano kills his father Folco instead. He seeks absolution by becoming a hermit in a cave near Jerusalem. Meanwhile, Arvino embarks upon the crusade. In Antioch, King Acciano's wife

140

Sofia consoles her son Oronte, who has fallen in love with Giselda, the daughter of Arvino, who has been captured by the Muslems. Pirro, who has also repented his sins, joins the hermit Pagano in guiding the crusaders to victory. Giselda, who has repudiated her father for his cruelty, becomes deranged and wanders in the Valley of Jehoshaphat, where she encounters the wounded Oronte, and they seek refuge in a grotto. Meanwhile, Arvino, not knowing the hermit's identity, seeks his help. Through a miracle, the fountain of Siloam flows, saving the crusaders, who are victorious in battle. Arvino forgives the fatally wounded hermit, as the cross of the crusaders is seen over the Holy City.

Major Roles. ARVINO (t). PAGANO (bs); high tessitura; top F3. VICLINDA (s). GISELDA (s); needs strength and flexibility; top Db5. ORONTE (t); top Ab3.

Lesser Roles. PIRRO (bs). PRIOR OF MILAN (t). ACCIANO (bs). SOFIA (s).

Chorus. SATB.

Orchestra. picc, fl, 2 ob, 2 cl, 2 bsn, 4 hrn, 2 trp, 3 trb, tuba, timp, perc (3), 2 harp, org (opt), strings.

Material. Bel (Ri).

Performances. Op. Orch. of N.Y.: 12.7.72 (conc).

◤ Lucio Silla

Music by Wolfgang Amadeus Mozart (1756–1791). Libretto in Italian by Giovanni di Gamerra. Premiere: Milan, December 6, 1772. Version realized and edited by Thomas Conlin, premiere: Baltimore, January 19, 1968 (this analysis based on that version). Drama. Highly melodious; set numbers, patter recitatives; conventional harmonies. Overture. Setting: In and near Rome ca. 80 B.C. Three acts, seven scenes (approx 125 min).

ACT I i: The Exile; ii: Silla's dwelling; iii: Hall of the Heroes. ACT II i: Silla's dwelling; ii: The Capitol. ACT III i: The prison; ii: The Capitol.

Synopsis. Mozart's opera is presented before the guests at the 18th-century court of a patron. A master of ceremonies assigns courtiers to various duties and introduces the visiting singers, while the resident Maestro leads the overture.

The despot Lucio Silla has banished the Roman Senator Cecilio and with the aid of his sister Celia seeks the favor of Cecilio's betrothed Giunia. Aufidio, Silla's tribune, advocates force. Cecilio returns secretly and meets his friend the patrician Cinna, who is betrothed to Celia. Cecilio is dissuaded by Cinna from killing Silla, who believes that Giunia will do the deed; if not, he himself will. Giunia pleads for Cecilio's life before the Senate, but the tyrant only demands that she become his bride, and when Cecilio rushes in with drawn sword, casts him into a dungeon. Tragedy is averted when Celia intercedes with her brother for the lovers. Rome hails the magnanimity of Silla.

Major Roles. LUCIO SILLA (t); needs power for sustained line. GIUNIA (s);

high tessitura; very florid; some sustained passages, trill; top Db5 (touches D5). CECILIO (t); florid; trill; A1 to B3. CINNA (col s); some lyric passages, also very florid; trill; top Bb4. CELIA (s); many florid passages; trill; top C5.

Lesser Role. AUFIDIO (t); trill.

Chorus. SATB. Guards, Senators, nobles, soldiers, people.

Orchestra. 2 ob, 2 bsn, 2 hrn, 2 trp, timp, strings.

Material. Pr.

Performances. Chamber Op. Soc. (Baltimore): 1.19.68 (Amer prem). Manh. Sch. (NYC): 12.13.68.

⚓ Lucrezia Borgia

Music by Gaetano Donizetti (1797–1848). Libretto in Italian by Felice Romani after Victor Hugo. Premiere: Milan, December 26, 1833. Melodrama. Highly melodious; conventional harmonies; lyrical and dramatic vocal line; set numbers. Brief prelude. Setting: Venice and Ferrara, beginning of the 16th century. Prologue and two acts, four scenes (135 min).

Prologue: Venice, terrace of the Palace Grimani. ACT I i: Square in Ferrara, the Borgia palace at one side; ii: Hall in Ducal palace. ACT II: Small courtyard in Gennaro's house; ii: Festive hall in Negroni palace.

Synopsis. Lucrezia Borgia, the terror of the Renaissance, has done away with three husbands and is now married to a fourth, Don Alfonso, Duke of Ferrara. After a masked ball in Venice, she seeks out Gennaro, in reality her illegitimate son, and attracts him deeply until his companions reveal her identity, each relating a horror story of her poisoning a relative. Back in Ferrara, the Duke is jealous of Gennaro, not realizing his true relationship to Lucrezia, and finds a pretext to condemn him when the youth chisels off the first letter of "Borgia" from the facade of the palace. Lucrezia demands the desecrator's death until she finds it is Gennaro, then manages to give him the antidote to the poison she has had to administer, bidding him to flee Ferrara. But the young man joins his friends at a banquet, only to share in the poisoned wine prepared for the company by his mother. When she reveals her identity, he repulses her violently and dies. She quaffs the poison cup and expires upon his body.

Major Roles. ALFONSO D'ESTE, Duke of Ferrara (bs); Ab1 to Eb3. LUCREZIA BORGIA (s); needs great flexibility for difficult coloratura passages; trill; Bb2 to B4 (many high notes, touches C5). GENNARO (t); top A3 (one Bb3). MAFFIO ORSINI, Gennaro's friend (c); needs considerable flexibility; has famous showpiece, Ballata, B2 to F♯4 (touches G4).

Lesser Roles. JEPPO LIVEROTTO (t). DON APOSTOLO GAZELLA (bs). ASCANIO PETRUCCI (bs). OLOFERNO VITELLOZZO (t). GUBETTA (bs). RUSTIGHELLO (t). ASTOLFO (bs).

Chorus. SATB. Cavaliers, gondoliers, ladies, swordsmen, pages, soldiers, etc.

142

Orchestra. 2 fl, 2 ob, 2 cl, 2 bsn, 4 hrn, 2 trp, 3 trb, tuba, timp, perc, bells, harp, strings.

Material. Bel (Ri). Map.

Performances. Phila. Lyr.: 1967–1968.

⚑ Luisa Miller

Music by Giuseppe Verdi (1813–1901). Libretto in Italian by Salvatore Cammarano, based on Schiller's *Kabale und Liebe* (*Intrigue and Love*). Premiere: Naples, December 8, 1849. Tragedy. Highly melodic, maturing Verdi style showing through early influences, notably Bellini. Set numbers, arias, ensembles, recitatives. Overture (Sinfonia). Setting: The Tyrol, first half of 18th century. Three acts ("Love," "Intrigue," "Poison"), seven scenes (131 min).

ACT I i: Village square, showing Miller's house; ii: Hall in Count Walter's castle; iii: Interior of Miller's house (53 min). ACT II i: Interior of Miller's house; ii: Walter's apartment in castle; iii: Castle garden (38 min). ACT III: Interior of Miller's house (40 min).

Synopsis. Luisa, the daughter of a retired soldier, is in love with Carlo, who is in reality Rodolfo, son of a local nobleman, Count Walter. Wurm, one of Walter's retainers, also loves Luisa, and when Miller refuses his suit, reveals Carlo's identity, warning Miller of disaster if he cannot marry Luisa himself. Count Walter plans to marry his son to the widowed Duchess Federica. Rodolfo throws himself on Federica's mercy, confessing his love for Luisa, but the Duchess is furious. Rodolfo convinces Miller of his sincerity, but Walter calls Luisa a seductress, inciting Miller to attack him. Both Luisa and Miller are seized by the Count's men. Rodolfo frees them by threatening to tell how his father came to power through murdering his cousin. But Luisa believes her father still to be imprisoned and yields to Wurm's demand that she write a letter saying she only loved Rodolfo for his money and intends to marry Wurm. Luisa must also tell this in person to Federica. Rodolfo reads the letter and believes it. He poisons Luisa, then learning the truth, drinks poison himself, retaining only enough strength to stab Wurm fatally. The two fathers are left to grieve.

Major Roles. LUISA (s); needs strength for sustained passages; some floridity; high tessitura; trill; C3 to (several) C5. RODOLFO (t); C#2 to B3 (one Cb4, lower passage opt). MILLER (bar); much high tessitura; needs flexibility; A1 to G3. COUNT WALTER (bs); needs strength at extremes of range; some florid passages; F1 to Gb3. WURM (bs); Bb1 to F3. FEDERICA (c); one florid passage; G2 to G4.

Lesser Role. LAURA, a peasant (m-s); C#3 to B4.

Bit Role. A PEASANT (t).

Chorus. SSTTBB. Federica's ladies, pages, villagers, servants, archers.

Orchestra. 2 fl, picc, 2 ob, 2 cl, 2 bsn, 4 hrn, 2 trp, 3 trb, tuba, timp, perc, harp, org, strings.

Material. Bel (Ri).

Performances. Amato (NYC): 5.22.60; 2.16.68. Natl Mus. Th. (NYC): 1.8.63. Cal. West. Univ. (San Diego): 12.6.63. Rittenhouse Op. Soc. (Phila.): 1.18.68. Met. 2.8.68; 9.20.69, 10.15.71, etc. Univ. of Ind.: 1.9.71.

🎵 Lulu

Music by Alban Berg (1885–1935). Libretto in German by the composer, adapted from two plays by Frank Wedekind: *Erdgeist* ("Earth Spirit") and *Die Büchse der Pandora* ("Pandora's Box"). Premiere: Zurich, June 2, 1937. Tragedy with elements of humor, irony, and both fantasy and stark realism. Music is completely dodecaphonic throughout, although lyric elements abound. As in *Wozzeck*, the orchestra is in set forms (canon, sonata, various dance forms, etc.) Employs a great deal of *Sprechstimme*, some dialogue. Voice parts extremely difficult. No overture. Scenes separated by orchestral interludes (between II i and ii a silent film or slides are generally used to show what happens to Lulu). Third act left unfinished, and although later discovered to be in full score in shorthand, never released by composer's widow for performance. Act III is generally played in pantomime to accompaniment of "Lulu Symphony," drawn for orchestra performance by composer, including Rondo, Ostinato, and Song of Lulu from Act II; Variations from Act III and Adagio from Acts I and III. Setting: a provincial German town, Paris and London; late 19th or early 20th century before World War I. Prologue, three acts, seven scenes (128 min).

Prologue: A circus troupe before the curtain. ACT I i: A painter's studio; ii: An elegant room in Lulu's house; iii: Lulu's dressing room in the theater (64 min). ACT II i: Palatial hall of Lulu and Dr. Schön; ii: The same in slovenly condition (52 min). ACT III i: An elegant house in Paris; ii: A room in a London slum (12 min).

Synopsis. In the Prologue, an animal trainer introduces his circus troup. His chief character is Lulu, dressed as Pierrot; she has been variously called the Eternal Feminine, a phenomenon of nature beyond good and evil, a female Faust, and a latter-day Lilith. We first see her as Lulu (though called Eva) in a painter's studio, sitting for her portrait. She has been married to the elderly Dr. Goll at the insistence of the newspaper publisher Dr. Schön, who discovered her in sordid surroundings and brought her up. As the painter makes passionate love to her, Dr. Goll enters and collapses of a heart attack. Lulu marries the painter. In her new home, she receives an old street musician, Schigolch, whom she believes to be her father. She learns that Dr. Schön is to marry again, and tells him that she will try to prevent it. Dr. Schön, who calls her "Mignon," cruelly reveals her past to the painter, who cuts his throat. Dr. Schön despairs of his marriage, fearing the scandal of the suicide. Alwa, Dr. Schön's son, creates a diversion by announcing that Paris is in revolution. Lulu's cold-bloodedness repels him; she announces nevertheless that he will marry her. And in a scene in her dressing room, she ensures his break with his fiancée, staging a fainting fit, fending off an African prince

144

who wants to marry her, and at last reducing the doctor to such a state that he forswears his marriage and marries Lulu instead. But although he is the only one she really loves, she cannot deny her nature and flirts with several others (Alwa, a schoolboy, a servant, an athlete, and even a lesbian, Countess Geschwitz). Schön can bear it no longer and hands her a revolver to shoot herself. Instead, she shoots him and is arrested for his murder. The film or slides used during the interlude can depict the court in which she is condemned, her confinement to hospital after contracting cholera, and the plan for her escape. This concerns the Countess Geschwitz, who in her love for Lulu has also become infected with cholera, and in an elaborate hoax, takes her place in prison. A scene in Dr. Schön's house involves Geschwitz, Schigolch, Alwa, the Schoolboy, and the athlete Rodrigo, who hopes to marry Lulu and put her in his act. She is, however, so wasted after her illness that he rejects her. Alwa is now her last resort; she persuades him to flee with her and Schigolch to Paris. (From here on, the action is in pantomime with orchestra accompaniment.) Lulu's degradation begins; a white-slaver suggests that she become a prostitute, but she escapes in men's clothing. In a tawdry London attic, she receives men callers, supporting Alwa and Schigolch by her earnings. Geschwitz at last finds Lulu just in time to share her fate—murder at the hands of her last client, Jack the Ripper.

Major Roles. LULU (s); extremely high tessitura; trill; difficult intervals; aria is very florid with a simpler melodic line opt; very exacting acting part; one passage contains sustained B4 with opt F5 top; otherwise Ab2 to many D5. DR. SCHON (heroic bar); difficult skips and tessitura; G1 (touches F#1) to F3 (one A3, opt Eb3). COUNTESS GESCHWITZ (dram m-s); masculine appearance; B2 to F#4. ALWA (young heroic bar); A1 to B3 (one C4, opt G3; one opt C#4). PAINTER (lyr t); C2 (touches B1) to B3. SCHIGOLCH (high char bs); G1 to E3 (one F#3 *Sprechstimme*). RODRIGO (ATHLETE), doubles with ANIMAL TRAINER (bs); Ab1 to (G1, Eb1, C1 with higher opt). SCHOOLBOY, doubles with WARDROBE MISTRESS (c); G2 to A4.

Lesser Roles. THEATER MANAGER (buf bs); one C1 with C2 opt. PRINCE (t); G2 to A3. SERVANT (t). DR. GOLL (sp). JACK THE RIPPER (mute).

Orchestra. 3 fl (2 picc), 3 ob (Eng hrn), alto sax, 3 cl, bs cl, 3 bsn (cont bsn), 4 hrn, 3 trp, 3 trb, tuba, 4 timp and perc, vib, harp, piano, strings. *Stage*: jazz band: 3 cl (ten sax), alto sax, 2 jazz trp, banjo (can be from pit).

Production Problems. Film or slides to be used in Act II interlude.

Material. Pr(UE). VS (g).

Performances. Santa Fe: 8.6.63 (Amer stage prem); 8.12.64. Bost. Op. Group (Op. Co. of Bost.); 1.17.64; 2.23.68; as Amer. Natl Op. (Indianap.): 9.16.67; Bklyn: 10.6.67. San Fran.: 11.6.71.

✄ The Makropoulos Affair · Vec Makropoulos

Music by Leoš Janáček (1854–1928). Libretto in Czech by the composer after the drama by Karel Capek. Premiere: Brno, Czechoslovakia, December 18, 1926. Drama of suspense. Unconventional harmonies; vocal line highly declamatory; strong atonal bent. Setting: Prague, early 20th century. Three acts (98 min).

ACT I: Lawyer's office (38 min). ACT II: Backstage at an opera house (32 min). ACT III: Emilia's hotel suite (28 min).

Synopsis. While reviving litigation over the inheritance of two families, which has dragged on for a century, the interested parties find the beautiful opera singer Emilia Marty strangely well informed about the will of a long-deceased baron. Albert Gregor, his adversary Jaroslav Prus, and the latter's son Janek all fall in love with the mysterious woman, who meanwhile presses her own aim of recovering certain lost papers from the estate. Ultimately she breaks down and reveals that she is in fact Elina Makropoulos, who has lived for 327 years (under various aliases) because her father, a Greek alchemist, discovered the elixir of youth, which she drank. Though his formula is recovered and returned to her, she renounces it, having grown weary of life and hardened to human feelings. No one else wants the formula either, and as Elina dies, it is symbolically burned by Christa, a young singer.

Major Roles. EMILIA MARTY (dram s); powerful figure combining allure with frigidity, dominant in every scene; high tessitura; top B4. ALBERT GREGOR (t); young man, gentle disposition. JAROSLAV PRUS (bar); middle-aged, strong character; top F3.

Lesser Roles. VITEK (t) and KOLETANY (bar), lawyers. JANEK (t). CHRISTA (m-s), Vitek's daughter. HAUK-SENDORF ("operetta" t), diplomat, former lover of Emilia.

Bit Roles. STAGEHAND (bs). TWO SERVANTS (c,c).

Chorus. TTBB. In orchestra pit, briefly toward end.

Orchestra. 4 fl (picc), ob, Eng hrn, 4 cl (bs cl), 3 bsn (cont bsn), 4 hrn, 4 trp, 3 trb, tuba, timp, perc, cel, harp, strings (vla d'amore solo).

Material. UE.

Performances. San Fran. 11.19.66 (Amer prem). Litt. Orch. (Bklyn.): 12.10.67 (conc). NYCO: 11.1.70; 9.2.71 etc.

⚜ Maria Stuarda · Mary Stuart

Music by Gaetano Donizetti (1797–1848). Libretto in Italian by Giuseppe Bardari after Schiller's play. Premiere: Milan, December 30, 1835. Historical drama. Highly melodious; conventional harmonies; set numbers, recitatives, ensembles. Intended for Naples, the opera was banned because of the horror of Maria Cristina, Queen of the Two Sicilies, at the execution of Mary. Donizetti then adapted his music to a new libretto, and as *Buondelmonte*, on the subject of the 12th-century Guelph-Ghibelline rebellion, it was heard in Naples on October 18, 1834. Even at its Milan premiere, the censors intervened after six performances and banned it. Thomas Scherman's performance was the first in America. Setting: Elizabethan England. Three acts, five scenes (145 min).

146

ACT I: Gallery in Westminster Palace (34 min). ACT II: Park of Fotheringay Castle (36 min). ACT III i: Same as I; ii: Mary's apartment in Fotheringay; iii: Anteroom to execution chamber (75 min).

Synopsis. Elizabeth, revealing that she is secretly in love with someone else, nevertheless thinks of marrying the King of France. She discusses Mary with Talbot, who asks her to be merciful, and with Cecil, who reminds her of Mary's perfidy. Leicester enters; it is soon apparent that he is Elizabeth's love. She orders him to be ambassador to France. Talbot gives him a letter from Mary, which impresses him deeply. When Elizabeth demands to see the letter, she realizes that Mary wants both her throne and her lover, but she consents to visit the imprisoned queen. Mary, with Anna, her companion, is in the garden when Leicester announces Elizabeth's arrival. The meeting between the two is electric with suppressed emotions. Mary is at first submissive, as Leicester has advised her, but when Elizabeth accuses her of having connived at the death of her husband Darnley, she furiously calls Elizabeth the bastard of Anne Boleyn. Her fate is sealed. Elizabeth signs Mary's death warrant after some indecision, and tells Leicester, who has spurned her love, that he must witness the death of the woman he loves. In the famous confession scene that stirred Maria Cristina, Mary thinks she sees Darnley's ghost, and tells Talbot that Darnley died because Elizabeth was jealous of him. Cecil announces that Elizabeth has granted Mary one last death wish; she asks that Anna accompany her as far as possible. Leicester bursts in despite Cecil's protests. Mary sings of her love for Leicester, protests her innocence, and avers her devotion to the good of both England and Scotland, then goes in dignity to her death.

Leading Roles. ELISABETTA (m-s or s); needs flexibility; trill; C3 to B4. MARIA (s); both sustained and florid; needs power at extremes of range; trill; several passages with more ornaments optional; Ab2 to B4 (several with F#5 opt). LEICESTER (t); high tessitura; some fioratura; trill; F#2 to B3. TALBOT (bs); F1 to F3. CECIL (bar); Bb1 to F3. ANNA (c); C#3 to A4 (Bb4 and B4 in ensemble).

Chorus. SATTB. Cavaliers, courtiers, hunters, ladies in waiting, officials, guards.

Orchestra. 2 fl, picc, 2 ob, 2 cl, 2 bsn, 4 hrn, 2 trp, 3 trb, timp, perc, harp, strings.

Material. Teatro Donizetti, Bergamo. VS: Gerard, Paris.

Performances. Litt. Orch. (NYC): 11.13.64 (conc—Amer prem). Amer. Op. Soc. (NYC): 12.6.67 (conc). San Fran.: 11.12.71, etc. NYCO: 3.7.72, etc. Chic. Lyr.: 9.21.73. Phila. Lyr.: 2.26.74. Conn. Op. (Hartford): 3.4.74.

🎵 Marina

Music by Emilio Arrieta y Corera (1823–1894). Libretto in Spanish by Francisco Comprodon and Ramos Carrion. Premiere: Madrid, March 16, 1871. Drama (Zarzuela). Conventional harmonies resembling Donizetti,

Rossini; set numbers; ensembles; vocal line melodious, often florid. Preludes to Acts I, III. Setting: Coast of Catalonia, contemporary. Three acts (approx 120 min).

Synopsis. Marina and Jorge, who have grown up as brother and sister, are secretly in love with each other. Marina tests Jorge by accepting a proposal of marriage from Pascual, a local shipbuilder, but insists he obtain Jorge's consent. Jorge, now a captain, returns from his ship with his friend Roque, a sailor, and reluctantly gives his consent to the marriage. Marina has obtained from her friend Alberto a letter her father had left before his death. Pascual intercepts this and, believing it to be from a lover, denounces Marina. Jorge intervenes; the true state of the young couple's affections is revealed, and all ends happily.

Major Roles. MARINA (lyr-col s); needs flexibility; trill; top C5. JORGE (t). PASCUAL (bs). ROQUE (bar); needs flexibility; top F3.

Lesser Roles. TERESA (s). ALBERTO (bar). A SAILOR (bar). A VOICE (bar).

Chorus. SSTTBB. Sailors, fishermen, populace.

Orchestra. (From notations in VS; FS not available.) fl, cl, 4 trp, strings.

Material. FS-P: Union Musical Espanola, Madrid, VS (i, span)*.

✎ Masaniello, or, La Muette de Portici · The Dumb Girl of Portici

Music by Daniel François Auber (1782–1871). Libretto in French by Scribe and Delavigne, based on historical events. Premiere: Paris, February 29, 1828. Drama. Melodious; set numbers; many ensembles; recitatives. Overture. Setting: Naples and Portici, summer of 1647. Five acts (115 min).

ACT I: Gardens of palace of Duke of Arcos, with chapel (30 min). ACT II: Portici, seashore between Naples and Mt. Vesuvius (25 min). ACT III: Public Square in Naples (15 min). ACT IV: Masaniello's hut in Portici (30 min). ACT V: Front of Viceroy's palace in Naples (15 min).

Synopsis. During the period when the people of Naples rose against the Spanish occupation, Alfonso d'Arcos, son of the Spanish Viceroy, has seduced a dumb Neapolitan girl, Fenella, who still loves him in spite of his decision to marry the Spanish princess, Elvira. Fenella disappears, but later returns to seek Elvira's protection. After the royal wedding, Elvira learns that it is her bridegroom who betrayed the helpless girl. Fenella's brother Masaniello and his friend Pietro call the fishermen to arms, both to rescue their country and to revenge Fenella. Alfonso has persuaded Elvira that he loves only her and wishes to redress the wrong he did Fenella. With the best intentions, Alfonso sends Selva, captain of the guard, to fetch Fenella, but the action is misunderstood, and Masaniello's peasant army revolts. Their victories lead to looting and excess bloodshed, which Masaniello deplores. Fenella comes home to her brother's hut, where soon Alfonso and Elvira appear, fugitives. The royal couple's pleas for mercy touch brother and sister, who vow to save them; Masaniello gives them safe conduct in spite of Pietro's objections. Pietro turns against his friend and poisons him. Already insane and dying, Masaniello leads his former followers against a new siege by Alfonso. He is able to save Elvira's life but is himself struck down. Fenella in despair kills herself (in one version leaping from the palace into the Bay of Naples, in another casting herself into the molton lava of the erupting Vesuvius). Note: Auber's celebration of the revolutionary hero (in reality Tommaso Aniello) contains a patriotic duet which is said to have caused the outbreak of Belgian revolution against the Dutch after a performance in Brussels in 1830.

Major Roles. FENELLA (dancer); needs strong mimic talent. ALFONSO (t); high tessitura; D2 to C4. MASANIELLO (t); considerable high tessitura; needs flexibility; D2 to B3. PIETRO (bar); high tessitura; trill; Bb2 to F3. ELVIRA (s); florid; trill; Bb2 to B4.

Lesser Roles. LORENZO, Alfonso's confidant (t). SELVA (bs). EMMA, maid of honor (m-s). BORELLA, MORENO, fishermen (both bs).

Chorus. SATTB. Nobles, dames, fishermen, soldiers. Very important; often divided.

Ballet. In I, III. As elaborate as desired.

Orchestra. 2 fl, picc, 2 cl, 2 or 4 bsn, 4 hrn, 2 trp, 3 trb, tuba, timp, perc, org, strings.

Material. Troupenas, Paris. Map.

🎭 Maskarade · Masquerade

Music by Carl Nielsen (1865–1931). Libretto in Danish by Wilhelm Andersen after Ludvig Holberg. Premiere: Copenhagen, November 11, 1906. Comedy. Set numbers; recitative; many ensembles; conventional harmonies; vocal line melodious. Brief overture; Prelude to Act II. Setting: Copenhagen, spring of 1723. Three acts.

ACT I: A room in Hieronimus's house. ACT II: Street; Hieronimus's house at right; lighted theater in left background; booth for masks in left foreground. ACT III: Large ballroom.

Synopsis. Copenhagen is agog with a new form of entertainment—masked balls. Hieronimus, a middle-class merchant, has denounced these revels, which take place close to his house, as a work of the devil, and flies into a rage when he learns that his son Leander has not only attended one of these orgies but fallen in love with a strange girl there. He has already betrothed his son to the daughter of Herr Leonard from Slagelse, but Leander refuses to marry her. When Leonard arrives, he confesses to the same problem—his daughter has fallen for an unknown. Hieronimus catches his wife Magdelone practicing dance steps, and in a fury bolts his doors and places a guard outside, to keep his wife and son from attending the ball. But the guard Arv is frightened by Leander's servant Henrik, posing as the devil, into confessing a liaison with the cook. Henrik blackmails Arv into letting Leander

149

and Magdelone slip out. Hieronimus follows them, buying a mask and costume to disguise himself, but is soon recognized by Henrik, who persuades a schoolmaster to distract him and get him drunk. In this pleasant state, he misses the ardent courtship of Leander and his mysterious Leonora as well as the flirtation of his wife with a distinguished gentleman. At unmasking time, all is discovered. Of course Leonora is Leonard's daughter and Leander's proper betrothed; Magdelone's partner is discovered to be Leonard himself and even Hieronimus is pacified.

Major Roles. HIERONIMUS (bs); F1 to F3. MAGDELONE (m-s); A2 to F♯4. LEANDER (t); top B♭3. HENRIK (buf bs-bar); some high tessitura; needs flexibility; F♯1 to A3 (fals B♭4 and B4). ARV (t); top A (fals B♭). LEONARD (t or bar); B1 to G3. LEONORA (s); top A♯4.

Lesser Roles. PERNILLE, Leonora's maid (s); A2 to A4. NIGHT WATCHMAN (bs). SERGEANT-MAJOR OF CAVALRY (bar). MASK SELLER (bar). SCHOOLMASTER (bar). FLOWER SELLER (s). STEWARD (bs-bar). DANCE MASTER (mute).

Chorus. SSATTTB. Some solos. Students, officers, young girls, maskers of both sexes.

Ballet. Act III.

Orchestra. 3 fl (picc), 2 ob, 2 cl, 2 bsn, 4 hrn, 3 trp, 3 trb, tuba, timp, perc, harp, strings.

Material. G Sc (Ha). VS (g, da)*.

Performances. St. Paul Op.: 6.23.72 (Amer prem—Tr: Gemi Beni).

🎭 May Night

Music by Nikolai Rimsky-Korsakov (1844–1908). Libretto in Russian by the composer, based on a tale by Gogol. Premiere: St. Petersburg, January 9, 1880. Rustic comedy with supernatural elements. Music takes on color of village life, alternating with exotic expressiveness for water nymph fantasies. Vocal line melodic. Chorus and ballet important. Setting: Village in Little Russia, very long ago. Three acts, four scenes.

ACT I: Village street near lake, with Hanna's cottage. ACT II i: Interior of Mayor's cottage; ii: Street with Village Clerk's house. ACT III: Haunted manor house by shore of lake.

Synopsis. The story has as its center the old theme of the Russalki, water nymphs who are drowned human girls. Such a story is that told by young Levko, son of the town's mayor, to Hanna, the village belle, after an interval of revelry celebrating Whitsuntide. The widowed nobleman who owned the deserted mansion nearby had remarried; jealous of Pannochka, her stepdaughter, the new wife proved to be a witch and drove the girl out. Drowning, she was welcomed by the water nymphs and became their queen. The wicked stepmother was enticed to the lake but escaped by turning herself into a nymph; from then on Pannochka sought to discover her identity by asking the mortals for whom she often danced to guess it. The human story resumes: Levko surprises his own father (who has refused to allow him to marry Hanna) as a lecherous suitor for the girl and resolves on revenge. Through various misadventures, Levko and his father alternately gain the upper hand, but at last the young man returns to his sweetheart. In the midst of his serenade, Pannochka and the nymphs appear; he plays for them as they dance. Then in a game of "raven picking chickens," the stepmother is revealed and the nymphs drag her into the lake. As a reward, Pannochka gives Levko a letter which purports to be from the Governor, ordering the mayor to allow his son to marry Hanna.

Major Roles. LEVKO (t). HANNA (m-s). MAYOR (bs). His fussy SISTER-IN-LAW (c). VILLAGE CLERK (bs). DISTILLER (t). KALENIK, the best dancer in the village; inclined to drunkenness (bar or bs).

Lesser Roles. NYMPHS; STEPMOTHER; HENS; RAVENS (all s).

Chorus. SATB. Youths, maids, guards, nymphs.

Ballet. Folk dances, Act I. Nymphs dance, Act III.

Orchestra. 2 fl, picc, 2 ob, 2 cl, 2 bsn, 4 hrn, 2 trp, 3 trb, tuba, timp, perc, 2 harp, strings. *Stage:* 2 picc, 2 cl, 2 hrn, trb, tamb, string 5-tet.

Material. Pet.

▨ Mefistofele · Mephistopheles

Music by Arrigo Boito (1842–1918). Libretto in Italian by the composer after Goethe. Premiere: Milan, March 5, 1868. Revised version, premiere: Bologna, October 4, 1875. Moralistic drama. Set numbers; conventional harmonies; melodic; vocal line both florid and declamatory. Setting: The realms of space, medieval Germany, and ancient Greece. Prologue, four acts and epilogue (136 min).

Prologue: Nebulous regions of space. ACT I i: Frankfurt-am-Main, Easter Sunday; ii: Faust's study (58 min). ACT II i: A rustic garden; ii: The Brocken, Witches' Sabbath (49 min). ACT III: Prison. ACT IV: Vale of Tempe, Greece. Epilogue: Faust's study (29 min).

Synopsis. Mefistofele boasts that he can turn the virtuous Faust to evil. He appears to Faust and offers him the world and peace in return for his soul. Faust says that if he can experience one moment that he wishes never to depart, he will gladly let Hell's depths engulf him. Mefistofele arranges Margherita's seduction by Faust in her garden, then spirits him off to the Witches' Sabbath. Margherita, abandoned, destroys her child and dies in prison as Faust returns to her. Faust falls in love with Helen of Troy, but having used up all his worldly pleasures, becomes aged again, and resists the Devil's tempting, calling on the Scriptures for salvation. He dies to the triumphant song of a choir of angels, leaving Mefistofele defeated.

Major Roles. MEFISTOFELE (bs); needs great dramatic power as well as vocal agility; Gb1 to F3. FAUST (t); sustained, lyric, some dramatic climaxes; D#2 to B3. MARGHERITA (s); requires acting ability; C3 to B4. MARTA (c); Bb2 to E4. WAGNER (t); E2 to G3. Additional characters in Grecian scene: ELENA (HELEN OF TROY) (s); A2 to Bb4. PANTALIS (c); G2 to C4. NEREO (t);

151

F2 to G3. (Occasionally the final three characters double with Margherita, Marta, and Wagner.)

Chorus. SATB, children. Heavenly host, cherubs (24 boys), mystic chorus, penitents, strollers, bowmen, hunters, students, plebeians, villagers, bourgeois, witches, warlocks, Greek dancers, sirens, gilded ones, warriors. Many and varied supers, including a Fool, a Bandit, the Principal Elector, the Executioner, etc.

Ballet. Elaborate. Act I i: general populace. Act II ii: witches and warlocks. Act IV: Grecian.

Orchestra. 3 fl (3 picc), 2 ob, Eng hrn, 2 cl, bs cl, 2 bsn, 4 hrn, 2 trp, 3 trb, bs tuba, timp, perc, 2 harp, organ, strings. (NYCO Orchestra: 2 fl, picc, 2 ob (Eng hrn), 2 cl (bs cl), 2 bsn, 4 hrn, 2 trp, 3 trb, tuba, timp, perc (2), strings. *Stage:* Eb cl, 2 cl, pist, 4 hrn, 2 Flügelhrn, tam-tam, 3 trb, bs tuba, dr, bells, cym, acc, Fogliello, genis. NYCO uses 4 trp, 2 trb, 2 hrn.

Material. Bel.

Performances. Phila. Lyr.: 1965–1966. Amer. Op. Soc. (NYC): 1966 (conc). Hartt. Coll. (Hartford): 2.26.69. Aspen: 7.24.69. NYCO: 2.21.69; 3.12.70; 9.9.70; 10.12.71; 3.1.72, etc. N. Or. Philh.: 10.22.70 (conc). San Diego: 9.7.73. Honolulu Sym.: 10.7.73.

🎭 Melusine

Music by Aribert Reimann (1936–   ). Libretto in German by Claus H. Henneberg after the play by Yvan Goll. Premiere: Berlin, April 29, 1971. Modernized fairy tale. Atonal; extremely dissonant; highly expressive use of orchestra; some aleatoric passages; vocal lines very difficult; declamatory; *Sprechstimme* and dialogue; considerable melisma. Setting: France, before World War I. Four acts, eight scenes (approx 91 min).

ACT I: A modest villa near a forest. ACT II i: In the forest; ii: Near a lake in the forest. ACT III i: In front of the castle; ii: A hall in the castle. ACT IV i: A road in the forest; ii: Bedroom in the castle; iii: The villa.

Synopsis. Melusine, although married to Oleander, a businessman, leads a dreamy, virginal life centered in the forest, where she sometimes even spends nights. Her husband complains to her mother, Mme Lapérouse (with whom he has evidently had a previous liaison), but she counsels patience. The existence of the forest is threatened when it is bought by Count Lusignan, who wishes to build a hunting castle there. A surveyor arrives, but Melusine so bewitches him that he falls to his death from a wall. Melusine seeks the aid of her mentor, Pythia, a wood spirit disguised as a fortune-teller, who, in order to save the woods, gives Melusine a magic fishtail which will make her irresistible to all men. But she herself must remain virginal, Pythia warns. The charm takes effect on a mason and an architect. The workers refuse to continue in the haunted place, but the castle is eventually built in spite of Melusine's efforts. At a reception in the new edifice, the Count and Melusine fall in love, spied on by the Ogre, a servant of Pythia. The architect tries to

152

warn the Count about Melusine, but he will not listen. Now Melusine has lost her innocence; the wood is doomed. Pythia sets a fire to destroy it and the castle, and Melusine rushes into the flames to save her lover. Both, however, are burned to death. Melusine's body is carried to her home, where Oleander is forced to recognize her as the Count's lover.

Major Roles. MELUSINE (col s); extremely difficult; high tessitura and wide skips; C3 to E5. OLEANDER, her husband (t); E2 to A3. MME LAPÉROUSE, her mother (m-s); B♭2 to G4. PYTHIA (char c); A2 to G♯4. COUNT VON LUSIGNAN (lyr bar); C2 to G♯3. SURVEYOR (bs-bar); A1 to E♭3. MASON (bs); A1 to E3. ARCHITECT (t); considerable difficult melisma; C2 to B3. OGRE (bs); G1 to F♯3.

Lesser Roles. FOREMAN (sp). WORKER (sp). SECRETARY (sp). THREE MEN. THREE WOMEN (guests).

Orchestra. fl (picc), alto fl, ob, Eng hrn, cl (E♭ cl), bs cl, bsn, cont bsn, 2 hrn, 2 trp, 2 trb, timp, cel, harp, strings (4.4.3.3.2).

Material. Bel (Sch).

Performances. Santa Fe: 8.21.72 (Amer prem—Eng).

✍ The Midsummer Marriage

Music by Sir Michael Tippett (1905–   ). Libretto by the composer. Premiere: London, January 27, 1955. Comedy-fantasy. Melodic; continuous texture embodying set numbers; complex orchestration, highly chromatic yet not atonal; vocal lines difficult, wide intervals, considerable melisma. Brief prelude. Setting: A wood, the present. Three acts.

ACT I: A wood, with group of buildings at back, a temple in the center, ascending stairway at right, descending stairs to heavy gates at left. ACT II: Set is turned to right, centering descending steps and gates. ACT III: Same as I, evening and night.

Synopsis. In the theme, the gradual self-knowledge of two pairs of young people, one spiritual, the other worldly, references to *Die Frau ohne Schatten* and *Die Zauberflöte*, as well as *Die Entführung aus dem Serail*, are obvious. On a midsummer day, Mark and Jennifer meet in a wood, where they confront a band of mysterious beings, the Ancients, who emerge from a temple. Jennifer, unrealistically high-minded, is partially transformed to Athena, and led up the right-hand staircase. Mark, earthy and somewhat vulgar, is conducted downward and becomes Dionysus. Later they compare experiences, and meet halfway between the ideal and the real. Meanwhile, the other young couple—Bella, secretary to King Fisher, Jennifer's materialistic father, and Jack, an employee, learn their better selves. King Fisher is punished for his harsh treatment of his daughter; there is a Ritual Ballet which embodies earth in the mating rituals of hound and hare, water (fish and otter) and air (bird and hawk). In the last act, the clairvoyant Sosostris reveals the meaning of life in a ritual dance of purification and fertility (fire) led by Mark and Jennifer. They are ready for marriage.

Major Roles. MARK (t); needs great flexibility for melisma; A1 to B♭3. JENNIFER (s); sustained; some high tessitura; trill; melisma; B♭2 to B♭4 (touches C5; two C5 with opt F4 and G♯4). KING FISHER (bar); high tessitura; needs flexibility; A1 (touches G1) to F♯3. BELLA, his secretary (s); difficult florid passages; C3 to C5. JACK, a mechanic (t); needs flexibility; C2 to A3 (one C4 with F3 opt). SOSOSTRIS (c); both sustained and florid; G2 to F4. PRIEST (He-Ancient) (bs); G1 to E3 (one F3 with F2 opt). PRIESTESS (She-Ancient) (m-s); B2 to F♯4.

Bit Roles. DANCING MAN (t); from chorus. HALF-TIPSY MAN (bar from chorus).

Chorus. SSAATTBB. Very important and difficult, often divided. Mark's and Jennifer's friends. Dancers attendant on Ancients (can be ballet).

Ballet. Very important. Act II: The earth in autumn; the waters in winter; the air in spring. Act III: Ritual fire dance.

Orchestra. 2 fl (picc), 2 ob, 2 cl, 2 bsn, 4 hrn, 2 trp, 3 trb, timp, perc, cel, harp, strings.

Material. Bel (Sch). VS*.

🎵 A Midsummer Night's Dream

Music by Benjamin Britten (1913–   ). Libretto by the composer and Peter Pears adapted from Shakespeare. Premiere: Aldeburgh, June 11, 1960. Romantic comedy. Melodious vocal line over complicated orchestra. No overture. Some dialogue. Setting: The palace of Theseus and the Wood, imaginary times. Three acts, four scenes (140 min).

ACT I: The Wood, twilight. ACT II: The Wood, night. ACT III i: The Wood, early morning; ii: Theseus's palace.

Synopsis. Shakespeare's play is followed closely.

Major Roles. OBERON, King of the Fairies (counter t or c); G2 to C♯5. TITANIA, his Queen (col s); florid; trill; C3 to C♯5. HIPPOLITA, Amazon Queen, betrothed to Theseus (c); B♭2 to F♭4. THESEUS, Duke of Athens (bs); F1 to E3. LYSANDER (t); B♭1 to B♭3. DEMETRIUS (bar); A1 to F♯3 (one G3 with C3 opt). HERMIA (m-s); A2 to G♭4 (one G4 with G3 opt). HELENA (s); B♭2 to B♭4. BOTTOM, the weaver (also PYRAMUS in play) (bs-bar); E1 (E2 opt) to F3 (B fals). PUCK (sp); acrobatic or dancing role.

Lesser Roles. QUINCE, carpenter (bs). FLUTE, bellows mender (t); some extended passages as THISBY in play, top B♭3. SNUG, joiner (bs); one difficult passage as LION in play. SNOUT, tinker (t). STARVELING, tailor (bar). PEASEBLOSSOM, COBWEB, MUSTARDSEED, MOTH (treb).

Chorus. Fairies (treb or s).

Orchestra. 2 fl (picc), ob (Eng hrn), 2 cl, bsn, 2 hrn, trp, trb, perc (2), 2 harp, harpsichord, cel, strings. *Stage:* sopranino recorders, small cym, wd bl.

Material. B & H. StS*. VS*.

⚜ The Mines of Sulphur

Music by Richard Rodney Bennett (1936–   ). Libretto in English by Beverly Cross. Commissioned by Sadler's Wells Opera. Premiere: London, February 24, 1965. Melodrama. Mostly atonal, with occasional twelve-tone passages, occasionally lyrical; voice patterned after speech. Brief prelude. Short overture to Act II. Setting: Hall of a manor house in the West County of England, about 200 years ago. Three acts (approx 101 min).

Synopsis. Braxton, the owner of the rundown mansion, is murdered by Bonconnion, an army deserter, who is in league with the gypsy Rosalind. Tovey, a tramp, has joined the reckless couple, who plan to escape to the New World with the jewels and finery belonging to Braxton's former wife. Rosalind dresses herself in a sumptuous gown, and the trio celebrates. A troupe of raffish actors arrive, headed by Sherrin (who can double for Braxton). They agree to give a play in return for shelter, and suggest "The Mines of Sulphur," inspired by Otello: "Dangerous conceits are in their own nature poisonous." The players prepare. Fenney jeers at Leda, who "once played Juliet." She storms out, followed by all but Jenny, who has ascended to the balcony. Rosalind enters and tries on Jenny's cloak; Jenny teaches her a song. As they exit, Trim appears with Boncannion's uniform, which he had discarded in favor of richer raiment.

The play shows a Count (Sherrin) who marries a young girl Haidee (Jenny), but neglects her, so that she turns to his servant Hugo (Fenney) for love. The Count intends to murder them, but cannot strike his wife, who takes the knife and bids Hugo kill her husband. At this point, Rosalind and Tovey, shaken with fear at the parallel to their own murder, interrupt the play. Jenny is ill and taken to Rosalind's room. Tooley (a player) arrogantly confronts the murderous trio with their real identities. Bonconnion decides to burn the house and the actors with it. He sends for Jenny, kisses her, and is about to stab her when she tells him about another company that had played here long ago and left behind them the plague brought from London. She shows him a black spot on her breast. The players go, leaving the trio, all infected, to cry for mercy from God.

Major Roles. BRAXTON-SHERRIN-COUNT (bar); dramatic and sustained, also needs flexibility; wide skips; A♭1 to F3. ROSALIND (m-s); B♭2 to B4. BONCONNION (t); dramatic, flexible, difficult intervals, some high tessitura; B1 to B3. TOVEY (bar); B♭1 to E3. JENNY-HAIDEE (s); needs flexibility; B♭2 to B4. LEDA–MRS. TRAXEL, Haidee's mother (m-s); A2 to F♯4 (A4 opt). FENNEY-HUGO (t); D2 to A3.

Lesser Roles. TOOLEY-FLUNKEY (bar); B♭1 to F♯3. TRIM, a player (mute). *Orchestra*. 2 fl (picc), alto fl, 2 ob, 2 cl, bs cl, 2 bsn, 4 hrn, 2 trp B♭, 3

155

trb, tuba, timp, xyl, glock, vib, piano, clavicembalo, cel, harp, perc (3), strings. *Stage*: hrn.

Material. Pr (UE). VS (e, g)*.

Performances. Juill. (NYC): 1.17.68 (Amer prem). UCLA: 6.5.70.

🎵 Mireille

Music by Charles François Gounod (1818–1893). Libretto in French by Michel Carré, after the poem by Frédéric Mistral. Premiere: Paris (Théâtre Lyrique), March 19, 1864. Revised same year in three acts with happy ending and additional coloratura aria for Mireille, but original version generally produced. Folk tragedy. Highly melodious; recitative and set numbers; flavor of Provence in local dances and imitation of musette; intricate ensembles and choruses. Overture; brief prelude to Act III. Setting: Provence, in and near Arles. Five acts, seven scenes (approx 150 min).

ACT I: Ramon's farm. ACT II: The arena at Arles. ACT III i: The Valley of Hell; ii: The Rhone. ACT IV i: Ramon's farm; ii: The Crau Desert. ACT V: The Church of the Saints of the Sea.

Synopsis. Mireille, daughter of the wealthy farmer Ramon, loves a poor young basket maker, Vincent, in spite of her father's choice of Ourrias, the bull tamer, as her husband. The benevolent sorceress Taven warns Mireille of impending misfortune, and the girl tells Vincent that if evil befalls them she will meet him at the chapel of the Saint-Maries. She laughs at Ourrias's rough importunities. Vincent's father, Ambroise, introduces his son and daughter Vincinette, and asks Ramon's advice about the love-sick Vincent. Learning that Mireille is the object of Vincent's devotion, Ramon swears that he shall never have her. Ourrias confronts Vincent in the fearful Val d'Enfer, strikes him, and leaves him for dead, growing more and more panic-stricken as he flees. He calls for the Boatman to ferry him over the Rhone, but the Boatman and supernatural creatures cause the boat to be swallowed up in angry waves. Meanwhile, Mireille, envying the carefree life of a wandering shepherd, is told by Vincinette that Taven has rescued Vincent, and goes to join him. Wandering through the desert of the Crau, she becomes crazed with heat and barely manages to reach the Saint-Maries. She dies of exhaustion in her lover's arms, as her father forgives her and a voice from heaven welcomes her.

Major Roles. MIREILLE (lyr-col s); needs flexibility, trill; D3 to C5 (one Db5). In added Valse, top D5 with trill; one E5. VINCENT (lyr t); considerable high tessitura; D2 to Bb3. OURRIAS (bar); needs strength; some high tessitura; C2 (one A1, A2 opt) to F♯3 (many F3's). RAMON (bs); needs command of wide range; G1 to E3. TAVEN (m-s); C3 to F♯4.

Lesser Roles. VINCINETTE (s); D♯3 to G4. AMBROISE (bs); A1 to E3. ANDRELOUN, a shepherd (m-s or t); D3 to G4 or D2 to G3. CLEMENCE (s); D3 to A4. BOATMAN (LE PASSEUR) (bs); Eb2 to C♯3. AN ARLESIEN (bar); Eb2 to D3. CELESTIAL VOICE (s); A3 to A4.

Chorus. SSTTBB. Farmers, supernatural beings, pilgrims, church choir.

Ballet. Peasant dance (farandole) in Act II; possible ballet in Act III ii (supernatural creatures around the Boatman).

Orchestra. 2 fl (picc), 2 ob (Eng hrn), 2 cl, 2 bsn, 4 hrn, 2 trp, 3 trb, tuba, timp, perc (3—includes tamb Provence), harp, strings. *Stage*: organ, trp.

Material. Pet (Chou). VS (f)*. Map. Ka. B & H* (i, e).

Performances. Manh. Sch. (NYC): 5.10.63.

🎵 Miss Julie

Music by Ned Rorem (1923–   ). Libretto in English by Kenward Elmslie based on the play by August Strindberg. Commissioned by New York City Opera and Ford Foundation. Premiere: New York City Opera, November 4, 1965. Drama. Melodic, some set numbers, recitative. Sophisticated vocal line of principals contrasts with simple lighter music for incidental characters. Brief prelude. Setting: a country estate in Sweden, midsummer night in the 1880's. Stage should show three parts: garden, facade and door of manor, and kitchen with doors leading to Christine's and John's rooms. Two acts (58 and 50 min).

Synopsis. Christine, the cook, is singing to herself, but is interrupted by a band of maskers accompanied by Miss Julie, the Count's daughter, who teases her fiancé Niels, commanding him to kiss her boot. He breaks off the engagement in disgust. In the kitchen Christine and her fiancé, John, the Count's valet, discuss Miss Julie's desperate mood. Miss Julie joins them and demands that John dance with her. They flirt in French while Christine pretends to sleep, and eventually retires. Each recounts a dream of frustration; John confesses he has loved Julie since boyhood. When the revelers approach, John draws Julie into his room. The revelers taunt them from the kitchen.

John awakes the revelers, who stumble out, then tells Julie that they can escape if she will lend him money. But she has none, and they quarrel. At last he orders her to prepare for the trip and find the money somehow. Christine enters, and soon realizes the situation, threatening to leave. Julie returns with money stolen from her father's desk. When she insists on taking her canary with them, he kills it. Christine leaves for church, refusing to help the now hysterical Julie, who tries to slash her wrists with John's razor. A bell signals the Count's return, and John is reduced to servility. Miss Julie walks into the garden to take her own life.

Major Roles. MISS JULIE (s); difficult melodic line; sustained; wide skips; constant use of extremes of range; some melisma; G2 (one F♯2 spoken) to C5. JOHN (bs-bar); needs flexibility; wide skips; high and considerable low tessitura; E♯1 to G♭3. CHRISTINE (m-s); G2 to A4. NIELS (t); C2 to F3.

Lesser Roles. WILDCAT BOY (s or boy s); needs flexibility; G2 to F4. YOUNG COUPLE (s and t); girl has D♭5 (D♭4 opt). STABLEBOY in death's-head mask (bs).

Chorus. SATB. S fairly difficult. May be omitted in Act II.

Orchestra. 2 fl (picc), 2 ob (Eng hrn), 2 cl (alto sax), 2 bsn, 3 hrn, 2 trp, 2 trb, timp, perc, harp, strings.

Material. B & H. VS*.

Performances. Ball St. Univ. (Muncie): 6.30.66.

⚑ Monna Vanna

Music by Henri Février (1875–1957). Libretto in French after the play by Maeterlinck. Premiere: Paris, January 13, 1909. Poetic drama. Continuous texture; vocal line patterned after speech; no wide skips. Overture with chorus; prelude to Act II; long prelude to Act III ("Guido's Anguish"); long interlude between Acts III and IV. Setting: Italy, end of 15th century. Four acts (approx 180 min).

ACT I: Palace of Guido Colonna at Pisa. ACT II: Prinzivalle's tent. ACT III: Large room and terrace in Guido's palace. ACT IV: A cell.

Synopsis. Guido of Pisa, besieged by the ruler of Florence, his city starving, waits the return of his father Marco, who has gone as a messenger to Prinzivalle camped nearby. The old man enters and relates that Prinzivalle will send reinforcements, food, and arms on one condition: Guido's wife Vanna shall visit him that evening, unclothed save for a mantle. Guido scoffs at the idea that his loyal wife would agree, but the old man says she will go. Vanna herself appears to reaffirm her decision. Guido raves, pleads, and finally casts her off as she goes to her infamous mission.

Prinzivalle is approached by Trivulzio, who accuses him of treachery to Florence in sparing Pisa. Prinzivalle shows him his own intercepted letters, wherein he has reviled Prinzivalle, and orders Trivulzio imprisoned, though sparing his life. When Vanna enters, he overwhelms her with professions of his love, for it appears he has loved her since they were children together. She claims to love Guido still. But as noise heralds the approach of the Florentines, she resolves that Prinzivalle shall come with her to Pisa. Voices from Pisa in the distance hail Vanna as their deliverer. Guido, determined to take revenge on Prinzivalle, curses his father and will not believe Vanna's protestations of innocence. He orders Prinzivalle imprisoned, whereupon Vanna, realizing his vindictive nature, employs a strategem to free Prinzivalle. Reversing herself, she claims Prinzivalle did indeed dishonor her, and demands that he be immured in a deep dungeon. She alone has an extra key to this cell, and as soon as possible, leads him to freedom.

Major Roles. GIOVANNA (known as MONNA VANNA) (dram s); A2 to Bb4; one B4 (G4 opt); touches Db5 on a cry; one Cb5 (Gb4 opt). PRINZIVALLE (t); D#2 to Bb3. GUIDO COLONNA (bar or lyr bs); G1 to F#3. MARCO (bs); A1 to Eb3. TRIVULZIO (bs); Bb1 to C3.

Lesser Roles. VEDIO, page (bar). BORSO (t). TORELLO (bs or bar).

Chorus. SATB. Often divided. Lords, soldiers, peasants, men and women.

158

Orchestra. 3 fl, 3 ob, 3 cl, 2 bsn, 4 hrn, 3 trp, 3 trb, tuba, timp, perc, harp, cel, strings.

Material. Pr (Heu).

▣ Montezuma

Music by Roger Sessions (1896–   ). Libretto in English by Giuseppe Antonio Borgese, based on the record by Bernal Diaz del Castillo of the Spanish conquest of Mexico. Premiere: Berlin Deutscher Oper, April 19, 1964. Historical tragedy. Extremely difficult, dense orchestral texture, intricate twelve-tone idiom; composer specifies that vocal line, except for some declamatory passages, should be expressive bel canto with rhythms according to natural English speech. Text is elaborate, archaic, often obscure. No overture; several interludes; long Prelude to Act II with chorus. Highly difficult demands on all performers. Setting: Mexico, from March 1519 to June 1520. Three acts, ten scenes (approx 150 min).

ACT I i: Open space on Mexican coast; ii: Villa Rica on Gulf Coast; iii: Marketplace of Tlaxcala. ACT II i: Causeway across Lake Texcoco to city of Tenochtitlan, at back curtain suggesting floating gardens and houses at outskirts; ii: Curtain rises to show "Zocalo," Great Plaza of Tenochtitlan, at right "skull rock," at back snow-capped volcano; iii: Gardens of Montezuma. ACT III i: Palace of Axayaca in outer circle of Tenochtitlan, loggia on main floor, at back square is visible, prepared for auto-da-fé; ii: Quiet corner quarter between palaces and gardens; iii: Great Hall of fortress; iv: Hall on upper floor of palace, showing roof surrounded by crenellated parapets.

Synopsis. Bernal the Elder is discovered writing before an inner curtain; the main stage is the Mexican coast. He recalls Hernán Cortez's arrival and watches his own young self help plant the crucifix in alien soil. His comments are interspersed with the action. Cortez the Conqueror chooses Malinche, the Aztec slave girl, as his own prize; she later becomes the intermediary between Montezuma's forces and the invaders. Montezuma is held hostage. When Cortez goes to the coast to capture the man sent to arrest him, he leaves the Aztecs under the worst possible governor, the firebrand Pedro de Alvarado, who soon provokes the slaves to revolt. In spite of Cortez, Montezuma is stoned to death by his own people, and twilight falls on the ancient kingdom.

Major Roles. BERNAL DIAZ DEL CASTILLO THE ELDER (bs); F1 (one E1) to F3. HERNAN CORTEZ (bar); extremely high tessitura; Ab1 to G3. PEDRO DE ALVARADO (t); needs flexibility; C2 to B3. MALINCHE (s); G#2 to B4 (one C5). MONTEZUMA (t); C2 to B3. BERNAL DIAZ DEL CASTILLO THE YOUNGER (t); Db2 to Bb3. CUANUHTEMOC, Aztec noble (bar); high tessitura; Bb1 to G3. AGUILAR (t); A#1 to Ab3.

Lesser Roles. (Some doubling possible.) FREY OLMEDO DE LA MERCED, Conquistidore (bs); B1 to E3. CACAMATZIN, Lord of Texcoco (t), Act III. NETZAHUALCOYOTL, old priest (bs), Act II. TEUHTLILLI, ambassador of Mon-

159

tezuma (t), sings only in native language, Act I. SOLDIER OF CORTEZ' ARMY (t, not seen).

Bit Roles (several may be doubled). THREE CONQUISTIDORES (t, bar, bs), Act I. VETERAN (bar), Act III. DEACON (t), Act III. SEVEN INDIAN GIRLS (s), Act I. TWO INDIAN PRINCESSES, daughters of Montezuma: ITLAMAL (s), CUAXIMATL (m-s), Act II. LORD OF TACUBA (t), Act II. CACIQUE OF CEMPOALLA (t), Act I. TWO PASSERSBY (bar), Act III. FOUR DRUMMERS, Act III. THE NEGRO GUIDELA (high bar; not seen), Act III.

Supers. CUITALPIROC, ambassador of Montezuma; Spanish Conquistidores and soldiers; Aztec nobles, warriors, priests, slaves, citizens; Indian sacrificial victims; Tlaxcalan warriors.

Chorus. SAATTBB. Very difficult; extremes of range; wide skips; tricky rhythms. Spanish soldiers, men of Narvaez, Aztecs; invisible above stage as Nephelai (Clouds).

Ballet. Ritualistic, some masks.

Orchestra. picc, 2 fl (picc), 2 ob, Eng hrn, cl Eb, 2 cl Bb, bs cl, 2 bsn, cont bsn, 4 hrn, 4 trp, 3 trb, tuba, timp, piano, cel, perc (6), harp, 2 xyl, marimba, vib, strings, teponaztli (Mexican drum), conch shells, rattles. *Stage*: Eb cl, Chinese dr, Guiro, claves, maracas, tam-tam.

Production Difficulties. Scenic changes; large crowds onstage; arrows and stones thrown at Montezuma; chorus of clouds.

Material. Mar.

Performances. Univ. of Mich. (partial): 11.71.

▨ Moses und Aron · Moses and Aaron

Music by Arnold Schönberg (1874–1951). Libretto in German by the composer, based on the Old Testament. Concert premiere: 1954; stage premiere: Zurich, June 6, 1957. Religious drama. Twelve-tone harmony; vocal line partly patterned after speech (*Sprechstimme*), declamatory, occasionally melodic. Continuous texture. Extremely difficult in all phases: orchestral, vocal, chorus, production. Setting: Egypt in 17th Dynasty; Valley of Canaan. Two acts (Schönberg did not finish the third act, but left a dramatic outline which can be played.) (Two acts, approx 120 min).

ACT I: The Exodus. ACT II: In the mountains.

Synopsis. The opera is a spiritual argument between Moses and his brother Aron on the nature of God. God speaks to Moses out of the burning bush, and he brings the message to the skeptical and inconstant people and performs various symbolic miracles. The Israelites become impatient at Moses' forty-day sojourn on the mountain of revelation and fall into sin. Aron tries to prevent their defection, but finally gives in and restores former gods in the form of a golden calf. The people worship the idol in three orgies, each wilder and bloodier than the last, till the stage is an abbatoir of animal and human sacrifice. Moses returns, and in terrible anger, destroys the calf with a curse. Aron remonstrates, distorting the situation because he does

160

not understand Moses' abstract vision of God, whereupon Moses smashes the tablets he has brought down from the mountain and cries "O Word, Word, Word that I lack!" Most performances end here. The third act presents Moses confronting Aron, now a prisoner. Moses draws clear distinctions between God's ideality and Aron's misrepresentations but Aron cannot defend himself. He is given freedom, but falls dead, signifying that the arbitrary bondage and falsehood he represents are self-destructive in the presence of the absolute truth and freedom signified by Moses.

Major Roles. MOSES (bs-bar); mainly *Sprechstimme*; must be able to sing accurate pitches occasionally and be rhythmically exact; F♯1 to C♯3 (spoken G3). ARON (t); pitch accuracy imperative; needs great flexibility in all registers; B1 to B3.

Lesser Roles. YOUNG MAIDEN (s); D3 to B4. FEMALE INVALID (c); A♭2 to F4. YOUNG MAN (t); F♯2 to A♭3. NAKED YOUTH (t); F♯2 to B3. MAN (bar); A♭1 to E3 (also *Sprechstimme*); EPHRAIMITE (bar); F2 to E3. PRIEST (bs); G1 to D♯3 (F3 with opt F2). FOUR NAKED VIRGINS (2 s, 2 c). VOICE FROM BURNING BUSH (s, boys, c, t, bar, bs).

Roles from Chorus. Beggars (6–8 c, 6–8 bs). Several elderly persons (t). Seventy Elders, one-third singers (bs); the balance supers. Twelve tribal leaders (1st and 2nd t, 1st and 2nd bs). Six solo voices in orchestra (s, m-s, c, t, bar, bs).

Chorus. SSAATTBB. Extremely difficult and important. Many supers.

Ballet. As elaborate as possible.

Orchestra. 3 fl (picc), 3 ob (Eng hrn), E♭ cl, 2 cl B♭ and A, bs cl B♭ and A, 2 bsn, cont bsn, 4 hrn F, 3 trp C, 3 trb, tuba, timp, perc (large variety including glock, xyl, flexatone), harp, piano, cel, 2 mandolin, strings. *Stage*: picc, fl, cl, Eng hrn, hrn, 2 trp, 2 trb, timp, bs dr, tamb, high and low gongs, cym, xyl, piano, 2 mandolin, 2 guit.

Material. Bel (Sch). VS (g, e)*. Tr: Allen Forte.

Performances. Bost. Op. Group (Op. Co. of Bost.): 11.30.66 (Amer prem). Chic. Sym. (conc): 11.11.71; in NYC: 11.20.71.

✠ The Most Important Man

Music by Gian-Carlo Menotti (1911–   ). Libretto in English by the composer. Premiere: New York City Opera, March 7, 1971. Revised for Trieste, January 17, 1972. Drama. Melodic; conventional harmonies; set numbers in tightly knit continuous texture; important ensembles. Setting: Colonial Africa, 20th century. Three acts, ten scenes (163 min).

ACT I i: Dr. Arnek's laboratory; ii: The same, next morning; iii: Dr. Arnek's living room; iv: The same, a week later; v: Dr. Arnek's laboratory (60 min). ACT II i: Conference room in nation's capital, two years later; ii: Dr. Arnek's living room, next day; iii: The same, some days later; iv: The same, a few days later (44 min). ACT III i: Dr. Arnek's laboratory, evening of same day; ii: A swamplike area on outskirts of city (19 min).

161

Synopsis. Toimé Ukamba, a promising protégé of the famous scientist Dr. Otto Arnek, discovers a formula which will change the world and thus becomes the "most important man." But any success he may hope for is thwarted by the cruelty and indifference of the "white state," and by his decision to run away with the doctor's daughter Cora. Meanwhile, Dr. Arnek's wife and his assistant Eric plot against him. Ukamba dies in disgrace.

Major Roles. TOIMÉ UKAMBA (dram bar); high tessitura; many Ab's. DR. OTTO ARNEK (dram t); forceful character and voice; top A3. LEONA, his wife (m-s); needs strength for taxing role; top Ab4. CORA, his daughter (lyr s); top Bb4. MRS. AGEBDA AKAWASI, native leader (dram s); needs strength at top of range; many Bb's.

Lesser Roles. ERIC RUPERT (bar). PROF. CLEMENT (t). PROF. RISSELBERG (t). PROF. BOLENTAL (bar). PROF. HISSELMAN (bar). PROF. GRIPPEL (bs). UNDERSECRETARY OF STATE (buff bs).

Orchestra. 2 fl, picc, 2 ob, Eng hrn, 2 cl, bs cl, 2 bsn, cont bsn, 3 trp, 3 trb, 4 hrn, tuba, harp, piano, organ, timp, perc (2), strings.

Material. G Sc.

☙ Mourning Becomes Electra

Music by Marvin David Levy (1932–   ). Libretto in English by Henry Butler, based on Eugene O'Neill's play, itself based on Aeschylus's tragedy. Commissioned by the Metropolitan Opera Ass'n under grants from the Ford Foundation, John Simon Guggenheim Memorial Foundation, Mrs. Henry L. Moses, and Christian Humann. Premiere: Metropolitan Opera, March 17, 1969. Drama. Complicated continuous textures, set numbers embedded. Vocal line lyric, often patterned after speech, often highly melodic, with florid passages. Prelude; interludes. Setting: New England, 1865. Three acts, seven scenes (153 min).

ACT I i: Exterior of the Mannon house on the outskirts of a small New England seaport town; ii: The Mannon master bedroom (48 min). ACT II i: Interior of the Mannon house; ii: Aboard Brant's clipper ship in Boston harbor; iii: Outside the Mannon house (60 min). ACT III i: Interior of the Mannon house; ii: Outside the Mannon house (45 min).

Synopsis. The O'Neill trilogy has been greatly compressed, and only a few lines of the text retained, although the subtitles for the acts remain the same: "The Homecoming," "The Hunted," and "The Haunted." Doom hangs over the Mannon family from the first moment we realize that Christine has no real welcome for her returning husband, General Ezra Mannon, an inexpressive man and too long absent at the war. Christine has taken as a lover sea captain Adam Brant, the illegitimate son of Ezra's brother. Lavinia, her daughter, is being courted by Adam as a blind, but the ugly truth is soon revealed. Mannon suffers a heart attack, and is given poison instead of medicine by Christine. Lavinia discovers this and plans revenge. With her brother Orin, who has returned wounded from the war, she visits Brant's ship and

162

spies on a rendezvous between the captain and her mother. Orin kills Brant with a dagger. Lavinia reveals the murder to her mother next morning, whereupon Christine shoots herself. Lavinia calmly tells Jed, the old servant, to inform the family doctor that grief for her husband caused Christine's suicide. Orin is overcome by his own guilt feelings, but Lavinia consoles him, promises to love him and to take him away. They are gone for a year; when they return, Helen and Peter Niles greet them. Helen hopes to marry Orin, while Peter finds Lavinia newly receptive to his love. Orin sees them embracing, and sends Peter away in a jealous rage. Then he threatens Lavinia with an envelope that contains the Mannon history, and sends Helen away. At last his latent incestuous love for his sister manifests itself, but only horrifies Lavinia. Overcome with his conflicting emotions, Orin shoots himself. Lavinia tries to recover, and to draw Peter to her, but her energy and will are sapped, and she retires into the darkened Mannon house, a prisoner of her own and her family's guilt.

Major Roles. All are difficult, with sustained dramatic passages, extremes of range, florid passages; all need extraordinary dramatic ability. CHRISTINE MANNON (dram s). LAVINIA MANNON (spin or dram s). JED (bs). ADAM BRANT (dram bar). PETER NILES (lyr bar). HELEN NILES (lyr s). GENERAL EZRA MANNON (bs-bar). ORIN MANNON (high bar or t).

Supers. Townspeople, soldiers, sailors, dockhands, servants, fieldworkers.

Orchestra. 3 fl (picc), 3 ob (Eng hrn), 3 cl (bs cl, sax), 3 bsn (cont bsn), 4 hrn, 3 trp, 3 trb, tuba, harp, organ, piano, cel, elec guit, perc, strings.

Material. B & H.

Performances. Dortmund, Germany, November 1969.

🎼 My Heart's in the Highlands

Music by Jack Beeson (1921–   ). Libretto in English by the composer, based on the play by William Saroyan. Premiere: National Educational Television: March 18, 1970. Drama. Melodic; vocal line patterned after speech. Continuous texture with several set numbers embedded. Brief interludes for scene changes. Television production was continuous, but division into three acts is possible. Setting: Fresno, California, August and November 1914 (105 min).

Scenes: A house on San Benito Avenue; Mr. Kosak's grocery; Living room of the house.

Synopsis. In their modest California home, Johnny, his father Ben Alexander, an unsuccessful poet, and his grandmother, who speaks and sings only Armenian, live precariously, getting a little food on credit from the reluctant grocer Kosak. One day they are visited by an old actor, MacGregor, who has escaped from the old people's home, and whose strong character, virtuosity on the cornet, and insistence that his heart is in the highlands wins the family and neighbors, who bring gifts of food. But after a few weeks, Philip Carmichael comes to take MacGregor back. The family misses

163

him; life grows harder as winter draws on. Henry, a newspaper seller, comes by, teaches Johnny to whistle and leaves a free paper, from which Johnny's father learns about the war in Europe. Some of his poems are rejected by the *Atlantic Monthly*; he tries to reassure himself by reading them aloud. His despair is deepened when Mr. Cunningham, a real estate man, brings a young couple to view the house, on which three months' rent is due. Ben gives his poems to Kosak in lieu of money. The grocer reads them (actually taken from other Saroyan works) to his young daughter Esther, who is Johnny's friend. Johnny steals fruit. The family barricades the door, fearing the farmer whose fruit was stolen, but joyfully opens the door as MacGregor reappears. His cornet draws neighbors, who again bring offerings of food. Esther gives Johnny some coins she has saved as payment for the poems. MacGregor obliges the neighbors with a grand reading from Shakespeare, then collapses as attendants come for him. The young couple appears to claim the house, and Johnny, his father and grandmother pack their pitiful possessions and take to the road.

Major Roles. BEN ALEXANDER (dram t); needs strength and flexibility; top B3. JASPER MAC GREGOR (bs-bar); needs stamina and character. JOHNNY (boy s). MR. KOSAK (deep bs); low D1. THE GRANDMOTHER (c).

Lesser Roles. HENRY, paper carrier (boy alto); must whistle. ESTHER (girl s). PHILIP CARMICHAEL (bar). MR. CUNNINGHAM; YOUNG MAN AND WIFE (with baby) (sp). From chorus: RUFE APLEY, carpenter; SAM WALLACE, lineman.

Chorus. SATB. Friends and neighbors.

Orchestra. 2 fl (picc, alto fl), ob (Eng hrn) A, B♭ cl (bs cl, alto sax), bsn, 2 hrn, corn, piano (harm, acc, cel) perc, 3 vln, 2 vla, 2 vcl, cb (with C extension), recorded dog barks and growls.

Material. B & H.

🎵 Nabucco

Music by Giuseppe Verdi (1813–1901). Libretto in Italian by Temistocle Solera. Premiere: Milan, March 9, 1842. Pre-biblical melodrama. Melodious; set numbers; conventional harmonies; important ensembles; notable Verdi progress in character delineation and orchestral coloring. Overture (Sinfonia). Setting: Jerusalem and Babylon, 586 B.C. Four acts, seven scenes (Met has three acts—106 min).

ACT I ("Jerusalem"): Interior of Solomon's Temple. ACT II ("The Blasphemer") i: Royal apartments in Nabucco's palace; ii: Large hall. ACT III ("The Prophecy") i: Hanging Gardens of Babylon; ii: Banks of the Euphrates. ACT IV ("The Broken Idol") i: Apartment in palace, same as II i; ii: Hanging Gardens, same as III i.

Synopsis. Zaccaria, a Hebrew prophet, brings the captive Fenena, daughter of Nabucco (Nebuchadnezzar), to the Temple of Solomon, where the Hebrews are bewailing their defeat by Nabucco. He gives Fenena in charge

164

to Ismael, nephew of the King. The two have already met and are in love; he offers her escape as she had done for him in Babylon, but her sister Abigaille, at the head of a band of Babylonians disguised as Hebrews, captures the Temple. Abigaille offers freedom to Ismael in exchange for his love, but he refuses. Nabucco arrives and plunders the Temple, taking the Hebrews as prisoners to Babylon. Abigaille discovers proof that she is in reality a slave adopted by Nabucco; she vows revenge on everyone and is easily persuaded to assume the throne when a rumor of Nabucco's death arrives. Fenena frees the Hebrews, converts Ismael, and defies Abigaille, whose villainy is thwarted by the arrival of Nabucco, who orders the Jews put to death, Fenena among them. He proclaims himself God, and is dashed to the ground by a thunderbolt. Abigaille again seizes the crown, but Nabucco returns, and is persuaded to sign the Hebrews' death warrant. Learning of Fenena's implication, Nabucco angrily reveals Abigaille's lowly birth, but she produces the proof and tears it into pieces. Abigaille triumphs for the moment. The Hebrews in chains sing of their homeland (the famous chorus, "Va pensiero" which so inflamed the patriotic and suppressed Italians at its premiere). Nabucco regains his strength and his sanity, and swears to worship only the Hebrew God, then saves Fenena and the Hebrews, orders a new Temple built for them, and announces that Abigaille has taken poison. Repentant, Abigaille asks Nabucco to bless Fenena and Ismael and dies.

Major Roles. NABUCCO, King of Babylon (bar); needs acting ability to simulate madness; flexibility; high tessitura; B1 to F3 (one G3). ISMAEL (t); B1 to A3 (one B♭3). ZACCARIA (bs); F♯1 to F♯3. ABIGAILLE (dram s); sustained, very emotional; wide skips, florid passages; B2 to C5. FENENA (s or m-s); B2 to A4.

Lesser Roles. HIGH PRIEST OF BAAL (bs). ANNA, sister of Zaccaria (s). ABDALLO, old officer of Nabucco's (t).

Chorus. SSATTBB. Very important, really center of the work. Babylonians and Hebrews, men and women.

Orchestra. 2 fl, 2 ob, 2 cl, 2 bsn, 4 hrn, 2 trp, 3 trb, tuba, timp, perc, 2 harps, strings. *Stage*: Band.

Material. Bel (Ri) VS*.

Performances. Met: 10.4.60 etc. Lyr. Op. of Chic.: 10.4.63, etc. Amer. Op. Soc. (NYC): 10.11.68 (conc). R.I. Civic Chorale (Providence): 11.2.68. Phila. Lyr.: 11.14.69. San Fran.: 10.10.70. Bob Jones Univ. (Greensboro): 3.25.71.

🖾 Natalia Petrovna

Music by Lee Hoiby (1926–   ). Libretto in English by William Ball based on Turgenev's "A Month in the Country." Commissioned by the New York City Opera and the Ford Foundation. Premiere: New York, October 8, 1964. Romantic drama. Continuous texture; traditional harmonies; vocal line partly patterned after speech with melodic passages called arias; some

165

spoken dialogue. No overture; short Prelude to Act II. Setting: Islaev estate in Central Russia, midsummer 1850. Two acts, four scenes (126 min).

ACTS I (64 min) and II (62 min): Winter garden.

Synopsis. The uncontrollable passion of an older woman (Natalia Petrovna) for a young tutor in her household (Belaev) acts as a centrifugal and destructive force on all around her. It drives away from his uncomfortable and compromising position in the circle her tame lover, Rakitin, leaving her husband Islaev with the impression that Rakitin's was the only guilt. When Natalia accuses Belaev and her niece Vera of being in love, Belaev determines to go away, but is persuaded to stay and to confess his growing passion for Natalia, then sadly departs the scene. Natalia's goading at last drives Vera to accept the marriage proposal of a foolish old suitor, and finally even Lisavetta, the companion of Islaev's mother, announces her departure to marry the cynical family doctor. Natalia is left alone with the nucleus of her family: husband, son, and mother-in-law.

Leading Roles. MIHAIL MIHAILOVITCH RAKITIN, author in love with Natalia (bs-bar); F1 to Gb3. NATALIA PETROVNA ISLAEVA (s); Bb2 to B4. ARKADY SERGEITCH ISLAEV, her husband (t); C2 to A3 (one short Bb3). VERA ALEX-ANDROVNA, Natalia's orphaned niece (lyr s); C3 to C5 (touches C#5). ANNA SEMYONOVNA, Arkady's mother (m-s); A2 to A4. LISAVETTA BOGDANOVA, Anna's companion (col s); C2 to E5. ALEXEI ALEXEIVITCH BELAEV, Kolya's summer tutor (bar); C2 to G#3.

Lesser Roles. DOCTOR, family friend (t); Bb1 to Ab3. BOLISOV, landowner (t); Db2 to A3. KOLYA, Arkady and Natalia's son (mute).

Chorus. SATB; eight servants.

Orchestra. 2 fl, 2 ob, 2 cl, 2 bsn, 3 hrn, 2 trp, 2 trb, timp, perc, harp, strings. *Offstage*: piano, piano accordion.

Material. B & H. VS*.

Performances. Op. Soc. of Wash.: 3.26.65, etc.

🎵 Nausicaa

Music by Peggy Glanville-Hicks (1912–   ). Libretto in English by the composer and Robert Graves, after the latter's novel, *Homer's Daughter*. Premiere: Athens, August 19, 1961. Drama. Music is largely based on Greek folk music, its varied modes and meters; highly melodious and rhythmic. Vocal lines melodious, considerable melisma. Setting: The palace of Drepanum, a Greek City State in Western Sicily, about the 8th century B.C. Prologue and three acts, six scenes, three interludes (120 min).

Prologue and ACT I i: The palace; Interlude and ii: A balcony above the courtyard; iii: The shore. ACT II i: The courtyard; Interlude and ii: The palace. Interlude and ACT III: The courtyard.

Synopsis. The story may be termed "variations on a theme by Homer." Penelope becomes Nausicaa; Odysseus is Aethon, a shipwrecked Cretan no-

166

bleman. The idea that the *Odyssey* was written not by Homer but by a woman is exemplified in the secondary plot. Nausicaa disputes with the minstrel Phemius the role of Penelope, and eventually succeeds in making her version, upholding Penelope's faithfulness, official. Alcinous, King of Drepanum, goes in search of his lost son Laodamus, leaving his queen Arete, his daughter Nausicaa, and his young son Clytoneus. Many courtiers seek Nausicaa's hand, but she and Clytoneus overhear them plotting to overthrow the palace. Aethon appears, like Odysseus, from the sea, and seems to Nausicaa like an answer to her prayer to Athene. Unable to control the suitors, Clytoneus goes to seek help from a banished brother, but returns not with an army but a gift of fifty arrows, which Nausicaa interprets as a sign from the goddess. She plans a contest in which the winner will be he who can shoot the Great Bow of Hercules hanging in the palace. The Queen consults the auguries, which pronounce that a wedding by night will save the day. Aethon and Nausicaa, who have come to love each other, are immediately married in a night ritual. Next day, Aethon wins the contest and fells each suitor with one of the arrows. Phemius, as a conspirator, is saved by Nausicaa, for the life of a minstrel is sacred. She demands in return for his life that in the future he shall sing her version of the Penelope story. The King returns, and all is jubilation.

Major Roles. NAUSICAA (lyr s); B2 to firm C#5 (touches D5, one opt E5). AETHON (bar); considerable high tessitura; C#2 to A#3. PHEMIUS (t); C2 to C4. CLYTONEUS; B#1 to C#4. QUEEN ARETE; G2 to E4. KING ALCINOUS (bs); needs flexibility; G1 (F1 with A1 opt, touches E1) to F#3. ANTINOUS, suitor (t); top A3. EURYMACHUS, another suitor (bar).

Lesser Roles. PRIEST (t). MESSENGER (bar).

Chorus. SATBB, also SM-SM-SA and TTBB.

Ballet. Girls in Act I iii.

Orchestra, 2 fl, ob, 3 cl, 2 bsn, 2 hrn, 2 trp, trb, timp, perc, harp, strings.

Material. Bel (Col).

☙ Nina, ossia, La Pazza per Amore · Nina, or, Mad for Love

Music by Giovanni Paisiello (1740–1816). Libretto in French by J. Marjollier des Vivetières, translated into Italian by G. Carpani and G. B. Lorenzi. Premiere: Caserta, June 25, 1789. Edited by Carlo Gatti for 200th anniversary of Paisiello's birth and performed at Milan, March 29, 1940. Comedy. Very melodious; set numbers, recitatives, ensembles; conventional harmonies. Overture (Sinfonia). Two acts.

Synopsis. Nina, in love with Lindoro, is forced by her father the Count into another marriage. Lindoro and his rival duel and Lindoro is wounded. Nina goes mad. Her father, in remorse, relents. Lindoro recovers, Nina recovers, and all ends happily.

Major Roles. NINA (s); D3 to A4. LINDORO, her lover (t); top Bb3. THE

COUNT, her father (bs); Bb1 to E3. SUSANNA, her governess (s); top Bb4.
GIORGIO, the Count's Bailiff (buf bs); Bb1 to E3.

Lesser Role. SHEPHERD (t). Top Bb3.

Chorus. SATB. Villagers. Many supers.

Orchestra. 2 fl, 2 ob, 2 cl, 2 bsn, 2 hrn, 2 clarini (or trp), continuo, strings.

Material. B & H. VS.

✉ The Nose

Music by Dimitri Shostakovich (1906–   ). Libretto in Russian by the composer after a tale by Gogol. Premiere: Leningrad, January 12, 1930. Satirical comedy. Music highly descriptive at times; difficult; astringent. Brief overture; many interludes to allow for scene changes, one scored for percussion only. Vocal line extremely difficult; patterned after speech, declamatory, considerable high tessitura. Intricate ensembles. Setting: St. Petersburg in the late 19th century. Three acts, fifteen scenes (one before curtain), two in epilogue.

ACT I i: Kovalioff's bedroom; ii: Ivan Yakovlevich's bedroom; iii: Street along Neva riverbank; iv: Same as i; v: Kazansky Cathedral. ACT II i: Police commissioner's house; ii: Newspaper office; iii: Kovalioff's living room. ACT III i: Posthouse on outskirts of St. Petersburg; ii: Double set showing living rooms of Kovalioff and Podtotchina; iii: Intermezzo in front of curtain; iv: Outside newspaper office; v: Outside Junker's department store; vi: Tavrichevsky Gardens. Epilogue i: Same as I i; ii: Same as I iii.

Synopsis. Ivan Yakovlevich shaves Platon Kusmich Kovalioff, and next morning finds the latter's nose in a breakfast roll. His wife, Praskovia, threatens his arrest, and he flees, attempting to dispose of the nose, but is arrested when he throws it into the Neva River. Kovalioff discovers his loss and on the way to the police stops at Kazansky Cathedral, where he recognizes his nose in the guise of a Councilor of State. He fails to get the nose to return. Discovering that the Chief of Police is not at home, Kovalioff wants to place an advertisement in the newspaper, but the editor refuses. In a rage, Kovalioff returns home, where his servant Ivan is playing the balalaika. Policemen at a posthouse on the outskirts of the city watch for the nose as travelers assemble. As the coach is about to depart, the nose appears and is set upon by the hysterical crowd. In the confusion it assumes its original shape. The Police Commissioner returns the nose to Kovalioff, who cannot get it to stick to his face. A doctor only offers to buy it for his collection of curiosities. Kovalioff, believing that he has been bewitched by Podtotchina, the general's wife, who wants him to marry her daughter, writes a letter with the help of his friend Yarizhkin. Podtotchina's reply convinces him of her innocence. Stories about the nose have begun to circulate and crowds gather to watch for it, first at the newspaper office, then at a department store, and finally in the park. Kovalioff wakes the next morning with the nose in place. Yakovlevich comes to shave him and is warned to be careful of the nose. Kovalioff goes for a stroll, encounters Podtotchina and her daughter, and when their backs are turned, thumbs his nose at them, then goes off, flirting with a pretty vendor.

Major Roles. PLATON KUSMICH KOVALIOFF (bar); very difficult; much high tessitura, difficult skips; flexible passages; C2 to G3 (2 Ab3, 2 D4—fals). IVAN YAKOVLEVICH (buf bs-bar); F♯1 to Ab3 (many D4—fals). POLICE COMMISSIONER (high t); extremely high tessitura; some wide skips; sustained; Ab2 to E3. IVAN, Kovalioff's servant (t); not long but difficult; high tessitura; E2 to Bb3. NOSE as COUNCILOR OF STATE (high t); not long but extremely difficult; very high tessitura; A2 to C4 (sustained C4 passage has C3 opt).

Lesser Roles. PRASKOVIA OSSIPOVNA (s); C3 to C♯5. ALEXANDRA GRIGORIEVNA PODTOTCHINA (m-s); Bb2 to G4. HER DAUGHTER (s); E3 to B4. ADVERTISING EDITOR (bs-bar); F♯1 to C3. DOCTOR (bs-bar); G1 to E3. YARIZHKIN (t); G2 to Bb3.

Bit Roles. PORTER, MATRON, PRETZEL VENDER, many others; several speaking roles.

Chorus. Very elaborate and difficult, SATB divided in many parts; many solo bits.

Orchestra. 2 fl (picc, alto fl), 2 ob (Eng hrn), 2 cl (small cl, bs cl), 2 bsn (cont bsn), hrn, trp (corn à pist), trb, 2 harp, piano, perc (3), strings, balalaikas.

Production Problems. Transposition of Russian comedy to American flavor very difficult; very short scenes make patchwork effect; several interludes quite long; chorus scenes extremely tricky.

Performances. Santa Fe, 8.11.65 (Amer prem).

Material. Pr (UE). VS (g). Separate tr by Merle and Deena Puffer.

⚼ Oberon

Music by Carl Maria von Weber (1786–1826). Libretto in English by James Robinson Planché, based on a poem by Wieland. Premiere: London, April 12, 1826. Many revisions; probably most successful is Gustav Mahler's (premiere: Cologne, April 10, 1913), on which this is largely based. Gustav Brecher prepared text, in three acts; Mahler inserted seven pieces, mostly declamation over music drawn from Weber, to preserve continuity. Romantic drama. Music is atmospheric, expressive of moods and natural phenomena; leading motives foreshadowing Wagner; orchestra very important. Overture has become famous. Some dialogue. Setting: Oberon's kingdom, Baghdad, France, Tunis; early 9th century. Three acts, ten scenes (140 min).

ACT I i: Oberon's kingdom; ii: Reiza's vision; iii: Hall in the Caliph's harem in Baghdad (50 min); ACT II i: Banqueting hall in palace; ii: Palace garden; iii: Deserted shore (50 min). ACT III i: Palace garden of Emir of

169

Tunis; ii: Hall in palace; iii: Open place before palace; iv: Charlemagne's throne room (40 min).

Synopsis. Oberon and Titania, fairy king and queen, have quarrelled and will not be reunited until they find a pair of unquestionably faithful lovers. Puck suggests Huon de Bordeaux, who is being punished by Charlemagne, required to kidnap the Caliph of Baghdad's daughter. Oberon shows Huon and Reiza visions of each other, and gives Huon a magic horn. The adventures of Huon and his squire Sherasmin begin. The kidnapping, including Fatima for Sherasmin, is accomplished, but in fleeing, Huon loses the horn. However, a ship of Oberon's saves the little company, but Puck summons a storm to wash them on a deserted shore. Huon goes for help. Reiza sings an apostrophe to the sea, the famous "Ocean, thou mighty monster." A boat arrives, but it is manned by pirates, who carry Reiza away and subdue Huon. Oberon rescues Huon to a great chorus of mermaids and spirits of the air. Fatima and Sherasmin have been sold as slaves to the Emir of Tunis. Puck brings Huon thence, and he learns Reiza is also in the palace. The Emir makes love to Reiza while his wife attempts to seduce Huon, both unsuccessfully. Huon is condemned to death; Reiza with him when she declares she is his wife. But Sherasmin has found the magic horn, which saves everyone. All the lovers are reunited and spirited to France, where Charlemagne forgives Huon.

Major Roles. OBERON (t); C2 (with opt C3) to G3. PUCK (c); C3 to E4. REIZA (sometimes spelled REZIA) (s); difficult role; needs great flexibility; sustained; dramatic; Bb2 to B4 (one great C5). FATIMA (m-s); needs flexibility; trill; A2 to F4. HUON OF BORDEAUX, Count of Guyenne (t); high tessitura; flexible; trill; D2 to Bb3. SHERASMIN (bar); trill; C2 to G3.

Lesser Roles. DROLL (c). FIRST AND SECOND MERMAIDS (s, s).

Speaking Roles. TITANIA; HAROUN AL RASCHID, Caliph of Baghdad; BABEKAN, Persian prince; MESRU, harem guard; ALMANSOR, Emir of Tunis; ROSCHANA, his wife; NADINE, slave; ABDULLA, overseer; FIRST AND SECOND GARDENERS; CHARLEMAGNE.

Chorus. SATB. Elves, nymphs, sylphs, genii, fairies, mermaids, spirits of the air, earth, water, and fire.

Ballet. As elaborate as desired.

Orchestra. 2 fl, 2 picc, 2 ob, 2 cl, 2 bsn, 4 hrn, 2 trp, 3 trb, timp, perc, strings.

Material. Pet. VS*. Pr (2 vers: adapt. by Gustav Mahler and Alfred Roller; adapt. by Karlheinz Gutheim and Wilhelm Reinking).

☙ Of Mice and Men

Music and libretto by Carlisle Floyd (1926–   ), based on novel and play by John Steinbeck. Commissioned by Seattle Opera. Premiere: Seattle, January 22, 1970. Tragedy. A few set numbers embedded in continuous texture; conventional harmonies with frequent dissonance; intricate rhythms. Vocal line both melodic and patterned after speech. Brief prelude; interludes between Act I i and ii; Act III i and ii. Setting: The Salinas Valley of California; the present. Three acts, five scenes (113 min).

ACT I i: A clearing in the woods; ii: The bunkhouse (52 min). ACT II: The bunkhouse (24 min). ACT III i: The barn; ii: Clearing in the woods (37 min).

Synopsis. George and Lennie, migrant workers, are fleeing the police because of one of Lennie's periodical transgressions. The big man is almost a psychopath, who inadvertently kills the pets he cherishes; his friend George has sworn to take care of him but experiences constant revulsion and resentment. Still, they dream constantly of a retreat, a small farm where they can be at peace. They arrive at a ranch where they have jobs, but the disagreeable owner comes into immediate conflict with them, especially when his flirtatious wife appears in the bunkhouse, where he has forbidden her to go. The ranchhands persuade old Candy to allow his miserable old dog to be shot by Carlson, one of them. The cynical Slim tries to dissuade George from pursuing his dream of a little house, but George finds an advertisement that encourages him. Candy begs to be allowed to join the two, and his offer of money convinces George. They are celebrating when Curley's wife enters, followed by her husband, who picks a fight with Lennie. George tells him to protect himself, whereupon Lennie crushes Curley's hand. Lennie kills his latest pet, a puppy, and is hiding it in the barn loft when Curley's wife enters with a suitcase. She and Lennie muse on their separate dreams, hers for a Hollywood life, his for pets he can stroke. She invites him to stroke her hair, and when he will not stop, struggles frantically, until his anger is roused and he breaks her neck. Slim urges George to find Lennie before Curley does, and George reluctantly takes Carlson's revolver to put his friend out of his misery before the certain revenge in store for him. Lennie hides in the clearing in the woods, where George overtakes him. Choosing the moment when Lennie is ecstatically absorbed in the vision of their little house, George shoots his friend as the posse arrives. Callous to the tragedy, all exit but George and Slim, while a Ballad Singer whistles a few bars from a song he has entertained the bunkhouse with previously.

Major Roles. GEORGE MILTON (bs-bar); written originally for bass, the role retains some extremely low tessitura; difficult intervals; F♯1 to F♯3 (one A♭3 opt to C3). LENNIE SMALL (t); should be large, with boyish face; C2 to B3. CURLEY (t); D2 to B♭3. CANDY (bs); G1 to F♯3. CURLEY'S WIFE (s); needs some flexibility; A♯2 to C5. SLIM (bar); A1 to F3. CARLSON (t); E2 to A♭3. BALLAD SINGER (t); E♭2 to A3; should whistle and play harmonica.

Chorus. TBB. Ranchhands.

Orchestra. 2 fl (picc), 2 ob (Eng hrn), 2 cl (bs cl), 2 bsn, 4 hrn, 2 trp, 2 trb, tuba, timp, perc (2–3), cel, harp, strings.

Production Problems. Need four dogs: one old, one puppy, two bloodhounds.

Material. Bel.

Performances. Central City (Colo.): 6.27.70, etc. Kansas City, Mo.: 1970–1971. St. Paul: 1970–1971. Fla. St. Univ.: 6.4.71. Cincin. Summ. Op.: 7.9.71.

🎵 Opéra d'Aran · Opera of Aran

Music by Gilbert Bécaud (1925–   ). Libretto in French by Jacques Emmanuel, Louis Amade, and Pierre Delanoë after Robert Flaherty's film, *Man of Aran.* Premiere: Paris, October 25, 1962. Tragedy. Musical style eclectic, melodic, some set numbers; vocal line mostly patterned after speech. Prelude with men's chorus. Brief prelude to Act II. Setting: The island of Aran in the archipelago west of the Irish Free State, olden times. Two acts, seven scenes (110 min).

ACT I i: A public house in the village; ii: A cliff overlooking the beach; iii: Mara's house; iv: The quai (68 min). ACT II i: Mara's house; ii: A small square before the village church; iii: The cliff by the beach (42 min).

Synopsis. In the old Ireland, wives and sweethearts of dead men are supposed to remain faithful, lest the dead return for vengeance. Nevertheless, Maureen, whose betrothed Sean is thought to be dead (having left to try his luck in the world outside), falls in love with a stranger. This Angelo has been cast up from a shipwreck and brought back to life by the drunkard, Mickey MacCreagh. He is handsome and says he is rich. Maureen is ready to be persuaded to go with him to his warm and lovely country, but the island censures her. Sean's mother Mara, who is blind, frees Maureen from her promise as she is dying, but just as the girl is about to board the steamer that calls occasionally at Aran and leave with Angelo, Sean appears. He and Angelo fight; Maureen, attempting to part them, receives a blow by Sean from a steel cable. Her eyes are both put out. Now her fate is bound up with Angelo, who takes her in a small boat that cannot possibly survive the dangers of the ocean. He has already confessed that his grandiose story was a lie, so that their lives would have been as miserable in his country as on Aran. The dire prophecies of the eerie Man with the Harp have come true.

Major Roles. MAUREEN (dram s); C3 to C5. MARA MAC EININ (m-s); A2 to F4. ANGELO (t); Bb1 to B3. MICKEY MAC CREAGH (bar); G1 (E1 in part speech) to G3; needs strength in extremes of range. SEAN MAC EININ (bs-bar); Bb1 to E3. MAC JORRY, a fisherman (bar); A1 to Eb3. MAC CREAGH, Mickey's father (bs); G1 to E3.

Lesser Roles. THE CURE (bs); G1 to D3. MAN WITH THE HARP (bar); D2 to E3. THREE GIRLS (s, s, m-s). BARMAN (bs); F1 to G3.

Chorus. SATBB. Islanders, fishermen.

Orchestra. 3 fl (picc), 2 ob, 2 cl, bs cl, 3 hrn, 3 trp, 3 trb, timp, perc (tri, cym, Basque tamb, side dr, big dr, gong, bells), xyl, glock, cel, vib, harp, steamer siren, strings.

Material. Sal.

Performances. Montreal: 8.9.65 (N. Amer prem).

172

🎭 L'Ormindo

Music by Francesco Cavalli (1602–1676). Libretto in Italian by Giovanni Faustini. Premiere: Venice, 1644. Comedy-drama. Conventional harmonies; set numbers; recitative. Brief sinfonias or ritornellos between some scenes. New realization by Raymond Leppard (see note below); premiere: Glyndebourne, June 16, 1967. Setting: City of Fez in North Africa. Two acts, nine scenes (approx 135–140 min). (The following is based on Leppard realization.)

ACT I i: City of Fez; ii: Royal garden; iii: Palace; iv: Harbor (Arsenal). ACT II i: Nerillo before the curtain; ii: Cave outside city walls; iii: Harbor (Arsenal); iv: On the way to prison; v: In the prison.

Synopsis. The friends Ormindo and Amida discover they are in love with the same woman, Erisbe; but instead of fighting, they decide to let her choose between them. Nerillo, Amida's page, comments ironically on the nature of love in the first of a series of comic interludes by servants. Sicle, princess of Susio, has come to Fez in search for Amida, who has abandoned her. She and her maid Melide and her old nurse Erice are disguised as Egyptians and tell Nerillo's fortune. He reveals that Amida's affections have been snared by Erisbe, the young wife of the old King Ariadeno of Morocco and Fez, also that Amida has a rival, Ormindo. Sicle swears vengeance, and Erice comments cynically. Erisbe plays one lover against the other and continues to deceive her husband.

Sicle, reading Amida's palm, reveals to Erisbe his faithlessness to herself, and Erisbe turns to Ormindo. From now on, the frivolous tone of the story deepens. Amida, believing Sicle dead when she appears as a ghost, is restored to his love for her when she reveals that she lives. Erisbe and Ormindo elope, but are blown back to Fez by an unfavorable wind and cast into prison. Ariadeno sends his captain Osmano with a dose of poison for which he substitutes a sleeping potion. The lovers awake to be greeted by a repentant King, who abdicates both throne and queen to his younger rival.

Major Roles. (Ornaments opt). ORMINDO, Prince of Tunis (t); D2 (C♯2 opt) to A3. AMIDA, Prince of Tremisene (bar); needs both strength and flexibility; C2 to F3 (G3 opt). SICLE (m-s); florid passages; C3 to G4. ERISBE (s); needs flexibility; C3 to A4. ARIADENO (bs); F1 (one E1) to E3.

Lesser Roles. NERILLO (m-s); two arias; C3 to F4. MELIDE (m-s); one aria; ornaments opt; C3 to G4 (A4 opt). ERICE (t); one aria; C2 to A3. MIRINDI, waiting woman of Erisbe's (m-s); needs flexibility; two arias; B2 to F4 (touches G4). OSMANO (bar); D2 to E3.

Orchestra. Strings; continuo: 2 harpsichord, harp, 2 lutes, guitar, flue org, 3 vcl, 2 cb.

Material. G Sc. VS (i, g, e—tr Geoffrey Dunn)*.

Performances. Juill. (NYC): 1967–1968. Univ. of Wash. Fest.: 8.14.68. Op. Soc. of Wash.: 5.22.69.

Note on Realization. The role of Ormindo was originally too low for 20th-century male altos, too high for tenors, so some transposition has been made.

173

In original, Ormindo was the son of the King he cuckolded; this version omits a letter that explains the matter, and allows the King to be motivated by conscience. The Sinfonia from Act I is inserted to allow for his reaction. A duet from Cavalli's *La virtu degli strali d'Amore* (1642) has been inserted where Ormindo and Erisbe elope to replace an incomplete duet. Leppard invented the witches' spell with words from the 17th century designed to cure a broken leg. The repeat of the duet by Ormindo and Erisbe at the end has been adapted for quintet; the original duet is also included as optional. Leppard occasionally wrote out a five-part string accompaniment for arias. The comic solo scenes were originally designed to cover scene changes, so played before drop curtain in 1967.

🎵 Otello

Music by Gioacchino Rossini (1792–1868). Libretto in Italian by Marchese Berio after Shakespeare. Premiere: Naples, December 4, 1816. Tragedy. Set numbers, accompanied recitative. Melodious; vocal line for principals very florid. Overture (Sinfonia). Setting: Venice, end of 15th century. Three acts, six scenes (approx 180 min).

ACT I i: The Piazza San Marco, Venice; ii: Room in palace of Elmiro; iii. A magnificent hall. ACT II i: Elmiro's rooms; ii: Otello's garden. ACT III: Desdemona's chamber.

Synopsis. The story differs from Shakespeare (and Verdi) by placing the entire action in Venice. Furthermore, it is a letter Desdemona has written to Otello, whom she wishes to marry in spite of her father Elmiro's plan to wed her to Rodrigo, that Iago intercepts and shows to Otello to rouse his jealousy, as he believes it to be written to Rodrigo, the son of the Doge. Also, Otello marries Desdemona only after interrupting the ceremony in which she is to marry Rodrigo. But Otello's aroused jealousy prompts him to a duel with Rodrigo, in which the latter is killed, and to murder his wife.

Major Roles. (The three tenors have extremely exacting demands.) OTELLO (dram t); very florid; needs strength throughout range, especially in middle; trill; A2 to C4 (touches D4). DESDEMONA (s); needs great agility for florid passages; strength and agility in middle register; considerable high tessitura; many Ab4's and Bb4's; sustained C5. RODRIGO (light high t); extremely florid; many Bb3's, also C4, touches D4. IAGO (t); slightly lower than Rodrigo but florid; needs strength in middle range; top D4 or E4. ELMIRO (bs).

Lesser Roles. EMILIA (m-s). THE DOGE (t). GONDOLIER (light t); one special song; D2 to G3. LUCIO (t).

Chorus. SATB. People of Venice, etc. Very important.

Orchestra. 2 fl, 2 ob, 2 cl, 2 bsn, 2 hrn, 2 trp, trb, timp, perc, strings.

Material. Map. Radio Italia (Lake George perf) Tr: Martha Winburn England.

174

Performances. Amer. Op. Soc., Bklyn and NYC: 11.54. Rome Op. (Met, NYC): 6.25.68. Lake George, N.Y.: 7.13.68.

🎭 Our Man in Havana

Music by Malcolm Williamson (1931–   ). Libretto in English by Sidney Gilliat based on the novel by Graham Greene. Premiere: London, July 2, 1963. Melodrama with comic, even farcical overtones. Orchestra full of dramatic effects; occasional set pieces; vocal line largely patterned after speech; Spanish-like dance tempos; street calls. Brief prelude; orchestral interludes; with lights down, short interlude in III ii while checkers game progresses; another to allow Carter to get to Hasselbacher's apartment. Setting: Cuba, shortly before Castro's regime. Three acts, eight scenes (135 min).

ACT I i: Shop and Wonder-Bar; ii: Shop and street (45 min). ACT II i: London, Foreign Office; ii: Shop and Wonder-Bar; iii: Shop; iv: Dr. Hasselbacher's apartment (60 min). ACT III i: Shop and Wonder-Bar; ii: Shop; Interlude; Dr. Hasselbacher's apartment (30 min).

Synopsis. All the characters except the hero, Bramble, are larger than life, therefore perhaps truly operatic. Bramble, an ex-patriate Englishman who makes a bare living as a vacuum-cleaner salesman in Havanna, is increasingly disturbed because his spoiled sixteen-year-old daughter Milly has fallen under the influence of the sinister police chief Segura, who promises her luxuries her father cannot afford. Bramble reluctantly accepts a job as a spy for England offered by the exceedingly British Foreign Office representative, Hawthorne. He has carte blanche to recruit at least three agents with all expenses paid. His closest friend and partner at checkers, the mysterious German Dr. Hasselbacher, suggests that he can fulfiill his detested duty by living a lie, sending false reports and using non-existent agents. Bramble is extraordinarily successful; the Foreign Office becomes highly excited over his descriptions of mysterious installations and drawings of a potential secret weapon (which suspiciously resembles an oversized vacuum cleaner). A female spy, Beatrice, is sent to join him, but soon forgets her officiousness in affection. Furthermore, her suspicions (and those of Hawthorne, who pops up as a member of a tourist party) are allayed by the accidents (one fatal) to persons who bear the names and characters Bramble believed to be his own invention—a night club dancer, a professor, and a drunken flier. Now Bramble realizes that he is the next target—the enemy takes him seriously as well. In the midst of a vacuum cleaner sales conference, the potential murderer is revealed as one Carter, who slips poison into Bramble's drink. Hasselbacher warns Bramble, thereby revealing his complicity in the plot—on the wrong side. He too is a reluctant recruit. His murder follows almost immediately. Bramble realizes that he shall have to murder Carter in turn, for so the game goes on. Segura comes to call formally on Bramble, to play a game of checkers and to ask for Milly's hand. Bramble employs a ruse to get Segura drunk to insensibility,

175

steals his pistol and meets Carter in Hasselbacher's apartment, but cannot bring himself to murder. Veiled references seem to implicate Segura in the plot as well. The matter is settled when Carter fires at Bramble. Bramble returns the fire and kills Carter. Bramble returns home to resume the game with the awakening Segura.

Major Roles. BRAMBLE (t); wryly humorous, patter aria, needs some flexibility; Bb1 to Bb3. DR. HASSELBACHER (bs); difficult role; wide skips; E1 (one D1) to F♯3. MILLY (s); D♯3 to C♯5. BEATRICE (MRS. WESTON) (s); needs flexibility; D3 to C♯5 (one D♯5 and two-octave glissando F♯5 to F♯3). SEGURA (bar); C2 to F♯3. (fals Ab4). HAWTHORNE (high bar); Bb1 to A3. CARTER (bar); A1 to A3 (one Bb3).

Lesser Roles. LOPEZ, Bramble's shop assistant (t). FOREIGN OFFICE CHIEF (bs). SAVAGE, Foreign Office (high t). MISS JENKINSON, in London (c). MCDOUGALL, salesman (t). WATERMELON SELLER (m-s). LOTTERY TICKET SELLER (bs). SHOESHINE BOY (t).

Bit Roles. WAITERS (t, bar). LADIES (s, m-s). TWO POLICEMEN (both bar). WAITRESS (s). SECOND WAITRESS, FLOWER SELLER (m-s—can double). TRAMP (t). THREE MUSICIANS (t, s, c). CUSTOMERS (t, m-s, mute). GUIDE (t).

Chorus. SATB. Double chorus, m-s solo, small solos offstage. Tourists, guests, peasants, policemen, etc.

Orchestra. fl (picc), ob (Eng hrn), cl (bs cl), sax, bsn (cont bsn), hrn, trp, 2 trb, harp, piano (cel), perc (2), strings. *Stage*: elec guit. *Alternate large orchestra.* 2 fl (picc), 2 ob (Eng hrn), 2 cl (bs cl), alto sax, 2 bsn (cont bsn), 4 hrn, 2 trp, 3 trb, harp, piano (cel), perc (2), strings. *Stage*: elec guit.

Material. B & H (Wein). VS*.

✐ Owen Wingrave

Music by Benjamin Britten (1913–   ). Libretto in English by Myfanwy Piper, after a story by Henry James. Premiere: television, Europe and U.S.A. May 24, 1971. Drama with supernatural overtones. Continuous texture; contemporary idiom; vocal lines patterned after speech and with some melisma; customary angular prosody; important ensembles; interludes. Setting: England; the present. Two acts, many scenes (105 min).

ACT I i: The study at Coyle's military establishment; ii (no pause between the following): The park, in Miss Wingrave's hotel, the park, Miss Wingrave's hotel; iii: Room in Coyle's home; iv: Exterior of Paramore; v: Interior; vi: The hall at Paramore; vii: The dining room. ACT II i: Ballad; vision of young Wingrave and old general; ii: Portrait gallery and hall; iii: Coyle's room and dressing room; iv: Outside the haunted room; v: Another part of the gallery.

Synopsis. Owen Wingrave flouts the rigid military pattern of his family and refuses to be a soldier in spite of the scorn of his grandfather General Sir Philip and his aunt Miss Wingrave, as well as the haughty family portraits. Even his fiancée Kate and her mother, a soldier's impecunious widow, who live at the Wingrave's mansion Paramore, turn against Owen. Kate even seems to accept the flirtatious suit of Lechmere, Owen's comrade in the military school of Coyle. The only sympathy offered him is from Mrs. Coyle.

A flashback in the form of a ballad reveals that an earlier Wingrave had similarly renounced war as a boy and had been struck by his father, both being found dead in a room thereafter haunted by their presence. Owen, after being disinherited by Sir Philip, claims peace as the only strength, but is goaded by Kate into showing that he is not a coward by sleeping in the haunted room. She locks him in. Lechmere, who overhears the pact, informs the Coyles, who discover Kate opening the door and blaming herself for what she finds. Owen is dead.

Major Roles. GENERAL SIR PHILIP WINGRAVE (t); needs great flexibility; has long wordless solo with horn obbligato offstage; D♭2 to B♭3. MISS WINGRAVE (s); B2 to A♭4. OWEN (bar); some dialogue on pitch; G♯1 to G3. MRS. JULIAN, a soldier's widow (s); D3 to B♭4. KATE JULIAN (m-s); needs flexibility; B♭2 (touches A2) to G♯4. COYLE (bs-bar); some floridity; A1 to F♯3. MRS. COYLE (s); C3 to B♭4. LECHMERE (t); top B♭3. NARRATOR; B1 to F3.

Lesser Roles. YOUNG WINGRAVE AND A FRIEND (mute). OLD GENERAL (mute).

Chorus. Trebles. Supers: servants.

Orchestra. 2 fl, 2 ob, 2 cl, 2 bsn, 2 hrn, 2 trp, 2 trb, tuba, piano, harp, perc (4), strings.

Production Difficulty. Swift changes of scenes.

Material. G Sc (Fa).

Performances. Santa Fe: 8.9.73 (Amer stage prem).

◪ Pantagleize

Music by Robert Starer (1924–   ). Libretto in English by the composer after the play by Michel de Ghélderode. Premiere: Brooklyn College, April 7, 1973. "A farce to make you sad" (Ghélderode). Some set numbers embedded in continuous texture; unconventional harmonies; vocal line both melodic and declamatory; some florid passages; singers require strong acting ability. No overture; interludes between scenes. Setting: A city in Europe, on the morrow of one war and the eve of another. Three acts, ten scenes (approx 95 min).

ACT I i: Pantagleize's garret; ii: A cafe; iii: A promenade. ACT II i: Rachel's room; ii: Central tower of State Bank with grilles and safe; iii: The cafe, with added palm tree; iv: Rachel's room. ACT III i: A street, filled with debris, a body prone in middle; ii: A bare courtroom; iii: Barracks yard with wall.

Synopsis. Pantagleize is the innocent catalyst of a revolution, brought about by his utterance of the password: "What a lovely day!" The conspirators, ineptly planning their action in the cafe right under the nose of the police spy Creep, are the Negro Bamboola (an Uncle Tom caricature rather out of date and absurd); Bianca, a poet; Innocenti, an intellectual masquerading as a waiter; and the lame Banger, who caps the proceedings by bringing in a fully equipped machine gun. Pantagleize believes the furor he creates by his utterance of the password to be due to an imminent eclipse of the sun, and is persuaded to make inflammatory speeches in the street. As the revolution breaks out in full force, Rachel takes Pantagleize to her room, where she declares her love for him and sends him off, still dazed, with a revolver to seize the Imperial treasure at the State Bank. After he leaves, Creep enters and in the ensuing struggle shoots Rachel. In the State Bank the ridiculous General Macboom, torn between pride and fright, struts about until Pantagleize coolly tricks him into handing over the treasure. In the cafe once more, the four revolutionaries rejoice in their victory, and only Innocenti realizes Pantagleize's wholly inadvertent participation and warns him to get out while he can. Creep and assistants dispose of the conspirators one by one, but Pantagleize escapes, carrying the treasure to Rachel. He can hardly believe that she is dead, and goes out into the street melee. Creep finds him and arrests him. In the courtroom, soldiers amuse themselves by singing a sentimental ballad until the dignitaries enter. One after another the conspirators are condemned and shot, until it is Pantagleize's turn. Still uncomprehending, he dies with the words, "What a lovely . . ." on his lips.

Major Roles. PANTAGLEIZE (t); top A3. RACHEL SILBERCHATZ (m-s). CREEP (actor). BAMBOOLA (bs); must be able to dance; top D3. BIANCA (col s). INNOCENTI (bar).

Lesser Roles. BANGER (bar). GENERAL MACBOOM (bs). BANK MANAGER (t); can double with DISTINGUISHED COUNSEL. BALLADMONGER (c); can double with ASSISTANT BANK MANAGER. GENERALISSIMO (bs). TWO SENTRIES (2 bar). TWO SOLDIERS (2 bar). OFFICER (actor).

Chorus. SATB. Revolutionaries in Act I; masked jurors in Act III.

Ballet. Modern dance in I iii; III i.

Orchestra. 2 fl (picc), 2 ob (Eng hrn), 2 cl (bs cl), 2 bsn, 2 hrn, 2 trp, trb, tuba, perc (2), piano, strings.

Material. MCA.

🎵 Les Pêcheurs de Perles · The Pearl Fishers

Music by Georges Bizet (1838–1875). Libretto in French by Michel Carré and E. Cormon (Pierre-Etienne Piestre). Premiere: Théâtre-Lyrique, Paris, September 30, 1863. Pseudo-Oriental romance. Highly melodious; set numbers. Prelude; brief entr'acte between Acts II and III. Setting: Ancient Ceylon. Three acts, five scenes (98 min).

ACT I: A beach on the island of Ceylon. ACT II: Ruins of an Indian temple. ACT III i: Zurga's Hindu tent; ii: "A wild place"; the scene of execution.

Synopsis. Zurga is made chief of a band of pearl divers. He welcomes the return of his boyhood friend, Nadir, who left many years before to make his living as a hunter. Nourabad, the high priest, introduces a woman from another island, who will remain veiled for a year and by her prayers and singing drive evil spirits away from the fishing boats. Nadir recognizes Léila, a Brahman priestess with whom both he and Zurga have been in love: he has been seeking her in all his wanderings. Léila also recognizes him, and the two meet at night in the ruined temple. Nourabad surprises them and condemns them to death. Zurga will not help, but when Léila gives him a necklace he had once given her for saving him from an angry crowd, he realizes who she is, and in spite of his love for her, helps her and Nadir to escape. He himself is killed by the angry priests.

Major Roles. LÉILA (s); florid passages; trill; C♭3 to C5. NADIR (t); D2 to B3. ZURGA (bar); B♭1 to G3 (one G♯3 with E3 opt; one A3 with F3 opt). NOURABAD (bs); C♯2 to F3.

Chorus. SATTBB. Plays important role. Fishermen and their women.

Ballet. In Act III ii.

Orchestra. 2 fl, 2 ob (2 Eng hrn), 2 cl, 2 bsn, 4 hrn, 2 trp, 3 trb, timp, perc, harp, strings.

Material. Pet (Chou). VS*.

Performances. Litt. Orch. (NYC): 4.30.52 (conc); 2.16.53 (conc). Hartt Coll. (Hartford): 2.17.60; 2.24.71. Manh. Coll. (NYC): 4.13.62. San Fran. Spring Op.: 5.15.62; 3.26.64. Wayne St. Univ. (Detroit): 5.25.67. La Puma (NYC): 1967–1968. Riverside Op. (Cal.): 4.17.70. N. Or.: 11.4.71.

📖 Pénélope

Music by Gabriel Fauré (1845–1924). Libretto in French by René Fauchois. Premiere: Monte Carlo, March 4, 1913. Lyric poem. Continuous texture, a few set numbers; vocal line patterned after speech. Prelude. Setting: Ulysses' palace in Ithaca, ancient times. Three acts (145 min).

ACT I: Anteroom to Pénélope's chamber. ACT II: Summit of a hill overlooking the sea. ACT III: Great hall of the palace.

Synopsis. Because Ulysses has not returned after many years from the Trojan war, his wife Pénélope is besieged by many suitors. She puts them off by promising to decide when the tapestry she is weaving shall be completed, but by night she unravels what she has done by day. Detected in it, she is forced to agree to choose a suitor. Ulysses meanwhile has returned in the guise of an old beggar, recognized only by the old shepherd Eumée and the nurse Euryclée. The suitors agree to Pénélope's condition that they try with Ulysses' bow to shoot through the rings of axes. One by one they fail. Ulysses then takes the bow and succeeds, disposes of the suitors, and is reunited with Pénélope.

Major Roles. ULYSSES (t); D2 to A3. EUMÉE (bar); G1 to E3. PÉNÉLOPE (s); B2 to B4. ANTINOUS, a suitor (t); C♯2 to A3. EURYMAQUE, a suitor (bar); C♯2 to F3. EURYCLÉE (m-s); B♭2 to D4.

179

Lesser Roles. CLÉONE, servant (m-s). Women at court: MÉLANTHO (s); ALKANDRE (m-s); PHYLO (s); LYDIE (s). EURYNOME, governess (s or m-s). Suitors: LÉODES (t); CTÉSIPPE (bar); PISANDRE (t or bar). HERDSMAN (t).
Chorus. SATB. Shepherds, servants, dancers, flute players.
Ballet. Act III.
Orchestra. 2 fl, 2 ob, 2 cl, 2 bsn, 4 hrn, 2 trp, 3 trb, tuba, timp, harp, strings.
Material. Pr (Heu).
Performances. Seattle: 3.70; 5.70.

📧 Phillip Marshall

Music by Seymour Barab (1921–   ). Libretto in English by the composer, partially based on Dostoevsky's *The Idiot.* Unperformed. Tragedy. Set numbers and recitative embedded in continuous texture. Vocal line patterned after speech; some dialogue. No overture. Brief Prelude to Act II. Setting: Virginia in 1866, at end of Civil War. Two acts, twelve scenes, prologue and epilogue (can be performed on unit set).

Prologue: Dr. Norris' office in sanitarium. ACT I i: Promenade; ii: Hannan's living room; iii: Bedroom; iv: Brothel; v: Hannan's living room. ACT II i: Brothel; ii: Hannan's living room; iii: Outside Hannan's house; iv: Brothel; v: Duelling ground; vi: Hannan's living room; vii: Brothel. Epilogue: The sanitarium.

Synopsis. The philosophical basis of the work explores the question of the effect of the activist, the principled man, upon society, in personal rather than political terms. Phillip Marshall, who has heroically served in the Confederate forces and been hospitalized for a year, returns home and is invited to be the guest of his old friends, the Hannans. He promises the mother to persuade the son, his best friend Jonathan, to return home from where the father has driven him because of his pacifist ideas. The daughter Maritha has always idolized Phillip, but realizes he will inevitably seek out Rosellen, to whom he was betrothed. Rosellen, however, has become the mistress of the brothel-keeper Lucius and refuses to see Phillip. Jonathan too has taken refuge in the brothel and will not go home. Defeated, Phillip allows Maritha to believe he loves her and to announce their marriage. But Rosellen sends for him, confessing she has always loved him but fears Lucius's revenge. Lucius learns that Phillip has been hospitalized for shell shock, but the news does not deter Rosellen. Jonathan fails to kill Phillip in a duel and in despair at his worthlessness returns home and commits suicide. Mrs. Hannan renounces her husband as the cause of all this misery; Maritha humbles herself before Rosellen but cannot win Phillip back. Lucius murders Rosellen in jealous fury, and Phillip returns, vacant and silent, to the sanitarium. His efforts to do good have resulted only in tragedy for everyone.

Major Roles. PHILLIP (bar); B1 to F3. MARITHA (s); C3 to B4. JONATHAN (t); C2 to G3 (one A3). MRS. HANNAN (m-s); B2 to F4. MR. HANNAN (bs);

180

B♭1 to E♭3 (touches E3). ROSELLEN (s); D♭3 to A4. LUCIUS (bar); B♭1 to
E3. WELLINGTON, old family retainer (bs); C2 to E3.

Lesser Roles. ANDREW (bar). Top F♯3. DR. NORRIS; NURSE (sp).

Chorus. SSATTBB. Can be small. Strollers, revellers, Very Drunk Man,
Liz, Army, etc., guests.

Orchestra. In preparation.

Material. Pr.

🎬 The Picnic

Music by Richard Cumming (1928–   ). Libretto in English by Henry
Butler. Unperformed. Drama. Continuous texture, traditional harmonies;
vocal line melodious, occasionally dramatic. No overture. Setting: Perhaps
Virginia, in the leisurely past. Two acts (approx 108 min).

ACTS I and II: A grassy spot surrounded by trees, a path leading into it
from a slightly higher vantage point.

Synopsis. The picnickers assemble slowly: Rebecca Ferris, strikingly
handsome but blind; her husband Shaun, mercurial and buoyant; Anna, the
young cousin whom Shaun has taken as a ward, still subdued from her
early life with stern aunts; Inah Ames, Rebecca's mother, a wise woman
who knows her daughter very well; Dr. Martin, the Scottish friend of the
family; and two youths, Carl and Mylo, dark and light brothers, wily, clever,
at times almost demonic. They taunt Anna cruelly, are smoothly imperti-
nent to the others, but fawn on Rebecca, who encourages them. On the sur-
face, it is a beautiful calm day. But dark rifts begin to appear; it is evident
that Shaun is deeply interested in Anna and that she worships him, while
Rebecca is becoming apprehensive. The boys tell the story of how Rebecca
was blinded when Shaun struck her horse, which threw her. Although Mrs.
Ames and Shaun are obviously upset, they say nothing. Rebecca purposely
twists her ankle, so that Shaun must help her. Then in rapidly mounting
tension, it becomes clear that though Shaun and Anna love each other, Rebecca will never give up her husband. The true story of her blindness is revealed. She had struck Shaun in anger, then tripped on the stairs and fallen.
Shaun and Anna renounce what might have been their future. The disastrous picnic is over.

Major Roles. ANNA FERRIS (s); C3 to B4. REBECCA FERRIS (m-s); needs
strength and character; G♯2 to A4. SHAUN FERRIS (bar); some difficult passages; B1 to G3. INAH AMES (c); G2 to F4 (F♯4 opt). DR. ANDREW MARTIN
(bs); G1 to D3 (F3 opt). MYLO (t); C♯2 to G♯3. CARL (t); A2 to
F♯3. Both boys should be dancers who can sing or singers who can mime
and dance; vocal line not difficult.

Orchestra. 2 fl (picc), 2 ob (Eng hrn), cl, 2 bsn, 2 hrn, trp, harp, perc
(2), cel, strings. *Stage:* 1 perc; guit to be played by Dr. Martin or from pit.

Material. B & H.

▶ La Pietra del Paragone · The Touchstone

Music by Gioacchino Rossini (1792–1868). Libretto in Italian by Luigi Romanelli. Premiere: Milan, September 26, 1812. Comedy. Highly melodious; conventional harmonies; some exotic touches; set numbers, recitative, important ensembles. Overture; storm interlude. Setting: Hunting castle of Count Asdrubal, 19th century. Two acts; scenes alternate between castle garden and interior; one hunting scene (approx 170 min, with some recitatives deleted).

Synopsis. The "touchstone" is poverty. Count Asdrubal determines to find out which of three attractive widows visiting him is really in love with him for himself; he suspects that at least two of them may be favoring him for his wealth. The ladies have arrived with escorts: two poets (Giocondo and Pacuvio) and a theatrical journalist (Macrobio), who play a large part in the comedy of several situations. The Count puts his widows to the test by pretending to be a creditor whose claims will bankrupt him. Marchesina Clarice proves to be the faithful one, luckily, for she is the Count's favorite. But still he hesitates. So she resorts also to a ruse, impersonating her brother who insists that she marry Giocondo. Thus prodded, the Count vows his love, and all forget their rivalry by joining in the celebration.

Major Roles. COUNT ASDRUBAL (bs or bs-bar); needs strength at extremes of range; flexibility for florid passages; G1 to F#3 (or G3). MARCHESINA CLARICE (c); a typical difficult Rossini role; needs strength through range; extreme flexibility; trill; A2 to Ab4. GIOCONDO (t); florid passages; lyrical line; trill; top Bb3. PACUVIO (bar or bs bar); top F3. DONNA FULVIA (s); needs agility; top Bb4. MACROBIO (buf bs); difficult char role; also needs vocal agility and strength; trill; top F3.

Lesser Roles. BARONESSA ASPASIA (m-s); on stage a great deal without a great deal to sing. FABRIZIO, servant to the Count (bs).

Chorus. TTB. Friends of the Count; hunters, servants, Clarice's soldiers.

Orchestra. 2 fl (2 picc), 2 ob, 2 cl, 2 bsn, 2 hrn, 2 trp, trb, perc, strings.

Material. Bel (Ri)—see note under Clarion Conc. performance.

Performances. Hartt. Coll. (Hartford) as *The Touchstone*: 5.4.55 (Amer prem). Berkeley Community Litt. Th.: 4.3.64. Clarion Conc. (NYC): 10.31.72 (conc). Material used was partially Ri score, mainly autograph score. Recitatives greatly cut, and also some ensembles which will be included in a Vanguard recording. Cadenzas were added, tailored to performers. Note: A Bä edition is unreliable.

▶ Il Pirata · The Pirate

Music by Vincenzo Bellini (1801–1835). Libretto in Italian by Felice Romani, based on the tragedy *Bertram, or the Castle of St. Aldobrand* by Rev. R. C. Maturin. Commissioned by Teatro alla Scale; premiere: Milan, October 27, 1827. Many revisions, notably for Paris, 1833, by Ed. Duprez; arranged by P. Cremont in French in three acts with added characters and innumerable changes (published by Pacini, Paris). Sentimental historical tragedy. Set numbers, accompanied recitative; early Bellini style with large measure of typical cantilena and romantic cadences, but limited structural harmonies. Vocal line melodic with many florid passages. Prelude (sinfonia). Setting: Castle of Caldare and vicinity, Sicily, 13th century. Two acts, six scenes (approx 135 min).

ACT I i: Seacoast near Caldara; ii: Loggia of Caldara Castle; iii: Illuminated exterior of castle. ACT II i: Antechamber of Imogene's room in castle; ii: Loggia of castle; iii: Vestibule of castle.

Synopsis. Ernesto, Duke of Caldara, and Gualtiero, Count of Montalto, both love Imogene, a Sicilian noblewoman. Because she chooses Gualtiero, Ernesto quits the service of King Manfred and joins Charles of Anjou, who defeats Gualtiero. The latter flees to Aragon and organizes a fleet of pirates, who are defeated at Messina by the Anjou forces; Gualtiero is shipwrecked near Caldara, where Imogene has married Ernesto to save her father's life. This has all happened before the curtain, which rises to show the local fisherfolk being led in prayer by the hermit Goffredo, who recognizes the shipwrecked Gualtiero as his former pupil, and Itulbo, a lieutenant. When Imogene comes to welcome the strangers according to the laws of hospitality, Gualtiero hides, and overhears his lost love lamenting to her lady-in-waiting, Adele, and recounting a dream in which her husband kills Gualtiero. The latter utters an involuntary exclamation, and Imogene thinks she knows the voice, but does not discover his identity until later. When he learns of her marriage and sees her son, he is about to kill the boy, but is prevented by Imogene's plea. He almost reveals himself to Ernesto when Imogene refuses to meet him again, and when she reluctantly does so only to warn him that he has been betrayed, he refuses to flee unless she will accompany him. They are discovered by Ernesto, who is killed in a duel with his rival. Gualtiro hands himself over to the Council of Knights, who condemn him to death. Imogene has lost her reason because of these misfortunes, and her mind gives way to terror and despair.

Major Roles. IMOGENE (dram s); needs strength at extremes of range; much high tessitura; very florid; C♯3 to C5. ERNESTO (high bar); very flexible; high tessitura; F♯1 to A3. GUALTIERO (dram t); many florid passages; high tessitura; D2 to D4. GOFFREDO (bs); noble in style; D1 to F3.

Lesser Roles. ITULBO (t). ADELE (s).

Bit Role. SON of Imogene and Ernesto (boy, mute).

Chorus. SSAATTBB. Substantial and varied work, both musically and in acting. Fishermen and women, pirates, knights and ladies, etc.

Orchestra. 2 fl (picc), 2 ob, 2 cl, 2 bsn, 4 hrn, 2 trp, 3 trb, tuba, harp, perc (3), timp, strings.

Material. Bel (Col).

Performances. Amer. Op. Soc. (NYC): 1.27.59; 4.25.66 (conc). Cincin. Summ. Op.: 7.5.69. Phila. Lyr.: 1967–1968.

🎵 The Plough and the Stars

Music by Elie Siegmeister (1909–   ). Libretto in English by Edward Mabley, based on the play by Sean O'Casey. Premiere: Louisiana State University, March 16, 1969. Drama. Set numbers in closely knit continuous texture. Music embodies conventional harmonies as well as polytonality, traces of ragtime, hymns, ballads, etc., as expressive of mood and character. Vocal line now melodic, now patterned after speech. Setting: Dublin in 1915–1916; the street, the bar, the apartment. Three acts (150 min).

Synopsis. Nora has intercepted a letter containing a commission to the Irish Citizens' Army for her husband John. Peter Flynn, her uncle, finds it and leaves it in plain sight, but Nora spies it again and burns it. On the street, Fluther, the carpenter, Peter, and Mrs. Gogan, mother of a young tubercular girl, Mollser, are joined by Bessie Burgess, the lone Protestant in this nest of Catholics. She picks a fight with Mrs. Gogan, but the men separate them; then Bessie accuses Nora of snobbishness, but her husband protects her.

In the pub, everyone is watching the crowds go to a rally. John sings of the "Plough and the Stars," the flag symbolizing the revolution. Rosie, a prostitute, counters with a bawdy song. Captain Brennan of the Citizens' Army comes after John, who learns of the intercepted letter, and leaves, as the crowd grows noisier.

Easter has come to the street. Nora, pregnant, is searching the barricades for John, who finally appears, weary and dirty, followed by the wounded Lieut. Langdon in the arms of Capt. Brennan, who leaves Langdon and drags John back to the fighting. Artillery fire is constantly heard. Fluther shoots his way into the pub, while Bessie helps Nora into the house. The scene becomes frantic as Mrs. Gogan refuses to leave Mollser, who is dying, and Bessie has to seek a doctor for Nora, who is giving birth prematurely.

A few days later, Peter, Fluther, and Covey, a young radical, are playing cards near the coffin that contains Mollser and Nora's dead baby. Bessie orders them out as Nora wanders in, almost mindless. Jack staggers in, and Bessie tries to prevent him seeing the baby. But Nora strikes him and calls him a murderer. Realizing she has slipped over into madness, Jack goes for help. The coffin is taken away. Bessie, worn out, sleeps heavily, but Nora awakes her at the sound of shots. Nora runs to the window; Bessie, trying to drag her back, is shot, and dies, cursing Nora, who does not understand her need for help. Nora runs into the street, but is brought back by Sergeant Tinley. Corporal Stoddard arrives, thinking he has shot a sniper, for whom he mistook Bessie. Jack runs down the street, still in uniform, and is dropped by a shot from the Corporal. Then the latter and the Sergeant sit down to the tea Nora had laid. The sounds of battle grow louder as the British open their final and decisive attack on the city. The two soldiers sing sentimentally of home as their comrades sweep down to consolidate their hold on the district.

Major Roles. NORA CLITHEROE (s); B2 to B4. JOHN CLITHEROE (bar); A1

184

to G3. BESSIE BURGESS (m-c); A2 to F♯4. LIEUT. JAMES LANGDON (t); E♭2 to B♭3. MRS. GOGAN (m-s); B2 to G4. MOLLSER (s); C♯3 to G4. FLUTHER GOOD (bs-bar); G1 to E♭3. THE COVEY (bs-bar); A1 to E♭3.

Lesser Roles. PETER FLYNN (t); D2 to A3. ROSIE REDMOND (c); A2 to E4. CAPTAIN BRENNAN (bs); B1 to C♯3. CORPORAL STODDARD (bar); C2 to F3. SERGEANT TINLEY (bar); C2 to F3.

Bit Roles. FISH PEDDLER (t). BARTENDER (bs). CHIMNEY SWEEP (t). GLAZIER (bs). SCISSORS-GRINDER (bar). FIRST AND SECOND MAN (t, bar). FIRST AND SECOND WOMAN (c, s).

Chorus. SSATBB. Moderately difficult. Townspeople, passersby, soldiers.

Ballet. Two dance numbers in Acts I and II.

Orchestra. 2 fl (2 picc), 2 ob (2 Eng hrn), 2 cl (2 bs cl), 2 bsn, 4 hrn, 2 trp, 3 trb, tuba, piano, harp, timp, perc (2—many dr, xyl, glock, cel), strings.

Material. MCA.

Performances. Grand Théâtre Municipal de Bordeaux, France: 3.13,15.70.

✒ Postcard from Morocco

Music by Dominick Argento (1927–   ). Libretto by John Donahue. Commissioned by Center Opera Association, Minneapolis. Premiere: Minneapolis, October 14, 1971. Psychological fantasy. Eclectic music, embodying serial technique, Viennese waltzes, jazz, baroque counterpoint, etc.; vocal line melodious; complicated ensembles. Divertimento during which puppets may perform; a small Algerian orchestra in costume seems to provide music. Characters change from one to the other with half-masks. Setting: a waiting room in Morocco; the present. One act (100 min).

Synopsis. Seven travelers in a dismal waiting room, all isolated from one another, pursuing their own fragmentary thoughts, displaying their inner fears and compulsions, try to discover each others' secrets, represented by the content of their luggage. Each guards jealously against the feverish yet shallow curiosity of the others. The soprano has hats, the baritone shoes, the bass a cornet, and so on. For a moment it seems that Mr. Owen (the only one with a name) and the soprano reach a sympathetic understanding, but she remains a dream of lost love. Mr. Owen is trapped into revealing an empty paint box, and the others revert to their own preoccupations, watch a puppet show, then depart for the train. Owen climbs to the puppet stage and begins to act with the puppet a drama on a ship of which he is captain. The ship sails away as all voices are heard from a distance, the puppet curtain closes, and the train whistle sounds far away.

Major Roles. LADY WITH HAND MIRROR, etc. (col s); florid; trill; sings sentimental German duet with tenor; C3 to D5 (G5, F5, E5 with opt E5, D5, C5). LADY WITH CAKE BOX, etc. (s); B♭2 to B4 (C5 with A4 opt, C♯5 with A♯4 opt). FOREIGN SINGER, etc. (m-s); does dance; G2 to G♯4. PUPPET NO. I; OLD LUGGAGE MAN, etc. (lyr t); sings duet with coloratura soprano;

high B3; trill on A3. MR. OWEN (lyr t); sustained; C2 to B♭3. PUPPET NO.
II; SHOE SALESMAN, etc. (bar); needs flexibility; whistles; high G3 (trill on
F3). MAN WITH CORNET CASE; PUPPET MAKER, etc. (bs); needs flexibility;
whistles; emulates cornet; F1 (D1 with D2 opt) to F♯3 (G3 with E3 opt).

Lesser Roles. TWO PUPPETS (mute or d).

Orchestra. cl (alto sax, bs cl), trb, guit, piano & cel (piano with top removed), perc (sn dr, bs dr with foot pedal, tom-toms, sock cym, ride cym,
tri, wd bl, temp bl, cow bell, etc.), vln, vla, cb.

Production Problems. Scene should suggest cartoon-like atmosphere of
railroad station, exotic as Morocco, like interior of glass-covered pavilion;
a small stage for entertainments. Cardboard figures on wheels represent puppets, an Italian or Greek priest, vendors, waiters, etc.

Material. B & H.

🖾 Le Postillon de Longjumeau · The Postilion of Longjumeau

Music by Adolphe-Charles Adam (1803–1856). Libretto in French by De
Leuven and Brunswick. Premiere: Paris, October 13, 1836. Comedy. Highly
melodic; conventional harmonies. Brief introduction. Setting: Longjumeau, a
French village; in and near Paris; time of Louis XV, 1776. Three acts (120
min).

ACT I: Longjumeau (50 min). ACT II: Madeleine's house in Paris (50 min).
ACT III: Madeleine's country house near Paris (20 min).

Synopsis. Chappelou, the postilion in Longjumeau, is persuaded to desert
his bride Madeleine, hostess at the inn, by the Marquis de Corcy, an opera
impresario, and go to sing in Paris. He becomes a noted singer under the
name of St. Phar. Madeleine also goes to Paris and becomes Mme de Latour,
and the wheelwright Bijou is likewise transformed to Alcindor. St. Phar
rivals De Corcy for Madeleine, not recognizing her. The double identities
are at last unscrambled, when St. Phar discovers he has married the same
woman twice.

Major Roles. CHAPPELOU (ST. PHAR) (high t); top sustained D4. BIJOU
(ALCINDOR) (high or low bass); top F3 if high; F2 if low. MARQUIS DE CORCY
(t); no range problems; needs acting ability. MADELEINE (MME LA TOUR)
(lyr–col s); needs flexibility; top C5.

Lesser Roles. ROSE, a maid (s). BOURDON (chor).

Chorus. SATTB. Peasants, nobles, etc.

Orchestra. 2 fl (2 picc), 2 ob, 2 cl, 2 bsn, 4 hrn, 2 trp, 3 trb, timp, perc,
strings.

Material. Map.

🖾 The Prodigal Son

Music by Frederick Jacobi (1891–1952). Libretto in English by Herman
Voaden, based on four early American prints. Revised at the request

of Gaetano Merola of San Francisco, but never performed. Data based on revised version. Parable translated into American setting. Melodious, conventional harmonies. Some dialogue; some pantomime. Prelude is pastorale with mime; brief preludes to Acts II and III. Setting: 19th-century America. Three acts, four scenes.

ACT I: Autumn scene outside prosperous farmhouse. ACT II: Private room in elegant "hot" spot of pre-Victorian America. ACT III i: Desolate landscape; ii: Same as Act I, in spring.

Synopsis. In the pastoral prelude, servants cross and recross the stage, carrying fruits and vegetables; Robert and his father enter from the garden, greeting Ruth, an adopted daughter, who enters from the house. The father enters the house as a trapper shows Ruth and Robert his furs, then leaves. John and Nancy, Robert's brother and sister, enter and the father returns to complete the family picture. It is the father's birthday, and neighbors come to congratulate him. Robert chooses this unpropitious time to announce that he is going away, and asks for his patrimony. He is lured by the peddler, an evil spirit. In spite of everyone's pleas, he takes his patrimony and goes. Later he is discovered among false friends, Hope Nightingale, her black maid Belinda, and the Cynic, who betray him and steal all his money. Destitute and ill, he makes his way toward home and is befriended by Johnny Appleseed and the trapper Tom Rice, who leads him home. His father, Ruth, and Nancy welcome him with open arms, but his brother John, who had hoped to marry Ruth, comes only reluctantly to the fact that Ruth still loves the prodigal.

Major Roles. ROBERT (t); B1 to A3. FATHER (bar); A1 (G1 in ensemble) to E3. JOHN (bs-bar); G1 to G3. NANCY (s); D3 to A♭4. RUTH (m-s); D3 (C3 in ensemble) to B♭4 (C5 in ensemble). HOPE NIGHTINGALE (s); needs flexibility; C3 to G4. BELINDA (m-s) needs flexibility; B2 to G♭4. PHILIP, the Cynic (bar); E2 to F3. JOHNNY APPLESEED (bar); D2 to E♭3 (one F3 with F2 opt).

Lesser Roles. TRAVELING PEDDLER (bar). TOM RICE (t). HIS NEPHEWS (s, m-s).

Dancers. SYLVIA SLENDER, DILDA FREDERICK.

Chorus. SATB. Neighbors, servants, boon companions, a waiter.

Ballet. Country dance, I, III ii. Several solos, II.

Orchestra. 2 fl (2 picc), 2 ob (Eng hrn), 2 cl (bs cl), 2 bsn, 4 hrn, 2 trp, 2 trb, tuba, harp, perc, timp, strings.

Material. From composer's widow: 1155 Park Ave., NYC 10028.

✍ Prometheus

Music by Carl Orff (1895–   ). Libretto in Greek after the tragedy of Aeschylus. Premiere: Stuttgart, March 24, 1968. Tragedy; called "world theater piece" by composer; third of trilogy, preceded by *Antigonae* (1949) and *Oedipus*, the Tyrant (1959). Enormous and complicated orchestra, used sparingly; vocal line mainly declamation, strongly rhythmic; considerable dialogue; rare melodic passages. Typical reiteration; driving rhythms. Intentionally primitive and elemental musically. No overture. Chorus of fifteen women's voices very important. Setting: A mountain crag in the Caucasus; ancient times. One act (110 min).

Synopsis. Prometheus, the arch-rebel and arch-martyr, is the Titan (one of the immortal race who were supreme rulers until defeated by the gods) who stole fire from the gods in order to give it to men. As a symbol of wisdom versus force, he ultimately represents Man against God, and is made to suffer for his bold intervention by being reduced to man's status. Three henchmen of Zeus, Hephaestus, Kratos, and Bia, forge Prometheus to the rocks, where he will be burned by the sun, and his body endlessly tortured by vultures and eagles. The one who might save him has yet to be born, Kratos tells him. Hephaestus is the only one to show pity. Later several daughters of Oceanus appear to commiserate with the hero, who laments that Zeus is determined to destroy Man. Oceanus himself arrives and offers to intercede for his old friend with Zeus. Prometheus refuses his help and recounts his benefactions to mankind. He also refuses to divulge to the Oceanids the fate of Zeus, but later reveals that the god's son, born of Thetis, the sea nymph (whose name, however, he will not tell Zeus's crafty son Hermes), will destroy his father.

Meanwhile, he is visited by Io, wearing the horns of an ox. This girl, half-crazed by a gadfly, has been condemned to wander the earth forever by Zeus, whose advances she has refused. She is also haunted by the vision of Argos, the herdsman with 10,000 eyes (it is really Hera, the wife of Zeus, who jealously caused her misfortune, according to mythology). She pours out her story to Prometheus (who knows it already), and he offers her little consolation. She will roam far and wide, but eventually find a home near the Nile; Zeus will relent, and she will bear him a son. Generations later, one of his descendants will free Prometheus. Madly, Io resumes her journey. After Hermes's visit, the earth and sea toss violently and overwhelm the bound immortal.

Major Roles. PROMETHEUS (bar); needs extreme flexibility and dramatic strength; cruelly high (and some low) tessitura and wide skips; G1 to G3 (one A3, and fals A's). IO (s); extremely dramatic role; many passages in very high tessitura verge on screams.

Lesser Roles (all declamation and speech). KRATOS, BIA, HEPHAESTUS, OCEANUS, HERMES.

Chorus. All soloists, SA; very complicated and difficult.

Orchestra. 4 piano with cym (8 players), 6 fl (6 picc), 6 ob (2 Eng hrn), 6 trp C, 6 trb, 4 ten banjo, 4 harp, organ, elec organ, 9 cb, 5 timp, perc (12–15—very complex).

Material. Bel (Sch).

Performances. Litt. Orch. (NYC): 10.14.69 (conc—Amer prem).

🎭 Le Prophète · The Prophet

Music by Giacomo Meyerbeer (1791–1864). Libretto in French by Eugène Scribe. Premiere: Paris, April 16, 1849. Melodrama, based on historical personages. Music of highly dramatic expressiveness, color and lyricism; conventional harmonies; melodic and dramatic vocal line. Important choruses, famous march. Setting: Dordrecht, Holland, and Münster, 1534–1535. Five acts, nine scenes (approx 210 min).

ACT I: Bank of the River Meuse, below Count Oberthal's castle (33 min). ACT II: Jean's inn at Leyden (35 min). ACT III i: Winter camp of the Anabaptists in Westphalian forest, a frozen lake; ii: Zacharias's tent; iii: The camp (54 min). ACT IV i: Public square in Münster; ii: Interior of the Cathedral (48 min). ACT V i: Room in the palace; ii: Banquet hall (40 min).

Synopsis. Jean of Leyden joins the Anabaptists after Count Oberthal threatens to kill his mother Fidès unless Jean relinquishes his fiancée Berthe. Because of his resemblance to King David, Jean acquires power and is named a prophet of God. He triumphs over the rabble he leads in spite of plots by the Anabaptists, who now believe he has assumed too much authority. In fact, he has himself crowned Emperor at Münster. Fidès, who has been told he is dead, imperils his new status by proclaiming him her son. However, he silences her by invoking her loyalty, and promises her full repentance. The German Emperor pardons the Anabaptists if they will betray Jean. Berthe seeks him out, believing that he has killed her lover, but recognizes him, too late, for she has set the palace afire, and kills herself. In the midst of his enemies, Jean dies in the holocaust, his mother beside him.

Major Roles (all need extraordinary dramatic force). BERTHE (dram col s); high tessitura; fioratura passages; trill; B♭2 to C5 (2 C♯5). FIDES (dram col m-s); needs strength at extremes of wide range; flexibility; trill; G2 to B♭4 (one B4, 2 C5's). JEAN OF LEYDEN (dram col t); needs strength at extremes of wide range; sustained; trill; D2 (one C2, one B1) to B3 (opt C4, C♯4.) COUNT OBERTHAL (bs or bs-bar); high tessitura; some fioratura passages; G1 to E3 (one F3). Three Anabaptists: JONAS (t); wide range; florid passages; C2 (one A1) to A3 (one C4). MATHISEN (bs); florid passages; G1 to E3 (one E♯3, one F3). ZACHARIAS (bs); florid; F♯1 (2 F1's) to E3 (one F3).

Bit Roles. TWO CHILDREN (s, m-s). TWO PEASANTS (t, bs). SOLDIER (t). TWO BOURGEOIS (t, t). TWO OFFICERS (t, bs).

Chorus. SSAATTBB. Very important. Sometimes divided. Also children. Several solos. Nobles, citizens, Anabaptists, peasants, soldiers, prisoners, children.

Ballet. Skating ballet, Act III.

Orchestra. picc, 2 fl, 2 ob, 2 cl, 4 bsn, 4 hrn, 2 corn à pist, 2 trp, 3 trb, tuba, timp (4), perc, 2 harp, strings. *Stage.* 2 small sax, 4 sop sax, 4 trp, 4 alto sax, 2 ten sax, 4 bs sax, 2 cont bs sax, drum.

Material. Map.

🎬 I Puritani · The Puritans

Music by Vincenzo Bellini (1801–1835). Libretto in Italian by Count Carlo Pepoli, based on a play, *Tetes rondes et cavaliers*, by F. Ancelot and X. B. Saintaine. Premiere: Théâtre Italien, Paris, January 25, 1835. Drama, based loosely on history. Conventional harmonies; set numbers, arias, ensembles, patter and accompanied recitatives; florid, melodic vocal line. Preludes and introductions to acts. Setting: In and near a fortress near Plymouth, England, after the death of King Charles I, during the struggle between Puritans and Stuarts. Three acts, five scenes.

ACT I i: Courtyard of the fortress; ii: Elvira's chamber; iii: Hall of Arms. ACT II: Hall in the fortress. ACT III: Garden near Elvira's home.

Synopsis. Lord Walter Walton, a Puritan governor, has promised his daughter Elvira in marriage to a Puritan colonel, Sir Richard Forth, who is stationed at a fortress near Plymouth. However, she loves Lord Arthur Talbot, a Stuart sympathizer. Her uncle, Sir George Walton, intercedes so that she is allowed to marry Arthur, who is escorted to the fortress. Lord Walton has been ordered to transfer a woman prisoner to London, and because no one can leave the fortress without his permission, issues a safe-conduct pass to Arthur and his wife. Arthur discovers that the prisoner is Queen Henrietta, widow of Charles I, and because his own father has been killed serving the Stuart cause, determines to save Henrietta's life. Using the safe conduct and letting the Queen wear the wedding veil Elvira has playfully placed on her head, Arthur takes the prisoner to safety, abetted by Richard, who thus sees his vengeance accomplished. The deserted Elvira goes mad, believing Arthur has jilted her. Some months later, Arthur returns, but though Elvira's sanity is restored at the sight of him, he is arrested and sentenced to death as a traitor. A messenger arrives reporting the defeat of the Stuarts and proclaims amnesty to all political prisoners. The lovers are reunited amid universal rejoicing.

Major Roles. ELVIRA (col s); extraordinarily florid, wide compass, two-octave runs, chromatic scales; sustained high tessitura; needs great endurance; C3 to C5 (touches Db5). ARTHUR (lyr t); sustained high tessitura; flexibility essential; needs inexhaustible endurance; touches F1 to F4 (touches B4). RICHARD (bar); high tessitura; flexibility essential; also sustained cantilena; A1 to E3 (touches F3). GEORGE (bs); sustained high tessitura; Bb1 to Eb3 (touches E3).

Minor Roles. LORD WALTON (bs); Ab1 to C3 (touches D3). HENRIETTA (s or m-s); C3 to E4.

Bit Role. SIR BRUNO ROBERTSON, captain of the Puritan guard (t).

Chorus. SSATTBB in many combinations; also doubled. Puritans, ladies, soldiers, nobles, men and women of the fortress.

Orchestra. picc, 2 fl, 2 ob, 2 cl A, 2 bsn, 4 hrn D, 3 trp D, 3 trp, 3 trb, timp, big dr, cym, strings. (Note: In an early score, other instruments are indicated, possibly to provide tones missing before modern instruments: Bb cl; hrn C, Eb, G, F; trp Bb, E, C; hunting bugles offstage.)

Material. Bel (Ri).

Performances. Amer. Op. Soc. (NYC): 1956; 4.24.63. Bost. Op. Group (Op. Co. of Bost.): 2.12.64. Lyr. Op. Chic.: 11.1.69. Phila. Lyr.: 1971–1972. Conn. Op. (Hartford): 12.15.73.

◪ Radamisto

Music by George Frideric Handel (1685–1759). Libretto in Italian by Niccolo Haym, based on an event in the Annals of Tacitus. Premiere: London, April 17, 1720. Two revisions (the first version is used here). Historical Oriental drama. Classical harmonic structure, set numbers, patter and accompanied recitative; vocal lines very difficult, sustained as well as florid. Requires expert cast. Overture. Setting: Mesopotamia, about 26 B.C. Three acts, nine scenes.

ACT I i: Royal pavilion; ii: Battle camp, view of beleaguered city, low river bed; iii: Royal square before palace of Radamisto. ACT II i: Near banks of Araxes River, with ancient ruins; ii: Royal gardens with arbor; iii: Royal hall. ACT III i: Inner courtyard of palace; ii: Royal chamber; iii: Temple.

Synopsis. Tiridates, King of Armenia, desiring Radamisto's wife Zenobia, deserts his own wife Polissena, daughter of Farasmane (King of Thrace) and sister of Radamisto. Tiridates besieges Radamisto; his brother Phaarte captures Farasmane and Zenobia, who has tried to escape by plunging into the Araxes River. Tigranes, presumably an ally of Tiridates, captures Radamisto but proposes they join forces against Tiridates. The latter offers a crown and jewels to Zenobia, who refuses. Radamisto meanwhile has tried to learn the location of Tiridates's tent from Polissena, but she remains loyal to her faithless husband. Eventually Radamisto reaches Tiridates's palace and, in disguise, brings news that Radamisto has been killed. In spite of her grief, Zenobia keeps faith, and it is her great love and the loyalty of his own wife that persuade the tyrant, after many changes in the fortunes of battle, to renounce Zenobia and take Polissena back.

Major Roles. RADAMISTO (s); Bb2 to A4. ZENOBIA (c); florid, sustained, needs agility in skips, high tessitura; Bb2 to Eb4. POLISSENA (dram–col s); florid, sustained cantilena, high tessitura; E3 to Bb4. TIGRANES (s); E3 to G4 (A4 opt). PHAARTE (s); very difficult; florid, needs extreme agility; E3 to G#4.

Lesser Role. TIRIDATES (t); high tessitura, florid; D2 to A3.

Bit Role. FARASMANE (bs).

Chorus. SATB.

Orchestra. 2 ob, 2 bsn, 2 trp, 2 harpsichord, strings. *Stage*: 2 ob, 2 bsn, trp, strings.

Material. German Handel Society, Leipzig. Reprinted by Gregg Press Inc.

⚐ Il Re Teodoro in Venezia · King Theodore in Venice

Music by Giovanni Paisiello (1740–1816). Libretto in Italian by Giambattista Casti. Premiere: Vienna, August 23, 1784. Comedy. Highly melodic; traditional harmonies; set numbers; dialogue; important ensembles. Vocal line often florid; ornaments and cadenzas may be used by principals. Very brief prelude. Setting: Venice, about 1740. Two acts, seven scenes (140 min).

ACT I i: King Theodore's apartment in Taddeo's inn; ii: Garden of inn. ACT II i: King's apartment; ii: A terrace overlooking Grand Canal; iii: King's apartment; iv: Terrace; v: Prison.

Synopsis. Based on the true story of a German adventurer who by stratagem gets himself appointed King of Corsica and eventually dies in debtors' prison, this merry tale centers on such a pseudo-king. Penniless in Venice, he courts Lisetta, the pretty daughter of the innkeeper Taddeo, who is reputed to be wealthy. Dazzled at the prospect of being a queen, Lisetta rejects her true love, the Venetian merchant Sandrino, but the inappropriate marriage is thwarted by Theodore's arrest for debts in Leghorn, Genoa, Rome, Paris, London, Hamburg, and Berlin. He is eventually bailed out by Acmet, deposed Sultan of Turkey, who falls under the spell of Belisa, an exotic lady who is in reality Theodore's sister.

Major Roles. KING THEODORE, using the name of COUNT ALBERTO (bar); G1 to E3. GAFFORIO, Prime Minister of Corsica, disguised as Theodore's servant (t); D2 to A3. TADDEO (buff bs); flexibility for patter song; G1 to F3. LISETTA (col s); florid passages; A♯2 to B♭4. SANDRINO (lyr t); several coloratura passages; D2 to A3. ACMET, under the name of NICEFORO (bar); B♭1 to F♯3. BELISA (s); D3 to A4.

Lesser Role. A VENETIAN COURT OFFICIAL (bs).

Chorus. SATB. Servants, gondoliers, police officials, Venetian ladies and gentlemen.

Orchestra. 2 fl, 2 ob, 2 cl, 2 bsn, 2 hrn, 2 trp, strings.

Material. Pr.

Performances. Tanglewood: 8.7.61 (Eng vers by Boris Goldovsky and Arthur Schoep—Amer prem). Amer Musicol Soc. for Internat'l Musicol. Soc. (NYC): 9.10.61.

⚐ Rienzi, der Letzte der Tribunen · Rienzi, the Last of the Tribunes

Music by Richard Wagner (1813–1883). Libretto by the composer after Bulwer Lytton's novel. Premiere: Dresden, October 20, 1842. Tragedy. Shows influence of Meyerbeer and Spontini, little of later Wagnerian development. Melodic; dramatic; conventional harmonies. Very important choruses and ensembles. Overture; introduction to Act II. Setting: Rome, mid-14th century. Five acts, six scenes (151 min).

192

ACT I: Street outside St. John's Lateran Church, Rienzi's house at one side (45 min). ACT II: Hall in Capitol (40 min). ACT III: Square in Old Forum (30 min). ACT IV: St. John's Lateran Square (16 min). ACT V i: Hall in Capitol; ii: Square in front of Capitol (20 min).

Synopsis. Irene, the sister of Niccolò Gabrini (a papal notary known as Cola di Rienzi), is about to be kidnapped by the nobleman Paolo Orsini when another noble, Steffano Colonna, intervenes, as does Colonna's son Adriano, who loves Irene. Only the entrance of Rienzi subdues the ensuing brawl; he is hailed as the people's leader and determines to curb the nobles' power. Adriano joins him, but after he conquers, begs clemency for Orsini and Colonna, which Rienzi grants against the judgment of his followers. The nobles mass against Rienzi, who still holds his people's loyalty, but who will not accept Adriano's allegiance. When Colonna's body is brought in after the battle, Adriano swears revenge on Rienzi and wins over his closest adherents, Baroncelli and Ceccodel Vecchio. Raimondo, the papal legate, tells Rienzi the church has excommunicated him; he is deserted by everyone but Irene, who determines to die with him. Brother and sister stand on the balcony of the Capitol as the populace throw firebrands into the building, and it carries them down in flames as Adriano attempts to rescue Irene and is himself buried in the ruins.

Major Roles. COLA RIENZI (dram t); extremely taxing role; some high tessitura; needs strength throughout range; trill; D2 to A3. IRENE (dram s); very high tessitura; both sustained and occasionally florid; trill; E3 to firm C♯5. STEFFANO COLONNA (bs); exacting role; needs strength at bottom of range; F1 (E♭1 and D1 with B♭1 and D2 opt). ADRIANO (m-s); needs strength and flexibility; difficult dramatic role; A♭2 (G2 with G3 opt) to B4. PAOLO ORSINI (bs); G1 to F3.

Lesser Roles. RAIMONDO (bs); G1 to F3. BARONCELLI (t). CECCO (bs). MESSENGER OF PEACE (s); trill; B2 to A4. HERALD (t).

Chorus. SSSATTBB. Very large, many divisions. With supers includes ambassadors from Lombardy, Naples, Bavaria, Bohemia, etc.; Roman nobles, citizens, messengers of peace, priests and monks, Roman soldiers, guards, characters in Pantomime.

Ballet. Act III: Pantomime, Pyrrhic Dance, Combat of Gladiators and Cavaliers, Dance of the Apotheosis.

Orchestra. 2 fl, picc, 2 ob, 3 cl, 2 bsn, cont bsn, 4 hrn, 4 trp, 3 trb, tuba, timp, perc, harp, strings.

Production Difficulties. Collapse and burning of Capitol.

Material. Fürstner.

Performances. Conc. Op. Ass'n (NYC): 11.25.63.

Rinaldo

Music by George Frideric Handel (1685–1759). Libretto in Italian by Giacomo Rossi, based on Tasso's *Gerusalemme liberata.* Premiere: London, February 24, 1711. Revised 1731. Medieval drama. Highly melodious; difficult vocal line with considerable floridity; set numbers. Overture. Setting: Jerusalem and Armida's enchanted premises, time of the Crusades. Three acts, seven scenes (118 min—Handel Society of New York perf).

ACT I i: City of Jerusalem besieged; ii: Within the city; iii: Garden with fountain, live birds in cages (57 min). ACT II i: Great sea, with rainbow and anchored ship; ii: Garden of the enchanted palace (37 min). ACT III i: Horrible mountain, stalactites and falls, castle of Armida at top, guarded by monsters; cave at bottom; ii: Armida's garden (24 min).

Synopsis. The Crusaders led by Rinaldo and Goffredo are opposed by the Saracens led by Armida and her lover Argante, King of Jerusalem. The Saracens capture Almirena, daughter of Goffredo and betrothed to Rinaldo. The latter goes to her rescue, but comes under the spell of Armida, managing to resist her even though she transforms herself into a semblance of Almirena. Meanwhile Argante falls in love with Almirena, and when Armida discovers this, she withdraws her magical powers from the King. A Christian magician helps Goffredo and his army ascend the dreadful mountain and defeat Argante. Rinaldo rescues Almirena; Armida and Argante repent; all ends happily.

Major Roles. GOFFREDO (c in first vers; t in second); some high tessitura. ALMIRENA (s); no range problems; trill for bird aria. RINALDO (c); lengthily sustained; needs volume and strength throughout range; extremely florid; C3 to E4. ARGANTE (bs in first vers; c in second); very florid. ARMIDA (dram s); needs large, agile voice; trill; firm C5. EUSTAZIO, brother of Goffredo (c in first vers; deleted in second).

Lesser Roles. CHRISTIAN MAGICIAN (c in first vers; bs in second); one aria. TWO MERMAIDS (s or m-s). HERALD (s); can double with mermaid.

Chorus. Combined solo voices, briefly at end.

Orchestra. Sopranino (high recorder), important solo; 2 recorders, 4 ob, 4 bsn, 4 trp, timp, harpsichord, strings. (NY Handel Soc. used only 1 bsn and continuo of vcl, cb, harpsichord.)

Production Problems. Fanatsy can be carried to high point, with transformation scenes, trapdoors, a chariot with dragons, birds, horses, a sailboat, a cloud descending, mermaids, many battles, and a practical mountain that splits and reveals an army, two men hanging from a rope, etc.

Material. NYC Handel Soc. obtained from Handel Opera Soc. of London (English).

Performances. Handel Soc. of N.Y.: 3.27.72—based largely on first vers, but using t for Goffredo).

🎵 The Rising of the Moon

Music by Nicholas Maw (1935–). Libretto in English by Beverley Cross. Commissioned by the Glyndebourne Festival Opera. Premiere: Glyndebourne, July 19, 1970. Comedy. Contemporary idiom; some set numbers in continuous texture; vocal line declamatory with considerable melisma; recitatives; complicated ensembles. Prelude; Intermezzo between I i and ii. Setting: Town of Ballinvourney in the Plains of Mayo, Ireland; 1875. Three acts, four scenes (approx 140 min).

ACT I i: Monastery of St. Brenden the Less; ii: The refectory. ACT II: Interior of Sweeney's inn. ACT III: The Monastery.

Synopsis. The British 31st Royal Lancers, commanded by Col. Lord Francis Jowler and with the advice of the Prussian Major Max von Zastrow are about to occupy County Mayo in Ireland. The two commanders are accompanied by their wives and Captain Lillywhite, next in command, has brought his daughter Atalanta. The Irish are of course rebellious, especially Donal O'Dowd, who urges Brother Timothy of the Monastery not to receive the invaders. But as the incursion is inevitable, they hope to stir up a rebellion. A better plan is conceived when they learn of the trials imposed on a new recruit, Cornet John Stephen Beaumont. The Prussian Major insists that the novice accomplish these feats: seduce three ladies and drink three bottles of champagne before dawn, bringing back proofs. Corporal of Horse Haywood assists in the plot that now goes forward. Beaumont is taken to the local inn run by the widow Sweeney and her winsome daughter Cathleen. However, the ladies he encounters are not local dames, but the wives of the two commanders, each of whom reacts favorably. The Prussian Major, seeking diversion in the same inn, is referred to the room of the daughter, in reality occupied by Miss Lillywhite. Cathleen herself is the third "victim" of Beaumont, and falls for him desperately, but cannot persuade him to remain with her. When at dawn the boy presents his trophies, the entire regiment is present. The horrified commanders, seeking to hush up a scandal, let Beaumont go his way to pursue his metier—observing nature. His only regret is Frau Elizabeth von Zastrow, with whom he has achieved a sincere relationship.

Major Roles. Most need strength at extremes of range. BROTHER TIMOTHY (high t); B1 to B3. DONAL O'DOWD, farmer (bar); C2 to G3. CATHLEEN SWEENEY (m-s); difficult intervals in melisma; Bb2 to Ab4 (A4 with lower opt). COL. LORD FRANCIS JOWLER (bs-bar); G1 to F#3. MAJOR MAX VON ZASTROW (high bar); difficult intervals; needs dexterity; D2 (Bb1 with Bb2 opt). CAPTAIN LILLYWHITE (t); Eb2 to A3. LADY EUGENIE JOWLER (s); G#2 to C#5 in one passage. FRAU ELIZABETH VON ZASTROW (m-s); G#2 to Ab4. MISS ATALANTA LILLYWHITE (s); needs flexibility for some melisma; C3 to C#5 (one Db5 with Bb4 opt). CORP. OF HORSE HAYWOOD (bs-bar); F#1 to D3. CORNET JOHN STEPHEN BEAUMONT (lyr t); sustained, melisma; C2 to A3. THE WIDOW SWEENEY (c); A2 to Eb4. LYNCH, Irish farmer (bs); G1 to E3.

Lesser Roles. YOUNG GAVESTON, officer (t). WILLOUGHBY (bar). From chorus.

Chorus. TTTBBBBBB. Several solos. Men of the 31st Royal Lancers.

Orchestra. 3 fl (picc), 3 ob (Eng hrn), 3 cl (bs cl, Eb cl); 2 bsn, 4 hrn, 3 trp (corn), 2 trb, tuba, timp, perc: side dr, ten dr, bs dr, cym, susp cym, tamb, tri, rattle, whip, 2 bongo, cowbell, glock; strings. *Stage*: (A) picc, 2 cl, Eb cl, 3 trp, 2 trb, tuba, perc: side dr, bs dr with pedal, Hi-Hat cym attached. (B) 3 cl, trb, tuba, perc: bs dr with cym attached.

Material. B & H.

♫ Robert le Diable · Robert the Devil

Music by Giacomo Meyerbeer (1791–1864). Libretto in French by Eugène Scribe. Premiere: Paris, November 21, 1831. Melodramatic legend with supernatural elements. Elaborate orchestration, novel (for the time) effects; scenic grandeur, dramatic recitative as well as melodious set numbers; mixture of allegory, heroism and legend. Overture; several orchestral passages and interludes. Setting: Palermo, Sicily, 13th century. Five acts.

ACT I: A tournament. ACT II: Isabella's palace. ACT III: The cavern of St. Irene. ACT IV: Isabella's apartment. ACT V: The cathedral.

Synopsis. Robert, son of Bertha, daughter of the Duke of Normandy (who has been seduced by the Devil), wanders to Palermo in Sicily, where he falls in love with the King's daughter, Isabella, and intends to joust in a tournament to win her. His companion, Bertram (in reality his satanic father), forestalls him at every juncture. A compatriot, the minstrel Raimbaut, warns the company about Robert the Devil, and is about to be hanged when Robert's foster sister Alice appears to save him. She has followed Robert with a message from his dead mother; Robert confides to her his love for Isabella, who has banished him because of his jealousy. Alice promises to help and asks in return that she be allowed to marry Raimbaut. When Bertram enters, she recognizes him and hides. Bertram induces Robert to gamble away all his substance. Alice intercedes for Robert with Isabella, who presents him with a new suit of armor to fight the Prince of Granada, but Bertram lures him away from combat, and the Prince wins Isabella. In the cavern of St. Irene, Raimbaut waits for Alice but is tempted by Bertram with money, which he leaves to spend. Alice enters on a scene which betrays Bertram as an unholy spirit, and in spite of clinging to her cross, is about to be destroyed by Bertram when Robert enters. The young man is desperate and ready to resort to magic arts. Bertram summons up the spirits of sinful dead nuns, who attempt to seduce Robert. Under their spell, he steals a talisman cypress branch, which he uses to bewitch Isabella. But her tears move him and he breaks the branch, whereupon the awakened soldiers seize him. Bertram saves him and the two go to the cathedral, where Bertram hopes to induce him to sign the fatal contract at last, revealing his parentage and appealing to his filial instinct. Thinking all lost, Robert is about to agree when Alice once more intervenes, producing his mother's will which entreats him to save his soul. The time is up for Bertram, who sinks defeated into hell, while Robert is restored to an honorable life.

Major Roles. ROBERT LE DIABLE, Duke of Normandy (dram-col t); long and exacting role; many florid passages, extremely high tessitura; trill; E2

196

to C4 (2 C♯4 and 3 D4 with lower opt). ALBERT, a cavalier (bar); A1 to E3. RAIMBAUT (lyr t); some fioratura; trill; C2 (1 B1) to A3 (1 B♭3). BERTRAM (dram-col bs-bar); long role; considerable floridity; high tessitura; wide skips; trill; E1 to F3. ALICE (lyr s); extremely florid; high tessitura; wide intervals; trill; C3 to C5 (1 C♯5). ISABELLA (lyr s); constant difficult coloratura passages; high tessitura; difficult intervals; trill; C3 (1 B2 with higher opt) to C5. Note: Isabella, Alice, and Robert all have many sustained high notes.

Bit Roles. HERALD (t). PRIEST (bar). PROVOST (t). LADY OF HONOR (m-s). HELEN (Abbess) (mime or d). FOUR SOLO CAVALIERS (2 t, bar, bs).

Chorus. SSATTBB. Separate male and female choruses important. Several solos.

Ballet. One number in Act II; several in Act III, including famous dancing nuns.

Orchestra. 3 fl (picc), 3 ob (Eng hrn), 3 cl, 2 bsn, 4 hrn, 3 trp, 3 trb, (bs trb), tuba, timp, perc, bells, 2 harp, org, strings. *Stage*: cym, tri, picc, 4 trp, 4 hrn, 3 trb.

Material. Bel (Ri). Map.

🎵 Roberto Devereux · Robert Devereux

Music by Gaetano Donizetti (1797–1848). Libretto in Italian by Salvatore Cammarano, based on François Ancelot's play, *Elisabeth d'Angleterre*. Premiere: Naples, October 29, 1837. Semi-historical tragedy. Highly melodious; conventional harmonies; set numbers; recitative. Setting: Elizabethan England, 1601. Three acts, six scenes (NYC Opera version; 140 min).

ACT I i: Reception chamber in Westminster Castle; ii: Sara's room in Nottingham Palace (66 min). ACT II: Great Hall of Westminster (27 min). ACT III i: Sara's private rooms; ii: Tower of London; iii: Reception chamber in Westminster (47 min).

Synopsis. Queen Elizabeth confides in Sara, Duchess of Nottingham, that her love for Robert, Earl of Essex, transcends even her suspicion that he loves another. Sara is the object of this love, unbeknownst to her aging husband, the Duke of Nottingham, and of course to the Queen. Robert's execution for treason in the recent campaign in Ireland is demanded by Lord Cecil and the Royal Council, but Elizabeth refuses, and receives Robert. Believing that she has uncovered the truth about his other love, although he denies it, she determines to put him to death. The assurances of help from Nottingham are received with reserve by Robert, who visits Sara and discovers that she still loves him, although in his absence the Queen has forced her to marry Nottingham. He tears off the ring Elizabeth has given him as a token that she will always come to his aid if it is presented to her, and leaves it with Sara. She in turn gives him a blue scarf she has been embroidering, and over which Nottingham has observed her weeping. Robert's execution is ordered by the Council, Sir Walter Raleigh having arrested him at the Queen's orders and found on him the blue scarf. When Nottingham identifies it, he would kill Robert, but the Queen stays him, interposing her own vengeance by signing the death warrant. Robert writes to Sara, begging her to take the ring to Elizabeth, but Nottingham prevents her, so that the execution takes place. Elizabeth, waiting either the presentation of the ring or the notice of the execution, is disposed to forgive Robert everything, but even Sara's hasty arrival with the ring is too late. Elizabeth turns on the Nottinghams and orders them led away. Then she longs only for death and for James' accession to the throne.

Major Roles. ELIZABETH (dram-col s); extremely difficult role, both for vocal and acting demands; needs strength at extremes of range; flexibility of high order; trill; Bb2 to C5. ROBERTO (t); needs strength and flexibility; some high tessitura; Eb2 to Bb3. SARA (m-s); sustained; dramatic; needs strength and flexibility; some high tessitura; B2 (B3 opt; otherwise C3) to Cb5. NOTTINGHAM (bar); powerful role; needs flexibility; high tessitura; C2 to F3.

Lesser Roles. LORD CECIL (t); G2 to G3 (A3 in ensemble). SIR WALTER RALEIGH (bs); C2 (B1 in ensemble) to D3 (F3 in ensemble).

Bit Roles. PAGE (bs). SERVANT (bs).

Chorus. SATTB. Ladies of the Court, courtiers, pages, royal guards, attendants of Nottingham.

Orchestra. 2 fl, picc, 2 ob (Eng hrn), 2 bsn, 4 hrn, 2 trp, 3 trb, timp, perc, strings.

Material. Bel (Col).

Performances. Amer. Op. Soc. (NYC): 12.16.65 (conc). NYCO: 10.15.70; spring 71; 10.13.71, etc.

⚜ Rodelinda

Music by George Frideric Handel (1685–1759). Libretto in Italian by Nicola Haym. Premiere: London, February 13, 1725. Drama of conjugal fidelity. Simple harmonic structure; set numbers with accompanied recitative; difficult vocal line. Overture; brief Prelude and Fugue before Act III (from G minor Concerto Grosso) in Oskar Hagen edition. Setting: Milan, 6th century. Three acts, seven scenes (130 min).

ACT I i: Rodelinda's chamber; ii: Cypress grove with monuments of Lombard kings (55 min). ACT II i: Cypress grove; ii: Rodelinda's chamber (40 min). ACT III i: Gallery in palace; ii: Dungeon; iii: Palace garden (35 min).

Synopsis. Bertaric, the Lombard king, has been dispossessed by the tyrant Grimwald and is presumed dead. His Queen, Rodelinda, comes to his grave and is approached by Garibald, Grimwald's confidant, who threatens to hold her son unless she marries Grimwald. She makes the condition that Garibald give his own life. Bertaric, who has secretly returned, overhears, and is discovered by his sister Hadwig. His friend Hunolf reassures him of Rodelinda's faithfulness and persuades him to reveal himself. Grimwald confronts

Rodelinda but will not sacrifice Garibald's life. She demands that he slay her son Flavius, as she will not be the mother of the rightful king. Hunolf is not able to get a word with Rodelinda, but follows her. Grimwald bewails his sweet bondage to love. Rodelinda, at last learning the truth about her husband, rejoices. Bertaric joins her in a rapturous reunion, but is recaptured by Grimwald, who is counseled by Garibald to kill the prisoner even though they are not sure of his identity. Meanwhile, a sword is smuggled to Bertaric, who strikes the first person to enter his cell—his friend Hunolf. Leaving his cloak behind, Bertaric flees with Hunolf, and is once more considered dead when Grimwald finds the blood and cloak. Hadwig and Rodelinda are similarly deceived. Grimwald, nearly demented, longs for peace, and falls asleep in the garden. Garibald attempts to murder him but is foiled by Bertaric and Hunolf, and chased and killed. Grimwald yields to Bertaric as the rightful king and the people join in a paean of praise and joy.

Major Roles. RODELINDA (s); both sustained and flexible; E3 to B4. BERTARIC (bar); needs flexibility; A1 to F♯3. GRIMWALD (t); very difficult; extreme flexibility; C2 to A3. HADWIG (c); C3 to D4. GARIBALD (bs); high tessitura; flexible; B♭1 to F3. HUNOLF (bs); A1 to E3.

Lesser Role. FLAVIUS (mute).

Chorus. SATB. Nobles, guards, etc.

Orchestra. 2 fl, 2 ob, 2 bsn, 2 hrn, strings, cembalo.

Material. Map.

☙ La Rondine · The Swallow

Music by Giacomo Puccini (1858–1924). Libretto in Italian by Dr. A. M. Willner, Heinz Reichert, and Giuseppe Adami. Premiere: Monte Carlo, March 27, 1917. Drama. Set numbers interwoven into continuous texture; vocal line melodious, also patterned after speech. Brief prelude. Setting: Paris in the Second Empire. Three acts (95 min).

ACT I: Elegant salon in Magda's Paris house. ACT II: Bal Bullier. ACT III: Small cottage on French Riviera.

Synopsis. Magda, a beautiful demimondaine, is supported in luxury by Rambaldo, but secretly longs for romance, which seems to be a new fashion in Paris. At a festive gathering in her salon, she recalls an earlier incident when for a few hours she experienced love with a student. The only sympathetic response comes from Prunier, a poet who is in love with Magda's pert maid Lisette. Ruggero, a young family friend of Rambaldo's, enters and is given advice on the pleasure spots of the city. He reminds Magda of her first love, and after the guests have gone, she dresses as a grisette and follows the boy to the Bal Bullier. Unrecognized even by Lisette, she joins Ruggero, and soon rouses Ruggero's love. Even when Rambaldo confronts her with her betrayal, she chooses to leave with Ruggero. They spend many happy days in the country, but when their funds run low and Ruggero seeks and gains permission from his mother to marry her, Magda realizes that

199

she must give him up. As has been predicted by Prunier, she returns like the swallow to her former life, leaving her lover in tears.

Major Roles. MAGDA DE CIVRY (lyr s); B♭2 to C5. LISETTE (high s); B♭2 to C5. RUGGERO LASTOUC (t); E♭2 to B♭3. PRUNIER (t); B♭1 to A3 (B♭3 in ensemble; fals passage with top C, A opt). RAMBALDO FERNANDEZ (bar); C2 to E3 (E2 opt).

Lesser Roles. Friends of Rambaldo: PÉRICHAUD (bar or bs); GOBIN (t); CRÉBILLON (bs or bar). Friends of Magda: YVETTE (s); BIANCA (s); SUZY (m-s). RABONNIER, painter (bs). A BUTLER (bs). A SINGER (s). A GRISETTE (s). A STUDENT (t).

Chorus. SSTTBB. Two soloists (s). Dancers, waiters, flower girls, students, artists, men-about-town, grisettes, demimondaines.

Orchestra. 2 fl, picc, 2 ob, Eng hrn, 3 cl, 2 bsn, 4 hrn, 3 trp, 3 trb, bs tuba, timp, perc, harp, cel, strings.

Material. Bel (Son). VS (i, e)*.

Performances. N. Eng. Th. (Bost.): 11.20.58. Denver Lyr. Th.: 11.9.63. Grant Park (Chic.): 8.3.68. San Fernando Vall. St. Coll. (Cal.): 11.15.68. Chatham Op. (Pitts.): 4.4.69. Spr. Op. San Fran.: 6.3.69. San Ant.: 4.11.70. Univ. of S. W. La. Op. Guild (Lafayette): 4.71. Cincin. Summ. Op.: 7.18.73.

🎵 The Royal Hunt of the Sun

Music by Iain Hamilton (1922–   ). Libretto in English adapted by the composer from the play by Peter Schaffer. Historical tragedy. Contemporary idiom. Vocal line mostly lyrical, partly declamatory; some song-speech, dialogue. Setting: Spain, Panama, and Inca Empire in Peru, June 1529 to August 1533. Two acts, multiple scenes (see Production Difficulties) (120 min).

ACT I i: A bare stage with huge medallion on back wall; ii: Cathedral Church of Panama; iii: Dark stage, medallion begins to glow, then opens out as golden sun with twelve rays, Atahuallpa in center; iv: Province of Tumbes; v: The jungle, night; vi: Beyond the forest in Inca fields, morning; vii: The March to the Andes (two levels; Indians above, Spaniards below); viii: Mime of the Great Ascent; ix: Cajamarca, a large empty square, night; x: Same; xi: Same, lighter; xii: Inca procession; xiii: Mime of the Great Massacre (60 min). ACT II i: Inca Lament; ii: Atahuallpa chained; iii: Robing of Atahuallpa and Feast; iv: First Gold Procession; v: Atahuallpa's Song, Dance of the Aylu; vi: Second Gold Procession and Rape of the Sun; vii–xii: Before the Sun Chamber (60 min).

Synopsis. The story begins and is told partly by the recollections of Martin Ruiz, Pizarro's page, and shifts to the actual time, when Martin was a young man accompanying Francisco Pizarro on the expedition to Peru. Also in the group are Hernando de Soto, second in command; Miguel Estete, the Royal Veedor; Fray Vincente de Valverde, chaplain; and Fray

Marcos de Nizza, Franciscan friar, as well as various subordinate commanders. Their object is the fabled gold of the Incas, disguised under the determination to bring the Incas to the Christian faith. Atahuallpa, who has killed his legitimate brother to ascend to the throne, shares this illegitimacy with Pizarro, as well as other sympathies. Pizarro, however, breaks his promise unwillingly to set the Sun-king free once the Sun-chamber is filled with gold brought from all over the kingdom. The Spanish soldiers slaughter the Indians and Atahuallpa is garroted. Pizarro is left alone to mourn his victory and his friend.

Major Roles. PIZARRO (bar); long and difficult role; G1 to Gb3. ATAHUALLPA (bar); Ab1 to G3. DE SOTO (t); C2 to A3. ESTETE (t); C#2 to G#3. MARTIN as old man (bs-bar); mostly declamation. VALVERDE (bs); low tessitura; G1 to D3.

Lesser Roles. PIEDRO DE CANDIA, commander of Spanish artillery (bar); Bb1 to E3. DIEGO DE TRUJILLO, MASTER OF HORSE (t). YOUNG MARTIN (t or s); D2 to G3 or D3 to G4. Soldiers: SALINAS (bar); RODAS (t); VASCA (t); DOMINGO (bar). NIZZA (t); C#2 to A3. VILLAC UMU, Inca high priest (bs); B1 to Eb3. CHALLCUCHIMA, Inca general (t); Db2 to A3. CHIEFTAIN (t). HEADMAN (bar).

Bit Parts. FELIPILLO, Indian boy, interpreter (t). MANCO, messenger (t). INTI COUSSI, stepsister of Atahuallpa (mute). OELLO, a wife of Atahuallpa (mute).

Chorus. Indians SATB (occasionally doubled). Soldiers TB.

Orchestra. 2 fl, 2 ob, 2 cl, 2 bsn, 4 hrn, 3 trp, 3 trb, tuba, harp, piano, perc (4), timp, strings.

Production Difficulties. Frequent change of scenes; can be accomplished largely by lighting, particularly in second act, where scene shifts do not necessarily call for change in setting. Handling of chorus and supers in large groups for processions and massacre.

Material. Pr.

◙ Rusalka, or, The Mermaid

Music by Antonin Dvořák (1841–1904). Libretto in Czech by Jaroslav Kvapil. Premiere: Prague, March 31, 1901. Fairy tale. Strong national flavor; set numbers. Short prelude. Setting: A mythical kingdom. Three acts (142 min).

ACT I: Glade near lake, with witch's cottage (52 min). ACT II: Palace garden with pool (40 min). ACT III: Same as Act I (50 min).

Synopsis. This is a variation on the Undine story. The water nymph Rusalka falls in love with a mortal Prince, and seeks advice from the Water-sprite, who sends her to the Witch Jezibaba. The witch promises to help her on condition that she remain mute, and that if the Prince prove unfaithful, Rusalka must return to the depths of the lake. As the nymph drinks a magic potion, a mysterious Hunter warns of doom. But Rusalka embarks happily on her new life when the Prince discovers and falls in love with her. All is not well at the Castle, however, in spite of the festive preparations for the wedding. The Gamekeeper and Kitchenboy gossip that the Prince seems to have transferred his affections to a foreign Princess, having become bored with his fiancée's dumbness. When Rusalka discovers this, she throws herself into the pond. The Watersprite rises to curse the Prince, who is abandoned by his new love. Rusalka, transformed into a will-o'-the-wisp, has returned to her own lake, where Jezibaba offers her another hope—if she will sacrifice her lover's blood, she may be free of the curse. But Rusalka still loves the Prince. He, in turn, is deeply burdened with guilt and returns to the lakeside to call for Rusalka. She appears, and warns him of the danger of her kiss, but he gladly atones by embracing her. Freed at last, Rusalka sinks into her own element.

Major Roles. RUSALKA (dram or spin s); needs strength throughout range; Bb2 to B4. PRINCE (t) C2 to Bb3 (one firm C4). WATERSPRITE (bs); G1 to F#3. JEZIBABA (c); Bb2 to Bb4.

Lesser Roles. FOREIGN PRINCESS (s); Bb2 to C5. HUNTER (bar). GAMEKEEPER (t). KITCHENBOY (s).

Chorus. SATB. Guests. SSAA. Water nymphs. Small solos: 3 elves (s, s, c).

Ballet. In each act: water nymphs, wedding guests, wood nymphs.

Orchestra. picc, 2 fl, 2 ob, Eng hrn, 2 cl, bs cl, 2 bsn, 4 hrn, 3 trp, 3 trb, tuba, timp, perc (2), harp, strings.

Material. B & H. VS*. Tr: Martins. FS: Ar*.

Performances. USC (Ducloux tr): 12.7.63. Cambridge Wksp (Mass.): 5.3.69. Ravinia (Chic.): 8.15.70 (conc). Wash. Civic Op. (D.C.): 9.15.72 (Martin tr).

🎵 Russlan and Ludmilla

Music by Mikhail Ivanovitch Glinka (1804–1857). Libretto in Russian by the composer and five writers based on fairy tale by Pushkin. Premiere: St. Petersburg, December 9, 1842. Melodious, with native touches, also oriental flavor. Overture and brief preludes to each act. Setting: Kiev and imaginary locales. Five acts, nine scenes (171 min).

ACT I: Palace of Prince Svietozar (35 min). ACT II i: Finn's cavern; ii: Solitary spot; iii: Misty battlefield; iv: Same, with giant head (38 min). ACT III: Naina's enchanted palace (42 min). ACT IV: Chernomor's dwelling (30 min). ACT V i: Moonlit valley near encampment; ii: Palace at Kiev (26 min).

Synopsis. Prince Svietozar is giving a grand ball in honor of his daughter Ludmilla's suitors, who include Russlan, a native nobleman; Ratmir, a Tartar Prince; and Farlaf, a Scandinavian warrior, who is a coward at heart. Russlan is Ludmilla's favorite. Lel, the god of love, is invoked, but a thunderclap intervenes and the lights go out. When they return, the Princess is missing.

Her father promises her hand to the man who shall bring her back. Russlan learns from Finn, the wizard, that Ludmilla is a captive of Chernomor, a villainous dwarf, and that Naina, the evil fairy, is also to be feared. Russlan searches for magic weapons. Naina has promised to aid Farlaf, and has imprisoned Ratmir, casting spells on him. Russlan is saved from the sirens' spells by Finn, and manages to penetrate Chernomor's dwelling, where Ludmilla, after refusing to be diverted by a ballet, has been plunged into magical slumber. Russlan rescues her with his magic sword, but cannot awaken her. He makes use of a magic ring, which wakens her. Her father bestows her hand upon the victorious suitor.

Major Roles. SVIETOZAR (bs); Ab1 to Eb3. LUDMILLA (col s); quite florid; C#3 to C5. RUSSLAN (bar); some high tessitura; flexible; F1 to F3. RATMIR (c); low tessitura; some flexibility; G2 to F4. FARLAF (bs); needs flexibility for patter song; F1 to Eb3. FINN (t); C2 to G3. NAINA (m-s); D3 to D4.

Lesser Roles. GORISLAVA, Ratmir's slave (s); D3 to Bb4. BAYAN, a bard (t); D2 to G3. CHERNOMOR (t). AEDO (t).

Chorus. SSATB. Sons of Svietozar, boyars and wives; maids of honor, nurses, pages, stewards, slaves, etc.

Ballet: Oriental, Acts III and IV.

Orchestra. 2 fl (picc), 2 ob (Eng horn), 2 cl, 2 bsn, cont bsn, 4 hrn, 3 trp, 2 trb, timp, perc, piano, strings. *Stage*: 2 trp, perc.

Material. AMP (SZ).

🎭 The Sack of Calabasas

Music by Grant Fletcher (1913–   ). Libretto in English by the composer. As yet unperformed. Historical drama. Set numbers, conventional harmonies, vocal line partly melodious, partly patterned after speech and declamatory. Choral prelude. Interludes between scenes. Setting: Calabasas, southern Arizona, 1882. Three acts, thirteen scenes (150 min).

Prologue: Chorus in pit describes Calabasas, "the meanest town in the West," on a Sunday morning in 1882. ACT I i: The Golden Fleece Bar; ii: Railroad Street, "The Creation of Abimelech"; iii: Abimelech turns a vacant bar into a chancel; iv: Railroad Street; v: The chancel (60 min). ACT II i: The Golden Fleece; ii: The saloon next door; iii: Railroad Street; iv: Sue's room; v (interlude): A desert fire (45 min). ACT III i: The Golden Fleece; ii (interlude, chorus in pit): A hill north of Nogales; iii: Railroad Street (45 min).

Synopsis. Into the sinful town of Calabasas, which is growing suddenly because of the prospect of a railroad coming through, rides a stranger, who announces himself to be Abimelach, a preacher. He sets up a chancel in an abandoned bar and wins approval by his sermon on playing cards. Sedalia Sue and Longhorn Charlie plan to get the preacher drunk and catch him at the "badger game," but Longhorn fails to show up and Sue willingly accepts the gold pieces of the overly tempted preacher. Slim Parr, the Sheriff from

Grizzly Paw, creates consternation by revealing that Abimelech is a con man, his money counterfeit. The men set out to catch the imposter, but meet the Chinese Ah Chin Honk, who gives them a letter from Abimelech which ironically thanks them and breaks the news that a railroad engineer has told them the railroad will bypass Calabasas. The people of Calabasas, enraged, get drunk and burn down the doomed town.

Major Roles. ABIMELECH JONES (high dram bar); long passages onstage; A1 to G3. DEUCES WILD (bs); F1 to D3. SEDALIA SUE (spin s); F♯3 to B♭4. LONGHORN CHARLIE (t); F2 to B♭3. SLIM PARR (bar); C2 to F♯3.

Lesser Role. AH CHIN HONK (t); E2 to G♯4.

Bit Roles. ALICE (s or m-s); G♯3 to F2. MEN FROM THE CROWD (t, bar). THREE MEN AROUND CAMPFIRE (t, bar, bar). ONE OVERLY SENTIMENTAL DRUNK (bar or t).

Chorus. Double qt (4 t, 4 bs). SATB (occasionally divided). Important. Waddies, dissolute cowpokes, barmen, gamblers, hurdy girls, tarts, gunmen, drovers, miners, etc. Offstage choir, SATB, narrates from descriptive portions of story; can be in pit or at one side with P.A. system. May be replaced by narrator.

Ballet. Act I, ii: Irish dances; street dances.

Orchestra. 2 fl (picc), 2 ob, 2 cl, 2 bsn, 4 hrn, 3 trp, 3 trb, tuba, timp, perc (3), piano, strings.

Material. Composer: 1626 East Williams St., Tempe, Ariz. 85281.

⚐ Sadko

Music by Nikolai Rimsky-Korsakov (1844–1908). Libretto in Russian by the composer. Premiere: Moscow, January 7, 1898. "Lyric legend." Fairy tale, with pervasive folk atmosphere, alternating between the lyrical and the spectacular, with little human drama. Highly colored and exotic orchestration. Vocal line melodic, in recitative style modeled on one of the last Russian bards. Orchestral interludes between Scenes 5 and 6, 6 and 7. Setting: Novgorod, by the sea and in the depths of the sea, legendary times. Seven scenes (166 min).

Scene i: Great hall in the palace of the merchants' guild (25 min). ii: Bank of Lake Ilmen (28 min). iii: Room in Sadko's house (13 min). iv: Port of Novgorod on Lake Ilmen (40 min). v: By the lakeside, with Sadko's ship, *The Falcon* (13 min). vi: Underwater palace of the King of the Sea (28 min). vii: A green meadow near Lake Ilmen (19 min).

Synopsis. The merchant princes of Novgorod are entertained by a guslee player, who sings of old heroic days. Then Sadko also sings, but he belittles the city's commerce and promises the ships great wealth if they will sail to far oceans. He is laughed to scorn, and roams the lakeside bewailing his unhappy condition. A flock of swans sails toward him; when they reach land they are transformed into beautiful maidens. One of them, Volkova, the daughter of the King of the Sea, offers him her love as well as riches.

He rushes home to his disconsolate wife Ljuba Busslajevna, but rejects her in favor of his new fortune. Interrupting the scene of great merriment and excitement at the port, where clowns are dancing and singing, Sadko boasts that he can catch gold fish in the lake and wagers his head against their ships. The magic of the princess ensures his success. With all the ships at his command, he plans to sail far away, but first asks three merchants to describe their respective countries: A Viking, a Hindu (the famous "Song of India"), and a Venetian. He decides on Venice as his destination, and over twelve years amasses a great fortune. But now his ships are becalmed, and the superstitious sailors believe they must propitiate the King of the Sea. Sadko is chosen by lot and flung overboard. But he is rescued by Volkova and wins her hand in a scene of great fantasy and spectacle. However, an apparition strikes the guslee from his hand and forces him to return to land. Volkova accompanies him, changing herself into a river so that she will always be near him. His wife receives him with joy, and when all his ships return with hoards of treasure, he is proclaimed a hero.

Major Roles. SADKO (lyr t); D2 to A3 (one B♭3). LJUBA BUSSLAJEVNA (m-s); B2 to A4. NEJATA, young guslee player from Kiev (c); G2 to E4; important song. VOLKOVA (s); needs considerable flexibility; top B♭4 and firm C5. KING OF THE SEA (bs); A♯1 to E3.

Lesser Roles. DUDA (bs), SOPIEL (t), clowns. VIKING MERCHANT (bs). HINDU MERCHANT (t); top B♭3. VENETIAN MERCHANT (bar); some high tessitura; top G3, one A3. FOMA NASARITCH (t), LUKA SENOVITCH (bs), Novgorod officials. (The above are important character roles.)

Other Lesser Roles. TWO MOUNTEBANKS (2 m-s). TWO SOOTHSAYERS (2 t). APPARITION (bs). PILGRIM (bar).

Chorus. SSAATTBB. Very important. Townspeople, merchants, clowns, mountebanks, pilgrims, young Sea Princesses as swans.

Ballet. As spectacular as possible. Clowns. Procession of wonders of the sea and dance of the gold and silver fish in Scene v.

Orchestra. 3 fl (picc), 2 ob, Eng hrn, 3 cl (bs cl), 2 bsn, cont bsn, 4 hrn, 3 trp (high trp), 3 trb, tuba, timp, perc, high and low bells, 2 harp, piano org, strings. *Stage:* 3 trp.

Material. Pet.

Performances. Chatham Coll. (Pittsburgh): 4.3.68 (conc).

🎵 Sappho

Music by Peggy Glanville-Hicks (1912–   ). Libretto in English by Lawrence Durrell. Commissioned by the Ford Foundation and San Francisco Opera. Unperformed. Greek drama. Literary, poetic text. Continuous texture, exotic harmonies, set numbers embedded; vocal line largely patterned after speech with occasional lyrical passages. Overture. Setting: The island of Lesbos, circa 650. Three acts, seven scenes (135 min).

ACT I i: Spacious room of rich Greek family with court or terrace outside; ii: The same room set for a banquet. ACT II i: A brief prelude; can be before curtain or on small section of stage; must merge into ii: House as in I i; iii: Can be before curtain. ACT III i: Cave of the Oracle; ii: The house.

Synopsis. Kreon, elderly husband of Sappho, the mature famous beauty, has hired a diver to find the family tablets (records), submerged after an earthquake in whose ruins the child Sappho had been found. The diver is Phaon, twin brother of the celebrated general Pittakos, who is now at war in Attica. Phaon has recovered in Egypt from leprosy. He and Sappho discover themselves to be kindred spirits, and she sings his poem at a symposium. A debate between Sappho's friend Minos and the drunken poet Diomedes ends in a ribald rout, leaving Sappho and Phaon, who declare their love. Next day Minos brings the news that Diomedes's son has been killed in battle, while Kreon celebrates Phaon's finding of the records. A great crowd welcomes the victorious Pittakos, who is delighted to find his brother and offers him an administrative post in Attica. Phaon refuses, however. Pittakos reveals that he has killed Diomedes's son for cowardice. Sappho, furious, bides him retire from public life and attempts to kill him. She has sent him away previously as his amorous attentions grew onerous. Now he is humiliated, and resolves to consult the Oracle. Sappho's jeers at this are well-founded; she herself is the Oracle in disguise, and has refused the drug in order to give him advice from her own judgment. Only Diomedes knows of her priestess role, as he tells her when she visits him. He has taken poison, not so much because of his son's cowardice, but because he has coveted his son's young wife. As Sappho prepares to assume the Oracle's duties, Kreon reveals that he has found a letter from his wife telling of the birth of their daughter Sappho. He has married his own daughter. The penalty is confiscation of all his possessions and either banishment or the sword, according to the people's vote. Sappho will share this fate. The vote is for exile. Pittakos retains Sappho's children as hostages, when she refuses his offer to act as a spy for him in Attica. She prepares for banishment. Note: Sappho's last aria is one of four original Sappho poems incorporated by Durrell in his story.

Major Roles. SAPPHO (m-s); G2 to Ab4. DIOMEDES (bar); B1 to G#3. MINOS (bs-bar); F#1 to G3. PHAON (lyr t); C2 to B3. PITTAKOS (dram t); Bb1 to (several) C4. KREON (bs); F1 (one E1) to E3.

Lesser Roles. Three maidens, CHLOE (s); JOY (s); DORIS (m-s). THREE SYBILS (s, s, m-s). TWO CHILDREN (mute).

Chorus. SAATBB. Solo: An Alexandrian (t).

Orchestra. 2 fl (picc), 2 ob (Eng hrn), 2 cl, 2 bsn (cont bsn), 4 hrn, 3 trp, 3 trb, timp, perc, harp, strings.

Material. Bel.

The Scarecrow

Music by Normand Lockwood (1906–   ). Libretto in English by Dorothy Lockwood, adapted from the play by Percy Mackaye, based on Hawthorne's story, "Feathertop." Premiere: Columbia University, New York, May 19, 1945. Fantasy-drama. Set numbers embedded in continuous texture; vocal line partly melodious, partly declamatory; considerable dialogue; conventional harmonies. Brief prelude with curtain raised. Settng: Early New England. Two acts, five scenes.

ACT I i: Interior of a smithy; ii, iii and ACT II i and ii: Drawing room of Merton house during the course of a day.

Synopsis. Justice Gilead Merton abandoned Bess Rickby and her child to die; the woman survived and is suspected of witchcraft. She sells Rachel, Merton's niece, a magic mirror which will reveal the truth about anyone who looks into it. Then with the help of Dickon, a Yankee Prince of Darkness, Goody Rickby fashions a scarecrow and imbues it with life, through the instrumentality of a corncob pipe. For revenge, she sends the Scarecrow in the guise of Lord Ravensbane to win Rachel from her fiancé, Squire Richard Talbot. The handsome "lord" is successful, but Richard shows Rachel the pumpkinhead of her lover in the mirror. Rachel, however, remains loyal to Ravensbane, who, through the power of her love, becomes a man, and dies as a man after the magic pipe is broken. The populace who came to hang him and the witch and the devil marvels at the miracle.

Major Roles. (No range problems.) GOODY BESS RIGBY (m-s). DICKON (t). RACHEL MERTON (s); top A4. RICHARD TALBOT (t). JUSTICE GILEAD MERTON (bs); low F♯1. SCARECROW (LORD RAVENSBANE) (t); top A3.

Lesser Roles. JEDIDAH, Merton servant (s or m-s). MINISTER DODGE (bs). SIR CHARLES (t.) FANNY, his daughter (s). AMILLY (m-s).

Bit Roles. REV. TODD. REV. RAND. MISTRESS DODGE. SCARECROW'S VOICE from mirror.

Chorus. SSAATTBB. Male quartet offstage.

Orchestra. fl, picc, ob, bsn, 2 hrn, 2 trp, trb, timp, perc, piano anvil, strings (3.2.2.2.1).

Production Problem. Transformation of scarecrow.

Material. ACA.

☙ The Secret · Tajemstvi

Music by Bedřich Smetana (1824–1884). Libretto in Czech by Eliška Krásnohorská. Premiere: Prague, New Czech Theater, September 18, 1878. Romantic comedy. Lyrical in folkloristic vein. Overture. Setting: a small Czech town in the mid–19th century. Three acts. (108 min).

ACT I: The town square. ACT II: A mountain gully near a ruined castle and cloister. ACT III: Room in Malina's house.

Synopsis. A feud has divided the villagers for twenty years because the spinster Róza feels that Councilman Kalina (now a widower) should have married her; he in turn recalls only that her parents denied him because he was poor. During construction of his new house a letter is found among the debris of the old. Written by a friar (since deceased) at the time of the original misunderstanding, it directs Kalina to a ruined abbey in the mountains to find a treasure map. Meanwhile, Kalina's son Vitek wishes to marry Róza's niece, Blazenka, adding further fuel to the controversy. Kalina follows the friar's directions only to discover that the treasure he was meant to find is Róza herself. The two couples are united.

Major Roles. ROZA (m-s). BLAZENKA (s). KALINA (bar). VITEK (t). MALINA, Róza's brother (bs). BONIFACE, an ex-soldier (bar). NIGHTINGALE, a singer (high t).

Lesser Roles. INNKEEPER (s). BUILDER (bar). JIRKA, bellringer (t). GHOST OF FRIAR BARNABAS (bar).

Chorus. SATB.

Orchestra. 2 fl, 2 ob, 2 cl, 2 bsn, 4 hrn, 2 trp, 3 trb, timp, bells, guit, strings.

Material: B & H.

☙ Semiramide · Semiramus

Music by Gioacchino Rossini (1792–1868). Libretto in Italian by Gaetano Rossi after Voltaire. Premiere: Venice, February 3, 1823. Tragedy. Highly melodious; extremely difficult vocal lines with pervading *bel canto* and demanding ornamentation. Setting: Ancient Babylon. Two acts (157 min).

Synopsis. Queen Semiramide has had her husband Nino killed, and has taken Assur for a lover. Her son, Ninia, whom she has not seen since he was a boy, enters her service under the name of Arsace; he is victorious in battle and she falls in love with him. But he is already pledged to Princess Azema. In the Temple, Semiramide is about to announce her choice for future King when the tomb of Nino opens and his ghost proclaims Arsace as his successor, summoning the boy to his tomb at midnight to learn the secret of his assassination. Assur, enraged, slips into the tomb and confronts Semiramide, who now knows from the High Priest Oroe that Arsace is her son. She takes a blow Arsace means for Assur and dies. Arsace is proclaimed King.

Major Roles. SEMIRAMIDE (s); extremely florid; trill; Bb2 to B4. ARSACE (c); equally florid; trill; G2 to G4. ASSUR (bar); needs flexibility; trill; F1 (F2 opt) to F3. IDRENO, Indian Prince (t); florid; high tessitura; trill; A1 to D4.

Lesser Roles. OROE (bs); F1 to F3. NINO (bs); C2 to Eb3. AZEMA (s); D3 to F#4. MITRANE, captain of the guard (t).

Chorus. SSATB, many four-part divisions. Satraps, wise men, Babylonians, strange woman, Egyptians, slaves, Indians, etc.

Orchestra. 2 fl, 2 ob, 2 cl, 2 bsn, 4 hrn, 2 trp, 3 trb, timp, perc, strings. *Stage*: picc, 2 fl, 2 ob, 4 cl, 2 alto sax, ten sax, 2 bsn, 4 hrn, 4 trp, 3 trb, 2 tuba, ten flicorno, bar flicorna.

Material. Scala archives, through Bel.

Performances. Am. Op. Soc. (conc) 2.18.64. Lyr. Op. Chic.: 9.24.71.

⚜ The Shoemaker's Holiday

Music by Dominic Argento (1927–   ). Libretto adapted with additional lyrics by John Olos from Thomas Dekker's 17th–century ballad opera. Commissioned by Minnesota Theater Foundation. Premiere: Guthrie Theater, Minneapolis, June 1, 1967. Comedy. Primarily intended for actors; ranges lie well for amateurs, except for Eyre. Set numbers; some dialogue; contemporary harmonies. Setting: London and environs, 17th century. Two parts. Prologue leads into overture and is resumed after.

Part I i: London street; ii: Garden at Old Ford, Sir Roger Oteley's house outside London; iii: Tower Street; iv: Open yard by Eyre's shop; v: Field near Old Ford House; vi: Eyre's shop; vii: Room in Lincoln's house; viii: Field; ix: Room in Lord Mayor's house; x: Street; xi: Old Ford House.

Part II i: Seamster's shop in London; ii: Eyre's shop (now Hodge's); iii: Garden of Lord Mayor's house; iv: Eyre's house; v: Street near St. Faith's church; vi: Banquet hall.

Synopsis. Simon Eyre relates the story: The love of young Rowland Lacy and Rose is thwarted by his kinsmen, who send Lacy to war, and by her father, Lord Mayor of London, who takes her out of London. Lacy deserts and returns to Eyre's house disguised as Hans, a Dutch shoemaker. But all ends well, for Simon becomes Lord Mayor of London and allows the lovers to wed.

Major Roles. SIMON EYRE (bar); A1 to F♯3. ROWLAND LACY (may be t); B♭1 to F3 (touches G3). ROSE (s). SIR HUGH LACY, Earl of Lincoln.

Lesser Roles. SIR ROGER OTELEY. RALPH, soldier (bar). FIRK, shoemaker (bs-bar). HAMMON, hunter (bs or bar). WARNER, hunter (sp). HODGE, shoemaker (bs). MARGERY, Simon's wife (s). JANE, seamstress (m-s). SYBIL, Rose's maid (c). FOUR VENDORS (t, 2 bar, bs). THREE MEN (t, bar, bs). TWO SEAMSTRESSES (m-s, c). SOLDIERS, SHOEMAKERS, HUNTERS (t, bar, bs). BOY (sp). KING (sp). Some street cries.

Chorus. SATB.

Ballet. Dances at beginning illustrate story; Morris dance.

Orchestra. fl (picc, alto fl), cl, bsn, hrn, 2 trp, trb (ten-bs), guit (amplified), perc. May participate in action.

Material. B & H.

⚜ Siebzehn Tage und 4 Minuten · Seventeen Days and Four Minutes

Music by Werner Egk (1901–   ). Libretto in German by the composer after Calderón's *El mayor encanto amor* ("Love the Sorcerer"). Premiere: Stuttgart, June 2, 1966. "Semi-buffa." Contemporary idiom; many lyrical passages; continuous texture with set numbers embedded; vocal line often highly melodious, occasionally patterned after speech; many ensembles. Setting: Circe's island; ancient times. Three acts, five scenes.

ACT I: Mountains and woods on seashore. ACT II i: Square in front of

209

Circe's "palace;" ii: Wooded glen. ACT III i: Seashore; ii: Shady place in environs of "palace."

Synopsis. Circe has deposed and humbled Arsidas, former king of the island, and transformed the island into a trap for seafaring men. She and her girls are on the seashore when Ulysses's ship is sighted; they conjure up a storm and the ship is nearly wrecked. Ulysses and four men come ashore. Two are immediately changed into beasts, but Ulysses resists Circe's wiles, and forces her to restore the men. However, she persuades him to remain a while to rest, and a mutual attraction soon develops. They try to best each other at various games, while the sailors undergo adventures. Klarin discovers a chest containing two strange creatures, which turn into jewels; he himself is turned into a monkey. Leporell tries to train the monkey to play the guitar with the view of giving concerts. Moro and Antistes try to bring Ulysses to his senses by displaying the sacred weapons of Achilles. Klarin, regaining his human form, warns the others they have only seventeen days and four minutes to remain, otherwise they will be captive forever. Ulysses decides Circe isn't worth the risk, and all return to the ship. Circe, at first crushed by defeat, soon rallies, and sets out to snare the next ship.

Major Roles. CIRCE (s); needs some flexibility; sustained in middle to high register; lyrical passages; top Bb4. ULYSSES (t); some lyrical passages with Circe; top A3. LYBIA (s), ASTRAA (m-s), BABA (c), Circe's companions; mostly in ensemble. ANTISTES, steersman (bar); top F3.

Lesser Roles. ARSIDAS (t). MORO (bs). AN OLD WOMAN (s). A DWARF (t). KLARIN (buf t). LEPORELL (buf bs). A LION (sp). BRUTAMONTE, giant brother of Polypheme (mute).

Ballet. Act II. Nymphs, satyrs, young gods.

Orchestra. picc, 2 ob, Eng hrn, 2 cl, bs cl, bsn, 2 hrn, 2 trp, trb, timp, harp, strings. *Stage:* 2 trp, small & bs dr with cym, guit on tape. Short tape, signal of Klarin.

Material. Bel (Sch).

Performances. Center Op. Co. (Minneapolis): 1.17.70 (Amer prem).

🎵 Le Siège de Corinthe · L'Assedio di Corinto · The Siege of Corinth

Music by Gioacchino Rossini (1792–1868). Libretto in French by Luigi Balocchi and Alexandre Soumet. Premiere: Paris, October 9, 1826. It is a revision of *Maometto II* (premiere: Naples, December 3, 1820). Revised for Italy. Several versions exist, of both *Le Siège* and *Maometto,* so that contemporary production can be very flexible. Latest version by Randolph Mickelson for La Scala, Milan; premiere: April 11, 1969. (See below for notes on various versions.) Lyric tragedy. Set numbers; conventional harmonies; important ensembles, recitatives; vocal line often florid; ornamentation depending on version. Setting: Corinth, 15th century. Three acts (Scala version, three acts, four scenes). Duration depends on version and ornamentation; La Scala version approx 145 min.

ACT I: Vestibule of the Palace of the Senate (La Scala, same; ii: Piazza at the harbor). ACT II: Pavilion of Maometto (La Scala: Maometto's ship, with castles in distance). ACT III: Tombs of Kings of Corinth (La Scala: same); destruction of Corinth.

Synopsis. Pamira, daughter of Cleomene, Governor of Corinth, has fallen in love with a stranger, who later returns as Maometto, the Mohammedan conquerer. Torn between love and patriotism, she reluctantly agrees to marry Neocle, a young Greek officer chosen by her father, but later changes her mind. In the destruction of Corinth she dies with her father and valiant compatriots.

Major Roles. MAOMETTO II, Emperor of Turkey (lyr bs or low bar); must have penetrating quality to carry over ensembles and orchestra; florid; G1 to F3; of two versions of Act I aria in score, top line is *Siège*, bottom line *Maometto.* PAMIRA (orig. written low, but preferably spin or dram s); taxing role, resembling Norma in tessitura (A–E); B2 (opt G♯2) to B4 (preferably C5); ornaments carry to E5 in La Scala version. NEOCLE (t or c— see note); t has low tessitura but high range, similar to Otello; Bb1 to firm C4; c has Bb2 (touches G2) to Eb4 in orig; La Scala version added G4's and in added aria Ab2 to Bb4. All require trill.

Lesser Roles. CLEOMENE (dram t or high bar); needs strength; one important solo in trio; florid passages; trill; Bb1 to B3. JERO, a guard (bs profondo); needs strength; one aria with chorus; G1 to F3. ISMENE, Pamira's confidante (m-s); one aria. OMAR, confidante of Maometto (bs).

Bit Role. ADRASTO, Greek warrior (t).

Chorus. SSTTBB. Important and dramatic. Turks and Greeks.

Orchestra. 2 fl, 2 ob, 2 cl, 2 bsn, 4 hrn, 2 trp, 3 trb, tuba, timp, perc, 2 harp, strings.

Production Problems. Fire and collapse of Corinth at end to accompany several minutes of orchestra alone.

Material. (Bel) Ri. VS (i)*. La Scala vers: copyright R. Mickelson.

Note on Revisions: Rossini made two versions of *Maometto II,* adding for the Venice performance the finale from his *La Donna del Lago* and a Sinfonia as Overture, which is printed in the Ricordi score of *L'Assedio.* Mickelson's version of *L'Assedio* restores two pieces from *Maometto,* a section of the Act III aria for soprano, and a scena for the mezzo-soprano near the end. The Ricordi score shows Neocle both as tenor and contralto; it was contralto in *Maometto* but tenor in *Le Siège;* when given in Italy in Rossini's period, the role was changed back to contralto. Ranges for both are given. A big duet in Act II in the Ricordi score (pp. 170–178) was cut by Mickelson; it was written and inserted by Donizetti for a performance he conducted, with Rossini's permission. A producer who has a bass of unusual quality could restore from *Maometto* a florid cavatina and an aria in Act I. In the period of the premiere, pitch varied from place to place, so that today's ranges could be transposed without violating tradition. For example, the important aria for Neocle inserted for La Scala was written in E, but a note in the original manuscript in Rossini's hand asks that it be transposed to D; La Scala did it in E♭ as best fitting the singer. The range is given above in that key. Pamira's range in the original shows a fairly low tessitura, but Mickelson's ornamentation for the Scala version carries it up to E♭, and it could go to any extreme, depending on the singer.

🎵 The Snow Maiden · Snegorotchka

Music by Nikolai Rimsky-Korsakov (1844–1908). Libretto in Russian by the composer after a play by Ostrovsky. Premiere: St. Petersburg, February 10, 1882. National epic alternating fairy tale and realistic scenes. Colorful orchestration; strong folk choruses; lyrical and pastoral vocal passages, often accompanied by the guslee, Russian stringed instrument. Setting: Legendary Russian province. Prologue and four acts.

Prologue: Moonlight night on Red Mountain, in the distance the village of Berendeys, ancient capital of the Tsar. ACT I: Outskirts of the village. ACT II: Hall in the Tsar's palace. ACT III: The sacred forest. ACT IV: Valley of the Sun God Yarila.

Synopsis. The Winter stays too long in the province of Berendeys because King Winter wants to be near his wife, Fairy Spring, and their daughter, the Snow Maiden. But at last he departs, leaving his daughter in the custody of a worthy peasant couple. The maiden attracts young men, but herself cannot love anyone, even the charming shepherd singer Lel. At the betrothal ceremony of the rich Tartar merchant Mizgyr and the maiden Koupava, Mizgyr notices the Snow Maiden and immediately deserts his betrothed for her. Koupava seeks justice from the Tsar, who sends for the Snow Maiden. The entire court is spellbound by her beauty, but the Tsar suspects that her coldness has something to do with the Sun God's displeasure, and offers a fortune to the suitor who shall warm her heart. At a festival celebrating the coming of summer, Lel chooses Koupava for a bride. The Snow Maiden, disgruntled and realizing her lack, asks her mother to allow her to love a human. Upon the reluctant consent of Fairy Spring, the Snow Maiden selects Mizgyr, who has been courting her in vain. But their happiness is short-lived; a ray of sun strikes the Snow Maiden and melts her away, while Mizgyr drowns himself. The sacrifice, however, has brought summer back to the land.

Major Roles. SNEGOROTCHKA, the Snow Maiden (s); has several charming songs. KING WINTER (bs). FAIRY SPRING (m-s). LEL (t or c); has one extended solo. KOUPAVA (m-s). MIZGYR (bar or t).

Lesser Roles. TSAR (t). VILLAGER (t). HIS WIFE (m-s). WOOD GHOST (t). CARNIVAL KING (bs). BERMYATA, a Boyar (bs). TWO HERALDS (t, t or bar). PAGE (m-s).

Chorus. SATB. Very important. Woodland sprites, villagers, courtiers, musicians, etc.

Ballet. Folk dances, Act III.

Orchestra. 3 fl, 2 ob, 2 cl, 2 bsn, 4 hrn, 2 trp, 3 trb, tuba, timp, perc, harp, cel, strings.

Material. Ka.

🎵 Die Soldaten · The Soldiers

Music by Bern Alois Zimmerman (1918–   ). Libretto in German by the composer, based on the play by Reinhold Lenz. Premiere: Cologne, February 15, 1965. Drama. Complex twelve-tone style overlaid with jazz and Bach chorales; extremely difficult. Vocal lines very exacting, awkward intervals; much *Sprechstimme*, dialogue. Strict musical forms observed. Production complicated by requirement that some scenes be performed simultaneously. Films and projections employed, demanding three projectors. Long Prelude; interludes between scenes (see below); preludes to Acts III and IV. Setting: Lille and Armentières in French Flanders; yesterday, today, tomorrow. Four acts, fifteen scenes.

ACT I i: Wesener's house in Lille; ii: Stolzius's house in Armentières; Tratto I (interlude); iii: Wesener's house; iv: Outskirts of Armentières; v: Marie's room in Lille. ACT II i: Coffeehouse in Armentières; Intermezzo; ii: Wesener's house. ACT III i: Officers' club in Armentières; ii: Marie's room; iii: Wesener's house; Romance (interlude); iv: Countess de la Roche's house in Lille; v: Wesener's house. ACT IV i: Coffeehouse; Tratto II (interlude); ii: Lt. Mary's room; iii: Bank of the River Lys.

Synopsis. Marie, daughter of the Lille jeweler Wesener, has fallen in love with Madame Stolzius's son, a young cloth merchant of Armentières. She evades her sister Charlotte's questions and a quarrel ensues. Stolzius returns Marie's love, but the girl is dazzled by the courtship of the young French officer Baron Desportes, although her father warns her that she will lose her reputation if she associates with him. A poem from Desportes convinces Wesener, however; still, he urges Marie not to break off with Stolzius.

In Armentières, Major Haudy and the moralistic chaplain Eisenhardt quarrel over the amorality in soldiers' lives. When Stolzius delivers cloth to the Officers' Club, he overhears shameless gossip about Marie and Desportes and writes her a reproachful letter. Desportes offers to answer the letter in kind, and his passionate entreaties induce her to yield to him. Stolzius receives Desportes's letter and the engagement is broken, much to the distress of Marie's grandmother. Stolzius still defends the girl to his mother. But her reputation is ruined as Desportes leaves her. Stolzius joins the army and has become the aide of Lt. Mary, a comrade of Desportes. He hopes to avenge Marie. Charlotte accuses Marie of being a camp follower. Another young man has fallen in love with Marie, the Count de la Roche, whose mother begs him to forget her, but when the Count abandons her, takes Marie into service.

Marie runs away, dishonored and broken. Desportes and Lt. Mary jest cynically about the girl. Stolzius poisons Desportes, then commits suicide. On the banks of the Lys River, old Wesener is approached by a prostitute. He does not recognize his daughter. The inhumanity of the Establishment (here the military) to the individual is brought home.

Major Roles. WESENER (bs); difficult intervals; sudden switch from speech to high sung notes; F1 to G3. MARIE (high dram-col s); difficult dramatic role as well as vocal; trill on D5, Eb5, and E5; B2 to F5. CHARLOTTE (m-s); G♯2 to Cb5. WESENER'S OLD MOTHER (low c); F♯2 to Bb4. STOLZIUS (high bar); G1 to Ab3. STOLZIUS'S MOTHER (high dram c); F♯2 (F♯3 opt) to Bb4 (Cb4 with F♯4 opt). OBRIST, COUNT OF SPANNHEIM (bs); E1 to G3 (G2 opt). DESPORTES (high t); wide skips; trill on D4; B1 to D3. PIRZEL, a captain (high t); B1 to D4. EISENHARDT (heroic bar); high tessitura; trill; F1 to A3. LT. MARY (bar); high tessitura; wide skips; A1 to Ab3. MAJOR HAUDY (heroic bar); F♯1 to Ab3. COUNTESS DE LA ROCHE (m-s); G♯2 to Cb5 (with lower opt). COUNT DE LA ROCHE (very high lyr t); B1 to Db4 (D4 with lower opt). THREE YOUNG OFFICERS (buf t or dram s); all have C♯4 (D4 with D3 opt).

Lesser Roles. Actors: YOUNG HUNTER, MME ROUX, LACKEYS, YOUNG ENSIGN, DRUNKEN OFFICER, THREE OFFICERS.

Chorus. Officers, ensigns, servants, etc. employ rhythmic speech.

Ballet. Dreamlike sequences in coffeehouse scene.

Orchestra. 4 fl (picc, alto fl), 3 ob (ob d'amore, Eng hrn), 4 cl (2A, bs cl, Eb cl); alto sax, 3 bsn (cont bsn), 5 hrn (5 ten tuba, bs tuba), 4 trp (F, B, 2A), bs trp, 4 trb (bs trb), tuba, timp, perc (8–9, very complex), 2 harp, cembalo, piano, cel, organ, guit, strings.

Production Difficulties. See above.

Material. Bel (Sch). VS*.

🎵 Summer and Smoke

Music by Lee Hoiby (1926–   ). Libretto in English by Lanford Wilson, based on the play by Tennessee Williams. Premiere: St. Paul, June 19, 1971. Drama. Contemporary harmony in continuous texture, very expressive, reticent; vocal line patterned after speech, occasional lyrical passages. Prelude to Act ii: several interludes for quick scene changes. Setting: the small town of Glorious Hill, early 20th century. Prologue, two acts, twelve scenes (132 min).

Prologue: The fountain in the park; ACT I i: Same; ii: The Winemiller parlor; iii: Same; iv: John's office; v: Moonlight Casino; vi: The fountain. ACT II i: The Winemiller parlor; ii: John's office; iii: The Winemiller parlor; iv: The fountain; v: John's office; vi: The fountain.

Synopsis. As children, John Buchanan, Jr., and Alma Winemiller are attracted to each other, but John is a realist, Alma a romantic, hampered by a narrow outlook and restricted by the unbalanced actions of her mother and the righteousness of her preacher father. John yields to the more accessible charms of Rosa Gonzales, and the local tavern, Moonlight Casino, while Alma becomes more introverted; although she makes one excursion to the Casino with John, it ends in disappointment, as she cannot meet his frankness. While John's father is away, the Gonzales family overflows the office to celebrate the wedding of John and Rosa. Alma surreptitiously phones the elder Buchanan, who returns to chase the wild party out of his house and is shot by Papa Gonzales. John blames Alma for the tragedy and goes away to resume serious study. Alma grows more and more to be a recluse, until when John returns as a successful doctor, she can hardly bear to meet him. At last she does confront him and boldly kisses him, but it is too late. He has just become engaged to young Nellie, a piano pupil of Alma's, who has come home for the holidays from a finishing school. In quiet despair, Alma accepts the invitation of a traveling man to visit the Moonlight Casino.

Major Roles. ALMA WINEMILLER (lyr-dram s); requires intensity of acting; C3 to B4. JOHN BUCHANAN, JR. (bar); B1 to G♭3 (one A♭3). ROSA GONZALES (m-s). REV. WINEMILLER (bs-bar); C♯1 to F3. MRS. WINEMILLER (sp); character actress; pitch notations are guide to spoken inflections. NELLIE EWELL (lyr s); C♯3 to B♭4. ROGER DOREMUS, Alma's friend (t); D2 to G♯3.

Lesser Roles. DR. BUCHANAN (bs-bar). PAPA GONZALES (sp); character actor; speaks only Spanish. MRS. BASSETT (m-s). ROSEMARY (s). VERNON (bar). ARCHIE KRAMER (bar). ALMA AS CHILD (sp). JOHN AS CHILD (sp).

Supers. Townspeople.

Orchestra. 2 fl (picc), 2 ob (Eng hrn), 2 cl (bs cl), 2 bsn, 4 hrn, 2 trp, 2 trb, timp, cel, harp, strings. *Stage*: piano; dance band including 2 vln, guit. Tape: military band.

Material. Bel.

Performances. NYCO: 3.19.72 etc.

✄ Susanna

Music by George Frideric Handel (1685–1759). Libretto in English anonymous. Premiere: London, February 10, 1749. Drama with comic interludes, after the Apochryphal story. Considered as an oratorio, yet with many operatic elements, *Susanna* fell between two stools and was neglected for a long time. Nowadays it seems to partake more of opera, although the mighty choruses belong to oratorio and somewhat contradict the simple, rural, tuneful setting of the story. Highly melodious; humorous in travesty of "trumpet" and "rage" arias; strong characterization of individuals. All are florid; those marked * extremely so, with trills. Three acts (the Barnard-Columbia performance cut two choruses and arias by lesser characters).

215

ACT I: Marketplace in Babylon. ACT II: Susanna's garden. ACT III: Court-room.

Synopsis. When her husband Joachim goes away on a business trip, Susanna is beset by the two aging Elders, both aflame with love for her. They spy on her bathing, then when she indignantly rejects them, denounce her as an adultress. Daniel intervenes, separates the Elders, and they betray themselves by differing on what tree they saw Susanna under. She is vindicated.

Major Roles. SUSANNA (s)*. DANIEL (s). JOACHIM (c). FIRST ELDER (t); has travesty on "trumpet" aria. SECOND ELDER (bs)*; wide skips; travesty on "rage" aria. CHELSEAS, Susanna's father (bs)*.

Lesser Roles. AN ATTENDANT (s). JUDGE (bs).

Chorus. SATB. Can be vital, if large choruses are given.

Orchestra. Barnard-Columbia version: fl, 2 ob, bsn, 2 trp, harpsichord, 3 vln, vla, vcl, cb.

Performances. Columbia Univ.-Barnard (NYC): 2.20.69.

🖝 A Tale of Two Cities

Music by Arthur Benjamin (1893–1960). Libretto in English by Cedric Cliffe, based on Dickens's novel. Premiere: London, 1953 (radio); 1957 (staged). Romantic melodrama. Set numbers knit into continuous texture; melodious; vocal line patterned after speech; some dialogue. Brief preludes to scenes; interlude between Scenes 5 and 6. Setting: Paris and London, 1783, 1789, and 1790. Six scenes.

Scene i: Wineshop in Paris, 1783. ii: Dr. Manette's garden in Soho, London, 1789. iii: Wineshop, Paris, 1789. iv: Revolutionary tribunal, 1790. v: Prison cell. vi: Place de la République.

Synopsis. The story closely follows Dickens's tale of the French Revolution, in which Mme Defarge plotted the downfall of her aristocratic enemies, one particular family who were responsible for the death of her brother, and how she is thwarted by the impersonation by Sydney Carton of the last member of that family, Charles Darnay. Both loved the same girl, Lucie, daughter of Dr. Manette, who had tended the peasant boy years before and had been imprisoned in the Bastille until smuggled out by the Defarges.

Major Roles. MME DEFARGE (dram s); needs strength and some flexibility (Cb3 to Bb4). LUCIE MANETTE (lyr s); needs some flexibility (top B4). DR. MANETTE (t); top G3. CHARLES DARNAY (t); C#2 to A3 (one C4 opt). SYDNEY CARTON (bar); needs dramatic power (Bb1 to F3).

Lesser Roles. MISS PROSS (char c). YOUNG COUNTESS (lyr s). LORRY (bar). DEFARGE (bs). MARQUIS DE SAINT EVREMOND (bar). GABELLE, his steward (bs). THE SPY (t). HURDY-GURDY MAN (bar). OLD MARQUIS (bs). THREE WOMEN (m-s, c, char c). JACQUES I (bar). JACQUES II, a cripple (bs). JACQUES III (bar). JACQUES IV (t). CORPORAL (sp). OLD COUNT (sp). OLD MARQUISE (sp). LITTLE SON OF JACQUES IV (mute).

216

Chorus. SM-SATB. Various solo voices. Flute player, fiddler, dancers.

Orchestra. picc, 2 fl, 2 ob (Eng hrn), 2 cl (bs cl), 2 bsn, 4 hrn, 3 trp, 2 ten trb, bs trb, tuba, timp, perc (tamb, side dr, bs dr, cym, gong, glock, harness chains, tri, ten dr, coconut shells), harp, piano & cel (1), strings. *Stage*: guit, fl, vln.

Material. B & H. VS*.

Performances. San Fran. St. Coll: 4.2.60 (Amer prem).

⛫ Tamerlane

Music by George Frideric Handel (1685–1759). Libretto in Italian by Nicolo Haym. Premiere: London, October 31, 1724. Medieval heroic drama. Highly melodious; patter and accompanied recitative and set numbers; much melisma; notable trio. Brief overture. Setting: the town of Prusa in Bithynien, 1400. Three acts, seven scenes (120 min).

ACT I i: Court of Castle of Prusa; ii: Dark, high room in tower; iii: Great hall (45 min). ACT II i: Gallery in Tamerlane's apartment; ii: Great hall (40 min). ACT III i: Inner court of harem; ii: Great hall (35 min).

Synopsis. Tamerlane is the English form of Timur Link, Mongol conqueror, born near Samarkand, died 1405. Called "Prince of Destruction." Bajazet, first Sultan of Turkey (1389–1403), overran Southeast Europe; defeated by Tamerlane near Angora in 1402 and made prisoner. Bajazet's daughter is engaged to the young Greek prince Andronico, but desired by Tamerlane, who, however, eventually decides to marry Irene, Princess of Trapezunt, and forgives the young couple. Bajazet meanwhile has taken poison rather than witness the conqueror's triumph and his daughter's disgrace. His death scene is extremely powerful.

Major Roles. TAMERLANE (bs-bar, orig. c); flexible, sustained; trill; Bb1 to D3 (E in ensemble). BAJAZET (t); very florid; impressive death scene; B1 to A3. ANDRONICO (c); very flexible; trill; A2 to D4. ASTERIA (s); flexible; trill; E3 to A4 (one Bb4). IRENE (c); florid; trill; A2 to E4.

Lesser Roles. LEONE (bs); servant of Tamerlane but confidante of Andronico. ZAIDE, lady-in-waiting to Asteria.

Orchestra. 2 fl, 2 recorders, 4 ob, 4 bsn, 2 trp, strings.

Material. BH.

⛫ Taverner

Music by Peter Maxwell Davies (1934–   ). Libretto in English by the composer based on John Taverner's life. Premiere: London, July 12, 1972. Historical drama. Intricate, complicated orchestration based on some Taverner themes but contemporary in idiom, employing dissonance and many modern devices. No overture; important interludes. Vocal line extremely difficult; most major roles consistently employing awkward intervals and considerable sustained melisma. Setting: England, 16th century. Two acts, eight scenes (130 min).

ACT I i: Courtroom; ii: Chapel; iii: Throne room; iv: The same (80 min). ACT II i: Courtroom; ii: Throne room; iii: Chapel; iv: Marketplace in Boston, Lincolnshire (50 min).

Synopsis. The text is drawn from contemporary records and widely assorted quotations. The musician John Taverner was accused in 1528 of heresy but released at the intervention of Cardinal Wolsey. After the religious changes brought about by Henry VIII, Taverner became a notorious agent of Cromwell. At his first trial Taverner is saved by the Cardinal although the Abbot seems bent on condemning him. The testimony of his father, his mistress Rose, a drunken priest, and a boy do not help his cause. John is persuaded to renounce his religion and his muse, saying that he "repented him very much that he had made songs to popish ditties in the time of his blindness." A second trial is a parody of the first with the roles reversed—John condemning the abbot.

Major Roles. JOHN TAVERNER (t); A1 to Bb3. RICHARD TAVERNER, his father, later ST. JOHN (bar); low E1. CARDINAL, later ARCHBISHOP (t); extremely florid; G#1 to Ab3. KING HENRY VIII (bs); needs flexibility; Eb1 to E3 (Gb4 fals). JESTER, later DEATH and JOKING JESUS (bar); difficult intervals; F#1 to F3. WHITE ABBOT (bar); G1 to F3. PRIEST CONFESSOR, later GOD THE FATHER (counter t); stutters; Bb1 to Ab3. ROSE PARROWE, later VIRGIN MARY (m-s); exceptionally difficult melisma and intervals; G2 to Bb4.

Lesser Roles. BOY (treb); needs flexibility; difficult intervals; Bb2 to Ab4. CAPTAIN (bs); low F1 (Eb1 with Ab1 opt). ANTICHRIST (high sp). ARCHANGEL GABRIEL (high t). ARCHANGEL MICHAEL (deep bs); low Eb1. FIRST MONK (t); top C4. SECOND MONK (t); top Bb3.

Chorus. TTBB. Council and monks. Treb (at least 16). Demons and choirboys. SATB. Townspeople.

Supers. Two priests, each with large silver cross. Two laymen with symbolic pillars, later hooded executioners. Two soldiers with pickaxes. Two acolytes, boys. A novice. Soldiers, dancers.

Ballet. Dance of Death, II ii.

Orchestra. 2 fl (2 picc), 2 ob (Eng hrn), 2 cl (2 Eb cl, bs cl), 2 bsn (cont bsn), 4 hrn, 4 trp (3 & 4 sometimes "Bach" picc F), 2 trb, 2 tuba, timp, perc (very elaborate, 5 players) harm, harp, strings. *Stage.* Act I: guit, 1 & 2 vln, 1 & 2 vla, 1,2,3,4 vcl, cb (or lute, 2 treb viols, 4 bs viols, violine), 2 keyless 18th-century ob (or 2 sopranino Rauschpfeifen), Tabor. Act II: Quintadecima (or sopranino recorder or picc), Discant schalmey (or corn or cl), great double quint pommer (or serpent or cont bsn), shawm (or trp or Rauschpfeife), alto sackbut (or alto trb), nakers (or timp high C), positive org, regal, descant, treb, ten, and bs recorders (SATB Blockflöten), soldiers dr.

218

Production Difficulties. Many apparitions, complex lighting effects, difficult props, masks and costume changes, burning pyre.
Material. B & H.

⚔ Die Teufel von Loudun · The Devils of Loudun

Music by Krzysztof Penderecki (1933–   ). Libretto in German by the composer, based on John Whiting's dramatization of Aldous Huxley's novel. English translation by Desmond Clayton. Commissioned by Hamburg Staatsoper. Premiere: Hamburg, June 20, 1969. Religious melodrama. Vocal lines extremely difficult, most with wide skips. *Sprechstimme*, more sung than spoken. Some dialogue. Important chorus. Setting: Loudun, France, early 17th century. Three acts, 30 scenes (approx 150 min).

ACT I i: Jeanne's cell; ii: Streets of Loudun; iii: Grandier with Ninon in tub; iv: Street; v: Church; vi: Church; vii: Street; viii: Confessional; ix: On town wall; x: Street; xi: Cloister; xii: Pharmacy; xiii: Jeanne's cell. ACT II i: Church; ii: Street; iii: Cell; iv: Cell; v: Grandier and Philippe; vi: Pharmacy; vii: Convent garden; viii: On the fortifications; ix: Church; x: Street and church. ACT III i: Three cells; ii: Third cell; iii: Public place; iv: Claire, Jeanne, Louise, Gabrielle; v: Upper room; vi: Procession; vii: St. Peter's Church and St. Ursula's Convent; auto-da-fé.

Synopsis. By a cumulation of many details, the Vicar of St. Peter's Church, Urbain Grandier, is brought to execution at the stake. The first cause is the belief of several nuns of the convent, especially the Prioress, Sister Jeanne, that they have become possessed of the Devil, holding Grandier responsible. Jeanne has a vision of Grandier in a heretic's shirt, a rope around his neck, his legs broken. The sisters are ridden with superstition and hysteria, and in Jeanne's case at least, a hopeless love for Grandier. The worldly vicar is involved with both the widow Ninon and the young Philippe—who is expecting his child. Adam, a chemist, and Mannoury, a surgeon, cynically plan to denounce Grandier. The latter falls in further trouble by siding against the King and Richelieu in their decision to demolish the city's fortifications, which have protected Protestants. In the second act, spiritual and secular dignitaries attempt to exorcise the demons possessing the nuns, but without success. Jeanne confesses that Grandier came to her as a demon; Father Barré and Father Rangier decide she is Grandier's innocent victim. De Cerisay, chief magistrate, is skeptical and orders the exorcism stopped. But the fanatics obtain permission for a public spectacle. Grandier is arrested as he is about to enter his church, is found guilty as being the source of the nuns' possession, and is tortured before going to the stake. Too late, Jeanne realizes that it is her unrequited love which has been the source of the possession.

Major Roles. SISTER JEANNE OF THE ANGELS (s); very difficult role; G#2 to Bb4 (one C5, one opt Db5) in own range; when possessed, should utter deep bass notes (G1 and C1). URBAIN GRANDIER (bar); dramatic, sustained; powerful acting; G#1 to Ab3 (A fals). FATHER BARRÉ, vicar of Chinon (bs);

219

wide skips; F1 to F3. DE LAUBARDEMONT, King's special commissioner to Loudun (t); B♭1 to B3 (one C4). FATHER RANGIER (deep bs); low D1; ADAM (t); C2 to A♭3; (A and C fals). MANNOURY (bar); difficult intervals; high tessitura; A♭1 to A3. NINON (c); B2 to F4. PHILIPPE (high lyr s); needs flexibility; first sung note is C5; also has D♭5; opt coloratura passages very difficult, with A5.

Lesser Roles. PRINCE HENRI DE CONDÉ, King's Special Ambassador; B♭1 to F♯3. GABRIELLE (s); needs flexibility; high tessitura; top E5 and G5. CLAIRE (m-s). LOUISE (c); low F2. FATHER MIGNON, Ursuline father confessor. FATHER AMBROSE, old priest (bs). BONTEMPS, jailer (bs-bar). MAYOR JEAN D'ARMAGNAC of Loudun (sp). GUILLAUME DE CERISAY, chief magistrate (sp).

Chorus. SATB, much divided; very difficult; some wordless "keening"; occasionally all voices singing different lines; contrapuntally complicated. Noblemen, pages, Ursulines, Carmelites, people, children, soldiers, etc.

Orchestra. 4 fl (picc, alto fl), 2 Eng hrn, cl E♭, 2 cl B♭, bs cl, contrabs cl, 2 alto sax, 2 bar sax, 3 bsn, cont bsn, 6 hrn, trp D, 4 trp B♭, 4 trb, 2 tuba, elec guit, harp, piano, harm, organ, strings, timp, perc (3—military dr, bs dr, whip, 5 wd bl, rattle, guiro, Cuban sapo, cym, 6 susp cym, 2 tam-tam, 2 gong, Javanese gong, tri, bells, tub bells, church bells, saw, flexitone, vib.

Material. Bel (Sch).

Performances. Santa Fe: 8.14.69, etc. (Amer prem).

▨ Tiefland · The Lowlands

Music by Eugen d'Albert (1864–1932). Libretto in German by Rudolph Lothar after Angel Guimerà. Premiere: Prague, November 15, 1903 (three acts). Present version, premiere: Magdeburg, January 16, 1905. Realistic drama. Continuous texture; vocal line occasionally highly dramatic, quasi-Wagnerian; also patterned after speech; occasionally melodic. Prelude, interlude between Prologue and Act I. Setting: The Pyrenees and Catalonian Lowlands, beginning of the 20th century. Prologue, two acts (130 min).

Prologue: A rocky slope on the Pyrenees (25 min). ACT I: Inside the Lowlands mill (60 min). ACT II: The same (45 min).

Synopsis. Pedro and Nando enjoy their solitude as shepherds in the Pyrenees, but Pedro has dreamed that he will have a bride. His dream seems to be coming true when the wealthy landowner Sebastiano brings Marta up the mountain, intending to marry her to Pedro to quiet scandal and allow him to marry a rich woman, while keeping Marta as his mistress. Marta is horrified at the arrangement but Sebastiano reminds her that he took her and her father off the streets and gave them the mill. She flees, refusing even to look at Pedro, who, however, is overjoyed at his good fortune. In the mill, the women are teasing the miller Moruccio to learn about the wedding, but he tells them nothing. Marta's young confidante Nuri innocently reveals the truth, however. Marta bewails her fate to Nuri. The village elder Tommaso at first refuses to believe in Sebastiano's perfidy, but is at last convinced by

220

Moruccio (who is dismissed) and tries to stop the wedding. It is too late. Pedro cannot understand his bride's coolness, and tells her the story of how he once strangled a wolf that was robbing the flock. In spite of herself, she is touched by his directness and simplicity. A light appears in the room adjoining, but Marta prevents Pedro from investigating, for she knows it is Sebastiano. Thoroughly disgusted at her master's arrogance, she spends the night in her chair, with Pedro at her feet. In the morning, Nuri awakens Pedro, who is extremely unhappy, and tries to console him. Marta, who has gone to her room, returns and shows her new feeling for him by an outburst of jealousy. Tommaso learns her story and insists she tell Pedro. After a tumultuous scene, she agrees to go to the mountains with Pedro, but they are stopped by Sebastiano, who carelessly orders Marta to dance. She betrays him to Pedro, but the shepherd's furious attack is thwarted by the villagers and he rushes out. Tommaso tells Sebastiano that he has revealed the whole story to his prospective father-in-law, and the rich marriage is off. Sebastiano determines to keep Marta anyway, but she calls for Pedro, and he, unwilling to leave her, appears to her rescue. He strangles Sebastiano, as he had once killed the wolf, and takes Marta to the mountains forever.

Major Roles. SEBASTIANO (bar); top F♯3 (one G♭3). MARTA (m-s); sustained, highly dramatic; top A♯4 (one B♭4, one B4). PEDRO (t); both lyric and dramatic; top A3. TOMMASO (bs); G1 to E♭3. MORUCCIO (bar); top E♯3. NURI (s).

Lesser Roles. PEPA (s). ANTONIA (s). ROSELLA (c). NANDO (t). A VOICE (bar, from chor). PRIEST (mute).

Chorus. SATB. Villagers, millers, etc.

Orchestra. 3 fl (3 picc), 2 ob, Eng hrn, 2 cl, bs cl, 2 bsn, cont bsn, 4 hrn, 3 trp, 3 trb, tuba, timp, perc, harp, strings. *Stage:* cl (can be from orch), bells.

Material. (BB).

Performances. Amer. Op. Soc. (NYC): 4.9.69 (conc).

🌃 Die Tote Stadt · The Dead City

Music by Erich Wolfgang Korngold (1897–1957). Libretto in German by Paul Schott based on Georges Rodenbach's play *Bruges-la-Morte*. Premiere: Hamburg and Cologne, December 4, 1920. Fantasy-drama. Music evocative of the bizarre and supernatural; colorful orchestration; vocal line often melodic. Preludes to Acts II and III. Setting: Bruges, end of 19th century. Three acts (145 min).

ACT I: Paul's house (50 min). ACT II: Deserted wharf before Marietta's boarding house; theater party passes in boats (Vision of dissolute nuns) (55 min). ACT III: Paul's room (Vision of procession, first religious, then menacing) (40 min).

Synopsis. The story is redolent of the macabre, the supernatural. The young widower Paul, obsessed by the death of his wife Marie, keeps flowers

221

before her portrait and lives only in her memory. A company of traveling players arrives, among them the dancer Marietta, who so strongly resembles Marie that Paul seeks her out. She comes to visit him, and to humor him puts on one of Marie's dresses and sings one of her songs. Paul follows her to her boardinghouse but finds her gone in a boat party, yielding flirtatiously to the advances of Count Albert of Brussels and even more taken by the charms of the Pierrot of the troupe, Fritz. Frank, Paul's friend, also seems to have gained her favors. Marietta assumes the habits of a nun and acts out a parody which horrifies Paul. Marietta persuades Paul to take her home with him, where once more the dancer impersonates the dead wife to Paul's growing distraction. She takes a long strand of Marie's hair which Paul has ghoulishly preserved and winds it about her throat, whereupon Paul strangles her in a rage. Then he awakes from what has been a cruel nightmare, to discover that the girl has just arrived to see him—all else has been a figment of his dream. He repulses her and joins his friend Frank to go to another city and begin a new life.

Major Roles. PAUL (t); brittle, feverish quality; top Bb3. MARIETTA (s) a coquette; C#3 to Bb4 (one C5). FRANK (bar); top F#3. FRITZ (t).

Lesser Roles. COUNT ALBERT (t). BRIGITTA, Paul's housekeeper (c). VISION OF MARIE (s). Dancers in Marietta's troupe: JULIETTE (s); LUCIENNE (m-s); GASTON (t); VICTORIN, the regisseur (t).

Chorus. SATB. Children behind scenes.

Orchestra. 3 fl (3 picc), 2 ob, Eng hrn, 2 cl, bs cl, 2 bsn, cont bsn, 4 hrn, 3 trp, bs trp, 3 trb, tuba, 2 harp, cel, piano, harm, mandolin, timp, perc (3–4), strings. *Stage:* org, 2 trp, 2 Eb cl, glock, wind machine, 2 trb, perc.

Production Problems. Visions and apparitions.

Material. Bel (Sch).

✠ Die Toten Augen · The Dead Eyes

Music by Eugen d'Albert (1864–1932). Libretto in German by Hanns Heinze Ewers after the story by Marc Henry. Premiere: Dresden, March 5, 1916. Biblical drama. Conventional, lush harmonies; vocal line both dramatic and melodious. Setting: Rome, early Christian days. Prelude and two acts (125 min).

Prelude: A bright landscape (25 min). Acts I and II: A Roman country house and Jerusalem (80 min).

Synopsis. A shepherd, his boy, and a reaper celebrate the advent of Palm Sunday. In the house of the Roman envoy Arcesius, his wife Myrtocle, a beautiful blind Corinthian, mourns that her "dead" eyes will not allow her to see her "handsome" husband (who is in reality very ugly). The Roman Lieutenant Galba advises her to appeal to Christ, who is making his way to the Holy City on this Palm Sunday. In Jerusalem the Mary Magdalen appears briefly, announcing Christ's coming. Myrtocle's sight is restored. On the way home with her Greek slave Arsinoë, she meets Galba, whom she mistakes for her husband. Finally yielding to her passionate approach, Galba is embracing her when Arcesius discovers them and strangles his friend. Myrtocle screams that her husband has been killed by a monster. Undeceived, she realizes the gift of sight has destroyed her happiness and stares into the sun until she becomes blind again. Her infirmity now allows her to accept her penitent husband once again.

Major Roles. ARCESIUS (bar); some high tessitura; top F♯3. MYRTOCLE (s); one rhapsodic aria; top B4. AURELIUS GALBA (t); top A3. ARSINOE (s); top A4.

Lesser Roles. SHEPHERD (t); top A3. REAPER (bar). SHEPHERD BOY (s). MARY MAGDALEN (c). KTESIPHAR, Egyptian sorcerer (buff t); top A♭3. Jewish women: REBECCAH (s); RUTH (m-s); ESTHER (s); SARAH (s). FOUR JEWS (t, t, bar, bar). AN OLD JEW (bs). A SICK WOMAN (s).

Chorus. SSATBB. Jews, slaves, reapers, shepherds.

Orchestra. 3 fl (picc), 3 ob (Eng hrn), 3 cl (bs cl), 3 bsn, 4 hrn, 5 trp, 3 trb, bs tuba, timp, perc, 2 harp, cel, org, strings.

Material. G Sc (BB).

🎵 Les Troyens · The Trojans

Music by Hector Berlioz (1803–1869). Libretto in French by the composer after Vergil. In two parts: I, "La Prise de Troie"; II, "Les Troyens à Carthage." The complete work was not given until December 5, 1890, in German, in Karlsruhe. Previously Part II was heard in Paris on November 4, 1863, Part I in Nice in 1891, Paris in 1899. Later "complete" performances: Cologne, 1898; Stuttgart, 1913; Paris (shortened version), 1921; Berlin, 1930; New England Opera Theater, Boston, 1955 (3½ hr); London (English), 1957, 1958; New York, Philadelphia, Baltimore (American Opera Society), 1959–1960 (concert); Milan, 1961; Paris, 1962; San Francisco, 1968; Opera Company of Boston, Part I, February 3, 6, 1972; Part II, February 4, 6 (American premiere of complete staging). Ancient drama of grand design. Brilliant, subtle, and colorful orchestration, severity of Part I yielding to richness of Part II; setting of text extremely felicitous and appropriate. The two parts are considered separately. Overall duration approx 4½ hr.

PART I. LA PRISE DE TROIE · THE CAPTURE OF TROY

Very brief prelude. "Trojan March." Setting: Troy, near the end of the Trojan War. Two acts, four scenes.

ACT I: The plains before the walls of Troy; ii: Outside the Citadel. ACT II i: Aeneas's tent; ii: The Temple of Vesta.

Synopsis. The Trojans are rejoicing at the apparent withdrawal of the Greek army after ten years of siege. They come out into the plain, examining with great curiosity the gigantic horse the Greeks have left behind. Cassandra, daughter of King Priam, who has been blessed by the gods with the gift of prophecy, and then cursed because no one will believe her, is the only one who foresees doom, except a priest, Laocoön. But when Laocoön tries to destroy the horse, he and his sons are crushed to death by two serpents. Learning of this, the people joyously drag the horse within the gates as a good omen. But Cassandra continues her prophecy of doom, unbelieved even by her lover Choroebus. When the Greeks contained within the horse have opened the gates to the returning army and Troy is sacked, only Aeneas, warned by the ghost of Hector, escapes with his son. Cassandra appears before the women of Troy and persuades them to take their own lives rather than become slaves to the Greeks. As the invading army enters, demanding the Trojan treasure, Cassandra stabs herself and all the women, except a craven few who are allowed to go, follow suit.

Major Roles. CASSANDRA (dram s); requires great stamina and sustained force; strength at extremes of range; Cb3 to B4. CHOROEBUS, her betrothed (bar); sustained, dramatic; B1 to F3 (F♯ in ensemble). AENEAS (dram t); E2 to B3.

Lesser Roles. These sing mostly in ensemble: HELENUS, son of Priam (t); ASCANIUS, son of Aeneas (s); HECUBA, wife of Priam (m-s); PANTHEUS, Trojan priest (bs); PRIAM, King of Troy (bs). GHOST OF HECTOR (bs). POLYXE-NA, daughter of Priam (s); sings only with chorus. ANDROMACHE, widow of Hector (mute). ASTYANAX, her son (mute).

Chorus. SSATTBB. Very important. Trojan warriors, magistrates, priests of Neptune and Jupiter, priestesses, Trojan men and women.

Ballet. Act I ii; celebration.

Orchestra. (Obsolete instruments are listed, their modern substitutes in parentheses.) 2 fl (2 picc), picc, 2 ob (Eng hrn), 2 cl (bs cl), 4 bsn, 4 hrn, 2 trp, 2 corn, 3 trb, ophicleide (tuba), timp, perc: bs dr, cym, tri, sn dr, ten dr, sistres; 3 harp (may be doubled), strings. *Stage*: Three groups. I: petit saxhorn suraigu (high Bb trp), 2 trp, 2 corn, 3 trb, ophicleide. II: 2 sop saxhrn, 2 alto saxhrn, 2 ten saxhrn, 2 bs saxhrn, cym. III: 3 ob, harp (Berlioz called for 6–8, but these double first, as orch harps double).

Material. Chou. Bä (Br); VS (2 vol)*.

Performances. See above. Met: 10.22.73 etc.

PART II. LES TROYENS A CARTHAGE • THE TROJANS AT CARTHAGE
Prelude. Important orchestral interlude, **The Royal Hunt and Storm**; Trojan March. Setting: Carthage, a new African city. Three acts, five scenes.

Synopsis. Queen Dido, who has fled from Tyre with her court, has established a flourishing city, Carthage, on the African coast. Her sister Anna counsels her to remarry (she is the widow of Sichaeus), but Dido resolves to remain faithful to her husband's memory and to give all her energies to the building of her city. The Trojans arrive under assumed identities and are warmly welcomed. When Narbal, Dido's minister, brings news that Iarbus and his Numidians have invaded, Aeneas reveals his true identity **and repels** the invaders. Dido falls in love with the Greek hero, much to the disquiet of Narbal.

In a symphonic interlude, The Royal Hunt and Storm, naiads and satyrs disport themselves in the forest until disturbed by the royal hunting party. Dido is dressed as Diana, goddess of the hunt. A raging storm drives Dido and Aeneas into a cave, where presumably their love is consummated. Peace is gradually restored.

The couple watch a celebration, including a ballet and a song by the poet Iopas, and Aeneas recounts the history of Troy's fall. After an extended love duet, the couple departs, as the figure of Mercury appears, strikes Aeneas's shield and cries out "Italy!" Both Dido and Aeneas have forgotten their duty.

Now the Trojans must depart on their mission, although Aeneas grieves to lose Dido. All her pleas are not proof against warnings from the ghosts of Priam, Choroebus, Cassandra, and Hector, however. The Trojan ships sail away, and Dido determines to die. She mounts a funeral pyre and stabs herself, as a vision of Rome triumphant appears to her and to the revengeful Carthaginians.

Major Roles. DIDO (m-s or s); dramatic, sustained; requires stamina as well as vocal agility; C3 to Bb4. ANNA (c); low G#2. AENEAS (dram t); dramatic, sustained; C2 to C4. ASCANIUS (s); top B4. NARBAL (bar); F1 to E3. PANTHEUS (bs); F1 to E3. IOPAS (t); top C4.

Lesser Roles. HYLAS, a Trojan sailor (t); one song; top G3. MERCURY (bar). TWO SOLDIERS (bar, bs). GHOST OF CASSANDRA (s). GHOST OF CHOROEBUS (bar). GHOST OF HECTOR (bar). GHOST OF PRIAM (bs). These may double with major roles.

Chorus. SATBB. Soldiers of Troy and Carthage, courtiers, hunters, sailors, naiads, fauns, satyrs, people of Carthage.

Ballet. As elaborate as desired.

Orchestra. See Part I.

Material. See Part I.

Performances. See above. Met: 10.22.73 etc.

🎼 Tsar Saltan

(Entire title: The Story of Tsar Saltan, of his Son, the Famous and Mighty Hero Prince Gvidon Saltanovich, and of the Beautiful Swan Princess) Music by Nikolai Rimsky-Korsakov (1844–1908). Libretto in Russian by B. E. Belsky after Pushkin's poem. Premiere: Moscow, November 3, 1900. Fantasy with new element for composer, satire. Uses folk themes, leitmotifs. Unusually copious employment of orchestra: long preludes to Acts I, II, III, several orchestral interludes, including famous "Flight of the Bumblebee." Set numbers in continuous texture; colorful harmonies; vocal line melodious. Setting: Partly in town of Tmoutarakany, partly on Bouyanye Island; legendary times. Prologue, four acts, seven scenes.

Prologue: A rural winter evening. ACT I: The Tsar's court in the town.

ACT II: The island, by the shore. ACT III i: The island, a forest; ii: The city, same as Act I. ACT IV i: The island, same as Act III i; ii: Town of Dedenets, interior of citadel; iii: Entrance to palace.

Synopsis. Of three sisters, Povarika, Tkachika, and Militrisa, the Tsar has chosen the youngest, Militrisa as his bride. The jealousy of the two elder sisters has driven the Tsaritsa and her son, Prince Gvidon, from the kingdom, but they find refuge on the magical island where they are befriended by a beautiful Swan—who of course turns into a Princess and marries the Prince. Gvidon is sent back to his father's court as a Bumblebee and the truth is revealed, with a happy ending including the Cinderella-like forgiveness of the elder sisters.

Major Roles. TSAR SALTAN (bs); top F3. TSARITSA MILITRISA (s); C♯3 to A4. POVARIKA, eldest sister (s); top B4. TKACHIKA, middle sister (m-s); C3 to F4. BABA BABARIKA, marriage broker (c); low G2. PRINCE GVIDON (t); top A3. SWAN PRINCESS (s); sustained, also needs flexibility; some high tessitura; top C5. OLD GRANDFATHER (t); top G3. SHOMORCH (bs).

Lesser Roles. COURIER (bar). THREE SHIPMASTERS: t, bar (top F3), bs.

Chorus. SSAATTBB. Very important. Often broken up into small groups: enchanters, 6–10 bs; spirits, 6–10 t; nurses, 6–10 s; guards, 4–6 t, boyars, 4–6 bs, etc.

🎭 The Tsar's Bride

Music by Nikolai Rimsky-Korsakov (1844–1908). Libretto in Russian by L. A. Mey, with added scene by I. F. Tumenev. Premiere: Moscow, November 3, 1899. Tragedy, based on historical characters, one of only two operas by the composer to use only real personages. Music is more truly vocal in style, lyrical and dramatic, with important ensembles, set numbers, recitatives. Overture; brief prelude to Act III. Setting: Environs of Moscow, autumn of 1572. Four acts (134 min).

ACT I: Great hall in Griaznoi's mansion, village of Alexandrovskay (45 min). ACT II: (The Love Philter) A street with the houses of Sobakin and Bomelius, mansion of Prince Gvosdeva-Rostovsky, entrance to monastery (35 min). ACT III: Room in Sobakin's house (27 min). ACT IV: Hall in the Tsar's palace (27 min).

Synopsis. The Opritchnik Griaznoi has fallen violently in love with Martha, but her father, the Novgorod merchant Sobakin, has promised her to the Boyar Lykov. At a party given by Griaznoi, his mistress Lyoubacha overhears him ordering a love philter from Bomelius, the Tsar's physician, and reproaches him, but in vain. She in turn buys a poison from Bomelius, paying his price, a kiss, unwillingly. The Opritchniki pour out of the Prince's house after a feast, singing their violent song. Within the Sobakin house, Lykov learns to his despair that his wedding has been put off, because Martha and her friend Dounyasha have been invited to a reception by the Tsar, who will choose his bride from the guests. Griaznoi hypocritically consoles his friend. Domna Ivanova Sabourova, Dounyasha's mother, arrives and describes the reception—the Tsar has talked a great deal to her daughter and only looked at Martha. While they wait for the girls, Griaznoi pours his potion into the glass intended for Martha. But while the company is toasting Martha and Lykov, the Tsar's messenger arrives with the stunning news that Martha has been chosen as the monarch's bride. She soon becomes ill, however. Griaznoi confesses to having named Lykov as the poisoner, and the Boyar has been executed. This drives Martha into madness. Lyoubacha confounds the company by telling how she had switched the potions; the infuriated Griaznoi stabs her and is led off to be executed.

Major Roles. VASSILY STEPANOVICH SOBAKIN (bs); A1 to E3. MARTHA, his daughter (s); needs both strength and flexibility; C♯3 to B♭4 (one firm C5). GREGORY GREGOROVICH GRIAZNOI (bar); dram role; B1 to F♯3 (one G♭3, one G3 with E3 opt, one firm G3). BOYAR IVAN SERGEICH LYKOV (t); top A3. LYOUBACHA (m-s); has unaccompanied song; B♭2 to G4. ELISAY BOMELIUS (t); top A3. DOMNA IVANOVNA SABOUROVA (s); has one aria.

Lesser Roles. DOUNYASHA (c); B2 to E4. PETROVNA, Sobakin's housekeeper (m-s).

Bit Roles. TSAR'S VALET (bs). SERVANT (m-s). YOUNG BOY (t). YOUNG MAN (bar). TWO COURTIERS (one is Tsar incognito) (mute).

Chorus. SATTBB. Very important. Opritchniki, singers, dancers, boyars, servants, people.

Ballet. Act I.

Orchestra. 3 fl (3 picc), 3 ob (3 Eng hrn), 3 cl, 2 bsn, 4 hrn, 3 trp, 3 trb, tuba, timp, perc, harp, piano (ad lib), strings.

Material. Pet.

🎭 Turandot

Music by Ferruccio Busoni (1866–1924). Libretto in German by the composer based on the drama by Gozzi. Premiere: Zurich, May 11, 1917. A Chinese fable; drama with grotesque episodes. Conventional harmonies but rich scoring; some set numbers in continuous texture; vocal line melodic; some dialogue. Brief overture; interlude, Act II between iv and v. Setting: Ancient Peking. Two acts, eight scenes (105 minutes).

ACT I i: A square; ii: Before the curtain with Truffaldino; iii: Throne room of palace. ACT II i: Chorus and singer; ii: Public place; iii: Turandot alone; iv: Before the curtain; v: Throne room.

Synopsis. The general story line is similar to Puccini's: the Chinese Princess will marry only the suitor who can guess the three riddles. (Answers: human understanding; manners or morals; art.) There are additions of commedia dell'arte characters, a confidante for Turandot, the mother of an executed prince, and a male companion for Kalaf instead of the faithful slave Liu. As in the other opera, Turandot discovers Kalaf's name, but yields to love.

Major Roles. TURANDOT (dram s); sustained; needs strength at extremes of range; very dramatic; B♭2 to B♭4 (one B4). KALAF (t); needs strength as well as flexibility; E♭2 to B♭3 (B3 with G3 opt). ALTOUM, the Emperor (bs); E1 to E3. ADELMA, Turandot's confidante (m-s); E♭3 to A♭4. BARAK, Kalaf's friend (bar); C2 to E3. MOTHER OF BLACK SAMARKAND PRINCE (m-s); top A♭3. TRUFFALDINO, head eunuch (t); high tessitura; requires agility; D2 to C4. PANTALONE, minister (bar); B1 to E♯3. TARTAGLIA, minister (bar); top F♯3.

Lesser Roles. EIGHT DOCTORS (4 t, 4 bs). A SINGER (s); C♯3 to G4. THE EXECUTIONER (mute).

Chorus. SSATTB. Slaves, dancers, complaining wives, eunuchs, soldiers, a priest.

Ballet. In Act II.

Orchestra. 2 fl (picc), 2 ob (Eng hrn), 2 cl (bs cl), 2 bsn (cont bsn), 4 hrn, 3 trp, 3 trb, timp, perc, harp, cel, strings. *Stage:* 2 trp, 2 trb, timp, dr, bells.

Material. (BH).

Performances. Litt. Orch. (Brooklyn): 10.8.67 (Amer prem).

⛴ Twelfth Night

Music by David Amram (1930–   ). Libretto in English by Joseph Papp after Shakespeare. Premiere: Lake George, N.Y., August 1, 1968. Comedy-drama. Conventional harmonies for set numbers, recitatives and ensembles; vocal line melodious. No overture; Prelude to Act II. Setting: Illyria. Two acts, five scenes (120 min).

ACT I i: Court of Count Orsino; ii: Olivia's garden; iii: Orsino's court; iv: Olivia's garden. ACT II: Olivia's garden.

Synopsis. The plot is the familiar Shakespearean comedy of mistaken identities: Olivia falling in love with Viola, who is disguised as a boy, and eventually accepting her brother Sebastian, rescued from a shipwreck. Viola meanwhile is in love with Orsino, who is wooing Olivia, but turns his affections to the stranger. The action is complicated by the intrigues of the comic figures, Sir Andrew Aguecheek and Sir Toby Belch, and by the pretensions of Olivia's steward Malvolio.

Major Roles. ORSINO (bar); A1 (touches G1) to F3 (one F♯3, one G3). FESTE, the Fool (t); D2 to A3 (D♭5 fals). VIOLA, disguised as Cesario (m-s); G2 to B♭4. SIR TOBY BELCH (buf bs); needs flexibility and strength in low range; E1 to D3 (B♭4 fals). MARIA (m-s); trill; B2 to A4. SIR ANDREW AGUE-CHEEK (buf t); C♯2 to A3 (C4 in ensemble; B♭3 with G♭3 opt; C5, D♭5, D5 fals); one passage *Sprechstimme.* OLIVIA (s); sustained; also needs flexibility; B2 to C5. MALVOLIO (bar); difficult intervals; flexibility required; trill; F1 to F3 (some fals).

Lesser Roles. ANTONIO (t); top A3. SEBASTIAN (t); top A♯3 (B♭3 in ens).
Bit Roles. TWO OFFICERS (t, bs). PRIEST (bs).
Chorus. SATB. Briefly in Act II.
Ballet. Dances in Act II. Sir Toby and Sir Andrew dance a galliard.
Orchestra. fl (picc), cl (bs cl), bsn (cont bsn), 2 hrn, trp, trb, timp, perc (2), strings. *Stage*: fl, vla, bsn, Eng hrn.
Material. Pet.
Performances. Hunter Coll. (NYC): 4.24.69. Bost. Univ.: 4.72.

📧 Der Vampyr · The Vampire

Music by Heinrich Marschner (1795–1861). Libretto in German by W. A. Wohlbrück, based on Polidori story attributed to Byron and on melodrama by Nodier, Carmouche, and De Jouffroy. Premiere: Leipzig, March 29, 1828. New version by Hans Pfitzner. Romantic melodrama. Elaborate, colorful orchestration; vocal line melodic, dramatic. Setting: Scotland, 17th century. Two acts, four scenes.

ACT I i: Wild rocky gorge with vampire's cavern; ii: Hall in Davenant castle. ACT II i: Square in front of Marsden's castle; ii: Hall in Davenant castle.

Synopsis. Lord Ruthven has become a vampire, and lives on the blood of his victims. For his sins, he is about to be condemned by the spirits, but is reprieved on the condition that he bring a pure maiden for each of three years as a sacrifice. The first of these is Ianthe, daughter of Sir Berkley, who finds his daughter and wounds Ruthven almost mortally. The vampire is saved, however, by Edgar Aubrey, a relative of Sir Humphrey of Davenant, who is forced to swear that he will keep silent about Ruthven on pain of becoming a vampire himself. The next victim is to be Malvina, Sir Humphrey's daughter. Aubrey, recognizing the Earl of Marsden, the bridegroom, as Ruthven, cannot intervene. Another victim presents herself in the person of Emmy, daughter of the Marsden bailiff, John Perth, who is about to be married to George Dibdin, in Sir Humphrey's service. Aubrey cannot prevent her doom either, but finally breaks the spell when Malvina is about to be wed to the vampire, who perishes by a stroke of lightning. Aubrey and Malvina are happily united.

Major Roles. SIR HUMPHREY (bs). MALVINA (s). EDGAR AUBREY (t). LORD RUTHVEN (bar). SIR BERKLEY (bs). IANTHE (s).

Lesser Roles. GEORGE DIBDINS (t). JOHN PERTH (sp). EMMY (s).

Bit Roles. Marsden folk: JAMES GODSHILL (t); RICHARD SCROP (t); ROBERT GREEN (bs) THOMAS BLUNT (bs); SUSE, Blunt's wife (m-s). VAMPIRE MASTER (sp). BERKLEY SERVANT (bs).

Chorus. Noblemen and women, hunters, servants, ghosts, devil's minions, etc.

Orchestra. 2 fl (picc), 2 ob, 2 cl, 2 bsn, cont bsn, 4 hrn, 2 trp, 3 trb, timp, perc, harp, strings. *Stage:* 2 hrn, trp.

Material. B & H.

🖾 Les Vêpres Siciliennes · I Vespri Siciliani · The Sicilian Vespers

Music by Giuseppe Verdi (1813–1901). Libretto in French by Eugène Scribe and Charles Duveyrier. Premiere: Paris, June 13, 1855. Many performances in Italy thereafter under various titles. Melodrama based on historical event, the massacre of the French by Sicilians on March 30, 1282. Melodious; conventional harmonies; set numbers; important ensembles. Overture (Sinfonia). Setting: Palermo, 1282. Five acts, six scenes (125 min).

ACT I: The great square, Palermo (27 min). ACT II: A valley outside the city (25 min). ACT III i: Di Montforte's room (16 min); ii: The ballroom (12 min). ACT IV: The courtyard of the fortress (30 min). ACT V: Garden of Di Montforte's palace (15 min).

Synopsis. Arrigo, a young Sicilian, and the Duchess Elena plot to overthrow the French, who rule Sicily rigidly. Guido di Montforte, governor, feels a strange sympathy for Arrigo (who is in fact his son), but the rebel spurns him. Giovanni da Procida, a noble physician, returns from exile and assists in preparing the Sicilian uprising. Elena demands that Arrigo shall kill the governor as the price of her hand in marriage. Arrigo is invited to a feast by the governor, but when he refuses, he is arrested, and brought before Di Montforte, who reveals their relationship. Torn between filial responsibility and patriotism, and realizing that as Montforte's son he may never marry Elena, he nevertheless protects his father when the conspirators attempt assassination at a ball. The governor offers to pardon Elena and Procida if Arrigo will acknowledge him as father, but Arrigo consents only when his friends are at point of death. Procida still plans revenge; the Sicilians will attack the French at the wedding of the young couple. Elena does not tell Arrigo, and the massacre takes place when the wedding bells ring. Arrigo dies with his father and Elena stabs herself—but Sicily is freed.

Major Roles. GUIDO DI MONTFORTE (bar); B1 to G♭3. ARRIGO (t); needs flexibility; C2 to B3. DUCHESS ELENA (s); florid passages; trill; A2 (touches G♯) to C5 (touches C♯5). GIOVANNI DA PROCIDA (bs); needs flexibility; F1 to F3.

Lesser Roles. BETHUNE, French official (bs). COUNT VAUDIMONT, French official (bs). NINETTA, Elena's lady-in-waiting (c). DANIELE, Sicilian (t). TEBALDO, French soldier (t). ROBERTO, French soldier (bs). MANFREDO, Sicilian (t).

Chorus. SATTB, also TB. Very important. Sicilian men and women, soldiers, Frenchmen, youths, pages, nobles, etc.

Ballet. Act II: Tranatella. Act III ii: "The Four Seasons."

Orchestra. 2 fl (2 picc), 2 ob, 2 cl, 2 bsn, 4 hrn, 4 trp, 3 trb, tuba, timp, perc, harp, strings. *Met Orch*: same except no picc, no perc; *Stage*: side dr, castagnetta.

Material. Bel (Ri).

Performances. Litt. Orch. (NYC): 1.13.64 (conc). Met (Newport): 8.23.67 (conc); 1.31.74 etc.

🖾 La Vestale · The Vestal Virgin

Music by Gaspare Spontini (1774–1851). Libretto in French by Etienne de Jouy. Premiere: Paris, December 16, 1807. Melodrama. Set numbers, recitative; highly dramatic; bold harmonies for the period; colorful orchestration; vocal line melodic. Overture (Sinfonia). Setting: Ancient Rome. Three acts.

ACT I: Roman Forum. ACT II: Interior of the circular Temple of the Virgins. ACT III: Field of Infamy; three tombs in large pyramid, one open for Giulia.

Synopsis. Although Licinio and Giulia love each other, she becomes a Vestal Virgin while he is fighting in Gaul. When he returns in triumph, she is chosen to place the wreath of laurel on his brow. He breaks into the temple to win her back; in her preoccupation with him, she allows the sacred fire to go out. In the ensuing confusion, Licinio is rescued by his friend Cinna, Captain of the Legion, but Giulia is condemned to death. The High Priest gives her a black veil as she is led to her tomb. But a flash of lightning rekindles the flame; Giulia is pardoned and reunited with Licinio.

Major Roles. LICINIO, Roman general (lyr-dram t); C♯2 to A3. GIULIA (dram s); sustained; florid; formally pathetic, also moments of high drama; C♯3 to B♭4. CINNA (t or bar); some florid passages; B♭1 to F♯3. HIGH PRIEST (Pontifex Maximus) (bs); B1 to E3. HIGH PRIESTESS (s or m-s); needs both strength and flexibility; B2 to A4.

Lesser Role. A CONSUL (bs).

Bit Role. A DIVINER (bs).

Chorus. SSATB. Important. Sometimes women alone. Vestals, priests, populace, matrons, senators, consuls, warriors, gladiators, dancers, children, prisoners. Many supers desirable.

Ballet. Act I, as extensive and elaborate as desired; also at end.

Orchestra. 3 fl, 2 ob, 2 cl, 2 bsn, 4 hrn, 2 trp, 3 trb, tuba, timp, perc, 2 harp, strings. *Stage*: band.

Material. Bel (Ri). VS*.

Performances. Conc. Op. Ass'n (Scherman-NYC): 1.12.63 (conc).

🖾 La Vie Parisienne · Parisian Life

Music by Jacques Offenbach (1819–1880). Libretto in French by Henri Meilhac and Ludovic Halévy. Premiere: Paris, October 31, 1866. Satirical comedy. Highly melodious; set numbers. Setting: Paris during the Second Empire. Four acts.

ACT I: La Gare du l'Ouest. ACT II: Gardefeu's apartment. ACT III: The apartment of Bobinet's aunt. ACT IV: A restaurant.

Synopsis. The story relies heavily on impersonation and concealed identities, with overtones of sociological revolution under the picture of glittering Paris life. Two young men, Bobinet and Raoul de Gardefeu, are rivals for the favors of the demimondaine Metella, but she spurns them for another man. Gardefeu bribes his former valet, Joseph, and takes his place as a tourist courier, conveying the wealthy Swedish Baron and Baroness Gondremarck to his own house, pretending it is the Grand Hotel. To maintain the masquerade, Gardefeu invites to a great supper his shoemaker, Frick, and a glove maker, Gabrielle, who bring along a crowd of their fellows, rather rude but enormously zestful. Metella is also present at the Baron's request. Bobinet takes over the following night with a party in the house of his absent aunt, when all the servants masquerade as nobility, to the enchantment of the Baron. The party ends in a riotous champagne supper and dance. The next night, a rich Brazilian, Pompa di Matadores, is host at Alfred's restaurant. Baron Gondremarck arrives for a rendezvous with Metella, but she tells him she is returning to Gardefeu and offers as a substitute a heavily veiled lady—the Baroness, of course. The Baron has discovered Gardefeu's deception and challenges him to a duel, but is pacified by recalling the fun the young men had arranged for him. Everybody is reconciled, everybody is happy.

Major Roles. All need attractive appearance, acting ability; range and difficulties not important. BARON DE GONDREMARCK from Sweden. BARONESS DE GONDREMARCK. RAOUL DE GARDEFEU, a boulevardier. BOBINET, his friend. JOSEPH, a courier. METELLA, a demimondaine. POMPA DI MATADORES, a wealthy Brazilian.

Lesser Roles. FRICK, shoemaker. GABRIELLE, glove maker. ALFRED, headwaiter.

Chorus. SATB. Railway officials, shop assistants, townsfolk, servants, restaurant guests.

Ballet. As elaborate as desired.

Material. Map.

✄ A Village Romeo and Juliet

Music by Frederick Delius (1862–1934). Libretto in German by the composer after a novel by Gottfried Keller. Premiere: Berlin, February 21, 1907. Premiere English version: London, February 22, 1910. Tragic fantasy. Set numbers knit into continuous texture; long, flowing melody; preludes of first five scenes; interlude has become well known as "A Walk to Paradise Garden." Setting: Seldwyla, Switzerland, mid 19th century. Six scenes (six years elapse between i and ii).

232

Scene i: Hillside between fields of Manz and Marti; ii: Outside Marti's neglected house; iii: The wild land; iv: Dream of Vrenchen and Sali; v: The Fair—all kinds of entertainment and a sideshow; vi: Paradise Garden, a delapidated but charming inn.

Synopsis. A bitter dispute between two rich farmers over a piece of land owned in reality by the Dark Fiddler ruins both. Their children—Manz's Sali and Marti's Vrenchen—were forbidden to visit the disputed land, but after six years meet there, where the Fiddler invites them to roam the world with him some day, then departs. Marti catches the children and Sali knocks him down, injuring him so severely that Vrenchen has to take him to Seldwyla. All his property is sold, and she must go away. Sali comes to her on the eve of departure, and they fall asleep, dreaming that they are being married in old Seldwyla church. When they waken, they decide to go to the fair at Berghald, but soon become embarrassed at the attention they arouse and start off for Paradise Garden. There they find the Fiddler and the vagabonds. But that life is not for them either, and when they hear the song of the boatman in the distance, they know they must go that way—and die together. They drift off in the boat, and as Sali pulls the plug, the boat gently sinks in the distance.

Major Roles. MANZ (bar); high tessitura; C♯2 to G3. MARTI (bar); G1 to F♭3. SALI (t); B♭1 to B3. VRENCHEN (s); B♭2 (opt A♭2) to B4 (opt C5). DARK FIDDLER (bar); high tessitura; B♭1 to F♯3 (opt G3).

Lesser Roles. TWO PEASANTS (2 bar). THREE WOMEN (s, s, c). GINGER-BREAD WOMAN (s). WHEEL-OF-FORTUNE WOMAN (s). CHEAP-JEWELRY WOM-AN (c). SHOWMAN (t). MERRY-GO-ROUND MAN (bar). SHOOTING-GALLERY MAN (bs). Vagabonds: SLIM GIRL (s); WILD GIRL (c); POOR HORN PLAYER (t); HUNCHBACK BASS FIDDLER (bs). THREE BARGEMEN (bar, bar, t).

Chorus. SATBB. Vagabonds, peasants, bargemen, church congregation.

Ballet. Folk dances in Scene v.

Orchestra. 3 fl (3 picc), 3 ob, Eng hrn, 3 cl, bs cl, 3 bsn, cont bsn, 6 hrn, 3 trp, 3 trb, tuba, 2 timp, perc (xyl, tam-tam, bells, cym), 2 harp, strings. *Stage*: vln, 6 hrn (from orch pit), 2 corn, 2 alto trb, wirbel dr, steel plates, church bells, organ.

Material. B & H. VS*.

Performances. Op. Soc. of Wash.: 4.28.72 (Amer prem). St. Paul Op.: 6.27.73. NYCO: 10.6.73 etc.

⚜ Le Vin Herbé · The Magic Wine

Music by Frank Martin (1890–   ). Libretto in French by Joseph Bédier after the romance of Tristan and Isolde. Premiere: Zurich, March 26, 1942. Legendary romance. Music of antique character, spare, mild dissonances, unusual harmonies; vocal line patterned after speech. Setting: Cornwall and Brittany, Arthurian times. Prologue, three acts, Epilogue (93 min).

233

Prologue: The chorus introduces the story. ACT I: The Love Potion (32 min). ACT II: The forest of Morois (21 min). ACT III: The death (40 min). Epilogue: Salutes all lovers in the names of great troubadours.

Synopsis. Follows the Tristan legend, including Isolde of the White Hands, whom Tristan marries after leaving Isolde.

Major Roles. (Divided between 3 s, 3 c, 3 bar, 3 bs—others from chorus). ISOLDE'S MOTHER (c); G#2 to Gb4. ISEUT-ISOLDE (s); sustained; some high tessitura; C3 to Bb4. BRANGHIEN-BRANGAENE (s); D#3 to C5 (A4 opt). TRISTAN (t); D#2 to A3 (one Bb3 with G3 opt; one B3 with G#3 opt). MARC-KING MARK (bar). LE DUC HOEL (bs). KAHERDIN-KURVENAL (t). ISEUT AUX BLANCHE MAINS–ISOLDE OF THE WHITE HANDS (c).

Chorus. See above. Comments and narrates between solos.

Orchestra. 2 vln, 2 vla, 2 vcl, cb, piano.

Production Problems. As the work is more an oratorio than opera, and thus rather static, a great deal can be done with lights and projections, to give a tapestry-like effect.

Material. Pr (UE). VS (f, g).

🎻 The Violins of Saint Jacques

Music by Malcolm Williamson (1931–   ). Libretto in English by William Chappell, adapted from the novel by Patrick Leigh Fermor. Commissioned by Sadlers Wells with the help of the Calouste Gulbenkian Foundation. Premiere: London, November 29, 1966. Exotic drama. Continuous texture with ariosos, and set numbers; complex orchestra with considerable atmosphere, West Indian and dance motives; vocal line melodic, fluent. Prelude with chorus. Setting: the Caribbean island of Saint Jacques, 1902. Prologue and three acts, six scenes (130 min).

Prologue: A boat on the Caribbean. ACT I: In the Liana jungle on Saint Jacques. ACT II i: Ballroom and garden of Beauséjour; ii: Near the harbor. ACT II i: The ball; ii: Interlude depicting the island's annihilation; iii: The open sea at dawn.

Synopsis. Fishermen hear the sound of ghostly violins, which play once a year as the volcanic island of Saint Jacques is supposed to rise from the sea. In the jungle, a complicated tangle of human relationships is revealed. Sosthène, son of Count de Serindan, is in love with his cousin Berthe, who is indifferent to him but infatuated with his sister Joséphine. Joséphine, however, has fallen in love with Marcel Sciocca, son of the despised Corsican governor. They plan to elope that night, when the Serindans' ball shall be in full swing. Mathilde, Countess of Serindan, receives with great boredom her guests, among them Captain Joubert, an elegant fop, the twin brothers Chambines, and the governor and his family. Sosthène tells Berthe about Joséphine's love for Marcel, and seeing her hurt, makes her a love offering in the form of a snake dance by Pierrot. The ball continues, as the volcano rumbles menacingly. A drunken guest insults Marcel, who challenges him, but runs away with Joséphine instead of fighting. The governor lets fall the information that Marcel is already married, whereupon Berthe and Sosthène hasten to intercept the elopers. Maman Zelie, the voodoo priestess, predicts that at dawn only one of the island's inhabitants will be alive, then she intercepts the runaways, and enables Sosthène to take them back. Sosthène has sent Berthe to the harbor to see if the lovers will try to escape by sea, so that she, in a little boat, is the only living soul when the volcano wreaks its violence on the entire island, which disappears beneath the sea.

Major Roles. BERTHE (s); Bb2 to Db5. SOSTHENE (t); needs flexibility; D2 to C4. JOSÉPHINE (m-s); A2 to A4. MARCEL (bar); Ab1 to G3. COUNT AGENOR DE SERINDAN (bs); F1 (touches E1) to F3. MATHILDE, Countess de Serindan (s); very florid; A2 to E5. MAMAN ZELIE (m-s); needs flexibility; wide skips; G2 to Gb4.

Lesser Roles. CAPTAIN HENRI JOUBERT (t); E2 to A3. GENTILIEN, butler (bar). FRANCOIS DE CHAMBINES (t). GONTRAN DE CHAMBINES (t). GOVERNOR SCIOCCA (t). MME SCIOCCA (s). OLD FISHERMAN (bar). BASKET MAN (t). FIRST OARSMAN (t). SECOND OARSMAN (bs). FIRST NETMAN (bar). SECOND NETMAN (bs). PIERROT (dancer).

Chorus. SATTBB. Very important; often divided; many soloists. Fishermen, servants, guests, maskers, revellers.

Ballet. Dancers and revellers at the ball.

Orchestra. 3 fl, 3 ob, 3 cl, 3 bsn, 4 hrn, 4 trp, 3 trb, tuba, organ, 2 harp, timp, perc (3), strings. *Stage*: fl, cl, 2 hrn, 4 trp, 3 vln, cb.

Material. B & H (Wein). VS*.

🎵 Der Waffenschmied · The Armorer

Music by Albert Lortzing (1801–1851). Libretto by the composer, based on Von Ziegler's "Liebhaber und Nebenbuhler in Einer Person" ("Lover and Rival in One Person"). Premiere: Vienna, May 31, 1846. Comedy. Highly melodious; set numbers, dialogue; many ensembles. Overture; brief entr'actes. Setting: Worms, 16th century. Three acts (135 min).

ACT I: Stadlinger's workshop (55 min). ACT II: Room in Stadlinger's house (50 min). ACT III: The same (30 min).

Synopsis. The Count of Liebenau loves Marie, daughter of the armorer and veterinary Stadlinger, and woos her both in his own person and disguised as Konrad, a journeyman smith. She falls in love with him in the latter guise, but her father will have none of this suitor: as a nobleman he is too high, as a journeyman, too low. He resolves to marry her to Georg, actually the Count's valet, posing as another journeyman. During the celebration of Stadlinger's jubilee, the whole matter is straightened out, when the father decides on Konrad as the lesser of two evils, and receives a pleasant surprise.

Major Roles. HANS STADLINGER (bs); has noted aria, "Auch ich war ein Jungling"; G1 to E3 (opt F3's). MARIE (s); D3 to A4. COUNT VON LIEBENAU (disguised as KONRAD) (bar); A1 (G1 in ensemble) to F♯3. GEORG (disguised as smith) (t); high tessitura; needs flexibility; D2 to E3.

Lesser Roles. COUNT ADELHOF AUS SCHWABEN (bs). IRMENTRAUT, Marie's governess (m-s). BRENNER, Stadlinger's brother-in-law (t). A JOURNEYMAN SMITH (bs).

Chorus. SATTBB. Citizens, armorers, knights, esquires, pages, heralds.

Orchestra. 2 fl (2 picc), 2 ob, 2 cl, 2 bsn, 4 hrn, 2 trp, 3 trb, timp, perc, strings.

Material. Pet. VS (g)*.

⚜ La Wally · The Wally

Music by Alfredo Catalani (1854–1893). Libretto in Italian by Luigi Illica after Wilhemina von Hillern's "La Wally d'Avvoltoio" ("Die Geyer-Wally"). Premiere: Milan, January 20, 1892. Lyric drama. Set numbers; recitatives; conventional harmonies; vocal line melodious. Brief overture; Preludes to Acts III, IV. Setting: The Tyrol, about 1800. Four acts.

ACT I: Broad square, crowded with little tables. Left, Stromminger's house; right, scattered houses and trees. At back, houses of Hochstoffe, gigantic cliffs above profound abyss, where River Ache runs. Bridge with crucifix. Mountains at extreme rear. ACT II: Piazza in Sölden. ACT III: Wally's room and street in Hochstoff. ACT IV: Murzoll.

Synopsis. Wally's suitors, Gellner and Hagenbach, quarrel. Her father turns her out for refusing to marry Gellner. A year later, Hagenbach meets her again, jilts Afra for her; but Gellner plants suspicion of Hagenbach. Wally, disillusioned, promises to marry Gellner if he kills Hagenbach, but Gellner fails. Wally, repentant, saves Hagenbach from the abyss; however, an avalanche overwhelms him. She leaps into it to join him in death.

Major Roles. WALLY (lyr s); needs some flexibility; top B4. STROMMINGER, her father (bs); top E3. WALTER, lyre player (s); needs flexibility; trill; sings "Eidelweiss" song; top A4. GIUSEPPE HAGENBACH OF SOLDEN (t); one firm B♭3; one firm B3. VINCENZO GELLNER OF HOCHSTOFF (bar); some high tessitura; some firm F3 and G3.

Lesser Roles. AFRA (m-s). WANDERER (bs).

Chorus. SSATTBB. Often divided. Alpists, shepherds, citizens, old women, peasants, hunters, youths of Sölden and Hochstoff. Supers: strolling musicians, peasants, hunters.

Ballet. Youths and hunters, Act I.

Orchestra. 3 fl, 3 ob, 3 cl, 2 bsn, 4 hrn, 3 trp, 3 trb, tuba, timp, perc, organ, harp, strings. *Stage:* band.

Performances. Op. Guide Theat. Co. (NYC): 1.5.58. Am. Op. Soc. (NYC): 3.7.68 (conc).

ᵂ War and Peace

Music by Serge Prokofiev (1891–1953). Libretto in Russian by the composer and Mira Mendelson based on Tolstoy. Premiere: Leningrad, June 12, 1946. Revised several times; originally conceived for two evenings; present edition makes one evening feasible. Historical drama. Music ranges widely over different styles; expressive, dramatic, lyrical, martial, with generally tonal harmonies, continuous texture. Vocal lines melodic as well as declamatory; often conforming to speech patterns. Overture. Some orchestral passages, as in ball scene; prelude to Scene 13. Setting: Russia, just before, during, and after Napoleon's invasion (1809–1812). Prelude and thirteen scenes (outlined in synopsis) (approx 240 min).

Prologue (Epigraph): chorus. Scene 1: In the garden of Count Rostov's estate, Prince Andrei Bolkonsky overhears a duet by Rostov's daughter Natasha and her cousin Sonya and is captivated by Natasha. 2: On New Year's Eve, 1810, at a ball in the palace at St. Petersburg, Andrei dances with Natasha and becomes more deeply infatuated. 3: In an anteroom in the palace of old Prince Nicolai, Andrei's father, Count Rostov and Natasha wait for an audience. Rostov has approved Andrei as Natasha's husband, but the old prince receives the Rostovs rudely in spite of the intervention of Andrei's sister, Princess Marie. Andrei is sent abroad to prevent the marriage if possible. 4: At a party in the salon of Prince Pierre Bezukov and his wife Hélène, the latter's dissolute brother Anatol, Prince Kuragin, is smitten with Natasha and she rather unwillingly returns his interest. 5: In Anatol's rooms, his friend Dolokhov tries to prevent the rash youth from eloping, pointing out that not only is he already married but that he will be deserting his present faithful mistress. 6: At the home of Princess Maria Akhrosimova, to whom the Rostovs have confided the care of Natasha, Pierre, who has already fallen under the girl's spell, enlightens her about Anatol's perfidy, and she expresses her remorse. 7: In Pierre's study, he orders Anatol to leave Moscow. But his personal affairs are banished from his mind as his friend Denisov brings news of Napoleon's invasion. 8: The hills near Borodino. Pierre arrives to witness the coming battle, and meets Andrei, who has already taken up arms. Pierre himself is excited by the conflict, and joins the army. General Kutuzov holds a review of his troops and asks Andrei to join his staff, but the prince refuses, preferring to go to the front. 9: In Napoleon's camp, the commander receives news of his defeat in battle, but decides to press on to Moscow. 10: A hut near Fili. Kutuzov holds a council of war and decides to abandon Moscow. 11: In a crowded Moscow street, refugees are fleeing. The Rostovs take several wounded officers in their entourage; one of them, unbeknownst to Natasha, is Andrei. Pierre and a soldier, Platon Karateyev, are arrested. Napoleon is deeply affected by the Rus-

237

sian spirit. 12: In a hut outside Moscow, Andrei lies delirious. Natasha appears and asks forgiveness. They are reunited, but too late, as Andrei dies. 13: On the road to Smolensk, the French are in full retreat. Pierre and Platon are freed by the Partisans. The unbeaten Russians sing a hymn to Kutuzov and to their country.

Major Roles. PRINCE ANDREI BOLKONSKY (bar); high tessitura; C2 to G3. ILYA, Count Rostov (bs). NATASHA, his daughter (lyr-dram s); D3 to Bb4; Cb5 with Eb4 opt. PIERRE, Prince Bezukov (dram t); C2 to A3; B3 has lower opt. HELENE, his wife (c or m-s). ANATOL, Prince Kuragin, her brother (t); D♯2 to Bb3. DOLOKHOV, his friend (bs). MICHAEL, Prince Kutuzov (bs); A1 to E3. VASSILI DENISOV, Pierre's friend (bar); top F♯3.

Lesser Roles. NICOLAI, old Prince Bolkonsky (bs); top G3. PRINCESS MARIE, his daughter (m-s). SONYA, Natasha's cousin (m-s); C3 to G4. PRINCESS MARIA AKHROSIMOVA (s). PLATON KARATEYEV (t).

Note. There are in addition more than 50 lesser or bit roles, mostly male singers, many of whom can be doubled.

Chorus. SSATTBB. Men's chorus very important. Peasants, soldiers, Cossacks, aristocrats, Napoleon's staff, Partisans, folk.

Orchestra. 3 fl, 3 ob, 3 cl, 3 bsn, 4 hrn, 3 trp, 3 trb, tuba, timp, perc, harp, strings. *Stage*: band for dancing.

Ballet. Ball in Sc. 2.

Production Difficulties. In addition to length, the scenes are played continuously, which should require sophisticated staging.

Material. MCA.

Performances. Only U.S. performance was an NBC-TV production, cut to approx. 150 min, 1.13.57. Bolshoi Opera gave a performance in Montreal 8.11.67, and a recent English production had a translation by Edward Downes.

🎝 The Whirlpool · Krútnava

Music by Eugen Suchon (1908–   ). Libretto in Czech by Stefan Hoza. Premiere: Bratislava, December 10, 1949. Rural drama. Strong nationalistic element in orchestra of continuous texture, highly dramatic. Vocal line partly melodic, partly based on speech patterns. Choral prelude may be omitted, with use of brief orchestral prelude directly into scene; interlude between Scenes i and ii; brief prelude to Scene iv. Setting: A mountain village of Slovakia, after World War I. Six scenes (107 min).

Scene i: A pastoral landscape. ii: Police station. iii: Simon's house. iv: The same. v: A forest. vi: A village feast.

Synopsis. Young Jan Stelina, betrothed to Katrena, is found dead in the meadow. The police are unable to discover his murderer, so his father Stelina vows to do so on his own. Katrena's stepmother Zalchika and her godmother Skolnica finally persuade the girl to marry Andrew, son of the wealthy Simon. But a year later, when her child does not resemble Andrew, the village gossips and Andrew takes to drink. Stelina quarrels with Andrew over his treatment of his wife and the child, and is delighted when Andrew accuses Katrena of adultery—the child may be his own grandson. In a drunken stupor, Andrew finds himself in the clearing where he had killed Jan and determines to give himself up. At a feast, Simon's young shepherd reveals that he saw Andrew hide a gun. Andrew confesses, whereupon Stelina represses his first instinct to kill him, and takes Katrena and the child to his own home.

Major Roles. STELINA (bs); considerable low tessitura; needs flexibility; can go as low as C1 and D1 (with G1 opt) to E3. KATRENA (s); B2 to B4. ANDREW (t); sustained, dramatic; important drunk scene; B1 to Bb3 (one B3, F3 opt).

Lesser Roles. SIMON (bs). SIMONKA, his wife (m-s). ZALCHIKA (s). SKOL-NICA (c). MARY (s), SUSAN (c), Katrena's friends. YOUNG SHEPHERD (s); several sustained B4's. KRUPA (t); one important scene. HRIN (bar); top F3. OLEN (bs). GROOM'S WITNESS (bs). BRIDE'S WITNESS (c). FIRST BRIDESMAN (t). WOMAN (s); top B4. COOK (s).

Bit Roles. POLICE CHIEF, POLICEMAN, TWO MEN (sp).

Chorus. SAATTBB. Villagers, wedding guests, musicians. Occasionally divided.

Ballet. In iii and vi. Folk character.

Orchestra. 3 fl (picc), 3 ob (Eng hrn), 3 cl (bs cl), 2 bsn, cont bsn, 4 hrn, 3 trp, 2 trb, bs trb, tuba, timp, cym, little dr, tamb, tri, bells, harp, cel, strings. *Stage:* cl.

Material. B & H.

🎭 White Wings

Music by Douglas Moore (1893–1969). Libretto in English by the composer after the Philip Barry play. Premiere: Hartt School, Hartford, February 9, 1949. Satirical comedy. Set numbers, conventional harmonies, continuous texture; vocal line melodic. Prelude. Setting: New York or any big city, 1895–1915. Three acts, four scenes (120 min).

ACT I: The Boulevard. ACT II i: The Parkway; ii: The same. ACT III: The Parkway.

Synopsis. The Inch dynasty, proud of their trade of street sweeping (euphemistically designated "White Wings"), is about to totter because of the invention of the "horseless carriage." Archie, the Inch scion, is in love with Mary Todd, who is inclined to despise his profession, but returns to him, sure the horse is obsolete, and clinching it by shooting the last of the breed. Archie takes willingly to driving a taxi, while his father less happily mounts a garbage truck.

Major Roles. (No range problems.) MARY TODD (s). MRS. FANNIE K. INCH (s). ARCHIE INCH (t). KIT CANARI (bar). HERBERT. MR. ERNEST INCH. MAJOR PHILIP E. INCH. CHARLIE TODD.

Lesser Roles. THREE WHITE WINGS. DR. BOWLES. DR. DERBY. TAXI DRIVER. CITY EMPLOYE. JOSEPH, a horse.

Chorus. SATB. Citizens.

Material. Not published.

✙ Der Wildschutz · The Poacher
or Die Stimme der Natur · The Voice of Nature

Music by Albert Lortzing (1801–1851). Libretto in German by the composer, based on a comedy by Kotzebue, *Der Rehbock.* Premiere: Leipzig, December 31, 1842. Comedy. Set numbers; very tuneful; some dialogue; conventional harmonies. Overture. Setting: Eberbach's castle and village, 1800. Three acts (140 min).

ACT I: Square before the village inn (55 min). ACT II: Elegant salon in Eberbach castle (50 min). ACT III: Park with pavilion (35 min).

Synopsis. Celebration of the betrothal of the schoolmaster Baculus to Gretchen is interrupted by the Count's order for Baculus's arrest for poaching. He has indeed killed a roebuck for the wedding feast. Gretchen offers to intercede, and is joined by the Count's own sister, the widowed Baroness Freimann, who arrives with her maid disguised as students. The Count arrives with Baron Kronthal, his brother-in-law (who is living on the Count's estate as a groom, unbeknownst to his sister, the Countess). Both men are immediately taken with Gretchen and the disguised Baroness, and invite everyone to a party. The Countess, reading Sophocles aloud to her bewildered but admiring servants, is approached by Baculus, but before he can plead his cause, the Count throws him out. Now the Count and the Baron begin a lively rivalry for the false Gretchen (the Baroness), playing a billiards game during which the Count knocks over the lamp and seizes "Gretchen" in the dark. The Countess enters, with Baculus, to whom the Baron offers 5,000 thalers for his supposed bride. The latter's identity is at last revealed, and all misunderstandings clear up, even the schoolmaster's poaching—he has killed his own donkey instead of a roebuck.

Major Roles. BACULUS (bs); G1 to F3. COUNT EBERBACH (bar); B1 to F3. BARON KRONTHAL (t); needs flexibility; top A♯3 (B3 in ensemble). GRETCHEN (s); C3 to A4. COUNTESS EBERBACH (c or m-s); needs flexibility. BARONESS FREIMANN (s); needs flexibility; C♯3 to B4.

Lesser Roles. NANNETTE, a maid (m-s). PANKRATIUS, a steward (bs). A GUEST (bs).

Chorus. SATTBB. Hunters, villagers, children.

Ballet. Folk dance in Act I.

Orchestra. 2 fl (2 picc), 2 ob, 2 cl, 2 bsn, 4 hrn, 2 trp, 3 trb, perc, tri, strings.

240

Material. Pet. VS (g) *.
Performances. UCLA: 5.17.68. Univ. of Wisc.: 5.17.70.

◤ Wings of the Dove

Music by Douglas Moore (1893–1969). Libretto in English by Ethan Ayer, based on the novel by Henry James. Commissioned by the Ford Foundation. Premiere: New York City Opera, October 12, 1961. (Revised with smaller ballet, 1962). Drama. Continuous texture, embodying set numbers, ensembles; melodic; conventional harmonies. Setting: London and Venice, 1902. Two acts, six scenes (117 min).

ACT I i: Parlor of Maud Lowder, London (16 min); ii: The same (18 min); A room in the National Gallery (17 min). ACT II i: Courtyard and balcony of the Palazzo Leporelli, Venice (31 min); Millie's apartment in the Palazzo (17 min); Maud Lowder's parlor (18 min).

Synopsis. Kate Croy, whose father has gambled away all their money, desperately loves Miles Dunstan and wants to marry him, but not without money. She and her aunt are visited in London by a rich and frail American heiress, Milly Theale, who has met Miles in America and fallen in love with him. It is not difficult for Kate to arrange a marriage between the two, believing that Millie will soon die and Miles inherit her wealth. The young couple live in a Venetian palace that belonged to a Doge's daughter whom Millie strangely resembles. Lord Mark, an evil, bitter man, tells Millie of the plot and that Kate is her husband's mistress. Millie refuses to see Miles at first, but they are reconciled before she dies. He has grown to care for her, and though he promises to marry Kate if she will renounce the money Millie has left him, they reach an impasse and Miles leaves her. Millie, the white dove who has stretched out her wings over them both, has sent Kate her white shawl. As Kate scatters the pieces of the envelope containing Millie's money, her aunt Maud enters and wraps the shawl about her in spite of her shrinking, and they are left to gaze at the portrait of the Venetian beauty who so resembles Millie.

Major Roles. KATE CROY (m-s); needs strong dramatic talent; commanding presence. HOMER CROY, her father (bar). MILES DUNSTER, young journalist (bar). AUNT MAUD LOWDER (c). MILLIE THEALE (lyr s). SUSAN STRINGHAM, her companion (s). LORD MARK (t); needs acting ability.

Lesser Roles. STEFFANS, servant (bar). LECTURER AT NATIONAL GALLERY (t). GUILIANO, majordomo at Palazzo Leporelli (bar). MUSEUM GUARD (mute).

Chorus. Madrigal chorus of 6 women (minimum) for ballet.

Ballet. Ensemble at Aunt Maud's party (I ii). Venice scene, 12 minimum (II iv).

Orchestra. 2 fl (picc), 2 ob (Eng hrn), 2 cl (bs cl), 2 bsn, 3 hrn, 2 trp, 2 trb, timp, perc, strings.

Material. G Sc. VS*.

241

Performances. Univ. of Wisc.: 8.21.67. Coll. of St. Benedict Op. Wksp.: 4.10.70.

◤ Yerma

Music by Heitor Villa-Lobos (1884–1959). Libretto in Spanish by composer after play by Federico Garcia Lorca. Commissioned by John Blankenship through Hugh Ross. Premiere: Santa Fe, August 12, 1971. Tragedy. Continuous texture with set numbers embedded; exotic and polytonal orchestration; some Spanish atmosphere; vocal line both melodious and patterned after speech. Brief prelude. Interlude between I i and ii. Setting: contemporary Spain. Three acts, six scenes (95 min).

ACT I i: Yerma's house; ii: A field (45 min). ACT II i: Near a river; ii: Yerma's house (24 min). ACT III i: House of Dolores; Hermitage in mountains (26 min).

Synopsis. Yerma's name means "barren," and this is the compelling theme of the story. Yerma and Juan are childless after two years of marriage. The new pregnancy of her neighbor Maria only increases Yerma's anguish, but she will not yield to the suggestion of old women that she take a lover in order to have a child. Her honor forbids her to associate with her old sweetheart, Victor; furthermore, the jealous Juan brings his two old sisters to watch over her. She steals out to join a pilgrimage to the hermitage of a saint who is supposed to bring fertility to the barren. When Juan makes it clear that he wants her only for her carnal attraction, she strangles him, crying that thus she has killed her own child.

Major Roles. YERMA (dram s); extremely taxing; character is seldom off stage; needs strength throughout range; great dramatic intensity; important aria; C3 to B4 (one high *ppp* note). JUAN (t); strong, powerful; most melodic among roles; dramatic duet with Yerma; E2 to A♭3. VICTOR (romantic bar); C2 to E3. MARIA (m-s); C3 to G4. DOLORES, a sorceress (m-s).

Lesser Roles. OLD WOMAN (char m-s). TWO SISTERS-IN-LAW. DOLORES'S DAUGHTER. SIX LAUNDRESSES (3 s, 3 m-s). MASKED MAN (t); MASKED WOMAN (s).

Chorus. SSSAATTBBB. Children. Acts as Greek chorus commentary.

Ballet. Opt. Ritual, Act III i and ii.

Orchestra. picc, fl, ob, Eng hrn, 2 cl (sax, sax, bs cl), bsn, cont bsn, 2 hrn, 2 trp, 3 trb, tuba, timp, perc (2), harp, piano, cel, strings.

Material. Tr: Reade Elastaire.

◤ Zar und Zimmermann · Tsar and Carpenter

Music by Albert Lortzing (1801–1851). Libretto in German by the composer, based on play, *Le Bourgmestre de Sardam* by Mélesville, Merle, and de Boirie. Premiere: Leipzig, December 22, 1837. Comedy. Highly tuneful;

set numbers; recitative; dialogue. Overture. Setting: Saardam, Holland, in 1698. Three acts (145 min).

ACT I: Shipyard (65 min). ACT II: An inn garden (40 min). ACT III: A room in Town Hall (40 min).

Synopsis. Tsar Peter I, masquerading as a shipwright in the yard of the widow Browe, befriends a young compatriot Peter Ivanov, who is in love with Marie, niece of Burgomaster Van Bett. The French Ambassador, Marquis de Châteauneuf, also pays attentions to Marie. The Russian Ambassador, Admiral Lefort, brings news of unrest in Russia, and Peter decides to return. Meanwhile, the French Ambassador has discovered Peter's identity, but the others suspect Ivanov. Controversy boils over at a wedding party for the widow's son, when soldiers enter to search all foreigners. The Tsar escapes, leaving Ivanov a promotion and permission to marry Marie.

Major Roles. PETER I, alias PETER MICHAILOV (bar); high tessitura; needs flexibility; D2 to F3. PETER IVANOV (t); C2 to A3. VAN BETT (buff bs); A♭1 (opt G1) to E3 (one G3). MARIE (s); C3 to A4. MARQUIS DE CHATEAUNEUF (high t); top B3.

Lesser Roles. ADMIRAL LEFORT (bs). LORD SYNDHAM, English Ambassador (bs); low E1 in ensemble. WIDOW BROWE (c).

Chorus. SSAATTBB. Dutch officers, soldiers, people of Saardam, carpenters, magistrates, beadles, sailors.

Ballet. In Act III.

Orchestra. 2 fl (picc), 2 ob, 2 cl, 2 bsn, 4 hrn, 2 trp, 3 trb, timp, perc, strings. *Stage*: picc, cl, 2 bsn, 2 hrn.

Material. Pet. Map. Ka. VS: Pet (g)*.

Performances: Montgomery Coll. (Rockville, Md.): 4.1.71(e).

✄ Der Zerrissene · The Split Personality

Music by Gottfried von Einum (1918–   ). Libretto in German by Boris Blacher after a play by Johann Nestroy. Premiere: Hamburg, September 17, 1964. Revised version premiere: Vienna, March 21, 1968. Farce-comedy; social satire with romantic elements. Set numbers; arias and ensembles in chromatic harmony; free, acrobatic vocal lines; mainly continuous texture; some *Sprechstimme* and dialogue. Setting: Austria in early 19th century. Two acts.

ACT I: Garden pavilion of Herr von Lips. ACT II: Tenant Krautkopf's farm.

Synopsis. Anton, Christian, and Josef, Lips's servants, bring champagne and comment on their master. They agree he is a split personality. Gluthammer, locksmith, begins work on a balcony railing over the pool but stops because of the noise. Kathi, Krautkopf's cousin and servant, comes to pay back money she has borrowed from Lips. Gluthammer tells how he had fallen for a pretty milliner, sold his locksmith business to invest in her shop, and been left bankrupt. He has started all over again, but will not listen to

Kathi's condemnation of his former love, Mathilde. They go out. Lips enters and bewails the fate of a rich man with no friends. His guests say that there is always marriage. He responds that he will marry the first available woman who appears. An unknown is announced: the widow Mme von Schleyer, who asks him to buy a ticket for a charity ball. She was a milliner, she relates, and her husband was an old scoundrel. Lips gives her 100 gulden, then proposes to her. While she is making up her mind, Kathi enters; then Stifler, who recognizes the widow as the vanished Mathilde. Kathi, remembering Gluthammer's tale, says nothing, but after the others go, and Gluthammer enters, she tells him Mathilde will marry Lips. Gluthammer refuses to believe any wrong and determines to rescue her from "kidnappers." He confronts her as she and Lips are arranging the marriage, struggles with Lips, and both fall over the damaged railing into the pool. Everyone presumes both are dead.

In Krautkopf's farm building are two trap doors. The farmer is haranguing two hands, as Kathi and Lips enter. The latter, disguised as a peasant, tells Kathi he does not want to be caught as the murderer of Gluthammer. Krautkopf hires him as a hand, and he and Kathi go off. Now Gluthammer enters and reveals himself to Krautkopf as a fugitive for murdering Lips. He hides in the cellar. Lips realizes that he loves Kathi, then learns that his legatees, three friends, are false. Unobserved, he adds a paragraph to his will, leaving everything to Kathi. After a great deal of misunderstanding, Lips reveals his identity, but the Judge orders him confined. He descends through the trapdoor and discovers Gluthammer. Each thinks the other a ghost, but both eventually emerge, to the joy of Kathi, who promises to marry her benefactor. Lips makes a generous gift to Gluthammer and gives him permission to remarry Mathilde. Gluthammer accepts the money but rejects the lady. (Several characters' names contain a punning connotation.)

Major Roles. HERR VON LIPS (bar); F1 to G♭3; a little *Sprechstimme.* MME SCHLEYER (veil) (m-s); considerable coloratura; F♯3 to A4. KATHI (lyr s); C♯3 to B4. GLUTHAMMER (glowing hammer) (t); high tessitura; wide skips; D2 to B3. KRAUTKOPF (cabbage head) (bs); A♭1 to E3.

Lesser Roles. STIFLER (t), SPORNER (bar), WIXER (bs), Lips's friends. JUSTICE (bs). ANTON, a servant (t); needs agility; F♯2 to A3. JOSEF (bar), CHRISTIAN (bass), other servants. FARMHAND, can double with Josef and Sporner (bar). FARMHAND, can double with Christian and Wixer (bs).

Orchestra. picc, 2 fl, 2 ob, 2 cl, 2 bsn, 4 hrn, 3 trp, 3 trb, tuba, timp, strings.

Material. B & H. VS*.

Short Operas

SHORT OPERAS

🎵 Amnon und Tamar · Amnon and Tamar

Music by Josef Tal (1910–). Libretto in German by Recha Freier from Samuel II, Chapter 13. Biblical drama. Exotic orchestration, some dissonance; vocal line declamatory. Brief prelude; interludes. One act, four scenes (approx 20 min).

I i, ii, iii: Amnon's room. iv: The feast.

Synopsis. Amnon, sickening for love of Tamar, sends for her. Through pity and by force of his exhortations, she yields to him, whereupon he denounces her as a whore before a festive gathering.

Major Roles. TAMAR (m-s); Ab2 to G4. AMNON (t); B1 to G3. ABSALOM (bs-bar) B1 to D3. JONADAB (bs); Ab1 to D3.

Chorus. TB. Slaves, shepherds.

Orchestra. fl (picc), ob (Eng hrn), cl (bs cl), hrn, trp, trb, harp, cel, piano, xyl, vib, timp, perc (3), vla, vcl, cb.

Material. Pr (Imp). Tr: Rahel Vernon.

🎵 Apollo and Persephone

Music by Gerald Cockshott. Libretto in English by the composer. Farce based on ancient Greek myth. Melodious; some dialogue. No overture. Setting: A mountaintop (perhaps Olympus?); ancient, ancient Greece. One act (approx 25 min).

Synopsis. Persephone, seventeen, is not allowed out after dark by her strict mother Demeter (goddess of the harvest) for fear of the god Pluto. One afternoon, after picking flowers on the plain, she climbs the nearby mountain, where Pluto appears and pays her marked attention. She is saved from a fate worse than death by the appearance of a strange shepherd (Apollo), rather to her disappointment. Apollo, who has become a realist, has decided to rewrite the legend that Pluto kidnaps Persephone, and succeeds in disillusioning the Dark God by showing him that Persephone is all too eager to be kidnapped. He decides to return to Hades a bachelor. Apollo suggests that Persephone marry him instead, but she is reluctant until he reveals his true self. Then even Demeter is won over. She decides to take a new husband

247

herself, and picks up the flower basket. Pluto will eventually grow lonely again.

Major Roles. PERSEPHONE (s); C3 to A4 (one C5 with C4 opt). STRANGER (APOLLO) (t); C2 to A3. PLUTO (bs-bar); F1 to E3. DEMETER (bs-bar or c; if former, can double with Pluto); G1 to E3.

Orchestra. String qt or str with piano.

Material. Af.

Performances. Af NYC: 2.22.56 (Amer prem).

🎵 Ba-Ta-Clan

Music by Jacques Offenbach (1819–1880). Libretto in French by Ludevic Halévy. English adaptation and translation by Ian Strasfogel. Premiere: Paris, December 29, 1855. Satirical comedy. Music unaltered in new version; dialogue replaced by narration; subtitles when original French is sung. Highly melodious; conventional harmonies; set numbers. Abrupt stylistic changes call for flexibility in production. Overture. Setting: The mythical island of Ché-Ni-Or; anytime. One act, four scenes (approx 45 min).

ACT I i: Throne room of King Fé-Ni-Han. ii: A Paris cafe. iii: The countryside. iv: A ship at anchor along the coast.

Synopsis. The original is a satire on many aspects of French life, easily translated to the problems and foibles of today. King Fé-Ni-Han (a pun on the French *fainéant*, roughly "lazy oaf") rules the Oriental island of Ché-Ni-Or, but cannot understand its language. A revolution is fomented by Ko-Ko-Ri-Ko, who holds a peace conference with the king and his advisor Ké-Ki-Ka-Ko and the Princess Fé-An-Nich-Ton, but no one can agree on anything in the jumble of French-Italian and Chinese noises that pass for but completely stymie communication. Fé-An-Nich-Ton and Ké-Ki-Ka-Ko discover, through surreptitious reading of French newspapers, that they are French, and decide to escape, but are intercepted by the revolutionists, who insist they be put to death. They are saved by the sudden realization of Fé-Ni-Han that he is also French, but their plans to escape are foiled by quarrels among themselves. By strange logic, they decide to join the revolutionaries since their rallying cry, the Ba-Ta-Clan, is irresistible. Some operatic heroics follow, after which Ko-Ko-Ri-Ko, remembering his student days in France, allows the Frenchmen to go, leaving the throne to him.

Major Roles. NARRATOR (sp). KING FÉ-NI-HAN (revealed to be Napoleon Buonaparte) (buf t); considerable comedy. PRINCESS FÉ-AN-NICH-TON (later Virginie Durand) (col s); many florid passages. KÉ-KI-KA-KO, Captain of the Guards (later Vicomte Alfred de Cérisy) (t). KO-KO-RI-KO, chief conspirator (bs-bar); dark voice, but with considerable high tessitura. TWO BA-TA-CLAN TRUMPETERS, conspirators (2 fals t).

Chorus. SATB. Conspirators, ladies-in-waiting.

Ballet. Polkas, waltzes, can-can for duets between Fé-An-Nich-Ton and Ké-Ki-Ka-Ko.

248

Orchestra. 2 fl, ob, 2 cl, bsn, 2 hrn, 2 trp, trb, timp, perc, strings.

Production Notes. Scenery should abound in satirical references to cur‧ rent political manifestations, burlesquing reactionaries, revolutionaries, etc. Subtitles may be vaudeville placards or cartoon bubbles held to singers' mouths. The three Frenchmen and four ladies-in-waiting must wear ample Chinese robes that can be stripped off to show European costumes.

Material. G Sc. VS*.

Performances. N. Eng. Cons. (Boston): 5.16.69 (Amer prem). TV: 4.1.70.

☙ The Bald Prima Donna

Music by Martin Kalmanoff (1920–). Libretto based on *La cantatrice chauve* by Eugene Ionesco, translated into English by Donald Watson. Premiere: West Side YMCA, New York, by Community Opera, February 15, 1963. Satire. Neoclassical style, not difficult; melange of various abstract forms to match various sections of the "play of the absurd." Setting: A typical middle-class English interior; present. One act (60 min).

Synopsis. The words of the surrealistic play are merely cloaks for emotions of the players—anger, boredom, amusement, etc. To describe the action realistically (which hardly does it justice), the scene shows Mr. and Mrs. Smith at home, discussing trivia. Mr. and Mrs. Martin arrive for dinner (which never eventuates). The four converse with alternate animation, boredom, antipathy, and curiosity. The advent of a fireman seeking fires to put out changes the course of the chatter; the fireman is persuaded to tell stories which are meaningless; the maid Mary enters and does her little recitation before being forced out. Animosity grows between the two couples until at the end they are shouting furiously at each other in phrases that convey more onomatopoeia than sense. After a blackout, the play begins all over again, with the lines formerly said by the Smiths now in the Martins' mouths.

Major Roles. (All need agility and clean articulation.) MRS. SMITH (s); trill; A2 to C5. MARY, the maid (col s); C3 to A4 (C5 opt). MRS. MARTIN (c); G2 to G4. MR. SMITH (t); trill; C2 to C4. MR. MARTIN (bs-bar); trill; wide skips; G1 to E3. FIRE CHIEF (bs) E1 to E3. NARRATOR: can speak or sing; moderate range.

Orchestra. Piano, clock chime, wd bl, cym.

Material. Composer: 392 Central Park W., NYC 10025.

☙ The Bear

Music by Sir William Walton (1902–). Libretto in English by Paul Dehn and the composer after Chekhov. Commissioned by the Koussevitzky Foundation. Premiere: Alderburgh Festival, English Opera Group, June 3, 1967. Comedy. "Extravaganza." Continuous texture with melodic passages embedded; satirical and witty orchestration; some Russian flavor; vocal line patterned after speech with melodic sections. Setting: A drawing room of Mme Popova's house in the country, Russia, 1888. One act (48 min).

Synopsis. Mme Popova, a young widow, is determined to remain faithful to her late husband's memory but is jolted out of her somewhat hypocritical mourning by the incursion of her neighbor, Smirnov, who demands payment for a debt incurred by her husband. In the ensuing argument she challenges him to a duel, but when he attempts to show her how to fire a pistol they discover feelings for each other that are stronger than hate. The servant Luka finds them embracing, and this battle between the sexes ends with a kiss.

Major Roles. MME POPOVA (m-s); needs acting ability; some melisma; G2 to Ab4 (A4 opt). SMIRNOV (bar); needs flexibility; trill; A1 to G3 (B4 fals).

Lesser Role. LUKA (bs); G1 to Eb3.

Bit Roles. COOK and GROOM (mute).

Orchestra. Single woodwind, hrn, trp, trb, perc, harp, piano, string 5-tet.

Material. Ox.

Performances. Juill. Sch. (NYC): 3.29.73.

⚜ Bertha

Music by Ned Rorem (1923–   ). Libretto in English by composer, based on play by Kenneth Koch. Legendary melodrama. Contemporary idiom; vocal line declamatory. One act, ten scenes.

ACT I i: Oslo, the ramparts. ii: A study in the castle. iii: Bertha's summer lodge. iv: Scottish frontier town. v: Council chamber. vi: Rose garden. vii: Bertha on the throne. viii: Throne room. ix: Public place. x: Throne room.

Synopsis. Queen Bertha of Oslo commands an attack, even though her garrison is surrounded by barbarians. She appears in a ring of white eagles, frightening the barbarians off. A teacher questions her, Are not the people themselves barbarians? She has him beheaded and higher learning thereby "disreinstated." Now the country is at peace, so the dissatisfied Bertha makes war on Scotland. The Counselor objects to such ceaseless wars, and Bertha dismisses the Council. Two young lovers meet in Bertha's garden and are shot dead—Bertha does not approve of lovers' trysts. As she grows older, her madness increases. She longs for new adventures and gives Norway to the barbarians in order to reconquer it. She succeeds, but falls dead on her regained throne. All hail her as a great queen.

Major Roles. BERTHA (m-s); needs sustained strength; some flexibility; Ab2 to A4. COUNSELOR (bs); F1 to C♯3.

Lesser Roles. NOBLE (t); C2 to G3. OFFICER (t). OLD MAN (bar or bs). TEACHER (t). MESSENGER (t). THREE SCOTS (t, t, bs).

Bit Roles. NORWEGIAN SOLDIER. GIRL (s). MAN (t). TWO NORWEGIAN CITIZENS (t, bs). BARBARIAN CHIEF (t).

Orchestra. Piano.

Material. B & H.

250

✍ The Big Black Box

Music by Sam Morgenstern (1911–   ). Libretto in English by Francis Steegmuller, based on an article in the Manila (Philippines) press. Premiere: Met Studio, New York, February 13, 1968. Comedy. Set numbers knit into continuous texture; contemporary idiom with Spanish flavor; vocal line patterned after speech. Setting: New Seville, Mexico, early 19th century. One act, four scenes (50 min).

ACT I i: Entrance hall in Don Augustin de Cordoba's house, Christmas Eve. ii: A street, later. iii: Don Fausto's office, still later. iv: Baptistery of the Franciscan church, Christmas morning.

Synopsis. Among the guests arriving for a ball at Don Augustin's are Manuel, a poor lawyer who loves Onita, daughter of the local usurer Don Fausto, and Onita's duenna, Dona Clara. When they have gone into the ballroom, two tipsy sailors bring a big chest into Don Augustin's house, telling him it is a gift. When they open it, he screams in horror and tells them to take it away. They try to deliver it at various houses, but the reaction is always horror; at last, a victim of Don Fausto's bids them take it to the usurer. The latter believes he is being pursued by an enemy, and his daughter and Dona Clara take advantage of his predicament to summon Manuel to help. He alone is able to read the Latin inscription on the box, and tells everyone to meet him at the Franciscan church next morning. The Abbot is overjoyed; the supposed "corpse" in the box is in reality a statue of St. John the Baptist sent as a present from Old Seville. Don Fausto, outwitted, is forced to give his consent to the marriage of Manuel and Onita, as well as a large donation to the monastery.

Major Roles. DON AUGUSTIN (bar); A1 to F3. ABBOT (t); D2 to A♭3. ONITA (s); C♯3 to B♭4. DONA CLARA (m-s); A2 to G4. MANUEL (t); C2 to A3. FIRST SAILOR (t); C2 to A3. SECOND SAILOR (bs); low A1. DON FAUSTO (bs); G1 to E3.

Lesser Role. PASSERBY (bar); B♭1 to E3.

Chorus. SATB. Guests, friars, etc.

Orchestra. Piano.

✍ Boccaccio's "Nightingale"

Music by Lester Trimble (1923–   ). Libretto in English by George Maxim Ross, based on Boccaccio's *Decameron*. Unperformed to date. Romantic comedy. Set arias and ensembles knit into continuous texture; modal/polychordal harmonies; vocal line melodic, often florid. Brief overture; longer overtures to Acts II and III. Setting: 14th-century Florence. Three acts (85 min).

ACT I: Night-time summer garden in Florence (42 min). ACT II: Caterina's balcony, with large tree nearby, curtained bed visible (23 min). ACT III: The same; morning (22 min).

251

Synopsis. This is a happy Boccaccio tale, told by young Filostrato on the Fifth Day. Two characters, the Count and the Friar, have been added. Caterina and her playmate since childhood, Ricciardo, slip away from the festive scene in her father's garden, and Caterina returns alone, to be approached by the Count, but to reject his advances. Her mother Giacomina, approves the Count, but her father, Lizio, abhors him, insults him, and breaks up the party. Ricciardo and Caterina plan a rendezvous on her balcony, where she persuades her mother to move her bed because of the heat. Lizio, protesting, is no match for his women, but thinks he has assured Caterina's safety by locking the door to the balcony. Caterina lights a candle as a signal to her lover, who duly appears and climbs the tree to her balcony. The lovers withdraw, but leave the candle burning. The Count returns, hears Caterina singing of love, and thinks the candle a welcome for him, but is restrained by the Friar, who also shows up. The ensuing scuffle wakes Lizio, who cudgels the Friar, but misses the Count, who climbs the tree, then finds Ricciardo's doublet and vows revenge. Caterina wakens, but cannot arouse Ricciardo; they are discovered by Lizio, who eventually consents to their marriage.

Major Roles. CATERINA (lyr s); D3 to Db5. RICCIARDO (lyr t); D2 to C4. GIACOMINA (m-s); D3 to G4. THE COUNT (bar); F1 to F3. THE FRIAR (t); C2 to A3. LIZIO (bs); F1 to F4.

Bit Roles. (Servants). ASSUNTA (m-s). ROBERTO (bar). ALFREDO (bar).

Chorus. SATB. Opt.

Ballet. Opt.

Orchestra. Chamber (16) or full (65).

Material. King Philip Press.

✍ The Boor

Music by Ulysses Kay (1917–   ). Libretto in English by the composer, adapted from the play by Anton Chekhov. Commissioned by the Koussevitzky Foundation in the Library of Congress. Premiere: University of Kentucky, Lexington, April 3, 1968. Comedy. Continuous texture; a few arias connected by accompanied recitatives; mostly conventional harmonies; vocal line melodic, occasionally declamatory. No overture. Setting: A Russian landowner's house, early 19th century. One act (approx 40 min).

Synopsis. A middle-aged landowner comes to collect a debt from a landowning widow, a debt incurred by her late husband. She refuses to pay, and they quarrel. She challenges him to a duel—if he will teach her how to shoot. In the course of the lesson he falls in love with her. Her old servant, Luka, who has gone to fetch help to throw the visitor out, returns to find the couple embracing and planning to marry.

Major Roles. ELENA IVANOVA POPOVA (s); spirited singing and acting. GRIGORY STAPANOVICH SMIRNOV (bar); same requirements.

Bit Parts. LUKA (t). THE GARDENER; THE COACHMAN (mute).

252

Orchestra. fl (picc), ob (Eng hrn), cl, bsn, hrn, trp, trb, piano, perc, 2 vln, vla, vcl, cb.
Material. MCA.

▶ The Brute

Music by Lawrence Moss (1927–   ). Libretto in English by Eric Bentley based on a play by Chekhov. Premiere: Yale Summer School of Music, New Haven, July 29, 1961. Comedy. Contemporary idiom in chromatic vein; vocal line patterned after speech. Brief prelude. Setting: Drawing room of a Russian country house. One act (approx 23 min).

Synopsis. A pretty young widow remains faithful to the memory of her late unfaithful husband. "The Brute," Smirnov, intrudes to demand payment for a huge quantity of oats purchased by the late master for his horse Toby. The two engage in heated conversation which culminates in a challenge to a duel. The widow unpacks her husband's pistols and demands that the brute teach her to shoot. During the lesson, he falls in love. The servant Luka returns with help to stop the duel only to find the combatants embracing.

Major Roles. THE WIDOW POPOVA (s); needs flexibility; top A4. GRIGORY S. SMIRNOV (b-bar); needs flexibility; top E3.

Lesser Roles. LUKA (t). GARDENER, COACHMAN (mute).

Orchestra. fl (picc), cl, bsn, vib, piano, perc (1), vln, vla, cb. Alternate vers: piano, perc (1).

Material. Pr. VS*. Tape available.

Performances. N.Y. St. Univ. (Buffalo): 4.24.68. Wash. Univ. (St. Louis): 11.22.68. S. Cal. Chamber Music Soc. (L.A.): 1.25.71.

▶ La Buffonata · Buffoonery

Music by Wilhelm Killmayer (1927–   ). Libretto in German by Tankred Dorzt. Premiere: Stuttgart, October 21, 1960 (radio); Heidelberg, April 30, 1961 (staged). Ballet opera. Contemporary idiom; vocal line often difficult; satirical. Setting: any version of commedia dell'arte, the more fantasy the better. One act, ten scenes (approx 40 min).

Scenes i, ii: March; the director (Pantalone) introduces the show; iii: Columbina rejects three Harlequins; iv: Lucia cools the Capitano's ardor; v: The virtuous Rosetta turns virago after marriage to the rich old Don Lisardo; vi: Pantalone calls a doctor for his daughter Isabella; she recovers immediately when the doctor (her lover Florindo) prescribes moonlight serenades and a thousand kisses; vii: The neighbors gossip about Zerbinetta and her lovers; viii: Polovardo fails to catch Lisetta and collapses; she immediately becomes lovingly solicitious; ix: Camilla thrice intrigues with harlequin lovers until her husband Pantalone disguises himself as a harlequin, beats her, and locks her into a cage; x: The director calls the female characters before the curtain—all seven are one.

Singers. Col s; trill on Bb4 and C5; needs extreme flexibility; top F5 (Db5 opt); m-s, 2 t, bs. DIRECTOR (PANTALONE) (bs-bar); Gb1 to Gb3 (two Ab3's opt).

Dancers. Columbina, Lucia, Rosetta, Isabella, Zerbinetta, Lisetta, Camilla, Capitano, Florindo, Don Lisardo, Polovardo, Harlequins.

Chorus. SATTTB. Briefly in Italian.

Orchestra. 2 fl (picc), 2 ob, cl (Eb cl), 2 bsn, 2 hrn, trp, tuba, timp, perc (3), piano, cel, strings.

Material. Bel (Sch).

✄ The Burning Fiery Furnace

Music by Benjamin Britten (1913–). Libretto in English by William Plomer, after the Old Testament story of Shadrach, Meschach, and Abednego. Premiere: Oxford Church, Suffolk, June 9, 1966. The second parable for church performance (see *Curlew River* and *The Prodigal Son*). Setting: Suggesting Babylon by costumes and props, 6th century B.C. One act (approx 65 min).

Synopsis. The Abbot introduces the play. Three young Israelites come to Babylon and are honored, appointed to rule over three provinces, and given Babylonian names, Shadrach, etc. When they refuse to eat Babylonian food, the Astrologer convinces Nebuchadnezzar this is an insult. The Herald announces the royal decree: a great golden image of the Babylonian god Merodak is to be set up, and the Babylonians sing a hymn. When the three Israelites refuse to worship, Nebuchadnezzar condemns them to the fiery furnace. However they stand unharmed in the fire with a fourth figure, an Angel. Nebuchadnezzar frees them, is converted to their god, and repudiates the Astrologer.

Major Roles. NEBUCHADNEZZAR (t). ASTROLOGER (bar); doubles with Abbot. MISAEL (Shadrach) (t). ANANIAS (Meschach) (bar). AZARIAS (Abednego) (bs). HERALD (bar); doubles with Leader of Courtiers.

Lesser Roles. CHORUS OF COURTIERS (3 t, 2 bar, 2 bs). ANGEL'S VOICE (treb). FOUR ASSISTANTS (treb); double with Acolytes.

Orchestra. fl (picc), hrn, alto trb, perc, harp (little harp), chamber org (little cym), vla, cb (Babylonian dr).

Material. G Sc (Fa). VS*.

Performances. N.Y. St. Univ. (Buffalo): 12.13.68. Wash. Univ. Op. Studio: 4.26.70.

✄ The Burning House

Music by Alan Hovhannes (1911–). Libretto in English by the composer. Commissioned by Broadcast Music, Inc. Premiere: Gatlinburg, Tenn.,

August 23, 1964. Fantasy. Exotic orchestration; vocal line declamatory. Setting: The Universe. One act (26 min).

Synopsis. Vahaken defies Death and is victorious over the Demon; is alone in the universe; proclaims himself fire; creates burning house; appears at last alone in outer space among billions of burning suns.

Major Roles. VAHAKEN (bar). DEATH (bar). DEMON (d).

Chorus. 8 bar or any multiple of 8. If more than 8, voices sing each part at own speed instead of simultaneously; the resulting "sound collisions must create mystery, confusion, and terror."

Orchestra. fl, perc (4—pedal timp, bs dr, tam-tam, xyl, marimba, glock, vib, chimes).

Production Problems. Fire on stage, developing from delicate flashes to holocaust; vision of outer space with billions of suns.

Material. Pet.

✎ Le Cadi Dupé · The Cadi Outwitted

Music by Christoph Willibald von Gluck (1714–1787). Libretto in French; German adaptation by Fritz Krastel. Premiere: Vienna, 1761. Comedy. Conventional harmonies; set numbers; melodic. Setting: a Turkish house. One act (approx 45 min).

Synopsis. Fatime, wife of the Cadi, complains to the young lovers Nuradin and Zelmire about the sad fate of Turkish women who are confined in the harem like slaves. The Cadi is meanwhile courting Zelmire, who seemingly consents to a marriage, but says she is Omega, daughter of Omar the dyer. When Omar brings his daughter to the Cadi, he is horrified to see that she is really an ugly shrew. Time has been gained for the marriage of Nuradin and Zelmire, and the Cadi must accept his "betrayal" with good grace, and apologize to his wife for philandering.

Major Roles. THE CADI (bar). FATIME (s). ZELMIRE (s). NURADIN (t).

Lesser Roles. OMAR (bs). OMEGA (s).

Orchestra. 2 fl, 2 ob, 2 cl, 2 bsn, 4 hrn, 3 trp, timp, perc, strings.

Material. Pr. VS (g—Eng tr, Ruth and Thomas Martin).

Performances. Hartt Coll. for Mus. Educ. Nat'l Conf., Phila.: 3.17.64 (prem Martin vers).

✎ Calvary

Music by Thomas Pasatieri (1945–   ). Libretto in English, exact setting of the play by W. B. Yeats. Premiere: Seattle, April 7, 1971. Religious music drama. Set numbers; conventional harmonies. Considerable symbolism. One act (33 min).

Synopsis. A timeless exploration of man's relationship to God and vice versa. A religious confrontation between Christ and Lazarus and Christ and

Judas. Wide possibilities of interpretation stress the position of religion in today's society.

Roles. THREE MUSICIANS: (1) s (heavier than 2); (2) s; (3) m-s. CHRIST (bar). JUDAS (t). LAZARUS (bs). THREE ROMAN SOLDIERS: 2 bar, bs.

Ballet. Dancers are optional; can be effectively used.

Orchestra. fl, ob, cl, bsn, hrn, harp, vln, vla, cel.

Material. Bel. VS*.

🎵 The Capitoline Venus

Music by Ulysses Kay (1911–   ). Libretto in English by Judith Dvorkin based on a story by Mark Twain. Commissioned by the Quincy Society of Fine Arts, Quincy, Ill. Premiere: University of Illinois Opera Group, March 12, 1971. Historical fantasy-comedy. Set numbers, accompanied recitatives embedded in continuous texture; traditional harmonies; vocal line melodious. Overture; brief interludes. Setting: Rome, late 1800's. One act, five connected scenes (45 min).

Synopsis. Mark Twain's "Legend of the Capitoline Venus" is his satirical parody on one of the more interesting stories in the history of American gullibility, written in 1869 at the time of the sensational swindle of the "petrified giant." Ostensibly as a joke upon a fundamentalist revival preacher with whom an argument over the existence of biblical giants had taken place, one George Hull had a stone giant carved in Fort Dodge, Iowa, transported to Cardiff, N.Y., buried on his brother-in-law's farm, dug up and "discovered," and exhibited for pay. The opera is a paraphrase of this tale, set in Rome, with young Americans involved.

Major Roles. GEORGE ARNOLD, earnest and capable (t). JOHN BARTON, his roommate; forceful, positive (bar). MARY PHILLIPS, rich and pretty, about 21 (s); one demanding aria, fairly chromatic. MR. PHILLIPS, Mary's father, rich, bustling, impatient; character actor (bs).

Lesser Roles. GEORGE'S ITALIAN NEIGHBORS; good voices and "hammy" acting (t, bs, 2 bar).

Orchestra. fl, ob, cl, bs cl, bsn, hrn, trp, trb, perc (1), vln, vla, vcl, cb (strings may be doubled).

Material. MCA.

🎵 Carmina Burana

Music by Carl Orff (1895–   ). Libretto, songs of traveling minstrels, partly in Latin, partly in Middle High German. Premiere: Frankfurt-am-Main, 1937. "Scenic cantata." Primitive, repetitive rhythms and tunes, important percussion, dynamic changes; impressive chorus. In staged performance, chorus may stand at sides, while dancers and small chorus mime meaning of songs. Prologue, three parts, Epilogue (65–70 min).

Synopsis. Prologue: introductory chorus in praise of the all-powerful Fortuna. Part I: Paean to spring, nature and joy of life. Part II: "In the Inn," grotesque solo songs, the "Roasted Swan," the "Abbot of Cucanien," and hymn to earthly pleasures. Part III: On love in its many aspects. Epilogue: Return of the Fortuna chorus.

Major Roles. s, t, bar.

Lesser Roles. 2 t, bar, 2 bs.

Chorus. SATB. Great and small divisions. Children.

Ballet. Solo dancers.

Orchestra. 3 fl, 3 ob, 3 cl, 3 bsn, 4 hrn, 3 trp, 3 trb, tuba, timp, perc (elaborate), cel, strings.

Material. Bel (Sch).

Performances. Numerous, many by symphony orchestras, since Amer prem: San Fran 1.10.54 (conc); 10.3.58 (stage). Recurrent in NYCO repertoire.

✄ The Carrion Crow

Music by Grant Fletcher. Libretto in English by Frances Wells, adapted from a radio play by John Jacob Niles. Folk tale. Conventional harmonies; melodious; folk flavor. Brief overture. Setting: Any mountain cabin, after World War I (can be staged very simply; with a few spoken interpolations is also possible for radio production). One act (43 min).

Synopsis. Ebenezer Botts, a poor tailor, is selling a coat to a mountain politician Snitch Crochett but is constantly bedeviled—by his wife Pansy, her father Grandpaw (a veteran of the Civil War), the local farm loan bank collector Gathe Geezle, and the loafer Enoch Alsop. Most irritating is the "Caw! Caw!" of the old crow behind him. Finally, Eb's son Luke, reveals that the coat is a madeover, and Snitch stalks off. Exasperated, Eb resolves to do away with the whole bunch. His daughter Doofie brings out his shotgun, and Eb decides to start with the crow, but misses and hits the family's pet sow Annabelle instead. Pansy grabs the rifle and stands over Eb, forcing the others to duck—and pray for Annabelle's soul.

Major Roles. EBENEZER BOTTS (t); Eb2 to G3. SNITCH CROCHETT (Eb1 to C♯3). ENOCH ALSOP (bar); Ab1 to E3. PANSY BOTTS (s); Eb3 to Ab4. GATHE GEEZLE (bar); A1 to F3. GRANDPAW (t); F2 to Gb3. LUKE (t or m-s or c); top Gb3 or Gb4.

Lesser Roles. DOOFIE (s); F3 to Gb4. THE CROW (c); only caws. ANNABELLE (any low voice; only grunts).

Orchestra. 2 fl, 2 ob, 2 cl, 2 bsn, 2 hrn, timp, strings (small number possible).

Material. Composer: 1626 E. Williams St., Tempe, Ariz. 85281.

📼 Catulli Carmina

Music by Carl Orff (1895–   ). Libretto in Latin by the composer after the poems of the Roman Gaius Valerius Catullus (87–54 B.C.). Premiere: Leipzig, 1943. Dance drama with vocal soloists. Typical rhythmic style, more sophisticated than *Carmina Burana* (See). Vocal line largely monotone. Chorus vitally important. Setting: Rome. One act, four scenes.

ACT I i, ii, iii, iv: Square with tavern and houses of principals.

Synopsis. As secondary action, girls and boys express their mutual affection while their elders soberly call to their attention the fate of the poet Catullus, who died of love. Catullus's love for Lesbia is mimed as the chorus sings his verses; Lesbia betrays him with his friend Caelius; he consoles himself with the courtesan Ipsitilla but again confronts Caelius. But he dies of love for Lesbia. The young people, not at all dismayed by this warning, return to their love making.

Major Roles. CATULLUS, CAELIUS, LESBIA, IPSITILLA (d). Singers (s, t).

Chorus. SSATTBB. Very important; a cappella.

Ballet. Youths and maidens.

Orchestra. 4 piano, 4 timp, elaborate perc (10–12 players).

Material. Bel (Sch). VS*.

Performances. Caramoor Fest.: 6.26.64 (Amer stage prem).

📼 Chanson de Fortunio · Song of Fortunio

Music by Jacques Offenbach (1819–1880). Libretto in French by H. Crémieux and Ludovic Halévy. Premiere: Paris, January 5, 1861. Comedy. Light, melodious; set numbers, dialogue. Overture. Setting: A large city, time of Louis XV; a garden pavilion. One act (50 min).

Synopsis. The Notary Fortunio, growing old, suspects his young wife of having a lover, perhaps his chief clerk Valentin. Valentin, indeed, is consumed by a hopeless passion for his employer's wife. The Notary's clerks discover Fortunio's secret: that in his youth he wrote a song that proved irresistible to women; thus he had won the heart of his employer's wife. But he forgot it after he married. All the clerks sing it, and all win favor but Valentin, who by a ruse is left alone with Laurette but is too shy to confess the object of his love. Fortunio himself, returning furious from his false errand, reveals the young man's passion. Laurette is not angry; on the contrary, she throws Valentin a rose from her balcony after Fortunio has forced her to retire.

Major Roles. (No vocal problems.) FORTUNIO, lawyer and notary (sp). LAURETTE, his wife (s); needs flexibility; trill. VALENTIN (s); some flexibility; trill on B4; one C5. PAUL FRIQUET, the youngest clerk (buff t).

Lesser Roles. BABET, the cook (m-s). GUILLAUME, LANDRY, SATURNIN, SYLVAIN, clerks in Fortunio's office (4 s).

258

Orchestra. 2 fl, 2 ob, 2 cl, 2 bsn, 4 hrn, 2 trp, 3 trb, timp, tri, strings.
Material. Pr (Heu). Map.

◢ Chanticleer

Music by Joyce Barthelson (Contemporary). Libretto in English by composer adapted from Chaucer's "The Nun's Priest Tale" (*Canterbury Tales*). Premiere: New York, at Biennial of National Federation of Music Clubs, as First Prize Winner, April 15, 1967. Comedy-satire. Continuous texture of conventional 20th-century harmonies; set numbers embedded; vocal line melodious. Setting: A chicken yard in medieval England. One act (45 min; 30 min for conc perf without chorus).

Synopsis. A boastful rooster, flattered by wily Mr. Fox into a display of his crowing prowess, is seized by the fox and carried off. Chanticleer's favorite wife, Partelote, begs the barnyard turkey Gobbler to rescue Chanticleer. Gobbler tempts Mr. Fox into dropping the rooster to pursue the larger, juicier bird, and the freed rooster joins his rescuer in a pine tree, while Mrs. Fox berates her husband for losing their dinner. Gobbler warns the chastened cock against any further boastful display.

Major Roles. NARRATOR, who sets the scene (sp). CHANTICLEER (t); F2 to A3. PARTELOTE (s); F3 to Bb4. GOBBLER (bs); G1 to D3. MR. FOX (Db2 to Eb3). MRS. FOX (c); B2 to E3.

Lesser Roles. THREE HENS, Chanticleer's other wives (2 s, c).

Chorus. SSATBB. Pilgrims, who act as commentators. Not difficult.

Orchestra. 2 fl, ob, 2 cl, bsn, 2 hrn, 2 trp, 2 trb, timp, perc, xyl, bells, harp, strings. Also 2 piano or piano 4 hands.

Material. Fi. Tape of conc. perf. available.

Performances. Nat'l Ass'n of Amer. Comp. & Cond. (NYC): 1.26.68. WNYC Amer. Fest. (NYC): 2.14.68. New Sch. Op. Wksp. (NYC): 2.1.68 (excerpts). Chaminade Club (Providence, R.I.): 2.18.68.

◢ Christopher Sly

Music by Dominick Argento (1927–   ). Libretto in English by John Manlove, based on Shakespeare's *The Taming of the Shrew*. Premiere: University of Minnesota, Minneapolis, May 31, 1967. Comedy. Melodic; set numbers; important ensembles; some dialogue. Setting: Rural England, 16th century. One act, 2 scenes, interlude (approx 70 min).

ACT I i: Exterior of the Garter Inn; Interlude: Lord's bedchamber; ii: Lord's bedchamber. (Note: Cadenzas in interlude indicate stage actions, and preparation of scene, accomplished with curtain up and no pause.)

Synopsis. Christopher Sly pursued by his creditors, Peter Turph and Henry Pimpernell, as well as the hostess of the alehouse Marion Hacket, is found in a drunken stupor by a Lord and his hunting party. As a joke, the Lord

259

takes him to his quarters, puts him in bed and when he is awake, pretends that he is a lord, with all amenities including a wife (simulated by a page). Sly is persuaded he has slept seven years, but eventually comes to himself and when the Lord goes out, strips the room of all its valuables and goes off with the Lord's two mistresses as well. The laugh is turned on the jokers.

Major Roles. CHRISTOPHER SLY, tinker (bs-bar); F♯1 (touches F1) to G♯3. PETER TURPH, tailor (t). HENRY PIMPERNELL, smith (bs-bar); F♯1 to F3. MARION HACKETT (m-s); top A♭4. A LORD (t); some flexibility; trill; C2 to A3 (B♭3 opt). PAGE (s); some difficult passages; A2 to B♭4 (touches C5 in ensemble). THREE HUNTSMEN, later SERVANTS (bar, t, bs); some difficult passages. TWO LADIES (2 lyr s); occasional difficult passages.

Lesser Roles. OFFICER OF THE LAW; MUSICIANS (mute).

Orchestra. fl, ob, cl, bsn, 2 hrn, trp, perc, harpsichord, string quintet. *Stage*: 3 recorders (opt).

Material. B & H. VS*.

Performances. Cambridge Op. (Mass.): 5.24.68. Western Op. Co. (San Fran.): 6.27.69 (conc). Ariz. St. Univ. (Tempe): 2.26.71, etc.

✠ El Cimarrón · The Cimarrón

Music by Hans Werner Henze (1926–   ). Libretto in German adapted by H. M. Enzensberger from Miguel Barnet's biography of Esteban Montejo. English version by Christopher Keene. Premiere: Aldeburgh Festival, England, June 22, 1970. "Recital for four musicians." All participants play percussion. Extremely difficult vocal and instrumental parts. Setting: Cuba, the past. Two parts, fifteen scenes (76 min).

Part I i: The world; ii: The Cimarrón; iii: Slavery; iv: Escape; v: The forest; vi: Ghosts; vii: The false freedom. Part II i: Women; ii: The machines; iii: The priests; iv: The rebellion; v: The battle of Mal Tiempo; vi: The bad victory; vii: Friendliness; viii: The machete.

Synopsis. The runaway slave was an aged resident of a remote Cuban village who claimed to be a survivor of Spanish slavery, Yankee imperialism, and other crimes. He said he was 104 at the time he was interviewed by Barnet. *Cimarrón* means "wild" or "fugitive slave." Henze has used fifteen excerpts from this biography. The conflict between the slave's love for the forest and wild animals and his longing for the civilization that offers women—the joy of his life—is effectively presented. Eventually the Cimarrón leaves the city to go back to his tranquil village.

Role. EL CIMARRON (bar); Extremely difficult tour de force; needs extraordinary vocal resources; strength throughout great range with top A♭3 in notation, fals A4; many passages half spoken, half sung. Where vocal passages are not fully notated choice of pitch is left to singer; intervals should be wider and more chromatic. Some fast improvisation and paraphrasing; some quarter tones.

260

Orchestra. fl, guit, perc (very elaborate and exotic). All play perc. Necessary doubling; picc, alto fl, bs fl, harmonica, trill whistle, jew's harp.

Material. Bel (Sch).

Performances. Univ. of Pittsburgh: 3.27.71 (Amer prem).

⊭ The Clock

Music by Vittorio Rieti (1898–   ). Libretto in English by Claire Nicholas. Unperformed. Drama. Occasional ariettas and ensembles in continuous texture of contemporary idiom; recitatives; short passages of speech over orchestra. Brief overture. Clock effects. Interlude between Act II and epilogue for change of scene. Setting: contemporary New England. Two acts and epilogue (approx 60 min).

ACT I: Mrs. Malone's living room. ACT II: Room in small seaside boarding house; flashback to Act I. Epilogue; same as Act I.

Synopsis. The New England matriarch, Mathilda Malone, dominates her family completely. Thirteen years before the opera begins, she has driven her son Richard's new wife from home. With Doda's departure, a valuable diamond necklace has disappeared. As the curtain opens, a shadowy figure enters the Malone living room, goes to the large clock, and deposits a package in it. As the day begins, Richard bemoans his futile life, railing at the clock for its erratic chimes and its marking of the passage of time. His sister Martha, her husband Phil, and son Bill arrive, expecting to find Mathilda gravely ill, as they have had a wire from Richard. Her ailment, however, has proved only minor indigestion; she is hale and hearty and plays cards every day with a boy who has been found stealing cherries in the orchard. Martha's contingent immediately suspects Dickie of alienating Mathilda's affections. Dickie, who has won several keepsakes already in the card game, plays for the clock, and when he wins, Richard offers to show him how to wind it. The necklace is discovered. In the confusion, Dickie escapes and returns to his mother in the boarding house—Richard's former wife. She has intended to go away without the boy, but when he discovers her preparations, she tells him the story of her marriage and her flight. In remorse, Richard has sent her the necklace, which he was supposed to deposit in the bank. Dickie rebels at returning to his grandmother, who has sent him a note of apology. Mathilda and Richard wait for the boy, meanwhile dismissing Martha and her family. But Dickie does not appear. Mathilda begins to lay out the cards by herself, admitting that the high cards are gone, and asking only for the joker. She has lost her gamble.

Major Roles. MATHILDA (c); Bb2 to G4. RICHARD (bar); B1 to F3. MARTHA (m-s); B2 to A4. PHIL (bs); F1 to E3. BILL, Martha's son (t); D2 to A3 (mostly in ensemble). DICKIE (m-s); C#3 to G4. DODA (s); D3 to B4.

Lesser Roles. LANDLADY (m-s). PEGEEN (m-s).

Orchestra. 2 fl, 2 ob, 2 cl, 2 bsn, 4 hrn, 3 trp, 3 trb, timp, perc, harp, cel, strings.

Production Problem. Flashback change of scene; time determined by short interlude.

Material. Composer: 1391 Madison Ave., NYC 10029.

◪ Le Convenienze ed Inconvenienze Teatrale · Opera: Italian Style

Music by Gaetano Donizetti (1797–1848). Libretto in Italian by the composer and (possibly) Jacopo Ferreti, based on two comedies by Antonio Simone Sografi. Premiere: Teatro Nuovo, Naples, November 21, 1827. Revised by Thomas Philips in English version by Philips and William Ashbrook. Premiere: University of New Mexico, Albuquerque, April 9, 1970. New version adds a trio, chorus, and finale drawn from other versions by Donizetti. Comedy. Highly melodious, set numbers, important ensembles; spoken dialogue. Setting: A typical provincial Italian theater. One act.

Synopsis. A madly temperamental prima donna and her fussy father, who is also a singer, make life miserable for their colleagues. Her chief rival is another soprano, Luigia, with an aggressive mother, Agata (sung by a buffo-bass), who tries to substitute for a defecting counter tenor (Musico) and throws the whole cast into confusion. At last the first tenor stalks out and the directors cancel the performance, leaving the Impresario and Maestro (composer) no choice but to abscond, since all the money is gone.

Major Roles. PRIMA DONNA (col s); very florid, many trills; B2 to B4 (2 C5's with lower opt). MAESTRO (Composer) (bs cantante); needs great flexibility; some high tessitura; G1 to F3. AGATA (buf bs); needs flexibility; trill (B♭1 to F3) (one G3). TENOR (t); F2 to A3. LUIGIA (s); B2 to E4. POET (librettist) (bar); A1 to E3.

Lesser Roles. MUSICO (count t or t); B1 to E3 if t. PROCOLO, Prima Donna's father (bs); G1 to E3. IMPRESARIO (bs); A1 to G3.

Chorus. SATB. Typical opera chorus.

Orchestra. fl, 2 ob, 2 cl, 2 bsn, 2 hrn, harpsichord, strings.

Material. From Thomas Philips, 3803 Aspen, NE, Albuquerque, N.M. 87110.

◪ Curlew River

Music by Benjamin Britten (1913–   ). Libretto in English by William Plomer, based on Noh play, *The Sumida River.* Premiere: Oxford Church, Suffolk, June 13, 1964. "A parable for church performance." Miracle story. Partly based on plainsong; linear harmony, polytonality almost absent; many harmonic clusters determined by prolongation of melodic line; highly stylized. Setting: transposed to the Fenlands of England; costumes highly stylized; important masks. One act (approx 70 min).

262

Synopsis. Monks are preparing for a Miracle play; the Abbot addresses the congregation and the actors receive ceremonial robes and masks. The play: A ferryman is about to take pilgrims to a shrine across the Curlew River. One remaining place is given to a weary traveler, but a Madwoman gains place after she sings wildly about strange birds in the Fenland; the pilgrims sympathize with her wish to cross in search for her kidnapped son. The Ferryman tells the story of the shrine: just a year ago he took a stranger and an ill child across the river; when the boy died, the people came to believe him a saint, whose spirit can work miracles. The Madwoman is bitter, realizing this must have been her son, but eventually throws herself before the child's tomb, and experiences a miracle. The child appears and promises they will meet in heaven. Her sanity is restored. Now the play is ended, and the Abbot and monks discard their robes and masks, and leave the church in procession, singing the hymn that was part of the entering processional.

Major Roles. MADWOMAN (t). FERRYMAN (bar). TRAVELER (bar). SPIRIT OF THE BOY (treb). CHORUS LEADER (bs); doubles with ABBOT.

Lesser Roles. CHORUS (3 t, 3 bar, 2 bs). THREE ASSISTANTS (Acolytes).

Orchestra. fl (picc), hrn, perc, harp, chamber org, vla, cb.

Material. G Sc (Fa). VS*.

Performances. Litt Orch (NYC after long tour): 11.27.67. Univ. Cal. Op. Th.: 5.2.69. Caramoor Fest.: 6.22.69. Kent St. Univ.: 10.28.69. Leverett House Op. Soc. (Harvard Univ.): 4.24.70. Many others.

🎭 Dantons Tod · Danton's Death

Music by Gottfried von Einem (1918–   ). Libretto in German by Boris Blacher and the composer after the play by Georg Büchner. Premiere: Salzburg Festival, August 6, 1947. Historical drama. Largely declamatory; conventional harmonies with added dissonances; vocal line patterned after speech; little melody. No overture; interludes between each scene. Important ensembles. Setting: Paris, March and April, 1794, during Reign of Terror. Two acts, six scenes (78 min).

ACT I i: A luxurious room (9 min); ii: A street (16 min); iii: A room (12 min). ACT II i: The Conciergerie—Inside the prison (15 min); ii: The Revolutionary Tribunal (15 min); iii: Place de la Révolution (11 min).

Synopsis. The theme of the opera, as of the play, is the opposite qualities and ambitions of Danton, former leading revolutionary who has become disillusioned and strives to inject humanity into the processes of government, and Robespierre, the abstract revolutionary who rules by terror. The opera opens with the news of execution of former heroes of the Revolution, filling with alarm the three deputies, Danton, Hérault de Séchelles, and Camille Desmoulins, who would like to end the terror. In a street, Simon and his wife quarrel violently and draw a crowd, which soon turns its fury toward passing aristocrats. A nobleman is about to be hanged from a lamppost when Robespierre enters and calms them down, inviting them to the Jacobin Club, head-

263

quarters of the Terrorists. Danton is critical of Robespierre, who decides to sacrifice his former friend with the assistance of St. Just, a member of the repressive Committee for Public Safety. Danton, learning of his doom, remains calm, but Camille, urged by his wife Lucille, determines to intervene, not realizing that his fate has been sealed along with Danton's. As Danton appears before the people in the square before the prison, he is acclaimed until Simon turns them against him. In prison, Danton shows his strength of mind, but Camille breaks down. Lucille, deranged, appears before the prison, calling for her husband. The trial seems to go in Danton's favor as the people hail him, but he is nevertheless sentenced to death, along with the other accused. In the Place de la Révolution, they are put to the guillotine. The crowd disperses. Lucille wanders in distractedly, crying "Long live the King." She is arrested and dragged away.

Major Roles. GEORGE DANTON (bar); long, sustained, difficult; needs dramatic force; strength at extremes of range; Ab1 to F#3 (several Gb3's with lower opt). CAMILLE DESMOULINS (t); D2 to B3. HÉRAULT DE SÉCHELLES (t); D2 to G#3. ROBESPIERRE (t); D2 to Ab3. ST. JUST (bs); A1 to E#3. LUCILLE (s); C#3 to Bb4.

Lesser Roles. HERRMANN, president of the Revolutionary Tribunal (bar). SIMON (buf-bs); A1 to D3. JULIE, Danton's wife (m-s). SIMON'S WIFE (c). YOUNG MAN (t—can be from chor). TWO EXECUTIONERS (t, bs). WOMAN (s).

Chorus. SATB. Very important. Citizens, guards, Terrorists, etc.

Orchestra. 3 fl (picc), 2 ob, 2 cl, 2 bsn, 4 hrn, 3 trp, 3 trb, bs tuba, timp, perc (tri, military dr, tamb, bs dr, ten dr), strings. *Stage*: tam-tam.

Material. Pr (UE). Tr: Martins.

Performances. NYCO (Amer prem): 3.9.66.

◪ Dark Waters

Music by Ernst Krenek (1900–   ). Libretto in English and German by the composer. Premiere: Los Angeles, USC, May 2, 1951. Melodrama. Unconventional harmonies, some dissonance; vocal line angular, patterned partly after speech; some dialogue; one duet. Setting: The deck of a riverboat, supposed to move parallel to footlights, from right to left; summer night. One act (56 min).

Synopsis. Joe, a bargeman tired of his mean life, agrees to smuggle diamonds across the border for two gangsters, hoping to meet the "big chief" and become rich. His downtrodden wife Claire and his restless son Phil try to dissuade him. A mysterious girl drops (presumably) from a bridge to the boat and steals one of the diamonds. She charms each of the family in turn, promising to run away with Phil and eliciting a promise from Joe to let her work with him. When a policeman boards the boat, Joe tells him the girl is his niece. Believing Phil has stolen the diamond, Joe shoots at him but hits the girl, who has attempted to shield Phil. The gangsters enter, confounding Joe by revealing the diamonds were fake, as a test of his first job for them, and taunt him with the information that this is his last trip—he has killed the daughter of "the big chief," Mendoza, the rich man who lives on the hill above San Pedro, from where the girl had tried to escape.

Major Roles. CLAIRE (m-s); A2 to E4. JOE (dram bar); C2 to F♯3. PHIL (t); top G♯3. A GIRL (Dolores Mendoza) (s); C♯3 to A4.

Lesser Roles. TWO GANGSTERS (bs, t). OFFICER (bs).

Orchestra. fl, ob, cl, bsn, 2 hrn, trp, trb, perc, piano, strings.

Material. G Sc (Bä).

✖ Une Demoiselle en Loterie · A Lady in Lottery

Music by Jacques Offenbach (1819–1880). Libretto in French by Jaime *fils* and H. Crémieux. Premiere: Paris, July 27, 1857. Comedy. Light, melodious; set numbers; conventional harmonies; dialogue. Overture. Setting: A middle-class drawing room; Second Empire. One act (approx 60 min).

Synopsis. Aspasie and Démeloir have quit their circus jobs as barker and equestrienne to raffle the lady off in marriage. So far, they have had no luck. But Aspasie has had a letter from her cousin Pigeonneau, who, ignorant of her identity, wants No. 100 in the lottery, sure it will win. The two conspirators trick Pigeonneau, who has become a wealthy goose merchant on the legacy Aspasie feels should be hers, into giving his fortune for the ticket, which is then proclaimed the winner. Everyone is happy, for Aspasie and the Goose-king have fallen in love, and Démeloir becomes their servant.

Roles. PIGEONNEAU (t). ASPASIE (col s); many florid passages; trill; top C5 (one E5). DÉMELOIR (bar).

Orchestra. 2 fl, ob, 2 cl, bsn, 2 hrn, 2 trp, trb, timp, perc, strings.

Material. Pr (Heu).

✖ La Divina

Music by Thomas Pasatieri (1945–   ). Libretto in English by the composer. Premiere: Juilliard, New York, March 16, 1966. Satirical comedy. Set numbers, conventional harmonies; vocal line melodic, moderately florid. Setting: Almost any theater, any time from 1800 to 1972. One act (25 min).

Synopsis. At the "farewell" performance of an aging diva, her maid and manager are not displeased to see an end to the confusion constantly created by their prima donna's temperament and "star complex." Left alone for a contemplative moment in her dressing room, the star reflects on the past and expresses fear of a future without the glamor of the spotlight. To the ecstasy of the crowd and the chagrin of her staff, she announces yet another "farewell" next week.

Roles. MADAME ALTINA (col s). CECILY, her maid (m-s or c). HAEMON, her manager (bar). A YOUNG CONDUCTOR (t).

Orchestra. 2 fl (picc), 2 ob, 2 cl, 2 bsn (cont bsn), hrn, trp, harp, piano and celesta (1), timp and perc (1), strings.

Material. Pr. VS*.

Performances. Many at colleges: Texas, Nebraska, Ohio, Boston, Georgia, California, etc. For Washington performance, see *The Women.*

🎵 Djamileh

Music by Georges Bizet (1838–1875). Libretto in French by Louis Gallet. Premiere: Paris, May 22, 1872. Opera-comique, with set numbers connected by dialogue. Highly melodious, with simple harmonic structure; oriental coloration. Prelude. Setting, the Court of Haroun, an oriental ruler; time unspecified. One act (65 min).

Synopsis. Haroun believes that he is incapable of love, but he is truly loved by Djamileh, one of his slaves. When he gives her her freedom, she reappears in disguise, and when he recognizes her, she says she prefers his love to liberty. Impressed by this, Haroun yields to love.

Roles. DJAMILEH (m-s); needs trill; B2 to Bb4; HAROUN (t) C2 to B3; SPLENDIANO, Haroun's friend, in love with Djamileh (bar) C2 to G3; A SLAVE-MERCHANT (sp).

Chorus. STTBBB.

Ballet. Dance of slaves.

Orchestra. 4 hrn, 2 trp, 3 trb, timp, perc, harp, strings (2.2.2.2). *Stage*: ob, tambour basque, harp.

Material. Pet. VS*. Tr: Jess Perlman.

Performances. Litt. Orch. (NYC): 1960. Cal. West. Univ. (San Diego): 1.67.

🎵 Le Docteur Miracle · Doctor Miracle

Music by Georges Bizet (1838–1875). Libretto in French by Léon Battu and Ludovic Halévy. Premiere: Paris, April 9, 1857. Bizet and Charles Lecocq were winners in a competition by Offenbach; both wrote on the same libretto. Comedy. Melodious. One act: the living room of the Mayor of Padua's house, Middle Ages (approx 60 min).

Synopsis. Aroused by the noise of a traveling quack doctor, the Mayor of Padua rushes out, leaving his daughter, Lauretta, and her stepmother, Véronique. He returns with a new servant to replace one who has acted as a go-between for Lauretta and her lover, Captain Silvio. The new servant, Pasquin, is as ugly as sin, and his first attempt at cooking a French omelet is disastrous; the Mayor hurries out with Véronique for a walk to restore his digestion. Lauretta comments offensively on Pasquin's appearance until he reveals himself as Silvio. They fall into each other's arms, but are surprised

266

by the Mayor, who throws Silvio out. Hardly has the young man departed when a letter is delivered to the Mayor, warning him that Silvio has poisoned his omelet. In horror, the Mayor sends for the quack doctor, who promises to cure him for 5,000 ducats and marriage to his daughter. Lauretta surprisingly agrees; the Mayor is foiled once more by consenting in writing to Lauretta's marriage to Silvio—for of course the miraculous doctor is he. His prescription reveals that he had never intended to poison his future father-in-law. The Mayor gives in, and the lovers are united.

Roles. THE MAYOR OF PADUA (bar); high tessitura; very florid; trill; A1 to G3 (one A3, A2 opt). LAURETTA (s); some florid passages; trill; D3 to C5. VÉRONIQUE (s); trill; B♭2 to G♯4. CAPTAIN SILVIO (disguised as PASQUIN, DR. MIRACLE) (t); trill; D2 to A3.

Orchestra. 2 fl (picc), ob, 2 cl, bsn, 3 hrn, corn à pist, 2 trb, 2 timp, tri, string 5-tet. *Stage:* cl, trb, bs dr, cym.

Material. Edit. Français de Musique, Paris SOFIRAD.

Performances. Univ. of Tex. (Austin): 11.11.67. San Fran. Op. Guild: 1.25.69. E. Cent. St. Coll. (Ada, Okla.): 3.19.69. Mannes Coll. (NYC): 3.24.71.

📽 Dunstan and the Devil

Music by Malcolm Williamson (1931–   ). Libretto in English by Geoffrey Dunn. Commissioned by the Cookham Festival Society. Premiere: Cookham Festival Society, May 19, 1967. Religious fable. Some conventional, some modal harmonies; occasional dissonance; very spare orchestration. Lyrical vocal line. Setting: Glastonbury, Winchester, and Rome, 10th century. Prologue and one act, four scenes (58 min).

Prologue: Miracle of the Candles, Church of the Blessed Virgin Mary, Glastonbury, Feb. 2, A.D. 925. Scene i: The Devil rises out of Hell; ii: The Devil's first fight, Palace of King Athelstan, Winchester, A.D. 943; iii: Vision of the Apostles, Mons Gaudii near Rome; The tweaking of the Nose, Dunstan's cell at Glastonbury. Note: The three levels, Hell, Earth, and Heaven, can be accomplished on unit set, necessitating no changes.

Synopsis. The story of Saint Dunstan, eventually made Archbishop of Canterbury, and his legendary encounters with the Devil, begins here with a miracle before his birth. His parents, Heorstan and Keondrud, visit the Glastonbury church to receive a blessing on their unborn son. God wrathfully blows out all the candles, but rekindles that of the mother-to-be Keondrud. Dunstan is thus predestined to a holy life. But as a young man he clings to worldly things, being a goldsmith of genius, and fond of a lady who embroiders him a stole. Hs uncle Alphege urges him towards a religious vocation, but the Devil tempts him away, until another miracle occurs: angels intercept a boulder the Devil is about to launch at uncle and nephew as they pray near Rome; Saints Paul, Peter, and Andrew come down to earth; and Dunstan enters the monastery. Here he works on objects for the church,

267

while the Devil attempts to turn him in vain to worldly pursuits. The Lady calls on the Devil for help to regain her love, but repents and Dunstan forgives her. He pursues the Devil, who assumes various animal forms, until at last Dunstan seizes the nose of the Devil's latest disguise, a fox, between red hot pincers. The Devil is defeated and humbled, and Dunstan is glorified.

Major Roles. DUNSTAN (t); E♭2 to A3 (one firm B♭3). THE DEVIL (bs); F1 to F3. ALPHEGE (bar); B♭1 to E3. THE LADY (s); D♭3 to B4.

Lesser Roles. KEONDRUD (m-s); C3 to D♭4. HEORSTAN (bar); C2 to E♭3. ST. PETER (t). ST. PAUL (bar). ST. ANDREW (bs).

Bit Part. OFFICER (t).

Chorus. SATB. People of Glastonbury. SSSA. Angels.

Orchestra. Piano duet, timp, perc (susp cym, large gong, small gong, chimes, xyl, glock, tri, bs dr, snare dr, ten dr, maraccas, bongos).

Material. B & H (Wein). VS*.

Performances. Princeton: 12.70 (Amer prem). St. John's Cathedral (NYC): 4.7.72.

♬ Eight Songs for a Mad King

Music by Peter Maxwell Davies (1934–   ). Libretto in English by Randolph Stow, suggested by George III's miniature mechanical organ which played eight tunes. Premiere: Pierrot Players, London, April 22, 1969. Monodrama. Contemporary, dissonant idiom, very expressive, often parodying; according to the composer, "a collection of musical objects borrowed from many sources, functioning as musical 'stage props,' around which the reciter's part weaves" (see below); vocal line extremely difficult (see below). Eight parts (33 min).

Song i: The Sentry; ii: The Country Walk; iii: The Lady-in-Waiting; iv: To Be Sung on the Water; v: The Phantom Queen; vi: The Counterfeit; vii: Country Dance; viii: The Review.

Synopsis. "The songs are to be understood as the King's monologue while listening to his birds perform, and incorporate some sentences actually spoken by George III" (Stow). The King has extended dialogues with the flute, clarinet, violin, and cello as the birds he attempted to teach to sing. His "madness" shows to varying degrees until, in No. vii, he snatches the violin through the bars of the player's cage and breaks it, giving in to insanity, "a ritual murder of a part of himself, after which he can announce his own death" (Davies). Many composers are "quoted," notably Handel's *Messiah.*

Role. KING GEORGE III (bs-bar); requires extraordinary range and command of unusual vocal sounds (howls, etc.); fals; wide variety of voice coloration; stamina.

Orchestra. fl (picc), cl, piano (harpsichord, dulcimer), vln, vcl, perc (railway whistle, side dr, susp cym, large susp cym, foot cym, large and small wd bl, very large bs dr, chains, small rachet, tom-tom, tam-tam, tamb, roto

268

toms, toy bird-calls, 2 temp bl, wind chimes, crotales, very small bells, glock, small steel non-resonant bars, crow—1 player). In addition, each player has mechanical bird-song devices operated by clockwork.

Material. B & H.

Performances. Aspen (1970). Buffalo: 1971. NYC: 12.9.71.

🎕 Elephant Steps

Music by Stanley Silverman (1938–   ). Libretto in English by Richard Foreman. Commissioned by the Fromm Foundation. Premiere: Tanglewood, Mass., August 7, 1968. Described by the composer as "occult music theater, dealing with perception and accomplishment." The music was an attempt to notate his spontaneous reaction to the text, later "ariculated into a strictly disciplined formal structure." No overture. Minimal staging is required. Setting: contemporary. One act, four scenes, one interlude (90 min).

Scene i: A bedroom; ii: Outside Reinheart's house; iii: Secret radio studio; Interlude; iv: Kitchen.

Synopsis. The story is symbolic, surrealistic, nightmarish. It involves the efforts of the ill Hartman, his wife Hannah, Max, Otto, and the Doctor to understand the mysterious Reinheart and penetrate his true nature. After being denied Reinheart's house while others have easy access, Hartman retreats to a comfortable kitchen with the Scrubwoman and the others, where he dreams that Elephant Angels urge him to climb a ladder to Reinheart's house. At its top, he sees the object of his search jumping seven times around the room, and is "illuminated."

Major Roles. HARTMAN (bs); needs dramatic force; E1 to E3. MAX (t); quality of nostalgic "pop" crooner; C2 to G3. DR. WORMS (high t); D2 to B♭3. SCRUBWOMAN (high s); D3 to B4.

Lesser Roles. HANNAH (s); high tessitura; D3 to C5. OTTO (pop bar). ELEPHANT ANGELS (s, c). CABARET SINGER (c).

Chorus. 3 s, 3 c.

Ballet. Rock dance in iv.

Orchestra. 2 fl (2 picc), 2 cl (s sax, cont bs cl), bsn (if no cont bs cl, doubles cont bsn), hrn, trp, trb, tuba, perc (3): xyl, cel, piano, harp, guit (banjo), 5 solo strings. *Stage*: 4-man elec rock band (guit, bs, org or 2 guit, dr).

Material. Composer: 185 West End, NYC.

Performances. Hunter Coll. (NYC): 4.23.70. Lake George: 8.12.70.

🎕 Das Ende einer Welt · The End of a World

Music by Hans Werner Henze (1926–   ). Libretto in German by Wolfgang Hildescheimer. Premiere: Hamburg Radio, December 4, 1953; Frankfurt (staged), 1965–1966. Serio-comic satire. Miniature musical forms (waltz, barcarolle, concertato, minuet, etc.); compact set numbers; contemporary idiom; some dialogue and *Sprechstimme*. Setting: The Lagoon of Venice, the present. One act (50 min).

ACT I: A man-made island in Amerigo, the Lagoon of Venice, built especially as a retreat for the Marchesa Montetristo, who could not bear the Continent. i: Hall of Palazzo Montetristo, eclectically decorated; ii: Outside the sinking palace.

Synopsis. Herr Fallersleben, arriving at a select soiree of the Marchesa, observes the guests in sophisticated chatter about music, books and antiques. He had sold her Marat's bathtub, of which she is very proud. A musicale ensues, consisting of a flute sonata by Antonio Gianbattista Bloch (1692–1756), "contemporary and friend of Rameau," revised by Wolfgang H. Weltli, and played by a descendant of Béranger and the Marchesa. The Majordomo explains that this "somewhat dull elegance, which clearly identifies the sonata as a second-class or newly discovered work," is the product of Weltli himself, Bloch being only imaginary. Fallersleben notices rats running at the side of the room and hears rumbling as the room shakes. The others see nothing, for their eyes are closed in rapt attention to the music. A servant informs the Marchesa that the foundation of the island and palace are afloat. The water begins to invade the room, but the music goes on. Fallersleben tries to escape, opening the double doors, which admit a wave that comes to the knees of the performers so that the Marchesa can no longer use the pedal "so essential to the cembalo," Fallersleben remarks. The cello also is impeded—"a cello full of water will never resonate as clearly." Fallersleben gains the exterior; as the palace sinks, he swims. The servants all flee; they feel no obligation to the true and noble cause of everlasting art. The guests finally rise and applaud the completed sonata with their hands over their heads, for the water has risen to their chins. A few cry, "Da capo!" Fallersleben seizes the only gondola and muses as he rows away that the end was truly unforgettable—but he mourns the loss of Marat's bath.

Major Roles. HERR FALLERSLEBEN (t); speaks prologue; difficult intervals; angular line; A1 to Cb4 (one C4 opt). MARCHESA MONTETRISTO (c); G2 to G4. MME DOMBROWSKA (t); a twofold talent, authority on modern dance and eternal youth; wide skips and difficult intervals; G#2 to B3; trill on A3. SIGNORA SGAMBATI (col s); astrologer; top D#5; trill on C#5. GOLCH (bs); famous connoisseur; very low in *Sprechstimme*; Eb1 (C1 with C2 opt) to G#3. PROFESSOR KUNTZ-SARTORI (bar); monarchist politician; high tessitura; Cb2 to G#3. MAJORDOMO (bar); top B3.

Chorus. SATB. Servants, guests. Sings sycophantly "sweet, sweet," parrot-like; or music by "Bloch."

Orchestra. recorder, fl, ob, cl, bsn, hrn, trp, trb, harm, grand piano, harp, guit, 3 timp, perc (bs dr, 2 tom-tom, 2 cym, tam-tam, rhumba bl, maracas, vib, glock, xyl, tub bells), strings (mostly solo).

270

Production Problems. Quick change of scene; simulation of flood and sinking of palace.

Material. Bel (Sch). VS*.

Performances. Peabody Cons.: 3.13.70.

✠ Erwartung · Expectation

Music by Arnold Schönberg (1874–1951). Libretto in German by Marie Pappenheim. Premiere: Prague, June 6, 1924. Monodrama. Dissonant, expressionistic, anticipates 12-tone principle; vocal line difficult. Setting: A forest, contemporary. One act, four scenes (30 min).

Scene i: Edge of a forest; ii: Deep darkness, a broad path through the dense forest; iii: Moonlight falls on a tree trunk; grass, ferns, and yellow fungus are visible; iv: Moonlit way out of the wood leading to a house.

Synopsis. In a forest at night a woman is searching for her lost lover. She experiences fear and terror almost to hysteria. Emerging from the forest, she stumbles over the body of her dead lover, bringing to a climax her hope, despair, and her hallucinations.

Role. A WOMAN (s or m-s); needs strength at extremes of range; suppleness for difficult intervals; highly dramatic, almost nightmarish quality; G2 to firm B4.

Orchestra. picc, 3 fl (2 picc), 3 ob, Eng hrn (ob), 4 cl, bs cl, 3 bsn, cont bsn, 4 hrn, 3 trp, 4 trb, tuba, harp, cel, perc (cym, bs dr, small dr, tam-tam, rachet, tri, glock, xyl), strings.

Material. Pr (UE).

Performances. Several since Amer prem: (NYC): 11.15.51 (conc); (Wash.): 12.28.60 (staged).

✠ Der Esels Schatten · The Donkey's Shadow

Music by Richard Strauss (1864–1949). Orchestrated and completed by Karl Haussner. Libretto in German by Hans Adler after Christoph Martin Wieland's novel, *The Abderites.* Premiere (private): Ettal, Bavaria, June 7, 1964; (public) Naples, October 28, 1964. Production devised by Dom Stephen Schaller. Musical numbers reduced from 18 to 14. *Singspiel.* Comedy. Setting: The city of Abdera in Thrace, the ancient version of "Gotham"; approximately 5th century B.C. Prelude and six scenes (90 min).

Prelude: The Frog Pond. Scene i: Road crossing the plain near Abdera; ii: Office of the Municipal Judge; iii: Kenteterion's workshop; iv: Hall in house of Agathyrsus; v: Frog pond of Temple of Latona; vi: Market square of Abdera.

Synopsis. The dentist Struthion, who has hired a donkey for a day disputes with the donkey's owner, Antrax, who denies that the payment allows the dentist to sit in the donkey's shadow to keep out of the sun. The quarrel goes through the courts and divides city opinion, even penetrating to the frog pond. The factions are finally reconciled, but the donkey has been left all the while tied in the sun without food or drink, and is in the end a skeleton. The people erect a statue in the beast's memory and reflect on their errors.

Major Roles. STRUTHION (bs); F1 to E3. ANTRAX (t); B1 to G3. KROBYLE, his wife (c); B2 to E4. GORGO, his daughter (s); needs flexibility; C3 to B4. PHILIPPIDES, municipal judge (bar); A1 to E3. PHYSIGNATUS, lawyer (t); D2 to G3. POLYPHONUS, lawyer (bs); D2 to E3. KENTETERION, leader of cobblers' guild (bs); A1 to F3.

Lesser Roles. AGATHYRSUS, head of Temple of Jason (sp). STROBYLUS, head of Temple of Latona (sp). MANSERVANT TO AGATHYRSUS. TWO PRIESTS OF LATONA. COURT USHER.

Chorus. TB. Frogs (monotone), people of Abdera, municipal guards.

Orchestra. 2 fl, 2 ob, 2 cl, 2 bsn, 2 hrn, 2 trp, timp, perc (xyl, castanets, side dr, bs dr, cym, bl, tri, tamb, gong, wd bl; frog's noises simulated), piano, strings.

Material. B & H. VS* (tr: Maria Pelikan; contains outline and analysis of revision and completion work done by Schaller and Haussner).

Performances. N. Ariz. Univ. Summ. Mus. Camp (Flagstaff): 8.14.70 (Amer prem).

🖾 Fables

Music by Ned Rorem (1923–   ). Based on fables by Jean de la Fontaine. Translated by Marianne Moore. Premiere: University of Tennessee, Martin, May 21, 1971. Four very short pieces; may be performed by singers or mimes illustrating the poems read from offstage. Chorus of two in final three pieces should try to sound alike from opposite sides of the stage. The order must be as follows if all are presented together: "The Lion in Love"; "The Sun and Frogs"; "The Fox and the Grapes"; "Animals Sick of the Plague."

Particulars. 1. The Lion in Love. The composer suggests one person dedicating the music to the haughty Mlle de Sévigné, seated in profile, then going to one side to explain the action; or the lines could be taken by two, three, or even four, each beginning at metronome change. The role ranges from Bb2 to G4 and needs flexibility.

2. The Sun and the Frogs. Performers: Two Frogs; Chorus of two soloists; no range problems.

3. The Fox and the Grapes. The Fox; Chorus of two soloists.

4. The Animals Sick of the Plague. Lion, Fox, Ass. Chorus of two soloists. Four voices for short final chorus: SATB.

Orchestra. Piano.

Material. B & H.

🎵 A Faun in the Forest

Music by Gerald Cockshott. Libretto in English by the composer. Premiere: After Dinner Opera Company, Westport, Conn., August 9, 1959. Commissioned by After Dinner Company. Satirical comedy. Set numbers; melodic; some dialogue. No overture. Setting: A medieval forest. One act (approx 30 min).

Synopsis. Convention demanded that the Lady should sit under the full moon on a hard rock in the forest until her lover, Sir Hugo the Dull, the dragon hunter, betrothed to her since childhood, came to her. Sir Hugo has been chasing dragons but has lost his horse. Dutifully, he proposes in a conventional love duet, but is interrupted by the entrance of The Faun, accompanied by an appropriate motif from Debussy's tone poem (may be played on recorder or flute, sung or whistled). This mythical being soon shows interest in the Lady's vital statistics, while she reciprocates his attentions. Confessing that he hasn't caught a nymph for years, the Faun proposes an exchange wih Sir Hugo, who hasn't caught a dragon. Each believes the other's métier will suit him better; the Faun gives Hugo his piccolo (for scaring dragons) and his goatskin with hooves attached, and leads the Lady off to live happily married ever after. The moral: Do not remain in the wrong occupation.

Roles. THE LADY (s); needs flexibility; C♯3 to A4 (one C♯5). SIR HUGO THE DULL (t); F2 to B♭3. THE FAUN (bs-bar); F1 to E♭3 (fals to D♭4 ad lib).
Orchestra. Piano.
Material. From Aft. Dinn. Co.

🎵 Feuersnot · Fire Famine

Music by Richard Strauss (1864–1949). Libretto in German by Ernst von Wolzogen. Premiere: Dresden, November 21, 1901. "Lyric poem." Free interpretation of old Dutch legend. Melodic; arias and important ensembles, set in continuous texture. Music reflects fantasy; highly colorful orchestration. Quotation of themes from Wagner's *Der Fliegende Holländer* and Strauss's *Guntram.* Very brief prelude. Setting: Munich, never-never time, during the summer solstice. One act (70 min).

Synopsis. Strauss intended his fable to chastise the little minds who drove Wagner out of Munich. His hero, Kunrad, represents Strauss himself, who as the successor of Wagner, will bring light and warmth through love once again to the benighted city. Children are gathering wood for the solstice bonfires, and after visiting the Burgomaster, decide to brave the occupant of the Wizard's House, a young dreamer called Kunrad. Waking from his chilly reverie, Kunrad cheerfully helps the children tear down his ramshackle house for firewood. Spying Diemut, the Burgomaster's daughter, he impulsively kisses her, to her shame. She represses her instinctive attraction to the stranger by vowing vengeance. The opportunity soon arises. Kunrad begs

273

her forgiveness; she pretends to relent and invites him to step into the large basket she had let down for the children's wood. When her suitor is halfway up to her balcony, she leaves him suspended there, the butt of the townsfolks' jeers. In rage, Kunrad calls on the Wizard to help. Suddenly, all fires in the town flicker and go out. To the lamentations and imprecations of the crowd, Kunrad, spotlighted by a sudden shaft of moonlight, cries that they do not know love; they have driven out genius. He, Wagner's follower, will triumph in spite of them. His chosen helpmate has also misunderstood. By now, Kunrad has ascended to the balcony, and the repentant Diemut draws him into her room, from where light begins to gleam softly. As their love is expressed, all the fires come once more to life.

Major Roles. SCHWEIKER VON GUNDELFINGEN, castle governer (t); E2 to B♭3. ORTOLF SENTLINGER, burgomaster (bs); needs flexibility; G♯1 to F3. DIEMUT, his daughter (high s); G♯2 to B4. Her playmates (mostly as trio, often in unison; A2 to B4): MARGRET (high s); ELSBETH (m-s); WIGELIS (c); has low E. KUNRAD (high bar); sustained, dramatic, consistently high tessitura; B1 to G3.

Lesser Roles. Mostly in ensemble. JOR POSCHEL, innkeeper (bs); E1 to F♯3. HAMERLEIN, haberdasher (bar); E2 to G3. KOFEL, smith (bs); A1 to F♯3. KUNZ GILGENSTOCK, brewer and baker; G♯1 to F♯3. ORTLIEB TULBECK, cooper (high t); E♭2 to B3. URSULA, his wife (c); G♯3 to F♯4. RUGER ASPECK, potter (t); E♭2 to A3. WALPURG, his wife (high s); B2 to B4.

Chorus. SATB. Also children. Townsfolk, servants.

Orchestra. 3 fl, 3 ob, 3 cl, 3 bsn, 4 hrn, 3 trp, 3 trb, tuba, 2 harp, timp, perc, strings.

Material. B & H. VS (g)*.

Performances. Indianapolis Sym.: 1.7.51 (conc). Northwestern Univ. (Evanston): 3.5.61 (scene).

🎬 Fiesta

Music by Darius Milhaud (1892–   ). Libretto in French by Boris Vian. Premiere (in German): West Berlin, October 3, 1958. Contemporary *verismo*. Melodious, exotic harmonies, some dissonance. Setting: A Spanish sea village; a quai with lighthouse in the distance; the near present. One act (23 min).

Synopsis. Onto the beach where the townsfolk lounge and drink, a small boat floats, bearing a shipwrecked man. The villagers bring him back to life and give him wine and fruit. Mercedes, who has been watching with her lover, the guitarist Fernan, makes up to the stranger, encouraging him to kiss and fondle her after she dances. Fernan stabs the interloper and walks away, followed by Mercedes, calling after him. Mario, Pedro, and Esteban chant a merry dirge, and leave the corpse to be taken back to the sea.

Major Roles. MERCEDES (m-s). NAUFRAGÉ (the Shipwrecked) (bar). NUNEZ (bs). JULIO (child). FERNAN (mute); guitarist.

Lesser Roles. MARIO (t). PEDRO (bar). ESTEBAN (bs). PIA (s). MARIA (m-s). CONCHITA (c).

Supers. CARACAS, ALBERTO, CORTEZ, RAPHAEL, RAQUEL.

Orchestra. fl (picc), ob, cl, bs cl, bsn, alto sax, trp, trb, perc, harp, 3 vln, 2 vcl, cb.

Material. Pr (Heu).

Performances. U.C.L.A.: 3.16.59 (Amer prem). Mannes Coll.: 4.6.60. Aspen: 7.31.69.

The Fisherman and His Wife

Music by Gunther Schuller (1925–). Libretto in English by John Updike, based on the Grimm fairy tale. Commissioned by the Junior League of Boston. Premiere: Boston, May 7, 1970. "A fairy tale for all ages." Contemporary idiom employing many devices (jazz combo, twelve-tone, rock, electronics, taped sounds); vocal line largely recitative, some brief melodic passages. Setting: A seaside, legendary times. Two acts (more effective if continuous), thirteen scenes.

Scenes i: Humble cottage; ii: Seaside. Thereafter, seaside, growing more ominous in aspect each time, alternates with a pretty cottage, a castle, a throne room, the papal residence, and the humble cottage.

Synopsis. The discontented wife of a simple fisherman prevails upon him to ask succeedingly more ambitious favors of a great fish he has caught but thrown back. First it is an improved cottage; next a castle; then she wants to be king, then pope; but when she demands to play God, she is restored to her original humble state and seems all the happier for it. A frisky cat is added to the original story.

Roles. THE FISH (bs-bar); C#2 to F3. THE FISHERMAN (t); C#2 to A3. THE WIFE (m-s); G2 to A4 (scream on B4). THE CAT (col s); needs flexibility; trill on A4; C3 to firm C5, D5, and touches E5.

Chorus. SSATB. Servants, courtiers.

Orchestra. 25–30, including (information from VS) 2 fl (picc, alto fl), 2 ob (Eng hrn), 2 cl (E♭ cl, bs cl), 2 bsn (cont bsn), alto sax, bar sax, hrn, trp, trb, tuba, perc (sn dr, bs dr, cym, tri, T bl, vib, guit, tam-tam, gong, chimes, glock, marimba), strings, elec bs.

Material. AMP.

The Flood

Music by Igor Stravinsky (1882–1971). Libretto chosen and arranged by Robert Craft principally from the book of Genesis and York and Chester cycles of Miracle plays. Premiere: CBS-TV (as *Noah and the Flood*), June 14, 1962; staged in final version, Santa Fe, August 21, 1962. Musical play. Astringent harmonies; difficult production. Brief prelude. Setting: Before and during the Flood. One act (24 min).

Synopsis. Noah and his wife quarrel during the building of the ark and she refuses to go aboard. But her sons persuade her. God makes a covenant of the rainbow with Noah.

Major Roles. LUCIFER, SATAN (t); C2 to A3. GOD (2 bs); No. 1: A♯1 to E; No. 2: low G1. NOAH, NOAH'S WIFE, NOAH'S SONS (sp). NARRATOR-CALLER; calls roll of animals (sp).

Chorus. SAT.

Ballet. Building of ark and flood are choreographed.

Orchestra. 3 fl (picc), alto fl, 2 ob, Eng hrn, 2 cl, bs cl, cont bs cl, 2 bsn, cont bsn, 4 hrn, 3 trp, 2 ten trb (alto trb), bs trb, tuba, timp, xyl, marimba, cym, bs dr, cel, piano, harp, strings.

Material. B & H.

📯 Flower and Hawk

Music by Carlisle Floyd (1926–   ). Libretto in English by the composer. Commissioned by the Jacksonville Symphony Association. Premiere: Jacksonville, Florida, May 16, 1972. Monodrama. Conventional harmonies with occasional dissonance, highly expressive; vocal line dramatic and lyrical. Brief prelude. Setting: Salisbury Tower, England, end of reign of Henry II. One scene (48 min).

Synopsis. The title is derived from the seal of the fabulous Eleanor of Aquitaine, who was imprisoned for all the last part of her life by her husband, King Henry. She has become desperate and very nearly considers suicide, but she begins to recall her past life and re-experiences the joys and torments of her husband's actions and her sons' tragic fates. As she regains her emotional freedom, she is able to reassume her role as Queen when the tolling of the bells announces the death of Henry and her liberation.

Role. ELEANOR OF AQUITAINE (s); needs great dramatic ability; considerable declamation; some wide skips; B2 to B4.

Orchestra. 2 fl (picc), 2 ob (Eng hrn), 2 cl (bs cl), 2 bsn, 4 hrn, 2 trp, 2 trb, tuba, harp, perc (4), strings.

Material. Bel.

Performances. Jacksonville Sym. (Wash.): 5.18.72; (NYC): 5.19.72.

📯 The Four Note Opera

Music by Tom Johnson. Libretto in English by the composer. Premiere: Cubiculo Theater, New York City, May 16, 1972. Comedy-farce. The four notes are A, B, D, and E. Upon these the composer has built a series of recitatives and arias which form the structure of the opera. Conventional harmonies, witty and expressive; many variations in rhythm, texture, and melodic shape. Setting: Any possible operatic room, the present. One act (approx 60 min).

276

Synopsis. The numbers indicate the plot: for example, the tenor's recitative reveals the fact that he will sing his only aria. There are conventional ensembles—the contralto sings repeatedly "I have a nice phrase," and the tenor complains that he "hardly has a thing." The various emotional moods end in mass suicide, as the singers become immobile and the music grinds slowly to a halt.

Roles. SOPRANO; top B4. CONTRALTO; A2 to E4. TENOR; B1 to E3. BARITONE; A1 to E3 (can be bs with low E1).

Orchestra. Piano.

Material. Composer.

Performances. Met. Op. Studio: 11.28.72. Several others at coll., TV.

The Franklin's Tale

Music by Noel Sokoloff (1923–   ). Libretto in English by Ted Hart based on Chaucer's tale. Premiere: Louisiana State University, Baton Rouge, November 10, 1961. Medieval drama. Melodious; conventional harmonies. Setting: A castle on the coast of Brittany, 1386. One act (approx 80 min).

Synopsis. The squire Aurelius is in love with the lady Dorigena, whose gentle husband Arveragus is away from the castle on a quest. Dorigena repulses Aurelius, who offers his fortune to the magician Cedasus if he will help fulfill the condition Dorigena has jestingly imposed: that she will yield only when all the rocks are removed from the coast of Brittany. Cedasus brings this about by a powerful incantation to the goddess of the moon. Arveragus returns just at this juncture and learning of Dorigena's foolish vow, bids her keep it. But Aurelius overhears and is moved to release the lady from her bargain. Cedasus suggests that each character saw what he wished to see and because each acted gently, the rocks are restored to the coast and "all is well restored by faith well kept."

Major Roles. ARVERAGUS (bs). DORIGENA (s). AURELIUS (t). RODOGONE, friend of Dorigena (m-s). CEDASUS (bs-bar).

Lesser Roles. THREE LADIES-IN-WAITING (s, s, c).

Orchestra. 2 fl, 2 ob, 2 cl, 2 bsn, 2 hrn, trp, trb, timp, perc (1), piano, strings.

Production Note. "Franklin's Tale" forms a complete double bill with the same composer's "Pardoner's Tale" (see).

Material. Pr.

Friedenstag · Peace Day

Music by Richard Strauss (1864–1949). Libretto in German by Josef Gregor. Premiere: Munich, June 24, 1938. Historical drama. Heroic expressiveness; orchestration dramatic; continuous texture; some melody. No overture. Setting: Citadel of a beseiged city during the Thirty Years War, October 24, 1648. One act (80 min).

ACT I: Circular room with arrow slits and staircases going up and down.

Synopsis. The Commandant refuses to surrender his garrison in spite of pleas from hungry townsfolk led by the Burgomaster and the Bishop, even when the ammunition is spent. But at last he agrees and tells the deputation to watch for a great sign of surrender at midday. He intends to blow up the citadel with himself and the garrison as the enemy arrives, and his young wife determines to die with him. But just as the fuse is about to be lit, the Burgomaster rushes in with news that the enemy wants to make peace. The Commandant at first refuses to meet the Holstein commander, but at last is persuaded to by his wife, and a great hymn of peace is sung by all.

Major Roles. COMMANDANT (bar); top Gb3. MARIA, his wife (s); Bb2 to several firm C5 (one Db5 with F4 opt).

Lesser Roles. BURGOMASTER (t); top B3. BISHOP (bar). A PIEDMONTESE (t). THE HOLSTEIN COMMANDER (bs). WATCHMAN (bs). RIFLEMAN (t). MUSKETEER (bs). BUGLER (bs). TWO OFFICERS (2 bar). CONSTABLE (bar). TOWNSWOMAN (s).

Chorus. SSATTBB (often divided). Soldiers of both armies, elders, women of a deputation, townspeople.

Orchestra. 3 fl, 3 ob, 3 cl, bs cl, 3 bsn, cont bsn, 6 hrn, 4 trp, 4 trb, tuba, timp, perc, strings. *Stage*: trp.

Material. B & H. VS (g)*.

Performances. USC (Los Ang.): 4.2.67 (Amer prem).

🎭 The Garden of Artemis, or, Apollo's Revels

Music by Daniel Pinkham (1923–   ). Libretto in English by Robert Hillyer. Commissioned by Miss Fanny Peabody Mason. Premiere: Cambridge, Mass., 1948. Comedy. "A tableau chantant in the antique manner." Neoclassic, tonal harmonies; set numbers; melodic. No overture. Setting: Mythological Greece. One act (30 min).

Synopsis. Clorinda, too young for love, is pursued by Apollo but changed to a flower by Artemis, patroness of virgins. Other virgins, also saved from their fate, are not so resigned, and Apollo changes them back to women, promising to free Clorinda also in a very short time.

Roles. CLORINDA (high lyr s); needs some flexibility; B2 to A4. ARTEMIS (m-s or c); some florid passages; Ab2 to E4. APOLLO (bar); top E3.

Chorus. SSA. Virgins. Character actresses.

Orchestra. fl, cl, vln, vla, vcl.

Material. E Sc.

🎭 A Gift of Song

Music by Mary E. Caldwell. Libretto in English by the composer. Premiere: Pasadena, December 3, 1961. Christmas opera. Melodious; conventional harmonies. Setting: Hallein, Austria, and Salzburg, 1853–1854. One act, three scenes (approx 65 min).

ACT I i: Living room of Gruber home in Hallein, a few days after Christmas, 1853; ii: Choir rehearsal room of Salzburg monastery of St. Peter, a year later before Christmas; Interlude: Stage coach; iii: Same as i.

Synopsis. Based on several historical facts about the composition of "Silent Night." Karl Gruber, in choir school in Salzburg, sings the song for the ambassador, and the choirmaster goes to the Gruber home to find the original.

Major Roles. KARL FRANZ FELIX, 12-year-old son of the composer (s). AN-NALISA, his older sister (s). PAPA GRUBER, in mid 60's (bar). MAMA GRUBER (m-s). CHOIRMASTER HERR DOKTOR GEHEIMRAT PROFESSOR VON SCHMALL-PLATZ, Ambassador from the King of Prussia (bar). CHOIRMASTER WILHELM, in his 20's (t).

Lesser Roles. RUDI, choirboy (s). PAGE (sp).

Chorus. Choirboys, villagers, 6 to 18; unison or SATB; three-part singing.

Orchestra. fl (picc), ob, 2 cl, bsn, 2 hrn, trp, timp, perc, harp, piano, strings. *Stage:* spinet (may be played from pit).

Material. B & H. VS* (contains full production suggestions).

Performances. Several in California churches and high schools.

▨ The Gift of the Magi

Music by Ruth Taylor Magney. Libretto by the composer after the story by O'Henry. Premiere: Minneapolis (for Minnesota Federation of Music Clubs), April 16, 1964. Comedy-drama. Set numbers; conventional harmonies; melodious vocal line. Brief prelude. Setting: A large city; contemporary. One act (approx 40 min).

ACT I i: A shabby upstairs apartment; ii: Mme Sofronie's hair shop; iii: The apartment.

Synopsis. The well-known Christmas tale of a poor young couple, each eager to buy a cherished gift for the other. Della has her beautiful long hair cut; Jim sells his watch to get enough money. Della buys Jim a watch fob; he buys her fancy combs.

Roles. DELLA YOUNG (s); C3 to G4. JAMES DILLINGHAM YOUNG (bar); Ab1 to E3. MME SOPHRONIE (c); Bb2 to Eb4.

Chorus. SSA. Small, offstage.

Orchestra. Piano.

Material. Composer: 1100 Missouri Ave., Duluth, Minn.

▨ The Glittering Gate

Music by Peggy Glanville-Hicks (1912–   ). Libretto in English after the play by Lord Dunsany. Premiere: YMHA, New York, May 15, 1959. A "curtain raiser"; comedy. Unconventional orchestration, vocal line patterned after speech with some aria-like passages, one difficult duet. Setting: Outside the Gate of Heaven, the present. One act (30 min).

Synopsis. The burglers, Jim and Bill, have found their way to the Gate of Heaven, but it is a lonely place, strewn with large black rocks. Jim, a drunk, is constantly plagued by beer bottles, which he finds in various nooks and crannies and which constantly descend through the air. The cause for his desperation: they are all empty. The two discuss what they hope to find in Heaven: Bill hopes to see his mother; Jim a girl named Jane. But when Bill at last opens the gates with "Old Nutcracker" (an implement which has cracked many safes and for which Lord Dunsany suggests an egg beater or similar foolish instrument), they are confronted by nothing but empty space studded with stars. There is no Heaven.

Roles. BILL (t); Bb1 to G3. JIM (bar); A1 to G3 (one A3).

Orchestra. fl, ob, cl, bsn, hrn, trp, timp, perc, harp, strings. Electronic tape simulates unearthly laughter, heard at frequent intervals, particularly when Jim discovers bottles are empty.

Material. Bel (Col).

⧫ Goodbye to the Clown

Music by Ezra Laderman (1924–   ). Libretto in English by Ernest Kinoy. Premiere: Neway Group, New York City, May 22, 1960. Fantasy-drama. Contemporary idiom with occasional set numbers; vocal line patterned after speech; some dialogue. Setting: can be suggested by simple props and lighting; contemporary. One act, five scenes (approx 45 min).

Scene i: A bench before a school; ii: Interior of school; iii: Outside house; iv: Dining room; v: Peggy's room.

Synopsis. Peggy has a clown, her own personal clown, who makes her laugh and on whom she blames all the tricks she does in school. He tells her stories and sings songs her beloved Daddy told and sang. She even insists on setting a place at table for him. But her Mother, in spite of Uncle George's remonstrances, breaks down and sends Peggy to her room. Then, eavesdropping, Peggy realizes at last that her father is dead and will never return, and that the clown was sent by him to bridge the gap between not understanding and growing up. Needed no longer, the clown disappears and Peggy falls asleep in her new maturity.

Major Roles. (No range problems.) PEGGY (s). MOTHER (m-s). CLOWN (bar); should be acrobatic; G1 to E3. UNCLE GEORGE (bs); F#1 to Db3.

Lesser Role. DR. BENSON, school principal (t).

Orchestra. fl, cl, hrn, perc, piano, strings.

Material. Pr.

🎼 The Grace of Todd

Music by Gordon Crosse (1937–   ). Libretto in English by David Rudkin. Commissioned by Friends of Covent Garden for the English Opera Group. Premiere: Aldeburgh, June 7, 1969. Comedy-satire on war. Contemporary idiom; considerable lyrical passages interspersed with sardonic scoring and expressive dissonance; vocal lines often difficult, declamatory, vigorous. Prelude (satirical military march). Setting: A summer afternoon; the present. One act, three scenes (75 min).

ACT I i: Muddy countryside with watercourse spanned by pipe; ii: Transition dream scene; iii: Same as i.

Synopsis. Todd, the lump, the slow-witted, looks on as Second Lieutenant Pratt and Lance Corporal Shard extol his buddies for their warlike qualities. Todd fails every test, finally falling into the mucky river as he attempts to cross the pipe. His officers revile him as useless. Left alone, he tries to clean up and dreams of becoming a pole vaulter or a judo expert. His buddies appear in the background, miming a map-reading exercise. Todd scorns them and they leave. Girls' voices are heard offstage as Todd continues to dream, watching a ball game and admiring Millichip's trumpet playing and Bowring's athletic dance. They come close to him as if to offer their gifts but really focus on the Lady, who appears behind Todd. She encourages Todd to believe he has a gift—his unique funny faces.

In an interlude, the Lady is left alone; then a blackout and orchestral interlude with offstage voices follow. Scene i returns and finds Todd still dreaming. Pratt determines to show how the pipe should be crossed, but falls in, endangering discipline. Shard finally brings the squad to order, all but Todd, who runs amok, butting the corporal like a bull and shouting "Charge!" All are frozen by a stroke of lightning and Shard regains control, ordering Todd to be taken prisoner. Pratt is left in the ditch, brandishing his fist at the sky.

Major Roles. SECOND LIEUTENANT PRATT (high t); both sustained and flexible; needs strength at high tessitura; difficult intervals; B1 to B3. LANCE CORPORAL SHARD (bar); G♯1 to F3. PRIVATE TODD (t or high bar); very high tessitura; needs strength, also flexibility; top A♭3 (one firm B♭3, others in song speech). PRIVATE BOWRING (t); C♯2 to A♭3. PRIVATE FURLONG (bar or bs); G♯1 to F♭3. PRIVATE MILLICHIP (bs); low G♭1. THE LADY (s or m-s); needs flexibility; B♭2 to G4. BOWRING'S GIRL (s); FURLONG'S GIRL (s); MILLICHIP'S GIRL (c); mostly in ensemble.

Lesser Roles. THREE GIRLS, as offstage chorus.

Orchestra. fl (picc), ob (Eng hrn), 2 cl (bs cl, E♭ cl), bsn, hrn, trp (B♭ corn), trb, perc (2), harp, piano (cel, elec org), solo string 5-tet. Three pre-recorded tapes: barrack square orders, marching, etc.

Material. Ox.

◢ The Great Stone Face

Music by Martin Kalmanoff (1920–   ). Libretto in English by the composer after Hawthorne's story. Premiere: Ball State University, Muncie, Ind., November 14, 1968. New England folk drama. Melodious; free tonality; folk flavor; vocal line patterned after speech. Brief prelude. Setting: New Hampshire valley, dominated by the natural phenomenon called The Great Stone Face; late 19th century. Prologue, five scenes (50 min).

Synopsis. Young Ernest's Mother tells him of the prophecy: that a child will be born in this valley who will become the noblest and greatest man of his time and grow to resemble The Great Stone Face. Through Ernest's life, one man after another seems to fulfill the prophecy, but all fail: the Man of Wealth, the Man of Valor, the Man of Diplomacy, and the Man of Art. Finally, in Ernest's old age, it is apparent that he, the Man of Character, has come to be the true man of the prophecy.

Major Roles. ERNEST as a boy (boy s); (all later act as villagers). ERNEST as a man (bar); Bb1 to F3. HIS MOTHER (m-s); C3 to G4. MR. GATHERGOLD; doubles as POET (t); F#2 to Ab3. OLD BLOOD AND THUNDER; doubles as HUSBAND and PHILANTHROPIST (bs); D2 to C#3. OLD STONY PHIZ; doubles as PROFESSOR (bar); C2 to F3.

Lesser Roles. Offstage voice of GREAT STONE FACE. TWO VILLAGERS (also BEGGARWOMAN and WIFE) (2 s).

Chorus. 2 s, boys, m-s, bar, bs.

Orchestra. Piano. Or 2 fl, ob, cl, bsn, 2 hrn, trp, 2 trb, timp, perc, strings.

Material. C Fi.

◢ Haircut

Music by Sam Morgenstern (1911–   ). Libretto in English by Jan Henry after a story by Ring Lardner. Premiere: Metropolitan Opera Studio, New York City, May 2, 1969. Drama. Set numbers knit into continuous texture, folk flavor with modern touch; vocal line partly melodic, partly declamatory. Brief prelude; interludes. Setting: Midwest American small town, around 1915. One act, three scenes (50–51 min).

ACT I i: The village square with barbershop; ii: The square at night with Doc Stair's house; iii: The square in misty morning.

Synopsis. Whitey the barber tells the visiting Circus Man about the practical jokes of Jim Kendall, the village bully. Kendall exemplifies this by relating how he has fooled his wife and children by leaving them stranded outside the circus; but the trick has backfired because Doc Stair has bought their way in. Kendall's anger is further inflamed by the sight of Doc talking to Julie Gregg, for whom Kendall has always cherished a passion. He takes out his rage on Paul, a homeless boy, promising to take him hunting next morning. Then he fools Julie by a phone call imitating Doc's voice and making an appointment that night. Julie, who loves Doc and cannot understand why he is cool to her, comes to the meeting and is jeered by all the men in town. Doc furiously confronts Kendall, but Julie protests that she is all right, and they part from each other. Next morning, Paul rushes in crying that Kendall has been shot—but that it was an accident. Mrs. Kendall wants vengeance on Paul, but Whitey persuades him to stay and face it like a man, then goes off to shave the corpse. Julie, who has discovered that Doc's restraint is caused by his being married to a hopeless invalid, also faces her future with a new maturity.

Major Roles. WHITEY (bs-bar); A1 to E3. JULIE GREGG (s); B2 to A4. PAUL (t); C2 to A3. JIM KENDALL (bar); A1 to G3. DOC STAIR (bar); Bb1 to E3.

Lesser Roles. MRS. SHEPPARD (m-s); B2 to E4. CIRCUS MAN (bs); F1 to B2. SHERIFF HOD MYERS (bs); Gb1 to E3. MILT SHEPPARD (t); Db2 to Bb3. MRS. KENDALL (m-s); B2 to G#4. CLEM SHEPPARD (mute).

Chorus. SATB. Townspeople, stretcher bearers.

Material. Composer: 40 Horatio St., NYC 10014.

☛ A Hand of Bridge

Music by Samuel Barber (1910–   ). Libretto in English by Gian-Carlo Menotti. Premiere: Spoleto, June 17, 1959. Comedy. Set numbers, conventional harmonies. Setting: Any American living room; the present. One act (9 min).

Synopsis. Two couples meet for their usual evening of bridge. Each, bored with his or her mate, indulges in a flight of fancy during the play.

Roles. DAVID, a businessman (bar). GERALDINE, his wife (s). BILL, a lawyer (t). SALLY, his wife (c).

Orchestra. fl, ob, cl, bsn, trp, perc, string quintet.

Material. G Sc. VS*.

Performances. Mannes Coll. (NYC): 4.6.60 (Amer prem). Many others.

☛ The Happy Prince

Music by Malcolm Williamson (1931–   ). Libretto in English by the composer after the story by Oscar Wilde. Commissioned by Watney Mann Ltd. Premiere: Farnham Festival, England, May 22, 1965. Fantasy. Melodious; specially singable by children. Generally conventional harmonies; some mildly contemporary idioms. Setting: A public square in a legendary city. One act (40 min).

Synopsis. The bejewelled statue of the Happy Prince looks down on his city with sadness, and confesses his despair of his people to a swallow on its way to Egypt. He sends the swallow on missions of mercy, using his jewels, until he is stripped of all worth and the swallow dies in exhaustion. The Prince's leaden heart breaks. The citizens take down the shabby statue and attempt to burn it with the bird's body. But the Prince's heart will not burn.

Four angels appear, proclaiming the heart and the bird the most precious things in the city, to a chorus of joy and praise.

Roles. THE SWALLOW (s). THE PRINCE (s). THE MAYOR (c). THE SEAM-STRESS (m-s). HER SON (high s). THE AUTHOR (m-c). THE MATCHGIRL (s). A RICH GIRL (s).

Chorus. Children: SSSA. Citizens: SSM-SA. Four Angels (S).

Orchestra. Piano duet, perc (as many as 4), string 5-tet (opt).

Material. B & H (Wein).

Performances. Newport (R.I.): 1967. St. John's Cathedral (NYC): 4.7.72.

⚜ Help! Help! the Globolinks!

Music by Gian-Carlo Menotti (1911–   ). Libretto in English by the composer. Commissioned by the State Opera of Hamburg. Premiere: Hamburg, December 12, 1968. Fantasy. Melodic; conventional harmonies; many electronic passages (realized by Eckhard Maronn); generally simple vocal line; some dialogue. Orchestral introduction. Setting: Contemporary America. One act, five scenes (70 min).

Scene i: A country road in deserted landscape; ii: Dean's office of St. Paul's school; iii: The country road; iv: The forest of steel; v: A vast empty plain.

Synopsis. A bus full of children returning to school after holidays breaks down and is menaced by a strange fog and the presence of globolinks, unearthly beings who can be fended off only by musical sound. The children have all left their instruments at school except Emily, who has brought her violin. She is persuaded by Tony the bus driver to find the way to school by playing the violin along the road, and departs. Meanwhile at the school Dr. Stone, the Dean, and Timothy, the janitor, worry about the absence of the children. Mme Euterpova, the flamboyant music teacher, confesses her love for Dr. Stone, but is repulsed. Left alone, the Dean becomes prey to the globolinks and is almost metamorphosed when Euterpova coaxes him to utter one musical note—a *la*, which remains the only sound he can produce. Three caricature-like teachers enter—Miss Penelope Newkirk, mathematics; Mr. Lavender-Gas, literature; and Dr. Turtlespit, science, and with Timothy take the children's musical instruments and march away as a rescue team. Emily is lost, and yields to the temptation to sleep. A globolink breaks her violin. Only the intervention of Dr. Stone with his *la* saves her, but the Dean himself is lost. Mme. Euterpova states the moral: only good music can save the world.

Major Roles. EMILY (s); needs facility; should play violin if possible; D3 to Bb4. MME EUTERPOVA (s); some dramatic and florid passages; C3 to Bb4. DR. STONE (high bar); C#2 to G3 (A3 with F#3 opt). TONY (bar); Bb1 to Gb3. TIMOTHY (t); D#2 to Ab3.

Lesser Roles. PENELOPE NEWKIRK (m-s). MR. LAVENDER-GAS (bar). DR. TURTLESPIT (bs); many F1's. Twelve children, several small solos.

284

Supers or Ballet. Globolinks in fantastic costumes.

Orchestra. picc, fl, ob, cl, bsn, 2 hrn, 2 trp, trb, tuba, harp, piano, timp, perc, strings, tape.

Production Difficulties. Globolink effects, eerie lighting, quick scene changes.

Material. G-Sc. VS (e, g)*.

Performances. Santa Fe (Amer prem): 8.1.69. NY City Center: 12.22.69.

✠ L'Ile de Tulipatan · The Island of Tulipatan

Music by Jacques Offenbach (1819–1880). Libretto in French by Henri Chivot and Alfred Duru. Premiere: Paris, September 30, 1868. Farce. Highly melodious; set numbers; dialogue. Overture. Setting: The unbelievable Island of Tulipatan, an incredibly long time ago. One act (48 min).

Synopsis. The Grand Majordomo of Tulipatan has no heir, only a daughter. He disguises her as a boy. The Duke has a son, but doesn't want to send him to the army, so disguises him as a girl. The result is foregone.

Roles. All need flexibility. CARATOIS XXII, Duke of Tulipatan (t); top A3. ALEXIS, his son (s); trill; B2 to A4. ROMBOIDAL, Grand Majordomo (t); important patter duet; top C♯4. THEODORINE, his wife (m-s); top A4. HERMOSA, their daughter (t); trill; patter aria and duet; some florid passages; top B3.

Chorus. SSTTB. A Palace Officer, officers, servants, a Page.

Orchestra. 2 fl, 2 ob, 2 cl, 2 bsn, 4 hrn, 2 trp, 3 trb, timp, bs dr, strings.

Performances. Mannes Coll. (NYC): 5.16.62.

✠ Introductions and Goodbyes

Music by Lukas Foss (1922–   ). Libretto in English by Gian-Carlo Menotti. Commissioned by Festival of Two Worlds, Spoleto, Italy. Premiere: Spoleto, June 1960 (staged); concert performance by New York Philharmonic May 6, 1960. Satire on cocktail parties. Set numbers in contemporary idiom. Setting: Any bachelor apartment; contemporary. One act (9 min).

Synopsis. The host receives nine guests; their comments are mimed; vocal comment is made by an invisible quartet seated in the pit. The conversation is typical "cocktail party," sharply satirized.

Roles. THE HOST (bar). NINE GUESTS (opt); actors or dancers. VOCAL QUARTET (SATB).

Orchestra. piano, harp, (opt), fl, cl, bsn, hrn (1 or more), xyl, strings (no cb).

Production Note. May be staged with complete cast or as bar solo; with full orch or piano and xyl or piano alone (1–2 players).

Material. C Fi. VS*.

Performances. Mannes Coll. (NYC): 5.16.62. Many others.

🎵 Iolanthe

Music by Peter Ilytch Tchaikovsky (1840–1893). Libretto in Russian by Modest Tchaikovsky after a play, *The Daughter of King René*, by Henrik Hertz. Premiere: St. Petersburg, December 18, 1892. Romance. Set numbers; highly melodious; nationalistic flavor; conventional harmonies. Brief prelude. Setting: Provence, in the South of France, mid-15th century. One act (approx 70 min).

ACT I: A lush garden of a small chateau; high walls; a door leading to bower.

Synopsis. Iolanthe, daughter of the King of Provence, was blinded so early in life by a narrow escape from a fire, that she does not realize her infirmity. Her father has kept her isolated, with only a few loyal companions, until it shall be time to consummate her engagement and marriage to the young Duke of Burgundy, a contract made between the two fathers in order to settle a long feud. King René fears the revelation of his daughter's blindness, and seeks a cure from a famous Moorish doctor, Ibn-Hakia, who holds out hope only on the conditions that she be informed of her condition and given a motivation to see again. These two conditions are immediately fulfilled by the unexpected advent of a young Burgundian nobleman, Count Vodemon, who has accompanied the Duke of Burgundy on a visit to René's court. They have lost their way, and as they venture into the strange secluded garden, Duke Robert says that he regrets his bargain, as he has fallen in love with the Countess Mathilde. As Iolanthe awakes and discovers the strangers, Robert retires, leaving Vodemon and the girl to discover a strong bond of sympathy and affection. When she picks a white rose after he has asked for a red one, Vodemon realizes that she is blind. They are discovered by the King and Ibn-Hakia; the former is furious, but the latter pleased that both his conditions seem to be fulfilled. Iolanthe responds to treatment and rapturously proclaims her new vision, and the King willingly releases Robert and accepts Vodemon as a son-in-law.

Major Roles. IOLANTHE (lyr s); sustained melodic line; top B4. KING RENÉ (bs); F1 to F3. COUNT VODEMON (t); top B♭3. DUKE ROBERT (bar); top G3.

Lesser Roles. BERTRAN, retainer of the King (bs). MARTA, his wife and Iolanthe's nurse (c). BRIGETTA (s); LAURA (m-s), Iolanthe's companions. IBN-HAKIA (bar); top F♯3. ALMERICH, King's weapon carrier (t).

Chorus. SATB. Servants, friends of Iolanthe, followers of King, Duke's soldiers.

Orchestra. 3 fl (picc), 3 ob (Eng hrn), 2 cl, 2 bsn, 4 hrn, 2 trp, 2 corn, 3 trb, tuba, timp, strings.

Material. Map.

Performances. Russ. Op. Co. (NYC): 1934. Paterson (N.J.): 1965. Natl. Orch. Ass'n. and Met Studio (NYC): 1.11.72 (conc).

📖 L'Ivrogne Corrigé · The Reformed Drunkard

Music by Christophe Willibald von Gluck (1714–1787). Libretto in French by Louis Anseaume after La Fontaine's fable. Premiere: Vienna, April 1760. Comedy. Highly melodious; conventional harmonies; dialogue. Overture. Setting: Provincial French town. Two acts (approx 60 min).

ACT I: Maturin's house. ACT II: Simulated courtroom.

Synopsis. Maturin continues to drink and carouse with Lucas in spite of his wife Methurine's objections. Lucas wants to court Maturin's niece Colette, but Methurine prefers Cléon as a suitor. In order to cure her husband's drunkenness, Methurine stages a mock trial with Cléon as Pluto. When the old sot is condemned to hell, he repents rapidly, and allows the two lovers to marry. Lucas decides that making and drinking wine is his métier, and gives up his idea of marriage.

Major Roles. MATURIN (t). METHURINE (m-s). COLETTE (s); trill; top G4. LUCAS (bar). CLÉON (bar).

Chorus. SATB. Farmers and their wives, players, Cléon's friends.

Orchestra. 2 ob, bsn, 2 hrn, strings, continuo.

Material. G Sc (Bä). Tr: Giovanni Cardelli.

Performances. Hartt Coll. (Hartford): 2.26.45 (Amer prem). Cal. St. Coll. (Fullerton): 1.14.69. Kath. Long Course (NYC): 4.9.69.

📖 Jeanne d'Arc au Bucher · Joan of Arc at the Stake

Music by Arthur Honegger (1892–1955). Libretto in French by Paul Claudel. Dedicated to Ida Rubinstein. Premiere: Basel, May 12, 1938. Dramatic oratorio, Atmospheric, expressive orchestra; vocal line declamatory; dialogue. Prologue and eleven scenes (75–80 min).

Prologue: Orchestra, chorus, solo sp. Scene i: Celestial Voices; ii: The Book; iii: The Voices of Earth; iv: Jeanne Delivered to the Beasts; v: Jeanne at the Stake; vi: The Kings, or the Invention of Playing Cards; vii: Catherine and Marguerite; viii: The King Who Goes to Reims; ix: Jeanne's Sword; x: Trimazo—Rehearsal of the Merry Month of May; xi: Jeanne d'Arc in Flames.

Synopsis. The most nearly intelligible description, according to Charles O'Connell in a Philadelphia Orchestra program booklet, was by Roger Secretain in Brussels in 1946. As abridged: Various representations of Jeanne's own life can be observed, as through her own eyes. Past and present are not differentiated. Jeanne exists at one and the same time in different parts of the world; she is in control of time and space. She sees the people disguised as beasts; there are strange kings, queens, and knaves. She herself is the pawn. She hears the voices of saints and giants; recalls her childhood in Lorraine when she hears the May Day song "Trimazo"; and ends her spiritual conflict in the flames.

Major Roles. JEANNE D'ARC (sp); sings few lines, B2 to A4. FRERE DOMI-

NIQUE (sp). VIRGIN (s); high tessitura; F♯3 to B4. MARGUERITE (s); F3 to A4. CATHERINE (c); G2 to E♯4.

Lesser Roles. A VOICE; PORCUS (top B3); FIRST HERALD; CLERK (t). A VOICE (low G1); SECOND HERALD; PEASANT (bs). A VOICE; VOICE OF A CHILD (s). FIRST RECITER; THIRD HERALD; DUKE OF BEDFORD; JEAN DE LUXEMBOURG; HEURTEBISE; PEASANT (sp). SECOND RECITER; USHER; REGNAULT DE CHARTRES; GUILLAUME DE FLAVY; PERROT; PRIEST (sp). THE MOTHER OF TONNEAUX (sp, from chor).

Chorus. SATB. Also children.

Orchestra. 2 fl (picc), 2 ob, 2 cl, bs cl, 3 sax, 3 bsn, cont bsn, 4 trp, 3 trb, bs trb or tuba, 2 piano, timp, perc (2), cel, Ondes martenot, strings. Howl of dog simulated.

Material. Sal.

Performances. Univ. of Colo. (Boulder): 7.27.62. Santa Fe: 7.24.63. NYCO: 10.3.63; others.

◢ The Judgment of St. Francis

Music by Nicholas Flagello (1928–   ). Libretto in English by Armand Aulicino. Premiere: Manhattan School, New York City, March 18, 1966. Based on the life of St. Francis of Assisi. Rondo form. Contemporary idiom; continuous texture; vocal line patterned after speech. Setting: Assisi, 1207. One act, seven scenes (approx 90 min).

Scenes i, iii, iv, vii: Episcopal palace of Bishop Guido II; ii: Garden of Pietro di Bernadone; iv: Church of San Damiano; v: Cellar of Bernadone's house. Scenes must be continuous, fading in and out.

Synopsis. Flashbacks from the trial of Francis (Francesco), who has been charged by his father Pietro of throwing away money to help the poor and suffering, show Francis kissing the hand of a leper, giving his father's money to restore a church (the priest later returns it), meditating in and being freed from his father's cellar by his mother and his friend Clara. Finally he casts off his rich clothing. Pietro renounces his son; the Bishop places his cloak on Francis's shoulders, acknowledging him as a true servant of God, and the Herald brings a gardener's shabby cloak for the saintly man to wear henceforth.

Major Roles. FRANCESCO (t); C2 to B3. MADONNA PICA, his mother (dram s); top B♭4. CLARA (lyr s); about 15 years; top B♭4. PIETRO, Francesco's father (bar); top F♯3 (one opt A♭3). PRIEST (bs); top E3. BISHOP (bs); top E3.

Lesser Role. HERALD (t).

Bit Role. LEPER (mute).

Chorus. SATB. Townspeople, heralds, attendants.

Orchestra. 3 fl, 3 ob, 2 cl, 2 bsn, 4 hrn, 2 trp, 3 trb, tuba, timp, perc, cel, harp, strings.

Material. Bel (Col).

288

🎭 The Juggler of Our Lady

Music by Ulysses Kay (1917–   ). Libretto in English by Alexander King, after Anatole France. Premiere: Xavier University, New Orleans, February 23, 1962. Historical drama. Set numbers, accompanied recitatives; traditional, occasionally modal harmonies; vocal line melodious. Prelude; very brief interludes. Setting: A fair in a small medieval town. One act (50 min).

Synopsis. During a medieval fair, the Juggler Colin is enchanted by the life and color and stays after curfew. With no place to sleep, he knocks at the monastery and is put up for the night. Unable to sleep, he wanders into the chapel and is enthralled by the statue of the Virgin. Being poor, he has nothing to offer the Virgin except his talents as a juggler. He performs for her as two monks watch him suspiciously. When he falls in exhaustion, the statue bends over and blesses him, much to the consternation of the monks. A transcendant chorus ends the opera.

Major Roles. COLIN (t); must act well, do elementary impression of juggling; E2 to A♭3. MARTIN, Colin's companion (bar); C2 to E3. CHRYSOSTOM, a monk (t); E♭2 to G3. NICODEMUS, a monk (bar); C2 to E♭3.

Lesser Roles. All very brief; they constitute chorus. FIRST STREET SINGER (bar). CHIEF BEGGAR (t). NOBLEMAN (bs). GYPSY WOMAN (m-s). YOUNG STREET SINGER (boy s). GYPSY GIRL (s). FIRST STREET VENDOR (c). SECOND STREET VENDOR (bar). MINE HOST (bs). HOSTESS (m-s). NIGHT WATCH (bs).

Orchestra. fl, ob, 2 cl, bsn, hrn, trp, perc (2), harp, vln 1 and 2, vla, vcl, cb.

Material. MCA.

Performances. UCLA (Los Ang.): Spring 1967.

🎭 Julius Caesar Jones

Music by Malcolm Williamson (1931–   ). Libretto in English by Geoffrey Dunn. Commissioned by the Finchley Children's Music Group. Premiere: London, January 4, 1966. Fantasy. Melodic; tonal; colorful orchestration. Brief prelude. Setting: Suburban England, the present. Two acts, four scenes (60 min).

ACT I i: Kitchen–living room at 37 Mortimer Rise, a Friday afternoon in early July; ii: The garden, later that afternoon; iii: The kitchen–living room, three weeks later, the night before the party. ACT II: The garden, next day.

Synopsis. The Everetts, an ordinary suburban family, decide to give a party. The children, however, play their own secret game, which involves a fantastic Polynesian Island, where Julius Caesar Jones, one of the characters they have created, rules strictly, under a secret sign which no grown-up must know. Unwittingly, the young Ambrose gives this sign away to their father, and runs off in fright, to be condemned by the fantasy court to death. As he is about to be executed, the children are summoned to the party, which breaks the spell, but Ambrose is left unconscious. This shocks the parents into an attempt to understand the children, but the children have been shocked into adolescence, and so the gap in understanding remains.

Roles. (Adults) MR. EVERETT (bar). MRS. EVERETT (s). MRS. WHYLEY, Mrs. Everett's widowed sister (m-s). (Children) JOHN EVERETT (treble). ELIZABETH EVERETT (s). AMBROSE EVERETT (treble). SUSAN WHYLEY (m-s). HARVEN, Ambrose's friend (treble). (Fantasy Children) ALOMA (m-s). JESS (s). BABS (s). JULIUS CAESAR JONES (boy m-s or boy bar). SILAS GAPTEETH (treble). THE LEOPARD (m-s). TOOMIE (treble). BIMBO (treble). TORTOISE (mute).

Chorus. SSA. Children, seen and unseen.

Orchestra, fl (picc), ob (Eng hrn), cl (bs cl), bsn, hrn, harp, piano, perc, string quintet. Scoring is lightened to accommodate children's voices.

Material. B & H (Wein). VS*.

🎝 Katya Kabanová

Music by Leoš Janáček (1854–1928). Libretto in Czech by Vincenc Cervinka, after the Russian play *The Storm* by Alexander Nikolaievich Ostrovsky. Premiere: Brno, Czechoslovakia, October 23, 1921. Romantic tragedy with social overtones: young blood stifled by reactionary mercantile mores. Vivid characterization, often by short, pungent musical ideas; declamatory style with little ensemble, many soaring melodic outbursts. Difficult orchestral score in late romantic style. Setting: outskirts of a small provincial Russian town on the banks of the Volga, about 1860. Three acts (88 min).

ACT I i: A park by the river; A room in the Kabanov house (34 min). ACT II i: Same as I ii; ii: Garden of the Kabanov house (26 min). ACT III i: A ruined house by the Volga; ii: A lonely spot on the riverbank (28 min).

Synopsis. The idealistic but weak-willed Boris, nephew of the overbearing old merchant Dikoy, secretly loves Katya, wife of Tikhon Kabanov. When Tikhon leaves on a business trip, Barbara, Katya's foster sister, arranges an assignation between Boris and Katya. In this love affair Katya finds temporary escape from her stifling provincial life, dominated by her harsh, old-fashioned mother-in-law, the widow Kabanikha. Guilt, however, leads her to confess publicly to her husband when he returns. Denounced by Kabanikha and the villagers, given up by her lover, she throws herself in the river. Her ineffectual husband, shocked into anger, brands his mother Katya's real murderer.

Major Roles. KATYA (lyr-dram s); youthful, capable of passionate expression and sustained high tessitura; top Bb4, touches B4. KABANIKHA (c or strong m-s); must be authoritative, vocally and dramatically. BORIS (lyr-dram t); top C4. DIKOY (bs); semicomic but frightening old man; drunken scene; top F3. BARBARA (lyr s) and VANYA (lyr t); secondary pair of lovers. TIKHON (t); passive, prematurely aged; top Bb3.

Lesser Roles. GLASHA, a servant; FEKLUSHA, a beggar woman (m-s); may

290

double. KULIGIN, friend of Vanya (bar). A BYSTANDER. A WOMAN IN THE CROWD (c).

Chorus. SATB. Briefly in Act III.

Orchestra. 4 fl (picc), 2 ob, Eng hrn, 3 cl (bs cl), 3 bsn (cont bsn), 4 hrn, 3 trp, 3 trb (bs trb), tuba, timp, perc, cel, harp, strings.

Material. Pr (UE). VS (cz)*.

Performances. Karamu: 11.26.57 (Amer prem). Empire St. Fest. (N.Y.): 1960. Juill. (NYC): 5.1.64. Eastman Sch. (Rochester): 3.23.73.

✄ The King's Breakfast

Music by Joyce Barthelson. Libretto in English by the composer, freely adapted from Maurice Baring's *Catherine Parr*. Premiere: Atlantic City, April 6, 1973, for National Federation of Music Clubs. Comedy. Highly melodious, occasionally appropriately modal; the melody of the King's song, "Alexander's Horse," adapted from Henry VIII's own composition. Setting: Breakfast room in King Henry's palace, 16th century London. One scene (approx 30 min).

Synopsis. At breakfast, Cathy, Henry's sixth wife, jealous of her predecessors, stirs up the peppery monarch. Their mutual pleasure in music effects several momentary reconciliations, until an argument over the color of Alexander the Great's horse leads to the threat of ultimate punishment; once again music soothes the savage Henry.

Major Roles. HENRY VIII (bar); C2 to G3. QUEEN CATHERINE PARR (s); Ab2 to A4.

Lesser Role. PAGE (sp).

Orchestra. P (4 hands).

Material. Composer.

✄ Die Kluge · The Wise Woman and the King

Music by Carl Orff (1895–   ). Libretto in German by the composer after a Grimm fairy tale, "The Farmer's Clever Daughter." Premiere: Frankfurt am Main, 1943. Comedy. Considerable dialogue, alternating with rhythmic, tuneful music over conventional simplistic harmonies. Setting: imaginary kingdom. One act, 12 scenes (90 min).

Synopsis. In spite of the advice of his daughter, who warned him that if he gave the King the golden mortar he found while ploughing, he would be suspected of having kept the pestle, the Farmer gave up his prize and was thrown into prison. The King insists on meeting the wise girl and promises mercy for her father if she will answer three riddles. This she does easily, and the King marries her. Now she is required to settle a puzzling case: While a muleteer and a donkeyman slept in an inn, the donkey bore a foal in the stable, but the man with the mule insists it belongs to him because it lay nearer his mule. In spite of being against the laws of nature, the King decides in favor of the muleteer, but the Queen tells the donkeyman to drag a net about on land, pretending that he can catch fish that way. The King accuses his wife of this trickery and sends her away, saying only that she may fill one chest with treasure. She gives him a sleeping potion and puts him in the chest as her most treasured possession; they are of course reconciled.

Major Roles. THE KING (bar); C2 to G3. THE FARMER (bs); G1 to E3. HIS DAUGHTER (The Clever Woman) (s); G2 to A4. JAILER (bs); low tessitura; D1 to G2. DONKEYMAN (t); D2 to A3. MULETEER (bar); high tessitura; trill; often in ensemble; D2 to G3.

Lesser Roles. VAGABONDS (t, bar, bs). Mostly in ensemble; normal ranges. *Note*: Fantastic costumes and masks should be used.

Orchestra. 3 fl (3 picc), 3 ob (Eng hrn), 3 cl (Eb, bs cl), 2 bsn, cont bsn, 4 hrn, 3 trp, 3 trb, tuba, timp (also small), perc (3—elaborate), harp, cel, piano. *Stage*: several dr, small bells, 3 trp, org.

Material. Bel (Sch). VS (g)*.

Performances. Karamu: 12.7.49 (Amer prem). San Fran: 10.3.58. Center Op., Minn.: 1.16.65; 12.3.69. Caramoor: 6.26.65. San Fern. Vall. St. Coll.: 11.17.67. Univ. of Cal. Santa Barbara: 3.1.68. Univ. of Ariz.: 12.3.69. Univ. of Wash. Fest. Op., Seattle: 3.11.70. Wash. St. Univ., Pullman: 5.1.70. Ambler Fest., Pa.: 7.29.70. Assoc. Artists Op., Dorchester, Mass.: 3.25.71.

✉ Krapp, ou la Dernière Band · Krapp's Last Tape

Music by Marcel Mihalovici (1898–   ). Libretto in French based on the play by Samuel Beckett. Premiere: Bielefeld, Germany, February 25, 1963. *Tour de force* drama for one voice. Complicated orchestra, expressive use of dissonance; intricate rhythmically and harmonically; vocal line patterned after speech with *Sprechstimme* and dialogue. Brief prelude. Setting: Krapp's lodgings somewhere in Europe; some time ago. One act (music alone 50 min; with staging 60 min).

Synopsis. Krapp is a disheveled, dirty old man, pasty-faced with a large red nose, disordered grey hair; nearsighted, hard of hearing, a cracked voice, heavy gait. He is seated at a table with microphone and tapes, in a crude light. The remainder of the room is in darkness. During the prelude, he eats two bananas, then reads from a diary, searches among the reels, puts one on, and accompanies it, talking to himself. He recalls other days, an old affair, philosophizes about his present state, while taking occasional nips from a bottle. He questions the word *viduity*, looks it up ("a state of widowhood"); is distracted for a moment and ponders the longed-for death of his mother; relives another love affair. His speech grows disjointed, he rambles about sexual experiences and religion, mumbles a hymn, drunkenly confused, with memories of Christmas. He finds a place on the tape and repeats the adventure of the girl in the boat, then stares into space as the reel rolls on in silence.

Role. KRAPP (bs-bar); very difficult; wide skips; glissandos; needs great flexibility and strength; F1 to G♯3 (B4 fals).

Orchestra. fl (or picc), ob, 2 cl, 2 bsn, 2 hrn, 2 trp, piano (cel), perc (4—including drums, cym, tri, wd bl, Chinese bl, gong, glock, xyl, vib), strings.

Material. Pr (Heu). VS (f, e, g).

☙ Ladies' Voices

Music by Vernon Martin. Libretto in English by Gertrude Stein. Premiere: Univ. of Okla. (Norman), June 3, 1956. Mock drama. Contemporary idiom; satirically expressive; vocal line patterned after speech. Brief overture. Setting: Can be picture gallery brought to life with moving cyclorama or with projected scenery: contemporary. One act (9 min).

Synopsis. A satirical comment on the problems of communication with the non sequiturs typical of Gertrude Stein. "Many words spoken seem to me to be English." "Yes, we do hear one another and yet what are called voices?" There is talk of masked balls, "poor Augustine," gossip and chatter with a philosophical undertone and name-dropping for the sake of sounds—"Mrs. Cardillac, archduke, Christ, Lazarus, Mahon, Genevieve, Caesar 'who kisses every day,' Mr. Richard Sutherland."

Roles. Originally for two s, two m-s or c. After Dinner Opera prod. used s, t, bs-bar.

Orchestra. Piano.

Material. Af.

Performances. Af. (Lake Placid, N.Y.): 7.29.71. others.

☙ Ein Landarzt · A Country Doctor

Music by Hans Werner Henze (1926–   ). Libretto in German based word for word on Kafka's story. Premiere: Hamburg Radio, November 29, 1951; revised for stage 1964. Hallucinatory drama. Highly expressive, supple orchestra; contemporary idiom; vocal line difficult, declamatory; may be produced as solo for Doctor. Setting: A country town in Europe. One act.

Synopsis. The story line proceeds through a series of nightmarish, surrealistic episodes and atmospheres. The country doctor must go to a faraway patient even though he has no horse. An animal is mysteriously provided by a stableboy who viciously assaults the doctor's housekeeper Rosa as the doc-

293

tor departs. His patient is a young boy, whose illness is not immediately apparent, but reveals itself to be a gaping wound in his side, glowing and alive with maggots. The doctor is ambivalent about trying to treat him, finds himself in bed with the boy, while the horse sticks his head through the window to observe, and the parents and a sister bemoan. At last the doctor escapes without his fur coat, dragging his clothes along, climbing on the horse, and riding off in a bitter snowstorm. The symbolism is heavy; the moral opaquely visible.

Major Role. COUNTRY DOCTOR (bar); a *tour de force*; highly declamatory; a good deal of monotone; some dialogue; A1 to G3 (one A3 with F2 opt).

Lesser Roles. STABLE BOY (t). THE PATIENT (boy c). THE FATHER (bs); ROSA (s); THE DAUGHTER (s); THE MOTHER (c); these utter only monosyllables.

Chorus. Children (s, c).

Orchestra. fl (picc), ob (Eng hrn), cl (bs cl), bsn, hrn, trp, trb, timp, perc (includes xyl, vib), piano (4 hands), organ (ad lib), strings.

Production Note. Color film especially prepared for Northwestern Univ. prod. Tr: Wesley Balk.

Material. Bel (Sch).

Performances. Northwestern Univ. (Evanston): 5.26.68 (Amer prem).

🎵 Das Lange Weihnachtsmahl · The Long Christmas Dinner
Music by Paul Hindemith (1895–1963). Libretto in English by Thornton Wilder, with a German translation by the composer. Premiere: Mannheim, December 17, 1962. Tragicomedy. Continuous texture, embodying set numbers. Short prelude. Setting: the dining room of the Bayard home, somewhere in America; the past century. One act (60 min).

Synopsis. The action depicts ninety years in the life of the Bayard family, somewhat in the manner of a morality play. Children are born and grow up and older people die, in the course of a long, continuous Christmas dinner, symbolic of many Christmas dinners over the years. The work is virtually plotless, but its themes are love and conflict between the generations, and the continuity of a family's life.

Roles. LUCIA (lyr s); C♯3 to G♯4. MOTHER BAYARD (c); B♭2 to F4. RODERICK (bar); D2 to F♭3. BRANDON (bs); A2 to D3. CHARLES (t); E2 to G♯3. GENEVIEVE (m-s); C3 to G♯4. LEONORA (s); high tessitura; E3 to B4. ERMENGARDE (c); A♭2 to E♭4. SAM (high bar); F♯1 to A♭2. LUCIA II (s); F2 to F♯4. RODERICK II (t); A♭1 to A♭3. Possible doubling of Lucia and Lucia II; Mother Bayard and Ermengarde; Roderick and Sam.

Orchestra. 2 fl (picc), ob, cl, bs cl, 2 bsn, cont bsn, hrn, 2 trp, 2 trb, tuba, harpsichord, perc, strings.

Material. Bel (Sch). VS*.

Performances. Juill.: 3.13.63.

¤ Der Langwierige Weg in die Wohnung der Natascha Ungeheuer · The Tedious Way to the Place of Natascha Ungeheuer

Music by Hans Werner Henze (1926–   ). Poem in German by Gastón Salvatore. Premiere: Rome, May 17, 1971. A revolutionary outcry, "spiritual odyssey in Marxist terms." Highly symbolical; each participant of 17 represents a political attitude. Orchestration is elaborate, colorful, rhythmically difficult, dissonant; many opportunities for improvisation; restless alternation of procedures and moods. One act, eleven parts (55 min).

i: Planimetry; ii: Attempts at molestation; iii: The veiled messengers; iv: The listless spy; v: Introduction to the difficult bourgeoisie: attempted return No. 1; vii: Attempted return No. 2; vii: Attempted return No. 3, German song; ix: Geodesy; x: Speech practice; xi: Metapenthes.

Synopsis. "Natascha Ungeheuer is the siren of a false Utopia. She promises the leftist bourgeois a new kind of security, which will permit him to preserve his revolutionary 'clear conscience' without taking an active part in class warfare" (Salvatore). The anxious, insecure leftist bourgeois sets out for her apartment, but refuses to go the whole way, realizing that he must turn back and begin all over again.

Role. VOCALIST (t); extremely difficult; wide range, difficult intervals; wears jeans, colored shirt, old army jacket, huge dark glasses; moves about in front space.

Orchestra. Each group represents political force: Brass ensemble wears tin helmets, upholders of law and order: hrn, 2 trp, trb, ten tuba. Piano 5-tet, sick bourgeois world: fl (picc), cl (B, Eb, bs cl), vln (vln with contact microphone, vla), vcl (vcl with contact microphone), piano; dressed in bloodstained hospital white, apparently maimed. Jazz group: bs cl (bs cl B, fl, ocarina), vib, small perc, sax (several sax, cl), trb, cb. Hammond org. Elaborate perc (1). Stereo tape with various noises, female voice. Two loudspeakers, small amplifying devices for strings.

Material. Bel (Sch).

Performances. New and Newer Music (NYC): 11.26.72 (Amer prem—Eng tr by Christopher Keene).

¤ The Last Puppet

Music by Anthony Strilko (1931–   ). Libretto in English by Harry Duncan based on a play by Grace Dorcas Ruthenburg. Premiere: for National Opera Association, December 1963. Tragedy. Basically tonal with dissonance as dramatic and motivational highlights. Vocal lines sometimes extreme in range; occasionally lyrical passages. Brief prelude. Setting: A puppet workshop looking into the street. One act (60 min).

Synopsis. The puppetmaker Kolar has been paid in advance for a puppet for the Margrave of Moonbourne, but has spent the money on a funeral for his wife. When on Shrove Tuesday the puppet is due, Kolar's daughter Tilda manages to stave off the Margrave's Herald, trying to sell their only possession, a rusty sword and a cracked emerald bottle, to an Old Clothes Man, who rejects them, and the family cat, which runs off, Tilda in pursuit. In her absence, Kolar attempts suicide, but is saved by Tilda, who determines to play the puppet herself. Kolar will not allow this, and assumes the puppet role himself, being led off in procession. The Margrave passes by, distributing gold pieces, some of which roll into the shop. But Tilda is unconsolable, even at the return of her cat.

Major Roles. KARL KOLAR (bar). TILDA (s). OLD CLOTHES MAN (buf t).

Lesser Role. HERALD OF THE MARGRAVE (bs).

Chorus. SATB. Townspeople, Margrave, his train, court drummer and buglers, soldiers, gypsies, children.

Orchestra. 2 fl (picc), 2 ob (Eng hrn), 2 cl, 2 bsn, 2 hrn, 2 trp, 2 trb, tuba, timp, perc, harp, strings.

Material. Composer.

🎶 The Ledge

Music by Richard Rodney Bennett (1936–   ). Libretto in English by Adrian Mitchell. Commissioned by Rostrum, Ltd. Premiere: London, September 12, 1961. Drama. Contemporary idiom; vocal line declamatory; some recitative. Very brief introduction. Setting: a ledge projecting from a large office building in big city; afternoon; interlude darkens to night. One act (35 min).

Synopsis. Joe, poised on the ledge ready to jump, is halted momentarily by another man who tells him of a similar experience. But when Joe remains obdurate the man leaves. Darkness falls and Joe is centered in a spotlight. His wife arrives, but all persuasion seems vain, until her laughter at something he says ironically brings him to his senses. He climbs slowly down to her.

Major Roles. JOE (t); C2 to B♭3. THE OTHER MAN (bar); A1 to E3. THE WIFE (s); needs flexibility; trill; A♯2 to B4.

Orchestra. fl (picc), ob, cl (E♭ cl, bs cl), bsn, 2 hrn, trp, ten trb, bs trb, tuba, perc (including timp—3), piano (cel), harp, 2 vln, vla, vcl, cb.

Material. Bel VS*.

Performances. Springfield, Mo.: 5.2.65 (excerpts).

🎶 The Lucky Dollar

Music by Ernest Kanitz (1894–   ). Libretto in English by Ann Stanford. Unperformed. Drama. Set numbers; free tonality mixed with atonality; vocal line melodic. Setting: Joe's cafe in small Nevada town; mid-1930's. One act, two scenes in same set (45 min).

Synopsis. A girl enters Joe's cafe, orders a quick meal, then leaves without paying as bus horn sounds. Joe seizes her suitcase, and she misses the bus. She confesses she is broke, and going west to find a better life. An Engineer who is present and acts as a *deus ex machina* suggests she stay as a waitress. Within two weeks the cafe is prospering, and Joe has fallen in love with the girl. The Engineer persuades her to put her money in the dollar jackpot, and she loses all, but when she ventures her lucky dollar, she wins a jackpot. Now she decides to resume her wandering, and the Engineer encourages her. She may return; no one knows.

Roles. JOE (t); D2 to A♯3. THE GIRL (s); E3 to C5. THE ENGINEER (bar); A♭1 to F♯3.

Orchestra. Piano.

Material. Composer.

⚜ The Man on the Bearskin Rug

Music by Paul Ramsier. Libretto in English by James Edward. Premiere: Northern State Teachers College, Aberdeen, S.D., April 13, 1969. Comedy. Continuous texture; contemporary idiom; vocal line patterned after speech. Setting: Henry's one-room apartment, "this year." One act (30 min).

Synopsis. Henry and his fiancée Doris are arguing over a party they just left; as she goes out to return to the party, the landlady, Mrs. Le Moine, arrives with a big package that contains a huge white bearskin rug. When unrolled and placed on the floor, it makes an enormous amount of difference in the atmosphere. Mrs. Le Moine practically throws herself in Henry's arms, and they are discovered by Doris. Henry persuades Doris to stand on the rug with him; its effect is immediate, and they are kissing when Mrs. Le Moine returns with the news that the rug really belongs to Sidney upstairs. With its departure, things settle down to the same dull reality; Doris resumes her nagging, and Henry subsides into subservience.

Roles. HENRY (bar); A♭1 to F3 (F♯3 and A3 opt). DORIS (s); D♭3 to A4 (B♭4 and C5 opt). MRS. LE MOINE (c); A♭2 to F4.

Orchestra. fl, ob (Eng hrn), 2 cl (bs cl), bsn, 2 hrn, trp, perc, harp ad lib, piano, solo strings or string orch.

Material. B & H. VS*.

Performances. Cham. Op. Group (Wilmington, Del.): 10.8.69. Univ. of Wash. (Seattle): 6.1.70.; others.

⚜ Many Moons

Music by Celius Dougherty (1902–   ). Libretto in English by the composer adapted from James Thurber's tale. Premiere: Vassar College, Poughkeepsie, N.Y., November 3, 1962. Fantasy for children. Conventional harmonies; melodic, although no formal set pieces; some ensembles. Brief introduction. Setting: Once-upon-a-time kingdom by the sea; three units: princess's bed to left; tall window in center; Throne at right. One act (40 min).

Synopsis. The Princess Lenore is ill from eating too many raspberry tarts and claims she will not be well until someone brings her the moon. The King angrily dismisses various suggestions that the moon is too far away, is too big, is made of bronze or of paste, and so on. Only the Jester suggests that Lenore herself be asked. She says the moon is only as large as her thumbnail, as far away as the branches of the oak tree, and made of gold. The goldsmith fashions a tiny moon on a chain which satisfies the Princess perfectly. Then the King realizes that the moon will still shine in the Princess's window and asks for advice. The Chamberlain suggests dark glasses, the Wizard black velvet curtains, the Mathematician fireworks—all rejected. Lenore again provides the solution: the new moon grows to replace the old, and so on and so on.

Major Roles. KING (bar); G1 to F♯3. LENORE, about 10 (s); top C5. JESTER (t); top B♭3.

Lesser Roles. ROYAL CHAMBERLAIN (m-s). ROYAL WIZARD (m-s). ROYAL MATHEMATICIAN (m-s). May be taken by one voice or three (s, m-s, c).

Orchestra. fl, ob, cl (bs cl), bsn, hrn, trp, trb, perc, piano, strings.

Material. G Sc. VS*.

Performances. Wilkes Barre (Pa.) Coll.: 1.30.70.

🎔 Un Mari à la Porte · A Husband at the Door

Music by Jacques Offenbach (1819–1880). Libretto in French by Alfred Delacour (Alfred Charlemagne Lartigue) and Léon Morand. Premiere: Paris, June 22, 1859. Comedy. Light, melodious; set numbers. Setting: Sitting room in an upstairs apartment in Paris. One act (45 min).

Synopsis. During a party in the apartment of Martin, a bill collector, a young man slides down the chimney of the dark sitting room and hides in a closet. Martin's wife, Suzanne, and her friend, Rosine, burst in, the former weeping because of a quarrel with her new husband. He has refused to show her what he claimed was a business letter. Rosine calms Suzanne and returns to the ballroom, whereupon Suzanne discovers the grimy young man. Rosine returns as the young man fails in an attempt to leave the room by means of a vine outside the window. He explains that he is a composer, Florestan, who has foolishly made love to the wife of a tailor to whom he is in debt. Surprising the couple, the tailor has beaten Florestan and threatened him with a bill collector, a monster named Martin. Suzanne reveals that this is her husband. At that moment, Martin is heard outside the door, which Suzanne has locked. Florestan seizes the key and inadvertently drops it into the garden. Martin goes out to search for it, but before he can enter the room, a house-painter's scaffolding miraculously appears at the window, holding a smock which Florestan dons, and escapes just as Martin unlocks the door.

Roles. MARTIN (t). SUZANNE (s). ROSINE (s). FLORESTAN DUCROQUET (t).
Orchestra. 2 fl, ob, 2 cl, bsn, 2 hrn, 2 trp, trb, timp, perc, strings.
Material. Pr (Heu).
Performances. Goddard Riverside Community Center (NYC): 3.8.70.

🎵 Le Mariage aux Lanternes · The Marriage by Lanternlight

Music by Jacques Offenbach (1819–1880). Libretto in French by Jules Dubois (M. Carré and L. Battu). Premiere: Paris, October 10, 1857 (produced in 1853 under the title *Le Trésor à Mathurin*). Pastoral comedy. Light, melodious, set numbers, dialogue. Overture. Setting: Outside a farmhouse; a large barn under the shade of a lime tree. One act (41 min).

Synopsis. The farmer Guillot has fallen in love with Denise, his young cousin-housekeeper, but he is pursued by two widows, Fanchette and Catherine. Denise and Guillot both write their Uncle Mathurin for advice. Mathurin replies to Denise that if she will sit under the lime tree that evening, a husband will appear, while he advises Guillot to dig for hidden treasure under the same tree. At the hour of Angelus, Denise waits under the tree. Guillot's digging produces nothing, but eventually he spies Denise asleep with Mathurin's letter in her hand. Reading it, he realizes he has found his love. The villagers' lanterns illuminate their betrothal.

Major Roles. GUILLOT (t); A1 to A3. DENISE (m-s); no range problems. CATHERINE (m-s); top A4. FANCHETTE (s); top C#5.

Lesser Role. NIGHT WATCHMAN (sp).

Chorus. SATB. Peasants.

Orchestra. 2 fl, 2 ob, 2 cl, 2 bsn, 4 hrn, 2 trp, trb, timp, bs dr, strings.

Material. AMP (BB). Pr. Map.

Performances. Karamu Th. (Cleve.): 2.27.62, etc. Sonoma St. Coll. (Rohnert Park, Cal.): 5.4.67. Univ. of Pacific (Stockton, Cal.): 1.12.68.

🎵 Markheim

Music by Carlisle Floyd (1926–   ). Libretto in English by the composer after the story by Robert Louis Stevenson. Premiere: New Orleans Opera Association, March 31, 1966. Melodrama. Angular, declamatory vocal line embedded in continuous texture of unconventional harmonies; two set numbers. Brief prelude. Setting: Interior of a pawnshop below street level, with many clocks and mirrors; London, Christmas Eve 1880. One act (80 min).

Synopsis. Pawnbroker Josiah Creach counts his money and puts it away as carolers sing for Christmas Eve. Markheim enters, haggard and ill-kempt, though obviously once handsome and elegant. Creach's maid Tess, leaving for her sister's Christmas celebration, awakens tender feelings in Markheim, but after she goes, the burden of his late call is revealed little by little. The amenities vanish as Creach refuses the money Markheim needs to evade cut-throat creditors, for the heirloom he offers as security is stolen. At Creach's insistent prodding and accusations, and crazed by the incessant ticking of clocks, Markheim confesses to thievery, bribery, lechery, and blackmail. Creach will still not lend the money, and Markheim murders him as the clocks strike eleven. Suddenly, a stranger appears on the stairs to an upper room. He resembles Markheim in a former elegant style. He offers to show Markheim where the pawnbroker's money is hidden and promises a life of unending pleasure if Markheim will only kill his conscience entirely. Markheim hesitates, but the Stranger tells him Tess is even now approaching the shop for a forgotten package—he will be branded a murderer. The only solution is to kill the girl. Markheim admits her, but cannot bring himself to murder again. He shouts at her to fetch the police. As she runs screaming away, the Stranger vanishes and Markheim kneels, joining the carolers, who have resumed their song as Christmas Day dawns.

Leading Roles. JOSIAH CREACH (t); B1 to A3. MARKHEIM (bs-bar); G♭1 to F3 (one G♭3). TESS (s); top B♭4 (touches C5). A STRANGER (t); top B3.

Chorus. SATB. Carolers offstage.

Orchestra. 2 fl (picc), 2 ob (Eng hrn), 2 cl (bs cl), 2 bsn, 4 hrn, 2 trp, 2 trb, tuba, timp, perc, harp, strings. Sleigh bells; clocks ticking and chiming.

Material. B & H. VS*.

Performances. Ball St. Univ. (Muncie, Ind.): 2.17.68.

🎵 The Martyred

Music by James Wade (1930–   ). Libretto in English by the composer, based on a novel by Richard E. Kim and a drama by Kim Ki-Pal. Korean version by David Youson Lee. Special lyric for Italian song by Valerio Anselmo. Premiere: Seoul, April 8, 1970. War drama. Mostly conventional harmonies, with some dissonance and a few twelve-tone passages to heighten dramatic effect; continuous texture in decidedly important orchestra; vocal line largely declamatory; some recitative. Brief overture. Setting: Pyongyang, Korea, 1950. Two acts, ten scenes; stage may be divided into three levels to facilitate quick scene changes; action is continuous within acts, with very brief interludes. Projections of flickering lights and noise of explosions may be used before II iv (90 min).

ACT I i: Refugee gathering in city; ii: Rev. Shin's home; iii: Army headquarters; iv: Shin's home; v: Meeting of clergy; vi: Outside Shin's house. ACT II i: Shin's house; ii: Memorial service; iii: Headquarters; iv: Church.

Synopsis. Pyongyang has been captured by United Nations and South Korean forces. A young Korean officer seeks in the ruined city for his long-estranged father, a Christian minister, only to learn that he was among a dozen clergymen brutally murdered by the Reds. The young Captain Park investigates, learning that one minister has survived, extolling the steadfastness of the twelve Christian martyrs and admitting his betrayal of them

300

to save his own life. A captured Communist officer, Major Jung, however, insists that the dead men "died like dogs, whimpering and denouncing one another an.1 their god," and that the survivor was spared because "he had the guts to spit in my face." Where does the truth lie? Park, who has renounced his faith because of his horror at the human condition, is nevertheless appalled at learning that his father had behaved similarly under torture. Col. Chang, Army chief of intelligence, is determined to make heroes of the ministers and arranges a memorial service. Park and Shin agree to uphold the martyrdom of the dead for the sake of the people's faith, regardless of its truth or falsity. A mob attempts to lynch Shin, but the result is the slaying of the demented son of Shin's housekeeper, Mrs. Hann—adding to Shin's guilt. The city is about to fall to the Reds once again, but Shin stays to comfort the hundreds of refugees who have no other hope than blind faith.

Major Roles. REV. SHIN (bar); dramatic role, highly charged; emotional; C2 to F3 (also touches F♯3, G3, A♭3). CAPTAIN PARK (t); C2 to A3 (one A♭3, one B♭3). COL. CHANG (bar); forceful, dramatic; high tessitura; G♯1 to G3. MAJOR JUNG (bs); top F3. MRS. HANN (m-s); B♭2 to G♭4.

Lesser Roles. REV. KIM (bs). REV. LEE (t). HANN (sp). ORPHANAGE DIRECTOR (s). CHANG'S AIDE (t).

Chorus. SSAATTBB. Citizens, refugees, penitents. Children: no more than 6, SSA. Ministers: 3 t, 3 bs.

Orchestra. 2 fl (picc), 2 ob (Eng hrn), 2 cl (bs cl), 2 bsn (cont bsn for one note only, can be cued elsewhere), 2 hrn, 2 trp, 2 trb, timp, side dr, cym, gong, strings. *Stage:* org (ad lib but desirable), guit, chimes.

Material. Comp.: Library Service Center, HO 8th U.S. Army, APO San Francisco 96301.

🎭 The Masque of Angels

Music by Dominick Argento (1927–   ). Libretto in English by John Olon Scrymgeour. Commissioned by the Community Center Arts Council of Walker Art Center, Minneapolis. Premiere: Minneapolis, January 9, 1964. Fable with religious implications. Melodic; humorous; conventional harmonies clearly differentiating between "sacred" and "secular." Setting: A church; the present (such as it is). One act (75 min).

Synopsis. A group of angels on routine inspection, find themselves in a church preparing to further the courtship of a young couple, Ann and John. Their captain, Metatron, instructs them; he is vexed at the small number of dancers and is told that the usual corps de ballet for such occasions has suffered an accident when too many tried to dance on the head of a pin. A soured Spinster and frustrated old Professor offer advice to the young couple, who are uncertain about their love. The angelic company finally accomplishes its mission as John and Ann embrace, even without the aid of the "Tie That Binds" dance, clumsily performed by the decimated ballet, and all move on to their next assignment: to promote improvement in the marriages of all heads of state, to the hoped-for benefit of the whole world.

Major Roles. METATRON (bar); G1 to F3. SANDOLFON, his aide-de-camp (t); needs some flexibility; C♯2 to B♭3. SADRIEL, company clerk (t). JEREMIEL, a Principality (t); B♭1 to A♭3. RAGUEL, another (bar); F♯1 to E♭3. JOHN, a young man (t); C♯2 to B3. ANN, a young woman (s); top B4. THE SPINSTER (m-s); A♯2 to E♭4. THE PROFESSOR (bs); F♯1 (F♯2 opt) to E3.

Chorus. SSAATTBB. Very important. Semi-chorus of Cherubim (Cherubiel, bs solo); semi-chorus of Seraphim. Semi-chorus of Powers (Abaddon, solo). Considerable melisma.

Ballet. Dominations: four Virtues who dance; four who dance comic "Tie That Binds"; eleven Virtues who play on instruments.

Orchestra. 2 ob, bsn, 2 trp, trb, perc, harp, 2 vla, 2 vcl.

Material. B & H. VS*.

Performances. Winifred Baker Chorale (San Rafael, Cal.): 12.11.65. Peabody Cons. (Baltimore): 3.19.65. Syracuse Univ. (N.Y.): 1.9.66. St. George's Church (NYC): 2.6.66. Other NYC churches: 1966–1968. St. Alban's Epis. Ch. (Los Ang.): 7.26.69.

◢ The Mermaid in Lock 7

Music by Elie Siegmeister (1909–   ). Libretto in English by Edward Mabley. Commissioned by the American Wind Symphony of Pittsburgh. Premiere: Pittsburgh, July, 1958. Fantasy with serious undertones. Conventional harmonies with jazz flavor; vocal line melodious; set numbers. Prelude. Setting: Pittsburgh, on the river; the present. One act, three scenes (50 min).

ACT I i: The lock; ii: The Catfish Club; iii: The lock.

Synopsis. Jack, the son of lock tender Cap'n Swabby, does not share his father's enthusiasm for his profession, and goes off to the Catfish Club to seek his latest flame, blues singer Monongahela Sal. In the darkness a strange figure appears; it is Liz the Mermaid, who has fallen in love with but been deserted by Jack when he was in navy maneuvers off Land's End in England. She has swum the Atlantic to find him. Cap'n Swabby sends her to the Catfish Club, but has a premonition of danger. Sal is singing a dirty blues, "Goosey Gander"; then Jack and Sal sing a parody on television commercials. The entry of Liz brings a romantic duet, "The Memory Is Green," but Sal soon stirs up the crowd in anger at the strange being who cannot join the dancing, and Jack and Liz are driven away. They return to the lock; soon Liz slips into the water and Jack joins her, to the sorrow of the Cap'n. Their voices are heard from afar, singing triumphantly "Land's End."

Roles. CAP'N SWABBY (bs-bar); B1 to E3. BONNY JACK (lyr bar); C♯2 to G3. LIZ (lyr s); C2 to G4. MONONGAHELA SAL (c); B♭2 to D♭4.

Chorus. SATB. Boys and girls at the Catfish Club.

Orchestra. 3 fl (2 picc), 2 ob (Eng hrn), 2 cl (E♭ cl, bs cl), 2 bsn, cont bsn, 4 hrn, 3 trp, 3 trb, tuba, piano, cel, harp, perc (2—including xyl, glock, vib, chimes, tam-tam), cb.

Material. Hen.

Performances. Hofstra Univ. (Hempstead, N.Y.): 5.4.62.

✄ Mr. and Mrs. Discobbolos

Music by Peter Westergaard (1931–   ). Libretto in English by Edward Lear. Premiere: Columbia University, New York, March 21, 1966. Comic opera of the absurd. Light, witty orchestration, using both twelve-tone and tonal harmonies; vocal line with wide skips; comic effects. Setting: the suggestion of a wall; Victorian costumes. One act (approx 17 min).

Synopsis. At sunset, Mr. and Mrs. Discobbolos carry a lunch basket and climb the wall. They introduce each other to the audience. It suddenly occurs to Mrs. Discobbolos that they may never get down from the wall. They agree that this might be a wonderful state of affairs, with no household worries. In the second scene, they have lived on the wall for twenty years, a month, and a day. Their twelve children (rag dolls) surround them as in a Victorian portrait. Now it occurs to Mrs. Discobbolos that it is very disadvantageous for their children to live on the wall—they never meet anyone or go to balls. What is their chance for marriage? Mr. Discobbolos slides off the wall, digs a trench, plants dynamite. After a little song, he sets it off, and the family disintegrates. The spirits of Mr. and Mrs. Discobbolos sing farewell as their children are raised to float in the air.

Roles. MRS. DISCOBBOLOS (s); B2 to B♭4. MR. DISCOBBOLOS (t); B1 to B♭3.

Orchestra. fl, bsn, vln, vcl, harpsichord, perc (1—marimba, vib, glock).

Production Problem. Machinery to hoist dolls for apotheosis; flash pots.

Material. Br. VS*.

Performances. Princeton Univ. Op. Cl.: 12.13.68. Washington Univ. (St. Louis): 4.27.69.

✄ The Mother

Music by Stanley Hollingsworth (1924–   ). Libretto in English by the composer and John Fandel after a Hans Christian Andersen tale. Premiere: Curtis Institute, Philadelphia, March 29, 1954. Fantasy. Conventional and modal harmonies; vocal line melodious as well as dramatic; very brief prelude and interlude. Setting: A northern country; old times. One act, four scenes.

ACT I i: Interior of Anna's peasant house; ii and iii: In the forest; (dissolve to) iv: The house.

Synopsis. Death, in the guise of the Old Man, takes Anna's sick child. She follows him into the forest, getting directions from Night, to whom she sings a lullaby; the Blackthorn, whom she warms in an embrace; and the Lake, for whom she weeps her eyes out. But Death convinces her that her child would have led a life of misery, whereas he is now at peace. She must return to life. (Alternate ending: Death leaves Anna alone in the forest.)

Roles. ANNA (s). THE OLD MAN (Death) (bs-bar). NIGHT (m-s). THE BLACKTHORN (t). THE LAKE (col s); trill; top C♯5. THE OLD WOMAN (m-s).

Orchestra. fl, ob, cl, bsn, hrn, trp, harp, piano, perc (2—timp, sn dr, bs dr, cym, wd bl, rachet, xyl, tri), strings (5-tet or full).

Material. Bel (Ri). VS*.

Performances. Neway Op. Gr. (NYC): 5.22.60.

🎬 Naboth's Vineyard

Music by Alexander Goehr (1932–   ). Libretto in Latin and English by the composer adapted from various versions of 1 Kings 21. Commissioned by the City Arts Trust for the 1968 City of London Festival. Premiere: London, July 16, 1968. Dramatic madrigal. Extremely difficult chamber orchestra of contemporary idiom; vocal lines angular; wide skips and awkward intervals. Setting: King Ahab's kingdom. One act (approx 25 min).

Synopsis. King Ahab weeps and won't eat because he cannot acquire Naboth's Vineyard. Jezebel attains his wish by lies; Ahab is forgiven by God, but his sons remain in trouble.

Roles. The action is mimed while three soloists (c, t, and bs) comment.

Orchestra. fl (alto fl, picc), cl (bs cl), trb, vln, cb, piano (4 hands).

Material. Bel (Sch).

Performances. Newport, R.I.: 7.25.69. Aspen: 1970.

🎬 La Navarraise · The Woman of Navarre

Music by Jules Massenet (1842–1912). Libretto in French by Jules Claretie and Henri Cain. Premiere: London, June 20, 1894. Melodrama (called "episode lyrique" by composer). Melodic, highly dramatic. Chief example of French *verismo*. Subtle use of Spanish and basque rhythms and harmonies. Overture. Setting: Spain during the war of 1874. Two acts (approx 55 min).

ACTS I and II: Village near Bilboa in Basque Province in the Pyrenees.

Synopsis. Anita, the Navarraise, who has lost parents and friends, falls in love with Araquil, a young sergeant of the Biscayan regiment, but his father Remigo does not consider her a proper match and sets a dowry far beyond her reach. She overhears the anti-Carlist general Garrido offering a large fortune to any soldier who will kill the Carlist general Zuccaraga. She decides to murder the general. Ramon, a Biscayan captain, sees her go to Zuccaraga's tent and informs Araquil. Believing her to be either the general's mistress or a spy, he follows her. A camp revel is followed by an intermezzo, after which Araquil returns, mortally wounded. Anita brings the dowry which has been paid her by Garrido for her deed, but Araquil dies denouncing her and she loses her reason.

Major Roles. ANITA (m-s or dram s); forceful, highly charged dramatic role; needs strength at extremes of range; C♭3 to A4, several high pitches have lower opt. ARAQUIL (t); E2 to A3; one B♭3. GARRIDO (bs); B♭1 to E♭3. REMIGO (bs); C2 to E3.

Lesser Roles. RAMON (t); F♯2 to G3. BUSTAMENTE, sergeant of the regiment (buff-bs).

Chorus. TB. Soldiers. Women and men of the village as supers.

Orchestra. 2 fl, picc, 2 ob, Eng hrn, 2 cl, bs cl, 2 bsn, cont bsn, 4 hrn, 3 trp, 3 trb, tuba, 2 harp, timp, perc (elaborate—3 players), strings. *Stage:* 6 trp, 3 mil dr, cannons, 2 bells.

Material. Pr (Heu). VS*.

Performances. Friends of French Opera (NYC—conc): 1.18.63.

🎵 Neues vom Tage · News of the Day

Music by Paul Hindemith (1895–1963). Libretto in German by Marcellus Schiffer. Premiere: Berlin, June 8, 1929. Satiric comedy, presenting fantastic view of German life, circa 1929. Set numbers, a few recitatives, woven into continuous texture; harmonic complexity; difficult vocal line. Prelude. Setting: Germany, late 1920's. Two acts, ten scenes.

ACT I i: Laura and Eduard's living room; ii: An office for divorce applicants; iii: The Office for Worldwide Opportunities; iv: Museum (room of the famous Venus); v: Bathroom in a great hotel. ACT II i: Divided between a hotel room and a jail cell; ii: Same as I iii; iii: Laura and Eduard's dressing room at a theater; iv: Projection room at a theater; v: The same.

Synopsis. Eduard and Laura, a newly married couple, return from their worldwide honeymoon, promptly quarrel, and decide to seek a divorce. Meanwhile, they are harassed by Frau Pick, a reporter, who sees them as "News of the Day." They seek the advice of the Baron d'Houdoux, president of "Universum," a corporation that claims to be able to do anything to make people happy, who offers the services of his employee, handsome Herr Hermann, a professional correspondent. After a rendezvous with Hermann in a museum, which so infuriates Eduard that he breaks a famous statue of Venus, and is sent to jail, Frau Pick plants Hermann in Laura's bathroom at her hotel, where he proceeds to take a bath. In the ensuing commotion, Laura realizes that she wants Eduard back, and they are subsequently reconciled. The chorus decides that Laura and Eduard no longer rank as "News of the Day," and set up two figures resembling them whom they can talk about, while Eduard and Laura escape to private life.

Major Roles. LAURA (s) needs power and flexibility; D3 to B4. EDUARD (bar); high tessitura; C2 to F♯3. HERMANN (t); must be handsome; E2 to A♯3. FRAU PICK (m-s); F♯2 to A♭4. BARON D'HOUDOUX (bs); A♯1 to E3.

Lesser Roles. Two divorcing couples: ELLI (s), OLLI (c), ALI (t), ULLI (bs). A MUSEUM-TOUR LEADER (bs). HOTEL MANAGER (bs). WINE STEWARD (bar). CHAMBERMAID (s). BYSTANDER (bs). SIX MANAGERS (2 t, 2 bar, 2 bs).

Chorus. SSAATTBB, very complex.

Orchestra. 2 fl (picc), ob, Eng hrn, 2 cl, bs cl, alt sax, 2 bsn, cont bsn, hrn, 2 trp, 2 trb, tuba, perc (2 players), piano, piano (4 hands), harp, mandoline, banjo, strings.

Ballet. Not indicated, but several opportunities for choreography.

Material. Bel (Sch).

Performance. Santa Fe: 1961.

🎵 One Christmas Long Ago

Music by William Mayer (1925–   ). Libretto in English by the composer, freely adapted from "Why the Chimes Rang" by Raymond MacDonald Alden. Premiere: Ball State Teachers College, Muncie, Ind., November 9, 1962. Christmas legend. Set numbers; conventional harmonies; vocal line melodious; some recitative, dialogue. Prelude with offstage voices. Setting: A remote land, in ancient times; Christmas Eve. One act, five scenes (70 min).

ACT I i: Old Man's cottage; ii: Triple scene: homes of Countess, Sculptor, Rich Merchant; iii: Snowy landscape outside town gate; iv: Interior of church; v: Snowy landscape.

Synopsis. Miraculous bells hung high in the church tower ring only when a good deed is done and ring only of their own accord. Various individuals try to influence the bells to ring: the Countess gives all her jewels; the Sculptor his self-portrait; the Rich Man his gold; the King his crown; but it is a little boy, who stays all night in the cold to care for an Old Beggar Woman, singing her a carol to keep up her spirits, who causes the bells to ring.

Major Roles. OLD MAN (bar); A1 to F3 (can double with RICH MERCHANT). OLDER BROTHER (boy s or s). PARSLEY THE PAGE (high bar); top F3. BEGGAR WOMAN (m-s); Ab2 to F4. YOUNGER BROTHER (boy s or s). SCULPTOR (t); C2 to Gb3 (can double with MINISTER). COUNTESS (s); needs flexibility; Bb2 to A4.

Lesser Role. KING (sp).

Chorus. SSATTB. Carolers, choir, congregation. Offstage s.

Orchestra. fl (picc), ob (Eng hrn), 2 cl (bs cl), bsn, 2 hrn, 2 trp, trb, perc, piano (cel), harm (opt), harp, strings. (Large orch. available.)

Material. Ga. VS*.

Performances. Phila. Orch.: 12.12.64.

🎵 The Opening

Music by Alec Wilder (1907–   ). Libretto in English by Arnold Sundgaard. Premiere: New England Conservatory, Boston, May 19, 1969.

Comedy, written especially for workshops. Conventional harmonies; melodic vocal line; dialogue. Brief overture. Setting: An intimate theater on the occasion of a world premiere. One act (28 min).

Synopsis. The play to be seen is called *The Reason Who.* The Prince announces that the leading lady, Marcia, has broken her ankle, hence the delay. He tries the glass slipper on various women in the audience. It fits the Usher. The Critic is enchanted. Marcia comes on stage, her leg in a huge cast, and is told the play is all over.

Roles. GERALD, the author, a prig (bar). ANTOINETTE, his wife (m-s). MRS. DOLLY FILAGREE (m-s). RONNIE (bar). ANNE (s or m-s). CLARENCE (bar, but dressed as aged 10). ALASTAIR FRONTENAC, critic (t). TRUDI, his patient wife (s or m-s). PRINCE CHARMING (bar). USHER (s). MARCIA (mute).

Orchestra. fl, ob, 2 cl, bs cl, bsn, 2 hrn, trp, trb, perc, cb.

Material. G Sc.

☙ Opera, Opera

Music by Martin Kalmanoff (1920–). Libretto in English by William Saroyan. Premiere: After Dinner Opera, New York City, February 22, 1956. "Opera Goofo"; satire. Conventional harmonies; melodious; voices should be in character rather than seek for beautiful tone; high notes may be falsetto. Setting: approximating a theater but all that is needed is a backdrop, a chair, and a gun; the present. One act (30 min).

Synopsis. The spoof is on the performance of "grand" opera and its surroundings: repetitions, florid decorations; clichés, cadenzas.

Roles. YOUNG WOMAN (s); needs flexibility; C3 to Db5. ELDERLY LADY (m-s); Db3 to F4. SISTER (m-s) B2 to A4 (these two roles may be doubled). BOY (t); C2 to C4. YOUNG MAN (bar or low t); C2 to G3. GORILLA-LIKE BOY (bs); F1 to D3. TWO OR MORE CANDY SELLERS (Bb1 to G3).

Orchestra. Piano.

Material. C Fi.

Performances. Many, including Nat'l Music Camp, Univ. of Minn., Ohio St. Univ., etc.

☙ The Other Wise Man

Music by Isaac Van Grove (1892–). Libretto in English by the composer, adapted from the story by Henry Van Dyke. Premiere: Bentonville, Ark., July 14, 1959. Biblical drama. Continuous texture of dramatic expressiveness; oriental, religious, Hebraic elements; vocal line partly melodious, partly declamatory. Interludes by chorus in pit. Setting: Bethlehem and Jerusalem, from A.D. 1 to 33. One act, four scenes (60–65 min).

ACT I i: Ecbatana; ii: Before the walls of Babylon; iii: Bethlehem-Judah; iv: Outside the Damascus Gate in Jerusalem (played without pause).

307

Synopsis. Artaban, one of the Magi, sells his possessions for three precious jewels which he intends to lay at the feet of the newborn Holy Babe, and follows the star that will show him the way to Babylon where the three Wise Men are awaiting him. Near the walls of Babylon, he encounters an aged Hebrew who has been cast out to die. He ransoms the slave with a jewel and hurries on to Bethlehem, having missed the three Wise Men. To save the baby of a young woman from Herod's soldiers, he bribes a Roman captain with his ruby. Then he wanders thirty-three years in his search for Jesus, arriving sick and half blind in Jerusalem on the day of the Crucifixion. He hopes to ransom Jesus with his remaining pearl, but gives it instead to Macedonian soldiers to save a young woman. At that moment, there is a convulsion of nature, and Artaban falls mortally wounded. He drags himself near the Cross, crying that he has failed in his mission. A Voice issues from above: "Verily, I say unto you, inasmuch as thou has done it unto the least of these my brethren, thou hast done it unto me." Artaban stretches his arms toward the Cross, then slowly sinks down and dies in peace.

Major Role. ARTABAN (t); a *tour de force*; needs strength throughout range, Puccini-like quality.

Lesser Roles. (All short, but needing strength.) ABGARUS, Artaban's father (bs bar). ATOSSA, Artaban's mother (m-s or c). ROXANA, Artaban's younger sister (lyr s). OLD HEBREW (t or high bar). YOUNG MOTHER OF BETHLEHEM (m-s or s). WOMAN MOURNER IN JERUSALEM (dram s or high m-s). SIX WOMEN MOURNERS (5 s, m-s). STORYTELLER (bs); some dialogue.

Bit Roles. ROMAN CAPTAIN (bar or bs). PARTHIAN MAID (s). TWO MACEDONIAN SOLDIERS (bar, bs). VOICE OF THE CRUCIFIXION (bar or bs, offstage); can double with STORYTELLER.

Chorus. SATB (in pit). People of Bethlehem and Jerusalem.

Orchestra. 2 fl, 2 ob, 2 cl, 2 bsn, 2 hrn, 2 trp, 2 trb, perc (2), harp and/or piano, strings.

Material. Unpublished. VS, CP (rent) from Joan Woodruff Van Grove, 1346 N. Laurel Ave., Hollywood, Calif. 90046.

Performances. Several (with P), including George Fox Coll. Op. Wkshp, Newberg, Ore.; Church Sanctuary, Oklahoma City, etc.

⚓ The Outcasts of Poker Flat

Music by Samuel Adler (1928–   ). Libretto in English by Judah Stampfer based on the story by Bret Harte. Premiere: University of North Texas, Denton, June 7, 1962. Western drama. Conventional harmonies with occasional folk flavor; expressive orchestration; vocal line often melodious and patterned after speech. Setting: Interior and exterior of a hut near Poker Flat "out West," middle 1800's. One act, two scenes (60 min).

Synopsis. Gambler Oakhurst and the Madam of Poker Flat, called Duchess, have been driven out of town by the righteous townsfolk and have stopped at a distant hut. They are joined by the girl Piney and the young man Innocent, who have eloped. Uncle Billy, the town drunk, makes off with their horses and packs in a snowstorm. Ten days later their situation is desperate. Duchess has given her slender rations to Piney, while Innocent has returned to town for help. Oakhurst shoots himself, and Innocent returns to find Duchess also dead and Piney in a faint. The townspeople repent and take Duchess and Oakhurst back for burial.

Major Roles. PINEY (s). DUCHESS (m-s). INNOCENT (t). OAKHURST (bar). UNCLE BILLY (bs).

Lesser Roles. THREE TOWNSMEN (t, t, bar).

Chorus. SATB. Townsfolk.

Orchestra. 2 fl (picc), 2 ob (Eng hrn), 2 cl, 2 bsn, 2 hrn, 2 trp, timp, perc, strings.

Material. Ox.

🎶 Padrevia

Music by Thomas Pasatieri (1945–). Libretto in English by composer, loosely based on a tale from Boccaccio's *Decameron*. Premiere: Brooklyn College, November 18, 1967. Revised version premiere: University of Washington, August 1971 (see also *The Women*). Drama. Continuous texture; conventional harmonies. Vocal line melodic. Setting: Fictional medieval Italian town, Padrevia. One act (52 min).

Synopsis. A present-day Narrator introduces us to the ruins of the domain once known as Padrevia. Here a castle was built by King Tancred for his beautiful daughter Gismonda, whom he wished to keep for himself isolated from the world. But the lonely girl meets a young gardener, Guiscardo, and their love grows through many secret rendezvous, until at last they are discovered in Gismonda's bedroom by the King, who throws the lover into prison, then has him killed. His heart, torn from his body, is brought to Gismonda in a golden chalice. Horrified, she pours poison into the chalice and drinks it. The distraught King finds her dying and kisses her with the passion repressed while she lived.

Roles. GISMONDA (spin s). GUISCARDO (t). TANCRED (bar). NARRATOR (sp). TWO GUARDS (mute).

Orchestra. fl, ob, cl, bsn, hrn, trp, trb, timp, piano, harp, 2 vln, 2 vla, 2 vcl, cb.

Material. Pr. VS*.

Performances. See *The Women*.

🎶 The Pardoner's Tale

Music by Noel Sokoloff (1923–). Libretto in English by Ted Hart based on Chaucer's tale. Unperformed. Melodrama. Contemporary idiom; vocal line patterned after speech. Setting: a town in Flanders, 1380. One act, two scenes (50 min).

ACT I i: Flemish tavern public room; ii: A room upstairs.

Synopsis. Three cronies meet for their nightly debauchery: Jankin, unhappily married drunkard; Symond, a miser, and Perkin, a lecherous apprentice. Incited by the tolling of a death knell for a fourth friend, they swear to seek out and kill death that very night. An old man tells them that death dwells in a room above them; when they burst into the room all they find is an old chest, filled with gold florins. Overcome with greed, Jankin and Symond send Perkin for wine and agree to murder him. But Perkin has poisoned the wine, and after the other two stab him to death, they celebrate in the fatal draught. The old man contemplates them philosophically.

Roles. JANKIN (bar). SYMOND (bs-bar). PERKIN (t). OLD MAN (bs). HOST OF THE TAVERN (t).

Orchestra. 2 fl, 2 ob, 2 cl, 2 bsn, 2 hrn, trp, trb, timp, perc, piano, strings.
Material. Pr.

Note: The Pardoner's Tale has also been set by Ernest Lubin to Hart's libretto; premiere Denver, 1966, available from ASCAP; by John Davis, premiere Univ. of Ariz., 1967; and by Alan Ridout to libretto by Norman Platt, premiere Kent Opera, England, 1971.

🎵 The Perfect Wife

Music by Giovanni Battista Pergolesi (1710–1736). Libretto, freely adapted from G. A. Federico's "La Serva Padrona," by Seymour Barab. Original premiere: Naples, August 28, 1733. Two versions: one with recitatives, the other with versified dialogue in the French manner in first scene. Light melodious line over conventional harmonies; set numbers. Added overture, Sinfonia, from another Pergolesi opera. Final duet added; was a substitute for the Italian in the French production of 1756. Can be used as encore. Comedy. Setting: early 18th-century Italy. One act, the home of Uberto (approx 40 min).

Synopsis. The bachelor Uberto and the maid Serpina are much attracted to each other, but cannot agree on a dowry, although Uberto begins to desire her more when she finally refuses him, saying that she wants to marry a prince. Stiffly, they pay each other extravagant compliments and descend to quarreling. The servant Vespone writes Serpina a letter purportedly from a prince looking for a bride, and shows up disguised as the suitor, becoming drunk and chasing Serpina. When he threatens Uberto with his sword, Serpina realizes the joke has gone too far. The hoax is revealed and forgiven.

Roles. SERPINA (s); needs flexibility; B2 to A4. UBERTO (buf bs-bar); needs agility over wide range; high tessitura in recitatives; F1 (one E♭1) to F3. VESPONE (mute).

Orchestra. Presumed medium.
Material. B & H. VS*.

310

✎ Perpetual

Music by Ernest Kanitz (1894–   ). Libretto in English by Ellen Terry. Commissioned by After Dinner Opera. Premiere: Lancaster (Calif.) Spring Festival, May 1961. Revised version: Premiere: UCLA Workshop, Los Angeles, February 1964. Lyric-fantastic love story. Set numbers; continuous texture; free tonality mixed with atonality. Vocal line melodic. Brief introduction. Setting: Antique mechanical music wagon, with three marionettes; approx 18th century. One act (16 min).

Synopsis. Three marionettes sing as they spin. From time to time the machinery stops with the singers in different relationships each time. The first stop, Colombina and Arlecchino face each other; Scaramuccio sings arietta, the other two a love duet. Next time, Colombina and Scaramuccio indulge in a frivolous duet while Arlecchino suffers agonies of jealousy; at the third stop, all three face forward and complain of being alone. Colombina is bored, Arlecchino in despair, Scaramuccio, as always, is cynical.

Roles. (Commedia dell'arte types.) COLOMBINA (lyr s); C3 to A♭4. ARLECCHINO (lyr t); D♯2 to B♭3. SCARAMUCCIO (bs-bar); G1 to E3.

Orchestra. Piano (1–2 players). Tri, tamb, small hand cym should be played by marionettes on downbeats when not singing.

Material. Pr for publ. Meanwhile, rent from composer.

Performances. Many at colleges; week with After Dinner Co. (NYC).

✎ Perséphone

Music by Igor Stravinsky (1882–1971). Libretto in French by André Gide. Premiere: Paris, April 30, 1934. Danced melodrama, based on Greek mythology. Music of exotic flavor though spare orchestration; vocal line difficult. Dancer takes chief role (Ida Rubinstein danced premiere). One act, three scenes (45 min).

ACT I i: Perséphone's abduction; ii: Perséphone in the underworld; iii: Perséphone reborn.

Synopsis. The story is that of Perséphone (Proserpine), daughter of Jupiter and Ceres, who was abducted by Pluto, King of Hades. Ceres, goddess of agriculture, forbade the earth to produce until Perséphone was released by Mercury. But even then, she had to return to Pluto for a third of each year, thus representing the seed that remains in the ground, then comes forth as corn.

Major Roles. PERSÉPHONE (d). EUMOLPE (t); E2 to B3. PLUTO (mute). NARRATOR (sp). MERCURY (mute).

Chorus. SAATTBB. Nymphs, Pluto's servants, adolescents, shades.

Ballet. Elaborate.

Orchestra. 3 fl, 3 ob, 3 cl, 3 bsn, 4 hrn, 4 trp, 4 trb, tuba, timp, perc, 2 hrp, piano, strings.

Material. B & H.

311

Performances. Many since Amer prem (Boston: 3.15.35—conc; Minn. Univ.: 11.56—staged), including Litt. Orch. (NYC): 10.19.62; Santa Fe: 1961, 1962, 1968. Ann Arbor Fest. (Phila. Orch.): 5.3.64; Los Ang. Mus. Fest.: 1966; Aspen: 1966.

⚑ Pharsalia

Music by Iain Hamilton (1922–   ). Libretto by the composer drawn from Lucan's Roman classic. Premiere: Edinburgh Festival, 1969. Dramatic commentary. Unconventional harmonies, largely drawn from opening 19-part chord; music closely connected with dramatic structure. Vocal line mostly declamatory, occasionally melodic. Setting: Not specified, although drama deals with the battle of Pharsalia and the doom of Rome. May be freely produced, with or without mime, and whatever action is desired. One act, 12 scenes without pause (approx 25 min).

Synopsis. There is no plot, no character development, but drama comments on tragedy of civil war and the battle of Pharsalia between Caesar and Pompey.

Roles. NARRATOR. Two s, one each c, t, bar, bs, often in ensemble, singing various roles; bar generally associated with Caesar, t with Pompey.

Orchestra. fl, cl, hrn, trp, trb, harp, piano, perc (snare dr, tam-tam, 3 cym, 3 wd bl, maracas, claves, 4 bongos, cassa, 2 tom-toms), vln, vla, vcl.

Material. Pr.

Performances. Washington Univ. (St. Louis—conc): 4.26.70 (Amer prem). Duke Univ. (Durham, N.C.): 4.6.73 (conc).

⚑ Philemon and Baucis

Music by Franz Josef Haydn (1732–1809). Libretto in German: first version (1773) as second part of *Der Götterath*, puppet opera; second (1776) differs in final chorus. Original story is found in Ovid's *Metamorphoses*, Book 8; Haydn's work probably adapted from a 1753 version by Gottlieb Conrad Pfeffel by Phillip Georg Bader. English version edited and translated by Cecil Adkins, based on 1776 libretto. Conventional harmonies; set numbers; vocal line melodious; some dialogue. Important overture and brief intermezzo between scenes. Setting: Ancient Phrygia. One act, two scenes (approx 50 min).

ACT I i: Phrygian village; ii: Philemon's hut.

Synopsis. The old couple, Philemon and Baucis, give succor to the gods disguised as beggars, and are rewarded by the restoration to life of their son Aret and his bride, Narcissa. Their humble hut is turned into a temple.

Roles. THE WANDERERS, Jupiter and Mercury (sp). PHILEMON (t); D♯2 to

312

B♭3. BAUCIS (s or m-s); B2 to G♯4. ARET (t); D2 to B♭3. NARCISSA (s); florid; needs considerable flexibility; trill; F3 to C5.

Chorus. SATB. Neighbors.

Ballet. Ad lib, in final chaconne.

Orchestra. 2 fl, 2 ob, bsn, 2 hrn, strings, continuo.

Material. Pr.

Performances. L'Ensemble du Sacre Coeur (NYC) as puppet opera: 2.25.73.

💌 Philémon et Baucis · Philemon and Baucis

Music by Charles François Gounod (1818–1893). Libretto in French by Jules Barbier and Michel Carré, after a legend. Premiere: Paris, February 18, 1860. Comedy-drama. Melodious; set numbers. Overture, Introduction (Pastorale); entr'acte between I and II. Setting: Phrygia, mythological times. Two acts (originally one, then three; revised for Opéra-Comique).

Synopsis. In a storm, Jupiter and Vulcan arrive on earth to punish the Phrygians for sacrilege. They ask for shelter at the cottage of the happy peasant couple, Philémon and Baucis, who receive them hospitably. Jupiter taunts Vulcan with the indiscretions of Venus, while their hostess, meditating on her long contented life with Philémon, nevertheless regrets her lost youth. At supper, Jupiter causes the water pitcher to remain miraculously full, thus betraying his godship to Baucis. Then the god grants Baucis's wish for restored youth, and woos her himself. She is flattered, and even consents to kiss the god, but Philémon is jealous. Vulcan tries to intervene, and the atmosphere becomes so quarrelsome that Baucis begs Jupiter to restore them to their former state. Touched by her piteous pleas, he does not renounce his gift of youth but vows to leave the couple in peace.

Major Roles. PHILÉMON (t); top C4. BAUCIS (lyr s); very florid; trill; D3 to B4 (touches several C5, D5). JUPITER (bs); can use extreme low tessitura; firm G1 (with E1 and other low notes given higher opt) to F♯3. VULCAN (bs); trill; G1 to E3.

Lesser Role. A BACCHANTE (s); one aria.

Chorus. SATTB. One passage divided. Bacchantes, blasphemers.

Orchestra. Presumed medium.

Material. Chou. Map.

Performances. Hartt Coll. (Hartford): 1956–1957.

💌 Photograph—1920

Music by Martin Kalmanoff (1920–). Libretto in English by Gertrude Stein. Premiere: Lake Placid, July 27, 1971. Comedy. Melodious, uncomplicated setting of witty Stein text. Single character sings and dances to accompany and double herself on sound film.

Double Role. TWIN I (s or m-s); B2 to B4 (C5, D5 opt); TWIN II (s or m-s); C3 to Bb4.
Orchestra. P.
Material. Composer.
Performances. After Dinner Co. (NYC): 10.4.72.

🎵 Pilate

Music by Alan Hovhaness (1911–   ). Libretto in English by the composer. Premiere: Pepperdine College, Los Angeles, June 26, 1966. Ballet opera. Exotic harmonies; chorus accompanied by percussion; vocal line mainly chant. Overture. Setting: a mountain. One act (30 min).

Synopsis. Pilate, after washing his hands of Christ's case, commits suicide on the summit of Mt. Pilatus, near Lucerne. He approaches the mountain as Silent Wings dances, and is torn between his conscience and the mob's cries to "Slay poverty and free the murderer." At last he releases his tortured soul and flings himself on the rocks below to the accompaniment of funeral chants.

Roles. PILATE (bs). SILENT WINGS (c); wears bird mask with beak, and black wings. CHORUS (bs). SACRED POVERTY (Vision of a Saint). MURDERER (Vision of a Murderer).
Orchestra. 3 fl, 3 trb, 5 perc (glock, gong; vib, ten gong; vib, bs dr; chimes; giant tam-tam).
Material. Pet. VS*.

🎵 La Poule Noire · The Weeping Widow

Music by Manuel Rosenthal (1904–   ). Libretto in French by Nino. Premiere: Paris, May 31, 1937. Drawing-room comedy. Melodious; traditional harmonies; set numbers; some dialogue. Setting: Constance's drawing room in Paris, 1920's. One act (45 min).

Synopsis. Constance is in a seemingly perpetual state of mourning for her late husband, and nothing can distract her from her show of grief. Her father Lajoie, her maid Madeleine, and a Spanish admirer Berbiqui (calling himself Fidelio), conspire to attract her attention by having Fidelio pose as a widow. He finally wins her completely, to everyone's delight.

Major Roles. CONSTANCE (s); Bb2 to Ab4 (B4 opt). BARBIQUI (Fidelio), Spanish nobleman (t); C#2 to Bb3. LAJOIE (bar); B1 to Eb3.
Lesser Role. MADELEINE (sp).
Chorus. SATB. Apartment hunters.
Orchestra. fl, ob, cl, bsn, 2 trp, trb, perc strings.
Material. Pr (Heu). Tr: Francis & Marion Lathrop; lyrics, Milton Feist.
Performances. Brooklyn Coll.: 4.2.54 (Amer prem–Eng).

🎵 Prima la Musica, Poi le Parole · Music First,
Then the Word

Music by Antonio Salieri (1750–1825). Libretto in Italian by Giovanni
Battista Casti. Premiere: Schönbrunn Palace, Vienna, February 7, 1786, in
double bill with Mozart's *Der Schauspieldirektor* (*The Impresario*; see *Opera
Production I*). Possibly not given again until resurrected by Károly Köpe
from Vienna Archives, revised and translated, and presented in Brooklyn
(see below). Satire. Conventional Italian style; set numbers, recitatives. Setting: A composer's studio in Vienna, 1786. One act (approx 60 min).

Synopsis. Like Mozart's opera, Salieri's deals with two capricious prima
donnas and their menace to the conductor, the composer, and the producer.
There is also a conflict between the musician and the poet about the relative importance of music or words (a foretaste of Strauss's *Capriccio*). Salieri may have been poking fun at himself as well as Casti's caricature of the
prima donnas.

Roles. COMPOSER (bar). POET (bar). ELEANORA (s). TONINA (s).
Orchestra. 2 ob, 2 cl, 2 bsn, 2 hrn, harpsichord, strings.
Material. Károly Köpe.
Performances. Brooklyn Coll. Op. Th.: 11.18.67.

🎵 The Prodigal Son

Music by Benjamin Britten (1913–   ). Libretto in English by William
Plomer after a New Testament fable. Premiere: Oxford Church, Suffolk,
June 10, 1968. Third of three "parables for church performance" (see also
Curlew River and *The Burning Fiery Furnace*). Music based on plainsong
with many echo effects; difficult because extremely exposed; vocal line largely chant. One act, three scenes: The son leaves; In the city; His return. Set
can be panorama, reversing direction for return.

Synopsis. A procession of monks forms as in the other two "parables,"
proceeds to the "stage," and the characters assume their costumes. The Abbot is not among them, since he plays the Tempter, coming out of the congregation. The Younger Son leaves his pastoral home; in the city the Parasites strip him; he returns to his Father's forgiveness, his Elder Brother's
envy and jealousy.

Roles. FATHER (bar). ELDER SON (high bar; wide skips). YOUNGER SON (t).
TEMPTER (Abbot) (t).
Chorus. TTBB. Parasites, beggars, servants, young servants, distant voices.
Orchestra. alto fl (picc), trp, hrn, vla, cb, harp, perc, organ.
Material. G Sc.
Performances. Caramoor Fest.: 6.29.69. Litt. Orch. (NYC): 12.14.69.

315

🎵 Punch and Judy

Music by Harrison Birtwistle. Libretto in English by Stephen Pruslin. Commissioned by the English Opera Group. Premere: Aldeburgh Festival, June 8, 1968. "Tragical comedy" or "comical tragedy." Polytonal idiom, varying from extremely dissonant to lyrical with colorful orchestration; many forms used, such as waltzes, lullabies, marches, serenades; vocal line patterned after speech; many ensembles. Highly stylized action. Setting: Includes Punch's travel frame, altar of murder, chorus gibbet, Pretty Polly's pedestal, and, before curtain, Choregos's booth and bandstand. One act (100 min).

Synopsis. The traditional Punch and Judy story is the basis for a psychic double life for Punch. On the one hand, he resorts to violence—throwing a baby into the fire, stabbing Judy to death, murdering the Doctor and Lawyer with syringe and quill pen respectively, and when condemned to hang, hanging the hangman instead. With the other part of his nature he seeks the ideal woman, Pretty Polly, and eventually wins her. Meanwhile there are many adventures, macabre, mind-wrenching, and clothed in rich and strange language. The fable may shine starkly through for children, but plays simultaneously on a demanding intellectual level for adults.

Roles. PRETTY POLLY, also WITCH (high s). JUDY, also FORTUNETELLER (m-s). PUNCH (high bar). LAWYER (high t). DOCTOR (low bs). CHOREGOS, also JACK KETCH (in the former role acts as narrator and commentator) (low bar).

Chorus. All soloists act as chorus at intervals.

Ballet. Mimes (3 male, 2 female).

Orchestra. trp, trb, harp, perc (2), string 5-tet. *Stage*: fl (picc), ob (C. A., ob d'amore), cl (bs cl, Eb cl), bsn (cont bsn).

Material. Pr (UE). Li contains full working directions.

Performances. Center Op. (Minneapolis): 1.30.70 (Amer prem).

🎵 Purgatory

Music by Gordon Crosse (1937–   ). Composer set the play by William Butler Yeats. Commissioned by BBC II for TV, and Cheltenham Festival. Premiere: Cheltenham Festival, July 7, 1966. Tragedy. Contemporary idiom reverting to tonality in last section; vocal line expressive, dramatic, declamatory. Brief prelude. Setting: a ruined house with bare tree in background. One act (35–40 min).

Synopsis. An old man returns with his young son to his former home, now in ruins, and begins to have visions of the past. His mother has died in childbirth, having married a drunken groom, who wastes her fortune and lets the house burn. In the fire his son kills him. When his own son tries to escape, the Old Man plunges his knife into the boy—the same knife that killed his father. But his hallucinations increase, his mother's ghost reappears, and he can only pray to God to let her soul rest.

Roles. OLD MAN (high bar); top A3. BOY (t); D♭2 to G3 (one A3).

Chorus. 9–12 women or 3 good solo voices. Wordless. Offstage throughout; occurs when Old Man hears hoofbeats and sees visions.

Orchestra. fl (picc), 2 cl (bs cl), bsn, hrn, trp, trb, harp, piano (cel), timp, perc (maracas, whip, wd bl, bongos, tamb, sn dr, mil dr, ten dr, cym, gong, hand bells in frame, glock, vib, marimba), strings.

Material. Ox. VS*.

Production Note. Tree grows light and should resemble human form when Old Man sings about his mother.

Performances. S. Meth. Univ. (Dallas): 4.70 (Amer prem).

⚑ Purgatory

Music by Hugo Weisgall (1912–   ). Setting of the play by Yeats. Premiere: Library of Congress, Washington, D.C., February 17, 1961. Tragedy. Difficult contemporary idiom; vocal line angular with difficult intervals. One act (35 min).

Setting and Synopsis. See entry above.

Roles. OLD MAN (bs); F1 (opt D♭ and E♭) to F3. BOY (high t or bar with high and strong fals); D♭2 (B1 opt) to C4.

Orchestra. fl (picc), 2 cl (E♭ cl, bs cl), bsn, hrn, trp, timp, perc, piano, strings.

Production Note. Vision of young girl and man.

Material. Pr. VS*.

Performances. N. Shore Comm. Arts Center (Great Neck, N.Y.): 4.20.63.

⚑ Rapunzel

Music by Richard Brooks (1942–   ). Libretto in English by Harold Mason, adapted from Grimm. Commissioned by Tri-Cities Opera, Inc. Premiere: Binghamton, N.Y., January 22, 1971. Folk fantasy. Set numbers; melodic; mixture of contemporary and traditional harmonies; some bi-tonality. Setting: Imaginary wood and tower. One act, three scenes (40 min).

ACT I i: Woods; ii: Rapunzel's tower, interior; iii: Deep forest.

Synopsis. The wandering Minstrel introduces each of the other characters, then his narration becomes the story. He leads the Prince to a tower where at an old woman's command, a strand of long golden hair descends. It belongs to Rapunzel, who is imprisoned by the Witch and guarded by a Strawman. The Witch enters and leaves the tower by means of the hair. The Prince learns the magic command, climbs to the tower, and is about to take Rapunzel away when he is attacked by the Strawman. Rapunzel hands him a torch to destroy the Strawman, but the Witch arrives in time to bewitch

317

and blind the Prince and carry off Rapunzel. The Minstrel and the Prince at last find Rapunzel, nullify the power of the Witch, and all ends happily.

Major Roles. RAPUNZEL (s); no difficulties; D2 to A4 (one C5). PRINCE (t); some high tessitura; E♭2 to B♭3 (one C4). MINSTREL (bar); needs comic acting ability; A♭1 to G♭3. WITCH (m-s); needs dramatic ability; highly chromatic passages, difficult intervals; G2 to G4.

Speaking Role. STRAWMAN. May be doubled by Minstrel if he can dance.

Orchestra. fl, ob, cl, bsn, hrn, trp, timp, perc, piano, strings.

Material. From composer: 69 Walnut St., Binghamton, N.Y. Performance fee.

📓 Renard · The Fox

Music by Igor Stravinsky (1882–1971). Libretto in French by the composer after a Russian folk tale. Premiere: Paris, May 18, 1922 (concert); June 2, 1922 (staged). "Burlesque for singing and acting." Music in a "popular" manner, touches of burlesque and improvisation, changing and subtle rhythms; departures from tonality. Acted by clowns, dancers, or acrobats, who enter and exit to a march, remaining onstage the entire time. One act (approx 25 min).

Synopsis. Everyone wants vengeance on Renard, who enters, disguised as a nun. He doesn't fool the Cock immediately, but eventually the bird jumps down from his perch and is seized by the Fox. The Cat and Goat force Renard to drop the Cock and run, but he returns and seizes the bird again; he escapes and remounts his perch. And the Fox tempts him again. The Cock prays in vain and passes out as Renard plucks out his feathers. The Cat and Goat serenade Renard, then threaten him with a knife, pull him out and strangle him. The other animals rejoice.

Roles. RENARD, COCK, CAT, BILLYGOAT (mimes). Singers (in orchestra): TENOR I; B♯1 to G♯3. TENOR II; needs flexibility; D2 to F♯3. BASS I; E♯1 to (many) G3; 2 B4 fals. BASS II: Consistently on F1 and E1; two firm D1; top C♭3.

Orchestra. fl, ob, 3 cl, bsn, 2 hrn, 2 trp, timp, perc, 2 cembalom, string 5-tet.

Material. G Sc (Che).

Performances. Several early. Univ. of Ill. (Urbana): 3.21.70. Experimental Th. Cl. of La Mama (NYC): 3.24.70.

📓 Romeo und Julia

Music by Boris Blacher (1903–   ). Libretto in German by the composer after Shakespeare, greatly compressed and cut. Premiere: Salzburg, 1950. Tragedy. Set numbers; ensembles; effective use of scene motifs. Three parts; scenes follow without interruption (65 min).

318

Synopsis. The chorus berates the Capulets and Montagues for their enmity. Lady Capulet tells Julia about the plans for her marriage to Paris. Capulet welcomes his guests. Romeo sees Julia; there is a conversation between the lovers, Capulet and Tybalt in ensemble. The Queen Mab song is taken by the chorus. The denouement is swift.

Major Roles. ROMEO (t); E2 to A3. JULIA (s); B2 to B4.

Lesser Roles (can be chorus in conc perf). LADY CAPULET (c). THE NURSE (c). CAPULET (bs). TYBALT (t). BENVOLIO (bs). PETER (s or t). THREE MUSICIANS (actors). (Peter and three musicians can be played by one actor, or the number in which they appear can be omitted.)

Chorus. SATB. Takes the place of Mercutio, Laurence, and others in narration and comment.

Orchestra. fl, bsn, trp, timp (perc), piano, string 5-tet.

Material. Pr (UE).

Performances. Univ. of Ill. (Urbana): 1.14.53 (Amer prem).

📖 Room No. 12

Music by Ernest Kanitz (1894–   ). Libretto in English by Richard Thompson. Premiere: UCLA Workshop, Los Angeles, February 26, 1958. Psychological tragedy. Continuous texture. Advanced tonality, considerable atonality. Melodic; also vocal line patterned after speech. No overture. Setting: Cheap rooming house; mid-20th century. One act (23 min).

Synopsis. In an old rooming house, a young man attempts suicide, but fails because a neighbor smells gas and intervenes. She calls the landlady, who sends for police, then waits in the hall for the ambulance. In Room 12, the inert young man struggles back to reality; figures from his past appear in a series of vignettes. At the end, they all merge in a kaleidoscope of mass accusation. In a last gesture of defiance, the young man crashes through a window to his death.

Major Roles. THE BOY (t); C2 to Ab3. MYRTLE (m-s); C3 to E4. THE MOTHER (c); C3 to F4. THE FATHER (bs); G1 to Eb3. BETH (lyr s). MAE (s). JOE (bar); may double with GEORGE (bar).

Minor Role. BOSS (speak).

Orchestra. 2 cl, 2 trp, trb, perc (1–2), piano, strings.

Material. Bel.

📖 Le Rossignol · The Nightingale

Music by Igor Stravinsky (1882–1971). Libretto in Russian by Stepan N. Mitusov after the fairy tale by Hans Christian Andersen. Premiere: Paris, May 26, 1914. Lyrical tale. Exotic harmonies, oriental coloring; first act, written previously, retains lyrical impressionism of earlier composition.

Brief prelude. Voices in orchestra; characters mimed. Setting: Ancient China. Three acts (45–50 min).

ACT I: Seashore near edge of forest, night. Entr'acte with chorus, veiled with curtains; Chinese march as curtains rise. ACT II: Porcelain palace of Emperor of China. ACT III: Emperor's bedroom.

Synopsis. The story closely follows the tale of the Emperor and the nightingale who enchanted him with song, then was banished in favor of a mechanical bird, but was finally brought back as the Emperor lay dying, and effected a cure by her song.

Major Roles. FISHERMAN (t); D♯2 to B3. NIGHTINGALE (col s); extremely florid; E♭3 to D5 (one F5). COOK (s); E♯3 to A4. EMPEROR OF CHINA (bar); B♭1 to E♭3. CHAMBERLAIN (bs); F♯1 to D♯3.

Lesser Roles. BONZE (bs). DEATH (c). THREE JAPANESE ENVOYS (t, t, bs).

Chorus. Act I: 4T, 4B; 2C, double SAT; short solos. Act II: SATB. Act III: C (Spectres).

Orchestra. 3 fl, 2 ob, 3 cl, 2 bsn, 4 hrn, 3 trp, 3 trb, tuba, timp, perc, 2 harp, cel, strings.

Material. B & H. VS*.

Performances. Many since 1926 Met prem, including Op. Soc. of Wash. (in Russ): 12.28.60; Santa Fe: 1962, 1963, 1969, 1970; NYCO: 10.3.63 etc.; Lyr. Op. of Chic.: 11.13.68 etc.; New Engl. Cons.: 1.14.70 etc.; NET Op. (TV): 9.71.

🖋 Royal Auction

Music by Ernest Kanitz (1894–   ). Libretto in English by Sidney Shrager and Alexander Chorney. Premiere: UCLA, February 26, 1958. Comedy, satire on mid-1950's. Set numbers, recitatives, dialogue; contemporary tonality, very free; occasional atonality; vocal line mostly melodious. No overture. Setting: A Chateau on the Riviera; mid-20th century. One act, two scenes (45 min).

Synopsis. Count Michael Massarotti, Pretender to the throne of Nicrotania, loves a commoner, the American schoolteacher Sally Jones, but is urged by his aide-de-camp, General de Luro, to marry one of two heiresses: Iris Stoner (pickle relish) or Kitty De Vries (Bean King's daughter). His efforts to keep the three women apart are in vain, but when he tells them (falsely) that the revolution in his favor has failed, the two rich women desert him, and he is left with Sally, his true love, for whom he intends to abdicate, becoming "Mike Massarotti," American citizen. A cynical Greek chorus debates with the pair of lovers over their chances.

Major Roles. SALLY (lyr s). MICHAEL (high bar). IRIS (s). KITTY (s).

Lesser Roles. GENERAL DE LURO (bar). BORIS, butler (bs). MRS. WARBURTON (dram s). CAPTAIN ANTONIO (t).

Chorus. Can be small.

320

Orchestra. 2 P.
Material. Bel.
Performances. Univ. of Wash. (Seattle): 12.61. Mich. St. Univ. TV.

✠ The Shining Chalice

Music by Isaac Van Grove (1892–   ). Libretto in English by Janice
Lovoos, based on her play. Premiere: Inspiration Point, Eureka Springs, Ar-
kansas, July 30, 1964. Fantasy. Set numbers; dialogue; conventional harmonies; vocal line melodic. Interlude between scenes. Setting: A remote little
kingdom, Middle Ages; Simon's humble cottage interior. One act, two
scenes (approx 50 min).

Synopsis. Timothy, the fifteen-year-old son of Simon and Mary, wastes
his time (according to his parents) making pottery no one can afford to buy.
But the Sad King (so called because he has not smiled since he lost his sight
in a Crusade and then lost his only son), hears of the boy and sends Sir Guy,
his troubadour, to commission a beautiful chalice, to be finished in five days.
Timothy accepts the challenge and has the chalice ready. The king is so enchanted by feeling the raised design of flowers that he smiles, makes Timothy Potter to the King, and gives his parents gold. When all have left, the
chalice shines in the darkness, lit from within, so that it appears to float in
space.

Major Roles. SIMON, a poor carpenter (bar); top E3. MARY, his wife
(m-s); top A♭4. TIMOTHY, their son (s); top A♭4. THE SAD KING (bs); top
E♭3.

Lesser Roles. SIR GUY (lyr t); top A3. OLIVER, his Jongleur (mute). SARAH
and ESTHER, neighbors (s, m-s). TWO GUARDS (bar or bs).

Chorus. Small. Villagers. SATB.

Orchestra. 2 fl, ob, 2 cl, bsn, 2 hrn, 2 trp, trb, perc (2), piano, strings.

Material. Composer, c/o Joan Woodruff Van Grove, 1346 No. Laurel
Ave., Hollywood, Calif. 90046.

✠ Signor Bruschino · A Son by Chance

Music by Giacchino Rossini (1792–1868). Libretto in Italian by Giuseppe
Poppa. Premiere: Venice, January, 1813. Comedy. Set numbers; conventional harmonies; vocal line melodious; some dialogue. Overture (Sinfonia).
Setting: Gaudenzio's castle in Italy; ground floor room giving on garden;
18th century. One act.

Synopsis. Florville, son of Gaudenzio's worst enemy, is in love with Gaudenzio's ward Sofia. When Gaudenzio decides to marry Sofia to the son of
Signor Bruschino, an irascible old aristocrat with the gout, Florville discovers that the son is locked in an inn for not paying his bills, and impersonates
him. Bruschino appears on the scene at the wrong moment, but Florville

321

cleverly befuddles him until Gaudenzio believes that the old man is repudiating his son for his bad behavior. Too late, after the lovers are married, does Gaudenzio discover his mistake.

Major Roles. GAUDENZIO (buf bs); difficult role; high tessitura; trill; very florid; Ab1 to F♯3. SOFIA (s); needs flexibility for florid passages; trill; top Bb4. BRUSCHINO, SR. (buf bs); some high tessitura; wide skips; considerable patter singing; C2 to F3. FLORVILLE (t); florid; trill; top A3.

Lesser Roles. BRUSCHINO, JR. (buf t). POLICE COMMISSIONER (bs). FILIBERTO, innkeeper (bar or bs); top F3. MARIANNA, servant (m-s).

Orchestra. 2 fl, 2 ob (Eng hrn), 2 cl, 2 bsn, 2 hrn, strings.

Material. Bel (Ri). VS*.

Performances. Mannes Coll. (NYC): 5.16.62.

▨ The Sisters

Music by Nicolas Flagello (1928–   ). Libretto in English by D. Mundy. Premiere: Manhattan School, New York City, February 22, 1961. Drama. Contemporary idiom; vocal line patterned after speech, occasionally dramatic, some lyrical passages. Brief prelude; interlude. Setting: Farmhouse in a Massachusetts coastal town, early 1800's. One act, two scenes (60 min).

Scene i: Interior of the farmhouse. ii: Clearing on a cliff, precipice at left, steep and hazardous path at right, sea in distance.

Synopsis. Three sisters live uneasily in their stern father's house. Martha, embittered, hates the younger Maryanna, while Hester is the peacemaker. Maryanna has fallen in love with a French sailor, Paul, and plans to elope with him. Martha, who has been rejected by Paul, tries to prevent them. But Maryanna gets safely away, and Hester meets at Martha's hands the fate intended for her younger sister.

Roles. MARYANNA (lyr s); D3 to Bb4 (one B4). HESTER (dram s); B2 to Bb4. MARTHA (c); Bb2 to G4. PAUL (lyr-spin t); top Bb3 (one B3). CALEB, the father (bar); D2 to F♯3 (one Gb3).

Orchestra. 3 fl, 3 ob, 2 cl, 2 bsn, 4 hrn, 3 trp, 3 trb, tuba, timp, perc, xyl, glock, cel, harp, strings.

Material. Bel.

▨ Le 66 · The Number 66

Music by Jacques Offenbach (1819–1880). Libretto in French by Forge and Laurencin. Premiere: Paris, July 31, 1856. Comedy. Highly melodious; set numbers, traditional harmonies; dialogue. Brief prelude. Setting: Road from Strasbourg to Steinach, 1860. One act (55 min).

Synopsis. A betrothed couple, itinerant singers Grittley and Franz, are on their way to Strasbourg to be with Grittley's sister Madeleine, whose husband has disappeared. Franz has bought a lottery ticket. A passing peddler offers to lend him money on the strength of winning. His number, 66, wins 100,000 thalers. Franz soon gets above himself, ordering new clothes and a carriage, and smashing Grittley's guitar. But before he can collect his winnings, the peddler discovers that the number is really 66 upside down, or 99. Now they are worse off than ever. But the peddler reveals himself to be Madeleine's errant husband, Berthold, and the three of them resume their journey to Strasbourg.

Roles. BERTHOLD (PEDDLER) (bs-bar); needs flexibility for patter aria; high tessitura; G1 to E3 (one F3). GRITTLEY (s); Bb2 to B4. FRANZ (t); E2 to A3.

Material. Pr (Heu). Af. Eng vers by Frances Barnard.

⚒ Sophie Arnould

Music by Gabriel Pierné (1863–1937). Libretto in French by Gabriel Nigond. Premiere: Paris, February 21, 1927. Romantic comedy. Conventional harmonies; set numbers; vocal line highly melodic; recitatives. Brief prelude. Setting: The great hall of a priory transformed by Sophie into a country home, at Luzarches; September 18, 1798. One act (45 min).

Synopsis. Sophie Arnould, a retired opera singer, has been spared by the revolutionary forces and lives in a redecorated priory. She is writing to her son when her former lover, Le Comte de Lauraguais, appears. This reunion is one of tender and teasing reminiscence. Seeing the letter, he learns of his son for the first time, and is tremendously moved. Babet, the servant, conducts him to a sleeping room while Sophie completes the letter, changing an admonition to beware of women to a plea for pity for the sex.

Roles. SOPHIE (s); trill; C3 to C5. COMTE DE LAURAGUAIS (Dorval) (t or high bar); D2 to F3 (Ab3, A3, Bb3 opt). BABET (m-s); A2 to G4.

Orchestra. 3 fl, 2 ob, 2 cl, 2 bsn, 4 hrn, 3 trp, 3 trb, timp, perc, harp, strings.

Material. Pr (Heu). Tr. Robert Gay.

Performances. Peninsula Fest. (Fish Creek, Wis.): 8.18.61 (Amer prem).

⚒ Sourwood Mountain

Music by Arthur Kreutz (1906–   ). Libretto in English by Zoë Lund Schiller. Premiere: University of Mississippi, January 8, 1959. Folk drama. Conventional harmonies; set numbers; vocal line simple and melodious; dialogue. Setting: The Appalachians, recent past; scenes can be very simple, with suggestive props. One act, five scenes.

ACT I i: A folk-dance gathering; ii: Judge's store; iii: The woods; iv: Lucy's garden; v: Lucy's room.

Synopsis. A mountain Romeo and Juliet. The feud of the Porters and Lovells is renewed by Danny Lovell's love for Lucy Porter. A previous

Porter, Nancy, has been betrayed by Robert Lovell. When Lucy flees with Danny, the women of both families join for peace against the men. The entire focus is changed when Ben Porter shoots and wounds Lucy, who is wearing Danny's cap. This brings Ben to his senses, and the families are reconciled as Lucy and Danny wed.

Major Roles. No range problems. THE JUDGE (bar). DANNY LOVELL (bar or t). LUCY PORTER (s). IDA PORTER (s). BEN PORTER (bar or bs).

Lesser Roles. LAVINIA LOVELL (sp). THREE MEN, THREE WOMEN (sp).

Chorus. SATBB. Important. Lovells and Porters.

Ballet. May be only square dance.

Orchestra. P. Or fl, ob, 2 cl, bsn, hrn, trp, piano, perc, strings.

Material. Bel (Col). VS*.

♭ Sterlingman, or, Generosity Rewarded

Music by Klaus George Roy (1924–   ). Libretto by composer translated and adapted from a short story by Arkady Averchenko. Premiere: Boston TV, April 18, 1957; staged version: Western Reserve University, Cleveland, May 26, 1960. Satirical comedy. Inventive and effective orchestration; light, humorous; vocal line patterned after speech. Setting: A small town in which saints' days are observed; November 10, the night before St. Martin's Day. One act, four scenes (45 min).

Synopsis. On St. Martin's Eve (before Martinmas), it was customary to prepare a "Martin's goose" in honor of the saint who divided his cloak with a beggar and was later known as the patron saint of feasting and conviviality. This story concerns an elderly couple who were visited on St. Martin's Eve by a mysterious stranger with an appealing proposition. The ensuing events strain severely the quality of mercy, and reveal a variety of human foibles—gullibility, avarice, and hypocrisy. No one comes off too well, but the moral is: the shoe need pinch only whom it fits.

Roles. JONATHAN, the old man (buf t). JACQUELINE, the old woman (m-s or s). A STRANGER (bar). A BEGGAR (bs).

Orchestra. fl, ob, cl, bsn, piano. Or P alone.

Material. Pr. Tape available.

♭ The Stronger

Music by Hugo Weisgall (1912–   ). Libretto in English prepared by Richard Hart after the play by August Strindberg. Premiere: Baltimore and Westport, Conn., Aug. 1952 (with piano); Composers' Forum, Columbia University, January 1955. Drama. A solo *tour de force*, with difficult soprano role; dissonant chromatic harmonies; some indication of popular tunes. Brief prelude. Setting: a contemporary cocktail bar. One act (approx 25 min).

324

Synopsis. Two actresses meet in a bar on Christmas Eve afternoon. Estelle, a chatterbox, joins Lisa without invitation, patronizingly gossips about her happy home and devoted husband. As she drinks more, she works up hostility, accusing Lisa of scheming to resume relations with her husband Harold, and plotting to dominate her. She paints Lisa as a monster of guile, then mercurially changes back to her artificially charming self. As she says goodbye and weaves out, Lisa sips her drink, and silently turns to the audience with an enigmatic smile.

Roles. ESTELLE (s); virtuoso role; calls for extreme flexibility, wide skips, declamation; tricky intervals; A2 to C5 (D5 opt). LISA (mute). WAITER and CAFE PATRONS opt.

Orchestra. E♭ alto sax (B♭ cl, E♭ cl), ten sax (B♭ cl, bs cl), trp, vln, vla, vcl, cb, piano.

Material. Pr. VS*.

Performances. Op. Wksp, Sewickley, Pa.: 8.15.69. Leag. of Comp. (NYC): 10.19.69 (among others).

ᴸᴬ Three Sisters Who Were Not Sisters

Music by Ned Rorem (1923–   ). Libretto in English by the composer based on the play by Gertrude Stein. Premiere: After Dinner Opera, Lake Placid, N.Y. July, 1971. Melodrama. Complex harmonies; vocal line patterned after speech; atmosphere of surreality. Setting: A room, alternately lighted and in darkness. One act, five sections (35 min).

Synopsis. Three sisters and two brothers play at murder. They are all both killers and victims. The only survivor is Jenny, who, because it is no good living alone, drinks poison. But no one is dead, which all agree is very nice, and so all go to bed.

Note. By John Malcolm Brinnen in his introduction to *Selected Operas and Plays by Gertrude Stein* (University of Pittsburgh Press, 1970): "Her plays call out to the imaginations of those who might make them 'work.' What she sets down on the page are but the stress, the shape, the tempos and the texture of a thing. Actors, musicians, scene designers and directors are invited to supply just about everything else."

Roles. JENNY (s); flexibility required; A2 to B4 (one C5). HELEN (s); B♭2 to A4. ELLEN (m-s); needs flexibility; G2 to E4. SAMUEL (also POLICEMAN and APACHE) (t); C2 to A♯3. SYLVESTER (bar); G1 to F3.

Orchestra. In preparation.

Material. B & H.

Performances. Af (Westport, Conn.): 7.31.71.

ᴸᴬ The Transposed Heads

Music by Peggy Glanville-Hicks (1912–   ). Libretto in English by the composer based on the novel by Thomas Mann, English translation by

325

H. T. Lowe-Porter. First opera commissioned by the Louisville Philharmonic Society, Inc. Premiere: Louisville, April 4, 1954. A legend of India. Many tunes and rhythms from Hindu folk and classical sources; exotic orchestration; vocal line melodious; text florid, patterned on Mann. Overture; brief interludes. Setting: India, ancient times. Two acts, six scenes (75 min—to add prelude to Act IV and interlude before scene vi add 6 min).

ACT I i: A bathing place on the banks of the Jumna River; ii: Same a few days later; iii: Sita's village on the wedding day. ACT II i: A forest glade with the ruin of the Temple of Kali; ii: The Guru's ashram in the Himalayas; iii: A hermit's retreat in the mountains.

Synopsis. A young Brahman, Shridaman, and his low-caste friend Nanda witness the ritual bathing of the lovely Sita. Shridaman falls in love and Nanda woos the girl on his friend's behalf, according to Hindu custom. After the wedding Shridaman leaves Sita and Nanda together while he prays, and it is apparent that there is an attraction between those two. Shridaman, hypnotized by the Goddess Kali, cuts off his own head as a sacrifice. Nanda blames himself and follows suit. Sita also blaming herself is about to commit suicide when the voice of Kali instructs her to place the heads back on. In her agitation Sita makes the Freudian slip of all times and reverses the heads. Now who is to say which is the legal husband? A Guru proclaims the head as rightful husband. The Nanda head with the husband body retires to a hermitage. Sita begins to long for the parts she lacks and goes in search of Nanda with Shridaman following. The three are united again and decide there is no solution but to "merge their separate essences in the universal whole" by jumping into the flames, but a wife may not commit suttee until she is a widow, so the two men kill each other in a duel. As they fall upon the fire Sita joins them and all are consumed.

Major Roles. SHRIDAMAN (t); needs flexibility; trill; C2 to C4. NANDA (bar); A1 to A3 (many high notes opt). SITA (s); Bb2 (F3 opt) to C5.

Lesser Roles. GODDESS KALI (sp). GURU KAMADAMANA (sp).

Chorus. SATB. Villagers.

Ballet. Wedding dance.

Orchestra. fl, ob, cl, bsn, hrn, trp, trb, harp, perc, string qt.

Material. AMP.

Performances. Phoenix Th. (NYC): 2.10.58.

🖎 Der Traum des Liu-Tung · The Dream of Liu-Tung

Music by Isang Yun. Libretto in German by the composer after a Chinese legend by Ma-Chi-Yuan (14th century). Premiere: West Berlin, September 25, 1965. Fantasy. Colorful orchestration; vocal line melodious and patterned after speech; Oriental flavor. Setting: China, 14th century. Intended as part of double bill under collective title *Traume* (*Dreams*) with the same composer's *Die Witwe des Schmetterlings* (see). Prelude, five scenes, epilogue (approx 60 min).

Prologue: In heaven. Scene i: The inn. ii: First dream scene, Palace of the Emperor. iii: Second dream scene, another room in the palace, a month later. iv: Third dream scene, the Emperor's hall of justice. v: Fourth dream scene, a lonely cottage. Epilogue: The inn.

Synopsis. The adventures of a frivolous student, Liu-Tung, who is converted to Taoism when a magician conjures up four dreams that chillingly depict his fate. The dreams idealize the renunciation of earthly values while striving for inner personal freedom. What has passed returns to nothingness if one gazes back at it. "Today is spring; tomorrow the flower wilts."

Major Roles. TUNG-HUA, an immortal (bs). CHING-YANG, a hermit (bar). FRAU WANG, innkeeper (m-s). PIEN-FU, trader (t). YU-CHAN, his wife (s). LIU-TANG (high bar).

Chorus. SATB. Ad lib. Heavenly beings.

Orchestra. 2 fl (alto fl, picc), 2 ob (Eng hrn), cl (bs cl), bsn (cont bsn), 2 hrn, trp, trb, tuba, timp, perc (4), harp, strings.

Material. AMP (BB).

◢ The Trial of Mary Lincoln

Music by Thomas Pasatieri (1945–   ). Libretto in English by Anne Bailey. Commissioned by NET. Premiere: NET, 1972. Drama. Continuous texture, melodious passages alternate with declamation; some dialogue. Setting: in and about Washington, Illinois, mid-19th century. One act, several scenes (50 min).

Synopsis. In a series of flashbacks, Mary Lincoln's early life is reviewed, the action always returning to the courtroom where she is on trial, and is finally judged insane and committed.

Major Roles. MARY LINCOLN (m-s); needs great acting ability; strength in extremes of range; one very high passage; one highly dramatic scene where she is accused of madness. ROBERT LINCOLN (bar). LEONARD SWEET, Mary's lawyer (bar). JOHNNY TODD (t). NINIAN EDWARDS (bar).

Lesser Roles. ELIZABETH EDWARDS. MRS. FAYE. STODDARD. ELIZABETH KECK-LEY. JUDGE. PARKER. TWO YOUNG SOLDIERS.

Orchestra. 2 fl, 2 ob, 2 cl, 2 bsn, 2 hrn, trp, trb, piano, harp, strings.

Material. Bel.

◢ Trois Opéras-Minutes · Three Tiny Operas

Music by Darius Milhaud (1892–   ). Librettos in French by Henri Hoppenot. Premieres: See under each title below. Satires on Greek myths.

Melodic; vocal line of moderate difficulty; unconventional harmonies heightening satirical aspect. Details under each title below.

L'ENLEVEMENT D'EUROPE · THE ABDUCTION OF EUROPA

Premiere: Baden-Baden, July 17, 1927. Setting: Thebes. One act: before the house of King Agénor (9 min).

Synopsis. Europa is betrothed to Pergamon but prefers "cattle" in the shape of a bull (the god Jupiter). Pergamon shoots the bull, but his arrow is deflected magically back to Pergamon's own breast—an unusual end to a bullfight. Jupiter bears Europa away on his back.

Major Roles. PERGAMON (bar); top F3. AGÉNOR (bs); low A1. JUPITER in the shape of a bull (t); top A♭3. EUROPA (s); top B♭4.

Lesser Roles. SERVANTS (s, m-s, c). SOLDIERS (t, bar, bs).

Orchestra. fl, ob, cl, bsn, trp, perc, vln, vla, vcl, bs.

L'ABANDON D'ARIANE · THE ABANDONMENT OF ARIADNE

Premiere: Wiesbaden, April 20, 1928. Setting: The island of Naxos. One act (10 min).

Synopsis. Thésée loves Ariane, who despises him, and is loved by her sister Phèdre. The god Dionysos, who has designs on Ariane, plies Thésée with wine until he sees double and thinks both sisters are boarding his ship. He will have to be content with Phèdre, while Dionysos whisks Ariane up to companion Diana in the sky.

Major Roles. ARIANE (s); no range problems. PHEDRE (s); no range problems. DIONYSOS (bar); top F3. THÉSÉE (t); top B♭3.

Lesser Roles. SHIPWRECKED SAILORS (t, bar, bs). BACCHANTES (s, m-s, c).

Orchestra. 2 fl, ob, 2 cl, bsn, hrn, 2 trp, timp, perc, 2 vln, vla, vcl, bs.

LA DÉLIVRANCE DE THÉSÉE · THE LIBERATION OF THESEUS

Premiere: Wiesbaden, April 20, 1928. Setting: The palace of Thésée. One act (6 min).

Synopsis. Thésée's son Hippolyte loves Aricie but is pursued by his stepmother Phèdre. In a rage at the youth's distaste, Phèdre accuses him to his father, who sends him off to death at the hands of a monster. His friend Théramène kills Phèdre in revenge, and is led off to execution. Only Aricie remains to console Thésée.

Major Roles. ARICIE (m-s). PHEDRE (s). HIPPOLYTE (bar). THÉRAMENE (bar). No range problems. THÉSÉE (t); top C4.

Lesser Roles. Chorus of voices from far away (s, c, t, bs). (This and the groups in the other two operas act as a Greek chorus of comment.)

Material. (UE). VS (f, g, e).

Performances. Europa, San Fran.: 5.18.55. *Ariane*, Urbana, Ill.: 3.6.55. *Thésée*, Iowa St. Univ. (Iowa City): 5.8.61. All three, Center Op. (Minneapolis). Mannes Workshop (NYC): 3.24.71.

328

◢ The Victory at Masada

Music by Martin Kalmanoff (1920–   ). Libretto and lyrics in English by composer. Premiere: Detroit Symphony and Opera, November 14, 1968. Drama. Conventional harmonies; occasional exotic flavor; vocal line melodious, set numbers. Setting: Masada in southern Israel, 1967 and A.D. 73. One act (60 min).

ACT I: Atop the natural fortress of Masada; flashback to exterior of Herod's villa; Roman camp; Masada fortress; return to the present.

Synopsis. The war of 1967 recalls to Rachel and Jacob, joined by Aaron and Rabbi Eleazar, the battle of Masada in A.D. 73, when, rather than be taken alive by the Romans, the entire garrison at Masada, men, women, and children, commit suicide. The story is told by Flavius Joseph, who confesses that through cowardice he defected to the Romans. He tells the three young people that they were present in that former battle, but shared the heroic fate of their companions. They pledge their courageous vow anew.

Major Roles. RACHEL (s). JACOB (t or bar). AARON (t). JOSEPH (bar). RABBI ELEAZAR (sp).

Lesser Roles. FOUR MEN (sp).

Chorus. SATB.

Orchestra. fl, ob, cl, bsn, hrn, trp, trb, timp, perc, harp, strings. Or P alone.

Material. Composer: 392 Central Park West, New York, N.Y. 10025.

Performances. Several, in NYC and Philadelphia, 1969.

◢ La Vida Breve · A Short Life

Music by Manuel de Falla (1876–1946). Libretto in Spanish by Carlos Fernandez Shaw. Premiere: Nice, April 1, 1913. Tragedy. Colorful harmonies; employs Spanish folk songs and powerful rhythms; vocal line both melodious and declamatory. Prelude and chorus; interlude and chorus, Act I ii; Bolero, Act II i; interlude, Act II, between i and ii. Setting: Granada, beginning of the 19th century. Two acts, four scenes (70 min).

ACT I i: Court of a gypsy dwelling in l'Albaicin, Granada, at left, entrance to a smithy; ii: Panoramic view of Granada from Mt. Sacree. ACT II i: Street in Granada, house of Carmela and Manuel, view of patio in fete for betrothal; ii: Patio.

Synopsis. Salud, a gypsy girl, considers herself betrothed to Paco, but her uncle and grandmother are suspicious of the young man. Indeed, he has deserted his gypsy sweetheart for the town girl Carmela, who lives with her brother Manuel in a fine house. Salud, followed by her grandmother and her uncle, goes to town and observes Paco in a betrothal feast, and rushes into the house, imploring Paco to kill her. Paco lies about his marriage, but this is too much for Salud, who drops dead at his feet.

329

Major Roles. SALUD (s); needs dramatic force as well as a lyrical line; B2 to B4. HER GRANDMOTHER (m-s or c); A2 to G4. PACO (t); D2 to A♯3. UNCLE SARVAOR (bs or bar); B1 to F3.

Lesser Roles. CARMELA (m-s). MANUEL (bar). A SINGER (bar); needs flexibility for melisma. FOUR PEDDLERS (s, s, s, m-s). VOICE IN BLACKSMITH SHOP (t). VOICE OF A PEDDLER (t). FAR-OFF VOICE (t).

Chorus. SSAATTBB. Blacksmiths, offstage voices, guests at feast.

Ballet. Act II, i and ii.

Orchestra. 3 fl, 3 ob, 3 cl, 3 bsn, 4 hrn, 2 trp, 3 trb, bs tuba, timp, perc, 2 harp, cel, strings. *Stage:* guit, bells.

Material. G Sc (Eschig). VS*.

Performances. Hartt Coll. (Hartford): 4.30.69. Aspen: 7.31.69. St. Paul: 10.9.69. Peabody Cons.: 3.13.70.

🎵 Le Villi · The Willis

Music by Giacomo Puccini (1858–1924). Libretto in Italian by Ferdinando Fontana, probably based on the legend related by Heine in an essay on German spirits and demons. Premiere: Milan, May 31, 1884. Fantasy-melodrama. Largely eclectic, but Puccini's future style apparent. Ten set numbers with choral prelude and prayer. Orchestral passages added when opera, compressed into one act, was expanded: "L'Abbandono" ("The Desertion") expressing Anna's grief and death lyrically, and "La Tragenda" ("The Specter"). The composer intended to have explanatory verses read throughout, but this was probably never done (it would have restored the account of Roberto's seduction and treachery and Anna's death, in the final version only referred to in passing). Instead, there is a spectral funeral procession and the ballet of the Willis, incongruously set to a lively tarantella. Also there are extended preludes and postludes to arias and duets. Setting: The Black Forest, olden times. Two acts (approx 62 min).

ACT I: The forest (25 min). ACT II: Door to the house (37 min).

Synopsis. Roberto leaves his village sweetheart Anna to collect an inheritance in Vienna. He returns penniless and broken in health from wild carousals with city sirens, and is greeted by Anna's funeral music. In a snowstorm the Villis appear (brides who have died in youthful bloom), with Anna at their head. They crowd around him in a death dance, mocking his dying pleas for forgiveness.

Roles. GUGLIELMO WULF (bar); high tessitura; B♭1 (G1 and E1 opt) to E3. ANNA, his daughter (s); C3 to B♭4 (one C5 with C4 opt). ROBERTO (t); one of longest *scenas* in opera; needs strength throughout range; C2 to B♭3.

Chorus. SATTB. Very important. Mountaineers, Willis, spirits.

Ballet. In Act II.

Orchestra. 3 fl, 3 ob, 2 cl, 3 bsn, 4 hrn, 5 trp, 3 trb, tuba, timp, perc, bells, harp, strings.

Material. Bel (Ri).

✍ La Voix Humaine · The Human Voice

Music by Francis Poulenc (1899–1963). Libretto in French by Jean Cocteau. Premiere: Paris, February 6, 1959. Drama. *Tour de force* for soprano with orchestra, practically a concerto. Orchestra of sensual atmosphere, dramatic highlights. Setting: A woman's bedroom, contemporary. One act (approx 40 min).

Synopsis. The woman, jilted by her lover who is about to marry another girl, engages in a farewell phone conversation, often interrupted by disconnections and other voices on the line. Her moods change quickly from anguish to a forced calm and back again. She discloses that she has taken sleeping pills to no effect, and we see her wind the telephone cord around her neck in a desperate gesture. She speaks standing, sitting, prone, supine, on her knees, roaming the room to the extent of the phone cord, finally falling on the bed, her head hanging, the phone receiver lying like a stone.

Role. THE WOMAN (s); should be young and elegant, not suggesting an old abandoned woman; the voice is often almost a monotone, like speech, some passages freely without accompaniment; C3 to A♭4 (one A4, one firm C5).

Orchestra. 2 fl (picc), ob, Eng hrn, 2 cl, bs cl, 2 bsn, 2 hrn, 2 trp, trb, tuba, perc, xyl, harp, strings.

Material. Bel (Ri).

✍ Volo di Notte · Night Flight

Music by Luigi Dallapiccola (1904–   ). Libretto in Italian based on Antoine de Saint-Exupéry's novel, *Vol de Nuit.* Premiere: Florence, May 18, 1940. Poetic drama. Music moves between tonality and atonality, highly expressive and emotional; long and occasionally lyrical vocal lines in continuous texture. Short prelude. Setting: A shabby airline office on the outskirts of Buenos Aires; early 1930's. One act (60 min).

Synopsis. Rivière, director of a small airline, is determined to prove that night flying is possible in commercial aviation, in spite of the many losses of lives and planes already suffered. Tonight a mail plane must take off for Europe. Three planes are inbound; two land in spite of fierce storms. The third, piloted by Fabien, is lost, in spite of the radio operator, who in trying to talk the pilot into safety, becomes his person for the listeners. Fabien's wife accuses Rivière of robbing her of happiness; the staff and fieldworkers also condemn him for all the disasters. Nevertheless, he sternly sends out the mail plane, "another crew up into the unknown . . . maybe to their death . . . certainly into the future."

Major Roles. RIVIERE (bs-bar); intense, brooding. ROBINEAU, a field inspector (bs). PELLERIN, a pilot (t). LÉROUX, a mechanic (bs). RADIO TELEGRAPHER (assuming identity of pilot Fabien) (t). MRS. FABIEN (s); has difficult dramatic aria. VOICE (s); heard offstage singing song of love.

331

Chorus. SATB. Staff officials, mechanics, fieldworkers.

Orchestra. 4 fl, 3 ob, 4 cl, ten, alto sax, 3 bsn, 4 hrn, 4 trp, 3 trb, tuba, timp, perc (8), 2 harp, cel, piano, strings. *Reduced vers:* 3 fl, 3 ob, 3 cl, 3 bsn, 4 hrn, 3 trp, 3 trb, tuba, timp, perc (4), harp, cel, piano, strings.

Material. Pr. (UE).

Performances. Stanford Univ. (Palo Alto): 3.1.62 (Amer prem—Eng). Manh. Sch. (NYC): 3.11.67.

🎵 The Wandering Scholar

Music by Gustav Holst (1874–1934). Libretto by Clifford Bax. Premiere: London, 1938. Edited by Benjamin Britten and Imogen Holst, for North American premiere, Toronto, Ontario, March 25, 1966. Comedy. Conventional harmonies; melodious; some dialogue. No overture. Setting: A 13th-century French farmhouse. Two acts (approx 30 min).

Synopsis. While her farmer husband Louis is away in town, Alison entertains the lecherous Priest Father Philippe, and is about to serve him pork, wine and cake—and something more precious—when they are surprised by a wandering scholar, Pierre. They get rid of him, but he returns with Louis, exposes them, and enjoys the feast while Louis beats his faithless wife.

Roles. ALISON (s); C3 to G4. LOUIS (bar); Bb1 to F3. FATHER PHILIPPE (bs); A1 to Eb3. PIERRE (t); C2 to A3.

Orchestra. picc, fl, ob, Eng hrn, 2 cl, 2 bsn, 2 hrn, strings.

Material. G Sc (Fa). VS*.

Performances. N.Y. St. Univ. (Potsdam): 8.1.68 (Amer prem). Cent. City (Colo.): 8.72.

🎵 What Price Confidence

Music by Ernst Krenek (1900–   ). Libretto in English by the composer. Premiere (as *Vertrauenssache*): Zurich, May 25, 1964. Comedy. Continuous texture of some dissonance; vocal line angular, patterned after speech. Setting: London, ca. 1900. One act, nine scenes (45 min).

ACT I i: Edwin's apartment; ii: Richard's apartment; iii: British Museum, near dinosaur skeleton; iv: Lobby of Aristeon Club; v: British Museum; vi: Waterloo Bridge; vii: Richard's apartment; viii: Edwin's apartment; ix: Richard's apartment.

Synopsis. Edwin, lacking confidence in himself and so being jealous of Gloria, promises her to trust the first person he meets who asks for trust. Gloria goes off to meet Richard, who wants her to run away with him. She temporizes, making the condition that he instill confidence in Edwin. He does this by inducing Edwin to accept a bad check for 1,000 pounds for a gambling debt. Then he "borrows" the jewels of his wife Vivian, pawning them to make the check good. Edwin, discovering the deception, tries to jump off Waterloo Bridge but is saved by Vivian, who invites him to tea. Gloria follows him there. Vivian gets the pawn ticket from Richard, gives it to Edwin, and turns the tables on Richard and Gloria by deciding to meet Edwin in Paris. One couple toasts "confidence," while the other ruefully questions its price.

Roles. EDWIN (bar); A♯1 to F♭3. GLORIA (s); needs some flexibility; D♭3 to B4. RICHARD (t); C2 to B♭3. VIVIAN (m-s); B2 to A4.

Orchestra. P only.

Material. G Sc (Bä).

Performances. Dartmouth Coll. (Hanover, N.H.): 8.2.68 (Amer prem). Western Op. Th. (San Fran.): 4.29.73.

🦋 Die Witwe des Schmetterlings · The Butterfly Widow

Music by Isang Yun. Libretto in German by Harald Kunz after a 16th-century Chinese story. Premiere: Nuremburg, February 23, 1969. Fantasy-comedy. Melodic, exotic flavor; vocal line patterned after speech, some *Sprechstimme.* Can be performed as double bill with same composer's *Der Traum des Liu-Tung* (see). Setting: Ancient China. One act, three scenes, interludes (52 min).

Introduction: The Butterfly's Dream (in "Chinese"). Scene i: Lao-tse's cottage. Orchestral interlude, The Long Way. ii: The cemetery. Funeral procession. iii: House of mourning. Epilogue: The Butterfly.

Synopsis. The high court functionary Tschuang-tse dreams each night that he is a beautiful giant butterfly. The sage Lao-tse says he was actually a butterfly in a former life. Unhappy with his nagging wife, he pretends to be dead. The widow visits the cemetery with her lover, whereupon the "corpse" rises up and scares her away. Then he becomes the butterfly he always wanted to be.

Major Roles. TSCHUANG-TSE (bar). MME TIAN, his young wife (m-s). LAO-TSE (t). A YOUNG WIDOW (s). PRINCE FU, follower of Tschuang-tse (high bar).

Lesser Role. OLD SERVANT (bs).

Chorus. SATB. Cemetery visitors.

Orchestra. 2 fl (alto fl, picc), 2 ob (Eng hrn), cl (bs cl), bsn (cont bsn), 2 hrn, trp, trb, tuba, timp, perc (4), harp, strings.

Material. AMP (BB).

Performances. N. West. Univ.: 2.27.70 (Amer prem—Eng tr by Robert Gay).

🦋 The Wizards of Balizar

Music by Normand Lockwood (1906–   ). Libretto in English by Russell Porter. Premiere: University of Denver, August 1, 1962. Comic fan-

333

tasy. Conventional harmonies with some oriental flavor; vocal line melodic, patterned after speech; some dialogue. Setting: The town of Balizar, a long time ago. One act, three scenes—single set possible.

ACT I i: Street in Balizar, Ismad's shop in center of row; ii: Interior of Ismad's shop; iii: Street.

Synopsis. Abdullah in the crowded street tells the story of how Ismad the tailor became a wizard at his wife's exhortation and learned from a book how to produce apparitions—only his were nothing but roses. The King's treasurer comes to ask help in seeking a lost ruby. Ismad gives up after numerous "spells" and goes to seek the ruby in the palace. His nephew Maki keeps on trying magic and brings the treasurer's wife to his door—she is the one who stole the ruby. She leaves it with Maki, who promises to set everything right. Ismad is caught snooping in the palace and is brought home, but Maki saves him by producing the ruby as Ismad pronounces a spell. Ismad gets a reward and also a law that he be master of the house and his wife wear only simple clothes. She is glad to change back to being the petted wife of such a great man, while Ismad and Maki resolve to use magic only as an occasional pastime.

Major Roles. ABDULLAH, a singer (bar). ISMAL (t). MAKI, aged 10–13 (unchanged boy's voice). ISMAD'S WIFE (m-s).

Lesser Roles. KAMAL, King's treasurer (sp). LADY, his wife (s).

Chorus. SATB. 4 vendors, slave dealer, blind beggar, thief, merchant, 2 men, 2 sailors, 3 women vendors, 2 women.

Material. ACA.

🎝 The Women

Music by Thomas Pasatieri (1945–   ). Libretto in English by the composer. Premiere: Aspen, August 20, 1965 (winner of Aspen Prize). Surrealistic drama. Continuous texture; conventional harmonies; vocal line both melodic and declamatory. Setting: Any place, any time after death. One act (14 min).

Synopsis. A powerful surrealistic struggle between a man, his wife, and his mother. By placing the opera in the afterlife, the composer has stressed "the eternal nature of the conflict."

Roles. MOTHER (s). WIFE (m-s). MAN (bar).

Orchestra. fl (picc), ob, cl, bsn (cont bsn), hrn, trp, harp, piano, timp and perc (1), vln, vla, vcl, cb.

Material. Pr.

Performances. The composer considers *The Women* part of a tryptych also including *La Divina* (see) and *Padrevia* (see). All three given at Univ. of Washington, August 1971.

334

🎭 Der Wundertheater · The Miracle Theater

Music by Hans Werner Henze (1926–   ). Libretto based on Miguel Cervantes's *El Retablo de las Maravillas*, translated into German by Adolf Graf von Schack. Premiere: Heidelberg, May 7, 1949, as an opera for actors. Revised for singers 1964, premiere in Frankfurt 1965. Satire. Contemporary idiom à la Berg, highly sophisticated, employing occasional parody (Strauss's "Dance of the Seven Veils"); mock overture; vocal line angular and difficult. Twenty-one self-contained numbers in various forms. Some dialogue. Setting: Spain "and everywhere; yesterday, today, tomorrow." One act (approx 40 min).

Synopsis. A variation on the theme of the Emperor's new clothes. Chanfalla, manager of the Miracle Theater, and Chirinos, his mistress, hoodwink the inhabitants of a small town by presenting a miracle theater in which fabulous sights are to be witnessed. Chanfalla proclaims that only bastards and other undesirables can't see these wonders. The result is foregone. Among the "sights" are Samson in the temple, a raging bull, a "herd" of mice, a cascade of water, Herodias (whom Chirinos miscalls the dancer for John the Baptist's head), and a dance in which the Alcalde's nephew joins. At last a Sergeant comes to requisition quarters for his troops, is treated to a display of "Herodias," and pronounces the whole town crazy. Everyone sets upon him, calling him the kind "who can't see." Then all leave the rogues to their triumph.

Major Roles. CHANFALLA (t); top A3. CHIRINOS (s). THE RUNT, a musician (t). THE GOVERNER (bar); top F♯3. BENITO REPOLLO, the Mayor (bs); top F♯3. TERESA, his daughter (s); top A4. REPOLLO, his nephew (d). JUAN CASTRADO, Councilman (bar); top G♯3. JUANA CASTRADA, his daughter (s); top A♭4 (B♭4 with D4 opt; B4 with F♯4 opt).

Lesser Roles. PEDRO CAPACHO, scribe (t). THE SERGEANT (sp). ROBED MAN WITH WHITE WIG (mute).

Chorus. SATB. Spectators.

Orchestra. 2 fl (picc), ob (Eng hrn), cl (bs cl), bsn, hrn, trp, trb, timp, perc (3—including tri, xyl, glock), harp, cembalo or harpsichord, string solos.

Material. Bel (Sch). VS (g, e)*.

Performances. Mannes Sch. (NYC): 2.5.70 etc. (Amer prem—Eng tr by Lesley Balk).

🎭 Yolimba, oder die Grenzen der Magie · Yolimba, or the Limits of Magic

Music by Wilhelm Killmayer (1927–   ). Libretto in German by the composer and Tankred Dorst. Premiere: Munich, May 9, 1970. Farce. Contemporary idiom employing popular and jazz tunes and rhythms in the style of *The Three-Penny Opera*, "classic turns," parody; loudspeaker and denatured sounds; vocal line difficult, mostly patterned after speech; some dialogue. Setting: contemporary Europe. One act and four "Hymns of Praise."

Synopsis. Möhringer, magician and moralist, endeavors to abolish the vice of love. To this end, he manufactures an enchanting artificial female in his laboratory. She is programed to seduce heads of families and other honorable citizens and to shoot anyone uttering the word *love.* Her first victim is Professor Wallerstein, archaeologist, who has just finished breakfast with his family. Yolimba arrives by parcel post (Grand Hymn of Praise to the Post Office), seduces, and shoots him dead. Next is the Tenor, who in an operatic scene with Yolimba sings a cadenza on the subject of amore—his fate is sealed. The policemen (Grand Hymn of Praise to the Police) and almost every male citizen in town are shot dead because they sing of love to the seductive Yolimba. At last she meets her fate in the person of the shy billposter Herbert: he is too bashful to utter the word *love.* Yolimba falls in love herself and cannot pull the trigger. She marries Herbert on the spot (Grand Hymn of Praise to Matrimony). The limits of magic are reached. The Magician blows up as the result of his ineptitude. The dead come to life and the dustmen (Grand Hymn of Praise to the Dustmen) remove the remains of magic.

Major Roles. MOHRINGER (bs-bar); A♭1 to G3 (E3 opt). YOLIMBA (col s); extremely difficult; many florid passages; many tr, one on B4; must dance; top E♭5. THREE MEN, as police clerks and postal clerks (t, t, bs); mostly in ensemble but very important.

Lesser Roles. PROFESSOR WALLERSTEIN (t or bar). HIS WIFE (s). THREE DAUGHTERS, 14–18. THREE SONS, 8–12. GERDA, housemaid (m-s); needs flexibility for solo. OPERA TENOR (t). HERBERT (sp). WIDOW (sp). ELEGANT WIDOW (sp). POLICE DOG. APPARITIONS (t, bs).

Chorus. SSATTB. Quite complicated, several solos. Citizens, post-office clerks, police clerks, street cleaners, children (possible children's chorus in last scene).

Orchestra. 2 fl (picc), 2 ob, 2 cl (alto sax), 2 bsn, 3 hrn, 2 trp, 3 trb, tuba, timp, perc (3–4), piano 4 hands, piano with amplifier, piano with cym, harm, strings. *Stage:* (from pit) fl (picc), 2 ob, 2 bsn, trp, trb, tuba, perc (1), harm. Noises on tape. Trp, 3 trb, tuba.

Material. Bel (Sch). VS (g)*.

Indexes

KEY TO ABBREVIATIONS

A: alto
ACA: American Composers Alliance, 170 West 74th St., New York, N.Y. 10023
acc: accordion
adapt: adaptation
Af: After Dinner Co., c/o Richard Flusser, 23 Stuyvesant St., New York, N.Y. 10003
Amer: American
AMP: Associated Music Publishers, 866 Third Ave., New York, N.Y. 10022
approx: approximately
arr: arranged, arrangement
Art: Artia, Prague (see B & H)
assn: association
B, b: bass
Bä: Bärenreiter, Germany (see G Sc)
bar: baritone
BB: Bote & Bock, Berlin (see AMP)
Bel: Belwin-Mills, 16 West 61st St., New York, N.Y. 10023
BH: Breitkopf & Härtel, Germany (see G Sc)
B & H: Boosey & Hawkes, 30 West 57th St., New York, N.Y. 10019
bib: biblical
bl: block(s)
BMI: Broadcast Music, Inc., 40 West 57th St., New York, N.Y. 10019
Br: Alexander Broude, 1619 Broadway, New York, N.Y. 10019
bs: bass
bs-bar: bass baritone
bs cl: bass clarinet
bs dr: bass drum
bsn: bassoon
buf: buffo

c: contralto
cb: string bass
cel: celesta
cent: century
char: character
Che: J & W Chester, London (see G Sc)
child: children
Chin: Chinese
chor: chorus
Chou: Choudens, Paris (see Pet)
cl: clarinet
co: company
col: coloratura
Col: Franco Columbo (see Bel)
coll: college
com: comedy
comp: composer
conc: concert
cont bsn: contra bassoon
corn: cornet
CP: chorus parts
cym: cymbal(s)
cz: Czechoslovakian
d: dancer
dan: Danish
dept: department
dial: dialogue
dr: drum
dram: dramatic
Du: Durand, Paris (see El-V, G Sc)
e: English
ed: edition
elec: electric, electronic
El-V: Elkan-Vogel (see Pr)
Eng: English
Eng hrn: English horn
E Sc: E. C. Schirmer, 600 Washington St., Boston, Mass. 02111

f: French
Fa: Faber Music (*see* G Sc)
fals: falsetto
fest: festival
Fi: Carl Fischer, 62 Cooper Sq., New York, N.Y. 10003
fl: flute
FS: full score
g: German
Ga: Galaxy Music Corp., 2121 Broadway, New York, N.Y. 10023
glock: glockenspiel
Gr: Gregg Press, 171 East Ridgewood Ave., Ridgewood, N.J.
G Sc: G. Schirmer, 866 Third Ave., New York, N.Y. 10022
guit: guitar
h: Hungarian
Ha: Wilhelm Hansen, Copenhagen (*see* G Sc)
harm: harmonium
Heu: Heugel, Paris (*see* Pr)
Hi: Highgate Press (*see* Ga)
hist: historical
HM: Hudebni Matice, Budapest (*see* B & H)
i: Italian
Imp: Impero-Verlag, Germany (see Pr)
inst: institute, institution
Ka: Edwin F. Kalmus Music Library, 14 East 60th St., New York, N.Y. 10023
L: long
Le: Leeds Music Corp. (*see* MCA)
Li: libretto
Lit: Henry Litolff, Frankfurt
LO: large orchestra
lyr: lyric
Map: Alfred J. Mapleson Music Library, 208 N. Broadway, Lindenhurst, L.I., N.Y. 11757
Mar: Edward B. Marks Music Corp., 136 West 52nd St., New York, N.Y. 10019
MCA: Music Corp. of America, 255 Park Ave. S., New York, N.Y. 10003
Met: Metropolitan Opera
Mi: Mills Music Co. (*see* Bel)
mil: military
min: minutes
MO: medium orchestra
m-s: mezzo-soprano
mu: mute
mus: music
NYC: New York City

NYCO: New York City Opera
ob: oboe
OO: Operation Opera, 392 Central Park West, New York, N.Y. 10025
op: opera
opt: optional
orch: orchestra(l)
org: organ
orig: original
Ox: Oxford University Press, 200 Madison Ave., New York, N.Y. 10016
P: parts (orchestra); piano
P: piano
perc: percussion
Pet: C. F. Peters Corp., 373 Park Ave. S., New York, N.Y. 10016
picc: piccolo
pist: piston
PP: 2 pianos
Pr: Theodore Presser, Bryn Mawr, Pa.
prem: premiere
qt: quartet
r: Russian
Ri: G. Ricordi (*see* Bel)
S, s: soprano
Sal: Editions Salabert, 575 Madison Ave., New York, N.Y. 10022
sax: saxophone
sch: school
Sch: B. Schott (*see* Bel)
Sh: Short
sn: snare
SO: small orchestra
soc: society
Son: Sonzogno (*see* Bel)
sp: speaker, speaking role
span: Spanish
spin: spinto
st: state
StS: study score
susp: suspended
T, t: tenor
tamb: tambourine
ten: tenor
th: theater
timp: timpani
tr: translation
trb: trombone
treb: treble
tri: triangle
trp: trumpet
tub: tubular (bells)
UCLA: University of California, Los Angeles
univ: university

UE: Universal Edition (*see* Pr)
USC: University of Southern California
vcl: cello
vers: version
vib: vibraphone
vla: viola

vln: violin
VS: vocal score
wd: wood
Wein: Josef Weinberger (*see* B&H, G Sc)
wksp: workshop
xyl: xylophone

INDEX BY COMPOSERS

L in parentheses following the name of an opera means that it is classified herein as long, Sh that it has been classified as short. LO means that a large orchestra is required, MO a medium orchestra, and SO a small orchestra, P or PP, piano or two-piano only. Where no orchestra entry appears, the information was not available. (See Introduction for more specific information.)

Adam, Adolphe. Le Postillon de Long-jumeau (L) LO, 186

Adler, Samuel. The Outcasts of Poker Flat (Sh) MO, 308

Albert, Eugen d'. Tiefland (L) LO, 220; Die Toten Augen (L) LO, 222

Amram, David. Twelfth Night (L) MO, 228

Argento, Dominick. Christopher Sly (Sh) SO, 259; Col. Jonathan the Saint (L) LO, 61; The Masque of Angels (Sh) SO, 301; Postcard from Morocco (L) SO, 185; The Shoemaker's Holiday (L) SO, 209

Arrieta, Emilio. Marina (L) SO, 147

Aschaffenburg, Walter. Bartleby (L) MO, 37

Auber, Daniel François. Le Domino Noir (L) LO, 76; Fra Diavolo (L) LO, 94; Masaniello (L) LO, 148

Barab, Seymour. The Perfect Wife (to Pergolesi music) (Sh) presumed MO, 310; Phillip Marshall (L) O in preparation, 180

Barber, Samuel. Antony and Cleopatra (L) LO, 29; A Hand of Bridge (Sh) SO, 283

Barraud, Henry. Lavinia (L) SO, 136

Barthelson, Joyce. Chanticleer (Sh) MO or PP, 259; Feathertop (L) MO, 86; The King's Breakfast (Sh) P, 291

Bécaud, Gilbert. Opéra d'Aran (L) LO, 172

Beeson, Jack. Lizzie Borden (L) MO, 139; My Heart's in the Highlands (L) SO, 163

Bellini, Vincenzo. Beatrice di Tenda (L) LO, 41; I Capuleti ed i Montecchi (L) LO, 55; Il Pirata (L) LO, 182; I Puritani (L) LO, 190

Benjamin, Arthur. A Tale of Two Cities (L) LO, 216

Bennett, Richard Rodney. The Ledge (Sh) SO, 296; The Mines of Sulphur (L) LO, 155

Berg, Alban. Lulu (L) LO, 144

Berlioz, Hector. Béatrice et Bénédict (L) LO, 42; Benvenuto Cellini (L) LO, 46; La Damnation de Faust (L) LO, 69; Les Troyens: La Prise de Troie, Les Troyens à Carthage (L) LO, 223–224

Birtwistle, Harrison. Punch and Judy (Sh) SO, 316

Bizet, Georges. Djamileh (Sh) MO,

342

Lesur, Daniel. Andréa del Sarto (L) LO, 26

Levy, Marvin. Mourning Becomes Electra (L) LO, 162

Lockwood, Normand. The Hanging Judge (L) MO, 107; The Scarecrow (L) MO, 206; The Wizards of Balizar (Sh), 333

Lortzing, Albert. Der Waffenschmied (L) MO, 235; Der Wildschutz (L) MO, 240; Zar und Zimmermann (L) MO, 242

Magney, Ruth Taylor. The Gift of the Magi (Sh) P, 279

Marschner, Heinrich. Hans Heiling (L) presumed MO, 108; Der Vampyr (L) MO, 229

Martin, Frank. Le Vin Herbé (L) SO, 233

Martin, Vernon. Ladies' Voices (Sh) P, 293

Martinu, Bohuslav. The Greek Passion (L) LO, 101

Mascagni, Pietro. L'Amico Fritz (L) LO, 25; Iris (L) LO, 117

Massenet, Jules. Cendrillon (L) LO, 60; Don Quichotte (L) LO, 77; Hérodiade (L) LO, 111; Le Jongleur de Notre Dame (L) LO, 121; La Navarraise (Sh) LO, 304

Maw, Nicholas. The Rising of the Moon (L) LO, 194

Mayer, William. One Christmas Long Ago (Sh) M or LO, 306

Menotti, Gian-Carlo. Help! Help! the Globolinks! (Sh) SO, 284; The Last Savage (L) LO, 135; The Most Important Man (L) LO, 161

Mercadante, Saverio. Il Giuramento (L) LO, 98

Messager, André. Béatrice (L) LO, 40

Meyerbeer, Giacomo. L'Africaine (L) LO, 21; Les Huguenots (L) LO, 113; Le Prophète (L) LO, 189; Robert le Diable (L) LO, 196

Mihalovici, Marcel. Krapp, ou la Dernière Band (Sh) MO, 292

Milhaud, Darius. Fiesta (Sh) SO, 274; Trois Opéras-Minutes (Sh): L'Abandon d'Ariane MO, La Délivrance de Thésée SO, L'Enlèvement d'Europe SO, 327–328

Moore, Douglas. Carry Nation (L) MO, 57; White Wings (L), 239; Wings of the Dove (L) MO, 241

Morgenstern, Sam. The Big Black Box (Sh) P, 251; Haircut (Sh) P, 282

Moss, Lawrence. The Brute (Sh) SO, 253

Mozart, Wolfgang Amadeus. La Finta Giardiniera (L) MO, 92; La Finta Semplice (L) SO, 93; Lucio Silla (L) SO, 141

Musgrave, Thea. The Decision (L) LO, 72

Mussorgsky, Modeste. Khovanshchina (L) LO, 126

Nielsen, Carl. Maskarade (L) LO, 149

Offenbach, Jacques. Ba-Ta-Clan (Sh) MO, 248; Chanson de Fortunio (Sh) MO, 258; Une Demoiselle en Loterie (Sh) MO, 265; L'Ile de Tulipatan (Sh) MO, 285; Un Mari à la Porte (Sh), 298; Le Mariage aux Lanternes (Sh) MO, 299; Le 66 (Sh), 322; La Vie Parisienne (L), 231

Orff, Carl. Antigonae (L) LO, 28; Die Bernauerin (L) LO, 47; Carmina Burana (Sh) LO, 256; Catulli Carmina (Sh) SO, 258; Die Kluge (Sh) LO, 291; Prometheus (L) LO, 187

Paisiello, Giovanni. Nina, ossia, La Pazza per Amore (L) MO, 167; Il Re Teodoro in Venezia (L) MO, 192

Pasatieri, Thomas. The Black Widow (L) MO, 48; Calvary (Sh) MO, 255; La Divina (Sh) MO, 265; Padrevia (Sh) SO, 309; The Trial of Mary Lincoln (Sh) MO, 327; The Women (Sh) SO, 334

Penderecki, Krzysztof. Die Teufel von Loudon (L) LO, 219

Pergolesi, Giovanni Battista. The Perfect Wife (adapted by Barab) (Sh) SO, 310

Thomas, Ambroise. Hamlet (L) LO, 106

Tippett, Sir Michael. King Priam (L) LO, 128; The Knot Garden (L) LO, 130; The Midsummer Marriage (L) LO, 153

Trimble, Lester. Boccaccio's "Nightingale" (Sh) SO, 251

Van Grove, Isaac. The Other Wise Man (Sh) MO, 307; The Shining Chalice (Sh) MO, 321

Verdi, Giuseppe. Aroldo (L) LO, 34; Attila (L) LO, 35; La Battaglia di Legnano (L) MO, 39; I Due Foscari (L) LO, 80; Ernani (L) LO, 82; I Lombardi alla Prima Crociata (L) MO, 140; Luisa Miller (L) MO, 143; Nabucco (L) LO, 164; Les Vêpres Sicilienne (L) LO, 230

Villa-Lobos, Heitor. Yerma (L) MO, 242

Wade, James. The Martyred (Sh) MO, 300

Wagner, Richard. Die Feen (L) LO, 88; Rienzi, der Letzte der Tribunen (L) LO, 192

Walton, Sir William. The Bear (Sh) SO, 249

Ward, Robert. The Crucible (L) LO, 64

Weber, Carl Maria von. Euryanthe (L) LO, 83; Oberon (L) LO, 169

Weill, Kurt. Aufstieg und Fall der Stadt Mahagonny (L) LO, 36

Weisgall, Hugo. Purgatory (Sh) SO, 317; The Stronger (Sh) SO, 324

Westergaard, Peter. Mr. and Mrs. Discobbolos (Sh) SO, 303

Wilder, Alec. The Opening (Sh) SO, 306

Williamson, Malcolm. Dunstan and the Devil (Sh) SO, 267; The Growing Castle (L) SO, 103; The Happy Prince (Sh) SO, 283; Julius Caesar Jones (Sh) SO, 289; Our Man in Havana (L) S or LO, 175; The Violins of Saint Jacques (L) LO, 234

Wolf-Ferrari, Ermanno. Il Campiello (L) LO, 54; Le Donne Curiose (L) MO, 79; I Gioielli della Madonna (L) LO, 98

Yun, Isang. Der Traum des Liu-Tung (Sh) MO, 326; Die Witwe des Schmetterlings (Sh) MO, 333

Zandonai, Riccardo. Francesca da Rimini (L) LO, 94

Zimmermann, Bern Alois. Die Soldaten (L) LO, 213